THE BRITISH POLITICAL TRADITION

VOLUME THREE
A MUCH GOVERNED NATION

Part 1

THE BRITISH POLITICAL TRADITION
in four volumes

I The Rise of Collectivism
II The Ideological Heritage
III A Much Governed Nation
IV The World Outside

THE BRITISH POLITICAL TRADITION

W. H. GREENLEAF

VOLUME THREE

A MUCH GOVERNED NATION
Part 1

METHUEN : LONDON & NEW YORK

First published in 1987 by
Methuen & Co. Ltd
11 New Fetter Lane, London EC4P 4EE

Published in the USA by
Methuen & Co.
in association with Methuen, Inc.
29 West 35th Street, New York NY 10001

© 1987 W.H. Greenleaf

Typeset by C. R. Barber & Partners
(Highlands) Ltd,
Fort William, Scotland
and printed in Great Britain
at the University Press, Cambridge

All rights reserved. No part of this book may be reprinted or reproduced or utilized in any form or by any electronic, mechanical or other means, now known or hereafter invented, including photocopying and recording, or in any information storage or retrieval system, without permission in writing from the publishers.

British Library Cataloguing in Publication Data
Greenleaf, W.H.
The British political tradition.
Vol. 3: A much governed nation.
Pt. 1
1. Great Britain—Politics and government—19th century 2. Great Britain—Politics and government—20th century
I. Title
320.941   JN216

ISBN 0-416-36820-4

Library of Congress Cataloging in Publication Data
Greenleaf, W.H.
The British political tradition.
Includes bibliographical references and index.
Contents: v. 1. The rise of collectivism—v. 2. The ideological heritage—v. 3. A much governed nation.
1. Great Britain—Constitutional history.
2. Great Britain—Politics and government. 3. Great Britain—Foreign relations. 4. Political science—Great Britain—History. I. Title.
JN118.G83   1983   320.941   82-18671
ISBN 0-416-15570-7 (v. 1)

We construct our world as an interpretation which attempts to restore the unity which the real has lost by our making its diversity explicit.
B. BOSANQUET, *Logic*, II. ix.1 (i)

CONTENTS

This volume has been divided into two parts. Part 2 forms a separate, but consecutively paginated, book. An index to both parts appears at the end of Part 2.

Part 1

LIST OF FIGURE AND TABLES ix
LIST OF ABBREVIATIONS xi
PREFACE xiv
ACKNOWLEDGEMENTS xv

1 THE CHANGE IN BRITISH POLITY 1

2 THE LABYRINTHINE MAZE 5
The old patchwork 7 A conflict of attitudes 19 The new patchwork 39 Little local difficulties 64 Central involvement and control 74 Search for a solution 88 Options 105 Intermediate government 109

3 IN DARK WONDER 130
Growth and its phases 130 Recruitment and organization 135 Rationalization and co-ordination 170 Managerial efficiency 195 Retrenchment and effectiveness 236

4 THE DEPARTMENT OF DEPARTMENTS 249
Collectivism and the crisis of public expenditure 250 Efficiency and organization 291 Steering the economy 313 The emperor's clothes 337

5 THE PUBLIC CONCERN – AND BEYOND 339
A parastatal world 339 Rationale 342 Public enterprises 351 Privatization 428 Fringe bodies 452 Issues and remedies 462 Beyond the fringe 483 Corporatism 499

viii Contents

APPENDICES 1–3 502

Part 2

LIST OF FIGURE AND TABLES vii
LIST OF ABBREVIATIONS ix
ACKNOWLEDGEMENTS xiii

6 THE SECOND YOKE 529
   The issue 529 Delegated legislation: origins 531 Modernists and Methuselahs 540 Delegated legislation: the position today 576 The new judicature 597 The debate about administrative justice 605 Tribunals: the position today 628

7 THE CENTRE OF THE GOVERNMENT MACHINE 643
   The Cabinet and collectivism 644 Size and composition 648 Committees 668 Ancillary agencies 691 Great Jove 719 Cabinet reform 752

8 THE NATIONAL PALAVER 762
   Increasing pressure 762 Procedural corollary 772 Response 816 The external catalyst 862

9 AN ORGANIZED QUARREL 874
   Factions no more 875 Democracy and party organization 881 Party and the positive state 907

10 THE REDRESS OF GRIEVANCES 918
   Channels of complaint 918 The Ombudsman family 924 Means of judicial control 946 Fundamental law and rights 958

L'ENVOI 992
APPENDIX 4 993
INDEX 1001

FIGURE AND TABLES

This volume has been divided into two parts. Part 2 forms a separate, but consecutively paginated, book.

FIGURE

1 Local authorities in England and Wales in 1955 and since 1974 96

TABLES

1 The main local institutions in England and Wales, 1800–1904 63
2 Receipts of local authorities in England and Wales, 1868–1984 72
3 Local government expenditure in England and Wales, 1870–1984 101
4 The growth of the Civil Service since 1797 132
5 Haldane revised, 1942 189
6 The structure of the non-industrial Civil Service, 1912–85 216
7 Treasury work and staff, 1805–1985 266
8 The nationalized industries in 1979 394
9 Other public corporations, 1984 400
10 NEB investments, 31 January 1979 408
11 Major utilities and services, 1985 412
12 Fringe bodies: functional areas 454
Appendix 1 HM Government as shareholder, 1928–85 502
Appendix 2 Privatization, 1979–86 512
Appendix 3 Central privatization proceeds, 1979–85 526

13 Administrative tribunals, 1985 632
14 Circulation of Cabinet papers, 1880–1954 647
15 Cabinet membership, 1782–1986 650
16 Size of Cabinets and governments, 1900–85 652
17 Types of ministerial appointment, 1906–86 664
18 Major standing Cabinet committees, 1945–85 678
19 Functions and membership of certain main committees of the Cabinet, 1949 682
20 Questions to ministers, 1847–1984 794
21 Urgency motions in the Commons, 1882–1986 800
22 Select committees of the House of Commons, 1864–1984 848

x Figure and Tables

23 Result of the general election, 1983 872
24 Cases referred to the Parliamentary Commissioner for Administration, 1967–85 936
25 The functions and cost of public authorities 1978–89 995

ABBREVIATIONS

ASI	Adam Smith Institute
BL	British Leyland
BMA	British Medical Association
BNOC	British National Oil Corporation
BT	British Telecom
BTG	British Technology Group
C., Cd., Cmd., Cmnd.	Command Paper
C & AG	Comptroller and Auditor General
CCR	Committee of Civil Research
CEB	Central Electricity Board
CEIS	Central Economic Information Service
CEPS	Central Economic Planning Staff
CID	Committee of Imperial Defence
CLA	Commission for Local Administration
CPC	Conservative Political Centre
CPRS	Central Policy Review Staff
CRD	Conservative Research Department
CSC	Civil Service Commission
CSD	Civil Service Department
CSO	Central Statistical Office
DEA	Department of Economic Affairs
DES	Department of Education and Science
DHSS	Department of Health and Social Security
DNB	*Dictionary of National Biography* (Compact edition, Oxford, 1975)
DOE	Department of the Environment
DSIR	Department of Scientific and Industrial Research
DTI	Department of Trade and Industry
EAC	Economic Advisory Council
FCO	Foreign and Commonwealth Office
GLC	Greater London Council
HC	House of Commons Paper
H.C. Deb.	House of Commons Debates
HL	House of Lords Paper

xii Abbreviations

H.L. Deb.	House of Lords Debates
HLRO	House of Lords Record Office
IEA	Institute of Economic Affairs
ILEA	Inner London Education Authority
ILP	Independent Labour Party
IRC	Industrial Reorganization Corporation
KCA	*Keesing's Contemporary Archives*
LCC	London County Council
LEA	Local education authority
LGB	Local Government Board
LPTB	London Passenger Transport Board
MPO	Management and Personnel Office
NEB	National Enterprise Board
NEC	National Executive Committee, Labour Party
NEDO	National Economic Development Office
Non-Parl.	Non-Parliamentary Paper
NUA	National Unionist Association
NUCA	National Union of Conservative Associations
O & M	Organization and Methods
OED	*Oxford English Dictionary* (Compact edition, Oxford, 1971)
OEDS	*A Supplement to the Oxford English Dictionary* (Oxford, 1972–86)
PAC	Public Accounts Committee
PAR	Programme Analysis and Review
Parl. Deb.	Parliamentary Debates
PCA	Parliamentary Commissioner for Administration
PEP	Political and Economic Planning
PESC	Public Expenditure Survey Committee
PLP	Parliamentary Labour Party
PPS	Parliamentary Private Secretary
PR	Proportional representation
PRO	Public Records Office
PSBR	Public Sector Borrowing Requirement
R. Com.	Royal Commission
Rep.	Report
RIPA	Royal Institute of Public Administration
SCE	Select Committee on Estimates
SCNE	Select Committee on National Expenditure
SCNI	Select Committee on Nationalized Industries
SDP	Social Democratic Party
Sel. Cttee	Select Committee
TIS	Treasury Investigation Section

TLS	*Times Literary Supplement*
Trans. R. Hist. S.	*Transactions of the Royal Historical Society*
UGC	University Grants Committee

PREFACE

This account of the emergence of contemporary political institutions in Britain follows volumes dealing with *The Rise of Collectivism* and *The Ideological Heritage*, both of which appeared in 1983. It shows how, in the perspective these other works describe, the traditional machinery of government expanded notably and was in many ways completely altered. As before I would like to express my gratitude to those who have helped in various ways. I am very indebted to the Leverhulme Trustees for the award of an emeritus fellowship and for generous financial help which enabled the present text to be completed. Professor T. A. Smith spared the time from a busy academic schedule to read a draft of chapter 5 and made helpful comments: I am much obliged to him. Mrs L. Johns typed successive drafts with skill and dispatch. I have been most impressed by, and thankful for, the very careful attention given to the text by Sarah Cahill of Methuen's editorial department and by Janet Tyrrell, the copy-editor. And, by no means least, at a time of particular difficulty, my wife gave invaluable help with the correction of the proofs: without her aid it would have been impossible to complete this task.

Two particular apologies are due. In the course of the first two volumes I referred from time to time to specific chapters or sections of the present study. These references related to an earlier draft of *A Much Governed Nation* which, as it happened, I had to revise more radically than I previously thought would be necessary. This involved *inter alia* altering the order of some of the chapters. However the original context of attribution makes fairly clear to which part of the present text attention has to be directed so, in practice, I hope no great difficulty should arise. The other point I must excuse is that (at the end of volume two) I promised the present book would appear in 1984. At the time I believed it would. But the process of revision and rewriting took very much longer than I had allowed for (not being completed until mid-1986) – which leads me once again to thank John Naylor and Nancy Marten of Messrs. Methuen for their considerable patience and understanding. It also prompts me to add that, though the fourth volume on 'The World Outside' will most definitely get done, I am as yet in no better position than Job to give much of an answer to the question, 'How long will it be ere ye make an end of words?'

May 1987

W. H. Greenleaf
Swansea

ACKNOWLEDGEMENTS

Some material used here is taken from previously published papers on 'The Character of Modern British Politics', 'Toulmin Smith and the British Political Tradition', and 'Urgency Motions in the Commons' which appeared respectively in the journals *Parliamentary Affairs*, *Public Administration*, and *Public Law*. I acknowledge with thanks the permission of the Controller of Her [Britannic] Majesty's Stationery Office to cite from various official publications and from Crown Copyright material in the Public Record Office.

W.H.G.

* * *

The author and publishers would also like to thank the following for their kind permission to use copyright material:

Allen & Unwin (Publishers) for material from H. Finer, *The British Civil Service*, for inclusion in Tables 4 and 7. A & C Black (Publishers) Ltd for extracts from Lord Hewart, *The New Despotism* (Ernest Benn, 1929). The British Broadcasting Corporation for material from their Annual Report and Handbook (1986), for inclusion in Table 9. The British Wool Marketing Board for material from the 1985 Annual Report and Accounts, for inclusion in Table 11. The Cable Authority for material from the Authority's leaflet, 'Cable is Coming', for inclusion in Table 9. Cambridge University Press for material from B. R. Mitchell and P. Deane, *Abstract of British Historical Statistics* (1962) and B. R. Mitchell and H. G. Jones, *Second Abstract of British Historical Statistics* (1971), for inclusion in Tables 2, 3 and 7. The Committee of Vice-Chancellors and Principals of the Universities of the United Kingdom and the Universities Statistical Record for material from the *Universities Statistical Record*, for inclusion in Table 11. Covent Garden Market Authority for material from their Annual Report 1984/85, for inclusion in Table 9. The Independent Broadcasting Authority for material from their Annual Report and Accounts (1984/85), for inclusion in Table 9. The Institute of Historical Research for material from J. C. Sainty, *Office Holders in Modern Britain I: Treasury Officials 1660–1870* (Athlone Press, 1972), for inclusion in Table 7. Keesing's Contemporary Archives for material for inclusion in Table 8 and Appendix 2. The Milk Marketing Board for material from their Annual Report and Accounts

xvi Acknowledgements

1985, for inclusion in Table 11. The Municipal Year Book for material for inclusion in Appendix 2. The Potato Marketing Board for material from their Annual Report and Accounts, for inclusion in Table 11. The Welsh Fourth Channel Authority for material from their Annual Report (1985) for inclusion in Table 9. Whitaker's Almanack for permission to reproduce material from *Whitaker's Almanack*, for inclusion in Tables 8, 9, 11 and Appendix 2.

I
THE CHANGE IN BRITISH POLITY

... influences of various kinds conspire to increase corporate action....
H. SPENCER, *The Man Versus the State*, 1884, Penguin 1969, p. 99

OVER THE past century and a half a revolution has occurred in our political affairs. From being a country in which there was no considerable array of public functions, we have become (in Maitland's phrase) 'a much governed nation' with councils, boards, departments, and authorities of many kinds exercising the numerous and extensive powers bestowed on them by modern legislation.[1] The purpose of the present volume is to describe some aspects of this notable fact on the assumption that the fullest understanding of the British political tradition as it has emerged in recent times requires a grasp of this institutional transformation.

The style of politics consistent with the older sort of civic order is one in which there is little continuing growth of public responsibility and political and administrative arrangements are by later standards relatively modest (and no doubt inefficient). They are characterized, too, by a diffusion of power with which is associated an acute disquiet about any manifest concentration of command and, too, a quick disposition to spring to the defence of personal liberty in the face of official interference. Naturally the role of government is often crucial but overall it is severely constrained.[2] Yet in time this concept of political office was fundamentally altered or, better, came to be accompanied and rivalled by a view of a very different sort. The shift of emphasis was recognized both by those who opposed and those who applauded it. Dicey, who was much disturbed by the trend, suggested that, in the early nineteenth century, the chief task of the ministry of the day was not the passing of laws to regulate the detail of communal affairs but rather what he called

[1] F. W. Maitland, *The Constitutional History of England* (1908; Cambridge, 1974), p. 501.
[2] Cf. Sir N. Chester, *The English Administrative System 1780–1870* (Oxford, 1981), p. 67.

2   A Much Governed Nation

'the guidance of national policy'. By this he meant two things: sustaining in the external world the country's broad collective interest; and establishing at home the general framework of domestic order within which individual citizens or groups of them could peacefully pursue their own concerns. The nature of government was determined by this vital but limited duty of defence and umpirage. But Dicey also believed that, by his own time, a great change was under way. Increasingly an administration was committed to a legislative programme involving more and more substantive intervention in economic and social life. In this way the last century witnessed the birth (or, more strictly, the recreation) of what one of his contemporaries called the 'Legislation-state'.[3] And, inevitably, a radical institutional response ensued. Some years later, W. A. Robson commented on the same trend (though his judgement of it was very different from Dicey's being notably more favourable). In a memorandum submitted to the Committee on Ministers' Powers he stressed that the 'scope and character of government have changed enormously in the last 50 years', that is, since about 1880. 'Formerly', he wrote,

> government was chiefly regulatory and negative: its main task (apart from defence) was to keep the ring and maintain fair play while private interests asserted themselves freely. Today, government is largely concerned with the administration of social services, and has become positive in a new sense.... The change from regulatory or *control* activities to *service* activities on the part of Government necessitates new forms of administrative authority.

It followed that institutional arrangements that were once suitable might no longer be so because expectations and purposes were different.[4] The process has also received clear official recognition in many places. For instance, in a report of the Government Organization Committee, written after the last war and so at the height of a more recent phase of collectivist expansion, it was taken as basic that the

> present-day complexities of Government arose mainly from the new responsibilities which had been assumed in the spheres of economic affairs and welfare, particularly the former. The need for further adaptations of the Government machine to deal effectively with these responsibilities seemed to be the question most urgently requiring investigation.

---

[3] A. V. Dicey, *Lectures on the Relation Between Law & Public Opinion in England During the Nineteenth Century* (1905; 2nd edn, London, 1920), p. 85; Sir J. Seeley, *Introduction to Political Science* (1896; London, 1902), p. 146.

[4] Ministers' Powers, Cttee, Memoranda ... and Minutes of Evidence, 1932 (Non-Parl.), vol. ii, p. 52 §3. This passage is cited more fully in Part 2 at p. 564.

And, it was concluded, this meant looking at all levels of government organization to see how it might be moulded to achieve more effectively the goals in view.[5]

In fact this tendency to assume a greater range of public duties began in a somewhat piecemeal and reluctant fashion, though later it became much more deliberate. It was often opposed and gave rise to an intense ideological debate; while the specific factors and occasions involved in its appearance and evolution were diverse.[6] But in the outcome no political institution existing at the beginning of the last century has been unaffected. Some traditional offices succumbed under the pressure and disappeared, while others were altered, perhaps quite radically, to enable them to cope more adequately with the growing burden of business. And naturally many new agencies of administration and control were also created to the same end. All this enhanced the need for probity and economy in an increasingly enlarged and costly system of policy formation and execution. It raised, in addition, numerous problems of efficiency concerning the recruitment, organization, and co-ordination of the pullulation of officials entailed. There was the further issue how to monitor the operation of *cette grande machine étatique* and specifically the question whether traditional instruments like Parliament and the courts were any longer sufficient for the purpose. And, as one aspect of this, means were necessarily sought of protecting more effectively the individual and his claims, of ensuring that, in the context of this enlarging and increasingly active medley of public authorities, he had a proper voice and the possibility of redress if his case should be neglected or ill-considered. For it was not only that the frontier between the private and public spheres altered markedly in favour of the latter but also that the territory formally left to the governance of personal choice had itself become less autonomous in important respects. The history of modern British polity thus reveals both a continuing parade of institutional modification and invention and a tendency to apply this machinery ever more widely. Nor has the process slowed in very recent times when there has been indeed a positive frenzy of reform and reorganization of many kinds.[7]

The general perspective, then, is one of the growth of government and of considerable institutional innovation. Old established bodies have

---

5 PRO, CAB 134/308, GOC(49) 3rd (14 October 1949), p. 5 §4(a).
6 On these matters, see volumes i and ii of this study of the British political tradition, namely, *The Rise of Collectivism* (London, 1983) and *The Ideological Heritage* (London, 1983).
7 Cf. G. K. Fry, *The Administrative 'Revolution' in Whitehall: a Study of the Politics of Administrative Change in British Central Government since the 1950s* (London, 1981), p. 1; T. A. Smith, *British Politics in the Post-Keynesian Era: Inaugural Lecture* (Acton Society Trust; London, n.d. [1986]), esp. §§IV–V.

4 A Much Governed Nation

been moulded to collectivist purpose (or cast aside) and new ones created to supplement them (or take their place). What follows here is specific description of this radical transformation. First there is an examination of changes in the machinery of administration, local, national, and quasi-governmental. Next, attention focuses on the central institutions of constitutional significance, Cabinet, Parliament, and party. Finally, in a kind of addendum, the issues are described which arise with respect to protecting the rights and interests of individuals, groups, and minorities at a time of increasing state power and intervention.

2
THE LABYRINTHINE MAZE

Year by year the subordinate government of England is becoming more and more important.
F. W. MAITLAND, *The Constitutional History of England*, 1908, repr. 1974, p. 501

IT MAY seem strange to begin consideration of our political institutions with an account of local government in that the subject is rarely, if ever, accorded such pride of place in general constitutional review. As examination of almost any recent textbook will show, to write about 'the government of modern Britain' often, perhaps usually, means to cover in some detail central politics in its various forms and aspects and, by comparison, to give local matters relatively brief attention or even none at all. Yet this emphasis reflects a very curious view indeed of British political life in that it fails to acknowledge either the historical significance of local bodies or the immense practical importance they still have. Certainly any such relegation or omission would be quite inappropriate in the present context. For it is the case that the growth of local intervention constituted the first thrust of a developing collectivism. The numerous local bodies of the time bore the brunt of the many problems created or exacerbated by the rise of modern industry, the increase of population, urban growth, and so forth. There were two reasons why this was so. One was that, even before the Great Change got under way, local authorities had acquired an array of protective, service, and welfare responsibilities. It is true the exercise of these functions was by no means general or systematic; nor, usually, was it adequate even by the best contemporary standards. But it was inevitable that, as agencies of social provision and control already in existence throughout the country, they should assume the burden of trying to cope with the difficulties resulting from the erection of factories and the massing of men. The second reason was quite simply the incapacity of central government. Not only was the accepted concept of its role moulded by the anti-interventionist ethos of the day but, as well, the administrative apparatus at its disposal was quite incapable of shouldering the tasks involved. In consequence these were largely taken in hand in the traditional way by local action. Of course this development was at first

6 A Much Governed Nation

only sporadic, being the result of initiatives to meet specific needs in particular places rather than a generalized response on a national scale. Yet in time the tendency did become more or less deliberate and uniform as the county and municipal authorities themselves acquired both greater experience and a positive conception of their office and as the demand for satisfactory public response intensified. It was with this in mind that the Webbs rightly stressed the significance of local institutions in the emergence of the positive state and devoted so much time and effort to their study producing, over many years, what is a very considerable work of scholarship indeed.[1]

The story is not a simple one. Thomas Madox, the legal antiquary, brought out in 1726 an historical survey of the English cities and boroughs. He commented at the outset of his essay that whoever wished 'to discourse in a proper manner concerning Corporated Towns and Communities, must take-in a great variety of matter'. The subject is, he added, 'extensive and difficult.'[2] Nor has it become less complex since. Writing in 1956, after a lifetime of experience in the fields of administration concerned, a senior civil servant referred to 'the labyrinthine maze of English local government.'[3] It is an apt description. But (to steal Pope's phrases) inquiry into this 'mighty maze' need not be 'without a plan'. The thread of guidance is provided, Ariadne-like, by the scheme of review adopted in the rest of this chapter. First there is a description of the old patchwork of local institutions on which the weight of the new industrial and social problems fell. The following section reviews the often shrill debate which arose in the course of initial local attempts to cope with the issues arising. Then there is an account of the increasing pressure for reform intended to make local institutions more able to deal efficiently and economically with the agenda in hand. But these changes, when completed, revealed in their turn intrinsic and

---

1 B. Webb, *Our Partnership* (London, 1948), pp. 149–50. Anyone exploring the subject must be deeply indebted to the Webbs' *English Local Government from the Revolution to the Municipal Corporations Act* (London, 1906–29): certainly I very frequently cite this work in the pages of this chapter, reference being to specific volume and page numbers. And a fuller indication of the whole may be appropriate on this first occasion: vol. i *The Parish and the County* (1906); vols ii–iii *The Manor and the Borough* (1908); vol. iv *Statutory Authorities for Special Purposes* (1922); vol. v *The Story of the King's Highway* (1913); vol. vi *English Prisons under Local Government* (1922); vol. vii *English Poor Law History (i) the Old Poor Law* (1927); vols viii–ix *English Poor Law History (ii) the Last Hundred Years* (1929). Two other volumes, originally published separately, were included in the series when it was reprinted in 1963 as vol. x *English Poor Law Policy* (1910) and vol. xi *The History of Liquor Licensing in England* (1903).
2 T. Madox, *Firma Burgi, or an Historical Essay concerning the Cities and Towns and Buroughs of England. Taken from Records* (London, 1726), sig. b[1] recto.
3 W. A. Ross, 'Local Government Board and After: Retrospect', *Public Administration*, xxxiv (1956), p. 23.

deep-seated deficiencies of a structural and financial kind and of which an increasing dependence on central government was a crucial mark. After discussion of these blemishes something is then said about the various attempts to improve matters which have been made in the period since the Second World War. The whole is thus a study in institutional adaptation, of the way in which local government bodies have been subject to the pressures of an increasingly complex society and have been continuously adapted so as to deal more effectively with the growing burden of responsibility placed on them. However one obvious limit to the account ought to be mentioned as a sort of confession. I refer (almost without exception) to the state of local affairs in England and Wales only. The position in Scotland and Northern Ireland diverges in sometimes fascinating ways but to deal with these differences would make the story even more complicated and lengthy than it is. However there is some general reference to these other places in the final section of this chapter which briefly reviews the experience and prospects of 'intermediate government', that is, institutions placed in the sphere between a local authority on the one hand and central government on the other.

THE OLD PATCHWORK

> Not chaos-like together crush'd and bruised,
> But, as the world harmoniously confused:
> Where order in variety we see,
> And where, though all things differ, all agree.
> A. POPE, 'Windsor Forest' (1713), ll. 13–16, in *Collected Poems*,
> Everyman, 1944, p.23

In their study of the unreformed local arrangements, the Webbs stress the absence of any system of local government properly so called and note that even the term did not come into common use until the middle of the last century.[4] None the less, whatever the diversity that prevailed from place to place, there was an implicit pattern in the sense that certain types of institution were to be found in all or most parts of the country. It is these bodies, to be described in this section, which constituted the old patchwork of local agencies and which had to cope as best they could with the problems created or exacerbated by a growing population and the rise of industry. Of course they were in due time substantially remoulded or replaced. Yet an interest in them is not merely antiquarian. For not only were they a crucial part of the story of developing collectivism in these islands, present arrangements themselves are very firmly rooted in those of the past: the shire county, established in 1974 as

---

[4] S. and B. Webb, *English Local Government from the Revolution to the Municipal Corporations Act* (London, 1906–29), iv. 353–5. Cf. B. Keith-Lucas, *The Unreformed Local Government System* (London, 1980), pp. 13, 154–5.

8   A Much Governed Nation

the main unit of local administration, has a continuous history going back more than a thousand years.

There were half-a-dozen types of institution involved.

First of all there were the justices of the peace in each county, a crucially important body of men. For to a great degree the conduct of civil affairs, in respect to what Maitland called 'police and social economy', rested on their shoulders: the magisterial system was truly the basis of government and administration throughout the country.[5] The justices were nominated on the advice of the lord-lieutenant though, as he always consulted leading members of the existing bench, appointment was in practice a matter of co-optation by the local squirearchy. Justices had to own freehold property in the county concerned, a requirement which in 1732 had been fixed in terms of land producing at least £100 a year. The reason for this rule was made quite explicit in the statute which said that 'the constituting Persons of mean Estates to be Justices of the Peace may be highly prejudicial to the Publick Welfare'. It was thus secured that the local government of the kingdom was government by country gentlemen, a category which in fact invariably included a good proportion of Anglican clergymen (because a clerical benefice was, in law, technically an estate in land).[6] In consequence, by the first decades of the nineteenth century, the county justices constituted a most exclusive class: they were principal landed proprietors within the county whose fathers and grandfathers had held their estates before them; there were no (or very few) persons of fortune from trade or manufacturing among their number; and they tended to be narrowly conventional in religion and political opinion, specifically they were Anglican and Tory (except, as the Webbs said, for those members of old Whig families of the governing class who could not decently be kept out).[7] In 1832 there were some 5,100 qualified justices in all though on average only about half of them played a regular part in the sessions (and it might be substantially fewer).[8]

Some idea of the range, complexity, and development of the magistrates' duties is given simply by turning the pages of their standard work of reference, Richard Burn's *The Justice of the Peace and Parish*

---

5   Maitland's phrase is from his *Justice and Police* (London, 1885), p. 80. Exactly what constituted a county, and so the extent of magisterial jurisdiction, was not easy to define: see S. and B. Webb, op. cit., i. 310–18 and Keith-Lucas, op. cit., pp. 40–2.
6   5 Geo. II, c. 18, Preamble; F. W. Maitland, *The Constitutional History of England* (1908; Cambridge, 1974), pp. 494–5; Keith-Lucas, op. cit., pp. 49–50. The county clergy had a very considerable role indeed in the local government of the day and in 1832 constituted a quarter of the entire magistracy: see S. and B. Webb, op. cit., i. 350–60, 384 n. 2, and Keith-Lucas, op. cit., pp. 151–2.
7   S. and B. Webb, op. cit., i. 382–6.
8   ibid., i. 581 n. 2; Keith-Lucas, op. cit., p. 49.

Officer which appeared in many editions after 1755.[9] And their responsibilities were necessarily augmented during and after the French Wars and in response to all the social and economic changes afoot. Thus they acted in respect to the prevention of crime and the treatment of criminals; drunkenness and the licensing of ale-houses; vagrancy, settlement, and the relief of destitution; the fixing of wages; the maintenance of roads, footpaths, and bridges; the assessment of local taxation; sanitary regulation; and even the permissible habits of life of whole sections of the community.[10] And there was always the catch-all responsibility for dealing with 'public nuisances', a concept capable of wide interpretation and application as Blackstone had shown in his *Commentaries*. All this, and more, was possible because the justices, in practically any detail of local administration, acted as a kind of legislature. They could convert their own opinions into 'mandatory enactments' by deciding particular cases and by virtue of being able to issue instructions to all the officers of townships and parishes within their jurisdiction.[11] And, of course, the quarter sessions had an unrestricted power to levy the county rate for all these purposes. It was only to be expected, therefore, that the justices should have become very closely involved in dealing with the problems of a nascent industrial society. In one way this was simply a continuation or extension of their existing functions, as with their long-standing duties relating to the Poor Law, the care of apprentices, or the regulation of relations between master and man. It was hardly surprising that suggestions for improvement or reform often looked to the extension of the justices' powers, for instance to secure better roads or to manage a system of proposed parochial schools. And it was to the justices, too, that Parliament entrusted the supervision of the statutory bodies being created to provide new services for the growing urban population. In a way the bench thus stood to other local authorities in the county as central government departments do today.[12]

While the ethos of county government was thus very much élitist, a degree of general participation was secured through the role of the grand jury. It was, for instance, involved in proceedings to determine whether, say, a parish had failed to repair its highways or maintain its bridges and whether money should be spent to remedy these deficiencies.[13] Equally

9 See also the documents cited in E. N. Williams, *The Eighteenth-Century Constitution 1688–1815: Documents and Commentary* (Cambridge, 1960), pp. 279–99. There is a detailed table showing the magistrates' concerns in two particular counties in Keith-Lucas, op. cit., p. 56.
10 S. and B. Webb, op. cit., i. 482, 534.
11 ibid., i. 539.
12 ibid., i. 554 and n. 1.
13 ibid., i. 446–56. Cf. the role of the hundred jury which seems, however, largely to have fallen into disuse by the early eighteenth century, ibid., i. 456–62.

county and town meetings survived, flourished even, as a mode of local political expression during the eighteenth and early nineteenth centuries. They were gatherings of all freeholders or ratepayers and so could be very large concourses of many thousands of people. Usually they were called by the high sheriff in the county and the mayor in a borough to discuss matters of either general or local moment. Thus such a meeting might consider a national issue like the level of taxation or Catholic emancipation, the abolition of slavery or Parliamentary reform; or a question of more restricted interest such as a proposal to establish a county scheme of social aid or to rebuild the gaol, to light the town streets with gas or how to prevent damage from riots. To give one particular instance: in October 1831 when cholera had broken out in Sunderland and the question arose of restricting the movement of both goods and persons, the Bishop of Durham called a county meeting to discuss the matter because of the outcry that had arisen about the epidemic.[14] The outcome of such an occasion was normally either a petition to Parliament or an instruction to the county or borough members, such addresses being widely canvassed and discussed. In their day these occasions were a traditional and constitutional means of expressing local opinion on a wide range of public affairs.[15]

There were some extra-parochial areas but the parish was the most numerous unit of local administration in both borough and county.[16] In the early nineteenth century there were no fewer that 15,635 parishes (or townships) as distinct centres of local government.[17] There were also considerable contrasts in their actual size and character. At one extreme the parish might embrace a large tract of empty moorland or have as its focus a handful of families in a rural hamlet; at the other end of the scale it could comprise a small but densely peopled area around a church in an ancient town or contain one of the closely packed urban slums created by

---

14 R. J. Morris, *Cholera 1832: the Social Response to an Epidemic* (London, 1976), p. 53. Cf. the vivid description of a county meeting in Kent in 1822 cited H. Jephson, *The Platform: its Rise and Progress* (1892; London, 1968), i. 571–5.

15 On these meetings, see S. and B. Webb, op. cit., i. 533 n. 3; Keith-Lucas, op. cit., pp. 20–1, 42–5; idem, 'County Meetings', *The Law Quarterly Review*, lxx (1954), pp. 109–14; also his *The English Local Government Franchise: a Short History* (Oxford, 1952), pp. 83–4; and J. H. Plumb, 'Political Man' in J. L. Clifford (ed.), *Man Versus Society in Eighteenth-Century Britain: Six Points of View* (Cambridge, 1968), pp. 13–14. In a good many parishes, the vestry meetings also often discussed general political issues: see S. and B. Webb, op. cit., i. 107–8.

16 I use here the simple term 'parish' but, in fact, there were many different types of parish: see M. D. Chalmers, *Local Government* (London, 1883), ch. III, and F. A. Youngs, Jr, *Guide to the Local Administrative Units of England* (London, 1979ff.), vol. i, pp. xiv–xv, xv–xvii. For a fascinating, if brief, picture of the parish, see the opening pages of Dickens' *Sketches by Boz* (1836).

17 First Annual Report of the Poor Law Commissioners, 1835, p. 6 cited S. and B. Webb, op. cit., i. 3 n. 1.

the new industry.[18] Most of them, however, were centred on a country village and, as late as 1831, nearly half had less than 300 inhabitants.[19] The parish was ruled by its vestry. Sometimes this body was 'open', access being allowed to all ratepaying householders. In a big town such a vestry could number several thousands and its proceedings be quite turbulent.[20] If so large, it would often appoint committees or boards to deal with major areas of concern especially if any salaried staff were employed. In some cases – in Liverpool for instance – an executive committee developed with a responsibility covering all parish affairs.[21] If not 'open' the vestry would be 'close' or 'select', that is, composed of a small, self-co-opting oligarchy of principal inhabitants (though a wider circle might be consulted on some issues).[22] Considerable hostility could arise between different political and sectarian groups in a vestry; or between a vestry and the justices where, say, the former was Radical and the latter Tory.

There was an array of duties which had to be undertaken by parishioners for the general good of the community. For example sixteenth-century legislation had imposed on them a responsibility for repairing roads in the parish, each inhabitant being obliged to spend six days a year on this work under the supervision of surveyors appointed by the churchwardens. The justices could 'present' to the sessions parishes that were remiss in this regard and force them to carry out the task more effectively. There was a range of parochial offices performance in which was technically the duty either of all parishioners or of those who paid the rates (and in some places at least women might hold certain of them as with the Widow Goe in Crabbe's poem.)[23] The chief posts were constable, churchwarden, overseer of the poor, and surveyor of the highways, the holders being personally responsible for the execution of the duties while in office. There might be other, salaried places as well, such as vestry clerk, beadle, or workhouse master.[24] Naturally the efficiency and honesty of the parish authorities varied considerably from place to place and time to time. A few achieved a high level of

---

18 ibid., i. 11; viii. 3.
19 First Annual Report of the Poor Law Commissioners, 1835, p. 9 cited S. and B. Webb, op. cit., i. 43 n. 1. Chalmers mentions the (apocryphal?) case of a parish where there was said to be only one ratepayer, op. cit., p. 34 n. 1.
20 See the examples given, S. and B. Webb, op. cit., i. 91–103.
21 ibid., i. 135–43.
22 See the examples cited ibid., i. 204–11.
23 G. Crabbe, 'The Parish Register' (1807), Part III, 'Burials', ll. 139ff., in *Poems*, ed. A. W. Ward (Cambridge, 1905), i. 202. The Webbs give examples of women holding parish office, op. cit., i. 17 and n. 4, 18 n. 1; but they were not always allowed to vote, ibid., i. 106–7.
24 For all these positions and their duties, see S. and B. Webb, op. cit., i. 15–35, 110–30, 163–6; and Keith-Lucas, *The Unreformed Local Government System*, pp. 83–90.

12 A Much Governed Nation

administration in terms of contemporary standards while others, perhaps most, were to some degree inefficient or even corrupt. A parish might obtain additional functions by private Act of Parliament so that in some places the range of parochial activity might be quite considerable. One case – which the Webbs believed to have been the best parochial government of its day – shows the range of responsibilities possible. At the end of the eighteenth century the select vestry in the wealthy London parish of St George's, Hanover Square, ran an infirmary; employed the poor; repaired highways; organized a salaried watch; paved, cleaned, and lit the streets; and dealt with sewage and the removal of night-soil.[25] For the purposes it undertook the parish might raise funds; and, in total, sums were involved that (given the public expenditure levels of the time) were very substantial. For instance from 1813 to 1815, at the end of the Napoleonic Wars, over £5 millions a year was spent, most of it on that primary parish responsibility, the maintenance of the poor; and twenty years later parochial expenditure came to nearly a fifth of the national budget.[26]

As the Webbs said, the county and the parish 'professedly covered all England and Wales'. But there were also other authorities – those of the borough and the manor – which 'stood out as islands of franchises, immunities or exceptions to the common rule and jurisdiction.'[27]

There was a diverse array of some 200 or so municipal boroughs whose status (where not dependent on prescription alone) was based on the grant of a charter by the Crown or, in some cases, a feudal lord.[28] Invariably there was a separate commission of the peace, drawn from members of the corporation, and which was one of a borough's most prized and potent features for it meant the right to conduct judicial, trading, and administrative affairs independently of the county justices, though the degree of autonomy entailed was not everywhere the same.[29] There was no requirement (as there was in the counties) that borough magistrates should own land of a certain value, but they were normally people of substance: Crabbe referred to 'our bench of wealthy, weighty men, Who rule our Borough, who enforce our laws'.[30] None the less during the early 1800s the quality of the borough magistracy showed signs of decline.[31] The burgesses or freemen who made up the

25 A. Aspinall and E. A. Smith (eds), *English Historical Documents 1783–1832* (London, 1959), p. 410; S. and B. Webb, op. cit., i. 239–41; iv. 377–8, 380–1.
26 Aspinall and Smith, op. cit., pp. 403, 411; S. and B. Webb, op. cit., i. 4. But cf. the useful and cautionary discussion in Keith-Lucas, op. cit., pp. 144–6.
27 S. and B. Webb, op. cit., iv. 1.
28 For the diversity of origin and character involved, see ibid., vol. ii, ch. VI esp. pp. 261–7.
29 ibid., ii. 278–9, 381–2.
30 G. Crabbe, 'The Borough' (1810), letter XVIII, ll. 34–5, in *Poems* (edn cit.), i. 450.
31 S. and B. Webb, op. cit., iii. 697–8, 719–20.

corporation were, then, a small, self-selecting oligarchy, usually professional men or major traders and craftsmen. In Swansea in 1831 (to take an example conveniently to hand) there were only 104 burgesses in a total population of over 13,000.[32] And the privilege of belonging to a corporation was seen as a kind of property which could be acquired by gift, marriage, or inheritance. These guild-like associations were clearly not intended to be representative of the town's inhabitants as a whole.[33] They were also invariably exclusive in political and religious terms. With only a few exceptions they were largely dominated by Tories and Anglicans who could and did use their funds and patronage (for example, the power to create freemen, that is, voters) in order to discriminate against other allegiances and, in particular, to control the election of borough MPs, the point which led ultimately to reform.[34]

The range of corporate functions varied. In theory it could be quite wide and what might be achieved by enlightened town government is shown by the case of eighteenth-century Hull where the corporation and the Town's Husband exercised a notable number of functions relating to such things as: building control; street paving, lighting, and scavenging; refuse disposal; sewerage; water supply; a fire service; police; poor relief; and more.[35] But usually the range of activities was more narrowly confined than this, of which state of affairs Swansea is again a convenient instance. Though there were occasions when the corporation there bestirred itself to attempt more, at the beginning of the last century its only executive functions were to regulate market facilities and to administer justice; beyond this the town relied on other bodies such as the Paving Commissioners established in 1809.[36] In practice a corporation's office, apart from providing a local magistracy (and so supervising the town vestries), was simply to administer communal property and charitable funds.[37] The position was one which could be turned to advantage: the wealth available could be put to privileged use; exclusive trading rights were enforced; tolls garnered (and exemption from them

---

32 G. Roberts, *The Municipal Development of the Borough of Swansea to 1900* (n.p. [Swansea], 1940), p. 17.
33 S. and B. Webb, op. cit., iv. 365–9; Aspinall and Smith, op. cit., pp. 403, 407–9; Keith-Lucas, op. cit., pp. 16–19, 25–7.
34 S. and B. Webb, op. cit., iii. 489–91, 699–705. Cf. F. W. Maitland, *Township and Borough* (Cambridge, 1898), p. 95.
35 G. Jackson, *Hull in the Eighteenth Century: a Study in Economic and Social History* (London, 1972), ch. XII. For a couple of similar cases, Wisbech and Liverpool, see S. and B. Webb, op. cit., ii. 138–48 and iii. 482–5.
36 T. Ridd, *The Development of Municipal Government in Swansea in the Nineteenth Century* (MA thesis, University College, Swansea, 1955), pp. 28, 35–40. On the variable range of corporate functions, see also E. N. Williams, *The Eighteenth-Century Constitution*, pp. 304–8; S. and B. Webb, op. cit., ii. 388–90, 393–4, 403.
37 S. and B. Webb, op. cit., ii. 394.

claimed); patronage exercised; and the like. It was this kind of financial advantage that lay behind Cobbett's pejorative reference to the 'snug' corporations and which led to widespread resentment of their privileges.[38] Clearly these municipal corporations are not to be thought of as if they were like a modern town council. They were in many respects private rather than public institutions. In any case they did not exist in all towns, only those which had a charter. This meant that many large urban areas such as Manchester had no corporation and depended on other bodies for the provision of such services as there were.

I do not know what Lewis Carroll had in mind when he wrote in *The Hunting of the Snark*, 'Let me tell you, my friends, the whole question depends On an ancient manorial right': but in some places local government certainly did. For, particularly in the townships of the north (though by no means only there), some at least of the functions performed elsewhere by the parish were carried out by manorial courts. These were either a court leet or a court-baron with a jurisdiction which covered a quite different geographical area from that of the parish.[39] The role in local affairs of the lord of the manor's steward, as aided by a jury, although generally declining, might still be considerable. This was the case, for instance, with the courts leet at Swansea and Manchester.[40] All the men of the village or township usually attended.[41] Like the parish these feudal survivals retained a number of unpaid offices and, through the judicial procedures involved, a wide array of functions could be undertaken, in particular concerning the suppression of nuisances, and ranging from regulating the use of common land, providing and clearing drains, and scavenging the streets, to supervising the quality of produce offered for sale in the markets and ensuring the abatement of smoke from factory chimneys as well as providing for the watch.[42] If reference to a celebrated instance from an early period may be permitted, it will be recalled that Shakespeare's father appears ingloriously in the rolls of the Stratford-upon-Avon court leet (in which he later held office) as having been fined for depositing refuse in the street in violation of the manorial by-laws.[43] And as late as 1843 an official report stated that the court leet at

38 W. Cobbett, *Rural Rides* (1830–2; Everyman, 1966–7), i. 99, 118.
39 In practice the Lord's court was often 'undifferentiated', see S. and B. Webb, op. cit., ii. 31–2.
40 G. Roberts, op. cit., pp. 5–6; Ridd, op. cit., pp. 13–14. The Webbs describe the Manchester court as 'an active local governing authority for a vast population ... right down to 1846', op. cit., ii. 99–113; and for their view of Swansea, ibid., ii. 239–40.
41 S. and B. Webb, op. cit., ii. 66, 101.
42 For a detailed account of manorial court business, much of it relating to agricultural management, see ibid., ii. 74–126.
43 S. Schoenbaum, *William Shakespeare: a Documentary Life* (Oxford, 1975), p. 14 and fac. 11. In Williams, op. cit., pp. 300–3, examples are given of the proceedings of a court-baron (in 1764) and of a court leet (in 1734 and 1805).

Ashton-under-Lyne was especially effective in dealing with sanitary matters such as 'dangerous tenements, defective sewerage, and filthy necessaries' and thus was able 'in no small degree to correct abuses and to punish...careless or avaricious landlords'.[44] Despite often considerable criticism, a manorial court might thus retain a notable local role and an important range of responsibilities during the first decades of the last century; moreover the influence of the lord of the manor on other local authorities could otherwise be considerable.[45] So far as such a court remained an effective local government unit, it continued (like the parish) to reflect, albeit incompletely, the old principle that the inhabitants themselves were to some degree involved in the conduct of affairs and obliged to give personal service.[46]

Finally there was a miscellany of bodies set up by local Act of Parliament to undertake particular duties which were, for one reason or another, being neglected by the array of institutions already described.[47] The Webbs estimated that there were something like 1,800 such special authorities and that in local government terms they were very significant indeed.[48] The range of tasks they undertook is easily indicated. Some of them were concerned with the care of paupers. There were in the early nineteenth century about 125 bodies of incorporated guardians set up in unions of parishes brought together for this purpose.[49] There were also up to a hundred old-established sewer commissions which dealt with the draining and protection of fens, marshes, and land liable to be flooded; and in days gone by these comprised very considerable areas indeed.[50] In some places there might, too, be bodies of trustees appointed under a Harbour Act or similar legislation to see to port facilities. Occasionally, as at Whitehaven, these harbour authorities might have wider responsibilities relating to the improvement of the town itself.[51] Also to be numbered among these *ad hoc* agencies were the 11,000 or more turnpike trusts. These mainly appeared after 1700 (when wheeled traffic

---

44 State of Large Towns and Populous Districts, R. Com. 1st Rep., 1844 (vol. xvii), Appendix p. 71. Cf. S. and B. Webb, op. cit., ii. 113–15 n. 1 where it is stated that this court was still active and effective as late as 1907. A few courts leet remain even today: see Keith-Lucas, op. cit., p. 30.

45 J. E. Williams, 'Paternalism in Local Government in the Nineteenth Century', *Public Administration*, xxxiii (1955), pp. 439–46. Cf. H. J. Perkin, 'The Development of Modern Glossop', in A. H. Birch, *Small-Town Politics: a Study of Political Life in Glossop* (1959; Oxford, 1967), pp. 16–18, 23.

46 Cf. S. and B. Webb, op. cit., ii. 124–6.

47 For examples of such statutes, see E. N. Williams, *The Eighteenth-Century Constitution*, pp. 314–22.

48 S. and B. Webb, op. cit., iv. 2, 9.

49 ibid., vol. iv, ch. II; vol. vii, ch. III.

50 ibid., vol. iv, ch. I. In London the various sewer commissions had also come to acquire functions relating to the disposal of sewage in the modern sense, ibid., iv. 105.

51 ibid., iv. 241; J. E. Williams, art. cit., pp. 440–2.

16 A Much Governed Nation

in particular began to increase) to provide on given sections of the highway a better road than the county and parochial system could ensure unaided. The payment of a toll was justified on the principle that travellers using the road should meet the cost of its repair and maintenance. By the mid-eighteenth century many of the main London routes were almost completely turnpiked; and by the late 1830s over 22,000 miles of road were thus serviced, that is, most of the main arteries of the kingdom and comprising a fifth of the total mileage. Moreover it is undoubtedly the case that without the trusts (and despite their many deficiencies) the highways would not have been improved sufficiently so as to handle the traffic necessary to the first stages of industrialization.[52]

However the most important group of special bodies of concern here was the 300 or so improvement commissions set up in particular places after 1748 when the first of them was authorized. In fact the specific name given to these bodies varied: improvement commission is a common generic term but they might equally be called paving, street, lamp, lighting, watching, police, or cleansing commissions.[53] As some of these titles indicate, the purpose of such bodies was, initially at least, a limited one, being perhaps simply to improve the streets of a town (or part of it) where conditions of growing population and passage seemed to require this, and to provide better protection therein.[54] But it was not unusual for a commission's responsibilities later to be widened: for instance the Birmingham Street Commission founded in 1769 had its powers extended by five further improvement Acts in the period up to 1828.[55] Some of these bodies assumed wider duties in respect of public health and protection as by laying on a water supply or providing fire engines. And in Manchester (as early as 1817) a gas works was built and run as a trading venture under such auspices. The Rochdale Improvement Commission was established as late as 1853 by private Act and had powers relating to such matters as road improvement, street widening, gas supply, and sanitation.[56] On the whole, however, these commissions

52 W. Albert, *The Turnpike Road System in England 1663–1840* (Cambridge, 1972), p. 56; S. and B. Webb, op. cit., iv. 205–6 and n. On the turnpikes, see as well ibid., vol. v, ch. VII; and the summary in Keith-Lucas, op. cit., pp. 121–30.
53 All these bodies are discussed in S. and B. Webb, op. cit., vol. iv, ch. IV.
54 ibid., iv. 273–5. Cf. ibid., iv. 309 on the process of development involved in street improvement. Keith-Lucas gives a detailed account of one commission established at Honiton in 1790, *The Unreformed Local Government System*, pp. 111–13.
55 D. Fraser, *Power and Authority in the Victorian City* (Oxford, 1979), p. 81. See also, S. and B. Webb, op. cit., iv. 252–6; and B. Keith-Lucas, 'Some Influences Affecting the Development of Sanitary Legislation in England', *Economic History Review*, 2s., vi (1953–4), pp. 293–5.
56 Parts of the Act (16 & 17 Vic., c. 210) are cited in E. J. Evans (ed.), *Social Policy 1830–1914: Individualism, Collectivism and the Origins of the Welfare State* (London, 1978), pp. 81–2.

were confined to a limited range of functions; and they could often be inefficient.[57] Nevertheless in some places – Birmingham and Manchester for example – they became the principal governing authority.[58] And their ultimate impact was considerable: they dealt with matters of daily life of importance to every household; they often set going public services of a new kind; and they levied a rate for such purposes. Their establishment was, in the opinion of the Webbs, 'the starting-point of the great modern development of town government.'[59] And it was their being merged later on with the borough councils created in 1835 that ultimately made these latter bodies the mainstay of urban affairs.[60]

In fact the relationship of the special purpose agencies to the other local authorities varied. Sometimes there was a more or less complete degree of overlap and common membership as when the additional powers were given to an institution, like a vestry or corporation, that already existed. But the improvement tasks could also involve the creation of a new administrative body quite separate in respect of both personnel and organization. Where thus distinct, membership of the new agencies might comprise either all those who contributed a certain subscription towards the cost involved or simply those who met a given property qualification or who were nominated by the lord of the manor; or (in a borough) there might be *ex-officio* membership for the mayor and aldermen of the corporation; and occasionally there was an element of election. In fact an improvement commission might be quite large and number many hundreds or even thousands; but in practice, appointment often being for life, it was usually a self-selected and self-renewing 'little clique of "principal inhabitants"', a sort of general meeting of interested local property-owners.[61] This helps explain why an improvement commission might only have been granted a limited jurisdiction or restricted rating powers.

At the beginning of the nineteenth century, then, there was a complex and varying array of local authorities, some of them feudal and medieval survivals, others recently established. They might have a common membership, at least in part, and often had shared responsibilities, though there was usually a substantial confusion of boundaries, rates, and powers, and often controversy and conflict. None the less between them they might undertake a not inconsiderable range of functions, tasks

57 On their restricted scope, see S. and B. Webb, op. cit., iv. 314–15, 343–4. And for an example of ineffectiveness, Ridd, op. cit., pp. 63–5.
58 S. and B. Webb, op. cit., iv. 252, 256–7, 273.
59 ibid., iv. 235–6.
60 ibid., iv. 347. When they were finally wound up in 1894, thirty-one improvement Act districts were still in existence: see 10 H.C. Deb. 4s., 21 March 1893, col. 681 (H. H. Fowler).
61 S. and B. Webb, op. cit., iv. 245.

that (for all the limits of purpose and administration involved) constituted a significant context of local action and which was well established even before the full demands of the Great Change were felt. Of course the nature and efficiency of the services rendered varied considerably from one place to another. And it is essential to realize that such basic provision was rarely seen as a matter of general local government responsibility as such but was rather regarded as activity affecting a restricted area or group of people. The questions faced were for instance: how to get these particular streets paved, lit, and cleansed; how to arrange for an adequate watch in a certain square or estate; how better to deal with the paupers or the sick in a given parish; how to repair that bridge; and always, of course, how to pay for these things (and who should pay). In a spirit of local voluntaryism, a group of citizens did not expect a general Act of Parliament to cope with such issues but, where necessary, applied for authority to deal with them themselves through the process of private legislation. Thus the powers of a parish vestry were increased or a body of commissioners created for a specific purpose. It was in this individualistic way, so admired and idealized by Toulmin Smith, that communities sought to cope with changing economic and social circumstances. Inevitably there was a wide variation of authority and achievement. Yet in assessing what was done it is merely foolish to judge by reference to some anachronistic latter-day standard which will inevitably lead to detraction. Given the expectations of the time the old patchwork of organizations was often good enough when the scale of things or problems was small, when each householder knew his neighbour, and so long as the simple needs of each locality could be satisfied by the traditional system of personal service given gratuitously and in rotation. But this sort of arrangement inevitably became more and more inadequate as needs increased.[62] Even so, relatively few people thought of general legislation as a solution, not only because this was not the usual way to tackle the matters in hand but also because no one could have forseen the scale and nature of the quite unprecedented development of industrial urbanization under way.

It was inevitable, then, that localities or groups of individuals should have tried to cope as they did, in a piecemeal fashion, adapting the old machinery and augmenting its powers as seemed appropriate. So,

> as the old towns increased in size, and villages grew rapidly into urban centres of industry, each town applied, if and when it thought fit, for an Act which allowed it to light, watch, pave, cleanse, and prevent nuisances in its streets, establish, enlarge or transfer its market, or perform for itself some of these or some other functions which the

---

62 Cf. ibid., i. 61–3; iv. 360–5, 398ff.

inhabitants, or often only an influential minority of them judged to be desirable.[63]

However the process of change was prolonged and diverse; and in the end (as will be seen) it led to a substantial reorganization of local authorities. It was also accompanied by a notable controversy about the nature and office of local government and which merits separate attention here not least because it exemplifies, in its own way and context, the contrast between libertarian and collectivist points of view.

A CONFLICT OF ATTITUDES

> Now, if the question of State-structure is in process of gradual solution by the friction of diametrically opposed theories, may it not be admissible that the question of State function should be solved in like manner?
> W. DONISTHORPE, *Liberty or Law?*, 1885, p. 5

The old patchwork of authorities failed to cope with the burgeoning problems of the day or otherwise became the object of criticism. Consequently during the nineteenth century, as the tasks assumed by or imposed on local government increased in scope, complexity, and cost, its structure and functions were revised from time to time to make it a more appropriate means of administration and control. The process was not an easy one and took a long time to complete. And about it there arose an often confused and invariably bitter debate about the proper nature and purpose of the various local bodies then existing or in prospect. Three main attitudes were struck in the course of this dispute. There were those who on principle or on grounds of the expense involved opposed most of the proposals to extend local responsibilities; those who believed that local bodies were corrupt or inefficient and that, in consequence, important duties should be transferred to some centralized system of administration; and those who rejected both these standpoints and stressed the capacity of local self-government itself to secure any necessary improvements. The first posture is one hostile to any extension of public functions; the other two both look favourably on a growing array of such responsibilities though they differ as to the public agencies appropriate to their exercise.

Opponents

It is customary nowadays to believe – or at least to say – that an effective and convenient system of local government is highly desirable, one that is

---

63 F. H. Spencer, *Municipal Origins...* (London, 1911), p. 315. This work stresses the crucial role of private Bill legislation in local attempts to cope with the contemporary

active in its own right and not merely as the agency of a centralized administration. Yet this is not a presumption which has always been accepted as undeniable and there were in the past those who opposed most vehemently the extension of local powers and responsibilities. The ground for objection might be one of principle, rest on criticism of a specific proposal, or simply reflect a desire to keep local expenditure as low as possible to avoid paying higher rates.

The major political theorists of the eighteenth century gave relatively little attention to questions concerning 'inferior' or 'subordinate' government though this is hardly surprising given their preoccupation, obsession even, with the avoidance of arbitrary power at the centre and the protection of property from its depredations. And their very silence has a certain significance. The local bodies of the day were largely dominated by men of means and status who easily fell, for instance, into the class of rational and industrious individuals approved by Locke or into the group described by Burke as men of 'light and leading', the natural superiors of civil society.[64] The counties, corporations, and parishes such persons dominated had functions administered (and usually acquired in the first place) through private initiative; which were largely serviced by voluntary and unpaid labour; and which, poor relief apart, entailed (by later standards) relatively little cost. In comparison with, say, the threat posed by the pretensions of the Crown or the existence of a standing army, there was little here to worry those who had at heart the interests of the ancient constitution and the traditional rights of the propertied individual. None the less certain aspects of 'public police and economy' did come to cause a great deal of concern.

The most prominent and troublesome of these questions was dealing with paupers. In fact this was the major task assumed by local agencies and the one which involved the most onerous financial burden. Consequently the responsibility never lacked critics. They argued that destitution was the result of God's will or was part of the natural order of things. To try to mitigate or eliminate it was, therefore, either impious or an attempt on the impossible. It was also excessively costly and as well entailed undesirable moral and practical consequences. For poverty was a spur to improvement, and public charity only encouraged idleness. When at the Board of Trade Locke had recommended the most severe treatment of the undeserving pauper and this was a view widely held for a long time afterwards.[65] One reverend commentator, writing nearly a

---

changes; see especially the superb summary in ch. VIII on which I have drawn here. Cf. p. 23 below.

64 Locke, *Of Civil Government*, §34; Burke, *The Works* (World's Classics, London, 1906–7), iv. 111.

65 J. Locke, 'Report of the Board of Trade ... Respecting the Relief and Employment of

hundred years later, urged that the labouring poor would only acquire habits of frugality and diligence under the spur of hunger. Consequently it would be best if 'the whole system of compulsory charity were abolished'.[66] In 1806 the Benthamite, Patrick Colquhoun, similarly described pauperism as 'a most necessary and indispensable ingredient in society', essential to the achievement of civilization: 'It is the lot of man – it is the source of *wealth*, since without poverty there would be no labour'.[67] Even after the Great War with France, when major social problems had begun to declare themselves (in the growth of unemployment, for example) there were still those who demanded that an end be made to public provision for the poor. Thus the Rev. Thomas Chalmers, a Scottish evangelical preacher and theologian, urged in 1818 that the Poor Laws were incompatible with the sanctity of property and were

> the result of a very bungling attempt, on the part of the Legislature, to do that which would have been better done had Nature been left to her own free processes, and man to the unconstrained influence of such principles as Nature and Christianity have bestowed upon him. We affirm, that the great and urgent law of self-preservation ought not to have been so tampered with....

Relief of destitution ought, therefore, to have been left to the family and voluntary charity.[68] Similarly Thomas Walker (who had been involved in local affairs at Manchester and was subsequently a London magistrate) suggested that the labouring class did not gain by parochial relief. In accordance with the economic theory of the day, he held that such payments were simply made from sums that would otherwise have gone in wages. The Poor Law was indeed 'a MORAL PESTILENCE' which made the able-bodied pauper's existence 'a lie':

> he lives by appearing not to be able to live; he will throw himself out of work, aggravate disease, get into debt, live in wretchedness, persevere in the most irksome applications, nay bring upon himself the incumbrance of a family, for no other purpose than to get his share from the parish.[69]

---

the Poor' (1697) in, *An Account of the Origin, Proceedings, and Intentions of the Society for the Promotion of Industry* ... (3rd edn, Louth, n.d. [1789]), esp. pp. 102–9.
66 [J. Townsend], *A Dissertation on the Poor Laws* (London, 1786), p. 87.
67 P. Colquhoun, *A Treatise on Indigence* ... (London, 1806), pp. 7–8.
68 [T. Chalmers], 'Causes and Cure of Pauperism', *The Edinburgh Review or Critical Journal*, xxix (1818), p. 270.
69 T. Walker, *Observations on the Nature, Extent, and Effects of Pauperism; and on the Means of Reducing It* (London, 1826), pp. 13, 18–19 (capitals in original). I first found

22 A Much Governed Nation

Of course, Malthus's theory of population confirmed these moral and social views out of the principles of demography: relief of poverty (whether by compulsory levy or philanthropy) will have at most a temporary or merely individual effect for, by aiding the subsistence of the poor at large, it will simply stimulate an increase in their numbers and so diminish their condition. Consequently the complete, if very gradual, abolition of the Poor Laws, coupled with a formal disclaimer that the pauper has any right to support, was the only logical policy to recommend.[70] The promotion of the health of towns by compulsory legislation – another major local concern – was equally subject to attack. Of the Act of 1848 *The Economist* said it was simply a 'pretext for interfering with all the pursuits and occupations' of their inhabitants. It was an attempt 'to regulate ... every business in every town' throughout the country, as reprehensible as the supervision of factory conditions and just as much to be deplored.[71]

Herbert Spencer was equally forthright and did a great deal to give this point of view a profound intellectual, and intendedly scientific, basis.[72] On the foundation provided by his system of 'Synthetic Philosophy', he broadened the attack on official intermeddling and was very firm indeed about the limits of 'state-duty' whether at central or local level and about the right to personal freedom from the claims of public authority. Thus in *The Proper Sphere of Government*, as in the later *Social Statics*, he is scathing about the Poor Laws and argues the inexpediency and impropriety alike of demanding contributions from citizens for the mitigation of distress or of imposing any scheme of compulsory charity. Nor may a state agency administer education.[73] And, while nuisances may be suppressed, there is no right to go beyond this to impose an entire sanitary régime save what is achieved by the voluntary effort of those directly concerned.[74] The conclusion in this respect is, if unpalatable to many, quite clear: 'Be it by general government or by local government, the levying of compulsory rates for drainage, and for paving and lighting, is inadmissible'. These are essentially affairs to be dealt with by

---

this and the immediately preceding references in S. and B. Webb, *English Local Government from the Revolution to the Municipal Corporations Act* (London, 1906–29), viii. 9–14.
70 T. R. Malthus, *An Essay on the Principle of Population* (1798; Everyman, 1967), ii. 48–51, 64–5, 200–9.
71 *The Economist*, vi (20 May 1848), pp. 565–6.
72 See *The Ideological Heritage* (London, 1983), pp. 48–82 for an account of Spencer's doctrine.
73 H. Spencer, *The Proper Sphere of Government* (London, 1843), letters II–III, VII; idem, *Social Statics...* (1851; Farnborough, Hants., 1970), chs xxv–xxvi.
74 Spencer, *Social Statics*, ch. xxviii esp. pp. 382–6.

commercial undertakings and so must rest with private initiative.[75] Nor did Spencer's views moderate much with the years: while he came to accept that there were some things local government must do, he continued to be sharply critical of the way it undertook tasks which, in his view, it should not, especially as the heavier burden of local taxation involved meant a greater restriction on the freedom of the individual to do as he will with his own.[76] Not uncharacteristically he wrote a paper on 'County Council Tyranny' for the Ratepayers' Defence League.[77] And, of course, from his early days he was always hostile to the aristocracy and landed classes who then dominated so many local institutions.

Spencer's followers were also radically critical of the extension of local responsibilities. Wordsworth Donisthorpe, for instance, said he feared the growth of officialism more at local than at central level: 'Local despotism is the worst despotism.'[78] Bodies such as the Liberty and Property Defence League, the Personal Rights Association, and the many ratepayers' defence organizations were very active in this cause. Their members were concerned about the establishment of municipal utilities, about slum-clearance developments, the provision of working-class housing, free libraries, about educational extravagance, and so forth.[79] And they took particular objection to the process of private Bill legislation by which local, and especially urban, authorities secured much enlarged powers to make so-called improvements by controlling the activities of citizens in 'every conceivable department of life.'[80] Thomas Mackay, an ardent Spencerian and a major figure in the libertarian cause, argued that local authorities, as monopolies, were simply less effective in the provision of services than would be 'a free state of enterprise'. 'They ... form a huge obstruction to beneficent

---

75 ibid., pp. 393–4. Cf. D. Duncan, *The Life and Letters of Herbert Spencer* (London, 1908), p. 468.
76 Spencer, *The Man Versus the State* (1884; Penguin, 1969), p. 59. See also on the Poor Laws, 'The Coming Slavery', ibid., pp. 83–8; and on the reformed municipal corporations, 'Representative Government – What Is It Good For?', ibid., pp. 238–41, 250–1. Also his 'Sanitation in Theory and Practice', in *Facts and Comments* (London, 1902), p. 157.
77 Duncan, op. cit., p. 313.
78 W. Donisthorpe, *Liberty or Law?* (London, 1885), pp. 60–1. Cf. idem, *Empire and Liberty: a Lecture on the Principles of Local Government* (London, 1886) esp. pp. 58ff. on the importance of securing the freedom of the individual from local trammels.
79 e.g. Lord Bramwell, *Laissez Faire* (London, 1884), pp. 20–1; W. C. Crofts, *Municipal Socialism* (London, 1885), pp. 35–44; T. Mackay (ed.), *A Plea for Liberty* (1891; 2nd edn, London, 1891), chs VII, X–XI; E. S. Robertson, *The State and the Slums* (3rd edn, London, 1884), p. 3.
80 Crofts, op. cit., pp. 3–27, 30–3, 56. On the process referred to, see the Earl of Onslow, '*The* Rise *and* Development *of* Local Legislation *by* Private Bill', *Journal of the Royal Statistical Society*, lxix (1906), pp. 1–31; also above pp. 18–19 and n. 63.

applications of capital to the service of mankind.'[81] Another publicist with similar views summarized the matter by saying that 'Local government is as good and necessary as imperial government, when there is not too much of it'; and municipal socialism is as harmful as state socialism, 'just as harassing to the individual and as hurtful to the common interests of the district.' He goes on to state in effect the gravamen of the charge against this tendency as it was revealed in the later part of the century:

> Since the Act of 1888 the scope of local government has been greatly widened. Old municipalities and new county councils find themselves clothed with ampler powers than their predecessors. On to their shoulders the State has shuffled many of its own responsibilities. At the same time, local bodies have taken over from the central government a corresponding share of it privileges. For many years previously these had been abused by the greater government, and personal liberty and property had suffered. With this precedent before them it was not likely that the lesser governments would restrict themselves in the use of their newly-acquired rights. It was more probable that the force of example would lead them into attempting to outdo the State, by means of their local institutions and officials, in the work of regulating and guiding the individual.[82]

In the end, however, this 'craze' for social reform and the official aggrandizement to which it leads will result in the councils and boards becoming a rival to the Great State itself which will then swallow them up; 'and the place of local self-government will know it no more.'[83] Dicey was also associated with the anti-collectivist organizations mentioned and clearly recognized the extent to which the growth in the powers of English government (which he deplored) was the result of the enlarged scope of local bodies.[84]

The extension of local functions was also fought by those who, in particular localities, objected specifically to the cost involved in, say, a proposal to widen a street, increase the police force, or improve the water supply. Writing in the early 1880s Sir Mackenzie Chalmers said that few people realized the extent of the sums spent each year by local authorities and 'the alarming rate' at which local expenditure and indebtedness were

---

81 T. Mackay, 'Investment', in Mackay (ed.), op. cit., p. 242.
82 F. Millar (ed.), *Socialism: its Fallacies and Dangers* (1906; 3rd edn, London, 1907), p. 70.
83 ibid., pp. 70–4.
84 A. V. Dicey, *Introduction to the Study of the Law of the Constitution* (1885; 10th edn rev., London, 1964), p. 389; idem, *Lectures on the Relation between Law & Public Opinion in England during the Nineteenth Century* (1905; 2nd edn, London, 1920), pp. 279, 284–8, 291–4.

increasing. Any ratepayer who did grasp the situation, he went on, probably regards it 'with feelings akin to those with which Frankenstein beheld the pranks of the monster of his own creation' and feels, too, there is little he can do about it.[85] By that time the thing had gone a long way and would indeed have been difficult to halt or reverse. But a rearguard action, unsuccessful in the outcome as it was, had been fought in different places by men who either objected to increased rates as such or felt that the expenditure proposed was too lavish, wasteful, or did not reflect the right priorities of policy. These people were often tradesmen and small manufacturers of whom it was – perhaps unfairly – said that 'in their private businesses they were not accustomed to deal with big transactions and high figures, so that spending large sums of money, if proposed, filled the brewer, the baker, and the candlestick maker with alarm.'[86] And, of course, frequent elections meant that heed had to be paid to their more or less constant cry for economy.[87] Chadwick was one who pilloried these critics mercilessly as did Dickens, Kingsley, and other literary supporters of 'improvement'.[88]

Sometimes it was urged that a task intended for a local authority was simply unnecessary. For example, one point made by opponents of the Bradford Improvement Bill in 1850 was that a grant of power to deal with river pollution was not needed: all that was required was that one alderman (who was supporting the Bill) should prevent his own factory from emptying its privies into the river.[89] Similarly it was often suggested that a proposed function should be left to the private initiative of those particularly involved: so fire-engines should not be maintained by the public but by those who felt it desirable to insure themselves against the risk concerned.[90] Again a distinction was often made between basic services, for which a local authority might properly accept responsibility (such as efficient sewage disposal or police), and others which were regarded as inappropriate. Thus at Liverpool in 1875 it was urged that it was not the task of a corporation 'to build labourers' dwellings.'[91] It was

85 M. D. Chalmers, *Local Government* (London, 1883), pp. 25–6.
86 T. Anderton, *A Tale of One City* (Birmingham, 1900), p. 6 cited E. P. Hennock, *Fit and Proper Persons: Ideal and Reality in Nineteenth-Century Urban Government* (London, 1973), p. 61. Cf. D. Fraser, *Power and Authority in the Victorian City* (Oxford, 1979), pp. 96, 159. On two different sorts of 'economist', see ibid., pp. 127–8.
87 Cf. Fraser, op.cit., pp. 69–70.
88 See the passages cited by S. E. Finer, *The Life and Times of Sir Edwin Chadwick* (1952; London, 1970), pp. 434–5.
89 A. Elliott, 'Municipal Government in Bradford in the Mid-Nineteenth Century', in D. Fraser (ed.), *Municipal Reform and the Industrial City* (Leicester, 1982), p. 118.
90 S. and B. Webb, op. cit., iv. 267 n. 1.
91 J. Rayner, *Sanitary and Social Improvement* (Liverpool, 1875), p. 8 cited Fraser, *Power and Authority in the Victorian City*, p. 48. Cf. the objections raised at Leeds in

widely believed, too, that where a service could be expected to produce a profit, running a gas or water works for instance, it should be left to private enterprise, the proper tasks of a local council being those in respect to which no such return could be expected.[92] And where a trading service was operated by a council there was often a bitter quarrel over the way it should be run. In the 1820s a prolonged battle was fought at Manchester over the price of the gas produced by the Police Commissioners. One group wanted it high enough to create a surplus to be used for further improvement; another, largely composed of Radicals and shopkeepers, wished the price to be kept as low as possible or, indeed, that the municipal works should be sold to the highest bidder.[93]

Above all it was the sheer cost of the extending local functions which was challenged especially if expensive capital projects (and so more municipal indebtedness) were involved. Objection was thus taken to many proposed changes, from the appointment of a medical officer of health to the compulsory purchase of houses for redevelopment, from building main sewers to an increase of official salaries. For many people so-called improvement was simply robbery, taking hard-earned money away from the ratepayers to provide services for others and, by enlarging the public debt, placing a greater burden on the future. For example, at Swansea at the mid-century the Public Health Act was adopted and the powers of the Paving Commissioners were extended (and amalgamated with those of the town council): but the ratepayers were simply not prepared to shoulder the increased charges in prospect. Even the threat of a cholera epidemic in 1853–4 was insufficient to overcome resistance to expenditure that would only (it was reckoned) be wasted given the level of incompetence and extravagance that had been usual.[94] Leeds provides another instance of the same sort.[95] It had a particularly large electorate with a higher than usual proportion of poorer voters with the result that local opinion was particularly sensitive to increases in spending and so in local taxation. There was resistance in the early 1840s on grounds of cost to carrying out new duties under a recently acquired Improvement Act. It was a Radical group, including Chartists (many of whom were small tradesmen), which attacked 'oppressiveness' and 'extravagance' in local

---

1851, and much later too, as described by B. Barber, 'Municipal Government in Leeds, 1835–1914', in D. Fraser (ed.), *Municipal Reform and the Industrial City*, pp. 98, 102.

92 See the passage from the *Leeds Mercury* (16 August 1851) cited B. Barber, loc. cit., p. 86; A. Elliott, loc. cit., pp. 122–3; Hennock, op. cit., p. 223.

93 S. and B. Webb, op. cit., iv. 266–7 and n. 1, 270.

94 T. Ridd, *The Development of Municipal Government in Swansea in the Nineteenth Century* (MA thesis, University College, Swansea, 1955), pp. 171–3, 193–4, 209 n. 37, 213, 217–219, 279 n. 3.

95 For what follows, see Barber, loc. cit., p. 105 and Hennock, op. cit., pp. 196–7, 209–10.

government and wanted to secure reductions in all departments of expenditure. Objections of this sort were not sustained in every case: a scheme of sanitary improvement was finally agreed because it seemed there was likely to be more economy in meeting its cost than in tolerating sickness. But as rates continued to rise – and they increased by over 40 per cent in the ten years after 1857 – opposition revived. In 1868 the Leeds Municipal Reform Association was founded largely to secure a reduction of expenditure and greater 'purity' in local administration (a firm connexion being assumed between temperance, economy, and social progress). The pressure for retrenchment led, for instance, to antagonism to the adoption of the Public Library Acts which entitled the council to spend the product of a penny rate. During all this period the machinery of local government in Leeds continued to be sustained, though with difficulty, and numerous activities were either not embarked on or were cut back. At the end of the century Mrs Webb described Leeds Liberalism as an extremely crude form of individualism, negative and destructive not least because it was so strongly 'anti-public expenditure'.[96]

But by then the position was changing. Partly – and paradoxically – this was because developments could often be financed out of the profits of trading services thus avoiding unacceptable rate increases; more importantly it was simply that the pressure for improvement was becoming so strong and widespread. In time the question was not, Can it be afforded? but, How efficiently can it be done? Challenges might still be made, as it were, at the margin, but basically the economists had been defeated and the activists and improvers were masters of the field. The extent of the failure is indicated by the fact that between 1870 and 1910 local government expenditure in England and Wales increased sixfold in cash terms and nearly trebled as a proportion of the national income; and over ensuing decades the growth continued.[97]

Centralizers

As well as the opponents of extensive local functions, there were others, equally vocal, who objected because they held the existing patchwork of institutions was corrupt, fragmented, and inefficient. On this view no improvement in the social condition could be achieved by reliance on the vestry, the municipal corporation, the improvement commission, and so forth. So what was required was enhancement of the role of national government for this alone would secure effective and economical administration of the necessary services. There were two possibilities.

96 B. Webb, *Our Partnership* (London, 1948), p. 157. Cf. her comments about similar views at Newcastle-upon-Tyne, ibid., p. 169 n. 1 esp. §(6).
97 See Table 3, p. 101 below.

28 A Much Governed Nation

One was the extension of central supervision of local bodies; the other was to by-pass or replace them by the creation of new centrally based agencies.

In fact elements of central control appeared quite early. What happened in respect of prison administration – a traditional function of the county and borough justices – was an earnest of things to come. The influence of reformers and of Parliamentary inquiry, the ending of transportation, and the increasing cost of the gaols all contributed to the demand for their more uniform and humane operation. The outcome was the Prisons Act of 1823 which (said the Webbs) was the first statute that

> dictated to Local Authorities the detailed plan on which they were to exercise a branch of their own local administration; the first that made it obligatory on them to report, quarter by quarter, how their administration was actually being conducted; and the first that definitely asserted the duty of a Central Department to maintain a continuous supervision of the action of Local Authorities in their current administration.[98]

Again in 1835 a further Act prescribed still greater uniformity of practice and authorized the Home Secretary to make binding regulations. It also subjected local authorities for the first time to constant inspection of their work in this respect by a staff of salaried professional experts. In due course central grants were made and this entailed further supervision until finally in 1878 the central government took over the whole system which was placed under the newly established Prison Commissioners. This was central intervention revealing in a few years its complete potential from supervision to supersession. As the general issue is reviewed later on in this chapter, nothing more will be said of it here save that the superintending role of central departments continually increased and that, as well, separate systems of administration under central guidance were set up in the major fields of the poor law, public health, and education.[99]

This centralizing tendency was supported by a considerable amount of general speculation. Jeremy Bentham, for one, rejected merely established institutions and wanted to fabricate a new system calculated to maximise utility. The argument was that men must be tutorially inclined by expert guidance into the right paths by following which their interests will be secured; and this meant local administration by salaried officials working according to a uniform and centrally prescribed plan. For instance, in his *Constitutional Code* (written between 1820 and

---

[98] S. and B. Webb, op. cit., iv. 462.
[99] On these matters, see below pp. 74ff.

1832), Bentham envisaged the creation of 'sublegislatures' subject in crucial respects to the oversight of functionally organized executive departments dealing with such subjects as indigence, health, education, trade, preventive services, and so forth.[100] Following this lead, the legal theorist John Austin argued that local bodies were necessarily dependent on the sovereign and performed only subordinate functions. In a later paper he urged the related point that centralized regulation was by no means necessarily synonymous with 'over-meddling' and could, on the contrary, conduce to good local administration.[101] Similarly J. S. Mill, although very much aware of the need to relieve pressure on the centre and to educate the people by cultivating a sense of local initiative and responsibility through a proper 'plan of representative sub-Parliaments', also enjoined that there should be a national organ to enforce the law and to act as adviser, co-ordinator, and critic.[102] Again Edwin Chadwick, possibly the most important figure of them all in practice, asserted the case for much greater centralized administration of services or, at least, control of the local agencies that carried them out. He not only found inspiration in Bentham's teachings but, as well, confirmation of these views in the administrative experience of France since the Revolution. This, he thought, showed the great practical advantage of centralized, co-ordinated, and professional authority as compared with a traditional patchwork.[103] Consequently he had little or no use for the existing array of overlapping, even conflicting, local bodies and their piecemeal powers. They were sinister interests, inefficient and wasteful, and dominated by petty oligarchies, no more than local 'job-ocracies' characterized by 'pertinacious blackguardism', fraud, and rapacity.[104] He did not like them; and he thought the first anti-centralizer was the Devil. Thus he definitely wanted to get rid of the existing local arrangements or, if that

100 J. Bentham, *Works*, ed. J. Bowring (1838–43; New York, 1962), ix. 640ff. For the later re-emergence in the Haldane Report of this idea of functionally organized central departments, see below pp. 176–7.
101 J. Austin, *The Province of Jurisprudence Determined...* (1832; London, 1968), lecture VI; 'Centralization', *The Edinburgh Review or Critical Journal*, lxxxv (1847), pp. 221–58, esp. pp. 255–6. I owe the latter reference to W. J. M. Mackenzie, *Theories of Local Government* (Greater London Papers no. 2; London, 1961), p. 8.
102 J. S. Mill, 'De Tocqueville on Democracy in America' (1840), *Collected Works*, ed. J. M. Robson *et al.* (London, 1963ff.), xviii. 169–70; 'Considerations on Representative Government' (1861), ibid., xix. 534–45; 'On Liberty' (1859), ibid., xviii. 309–10; 'The Regulation of the London Water Supply' (1851), ibid., v. 436. Cf. the discussion in J. Redlich and F. W. Hirst, *Local Government in England* (London, 1903), i. 182–90 esp. 184 where it is suggested that Mill's arguments and influence led in the 1860s to a weakening in the resistance to central control.
103 Finer, op. cit., Book One, ch. II.
104 [E. Chadwick], 'The New Poor Law', *The Edinburgh Review or Critical Journal*, lxiii (1836), p. 524. Cf. Finer, op. cit., pp. 302, 477.

were not possible, to by-pass them. He seems to have thought, so far as the Poor Law was concerned, that the ideal would involve the creation of a complete hierarchy of salaried officials, comprising a single national service from the minister down to the workhouse porter with elected boards of guardians serving as no more than supervisory or advisory committees.[105] But a single administrative system of this sort, run from London, was hardly feasible, (given the interests and pressures involved), so he had in mind rather a series of local bodies regulated within broad limits by a strong central board, the whole imbued with the spirit of professionalism and dedicated to a policy of radical improvement.[106] Hence his specific proposals not only for the Poor Law but also for the fields of public health and police.

Some centralists were reluctant converts. Tom Taylor, for instance, was a firm believer in local self-help but his experience at the Central Board of Health and later at the Local Government Act Office persuaded him that local affairs had fallen into the hands not of those best qualified to deal with them but of persons dominated by mob oratory, self-seeking, and ignorance. Thus was he led to justify central direction and control as a necessary alternative.[107] J. F. Stephen similarly acquired a rather jaundiced view of the 'internal government of England'. Local government, he said, 'not unfrequently means the right to misgovern your immediate neighbours without being accountable for it to any one wiser than yourself.' Moreover there was 'a chaos of acts, charters, commissioners, boards, benches, courts, and vestries of all sorts and conditions, which have no unity' and, in most instances, 'are subject to no central control'. Who can doubt, he asks, that the situation requires radical attention and that all the many problems relating to 'education, crime, pauperism, health', and numerous other subjects would be treated much more quickly and better 'if the consent of fewer people was required'? The emphasis here and the context of this specific reference alike make clear Stephen's belief that these are matters not for popular (or elective) but educated and professional determination by a body of full-time public servants in the Home Office.[108]

A final instance of this centralizing propensity may be cited: the Webbs' own study of the development of English local government (in the period between 1688 and 1835) which was published in the years after

---

105 S. and B. Webb, op. cit., viii. 235.
106 Finer, op. cit., pp. 77–80, 91–3, 434–6.
107 T. Taylor, 'On Central and Local Action in Relation to Town Improvement', *Transactions of the National Association for the Promotion of Social Science 1857* (London, 1858), esp. pp. 475–8. Cf. S. and B. Webb, op. cit., iv. 481–2; and *The Rise of Collectivism*, pp. 225–6.
108 J. F. Stephen, *Liberty, Equality, Fraternity* (1837; 2nd edn, 1874; Cambridge, 1967), p. 218.

1906. The pair's main concern in this, as in many other of their works, was to examine the institutions important to a collectivist age: hence their interest also in trade unionism, the co-operative movement, and the kind of constitution appropriate to a Socialist commonwealth. Their basic line of argument is revealed in various ways but may here be exemplified by reference to their analysis of the municipal corporation. In what they call their 'Alternative Judgement', presented in the course of a review of events leading up to the reforms of 1835, they note certain key deficiencies in the old municipal arrangements and indicate the main criteria for improvement suggested by these defects. Being always concerned above all to secure administrative efficiency in the achievement of Socialist purpose, they believed that what was required was a proper adjustment of structure, functions, areas, and relationships. The specific point was that the old municipal corporations failed badly in these respects.[109] Furthermore – and here the Webbs' basic political views begin to appear – it was the freedom claimed by the boroughs from central control which was suspect; for local autonomy of any significant kind and the variation it inevitably entails are alike unacceptable. They put this in terms directly contrary to those used by supporters of local autonomy:

> We cannot afford to let a town have what police it wishes, what trade regulations it prefers, what administration of justice it choses to provide, what highways, markets, or sanitation it elects, or what degree of physical health, of education, and of social order it happens to appreciate. The very conception of the Municipal Corporation was defective in not providing for it ... a place in a National Hierarchy of authorities, in which, by external audit, inspection, and control, provision might have been made, not only for the protection of individuals and minorities from injustice and tyranny, but also for the enforcement, in every department of social life, of that National Minimum of efficiency without which the well-being of the whole will be impaired.[110]

Despite the ritual reference to individual and minority claims, the emphasis is undoubted: local authorities are seen simply as part of a national arrangement of agencies under central control and dedicated to national purposes of a welfare kind. This is true even in the Socialist commonwealth they envisaged.[111] It is a view wholly at one with the Webbs' general political attitude.[112]

109 S. and B. Webb, op. cit., iii. 722–7, 729–37.
110 ibid., iii. 728–9. Cf. ibid., iii. 752–3.
111 S. and B. Webb, *A Constitution for the Socialist Commonwealth of Great Britain* (London, 1920), Part II, ch. IV.
112 On which see *The Ideological Inheritance*, pp. 381–411.

Improvers

However cogent the case made by those who would thus have recourse to London as the only locus of power capable of ensuring effective and worthwhile progress, the argument was frequently repudiated and with scorn: '"Ah!" said Mr. Podsnap. "...I see what you are driving at. I knew it from the first. Centralization. No. Never with my consent. Not English."' It was a view widely held, and not only by Englishmen: for instance, Tocqueville had influentially urged that the strength of a free people 'resides in the local community'; for though a nation may give itself free government, without local institutions it will lack 'the spirit of liberty.'[113] Half a century later one commentator asked whether local authorities should have the freedom from central control even to mismanage their own affairs; and answered that if they were placed 'in leading strings' they were 'not likely to learn aright the lesson of self-government.'[114] Opinion thus sustained the idea of the English state 'as an association or federation of self-governing communities.'[115] It was, therefore, necessary most strongly to defend these institutions especially against any proposal to replace them with some other arrangement which, however rational, was centrally imposed. And the threat itself was often a stimulus to local action: for instance, a good number of authorities sought extra powers so they could avoid (what would otherwise have been necessary) the adoption of the 1848 Public Health Act.[116] If private enterprise was not an acceptable means of providing essential services, and if centralization was rejected, then effective local action was indicated as the only possible alternative.[117]

The views of Dickens's staunch defender of the traditional local polity were possibly modelled on those of Joshua Toulmin Smith, one of the most ardent mid-century publicists in the cause of active local self-government.[118] He was long embroiled in the often bitter controversy over the respective roles in a constitutional state of local and central authorities. The aspect of the debate with which he was primarily concerned turned on the degree and type of autonomy which should be allowed to the localities as against the centralizing tendencies of the day.

---

113 C. Dickens, *Our Mutual Friend* (1865; London, 1963), p. 140; A. de Tocqueville, *Democracy in America* (1835–40; Fontana, 1968), i. 74.
114 Chalmers, op. cit., p. 159.
115 Redlich and Hirst, op. cit., ii. 9.
116 Elliott, 'Municipal Government in Bradford in the Mid-Nineteenth Century', loc. cit., p. 117. Questions of patronage were also involved, of course, ibid.
117 For the frequent rejection of private enterprise, see Fraser, *Power and Authority in the Victorian City*, pp. 31–2.
118 For the suggested affinity, see G. Chapman, 'The Onus of State Action', in H. Grisewood *et al.*, *Ideas and Beliefs of the Victorians: an Historic Revaluation of the Victorian Age* (1949; Dutton, 1966), p. 385.

Smith was in the vanguard of the counter-attack against Chadwick and his followers: he was described, for instance, by one contemporary opponent as 'the organ and type' of those who 'write passionately' in praise of local independence; while a modern commentator has plausibly urged that Smith produced the most elaborate theoretical vindication of that cause ever to appear in Britain.[119] He fervently believed that 'the History of England' was 'incapable of being reconciled with either the theory or the arguments of the favourers of Centralism' and that local self-government was the sole effective basis of both freedom and happiness.[120] As he succinctly put it in one of his many works:

> There are two elements to which every form of Government may be reduced. These are, LOCAL SELF-GOVERNMENT on the one hand, and CENTRALIZATION on the other. According as the former or the latter of these exists more or less predominant, will the state of any nation be the more or less free, happy, progressive, truly prosperous, and safe.[121]

It was a stance supported with a considerable and learned range of argument drawn from a disparate scholarly paraphernalia. The case rested on an analysis of moral and psychological fulfilment as well as a great deal of constitutional and administrative history, together with a detailed examination of the impropriety and deficiencies of centralized bureaucracy or (what Smith often called) 'Functionarism'.[122] Of this last point he was (as a leading member of the Anti-Centralization Union) most certainly convinced. Centralization and the reliance on others it entailed had, he held, inevitably led to 'the smothering of the primary Institutions' of the realm and was thus not only unconstitutional but also had undesirable moral, administrative, and social consequences.[123] It prevented local freedom of choice and was thus incompatible with the liberty of citizens. As a result it inhibited that development and satisfaction of the individual faculties on which alike personal fulfilment

---

119 T. Taylor, op. cit., p. 475; H. Whalen, 'Ideology, Democracy, and the Foundations of Local Self-Government', *Canadian Journal of Economics and Political Science*, xxvi (1960), p. 382. Cf. Mackenzie, op. cit., pp. 9–12.
120 J. T. Smith, *Local Self-Government Unmystified...* (London, 1857), p. 3. Cf. ibid., pp. 30–1, idem, *Parallels between...England and Hungary* (London, 1849), p. 24; idem, *The People and the Parish* (London, 1853), p. 8; idem, *Local Self-Government and Centralization...* (London, 1851), p. 28.
121 idem, *Local Self-Government and Centralization...*, p. 11 (capitals in original).
122 For a general account of Smith's case, see my 'Toulmin Smith and the British Political Tradition', *Public Administration*, liii (1975), pp. 25–44.
123 *The Parliamentary Remembrancer*, ii (1859), pp. 58–9; J. T. Smith, *The Parish, its Powers and Obligations at Law...* (1854; 2nd edn, London, 1857), pp. 614–16. For the Anti-Centralization Union (founded in 1854), see O. Anderson, *A Liberal State at War: English Politics and Economics during the Crimean War* (London, 1967), pp. 134–62.

34   A Much Governed Nation

and social progress depended.[124] Moreover centralization was likely to lead not only to corruption and inefficiency but also to be dangerous to life and health, the very objects it was supposed to sustain. Thus, after the enactment of legislation concerning sewers in 1848, the central policy pursued merely led, in a number of cases, to rivers being fouled by the effluent and so to the pollution of the water supply. Local action based on local knowledge would be more likely to prevent dangerous (and costly) absurdities of this kind.[125] In particular, Smith's beloved parish

> must be always felt to be a complete *Unit* in itself; of some one of which, each man forms a part. Men must realize the universally-proved truth, that no people, nor any neighbourhood, nor any set of men, nor any man, was ever yet made good, moral, clean, or safe by Act of Parliament, or by the appointment of salaried functionaries; but that the only hope and assuredness lie, in every man feeling and acting up to, the obligations of the relation in which he stands to the neighbourhood where he inhabits.[126]

The principle was, therefore, that 'ALL *local affairs* shall be managed and controlled *by local bodies only*', by the men of a given place and not by London-dominated boards and commissions.[127]

Smith was certainly no simple exponent of local quietism or *laissez faire* which, indeed, he specifically repudiated.[128] As a man of affairs, one who had been practically involved, too, in vestry business, he knew very well there were complicated communal needs to be met such as those concerning public health and especially in the large urban areas. But he did urge most vehemently that these problems could and should be tackled directly by the citizens involved through the traditional local authorities, deploying their considerable array of powers concerning public order, highways and bridges, lighting, paving, relief of poverty, sanitation, and so forth. Smith was thus convinced that these institutions, if properly reformed (to eliminate, for instance, the corrupt control of a local oligarchy), could cope, either singly or jointly, with the difficulties of the day. In fact many of his works are handbooks showing the reader how to deal with these problems, as with his *Practical Directions for the Formation of Sewerage Districts* (1854), *Practical Proceedings for the*

---

124 See e.g. J. T. Smith, *Government by Commissions Illegal and Pernicious...* (London, 1849), pp. 353ff., 368–9; idem, *Local Self-Government and Centralization...*, pp. 37–51.
125 idem, *Local Self-Government and Centralization...*, p. 345.
126 idem, *The Parish*, p. 617 (italics in original).
127 idem, *Parallels between...England and Hungary*, p. 28 (capitals and italics in original); idem, *The Metropolis and its Municipal Administration...* (London, 1852), p. 10.
128 idem, *Local Self-Government and Centralization...*, p. 69.

Removal of Nuisances and the Execution of Drainage Works (1855), or *The Laws of England Relating to Public Health* (1848).[129] If he may have under-rated the extent, complexity, and expense of coping with the issues increasingly faced in his day and after (he died in 1869) — and I am far from sure he did — he was manifestly a champion of local institutions as the best means of dealing with them as opposed to the solutions offered by the centralizers like Chadwick. As well he was the persuasive and assertive apostle of a tradition of local action that, however different, was the obvious forerunner of an extensive interventionism later to be dubbed 'Municipal Socialism': it is no accident that the Fabians cited Smith as an authority on local affairs. And the Webbs, though often critical of the historical basis of many of his claims about the parish, nevertheless recognized the power of the ideal and accepted that, if the many difficulties faced (and they were considerable) could have been overcome, then an 'extraordinarily wide and far-reaching' provision of services might have been established. It would have constituted, they said a restoration of the 'free and autonomous English village community' under the aegis of which the provision of almost any service and the enactment of practically any regulation desired by a majority of parochial inhabitants would have been feasible.[130] Smith's point of view was also found congenial by those who urged (for all sorts of reasons) that the functions of government should be decentralized as much as possible. This was one factor behind the attempt, late in the last century and early in this, to revive the parish as embodying self-government at local level.

In fact an extensive local interventionism developed quite rapidly as urban leaders addressed, in the first instance, the basic problems of sanitation, street improvement, slum clearance, and so forth, and then, once the treatment of such matters was in hand, the provision of additional amenities like swimming baths, parks, and libraries. Thus a widening range of social and environmental improvement was involved. This development was to a degree quite unconscious in the sense that it was not always or even usually motivated by any ideology, at least at this stage. Many towns were simply led to take action by practical problems, such as those concerned with sewage disposal, epidemics, bad housing, a high death rate, and so forth. But to deal with these required more money than the rates could easily provide and this deficiency might lead in turn

---

129 And cf. the other detailed references in my 'Toulmin Smith and the British Political Tradition', loc. cit., p. 43 n. 17.

130 S. and B Webb, op. cit., i. 37–8 n. 6, 146–8. Cf. J. W. Burrow, '"The Village Community" and the Uses of History in Late Nineteenth-Century England', in N. McKendrick (ed.), *Historical Perspectives: Studies in English Thought and Society* (London, 1974), ch. IX.

to proposals to take over, say, local gas or water companies so that the profits could be used for these other purposes: that is, the need for money for town improvement in certain specific respects could itself lead to more intervention and control beyond the problem areas immediately at issue. Yet overall the changes that occurred did not constitute a persistent and uniform current of advance being rather of varying pace, intermittent, patchy, and piecemeal: there was no universal or uniform provision throughout the country. Such variety was, of course, the inevitable result of differing local circumstances and of the haphazard impact of private legislation and the model clauses and adoptive Acts. But, although thus characterized by what F. H. Spencer called 'sporadicity', a more general pattern did begin to emerge and the cumulative effect was considerable.[131] Nevertheless what ensued was not what Toulmin Smith had anticipated or desired. He always stressed individual participation, being prepared to accept a great range of parochial and other local responsibilities so long as they were carried out by the inhabitants of the area concerned. However it did not happen this way. Instead, elected assemblies created a hierarchical body of salaried experts and officials, that is, what he most feared, 'the system of Bureaucracy and Functionarism.'[132] And rather than himself undertaking a duty, the citizen became a passive ratepayer content to see his representatives and an increasing array of clerks, inspectors, engineers, architects, and all the rest do the work in his behalf and increasingly under central direction.

Certainly local intervention was widely accepted and defended. J. A. Roebuck believed the town councils created in 1835 should take under their wing 'everything affecting the well being of the neighbourhood.' Francis Place held a similar view and outlined the extensive range of functions he envisaged.[133] The Christian Socialists also – in the guise, for instance, of Kingsley's 'Sanitary Reformer' – had a vision of improved cities in which the life even of the poorest could be fulfilled through radical improvement of basic living conditions, 'by abolishing foul air, foul water, foul lodging, overcrowded dwellings, in which morality is difficult and common decency impossible.' The city must thus be made to become what it ought to be. And specifically Kingsley was prepared to argue for corporate ownership and management of gas and water supply, the provision of proper sewerage, 'public baths and lavatories', 'and other matters besides'.[134] Sheldon Amos, in one of the first modern

131 For the term cited, see F. H. Spencer, *Municipal Origins...* (London, 1911), p. 318.
132 Smith, *The Parish*, p. 211.
133 See the references cited in Fraser, *Power and Authority in the Victorian City*, pp. 19–20.
134 C. Kingsley, 'Great Cities and Their Influence for Good and Evil' (1857), *Sanitary and Social Lectures and Essays* (1880; new edn, London, 1889), pp. 205, 216–17, 219;

reviews of political science, discussed the question and concluded that a quite numerous array of matters was appropriate to local administration: sanitation, education, water supply, lighting, bridges, roads, and much else, police forces being jointly in the hands of both national and local authorities.[135] There were naturally expressions of approval for active local government developed in the municipal centres themselves. For instance, at Manchester in 1834 a spokesman for the majority on the improvement commission argued it was highly desirable, for financial and other practical reasons, that the inhabitants of a town should own the gas and waterworks and similar facilities: profit was not a proper motive in these matters.[136] And most emphatic declarations of this sort were later developed.

The so-called 'Municipal Gospel' espoused in Birmingham was inspired by the Nonconformist conscience.[137] It urged service to the local community as a Christian and municipal duty, the corporation being seen as the contemporary expression in this regard not simply of the general interest of the town and its citizens but as much more, the embodiment of God's will and purpose and a means of giving them practical effect.[138] Nor was any merely limited task thus envisaged for the prosperous and leading inhabitants. A Birmingham Congregational minister, R. W. Dale, said in a sermon (published in 1867) that substantial ratepayers

> ought to feel 'called of God' to act as 'Guardians of the Poor.' They ought to work on the Committees of Hospitals. They ought to be Aldermen and Town Councillors. They ought to give their time as well as their money to whatever improvements are intended to develop the intelligence of the community. They ought to be reformers of local abuses. They ought to see to it that the towns and parishes in which they live are well drained, well lighted, and well paved; that there are good schools for every class of the population; that there are harmless public amusements; that all parochial and municipal affairs are conducted honourably and equitably.[139]

---

idem, 'The Air-Mothers' (1869), ibid., esp. pp. 146–50, 156. Cf. Kingsley's plea for sanitary reform in '"A Mad World, My Masters"' (1858), ibid., pp. 271–300.

135 S. Amos, *The Science of Politics* (London, 1883), ch. VII, 'Local Government', esp. pp. 298–9. Cf. H. Sidgwick, *The Elements of Politics* (1891; 2nd edn rev., London, 1897), ch. XXV.

136 See the passage from the *Manchester Times* (25 January 1834) cited in S. and B. Webb, op. cit., iv. 270–1.

137 For what follows I draw on Hennock, op. cit., Book I, Part II; also the summary in Fraser, *Power and Authority in the Victorian City*, pp. 101–10.

138 e.g. Hennock, op. cit., pp. 74–6.

139 R. W. Dale, 'The Perils and Uses of Rich Men', in his *Week-Day Sermons* (1867), pp. 175–6 cited ibid., p. 158. Cf. the passages cited ibid., pp. 78–9.

38 A Much Governed Nation

He thus urged the sacredness of secular business and the religious significance of local government action to diminish sickness and death, improve living conditions, and suchlike.[140] In this fashion municipal intervention acquired a moral and religious justification, became a civilizing mission, involving 'a new vision of the function and nature of the corporation' which attracted men of position and ability and which made administrative improvements possible. If an interest in popular education in particular first drew such men into public service, their involvement was quickly widened to take up other tasks.[141] The early career and mayoral activities of Joseph Chamberlain also did much not only to sustain this point of view but also to give it practical embodiment. He asserted, in a speech made in 1885, that

> the most fruitful field before reformers at the present time is to be found in an extension of the functions and authority of local government. Local government is near the people. Local government will bring you into contact with the masses. By its means you will be able to increase their comfort, to secure their health, to multiply the luxuries which they may enjoy in common, to carry out a vast co-operative system for mutual aid and support, to lessen the inequalities of our social system, and to raise the standard of all classes in the community.[142]

Referring to this passage Professor Hennock observes that it is prophetic of much subsequent domestic history. The Birmingham municipal reform movement was thus 'a form of collectivism' that 'lies at the root of the major developments in modern British history.'[143] Another contemporary encomium may also stand for the spirit of what was intended and achieved. In 1878 the state of civic affairs in Birmingham was appraised – and praised – in this way:

> The government of the town is in its own hands free, unfettered and complete. We have public edifices not unworthy of the place. Our streets are well kept, lighted, drained and watched. We have the means for the administration of justice by our own magistrates and in our own courts. The monopolies of gas and water have ceased to exist: these undertakings have passed into the hands of the community. The health of the population is cared for by an efficient system of sanitary measures; the means of cleanliness are afforded by baths and wash-

---

140 See the sermon quoted ibid., pp. 161–2.
141 ibid., p. 172 and Part II, chs 2–3.
142 C. W. Boyd (ed.), *Mr. Chamberlain's Speeches* (London, 1914), i. 165. On Chamberlain's collectivist doctrine, see also *The Ideological Heritage*, pp. 213, 223–31, 238–43, 376–7.
143 Hennock, op. cit., p. 175.

houses; recreation is provided by parks and pleasure grounds; and the opportunities of culture are offered to all classes in free libraries and museums of art. These benefits result directly from the institution of corporate government, and by such an agency alone could the force and the means of the community be directed to purposes of general advantage.[144]

Nor was Birmingham alone in developing an activist doctrine of this sort. The so-called 'new era' in the civic life of Leeds provided another such instance of the motivation behind the notable extension of local government functions that occurred and this despite the considerable cost involved.[145] One enthusiastic supporter epitomized the true accents of this local interventionism which emerged during the last quarter of the nineteenth century. The point had been reached, he wrote, at which it could be said that the 'true municipality should completely grasp the life of the community'. An authority's work 'should be done with such completeness as to leave no source of danger or evil unchecked, no material defect uncured, no intellectual want uncared for.'[146]

But, of course, a necessary preliminary to, or part of, this process of improvement was the creation of a more adequate local administration than that provided by the old patchwork of bodies, one more capable (according to the feelings and standards of the time) of dealing with contemporary problems in the complete way intended.

THE NEW PATCHWORK

... what we observe, in and after 1834, is not order rising out of chaos, but only a new patchwork taking the place of the old one.
E. HALEVY in H. J. Laski et al., A Century of Municipal Progress, 1935,
p. 35

The pressure for reform

Inevitably the array of local authorities existing at the beginning of the nineteenth century was often the subject of criticism. Their exclusive or partisan nature was one feature that led to early demands for change. For instance Whigs objected to the existing municipal corporations because

---

144 J. T. Bunce, *The History of the Corporation of Birmingham* (1878), i. 355 cited Fraser, *Power and Authority in the Victorian City*, p. 169. This passage is remarkably similar to that from S. Webb's *Socialism in England* (1890) cited in *The Rise of Collectivism*, p. 100.
145 See Hennock, op. cit., Book II, Part II and Barber, loc. cit., *passim*.
146 J. T. Bunce, 'Municipal Boroughs and Urban Districts', in J. W. Probyn (ed.), *Local Government and Taxation in the United Kingdom: a Series of Essays*, (2nd edn, 1882), p. 302 cited Hennock, op. cit., p. 321.

most of them were Tory strongholds, Radicals because they were not elected or otherwise representative, and Nonconformists because they were bastions of Anglicanism. Corruption, inefficiency, or abuse provided other occasion for censure though this was equally liable to be self-interested, the accusations being directed rather to the replacement of existing office-holders by the critics or their nominees than to the elimination of the deficiencies as such. Then there was the failure to cope with the growing practical problems of the day. The various local agencies, both survivals and innovations, were able at their best to deal with the communal difficulties of a relatively slow-moving agricultural society and even with the initial phases of social and industrial change. But in time the consequences of 'the massing of men' often proved overwhelming. The Webbs graphically pictured the situation in its most acute form:

> ...the Juries of the Lord's Court or the Church-wardens and Overseers and principal inhabitants in Vestry assembled, found themselves dealing, not with a little group of neighbours centring round church and manor-house, but with uncounted hordes of unknown men, women and children, crowded together in hastily built tenements; with the ancient King's highway, which had become encumbered with wagons and travelling beasts, transformed into streets lined with warehouses, with here and there a factory, forge or mine, each employing hundreds, and even thousands of 'hands,' and contaminating the ground, the streams and the air with its output of filthy refuse – a neighbourhood from which the country gentleman and the incumbent, who alone were Justices of the Peace, had usually withdrawn to more agreeable places of residence.[147]

It is not surprising that in 1832 a Whig newspaper in Manchester should have expressed the editorial view that the 'ancient forms', which may have been 'suited to the small towns and sluggish habits of bygone days', were 'worse than useless among our immense masses of population at the present time'.[148]

Yet, as implied by Halévy's remark (cited as epigraph to this section), what was achieved in response to this challenging state of affairs was really only an adaptation, amendment, or partial replacement of the existing structure. There was little or no sense of the need for a more uniform arrangement of local authorities as a whole with a planned hierarchy of officials and functions; and it is wholly misleading to see the

---

147 S. and B. Webb, *English Local Government from the Revolution to the Municipal Corporations Act* (London, 1906–29), iv. 399–400. See also ibid., vol. i, ch. II *passim*. For the phrase 'the massing of men', see ibid., iv. 398.
148 *Manchester Guardian* (6 October 1832) cited ibid., i. 102.

tendency to reform in the early and mid-nineteenth century as though this were the leading purpose in view. No doubt such a motive did exist – among Benthamites perhaps – but it hardly dominated any general body of opinion until later on in the century, if even then. The innovations have to be seen, rather, as a series of piecemeal responses to particular issues or areas of policy and not as the deliberate incremental establishment of a symmetrical, nation-wide system of local government. Of course with hindsight it is possible to detect certain general tendencies such as those the Webbs described as the emergence of the salaried official and the coming of the ratepayer. There may be discerned, as well, two main lines of institutional development which emerged as the 'new patchwork' appeared. One was the establishment of specialist bodies to deal with a particular segment of local administration; the other the creation of new or reformed general-purpose authorities. Moreover it appeared in time that the former were to be absorbed by the latter so that the generalist institutions came largely to dominate the field. Yet the story is complex and (as present-day experience shows) not without elements of retrogression in this regard. Illustration rather than a complete account is all that is possible – or necessary – here. Yet these matters are not only intrinsically important as one vital part of public response to the problems of a growing and increasingly complex society: they are also the essential perspective in which to view the local government changes of the more recent past. Certainly they are a major aspect of the growth of the positive state.

The specialist boards

One late-nineteenth-century observer commented that, as population and wealth 'advanced by leaps and bounds', new local authorities were 'created wholesale' to 'provide for the growing requirements of the nation'. Each special need, he went on, has been met 'by calling into existence a new special authority to deal with it' and this was done 'without any regard to previously existing divisions or authorities.'[149] For instance, after legislation in 1835 and again in the 1860s, there were in a number of parishes (or, especially in the rural areas, unions of them) highway boards to maintain the roads in the district concerned. Equally, *ad hoc* bodies might exist for various other purposes: lighting and watching; the provision of baths and washhouses; the supervision of burials; to run turnpikes or harbour facilities; and (from 1870 to 1902) to establish elementary schools (where these were not adequately furnished by the voluntary societies). There was a complex mosaic of such bodies and the whole gamut cannot be reviewed here. However during the last

149 M. D. Chalmers, *Local Government* (London, 1883), p. 24 n. 1.

century the two main subjects of local concern handled through this device of a special board were pauperism and public health and what happened in those spheres will be described because of its significance and exemplary character.

The problem of pauperism

The relief of destitution had long been a matter high on the agenda of government both as a charitable duty proper to a Christian state and as a matter of political prudence. And the role of the traditional local bodies was inevitably a substantial one because they constituted the only administrative machinery nationally available to deal with the question, the responsibility being shared by the justices and the parish officers. The former, in effect, legislated on these matters, establishing the local rules for mitigating indigence as with the so-called Speenhamland system promulgated in Berkshire in 1795. Practice (and the degree of success achieved) naturally varied from one place to another. In a large and well-ordered parish like Liverpool there would be a workhouse with a paid staff, overseers to administer outdoor relief, and collectors to gather the rates and taxes. Smaller parishes might form a union to provide such facilities by joint action; but this was not obligatory and the initiative remained in local hands. Attempting to cope with the poor and needy proved indeed to be more troublesome and expensive than all other local responsibilities combined. Circumstances were difficult: population was growing and, especially after the French wars, so was unemployment; in the rural areas a still unrepealed law of settlement created pools of redundant labour, and the extending process of enclosure made things worse; the Speenhamland system, despite the good intentions behind it, tended to depress wages and increase pressure on the relief fund (and so on the ratepayers) while having a demoralizing effect on the agricultural worker driven to ask for assistance; nor were corruption and abuse unknown. As to the cost, the total poor rate levied in England, at the beginning of the eighteenth century, stood at just £1 million; but it had risen slowly so that by 1775 it was nearly doubled. Then, in a mere decade, it bounded up by 25 per cent and, by the turn of the century, had reached £4 millions. In another twenty years it had doubled yet again to nearly £8 millions.[150] The task had in most places outgrown the traditional machinery and its resources; and, yet, as the matter was regarded as one of local concern, there was no central authority to secure a uniform policy of improvement. So Parliamentary action seemed imperative.

Agrarian disturbances heightened the call for reform and in 1832 the

---

150 S. and B. Webb, op. cit., iv. 406–7. There are slightly different figures, ibid., iv. 466 and viii. 1–2.

Whig government appointed a royal commission whose report appeared two years later. The principles of relief proposed were severe and, as it would be difficult to secure their effective application through the existing local bodies, new administrative arrangements were deemed necessary. The idea of a completely centralized service on the lines of the Post Office was considered but rejected. What was proposed instead was (in the Webbs' words) 'a new form of government ... destined to spread to other services', one based on the combination of a specialized central department to exercise executive control and elected local bodies covering the whole kingdom to administer the policy laid down.[151] The degree of central supervision envisaged was unprecedented; and the new local agencies to be created would dethrone the justices and by-pass the traditional parish. The establishment of a Poor Law Commission and the local boards of guardians was authorized by the Act of 1834 though it took three decades or so to put the entire country on the same basis of administration.[152]

Of course these changes concerned the treatment of one major problem only but there were points of considerable general significance involved. There was the idea of a uniform provision of poor relief throughout the country. And it was based on recognition of the need to replace the diverse and usually small parishes with larger units of administration in which size and resources were more appropriately adapted to function. In time the country was covered by these 'unions', their boundaries sometimes cutting completely across historic county, borough, and parish areas. There was also the concept of central supervision of policy and expenditure. Moreover the boards of guardians, although primarily concerned with the mitigation of indigence, acquired a diverse and not insubstantial array of related responsibilities to do with the causes of destitution such as old age, illness, and lack of education. For instance the workhouse hospitals and the outdoor medical treatment provided by the poor-law dispensaries were the only system of medical care operating on anything like a national scale. Indeed by the 1860s the great majority of the hospital beds in England and Wales were provided under these auspices and, in practice, increasingly administered on principles rather more generous than those supposed to operate in respect of the relief of poverty. This was in effect an important stage in the development of a public health service.[153]

151 ibid., viii. 57.
152 ibid., viii. 225–6. For examples of the long continuation of pre-1834 practice, see E. C. Midwinter, 'State Intervention at the Local Level: the New Poor Law in Lancashire', *Historical Journal*, x (1967), pp. 106–12.
153 O. MacDonagh, *Early Victorian Government 1830–1870* (London, 1977), pp. 117–20.

It was perhaps inevitable that difficulties should arise in the operation of these arrangements, symbolized by the conventional dislike of the workhouse and all it stood for and culminating in the inquiry conducted by the Royal Commission on the Poor Laws which sat between 1905 and 1909 and which, while disagreeing on important issues, envisaged substantial changes. The conventional range of the boards of guardians' responsibilities was being affected in various ways by the direct intervention of central government as by the establishment of national unemployment and health insurance schemes and the provision of old-age pensions. As well certain duties (such as the care of pauper mental defectives) had been transferred to other public authorities. There were also difficult issues of internal policy and administration largely arising from changes in the composition of the boards in some places. The property qualification for membership had been abolished, the *ex-officio* magistrates removed, and a new electoral procedure instituted. The result was that working-class representation and even control developed especially in high poverty areas like Poplar in East London and Bedwellty in the Welsh mining valleys. In such places the boards decided to repudiate the restrictive principles of 1834 and embarked on a policy of much more open-handed relief than usual which, of course, led to a substantial rise in the poor-rate.[154] This, coupled with other financial difficulties – not excluding cases of corruption – and instances of mismanagement (of contractual procedures for instance), led in some influential quarters to increasing criticism.[155] And the flood of pauperism created by the slump after the Great War placed a fresh burden on the boards, overwhelmed them indeed in some of the industrial areas most affected: nor was their response uniform.[156] Whatever their differences, both the majority and minority on the Poor Law Commission had agreed that the *ad hoc* elected guardians should go and that the principle of concentrating local responsibilities on the general authorities (which had been followed in the case of education in 1902) should be adopted in this instance also. But the change did not occur until the passage of the Local Government Act of 1929. Responsibility was then transferred to county and county borough councils whose duties were thus considerably enlarged. This resulted in the areas of administration becoming much bigger in that over 600 boards of guardians were thus replaced by 144 general local authorities. The Poor Law itself, however, technically

---

154 This particular story is told by e.g. B. Keith-Lucas, 'Poplarism', *Public Law*, vii (1962), pp. 52–80, a paper largely reprinted as ch. IV of B. Keith-Lucas and P. G. Richards, *A History of Local Government in the Twentieth Century* (London, 1978). N. Branson, *Poplarism 1919–1925: George Lansbury and the Councillors' Revolt* (London, 1979), is a full but somewhat partisan account.
155 e.g. B. Webb, *Our Partnership* (London, 1948), p. 337.
156 Cf. S. and B. Webb, op. cit., ix. 852ff.

remained in being until 1948 when responsibility for 'public assistance' was finally removed from local hands and given to a new National Assistance Board. By that time, the various aspects of the old Poor Law had been split up: hospitals, maternity and child welfare, unemployment insurance, aid to deprived children, care of the blind and crippled, and so forth had all been hived off in different ways from the parent stem legislatively planted in 1834. Nevertheless for something like a century the 'new Poor Law' arrangements with its special structure were a major part of local government as it responded to the widespread indigence and the many cognate problems of both traditional agrarian and new industrial circumstances.

The public health issue
The Poor-Law precedent was followed in coming to terms with the many problems of public health arising in the course of industrialization and urban development: that is to say, a combination of central supervision and an elected local body set up for this particular purpose. Of course there were previous attempts at sanitary reform. A local health board might be created or appropriate powers sought under an improvement Act but such steps, being dependent on particular initiative, could hardly be an adequate response to the overall needs of the growing towns, not least given the incredible sanitary habits of our ancestors and the fact that it was often only the better class urban areas in which such attempts at amelioration were made.[157] Emergencies had often been the stimulus to action as with the cholera epidemic of the early 1830s though the arrangements made invariably lapsed after the crisis was over.[158] Medical treatment was available at the old voluntary hospitals and dispensaries, at those provided by the Poor-Law boards, or through sick clubs and provident associations. Nevertheless in 1815 a shrewd contemporary observer of the British scene, the Prussian statesman Baron von Vincke, described the utter want of a systematic code of health law as one of the worst defects of English administration.[159]

However developments were afoot in the 1830s and '40s which

157 See the discussion of these and cognate issues by B. Keith-Lucas, 'Some Influences Affecting the Development of Sanitary Legislation in England', *Economic History Review*, 2s., vi (1953–4), pp. 290–6; and E. P. Hennock, 'Urban Sanitary Reform a Generation before Chadwick?' ibid., x (1957–8), pp. 113–20.
158 For what was done then see R. J. Morris, *Cholera 1832: the Social Response to an Epidemic* (London, 1976), esp. pp. 31–5, 51, 59, 73–4. This account is particularly valuable because it considers the social, religious, and scientific context of the attitudes revealed: see esp. ch. 6. For a detailed review of the administrative problems, see F. Brockington, 'Public Health at the Privy Council 1831–34', *Journal of the History of Medicine*, xvi (1961), pp. 161–85.
159 See the reference in J. Redlich and F. W. Hirst, *Local Government in England* (London, 1903), i. 134–5.

intensified concern with the public health issue and led to more general attempts to cope with it. There were all sorts of exigencies emerging on a large scale concerning such matters as drainage and sewage disposal, control of burial grounds, street cleaning, the supply of water, and so on. Nor was it any good, as people like Chadwick and Simon realized, only trying to improve the sanitation of the individual dwelling-house for this would simply worsen the problem of waste disposal. And it was little use overcoming key technical problems (such as the production of an effectively non-porous sewer pipe and the provision of a continuous water supply) if these advances were ill applied or not introduced at all because of their cost. It was being increasingly grasped that sanitation and other public health questions were all interconnected and demanded overall administrative treatment. It was also more and more appreciated that there could be a close link between disease and destitution each exacerbating the other. Chadwick, as secretary to the Poor Law Commission, examined the registration statistics compiled after 1837 (at his instance and for just such a purpose) and concluded that the condition of the poor would be eased by preventing ill-health and treating its causes. There were some major inquiries in the early 1840s into such questions as the health of towns and the sanitary condition of the labouring poor; and there was substantial pressure, for instance from the Health of Towns Association, to introduce radical administrative changes under the supervision of a central authority. Certain steps were taken. For instance there were the various 'Clauses' or 'Model' Acts of 1845–7 which contained detailed provisions on a wide range of matters relating to public health and which might be adopted by local authorities. A Nuisance Removal Act of 1846, the first of its kind, recognized the boards of guardians as a kind of rural sanitary authority for the purpose in view. A few places appointed a medical officer of health as Liverpool did in 1847. And the numerous local Acts often made provision for various forms of sanitary control. But whatever was done in this sporadic way fell a good deal short of what the more radical reformers envisaged: that is, a rationalization of areas and agencies on Poor-Law lines with a single health authority in each place under the general supervision and inspection of central government.

A renewed cholera alarm in 1848 provided the occasion; and the Public Health Act passed by Russell's government in that year was an attempt to implement such policies. It set up a General Board of Health, including a ministerial member as President, with power to create a local health district either if a given proportion of the ratepayers petitioned for this or if the local death rate was above average. A different procedure was followed in the boroughs and the rural parishes, thus initiating a separation between town and country that remained basic to the structure of local government until very recently. In the towns the local sanitary authority (subject in this respect to the General Board) would be either the town council, commissioners, or an elected board. Outside the urban areas a completely new, elected authority would be established with a jurisdiction closely related to that of the Poor-Law union. Any such local health authority would have a quite wide range of duties in the field of public sanitation and would dispose of powers that hitherto had largely been available only after obtaining an expensive local Act of Parliament.[160] As R. Lambert has said (in a classic study), for the first time

> England possessed the framework of a local sanitary organisation and a central authority charged with a general responsibility for the nation's health. The process of common sanitary legislation, by which the state was gradually to restrict individual *laissez faire* and extend the action of public authorities in the interest of general health welfare, had at last got fully under way.[161]

However the immediate outcome was in many respects disappointing to the reformers. The central board itself had only limited powers and was dissolved in 1858 though its duties were reallocated to the medical department of the Privy Council and to the Home Office. In addition the Act's provisions were only slowly implemented. By the mid-1850s local sanitary boards had been set up in places covering only about two of the eighteen million inhabitants of England and Wales and rural areas had hardly been touched at all. Subsequently, however, the sanitation of the countryside did tend to improve often as a result of the efforts of members of the business and professional classes who had moved into the country surrounding the towns where they worked.[162] None the less the general mortality rate did not show any improvement being, in fact, slightly worse in the early 1870s compared with what it had been thirty years before; though, in so far as the population and the size of towns had increased notably, a certain negative achievement was involved even in this.[163] Continuing attempts were made to tackle specific problems, and *ad hoc* responsibilities of different kinds were created from time to time. For instance in 1855 'nuisance authorities' were provided for and, ten years afterwards, 'sewer authorities', duties in these respects being given to existing local bodies such as a board of health, commissioners, town council, or vestry. But the assumption of authority was permissive and opposition to increasing the rates intense so that the impact was again limited. But a fresh cholera outbreak in the mid-1860s stimulated

160 See the exemplary list of powers in Chalmers, op. cit., p. 108.
161 R. Lambert, *Sir John Simon, 1816–1904, and English Social Administration* (London, 1963), pp. 71–2.
162 J. M. Lee, *Social Leaders and Public Persons: a Study of County Government in Cheshire since 1888* (Oxford, 1963), p. 26.
163 MacDonagh, *Early Victorian Government*, p. 160.

renewed activity and the Sanitary Act of 1866 gave special powers of enforcement.

Yet to many of those involved, these arrangements hardly seemed systematic or effective enough. Sir John Simon described them as 'a parquetry which was unsafe to walk upon', while G. J. Goschen told Parliament that the truth is 'we have a chaos as regards authorities, a chaos as regards rates, and a worse chaos than all as regards areas.'[164] This judgement about the mass of overlapping or conflicting public health jurisdictions which existed – poor law, registration, sanitary, vestry, burial, bath and washhouse, highway, water, nuisance, and other local authorities involved – had been confirmed by the reports of the Royal Commission on the Operation of the Sanitary Laws which appeared in 1871. It was established, for instance, that in 1870 there were as many as 670 boards of health and 114 improvement commissions with public health powers not to mention the many other local bodies concerned.[165] And the substantial use of the adoptive or voluntary principle meant that the benefits of sanitary science and law had only been partially and not always actively applied. Nor was the central supervision effective, such powers as there were being divided among a number of offices. So the commission recommended the creation of a single, strong department with powers of compulsion to oversee an efficient and energetic execution not only of public health policy but also of the Poor Law. Equally it stressed the importance of a uniform code of sanitary legislation to meet the requirements 'necessary for civilized social life': a good water supply, an efficient sewage system, properly clean streets, regulation of markets, food inspection, provision of lighting, control of burials and cemeteries, the prevention of nuisances, and the removal of refuse. Further the commission believed there was need for a radical revision of the complex array of local health authorities to ensure the concentration of responsibility. So its report suggested that in urban areas the agency concerned should be, in a municipal borough, the town council, and elsewhere a local board; in rural districts the area should be that of the Poor-Law union and the board of guardians should be the sole sanitary agency.[166] In the outcome the years 1871–5 saw a major series of statutes which made the work of the public health authorities more effective and which undoubtedly contributed to the decline in the death rate over the following years. By the first decade of the new century, it had fallen by some 30 per cent.[167] Thus in 1871 the

164 Sir J. Simon, *English Sanitary Institutions Reviewed in Their Course of Development and in Some of Their Political and Social Relations* (1890; New York, 1970), p. 322. For Goschen's remark, see 205 Parl. Deb. 3s., 3 April 1871, col. 1116.
165 Redlich and Hirst, *Local Government in England*, i. 147 n. 2.
166 Sanitary Laws, R. Com. 2nd Rep., 1871 (vol. xxxv), C. 281, pp. 23–4.
167 MacDonagh, op. cit., p. 160.

Local Government Board was created to take over a previously divided responsibility: the public health business of the Privy Council; the work of the Poor Law Board; and also the supervisory authority of the Local Government Act Office in the Home Department. Important changes were at once set in hand. In 1874 the sanitary tasks of the local authorities were extended; then, the year after, a consolidating Act was passed by Disraeli's government which completely revised and codified existing public health law and set out a lengthy sanitary code for the guidance of the LGB. It also established, broadly on the lines suggested by the royal commission, a simplified pattern of urban and rural sanitary authorities with a substantial range of powers and which remained in being until transformed in 1894.[168] But, even if there was thereby created 'a comprehensive and fairly intelligible system of administrative authorities suited to modern requirements', much still remained to be accomplished over ensuing decades in respect not only of the external environment but also of personal hygiene and the prevention and detection of disease.[169] For instance, even in 1915 nearly half the houses in Manchester had no water sanitation; and money for health improvements was still difficult to come by whether from local sources or central aid.[170] Nevertheless what had begun in varied ways nearly a century before was becoming a very wide and costly, but well accepted, national and local responsibility.[171]

It is clear, therefore, how close and important has been the link between the history of the Poor Law and of public health on the one hand and the development of local government on the other. Poor relief was the ground on which the parish had been transformed into an institution of secular administration; it was also that in which above all the justices established themselves as a local governing authority after 1700; and it was in this sphere that, in 1834, a new régime of specialized local bodies and of their central supervision first appeared. Then it was the Poor-Law unions on which the rural sanitary authorities were built and so the county districts created late in the last century. But these districts were general-purpose bodies of a qualitatively different kind and it is the emergence of this sort of authority that must now be reviewed.

---

168 38 & 39 Vic., c. 55. For a full review, see Chalmers, op. cit., ch. VII.
169 The citation is from Redlich and Hirst, op. cit., i. 155. On the later developments, see Sir George Newman, 'The Health of the People' in H. J. Laski *et al.*, *A Century of Municipal Progress 1835–1935* (London, 1935), esp. pp. 165ff.
170 A. Redford, *The History of Local Government in Manchester* (London, 1939–40), iii. 315–19.
171 The administrative aspects of these and subsequent developments are summarized in P. R. Wilding, 'The Genesis of the Ministry of Health', *Public Administration*, xlv (1967), pp. 149–68.

The general authorities

Of course the agencies created to deal with particular fields of policy were additional to or superimposed on the traditional, general-purpose authorities already in existence, that is, the municipal corporation, parish vestry, manorial court, or bench of county magistrates. In such circumstances there was inevitably some overlap or tension and the long-term tendency was indeed for the specific responsibilities to be formally transferred from the specialist bodies to the generalist authorities though not without the latter being substantially reformed. There was at work the idea of concentration J. S. Mill had in mind when he wrote, in *Representative Government* (1861), that 'in each local circumscription there should be but one elected body for all local business, not different bodies for different parts of it.'[172] There was also a growing understanding (never fully realized in practice) of the importance of relating a given array of functions to an appropriate area and range of resources.

The emergence of the town council

The many pressures making for increased intervention in the life of a local community appeared most strongly on the urban scene. It was there that the communal provision of such services as water supply, sewage disposal, housing, policing, and so forth seemed most requisite. The problems often led in the first instance to the establishment of an improvement commission which may thus be seen as the progenitor of the modern municipality.[173] Yet for long now these local services have, in the built-up areas, been most closely associated with the activities of the town council which emerged as the dominant authority from amid the welter of bodies which formerly existed and thus as the main instrument of urban collectivism. This development went through three phases.

The first relates to the Municipal Corporations Act of 1835. This was a piece of legislation of great symbolic significance and which proved in the outcome to have considerable potential for development. But its intrinsic nature is misconstrued if it is seen as a deliberate first step on the way to the changes which ultimately occurred. If the modern town council lay concealed in its provisions, it would be merely anachronistic to suppose that the creation of such an authority was the specific object in view at the time. In fact the measure was largely political in motive and has to be seen in the context of the partisan issues of the day.

The Whig government was dedicated to a series of reforms intended to undermine the power of its Tory opponents who, through various administrations, had been in office for more than twenty years. The Act

---

172 J. S. Mill, *Collected Works*, ed. J. M. Robson *et al.* (London, 1963ff.), xix. 538.
173 S. and B. Webb, op. cit., iv. 236, 346–7; and cf. pp. 16–17 above.

of 1835 was part of this programme. A royal commission was appointed to prepare the ground and its membership and terms of reference alike invited a report severely critical of the municipal bastions of Tory influence. Those aspects of the chartered boroughs were stressed which indicated their general improbity, the misuse of corporate property and revenues, a decline in the quality of the magistracy, and so forth. But the gravamen of the charge levelled was the 'perversion of municipal privileges to political objects' especially in connexion with the election of MPs and with 'rewards for political services'.[174] Consequently the major purpose of the Act was to undermine this political exclusiveness; and Creevey at least thought it was 'a much greater blow to Toryism than the Reform Bill itself'.[175] The commission considered that 246 places in England and Wales fell within its remit as possessing municipal powers. The City of London was held to merit separate attention; sixty-seven boroughs were disregarded because they were so small, being subsequently swept away; and the remaining 178 were dealt with by the Act.[176] In these boroughs it was provided that there should be a council elected by all householders of three years' residence liable for the poor rate and not in receipt of relief. This was a wider franchise than that established for Parliamentary elections three years before and created what Halévy has described as 'nothing less than islands of representative democracy.'[177] The municipality was to be separated from the administration of justice, the town magistrates being appointed in future by the Crown, a device which, it was hoped, would enable Whig governments to bring into being benches of more congenial political affiliation. These changes were primarily designed to secure a new

---

174 See e.g. Municipal Corporations in England and Wales, R. Com. 1st Rep., 1835 (vol. xxiii), p. 34 §73. On the partiality of the commission and the political significance of its work, see G. B. A. M. Finlayson, 'The Municipal Corporation Commission and Report, 1833–35', *Bulletin of the Institute of Historical Research*, xxxvi (1963), pp. 45–52; W. I. Jennings, 'The Municipal Revolution', in H. J. Laski et al., op. cit., pp. 57, 59–60; B. Keith-Lucas, *The English Local Government Franchise: a Short History* (Oxford, 1952), pp. 48ff.; N. McCord, 'Some Limitations of the Age of Reform', in H. Hearder and H. R. Loyn (eds), *British Government and Administration* (Cardiff, 1974), pp. 199–200; and S. and B. Webb, op. cit., iii. 714, 718–21.
175 Sir H. Maxwell (ed.), *The Creevey Papers* ... (1903; London, 1904), ii. 308. On the general background to the Act, see S. and B. Webb, op. cit., iii. 703–5; iv. 381–4. See also Finlayson, art. cit., esp. pp. 37–8, 49–52; idem, 'The Politics of Municipal Reform, 1835', *English Historical Review*, lxxxi (1966), pp. 674–80, 688–92.
176 5 & 6 Will. IV, c. 76. Reform of the Scottish and Irish corporations was effected in 1833 and 1840 respectively: on these statutes, see E. Halévy, *A History of the English People in the Nineteenth Century* (1913–46; 2nd trans. edn, London, 1961), iii. 214–15.
177 ibid., iii. 215. For the various changes in the franchise and their impact, see *The Rise of Collectivism* (London, 1983), pp. 201–21.

political balance by eliminating or restricting rival – that is, Tory and Anglican – influence in places that hitherto had largely been its strongholds. Given that this was the purpose in view, it was not thought necessary to impose on the reformed corporations any particularly wide sphere of action or the duty of implementing an enlightened or advanced conception of social utility (though some Radicals such as Place and Roebuck may have envisaged this).[178] So the new councils received no more authority than it had been usual to bestow by private Bill over the previous half century or so. Moreover no forceful attempt was made in the Act itself to transfer to the boroughs the powers and duties of the trading companies, improvement commissions, and other such bodies already providing local services.[179] In the outcome the town council remained as simply one institution among several that might be constitutionally distinct and continue side by side for some or many years. For example by the half century only twenty-nine such councils had exclusive powers of draining, cleansing, and paving; and as late as 1879 there were still fourteen boroughs in which the sanitary authority was independent of the council.[180] Nor was there any attempt (as there had been in the Poor-Law changes of the previous year) to ensure a national uniformity in the size and resources of the boroughs as units of administration. A wide disparity in these respects remained. Again the Act left quite untouched the government of many large and important towns like Bolton, Birmingham, Manchester, and Sheffield: because these were not already incorporated they were not directly affected by its provisions. In fact the boroughs dealt with in the Act composed a relatively small part of the then total urban area of the country and their inhabitants numbered only one-seventh of the population of England and Wales as a whole. Clearly if the 1835 Act was intended to reorganize municipal government in the country on a systematic and unified basis, as a means of providing effective urban services, it was hardly well conceived. This was no doubt one reason why the reform of a corporation sometimes created little local excitement or anticipation. It was also why a better prospect of advance might be offered by, say, the enhancement of the powers of an existing court leet or improvement commission.

The Act thus left the major problems of urban government unresolved. Indeed it was not intended to deal with them and so cannot reasonably be

---

178 Cf. McCord, loc. cit., p. 199. For the possibilities anticipated by the philosophical radicals, see Fraser, *Power and Authority in the Victorian City*, pp. 18–21.
179 Any such transfer was to be left to the trustees of the bodies concerned, 5 & 6 Will. IV, c.76, §lxxv.
180 J. L. and B. Hammond, *The Age of the Chartists 1832–1854: a Study of Discontent* (London, 1930), p. 53; Redlich and Hirst, *Local Government in England*, i. 132. For the gradual process of assimilation, see S. and B. Webb, op. cit., iv. 346–7.

seen as a step deliberately taken to sustain local interventionism. Yet the statute did contain elements capable of such development. And it was on this, as it were, unintended potential that the second phase of the change (which saw the emergence of the town council to pre-eminence) depended. Three particular provisions of the Act proved important in this regard. One was the clause which gave to the reformed councils a general authority to make by-laws for 'the good Rule and Government of the Borough'.[181] While not intended to mean much at the time it was obviously a duty capable of wide application if ever the will existed to press it or if circumstances seemed to require this (as they did as the century wore on). Moreover the powers at the disposal of many town councils to fulfil this responsibility did increase quite substantially though the development was intermittent and of varying effect. The reason it was not uniform was simply that it proceeded *ad hoc* through, on the one hand, the acquisition of special or adoptive powers and, on the other, the absorption of the functions of other local institutions as by taking over the environmental tasks of an improvement commission. In any event the result was a cumulative accretion of both authority and duty. This process was made feasible, too, by another – and practically more important – provision of the Act which conferred authority to levy an unlimited rate for general purposes.[182] This was the one thing perhaps which ultimately ensured the triumph of the municipal corporation. For other bodies, such as the improvement commissions, had only limited financial powers. Not – again – that it was originally intended or expected that this provision would be widely used as a basis for extensive social improvement. For one thing ratepayers themselves could be counted on to resist this. For another, in many places the revenue accruing from corporate property (now under new management) or from an improvement rate otherwise sanctioned was sufficient to cover the cost of the limited municipal tasks then in prospect. In Swansea, for instance, no borough rate was levied until 1872 nearly forty years after the power was granted.[183] It is possible indeed that one aim of the Municipal Corporations Act in 1835 was to reduce, rather than to increase, local expenditure or at least to restrain any extravagance in the use of funds of which the councils were to be considered trustees.[184] But this rating power was one in which considerable possibilities of municipal intervention were implicit. Thirdly there was also provision in

---

181 5 & 6 Will. IV, c. 76, §xc.
182 ibid., §xcii.
183 G. Roberts, *The Municipal Development of the Borough of Swansea to 1900* (n.p. [Swansea], 1940), p. 33.
184 Barber, 'Municipal Government in Leeds, 1835–1914', in Fraser (ed.), *Municipal Reform and the Industrial City*, p. 64; Keith-Lucas, *The English Local Government Franchise*, p. 9.

the Act for the future incorporation of towns other than the chartered boroughs specifically listed in its schedules.[185] The process was complex and costly, however, and this must have inhibited applications. Nevertheless in the first two decades of its operation twenty-two towns, most of them industrial cities, were granted charters.[186] By the late 1870s over sixty new boroughs had been created. A more rapid rate of applications followed after 1877 when the costs of a petition were allowed to be borne on the rates (instead of being met privately as hitherto). And in 1882 a consolidating statute applied the municipal system to twenty-five more towns. The result was that by the turn of the century there was a total of 313 incorporated boroughs. A cumulative momentum built up therefore. As a town council's powers increased and its rating potential came into play, so corporate status seemed more advantageous in dealing with a growing range of urban problems. But the development was none the less often opposed.[187]

Later stages in the emergence of the town council relate to the developments of a general order which occurred during the last three decades of the century. In the 1870s the Public Health Acts confirmed the town councils as urban health authorities; the Artizans' and Labourers' Dwellings Acts passed in 1868 and 1875 made considerable activity possible in housebuilding and redevelopment as J. Chamberlain's mayoralty at Birmingham showed.[188] In 1888 the largest and most important towns (and some others) were given the new status of county borough, thus becoming all-purpose authorities combining the powers and duties of both county and municipality. And in 1902 the responsibilities exercised since 1870 by the school boards were in the towns transferred to the county boroughs, which thus also became local education authorities: a most important shift because these matters were subsequently by far the most costly task shouldered by modern local government.[189]

The result of all this was the creation of what has been called 'the municipal leviathan'. By absorbing the powers of other local bodies, adopting permissive legislation, securing an extension of authority or area by private Act, and through generally applicable statute, the town councils grew in stature and were increasingly involved in treating the

---

185 loc. cit., §cxli.
186 See the list in Fraser, *Power and Authority in the Victorian City*, p. 150.
187 The central chapters of Fraser, *Power and Authority in the Victorian City*, constitute a fascinating series of case-studies relating to municipal development in various midland and northern towns.
188 Cf. *The Rise of Collectivism*, pp. 97–8 and *The Ideological Heritage* (London, 1983), pp. 223–5.
189 The county councils created in 1888 as well as some county districts also became LEAs.

problems of urban life. First of all the basic environmental issues were tackled. Then attention began to turn to other fields of activity. As well as any special powers and an often considerable element of municipal trading (gas and water especially), the typical functions of a town council ranged over roads, drainage and sewerage, public health (including asylums and hospitals), cleanliness and recreation (for instance, baths and washhouses, parks, and such-like), markets, libraries, museums, fire brigades, police and housing.[190] Many of these functions were, of course, traditional local responsibilities; but, by the end of the century (or at least shortly after), the activity they represented was not only much intensified and extended in itself but also by then concentrated on the one body, the municipal council which had emerged to pre-eminence. Thus the borough corporations, from being trustees of a rate fund to be frugally and partially administered, became the providers of a wide and growing range of public services to be conducted with initiative and enterprise: from forms of property they became major instruments of government drawn continually 'further along the collectivist road'.[191]

County reform

At the beginning of the nineteenth century the country gentlemen and clerics, protected in their exclusive occupancy of the magisterial bench by a high property qualification and by their own control over its membership, constituted what the Webbs called 'an autonomous County oligarchy'.[192] As such they were the effective rulers of rural England. But their position and the administrative structure over which they presided increasingly became the subject of depreciatory comment. First of all there was the dislike of many of the policies with which the bench was traditionally associated: the licensing of ale-houses, the enforcement of the game laws, the closing up of footpaths, and so on. Secondly there was the important point that, at a time when the franchise was being extended in other political contexts, the magistrates were not elected or in any formal way representative of or responsible to the citizens of the county. They were a social élite and their exclusive position was emphasized, too, by the practice of meeting in private to conduct much of their business. Of course, in deferential rural society the situation was often accepted as proper; but in the developing political circumstances of the day it did open the bench to the suggestion that its role was an anomaly or anachronism. To these criticisms of the justices themselves had to be added comment directed at the very untidy, indeed confused, array of many bodies dealing with county affairs, a diversity which

---

190 Cf. pp. 38–9 above and n. 144.
191 Fraser, *Power and Authority in the Victorian City*, p. 168.
192 S. and B. Webb, op. cit., iv. 388.

hardly conduced to efficiency. Thus one observer remarked in the early 1880s that the local government of Bedfordshire (selected simply as first in the alphabetical list but by no means untypical) consisted, in addition to the justices in quarter-sessions, of the following bodies, some of them traditional, many created in response to particular pressures and statutory requirements:

> 3 municipal boroughs; 3 urban sanitary districts; 6 rural sanitary districts, some of which stretch into adjoining counties; 6 highway districts, two of which stretch into adjoining counties; 6 burial-board districts; 4 lighting and watching districts; 45 school districts, four of which run into adjoining counties; 6 [poor-law] unions, some of which overstep the county borders; 134 entire poor-law parishes, and portions of three more. All these divisions overlap and interlace. Each of them is governed by its own petty authority, which for the most part wholly ignores the existence of any other division or authority.[193]

There was indeed a chaos of areas, authorities, franchises, and rates.[194] And this alone might account for much of the adverse comment on county government.

There was yet another dimension to this. In the larger towns a similar diversity was (as previously indicated) giving way to the dominance of the elected borough council. But, given the county arrangements as they were, there was no body which might achieve a similar local paramountcy. It was not a role which could be assumed by magistrates who were not responsible or representative in the wider sense then coming into vogue. In particular most of those citizens who paid the county rate had no share in the justices' decisions about expenditure and the policy it reflected. And this was troublesome at a time when otherwise it might have been desirable to increase the functions of the county and to help it in the discharge of this added burden by central aid in relief of the rates. In fact, as the century wore on, the duties of the bench had in some respects been eroded either by the transfer of responsibilities to central government (prison administration is an obvious example) or, as with the Poor-Law, and education after 1870, when the normal county administration was by-passed by the creation of a new elective structure. The anomaly was further emphasized after 1884 when the third Reform Act gave the Parliamentary vote to the agricultural labourer. It was thenceforth difficult (if not impossible) not

193 Chalmers, op. cit., pp. 19–20. Cf. the similar enumeration in respect of Somersetshire cited in C. H. Wilson (ed.), *Essays on Local Government* (Oxford, 1948), p. 4.
194 The variations in respect of date of election, scale of voting, tenure of office, method of election, and candidate qualifications are detailed in a table in Chalmers, op. cit., pp. 29–31 and also in V. D. Lipman, *Local Government Areas 1834–1945* (Oxford, 1949), pp. 74–6.

to extend to him fairly quickly the same right in respect of county government, especially as it could be, and was, urged that the exercise of the local franchise might aid and prepare him in the discharge of his national responsibility. Nor was the issue of principle diminished by the reduction in the mid-seventies of the property qualification for appointment to the county bench.[195] Change seemed inevitable in order to secure some degree of institutional rationalization and also to create a single, representative, that is, elected, body which could oversee the work of the other county agencies and to which further responsibilities, and funds to help meet them, might reasonably be entrusted in an increasingly democratic age. Reform along these lines had often been suggested but nothing came of the various schemes put forward until 1888 when the Salisbury government secured the passage of a Local Government Act for this purpose.[196] Maitland at least had high hopes of this statute – or some aspects of it – and believed it would mark the beginning of the end of the existing 'weltering chaos' among county authorities.[197]

This statute introduced four major changes. First, most of the administrative and financial (but not the judicial and licensing) duties of the JPs were transferred to newly created county councils two-thirds of the membership of which was to be directly elected the remainder being co-opted aldermen. Secondly control of the county police, a matter regarded as having judicial as well as administrative aspects, was put into the hands of a standing joint committee of the county council and quarter-sessions. Thirdly there was some rearrangement of the old geographical counties for administrative purposes (though the divisions chosen were not themselves new). For instance the 'ridings' of Yorkshire and the 'parts' of Lincolnshire each became an administrative county with its own council. Sixty-two such units were created in all (in addition to the special provision that was made for London). Finally sixty-one towns were excluded from the jurisdiction of the new county councils and given 'all-purpose' status as county boroughs. The original conception was of counties as mixed urban and rural areas with only the

---

195 Ownership of real estate producing £100 p.a. (a requirement admittedly sometimes ignored in practice) was replaced by two-year occupation of a dwelling house rated at £100. After 1906 there was a residence qualification only.

196 51 & 52 Vic., c. 41. For the immediate context of the 1888 reforms, see J. P. D. Dunbabin, 'The Politics of the Establishment of County Councils', *Historical Journal*, vi (1963), pp. 226–52.

197 F. W. Maitland, *The Constitutional History of England* (1908; Cambridge, 1974), p. 499. Yet compare the comment on the impending demise of the justice as ruler of the county in his 'The Shallows and Silences of Real Life' (1888), in H. A. L. Fisher (ed.), *The Collected Papers of Frederic William Maitland* (Cambridge, 1911), i. 468–79, the phrase cited being at p. 472.

ten very largest towns in the country excluded from their authority: an idea in some ways like the new 'shire' counties introduced in 1974 and from which only the major conurbations were separated. But the Bill was substantially amended in this regard and six times the number of county boroughs created (with a lowering, too, of the population minimum from 150,000 to 50,000). As a result, eighteen counties were severed from their county towns; and in the big industrial areas the effect was considerable, Lancashire, for example, losing seventeen major centres of population. As finally passed, therefore, the Act established a major division between large towns and the counties which proved to be the cause of a long-standing, indeed fatal, difficulty in the new arrangements.

Apart from police functions (which absorbed roughly a third of county expenditure) the most important tasks of the new administrative county councils concerned highways and bridges; though in 1902, with the abolition of the school boards, they also became local education authorities thus acquiring a function which quickly became by far the most costly of the services for which they were responsible. One purpose which the architects of the new scheme of county government had in mind was that it might be possible to relieve some of the pressure on central government by transferring to the counties certain of its functions; and authority was given in the Act to allow for this though the provision was never effectively used.[198] No doubt this was due in some degree to the difficulties created by the considerable diversity in size and resources between the new administrative counties. For, apart from the division of a few of the traditional geographical counties (already referred to), nothing was done – any more than it had been half a century before with the new boroughs – to secure any uniformity of acreage, population, or rateable value among the new county units. Clearly the continuity of established areas was regarded as more important.[199] And, in fact, despite the introduction of elections, the new counties (except those in Wales or near large towns) were for long still dominated by the same sort of person as before, the traditional 'social leaders'.[200]

Further reforms, this time of the lower tiers of county government,

---

198 51 & 52 Vic., c. 41, §10; and see J. Willis, 'Parliament and the Local Authorities', in H. J. Laski *et al.*, *A Century of Municipal Progress*, p. 414.

199 Some details of these disparities and the difficulties to which they led are to be found at pp. 68–70 below.

200 On the issues, results, and effects of the first county council elections, see J. P. D. Dunbabin, 'Expectations of the New County Councils, and their Realization', *Historical Journal*, viii (1965), pp. 353–79; Keith-Lucas, *The English Local Government Franchise*, pp. 114–15; and Lee, op. cit., *passim*. For Wales where, in the aftermath of 1888, the landed gentry were, on the contrary, routed nearly everywhere, see K. O. Morgan, 'The New Liberalism and the Challenge of Labour: the Welsh Experience, 1885–1929' (1973), in K. D. Brown (ed.), *Essays in Anti-Labour History: Responses to the Rise of Labour in Britain* (London, 1974), p. 160.

followed in 1894 though not without considerable opposition. But the need for some alteration was clear if only to reduce the tangle of existing arrangements and to meet the demand (from Nonconformists for instance) for some democratic change at the lower levels where Anglican vestries and churchwardens tended to dominate affairs. This further legislation complemented the earlier statute in a number of ways.[201] In the first place the existing sanitary and similar authorities were consolidated and replaced by urban and rural districts with their own elected councils (so that bodies originally set up for a special, public health, purpose thus provided the foundation for new general authorities at this level). The non-county (or municipal) boroughs remained in being as county districts. At the same time the parish was abolished as a local government unit in urban districts but retained in the rural areas where there was to be (depending on the population) either a general meeting of ratepayers or a council elected by them. In fact the parishes had in most places long been declining in importance: they had lost functions to the Poor-Law guardians in 1834 and to the more or less independent boards created from time to time to deal with specific tasks.[202] And though one body of opinion held that, in view of this decay, they might as well be abolished, others hoped for a measure of parochial renewal. The clauses of the 1894 Act dealing with the parish were intended to sustain a sense of responsibility for local affairs at this grass-roots level through village Parliaments which would govern themselves. To this extent at least the spirit of Toulmin Smith survived.

London
As by far the largest built-up area, and because it was also the capital, London was treated as an exception in local government terms. This was something of a disadvantage, however, for the metropolis was thereby withdrawn from the general stream of urban advance. Indeed much of the activity of groups such as the Progressive Party and the Fabians at the turn of the century may be regarded in essence as an attempt to secure for London the advantages already achieved in other more go-ahead places such as Birmingham and Manchester. As Sidney Webb wrote: 'Accepting the principle of "Municipal Co-operation", which has proved so advantageous in the larger provincial towns', the question for Londoners is what as citizens they can collectively do for themselves similarly to improve the metropolis and make it 'a pleasanter home for its million families'.[203]

Of course in 1829 the Metropolitan Police district had been created but

201 56 & 57 Vic., c. 73.
202 This loss of powers is described by Keith-Lucas, op. cit., pp. 38-9.
203 S. Webb, *The London Programme* (London, 1891), pp. 207-8.

the force was, as it still uniquely is, placed under the direct control of the Home Department. This respect apart London was (at mid-century) governed by a medley of bodies with no common area, without means of co-ordination, and having no combining authority. Thus there was the City itself, then as now a separate local government unit.[204] In addition there were various groups of justices, eight sewer commissions, a hundred or so paving, lighting, and cleansing boards, and getting on for 180 parish vestries, boards of guardians, commissions of highways and bridges, turnpike trusts, and so on. What was said some decades later applied then: that to give 'a methodical account of London government would be as difficult as to describe the pattern on a patchwork quilt.'[205]

Early attempts to bring some sort of system to this state of affairs – as with the amalgamation in 1826 of the turnpike trusts north of the Thames under a body of commissioners, or with the new Sewer Commission set up in 1848 – had relatively little effect.[206] But, after an inquiry, a Metropolitan Local Management Act brought another arrangement in 1855, creating a Metropolitan Board of Works whose central task (soon supplemented by other functions concerning town improvement) was to build a new sewage system to cope with the formidable sanitary problem posed by what was then the largest urban conglomeration in the world.[207] The area of operation was that covered since 1848 by the Sewer Commission. The MBW was an indirectly elected body its members coming from a second tier of authorities established at the same time. These were elected by all rated householders and, in addition to the City, comprised twenty-three vestries ruling large parishes and fifteen district boards made up of the other fifty-five parishes in the area concerned. The vestries and district boards were the sanitary and nuisance-removal authorities and looked after such matters as minor drainage, street lights, cleaning, paving, and so forth. The MBW achieved a number of improvements.[208] But it was itself under no supervision; and it had no real control over the district boards which tended, therefore, to grow in importance and go their own way. Moreover other *ad hoc* authorities existed or were created: the Common Poor Fund; the City of Westminster; the Metropolitan Asylums Board (1867); the London School Board (1870); the Port of London Sanitary Authority (1872); the various burial boards; the

---

204 The City's traditional institutions and their working are described by S. and B. Webb, op. cit., vol. iii, ch. X.
205 Chalmers, op. cit., p. 141.
206 The first known attempt to establish a municipal authority for the metropolis as a whole was the abortive Bill of 1814 which proposed to set up a Metropolitan Board of Paving Commissioners: see S. and B. Webb, op. cit., iv. 290–2.
207 18 & 19 Vic., c. 120.
208 A. Briggs, *Victorian Cities* (1963; Penguin, 1968), pp. 322–4.

Thames and Lee River Conservancy Board; and so on. Water and gas supply was in the hands of private companies with special statutory powers. It was hardly surprising, therefore, that a further bite of change came in 1888 when the first stage of county reorganization was enacted.[209] A new London County Council was then created with the same area of operation as the MBW but with some extra powers (ranging from tramways to parks, from highways to main drainage). The vestries and district boards remained as executive authorities for the basic services but in 1899, as a means of their reform and also as a kind of counterweight to the power of the LCC, these were themselves reorganized into twenty-eight metropolitan borough councils which were, in fact, somewhat varied in area, population, and rateable value.[210] These changes are another good example of how the apparently new is often little more than a reincarnation or refurbishing of the old. As earlier explained, the parish was generally in decline; but the London vestries, on the contrary, underwent a renaissance. There were no other bodies in the metropolis on whom the administration of the new services might be imposed; and so, after some reorganization, it was to the London vestries that Parliament gave more and more powers of sanitation and control; and, again, it was they which, after further change, were (in the Webbs' words) 'raised to the dignity of Metropolitan Borough Councils, sharing with the London County Council the whole municipal government of the greatest city in the world.'[211]

Under these arrangements, then, London as a whole remained a somewhat diverse entity. There was the single square mile of the old City; the 117 square miles of the LCC, the administrative county; in addition there was the Metropolitan Police district, that of the Metropolitan Water Board (set up in 1904) which was nearly five times the size of the LCC area; and so on. In fact the capital's new government was hardly established when voices were raised demanding its extension to cover the much larger area of Greater London, some 700 square miles of urban sprawl and its semi-rural hinterland as the only real and effective unit. This was a plea reflecting a growing body of opinion that, despite the creation of the LCC, all was still not well, not least because of the growing scope of the problems caused by the improvement of communications, the shift and growth of population, and so on. It was symptomatic of the difficulties that, when the question of London's transport was being tackled after the Great War, the solution found was

---

209 51 & 52 Vic., c. 41, §40. For a review of the various possibilities canvassed, both localist and centralist, see K. Young, 'The Conservative Strategy for London, 1855–1975', *The London Journal*, i (1975), esp. pp. 57–64.
210 62 & 63 Vic., c. 14.
211 S. and B. Webb, op. cit., i. 275–6.

the creation of an *ad hoc* body, the London Passenger Transport Board, with a substantially larger operating area, than through the existing local government system. All the problems besetting London government were obvious but were glossed over in favour of retaining the *status quo*, as in the royal commission report of 1923.[212] And decades were to pass before this nettle of reform was grasped, for there were powerful interests concerned to oppose change in the name of some form of metropolitan decentralization, as with the Conservative proposals for 'tenification'.[213]

Twentieth-century arrangements

Towards the end of the last century, when the new structure of local authorities was taking shape, Maitland commented: 'we have a pretty wild confusion not easily to be described in elementary lectures.'[214] It is indeed difficult to represent the changing position in a clear and brief form; but a somewhat simplified outline of the bodies so far reviewed is indicated in Table 1 which shows the main local authorities at three points in the period 1800–1904.

The major functions of the different types of authority established by the beginning of this century may be easily described. The main responsibilities of the county councils were education (after 1902), highways, and police which between them accounted for 90 per cent of county expenditure. The services provided by the district councils and municipal (or non-county) boroughs varied according to their population but basically related to housing (and slum clearance) and public health. The latter concern reflected the origin of most of these authorities in the nineteenth-century sanitary districts and comprised such things as sewerage, drainage, water supply, baths and washhouses, refuse collection, food and drugs inspection, and such like. After 1919, with the growth of the council estates, the former task – housing – became the districts' and municipalities' politically most vital function.[215] The county districts might also have an additional and substantial miscellany of duties ranging from streetlighting and gas supply to the provision of markets and transport facilities.[216] Parishes, which now

---

212 Local Government of Greater London, R. Com. Rep., 1923 (vol. xii), Cmd. 1830, pp. 113–14 §428.
213 These and later aspects of the matter are reviewed in Young, art. cit.; and see below pp. 91–2.
214 Maitland, *The Constitutional History of England*, p. 499.
215 Some indication of the scale of building involved is given in *The Rise of Collectivism*, p. 99.
216 For something of the range of functions involved, see Keith-Lucas and Richards, *A History of Local Government in the Twentieth Century*, ch. III.

Table 1 *The main local institutions in England and Wales, 1800–1904*

The old patchwork (1800)	The new patchwork (1870)	The reorganization[a] (1904)
parishes	largely as in 1800	administrative counties
manorial courts	*plus:*	non-county boroughs
county justices		urban districts
town and county meetings	poor-law boards	rural districts
	health boards	parishes
municipal corporations	burial boards	county boroughs
improvement commissions	school boards	poor-law boards (until 1930)
	highway boards	
sewer commissions	etc.	
incorporated guardians		
turnpike trusts		
etc.		
London:	*London:*	*London:*
parishes	Metropolitan Board of Works	London County Council
various boards and commissions	district boards	metropolitan boroughs
City of London	School Board	City of London
	Asylum Board	Metropolitan Water Board
	etc.	
	City of London	

a Two points should perhaps be noted: (i) there were also numerous joint authorities, on which see below pp. 111–15; (ii) the structure in Ireland was on the same model; in Scotland there were certain variations provided for in the 1889 Act but the family resemblance with English arrangements is striking. For a diagrammatic representation of the reorganization in England and Wales in the 1950s and since, see Figure 1, p. 96 below.

existed in local government terms only in the rural districts, had fallen far from their original position of importance and dealt with a few minor matters like allotments, footpaths, and (again increasingly significant after the Great War) the allocation of council houses. The county boroughs, as all-purpose authorities, combined the functions of county and county district. In London the LCC had broadly the same responsibilities as a county (except, of course, for police) while the metropolitan boroughs were in a roughly similar position to the county districts elsewhere. The functions of the school boards were in 1902 transferred to the counties, county boroughs, and some of the larger county districts. The boards of guardians were abolished in 1929, their Poor-Law tasks being allocated to the counties and county boroughs.

By the beginning of the present century, then, a new structure of local authorities had been established, one which subsisted without fundamental change until the 1970s. It was all more homogeneous or regular than it had ever been but there was still considerable variety and disparity to be observed. Nor is this surprising when it is recalled that the arrangements were the result of a series of more or less *ad hoc* administrative and political responses spread over three-quarters of a century and in no real sense the outcome of general principles and their considered application. In 1919 C. B. Fawcett commented:

> Our local government garb is inherited from the days of the small self-contained borough, jealous of its independence of the feudal lord, and the isolated village, which was under his control. It has been strained and torn in innumerable places by the growth and shifting of our population and the changes in our modes of life and association. And to meet these difficulties it has been darned and patched at frequent intervals, without any system or regularity. The problem of adjusting the local government divisions to the needs of the people has never been viewed as a whole; but until it is so considered there can be no hope of any real solution of it.[217]

Naturally the increasing pressures and problems of the present century put this new patchwork of local authorities under considerable strain. Notable defects emerged; and the changes that ensued are an important further reflection of the way our political institutions have had to be adapted, even transformed, to try to meet more effectively the needs of the modern age.

LITTLE LOCAL DIFFICULTIES

> ...and now remains
> That we find out the cause of this effect,
> Or rather say, the cause of this defect,
> For this effect defective comes by cause;...
> *Hamlet*, II. ii. 100–3

Only a few decades after it was completed, the changed local government structure was deemed to be 'in grave need of reform'; by 1947 it was said to be facing 'a crisis of the first magnitude'.[218] Certain basic flaws did indeed appear in its structure and operation especially as these were affected by such important social changes as the growth and shift of population, technological development not least the speeding-up of communications, and the enhancement of public expectations in respect of the level and range of services. There was also the impact of war and of economic distress on a large scale. In short the local government arrangements no longer corresponded to the new pattern of life, work,

---

217 C. B. Fawcett, *Provinces of England: a Study of Some Geographical Aspects of Devolution* (London, 1919), p. 29.
218 W. A. Robson, *The Development of Local Government* (London, 1931), p. 124; op. cit. (2nd edn, London, 1948), p. 7.

and needs which was emerging. Some adjustments were made as with the series of palliative statutes sponsored by N. Chamberlain after the Great War culminating in the Local Government Act of 1929. In retrospect it can be seen that these measures left the main problems largely untouched.

The principal difficulties which appeared over the years were as follows.

The first may baldly be described as town versus country, a conflict which (almost from the beginning) had 'been gnawing at the vitals of local government'.[219] There were two aspects to the problem. One concerned the extension of the boundaries of existing county boroughs. These were usually large and thriving towns that tended to grow through a proliferation of housing and industry and, as the land available for development within their jurisdiction was limited, there was always pressure to expand by taking over adjacent parts of a neighbouring county. Alternatively various built-up areas would merge and become a single urban agglomeration with a common pattern of work and living and with a county borough as its focus. Inevitably that centre would urge the advantages of a single local government unit to administer the services of the whole. As well the surrounding rural areas tended increasingly to be drawn into the ambit of the towns in terms both of work and the provision of facilities. But, of course, the wish to absorb land or urban outgrowths was a major cause of tension for to grant it would be to impose a severe loss on the county affected. None the less in the half-century after 1889 nearly 230 such extensions were permitted involving in total the transfer of an area of some 360,000 acres, population of nearly $1\frac{3}{4}$ million people, and property with a rateable value of more than £8 millions.[220] All this obviously constituted a considerable blow to the counties concerned. But, in addition to this there was the second dimension of the problem, for the counties were, and for similar reasons, also threatened (as it were) from within. A flourishing municipality or urban district would naturally wish to achieve independence of the county in which it was situated by promotion to county borough status. But at one blow this would deprive the county of a substantial proportion of the resources on which the viability of the services it provided, not least to the rural areas, depended. Between 1889 and 1922 thirty-three such proposals for promotion were made but, in recognition of the potential effect on the counties involved, a net increase of only twenty-one county boroughs was permitted. Thus their total number rose from sixty-one to eighty-two; and the loss

---

219 Robson, op. cit. (3rd rev. edn, London, 1954), pp. 58, 79.
220 V. D. Lipman, 'The Development of Areas and Boundary Changes (1888–1939)', in C. H. Wilson (ed.), *Essays on Local Government* (Oxford, 1948), pp. 28–9, 37, 43–4.

involved for the counties was 100,000 acres, population of over 1¼ millions, and rateable value of £6½ millions.[221]

Continuation of these two trends would clearly be disastrous for the counties affected, not least since they were increasingly being expected to assume costly functions. As it was, Lancashire County Council, for instance, had lost population of 667,000 and Staffordshire C.C. of nearly 400,000. Not surprisingly the local authority associations themselves could not agree how to resolve the issue, an impasse largely reflected in the reports of a royal commission which sat from 1923 to 1929 and whose final recommendations were largely concerned with matters of administrative detail.[222] However one positive outcome of its deliberations was embodied in an Act of 1926 which made promotions to county borough status more difficult: the minimum population requirement was raised from 50,000 to 75,000 and application became a more lengthy and costly process.[223] The result was that, after the promotion of Doncaster in that same year, no further advancement to county borough status occurred for a long time. After the last war there were numerous requests for boundary extensions and promotions (while, for their part, the county councils wanted nearly all the existing county boroughs demoted).[224] In fact the county borough population minimum was again raised substantially to 100,000; and the few actual attempts that were made to achieve the higher status were opposed or discouraged. There was a handful of successes in the 1960s – Luton and Solihull were advanced in 1964 as were Teesside and Torbay four years later – but by then it was becoming clear that some radical alteration to the whole local government system was impending. The crucial difficulty of the situation may be exemplified by the position of Cambridge which had been seeking county borough status since before the Great War. It had become a quite large, bustling town with a population (in 1971) of about 100,000 and a rateable value of £6¼ millions, the former being roughly a third and the latter a half of those of the entire administrative county of Cambridgeshire. The effect of the town's loss on the county's revenue and services may be imagined; and this single instance alone makes very clear the reasons why it was increasingly difficult for a growing town to be allowed the promotion in view. Given the increasing actual fusion of town and countryside in many places, it might seem that an effective local government system could function only on the basis of an integrated administrative structure reflecting this fact of social life. But it was hardly possible so long as, in particular, the separate county

---

221 ibid., p. 28.
222 Local Government, R. Com. Final Rep., 1929–30 (vol. xv), Cmd. 3436.
223 16 & 17 Geo. V, c. 38, §1.
224 Sir M. T. Eve, *The Future of Local Government* (London, 1951), p. 3.

and county borough areas remained as the twin, but distinct, bases of the existing arrangements. For, as R. H. S. Crossman said in the mid-sixties, this created a conflict 'inherent' in the established state of affairs and which was, in his view, 'one of the most stultifying things in our whole governmental system.'[225]

A similar difficulty concerned the large metropolitan places. 'Conurbation' was a word invented in 1915 by the Scottish botanist and sociologist, Sir Patrick Geddes, who used it to describe 'city regions' or 'town aggregates', extensive and continuous urban development which included and connected two or more substantial towns.[226] In local government terms such places were often seen as a problem that could not easily be tackled within the legal structure of the reorganized nineteenth-century arrangements. It is true that London had been treated as a special case from the outset though even there the built-up area exceeded the administrative boundaries established. But what of the other conurbations such as Greater Manchester or Birmingham, the West Riding, Tyneside, or the large urban conglomerations which had developed along the banks of the Clyde and the Mersey? These were equally single communities in many respects; but it would be difficult to treat any of them as a unit of administration except in the context of a general and radical process of local government reform. For example, in the greater Manchester area with a population of nearly 3 million people there were seventy-five different local authorities (more if the rural parishes were included). Being in some ways a unity, such a conurbation needed (it was often urged) to be treated accordingly, in respect of at least such major and costly services as planning, transport, and education. As well, this kind of situation constituted a special instance of the conflict between town and country already referred to: housing needs, urban overcrowding, the development of communications, and so on led to increasing encroachment and pressure on the rural periphery of the conurban area as a whole; yet to create a single metropolitan authority would diminish, perhaps substantially, the counties from which its parts would be withdrawn.[227]

A third set of problems arose from the two- or three-tiered structure of authorities and the distribution of functions between the different levels. The allocation of responsibilities had occurred in a piecemeal, even haphazard, way. Professor Robson believed it was 'so devoid of plan or order as to appear almost anarchical.' There had been a 'formless scattering of powers' merely; and this was certainly not conducive either

---

225 R. H. S. Crossman, *The Diaries of a Cabinet Minister* (London, 1975–7), i. 65, 440. Cf. ibid., i. 132, 300, 509, 622; ii. 255.
226 See the citations in *OEDS*, i. 626.
227 On the conurbation, see also pp. 95, 97 below.

to efficiency or good government.[228] Thus sometimes a county council was authorized to act throughout the whole county but at others in part of it only. Sometimes its powers were compulsory, at others not. In regard to certain functions the county could proceed only if it were of a certain size. A duty might be held concurrently with the districts; or the county might (or might not) have delegated a particular task to them. In some cases it had a supervisory power over the work of the districts; in some, but not others, it might even act in default; sometimes it could only persuade. What this complex state of affairs often meant in practice was that what was really a single function – such as education or public health – was split up, and the administrative power that should deal with the service was fragmented or diffused so that the formulation of a coherent policy, let alone its implementation, was rendered almost impossible. 'Could confusion be worse confounded?' Robson asked after a detailed review of these matters.[229] And the issue was further compounded by an intrinsic deficiency in the position of the smaller county districts. This appears as one aspect of the fourth general difficulty which concerns the disparity of cognate institutions.

There was indeed much diversity. In the same legal class of authority (say, the county borough or urban district) there was a most significant variation of area, population, and rateable value, and this resulted in what was recognized in between the wars as a notable 'asymmetry of structure'.[230] The kind of dissimilarity involved is easily indicated. In 1971 the most populous county in England and Wales, Lancashire, contained $2\frac{1}{2}$ million people while the least, Radnorshire, had only just over 18,000; and their respective rateable values were £94 millions and £617,000. Dramatic differences of this sort also existed in respect of the municipal boroughs and county districts. Even the county boroughs showed a notable contrast in respect of the main indicators concerned: Birmingham, for instance, had a rateable value of £55 millions while Merthyr Tydfil's was only £$1\frac{1}{2}$ millions.[231] The problem that arose from this state of affairs was twofold.

It was, first, that many of the smaller or poorer authorities in a given class were unable to perform with reasonable effectiveness the duties imposed on them by Parliament. A given responsibility might require a technical staff and area of operation not attainable by all councils within the category to which the function was allocated. Thus some trading services, to be run economically, require a densely populated area as a

---

228 Robson, op. cit., pp. 191–2, 216–17.
229 ibid., p. 192.
230 Local Government, R. Com. 2nd Rep., 1928–9 (vol. viii), Cmd. 3213, p. 8 §23.
231 I take these figures from P. W. Jackson, *Local Government* (3rd edn, London, 1976), pp. 35–6 where a full range of examples is given for each type of authority. Cf. W. A. Robson, *Local Government in Crisis* (1966; rev. 2nd edn, London, 1968), ch. XI.

basic market: many smaller and, especially, rural authorities, therefore, either relied on other public undertakings or on private enterprise. In some cases they had to join together with other authorities similarly placed which simply reinforced the point that, taken individually, their resources or areas were too small. Or, of course, they went without or accepted an inferior service: for the diversities could lead to a great and (it seemed to many observers) intolerable variation in standards. The smaller county districts were particularly vulnerable in this regard many of them being quite unable to provide adequately even a minimum array of the sometimes costly and complex services required by law. It was noted in 1927, for instance, that nearly 500 districts had a population of less than 5,000; while twenty-seven were responsible for the interests of fewer than 1,000 inhabitants.[232] Over the years something was done to alleviate the problem by the process of 'county review', that is, the rectification of district boundaries under powers authorized by the Act of 1888; and, after the Onslow inquiry in the 1920s, a considerable number of district amalgamations was imposed with a view to creating more viable authorities.[233] Even so, as late as 1950 there was one small UDC with a population of 2,200 and where the product of a penny rate was only £45.[234] The municipal boroughs and county districts (together with the rural parishes) constituted the great majority of local authorities in the country and represented government at grass-roots level. But so long as there was a considerable variation in their size and resources, and so in the adequacy of their services, the whole structure was bound to be weakened for many of them were simply not capable of operating as effective independent units. This is why some of their functions were transferred to the counties: elementary education (save for the few 'excepted' districts), police and fire brigades, the youth employment service, town and country planning, and maternity and child welfare among them.[235] The second problematic consequence was that a systematic allocation of functions was clearly impossible so long as there was an enormous disparity in population, size, and resources between individual authorities of the same legal type. There were numerous difficulties in giving a new task to a given class of council because so many of the particular bodies concerned would be unable to carry out the duties efficiently. The job might be within the resources and capacity of the larger members of the class; but the smaller would find it either

232 Local Government, R. Com. 2nd Rep., 1928–9, Cmd. 3213, p. 7 §19. For the origins of these small districts, see ibid., pp. 7–8 §20.
233 For details, see V. D. Lipman, *Local Government Areas 1834–1945* (Oxford, 1949), pp. 187ff.
234 Eve, op. cit., p. 2.
235 See the account of one municipal borough in A. H. Birch, *Small-Town Politics: a Study of Political Life in Glossop* (1959; Oxford, 1967), p. 126.

impossible or terribly burdensome. Because of this, responsibilities which might have been given to local government were not so allocated; and others were taken away.

This, indeed, was the fourth unsatisfactory aspect of the system: the tendency for functions to be transferred, or given, either to central government or (in ironic reversal of earlier trends) to *ad hoc* bodies subject to a varying degree of public control. This was a most disturbing feature because it involved not just the transfer of a duty from one authority to another but a loss of responsibility by elected local government as a whole. It occurred, for instance, in the case of substantial and costly services that needed a big area of operation or a large pool of resources for optimum efficiency or where there was difficulty in otherwise ensuring nation-wide co-ordination and uniformity of operation or treatment. Thus certain public utilities, though originally pioneered perhaps by many local authorities or even substantially owned by them – like telephones, electricity generation and distribution, gas undertakings, water supply, and road passenger transport – were, in time, largely nationalized or otherwise transformed in respect of ownership and operation. Again, for reasons of political sensitivity, as well as of cost and the need for uniformity of treatment, assistance to the unemployed who had exhausted their insurance rights ceased to be a primary local concern in the 1930s, as did general public assistance to the needy a decade or so later, thus breaking a traditional link between local authorities and the relief of destitution which had existed since the time of the Tudors. Similarly some health and welfare functions were lost as with the transfer of the local hospitals to the new health service in 1948. This was justified because, it was said, they needed larger catchment areas if they were to provide adequate specialist resources; but it was none the less 'a shattering blow'.[236] In the later 1940s too, the task of valuing property for rating was (after more than three centuries) transferred to the Board of Inland Revenue. Again the growing importance of trunk roads and later the development of the motorway system reduced the local role in this particular respect to that of agent merely.[237] And after the Second World War the new towns were developed outside the ambit of the local government system within which they might have been expected to be placed. Nor are these isolated instances of the loss of important functions by local government, a diminution hardly offset by the extensions that occurred in other fields.

As already implied, many of the matters mentioned had crucial financial aspects, and these may be seen to constitute a fifth major defect

---

236 Robson, *Local Government in Crisis*, p. 15.
237 Though, of course, well over 90 per cent of total road length remains a local responsibility.

revealed by the local government system. Its autonomy and efficiency were threatened because the range and expense of its duties increased more rapidly than the revenue at its disposal. Its financial basis, the rating system, proved inadequate. A rate is a tax on the assessed value of occupied land and buildings and for long provided the measure of taxable capacity for local purposes. But, over the years, rateable values grew relatively slowly, some hereditaments (dwelling-houses in particular) being especially undervalued. Moreover from 1875 on, certain properties were derated by law, that is, wholly or partly exempted from the tax; and though compensation was provided it was also the case that henceforth the rate was not fully in local hands. As well, rates were (like all taxes) a politically sensitive issue so that any proposal to increase them always aroused opposition. Consequently, as compared with rising costs, a shortfall could appear in the rate fund. Of course a deficiency might be met or diminished by imposing charges of various kinds, from rents or the interest on securities, by the transfer of any profit made by trading services, and so forth. Such miscellaneous sources were an increasingly significant part of the current revenue of local authorities. Even so, as the pressure of costs mounted, councils were invariably loath to embark on new enterprises or else became extremely concerned with economy. The result was that there seemed sometimes, or often, to be a failure to establish or continue services or to undertake improvements regarded by many as desirable or necessary.[238] It was in this context that local agencies began to receive help from national funds whether as a stimulus to provision, a subsidy to poorer areas, or in relief of the ratepayer.

This financial aid began in a very small way and on an *ad hoc* basis. Some of the earliest subventions related to prisons, the cost of criminal prosecutions, and police, these being services of national significance in respect to which uniform standards were deemed desirable. Certain Poor-Law grants were made as part of the package deal accompanying the repeal of Corn Laws as a means of lightening the rate burden on the agricultural interest which had lost the protection of a tariff. And loans were available for various capital purposes. In due course a whole range of local activities and services was thus aided and stimulated to some degree or other; and over the years the amount involved grew inexorably (as Table 2 shows). This aroused some concern because it was widely felt that local government should not be so dependent on central funds. The problem was grasped quite early in the process of grant giving. As part of the restructuring of the local system in the 1880s, it was proposed to replace most of the existing specific grants-in-aid with a general subsidy

---

[238] E. P. Hennock, 'Finance and Politics in Urban Local Government in England, 1835–1900', *Historical Journal*, vi (1963), pp. 212–25.

Table 2 Receipts of local authorities in England and Wales, 1868–1984[a]

(all amounts £m current prices)

Year	Total receipts	Rates amount	Rates %	Government grants amount	Government grants %	Loans amount	Loans %	Other[b] amount	Other[b] %	% of grants to rates
1868	30.4	16.5	54.3	0.8	2.6	5.5	18.1	7.6	25.0	4.8
1880	53.0	22.5	42.5	2.7	5.1	13.7	25.9	14.1	26.6	12.0
1900	100.6	40.7	40.5	12.2	12.1	23.4	23.3	24.3	24.2	30.0
1920	282.2	105.6	37.4	48.3	17.1	24.3	8.6	104.0	36.9	45.7
1940	711.8	201.3	28.3	181.9	25.6	89.4	12.6	239.2	33.6	90.4
1960	2,530.9	649.9	25.7	705.6	27.9	513.5	20.3	661.9	26.2	108.6
1979–80	29,979.7	6,122.5	20.4	12,096.5	40.4	3,135.9	10.5	8,624.8	28.8	197.6
1983–4	46,069.5	11,913.3	25.9	16,875.7	36.6	3,806.3	8.3	13,474.2	29.3	141.7

a Data up to 1960 are from B. R. Mitchell and P. Deane, *Abstract of British Historical Statistics* (Cambridge, 1962), pp. 414–15 and B. R. Mitchell and H. G. Jones, *Second Abstract of British Historical Statistics* (Cambridge, 1971), p. 163 (any discontinuities are explained in footnotes to the relevant tables). Figures for 1979–80 to 1983–4 are from the CSO's *Annual Abstract of Statistics*. Percentages are rounded up and so may not always total exactly 100. The totals in this column are estimated by calculation from the other data given.

b e.g. receipts from fees, interest, rents, sales, etc.

in the form of the proceeds of certain national taxes collected in each area, for instance the monies accruing from given licences and duties. These 'assigned revenues' were intended to place the newly created authorities on a more viable financial footing.[239] Although at the time the scheme produced more than twice the value of the grants foregone, it failed simply because once more the cost of services came to exceed the revenue collected. In the circumstances authorities clamoured for more and more central aid not least as many of the expensive services they were responsible for – education, housing, police, main roads, and the like – were of major national consequence and not simply of local benefit. As Table 2 shows, currently something like a third of local receipts comes from grants (about 20 per cent of these being specific, the rest the general rate support grant).[240] Happily it is not necessary here to follow the very complex details of the way in which this grant system has evolved or operates.[241] It is sufficient to note that the crucial role it has come to play in local government finance is a mark of the extent to which authorities have ceased to be autonomous as the growing burden of the duties they have acquired outstripped their own sources of income. It follows that financial independence could only be restored either by reducing the level or scope of locally provided services or by reforming the system of local finance so as to provide other sources of revenue.[242] Part of the problem is that local authorities undertake something like a third of public expenditure as a whole so that the more they are financially autonomous the less easy it will be for central government to influence the general pattern of demand and investment or to bring spending under control. Moreover a diversity of local provision (and taxation) would be likely to ensue to the detriment of nationally uniform standards of service which, rightly or wrongly, people have come to expect. With this in mind, there is a sense in which those of some collectivist persuasion will welcome the tendency to financial dependence; while libertarians may find themselves in a quandary: they ought perhaps to believe in the decentralization of initiative, yet to bring about a decline in public spending and activity as a whole a massive degree of control over local government is necessary.

But, in fact, the degree of central government supervision that has

---

239 R. J. Bennett, *Central Grants to Local Governments: the Political and Economic Impact of the Rate Support Grant in England and Wales* (Cambridge, 1982), p. 262.
240 Of course if loans are excluded the proportion of grants to the total is slightly higher: in 1983–4 it was 39.9 per cent.
241 See e.g. M. Schulz, 'The Development of the Grant System', in C. H. Wilson (ed.), op. cit., pp. 113–60; Bennett, op. cit., chs 2–3; B. Keith-Lucas and P. G. Richards, *A History of Local Government in the Twentieth Century* (London, 1978), pp. 141–9; and T. Burgess and A. Travers, *Ten Billion Pounds: Whitehall's Takeover of the Town Halls* (London, 1980).
242 For the various revenue proposals, see below pp. 100–5.

grown up, basically (though by no means entirely) as a result of increasing financial dependence, is the focus of all the many difficulties which the local government system revealed.

CENTRAL INVOLVEMENT AND CONTROL

> There is nothing about a borough council that corresponds to autonomy.
> SUMNER, L. J. in *Roberts* v. *Hopwood*, [1925] A. C. 578 at 607

The growth of centralization may indeed be seen as the most fundamental problem to emerge within the context of the reorganized local government arrangements established at the end of the last century. It is, so to say, the culminating tendency to which all the other deficiencies lead: if they had not existed there would have been notably less pressure of a centralizing kind. And the tendency is crucial because (if carried too far) it becomes the manifest nemesis of local self-government as such. Nor is this a matter of formal authority simply. As Professor Robson wrote, it is in Britain

> seldom necessary for administrative authorities to invoke their legal powers when dealing with one another. Matters are discussed in a gentlemanly and urbane manner, with the stronger party often being the first to suggest a compromise in the gentlest manner. But everyone knows where the whip hand lies – and acts accordingly.[243]

Throughout the whole history of government organization in these islands, there has been a fundamental ambivalence about the status and role of local offices: they have been seen both as subject to central government and as independent of it.[244] The basis of their subordination was the suzerainty of the king. It was usually he who created a corporation by the grant of a charter; and the various local bodies were (in the Webbs' phrase) essentially units of obligation liable to render public service, to maintain the King's Peace, to repair his bridges and highways, to exact and pay the revenue due to him, to suppress 'nuisances', and so forth.[245] And the senior local functionaries – lord-lieutenants, sheriffs, and magistrates – were nominally royal officers whose actions were subject to review. Yet the formal authority of the monarch and his ministers was substantially mitigated in practice. There was a strong sense that local rights were independent claims long-

---

243 W. A. Robson, *The Development of Local Government* (1931; 3rd rev. edn, London, 1954), p. 40.
244 Cf. J. Redlich and F. W. Hirst, *Local Government in England* (London, 1903), i. 10.
245 S. and B. Webb, *English Local Government from the Revolution to the Municipal Corporations Act* (London, 1906–29), i. 40–1, 306–7; iv. 356–8; J. S. Watson, *The Reign of George III 1760–1815* (Oxford, 1960), p. 45.

recognized; and, in many respects, local officers acted as a self-appointing oligarchy exercising a large discretion in the administration of the law. After the civil war and the revolution of 1688, the centre invariably abstained from intervention in local matters.[246] And if Parliament exercised a certain supervision through the scrutiny of local Bills, its members were (it must be remembered) the same sort of people who dominated the affairs of the county and the borough: it consisted of the 'consuls of the county republics'.[247] And, by the eighteenth century, the formal authority of the king's ministers was diluted into 'an anarchy of local autonomy.'[248] Hence the major centres of effective public direction which faced the first consequences of the Great Change were located not at Westminster or Whitehall but in the counties, boroughs, and parishes throughout the land. The tradition of autonomous communal responsibility thus antedates the substantial modern growth of central intervention; and the structure of our general government was almost a kind of superficies based on the underlying reality of local administration. Yet, as the pressures of modern life intensified and local institutions proved by themselves unable to cope with the problems facing them, this sense of primacy diminished. The structure of local bodies had radically to be adapted by legislation; and their mode of operation came to be increasingly dependent on central advice, regulation, and financial support. The contrast was reflected in a classic passage in the report of the Royal Sanitary Commission of 1868–71. In acknowledgement of the traditional view, it is boldly avowed that 'local self-government has been generally recognized as of the essence of our national vigour.' But then it is stated, just as firmly, that 'local administration, *under central superintendence*, is the distinguishing feature of our government.'[249] The two principles are hardly compatible, as Toulmin Smith for one would quickly have pointed out.

The 'drift towards centralization', or the 'concentration process' (as it has also been called), is reflected in the three main channels of oversight.[250] These are Parliament, the courts, and the central executive departments.

246 Cf. F. W. Maitland, *Township and Borough* (Cambridge, 1898), p. 95; S. and B. Webb, op. cit., vol. i, p. vi. A more recent study also makes clear that any pressure by central government was rarely long sustained and that local initiative was crucial: see G. C. F. Forster, 'Government in Provincial England under the Later Stuarts', *Trans. R. Hist. S.*, xxxiii (1983), esp. pp. 35, 40, 48.
247 J. H. Grainger, *Character and Style in English Politics* (Cambridge, 1969), p. 6. Cf. Bacon's apt remark in *The Works*, ed. J. Spedding *et al.* (London, 1858–74), xiii. 304; and S. and B. Webb, op. cit., i. 554–6.
248 S. and B. Webb, op. cit., iv. 353. Cf. ibid., i. 535, 556; iv. 395; and viii. 73.
249 Sanitary Laws, R. Com. 2nd Rep., 1871 (vol. xxxv), C. 281, p. 16 (my italics).
250 For the terms cited, see A. T. Peacock and J. Wiseman, *The Growth of Public Expenditure in the United Kingdom* (rev. new edn, London, 1967), pp. xxxiv–xxxv,

Parliament has always been closely involved with this superintendence in the sense that, in the absence of a charter, local authorities needed legislative sanction to authorize their activity. Originally Parliament acted largely at the request of individual localities, passing local Bills with provisions relating to the sponsoring body. During the eighteenth century these Bills were invariably approved without much scrutiny. But, as their number increased and as their broader significance and cumulative effect became more obvious, various changes occurred. Thus, as Parliament found it was dealing with the same sort of provision in many separate such Bills, the time-saving device was adopted in the 1840s of passing model clauses Acts which could be incorporated wholesale in particular local statutes, as with the Town Improvement and Town Police Clauses Acts which were both enacted in 1847.[251] This procedure entailed a kind of control in that it established indirectly the detailed form of a great deal of local legislation (much of it concerning services of an environmental kind) and was a way, too, of ensuring a degree of uniform provision in this regard. A cognate development was the so-called adoptive or enabling Act by which powers and functions could be given to any appropriate local authority that wished to take them up. Then there was the growing tendency for Parliament to gather together an array of municipal initiatives and to pass general legislation concerning these matters instead of just responding to individual petitions for a local Bill. An early example of this was the Health of Towns Act (1846).[252] And while a private Bill might, of course, be subject to considerable inquisition during its passage, public legislation of this sort would be more scrutinized still because it was concerned not with the affairs of a particular area or authority, but gave wider powers. Moreover, as compared with the clauses and adoptive Acts, the 'may' was replaced by 'shall' and local bodies thus seemed more like agents of national policy than before. Parliament was no longer reacting to their particular initiatives simply; rather they all had to respond to its will. This was manifest, too, when new forms of local authority were created by the legislature, as with the boards of guardians (1834) and the school boards (1870); or similarly when an existing array of local bodies was transformed as the municipal corporations were in 1835 or the counties half a century later.

29–30, 104, 118–20; M. Abramowitz and V. F. Eliasberg, *The Growth of Public Employment in Great Britain* (Princeton, N.J., 1957), pp. 83–4.
251 There were fourteen 'Clauses Acts' passed between 1845 and 1847 about half of which concerned local authorities: see the list in W. I. Jennings, *Parliament* (1939; 2nd edn, Cambridge, 1957), p. 463 n. 3.
252 R. M. Gutchen, 'Local Improvements and Centralization in Nineteenth-Century England', *Historical Journal*, iv (1961), pp. 87–8.

Judicial supervision arose in two ways. One was that a traditional local authority might itself be a court acting in a form of legal procedure – as with a court leet or magistrates meeting in quarter-sessions – and from its decisions appeal might lie to a superior tribunal (though the remedy was rarely sought). The other was that a local body would have duties imposed by charter or statute and failure to fulfil them could also lead to legal action. But major developments in this regard did not occur until the middle of the nineteenth century and after when Parliament was beginning substantially to extend local responsibilities. In particular the doctrine of *ultra vires* then came into its own to the effect that, if a council or its officials acted beyond their powers, an action at law would lie.[253] Naturally the result was of a negative sort, for the purpose was usually to delay or obstruct local activity, as for instance, in 1920 when, in a famous case, Fulham corporation was forbidden by the courts to provide a laundry service.[254] Of course a legal action is an expensive business and depends, in the first instance, on the initiative being taken by some individual or group. In fact, allowing for the range and cost of their activities and the number of persons and interests they affect, local authorities are not often taken to court.[255] Perhaps the most obvious way in which the *ultra vires* rule is enforced is by the action of the district auditor who, if he finds that funds have not been properly administered and accounted for, may take action against those who improperly authorized the expenditure concerned, as in the well-known Clay Cross case which arose over a refusal to raise council house rents.

The main supervision over local authorities of a continuous and detailed kind has necessarily been exercised by ministers and the central boards and departments. An early aspect of this was the way in which government offices were increasingly drawn into the process of private legislation. The Home Office monitored turnpike Bills and the General Board of Health kept a watchful eye on sewerage legislation. Similarly in the Preliminary Inquiries Act of 1846, Parliament provided that, when a locality wanted to submit an improvement Bill, the Commissioners of Woods and Forests might send a 'surveying officer' to make a preliminary report. And the departments' enabling role became increasingly important as the use of provisional orders became more common. Similarly, under the 1835 Municipal Corporations Act, Treasury sanction was required for the raising of loans or the alienation of corporate property; and local by-laws had to be approved by the Privy

---

253 S. Brice, ...*A Treatise on the Doctrine of Ultra Vires*...(3rd edn, London, 1893), p. 192.
254 *Att.-Gen.* v. *Fulham Corporation*, [1921] 1 Ch. 440.
255 T. Byrne, *Local Government in Britain: Everyone's Guide to How It All Works* (Penguin, 1981), p.219.

Council. What more particularly has been involved may be instanced, in the brief fashion possible here, by reference to some specific forms and aspects of local activity, functions both old and new, which relate in various ways to the fundamental responsibility of the Crown to sustain order and good government throughout the kingdom.

This is most clearly the case, of course, in respect to matters of public security. Like his predecessors the Secretary of State for the Home Department issued instructions to the lord-lieutenants and justices concerning the maintenance of law and order, just as the Secretary-at-War issued a 'route' for the movement of troops requiring the assistance of local communities in the provision of transport for this purpose. And as, with the growth of the industrial towns, crime and disorder mounted, central interest in police and criminal administration was also enhanced. For example, in the 1820s the Home Office required an annual report on the state of county gaols and there were also attempts to standardize prison procedure. As the costs were high and fell on the county rate, one of the first government grants to be given was for the mitigation of this burden. But at the same time the regulation of magistrates' powers was tightened and an inspectorate established. And, as Professor Keith-Lucas comments in a review of these matters, by accepting 'this bounty from the Exchequer the country gentlemen gave to the central government the right to claim supervision over the way that local funds were spent.'[256] Control over local police was similarly tightened though the process was slow. In return for financial help, the Home Office was able to stimulate the establishment of a force and gradually acquired power over its numbers, pay, clothing, the regulations by which it was administered, and the appointment of its chief constable, while the creation of a central inspectorate enabled it to assess whether a force was being efficiently maintained. Yet the extent and effectiveness of this supervision, especially in the early days, must not be exaggerated. By later standards it was quite loose: for instance the Home Office was for a long time unable to enforce uniform pay scales.[257] Nor did the power to withhold the police grant (before 1900 a threat which was on average made almost once a year) always have the intended effect despite the consequences it implied for the rates. The smallness of the Home Office staff was one reason for the relatively lax control which existed in practice and for the failure sometimes even to respond to local requests for advice.[258] But

---

256 B. Keith-Lucas, *The English Local Government Franchise: a Short History* (Oxford, 1952), p. 97.

257 J. Hart, 'The County and Borough Police Act, 1856', *Public Administration*, xxxiv (1956), pp. 407–8. Cf. A. Elliott, 'Municipal Government in Bradford in the Mid-nineteenth Century', in D. Fraser (ed.), *Municipal Reform and the Industrial City* (Leicester, 1982), pp. 126–33.

258 Hart, art. cit., pp. 408–9; H. Parris, 'The Home Office and the Provincial Police in

perhaps the main factor was the generally rather libertarian ethos of the day as reflected in the following minute written in 1883 by Sir William Harcourt, then Home Secretary, when his officials had proposed not to pay the grant to one authority because, in HM Inspector's opinion, its police force was not large enough:

> The view I have always taken on this matter is that if local self-government means anything at all it means that the Local Authority and not the Government Inspector is the proper judge of the number of police required by them. On this ground I stated to a deputation of the Corporation of Manchester in 1880 that I should certainly not compel them to keep on foot more police than they thought requisite, for that it was they who would suffer from the deficiency.
>
> I have on two occasions seen the Inspectors of Constabulary on this subject collectively and explained to them that I considered it no part of their duty to increase the charge on the Exchequer by insisting on Boroughs and Counties keeping up a force according to the standard of the Inspectors and not according to their own view of their local wants. One of the great evils of centralised government is this tendency to apply an artificial standard to all cases regardless of local wants....[259]

Perhaps this attitude was exceptional even then; but it seems that down to 1914 at least there was in practice little continuous and detailed central supervision of local police forces.[260] But at the end of the Great War the central grant was increased to half the total of all police expenditure and, as if in token of the meaning of this step, the following year the Police Act reinforced the Home Office's power (after consultation with the Police Council) to make regulations about the government, mutual aid, pay, and conditions of service of all police forces. Of course, this authority has since been further augmented.

Another major increment of central executive control was represented by the Poor Law Commission set up in 1834 which was, in fact, the first government office created exclusively to control and direct local authorities in the execution of their work.[261] As it happened this body never became the central autocracy its critics feared and, during its brief life, it always had to exercise its authority with great restraint.[262] So, as in

---

England and Wales – 1856–1870', *Public Law*, vi (1961), p. 236.
259 Cited Hart, art. cit., p. 411.
260 ibid., pp. 414–16. Parris, however, attributes to the inspectors a notable influence in some matters, art. cit., pp. 238, 242, 243: but, though this was undoubtedly the case, it is not incompatible with a general looseness of control by later standards.
261 S. and B. Webb, op. cit., iv. 466–7.
262 ibid., viii. 239–44.

the case of the police, it is necessary not to exaggerate the extent of effective supervision involved by its establishment or exercised by its successor. Yet its significance as an early symbol of the central oversight of local administration and of the endeavour to secure national uniformity by this means was undoubtedly considerable.[263] Similarly an important step was taken with the creation in 1848 of the General Board of Health, the body that so much aroused the ire of Toulmin Smith because he believed it was incompatible with local self-government. The matter of public health was none the less one of the main foundations on which the modern system of central involvement and control rests and conveniently signals the main lines of institutional development that later occurred.

According to the letter of the law the General Board had quite substantial powers; yet their application lacked a certain effectiveness. One reason was that its officials were often staunch believers in the propriety and efficacy of local rather than central action and expected the latter to be confined to aid and advice: any pressure beyond this would be 'mischievous and mistaken'.[264] Other factors were simply the practical difficulties in the board's way and the considerable opposition it encountered. In the outcome it was wound up in 1858 and its powers divided and transferred elsewhere as a means of sustaining a greater degree of voluntaryism and local autonomy. What subsequently happened is a good instance of the way in which, despite intentions of this sort, central help was increased and control strengthened. Partly this was a matter of personalities, partly of circumstance. Some officials deliberately sought to extend central involvement as in the case of Sir John Simon, a most forceful and able public servant, who was able to continue his very active work from the Medical Department of the Privy Council to which he went after the reorganization.[265] Similarly the Local Government Act Office, also then set up in the Home Department, came to be a focus of central supervision and advice notwithstanding its officials' belief in the virtues of local self-government. For they found that the pressure of administrative necessity and the insistent demands from the localities nullified the change of direction the Act of 1858 was supposed to have introduced.[266] Toulmin Smith and those who thought

---

263 On the Poor Law system, see above pp. 42–5.
264 T. Taylor, 'On Central and Local Action in Relation to Town Improvement', *Transactions of the National Association for the Promotion of Social Science 1857* (London, 1858), p. 480. Cf. Sir A. Helps, *Thoughts upon Government* (London, 1872), pp. 55–60.
265 R. Lambert, *Sir John Simon, 1816–1904, and English Social Administration* (London, 1963), ch. xiv; also his 'A Victorian National Health Service: State Vaccination 1855–71', *Historical Journal*, v (1962), pp. 1–18.
266 Cf. *The Rise of Collectivism* (London, 1983), pp. 225–6.

like him saw this increasing connexion as due only to the 'vexatious intermeddling' of the centre.[267] But this was hardly the sole reason; and in any case it continued to grow. Indeed in 1866 the Sanitary Act (29 & 30 Vic., c. xc) took a considerable step further. Sir John Simon's reports had revealed an often appalling position in respect of public health in many places and this led to pressure not only from some Parliamentary quarters but also from many of the local authorities themselves for central government to assume greater powers of intervention. The outcome was the famous clauses 16 and 49 of this statute by which the LGAO was given the most extreme possible sanction, being authorized to supersede a local office where it deemed this necessary. It was thus empowered to replace the local officials, to do work where the locality was in default, and to direct the negligent authority to pay. So strong, however, was the contemporary sentiment in favour of local self-government that the Act was glossed not as a basis for central control but rather as a means for securing uniformity of local administration.[268] None the less the powers thus granted went much beyond any that Chadwick ever had and were described by one observer at the time as 'perhaps the largest inroad on constitutional principle that Parliament has ever sanctioned.'[269] The authority thus granted was, it is true, limited in some respects and delayed in its full implementation because of intrinsic legal defects and the small central staff involved. But the powers were used and indeed quickly extended. Even in so short a period as that between 1868 and 1871, nine local authorities were superseded for default and in some of these cases the entire work concerned was undertaken by central government thus indicating where the ultimate responsibility for public health lay.[270] There is perhaps a tendency to imagine that central supersession of this kind, still quite rare, is a wholly modern phenomenon (as witnessed, for instance, by some recent civil defence and housing cases). But this power was introduced and used over a hundred years ago in the hey-day of ideas about local self-government and of hostility to centralization.[271] In sum, then, so soon as the localities, especially the smaller ones, began to tackle their public health problems, they themselves, because in various respects they were forced to acknowledge their own incapacity, opened the way to and pressed for aid and supervision from the centre where alone a convenient fund of scientific knowledge, legal training, and practical experience could easily

267 See e.g. J. T. Smith, *Local Self-Government Unmystified...* (London, 1857), p. 27.
268 Gutchen, art. cit., pp. 91–4. Cf. D. N. Chester, *Central and Local Government: Financial and Administrative Relations* (London, 1951), pp. 66–7.
269 Cited R. Lambert, 'Central and Local Relations in Mid-Victorian England: the Local Government Act Office, 1858–71', *Victorian Studies*, vi (1962–3), p. 139 n. 96.
270 ibid., pp. 143–4.
271 But cf. the diffident remarks about supersession in Helps, op. cit., pp. 57–9.

be found. And, of course, given the disparity of size and resources among local authorities, in no other way than by central help and pressure could a uniform provision of environmental services be anticipated. By the late 1860s the ground for further development of central control was already well prepared; and the growing feeling that a more co-ordinated set of arrangements for the administration of local policies and backed by the provision of grant-aid and its corollary, inspection, could draw on these preliminaries and precedents. Some degree of concentration in central departmental authority followed.

As early as 1853 Simon had argued the need for a single central department to be in charge of all these matters.[272] The Royal Sanitary Commission, set up in 1868, reported that the existing array of local bodies was no less than a chaos of areas and functions of widely varying efficiency and that a greater degree of central initiative and control than already existed was required to ensure uniformity and progress. It recommended for this purpose the creation of 'one Central Authority' under a minister to consolidate central responsibilities relating to the Poor Law, public health, and, indeed, local government as a whole. Despite this the formal stress was still on localism however: the proposed body and its chief were to be made more powerful 'not to centralize administration, but on the contrary to set local life in motion'.[273] In the outcome the Local Government Board was created in 1871 by merging the three main central departments which had hitherto been involved: the Poor Law Board, the Medical Department of the Privy Council, and the Local Government Act Office of the Home Department. The Registrar-General's Office was also absorbed as, a year or so later, were the responsibilities entailed by the administration of the Highways, Alkali, and Metropolis Water Acts.[274] In many ways this was a notable step forward in the direction of central control (though the notion that the board might become a kind of Ministry of the Interior was not widely held).[275] Even so there were many difficulties in bringing these agencies together as a single office of government and this was reflected in the way the affairs of the LGB were conducted.[276] It was criticized for being

272 Simon's *Reports*, p. xxvii cited P. R. Wilding, 'The Genesis of the Ministry of Health', *Public Administration*, xlv (1967), p. 149.
273 Sanitary Laws, R. Com. 2nd Rep., 1871 (vol. xxxv), C. 281, pp. 31–2. And cf. p. 81 above.
274 R. M. Macleod, *Treasury Control and Social Administration: a Study of Establishment Growth at the Local Government Board 1871–1905* (London, 1968), p. 10.
275 ibid., p. 12 and n. 12.
276 The detailed extent of its powers and the manner of their exercise are indicated in Macleod, op. cit., *passim*; and in M. D. Chalmers, *Local Government* (London, 1883), pp. 150–60.

dominated by the negative ethos of the Poor Law.[277] It never had a monopoly of supervisory power over local government, and other central departments jealously maintained their rights over such important matters as police, roads, elementary schooling, and much else. Even in respect of public health it shared authority with, for instance, the Home Office and the Board of Trade. And the Treasury of course was always much involved in many ways. Nevertheless the LGB's work, as the central focus of advice and administrative supervision over local government, continued to grow significantly. This may be roughly measured in terms of the letters and papers dealt with. In 1870, the first year of operation, the former totalled some 58,000 but after twenty-five years the number had risen to 160,000; while registered papers increased from nearly 82,000 in 1875 to 168,000 in 1896.[278] In 1883 *The Times* commented 'how vastly' the board's functions had grown and noted that they continued to enlarge year by year.[279] Notwithstanding this the degree or manner of LGB control varied considerably from one field to another; there were staffing difficulties; and the board's standing in Whitehall (and other quarters too) was not of the highest. One result was that, when a system of health insurance was introduced in 1911, the responsibility for its organization was deliberately bestowed elsewhere.[280] The need to replace the board by a properly organized Ministry of Health was urged by the Haldane Committee towards the end of the Great War.[281] And when this step was taken in 1919 the new department also assumed the main supervision of local government having considerable powers at its disposal for this purpose. Of course in the period since 1945 some reshuffling of central responsibilities has occurred; but in 1970 the major concern fell to the Department of the Environment where it still rests.

Education is another important local government service, not least because it has become by far the most expensive of all those provided. It is the case, too, that central government had a prior role in this field with the result that an office to oversee educational issues existed (within the Privy Council) before local government became fully involved which did not occur until the school boards were set up in 1870.[282] The supervisory

---

277 S. and B. Webb, op. cit., viii. 197–200.
278 Macleod, op. cit., pp. 11–12, 19, 33–4.
279 *The Times* (16 October 1883), cited ibid., p. 19.
280 S. and B. Webb, op. cit., viii. 218–20. For its part the LGB was hostile to the proposed insurance scheme: see e.g. Sir H. N. Bunbury (ed.), *Lloyd George's Ambulance Wagon: Being the Memoirs of William J. Braithwaite 1911–1912* (1957; Bath, 1970), pp. 17, 70, 128, 133–4.
281 For the Haldane Committee's view, see Machinery of Government, Ministry of Reconstruction Cttee, 1918 (vol. xii), Cd. 9230 esp. ch. IX.
282 See *The Rise of Collectivism*, pp. 188–9.

department administered the education grants and had extensive authority over the board school system, a power inherited by the Board of Education when it was established in 1899. Three years later when the local education authorities were created they were put under its aegis. And by the Act of 1918 the board was, for instance, charged with co-ordinating all forms of education and to this end empowered to require the submission of schemes from the LEAs. The continual extension of central authority in this regard was symbolized when the board was replaced in 1944 by a ministry. Whereas in 1899 the former had been charged with the 'superintendence' of local educational duties, the task of the new ministry was stated in much more positive terms: it was to secure effective execution by local authorities, under the minister's 'control and direction', of the 'national policy' the government had determined. Significantly this is the language of the old Poor-Law system; and the new emphasis notably reduced the status of LEAs, partnership being replaced by the domination of principal over agent as the centre of the relationship.[283] The existence of the power to give directions on policy indicates the ultimate realities of the situation even though it has rarely been used. During the quarter-century after 1944 it was actually applied eight times, first of all in 1951 when Durham County Council was instructed to give up the policy of the closed shop in employing teachers. And of course as educational expenditure has increased (as it has done enormously) so has central interest in efficiency and economy in administration. This can mean in practice very detailed supervision indeed. For example in the early fifties Cheshire County Council was to a large extent forced by the ministry to adopt a particular plan of primary school building.[284] And Sir Norman Chester cites a slightly earlier instance in which a large county borough, with its own highly qualified technical staff, was subjected to a prolonged inquisition about a project to erect a hutted day nursery and which involved central inquisition about even such things as the hot-water arrangements and the placing of particular rooms.[285] The degree of technical 'guidance' might thus be considerable.[286] In 1967 the Department of Education and Science (as it had become three years earlier) described its duties by saying that, in addition to advice by means of pamphlets, circulars, and White Papers, it

---

283 Robson, op. cit., pp. 38–40.
284 J. M. Lee, *Social Leaders and Public Persons: a Study of County Government in Cheshire since 1888* (Oxford, 1963), p. 152.
285 Chester, *Central and Local Government*, pp. 24–8.
286 See the supplementary memorandum on unnecessarily detailed control and advice submitted by the Society of Local Authority Chief Executives to the House of Commons Expenditure Committee, repr. in its 11th Report, 1976–7 (vol. xxxii), HC 535-III, Appendix 46.

sets minimum standards of educational provision; controls the rate, distribution, nature and cost of educational building; controls teacher training and supply and determines the principles governing the recognition of teachers as qualified; administers a superannuation scheme for teachers; arranges for the incorporation of estimates of local education expenditure in provision for general grant; supports financially by direct grant a limited number of institutions of a special kind; supports research; and settles disputes, for example, between a parent and a local education authority or between a local education authority and the managers of a school.

As Professor Mackintosh said, after citing this passage, it may well be wondered, given all this, in what sense education can be described as a local authority function.[287] Nor is the position basically different in many other fields in which the local bodies are in effect simply agents used to carry out central schemes and policies: 'a common pattern of *dirigisme*' had thus become very clear.[288]

As these examples indicate, then, central control, aid, and advice have increased and may be very detailed, taking stock of even the minutest aspect of affairs. The supervision is exercised in numerous ways. There are, for instance, controls over the borrowing powers of local authorities whether the money is obtained from the Public Works Loan Board or on the open market. As in modern times councils have increasingly had to undertake capital expenditure (with respect to roads, water supply, drainage, sewage, housing, schools, and so forth) this has been a not unimportant monitor of their activity.[289] Another such power lies in the audit of local authority accounts with the possibility of surcharging council members and officials who have authorized expenditure or made payments deemed to be *ultra vires* or even unreasonable. This may be a most severe restriction indeed on the policies thought appropriate by locally elected representatives.[290] Then there are other manifestations of central power and influence: issuing orders and regulations; letters, memoranda, and circulars of various kinds; informal discussions; the approval of schemes, by-laws, and the appointment of certain officials (such as chief constable or director of social services); through a requirement to submit reports and returns; inspection; arbitration in

---

287 J. P. Mackintosh, *The Devolution of Power: Local Democracy, Regionalism and Nationalism* (Penguin, 1968), p. 28.
288 B. Keith-Lucas and P. G. Richards, *A History of Local Government in the Twentieth Century* (London, 1978), p. 169.
289 There is a good, detailed account in M. Schulz, 'The Control of Local Authority Borrowing by the Central Government', C. H. Wilson (ed.), *Essays on Local Government* (Oxford, 1948).
290 See the comments in Keith-Lucas and Richards, op. cit., p. 153.

disputes; the exercise of appellate powers; rate-capping; and, of course, ultimately the threat to withhold grant or to act in default and impose commissioners, as recently with councils which refused to carry out civil defence functions (St Pancras in 1951, and Coventry in 1954) or to implement rent legislation (Merthyr, Bedwellty, and Clay Cross in 1972). But of course this severe sanction (usually arising from extreme political opposition to a given policy) reflects a very unusual situation.[291] The sort of control that really matters is an ordinary, day-to-day affair. One local official (who has commented most effectively on these questions) referred, as an instance of the extent and range of central supervision and instruction, to the experience of a 'certain small county', presumably Pembrokeshire. During the twenty-two working days of December 1969 the clerk to the council 'received no less than 135 communications of substance from the central government proper and a further 95 from quasi-governmental bodies such as the Industrial Training Boards and the Countryside Commission.' He adds that while one or two of these circulars and letters were 'invaluable' and many 'useful enough', most were 'the product of that presumption of incompetence which is the traditional central government attitude towards everything local.'[292] The reality of the situation is revealed, too, in the following passage from a paper by W. A. Ross who had worked as a senior civil servant in both the LGB and its successor the Ministry of Health. He is describing the manner of Sir Gwilym Gibbon who presided over the local government division of the ministry in the 1920s and early thirties:

> Theoretically he was all for liberty and independence of local authorities.... In practice when he dealt with particular cases he was something of a bureaucrat, that is in cases where the Ministry had control, as in the sanctioning of loans. The local authority might wish to carry out a work by direct labour. No, they must go to contract. They might wish to install in a proposed swimming bath a certain method of filtration. No, they must install a method more favoured by the Ministry's engineering staff. Being inclined to support the local authority, I would murmur in discussion 'government with the consent of the governed,' but this interjection was impatiently brushed aside.[293]

291 For some account of recent cases affecting a Secretary of State's power to act in default, see S. H. Bailey, 'Central and Local Government and the Courts', *Public Law*, xxviii (1983), pp. 8–16.
292 I. B. Rees, *Government by Community* (London, 1971), pp. 50–1. The same feeling is reflected in the evidence presented to the Expenditure Committee, 11th Rep., 1976–7 (vol. xxxi), HC 535-II, pp. 725ff. esp. p. 740 q. 1790 and Appendix 46 pp. 1082–6.
293 W. A. Ross, 'Local Government Board and After: Retrospect', *Public Administration*, xxxiv (1956), pp. 23–4.

Of course this sort of attitude often led to strained relations between central and local authorities and, as well, inhibited developments of a sort regarded by many people as highly desirable.[294] Nor are the arrangements otherwise trouble-free of course. One problem for a local authority is that it often seems to be dealing not so much with central government as a unit but with an uncoordinated series of independent contractors, 'some oblivious of one another, others in competition.'[295] But about the general position there has long been no doubt. Sir Ivor Jennings wrote, even before the last war, since when things have moved on apace, that nowadays the central government was the essential factor in local affairs:

> Foreign commentators on our system continue to speak of England as a country of 'local self-government.' It is clear that it is nothing of the kind. It is true that we have elected local authorities exercising a discretion according to the opinions which meet the approval of their own electorate. It is true also that they can do a great deal, within their powers, to improve the health and happiness of their constituents. But they are rigidly restricted to the powers conferred upon them by Parliament; their organization and their proceedings are determined by statutes..., and above all they are controlled more or less closely in all their activities by organs of the Central Government.[296]

It is hardly necessary to stress the point in these days of rate-capping: Liverpool and other places have learned the lesson the hard way. But is it too fanciful to imagine Toulmin Smith (and J. Podsnap) applauding D. Hatton and his colleagues from the elysian shades where opponents of centralization rest?

Of course it is necessary even so not to exaggerate the degree of central government dominance in this regard. Local authorities do possess statutory powers and revenue of their own; they exercise a degree of initiative that is often important, as in applying compulsory, or deciding whether to act on adoptive or persuasive, powers; and they can decide how to spend general grant money. And after all they are elected bodies albeit ones created by central government. They may, too, have a notable informal influence on government policy (and intervention itself) for the councils and their associations are in continual contact with the central

---

294 See e.g. the instances cited in A. Redford, *The History of Local Government in Manchester* (London, 1939–40) ii. 296–302; iii. 227, 258–9, 316–19.

295 Rees, op. cit., pp. 55–9. Cf. the summary of the Maud Committee review in Robson, *Local Government in Crisis*, pp. 56–8, and the criticisms in Expenditure Cttee, 11th Rep., 1976–7, HC 535-II, pp. 725–7 §§5, 7, 10–11.

296 W. I. Jennings, 'Central Control', in H. J. Laski et al., *A Century of Municipal Progress*, p. 450. As an ardent centralist, Jennings looked forward indeed to wider and more effective control of local authority activities, ibid., pp. 453–4.

departments on a whole range of issues.[297] This is not to say, of course, that more contact and consultation would not be desirable, or a greater degree of trust might be shown in the ability of an authority to get on with its tasks with less interference than usual.[298]

Thus the growth of central control and influence over the years has been a major aspect of local government affairs, one arising in good part because of the deficiencies of the institutions themselves and of the increasing scale, cost, and complexity of the tasks they had assumed or were given. These institutions were, in any case, a major part of the country's system of politics and administration. It is no wonder that since the last war there has been a continuing series of attempts to find an answer to the many difficulties which the late-nineteenth-century arrangements raised.

SEARCH FOR A SOLUTION

> ... I had the idea of introducing the theme of a radical reform ... and I told them that the dinosaurs would have to give way to modern animals....
> R. H. S. CROSSMAN, *The Diaries of a Cabinet Minister*
> (entry for 30 January 1966), i. 440

The range of problems and difficulties already described constituted, when seen obversely, a set of criteria for any rational reform of local government. A properly organized system would so far as possible eliminate, or at least ameliorate, the clash between town and country; it would provide in some way for the special problems of the conurbations in general and of the growth of London in particular; it would deal with the variation between authorities of the same class and the decline of the minor districts; and, crucially, the reform would treat the basic and related questions of central control and the provision of adequate independent sources of revenue. This last is, of course, vital; and the response to it will largely be determined by the general attitude adopted to the fundamental issue about the proper role of local authorities in modern circumstances: that is, whether they should be nourished by their tradition of autonomy and self-help or regarded as instruments for the execution of national policy. In which direction should the emphasis of reform lie: more independence or more effective agency? If to neither

---

297 e.g. as a matter of routine, circulars may be sent to local authorities for their comments before they are formally issued, or may be issued at the behest of the localities: see Expenditure Cttee, 11th Report, 1976–7, HC 535-III, Appendix 47 p. 1087 §§2–4.

298 See Byrne, op. cit., pp. 229–30 citing the Maud and Layfield reports; also Expenditure Cttee, 11th Rep., 1976–7, HC 535-II, esp. p. 725 §§1–3, p. 728 §19, and pp. 736–7 q. 1778, p. 742 q. 1804; ibid., HC 535-I, ch. XII.

extreme, at what point should a proper balance be achieved? Various schemes for change were urged. But successive governments blenched at the problems and prospects revealed; and quite some time passed before anything effective was done. It must be sufficient here to summarize developments since the last war in terms of a pattern of events and ideas falling into four phases.

First there was the tentative or, better, half-hearted effort of the period immediately after 1945 leading up to the abortive proposals of the Local Government Boundary Commission. During the war it had been obvious that the burden falling on local government would increase during the period of reconstruction as, for instance, the housing shortage was tackled and other locally based services were restored or developed. But no obvious or agreed policy existed about how local institutions should be improved to meet this challenge. So the coalition government, and the Labour administration which succeeded it, fell back on the idea of a special advisory body to suggest adjustments to the existing arrangements.[299] A deluge of discussion followed the establishment of this inquiry but it soon became apparent that there was no general agreement about what to do and that the Local Government Boundary Commission itself felt its remit to be inadequate: it was allowed only to tinker whereas something much more radical was required. In the end it made no piecemeal suggestions of the kind permitted to it about boundaries or status but went beyond its restrictive terms of reference to propose a systematic reshaping of the entire system. The details of this plan do not matter here save to note that it was based on an intendedly more symmetrical relation between area and resources on the one hand and responsibilities on the other.[300] Nevertheless critics were not slow to point out difficulties in what was suggested, the absence of any special treatment of the conurban areas for instance. However the government of the day was not prepared to grasp the nettle and, the truth be told, was not much concerned with sustaining the virtues of local self-government. For this meant diversity, possibly opposition, and might thus inhibit the planned achievement of the national minimum. The general effect of Labour Party policies had indeed been to diminish the local role: witness

---

299 See Local Government in England and Wales during the Period of Reconstruction, 1944–5 (vol. x), Cmd. 6579; also the Ministry of Health statement of November 1945, in *KCA* (1943–6), p. 7574B. The background of the coalition discussions is described in J. M. Lee, *Reviewing the Machinery of Government, 1942–1952: an Essay on the Anderson Committee and its Successors* (n.p. [London], 1977), pp. 130–1. And for astringent comment, see W. A. Robson, *The Development of Local Government* (1931; 3rd rev. edn, London, 1954), pp. 46–9.
300 Report of the Local Government Boundary Commission for the Year 1947, 1947–8 (vol. xiii), HC 86, p. 2 §1, pp. 19–21 §§39–41. For a summary, see *KCA* (1946–8), p. 9299A; also Robson, op. cit., pp. 52–62.

the weakening effect of depriving local authorities of their gas and electricity undertakings, their hospitals, their part in the provision of public assistance, and so forth. As well the minister, A. Bevan, was indifferent; and an election loomed not far ahead making it desirable to avoid contentious issues where possible. In the outcome the LGBC was wound up in 1949 and its report shelved, though interested academics at least chewed its recommendations over and over for many years. In repealing the Act which had set up the commission, the government implied it would review generally the structure and functions of local authorities. But the years passed; administrations changed; and nothing was done. In a way this was understandable because, inevitably, the various types of local council could not agree, their associations putting forward proposals which were diametrically opposed; so in whichever direction government leaned there would be a political rumpus. Meanwhile *ad hoc* decisions about functions, boundaries, and finance continued in the usual way adding yet more complexities to the traditional patchwork. But finally some search for a policy was initiated afresh in the mid-fifties and after, this time by the Conservatives.

Again a good deal of the detail relating to this second phase does not matter now as much of the impetus behind the exercise was lost after a few years and once more a fresh start had to be made. White Papers were issued in 1956–7 and followed by legislation in 1958.[301] This set up two investigatory commissions to make specific recommendations about England and Wales respectively, concerning such issues as promotion to county borough, reducing the number of county districts, and the treatment of the 'special review areas' (that is, the conurbations). A royal commission was also announced to explore the question of London government. All this was presented as a comprehensive package but everything obviously depended on the outcome of the detailed inquiries, not least as it was assumed that no radical reshaping of the structure was required.[302] In fact the terms of reference of the two commissions were once more rather restrictive and their work proceeded slowly; while the proposals put forward were of a piecemeal nature, led to protracted discussion, and, often, notable opposition. The Labour government which took office in 1964 lost patience and, in effect, swept the commissions aside (fearing, too, the potential impact of the proposed

---

301 Local Government: Areas and Status of Local Authorities in England and Wales, 1955–6 (vol. xxxvi), Cmd. 9831; Functions of County Councils and County District Councils in England and Wales, 1956–7 (vol. xxvi), Cmnd. 161; and Local Government Finance (England and Wales), 1956–7 (vol. xxvi), Cmnd. 209; 6 & 7 Eliz. II, c. 55.

302 Local Government: Areas and Status of Local Authorities in England and Wales, 1955–6, Cmd. 9831, p. 6 §17.

changes on some Parliamentary seats).[303] Nevertheless there had been some movement since the mid-1950s. Tackling the question of London had made it possible to look at the remainder of the problem more rationally; and the English commission had, in fact, cleared a fair amount of ground especially in its review of the conurbations. Some alterations had also been undertaken: quite a number of county borough extensions, a few creations, and a couple of county amalgamations. Specific proposals for local government in Wales were also promulgated.[304] And when the government determined, early in 1966, that the existing machinery of investigation was to be wound up, it was replaced by a royal commission to undertake a comprehensive review of English local government together with a similar inquiry for Scotland. Thus the scene was set, it was hoped, for a further and more effective stage of development.

The third phase begins with the changes effected in London government in the sixties. The report of the Herbert commission had appeared in October 1960.[305] Its major concern was with the untidy and anomalous machinery of local administration in the capital and with the fear that, unless the metropolitan arrangements were substantially improved and extended, central government might have to supersede them; and this would be disastrous for local government as a whole. The main recommendation was a nearly sevenfold extension of the area under the London authority involving a population increase of from $3\frac{1}{4}$ to $8\frac{3}{4}$ millions. The scope of the proposed changes is indicated by the effect they would have on neighbouring counties: Surrey, for instance, would lose nearly two-thirds of its population, almost a quarter of its area, and a third of its rateable value; while Middlesex would simply disappear. The new counterpart of the old LCC which was to govern this enlarged area was to be called the Greater London Council; and the ninety-five existing authorities in the area were to be reorganized as fifty-two Greater London Boroughs. The City of London was to be kept in being with the same powers as one of the new boroughs. The GLC was to have responsibility for those functions thought to require a single authority for the entire metropolis: education, planning for the area as a whole, main roads and traffic management, and fire and ambulance services (water supply was added later); while the new boroughs were to

---

303 R. H. S. Crossman, *The Diaries of a Cabinet Minister* (London, 1975–7), i. 87–8, 439–41. There is a good summary account of these matters (based on Crossman's diaries) in D. Peschek, 'The Man Who Started It All', *Municipal Review*, xlvi (1975–6), pp. 300–2, 322; cf. W. A. Robson, *Local Government in Crisis* (1966; rev. 2nd edn, London, 1968), ch. XXX.
304 Local Government in Wales, 1966–7 (vol. lix), Cmnd. 3340.
305 Local Government in Greater London, R. Com. Rep., 1959–60 (vol. xviii), Cmnd. 1164.

carry the main burden of the usual local and personal services (which had not been true of the old metropolitan boroughs). There was a great deal of opposition much of it political: for instance the Labour Party, which had tended to dominate LCC affairs, feared it would permanently lose control of a GLC embracing large suburban districts of presumed Conservative inclination (some of which were, in fact, ultimately excluded from the GLC area as finally established which was thus somewhat smaller than originally proposed). But there was also concern about the possible effect of the fragmentation of some services especially education in which the LCC had (it was said) maintained high standards; and here a major change was made by the Macmillan government when in late 1961 it announced its general acceptance of the recommendations.[306] In the end the existing education service was kept in being to serve the old LCC area under the new name of the Inner London Education Authority (technically as a special committee of the GLC). As well the number of London boroughs was reduced to thirty-two so that those outside the ILEA would be large enough to be education authorities, and also so that the new boroughs could effectively be the 'primary unit' of administration 'well equipped to provide a fully adequate standard of local services.'[307] Thus modified the proposals became law in 1963 and the first GLC election was held in April 1964. The Labour Party won, proving its earlier fears false.[308]

The terms of reference of the Redcliffe-Maud inquiry set up in February 1966 did not specifically preclude finance though (for some reason) it was not expected this would be a major concern; but otherwise the royal commission was directed to make recommendations 'for authorities and boundaries, and for functions and their division, having regard to the size and character of areas in which these can be most effectively exercised and the need to sustain a viable system of local democracy' in England.[309] The Scottish Commission under Lord Wheatley had a similar remit. Proposals for Wales (as noted above) already existed. The review was intended, in the words of the Prime Minister, to be 'the biggest...this century'; and R. Crossman, the minister concerned, thought the enterprise was 'the most important piece

---

306 London Government: Government Proposals for Reorganisation, 1961–2 (vol. xxxi), Cmnd. 1562.
307 ibid., p. 3 §8, p. 6 §19. The actual administrative area of Greater London as finally established was some 610 square miles with a resident population of 6.76 millions. The GLC budget for 1984–5 amounted to £3,570 millions (of which £507 millions was capital expenditure): see *Whitaker's Almanack* (1986), pp. 630, 660.
308 For subsequent experience of the new London system, see G. Rhodes (ed.), *The New Government of London: the First Five Years* (London, 1972).
309 Local Government in England, R. Com. Rep., 1968–9 (vol. xxxviii), Cmnd. 4040, p. iii.

of modernization the Labour Government has launched.'[310] The starting-point was indeed the inappropriateness to present-day conditions and needs of the existing local arrangements based as they were on survivals from medieval and early modern times as amended during the previous century. The system was in many respects the outcome of a merely random growth needing radically to be overhauled and a quite new structure and map created so that there could be a proper treatment of social deficiencies and effective planning of vital services. Efficient local government was crucial, the commission believed, to the reality of democratic freedom. It must, therefore, be nourished so it can fulfil its essential duties.[311] It must be able

> to perform efficiently a wide range of profoundly important tasks concerned with the safety, health, and well-being...of people in different localities; to attract and hold the interest of its citizens; to develop enough inherent strength to deal with national authorities in a valid partnership; and to adapt itself without disruption to the... unprecedented process of change in the way people live, work, move, shop and enjoy themselves.[312]

This led to the posing of a single basic question: 'What size of authority, or range of size, in terms of population and of area, is needed for the democratic and efficient provision of particular services and for local self-government as a whole?'[313] In this general context the commission considered two possible lines of reform. One envisaged a rearrangement in terms of thirty-five 'city regions' focused on the large towns and their natural hinterland and with a second tier of district authorities. The other was a scheme based on fifty-eight all-purpose bodies covering town and country (plus special treatment for three conurban areas). In each case there was provision for a regional (or provincial) structure to settle the strategy and planning framework within which the major units would operate. The majority of the commission preferred the second set of recommendations which was subsequently adopted in principle by the Labour government. The Prime Minister said its implementation would involve 'the most far-reaching reorganisation of local government the country has ever seen.'[314] Legislation was being prepared when the

---

310 729 H.C. Deb. 5s., 24 May 1966, col. 294; Crossman, op. cit., i. 527. Something of the problems in setting up the commission and arranging its membership is indicated in Crossman, op. cit., i. 400, 452–3, 457–8, 494, 504, 519–20.
311 See Local Government in England, R. Com. Rep., 1968–9 (vol. xxxviii), Cmnd. 4040, ch. I esp. p. 2 §6.
312 ibid., p. 1 §1.
313 ibid., p. 3 §8.
314 784 H.C. Deb. 5s., 11 June 1969, col. 1463. A White Paper later proposed certain changes, e.g. to defer the recommendations about the proposed provinces until the

94   A Much Governed Nation

general election of 1970 took place. The Labour Party was unexpectedly defeated and the incoming Conservative administration produced its own proposals for reform which were cast in a notably different mould.

The Heath government rejected the two possibilities considered by the commission because it suspected them of being ways simply of establishing more effective local and regional planning agencies and of stressing the towns (where Labour was strong) at the expense of the counties (usually bastions of Conservative support). It was pledged to 'a genuine devolution of power from the Central Government' and to the provision of a two-tier structure in the localities (to avoid the likely remoteness of the unitary authorities favoured in the commission reports).[315] In February 1971 two White Papers were published announcing the government's detailed intentions in respect of England and Scotland; there was also a consultative document on Wales.[316] The upshot was a scheme differing radically from that supported by the Labour Party. For whereas the latter would have involved the almost complete disappearance of the county the Conservative proposals were founded on it. There was inevitably some amendment of details after the promulgation of the proposals but the main features of the new system established in the mid-1970s are as follows.[317]

There are thirty-nine non-metropolitan (or shire) counties in England and eight in Wales. Basically this unit is the traditional administrative county created in 1888 though without any areas excluded from its jurisdiction as was the case with the former county boroughs (which were thus reabsorbed by the counties from which they were originally separated). The new county councils are responsible for all the main services: education, structure planning, traffic policy, highways, fire hazards, refuse disposal, and so forth. The maintenance of a police force is (subject to the amalgamation of areas) the responsibility of a

---

Commission on the Constitution had reported; and to increase the number of metropolitan areas to five: see Reform of Local Government in England, 1969–70 (vol. xviii), Cmnd. 4276. There was also a further White Paper on Wales dealing specifically with Glamorgan and Monmouthshire, ibid., Cmnd. 4310.

315 *A Better Tomorrow* as cited in *KCA* (1969–70), p. 24008A (24011).
316 Local Government in England: Government Proposals for Reorganisation, 1970–1 (vol. xxxii), Cmnd. 4584; Reform of Local Government in Scotland, ibid., Cmnd. 4583; Welsh Office, The Reform of Local Government in Wales: Consultative Document, 1971, (non-Parl.).
317 The account is very summary. Precise details as to functions are to be found in the specialized textbooks e.g. T. Byrne, *Local Government in Britain: Everyone's Guide to How It All Works* (Penguin, 1981), ch. 4. H. Elcock (and M. Wheaton), *Local Government: Politicians, Professionals and the Public in Local Authorities* (London, 1982), Part III; P. W. Jackson, *Local Government* (3rd edn, London, 1976), ch. 7; and P. G. Richards, *The* Reformed *Local Government System* (1973; 2nd edn, London, 1976), ch. III.

committee consisting of councillors and, in England and Wales, magistrates.[318] In order to establish authorities of appropriate size and, as well, to meet political pressures there was some adjustment of existing county areas. For instance a number of the old Welsh counties disappeared into such (to me) unrememberable creations as Gwynedd, Powys, and Gwent; while Glamorganshire was split into three separate counties (one of them merely a late concession to feeling in Cardiff). In England the changes included, for example, the merging of Westmorland, Cumberland, and part of Lancashire in the new county of Cumbria; and Humberside was constituted of the old East Riding of Yorkshire and a part of north Lincolnshire together with Hull. There was also a number of smaller boundary adjustments: in fact only five counties retained their territory unaltered. Similarly in Scotland nine new 'regions' were established from a fusion of the older counties while three sets of islands – Orkney, Shetland, and the Western Isles – are virtually all-purpose authorities. Then, secondly, there are the county districts. Each of the new counties is divided into a number of second-tier authorities, 296 in England and 37 in Wales. Their functions (which differ slightly in Wales) embrace housing, environmental health (including such matters as refuse collection, clean air, slaughterhouses, and so forth) plus some powers concurrent with those of the county such as airports, parks, museums, and swimming baths. All this was a death-blow to the once-mighty county boroughs. These, from being all-purpose authorities in their own right, became mere districts within the new counties and with a relatively limited range of powers. Naturally, because of their large populations, the areas concerned might still be very significant electorally and, therefore, politically within the counties; but in local government terms they are much weaker than before. In Scotland there are fifty-three districts and the division of functions, though broadly the same as in England and Wales, is different in some respects. Thirdly there are (in England) the parishes which continue in the rural (and some urban) areas with such minor functions as allotments, cemeteries, and community halls; in Wales and Scotland there are 'communities' instead. One important role of these bodies is to act as a kind of pressure group in defence of grass-roots interests where these are affected by the plans and decisions of other bodies. Finally there was special treatment for the conurbations. Six such areas were singled out – Greater Manchester, Merseyside, South Yorkshire, West Yorkshire, the West Midlands, and Tyne and Wear – and in each there was established a so-called metropolitan county with a two-tier structure. This was like the new shire county arrangement but there were two major differences. First the

---

318 In the Metropolitan district the Police Authority is the Home Secretary and in Northern Ireland is appointed by the Secretary of State.

Figure 1 Local authorities in England and Wales in 1955 and since 1974[a]

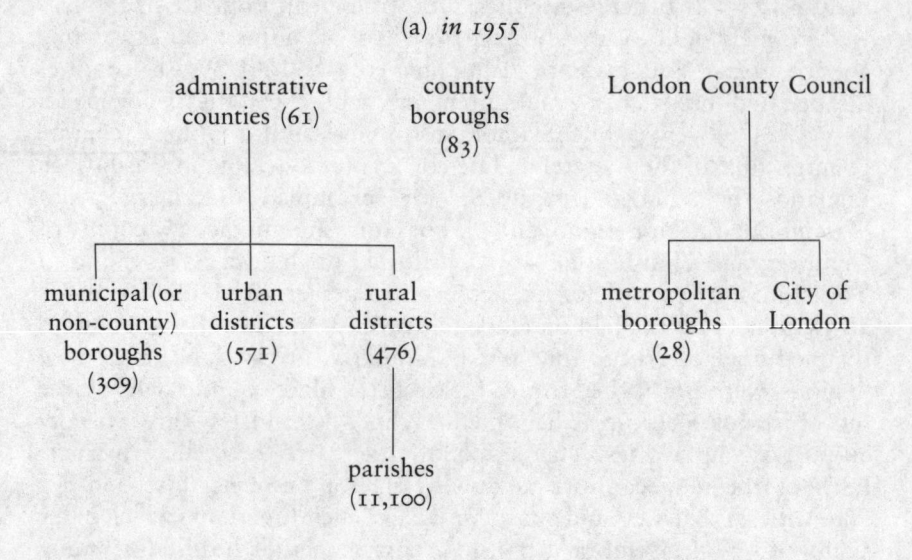

(a) *in 1955*

- administrative counties (61)
  - municipal (or non-county) boroughs (309)
  - urban districts (571)
  - rural districts (476)
    - parishes (11,100)
- county boroughs (83)
- London County Council
  - metropolitan boroughs (28)
  - City of London

(b) *since 1974*[b]

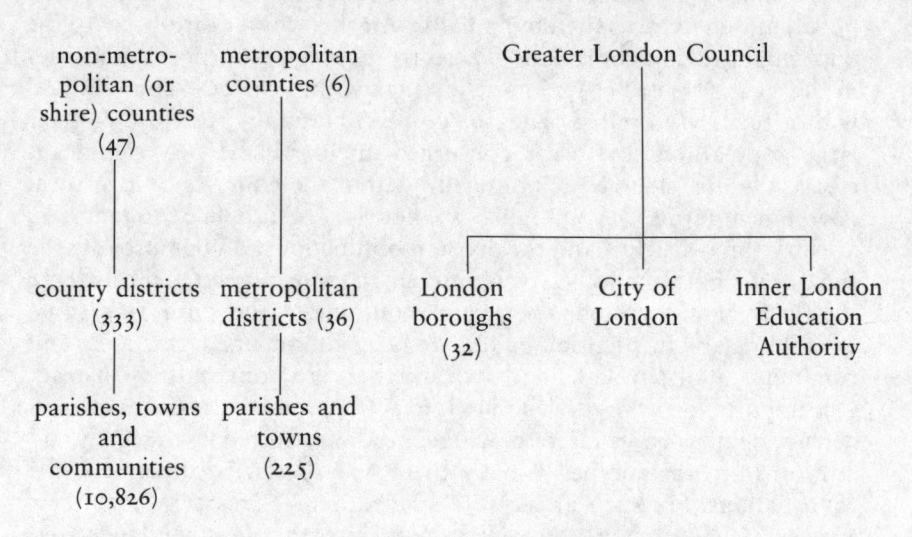

- non-metropolitan (or shire) counties (47)
  - county districts (333)
    - parishes, towns and communities (10,826)
- metropolitan counties (6)
  - metropolitan districts (36)
    - parishes and towns (225)
- Greater London Council
  - London boroughs (32)
  - City of London
  - Inner London Education Authority

a Based mainly on details in two Central Office of Information reference pamphlets on *Local Government in Britain* (edn 1955), p. 1 and (edn 1980), pp. 3, 5. The figure shows clearly enough the disappearance of the county borough, the emergence of the conurban metropolitan county, and the overall reduction in the number of major authorities (and so their increase in size) as the main features of the 1974 reorganization.

b As explained in the text, the metropolitan counties and the GLC were abolished as from 1 April 1986.

lower-tier body was normally the education authority in addition to having the usual district functions; and secondly, because of this, it was larger, usually with a population of at least 200,000.

Clearly these were crucial changes which are (in the case of England and Wales) diagrammatically shown in Figure 1. They constituted the first single, comprehensive measure of local government reform in our history.[319] Yet interestingly enough there is an air of reversion rather than revolution about the new arrangements. It is true there was the major innovation of special treatment for the large conurban areas outside London (though the experiment has proved short-lived); and there were numerous changes of boundary and size affecting sometimes long-established places. But in principle the new structure is based on a unit, the shire or county, which is well over a thousand years old; while the districts may perhaps be seen as no more than that revival of the old hundred or wapentake on the possibility of which Maitland mused.[320] It seems it was with some justice that the Webbs observed that the county boundary is 'the deepest and most enduring of English divisions.'[321] So much, one might think, for all the blueprints for completely new and very radical local government reform canvassed over the previous forty or so years. Instead of any of these we simply had, in effect, another new look given to the old inherited patchwork. On the whole Labour supporters did not like it and in particular saw the new system as being incompatible with a planned series of services for, and controls over, community life as a whole. 'Power to act comprehensively is absent' was one comment and it was feared, for instance, that the authorities would be 'too many and too small' for such a function as land-use planning.[322] Professor G. W. Jones wryly observed that the new system was designed to frustrate 'planning of any sort'; and he went on to comment:

> One might suggest that it reflects Conservative ideology: where Labour is committed to planning and emphases [sic] co-ordination, the Conservatives stress decentralised decision-making, partisan mutual adjustment and a system of administrative competition similar to the classical market economy. A basic political approach or style is

---

319 Cf. Lord Redcliffe-Maud's remarks in CCCXXXV H.L. Deb. 5s., 19 October 1972, cols 2040–1.
320 F. W. Maitland, *The Constitutional History of England* (1908; Cambridge, 1974), p. 500.
321 S. and B. Webb, *English Local Government from the Revolution to the Municipal Corporations Act* (London, 1906–29), i.283.
322 G. W. Jones, 'The Local Government Act 1972 and the Redcliffe-Maud Commission', *Political Quarterly*, xliv (1973), pp. 159, 161–2. Cf. the remarks of the secretary of the Welsh Council of Labour cited in J. Osmond, *The Centralist Enemy* (Llandybie, 1974), p. 146.

apparent in the shape and structure of the new local government system.[323]

The antithesis central to the present study could not be more nicely observed.

The latest, and fourth, phase of development relates to changes since 1974. As part of the scheme then completed, provision was made for a continuing review of areas and electoral arrangements through two permanent Local Government Boundary Commissions for England and Wales. Plans for the first review of English shire county boundaries were announced late in 1984.[324] In addition one very major change took place at the beginning of April 1986, that is, the abolition of the GLC and of the six metropolitan counties. There had naturally been dissatisfaction with the 1974 reorganization on the part of the big county boroughs which had been demoted to the limited status of districts in the new counties; and there was a demand for what was sometimes called 'organic change', that is, returning to the larger districts some of the functions they had lost.[325] For obvious reasons the Conservatives had never relished this idea but, after assuming office in 1979, they did increasingly consider a scheme in some respects not dissimilar but more radical and confined to the conurban areas. During the 1983 election their manifesto announced that the GLC and the metropolitan counties had been shown to constitute a 'wasteful and unnecessary tier of government' which should be disposed of, their functions being returned to the boroughs and districts which were, in any case, the major providers of services in London and the conurban areas. A White Paper followed setting out the government's proposals in more detail.[326] It was apparent the government believed the conurban counties were both anachronistic and impediments to public policy. They had been conceived at a time when strategic planning was the fashion and when it was thought that resources would be available to allow for increasing redevelopment. As neither consideration obtained any longer these Labour-controlled authorities and their free-spending habits had simply become a barrier alike to the limitation of public expenditure, the reduction of inflation, and the achievement of greater efficiency in national life. After some difficulty (not least concerning the cancellation of the elections concerned), the necessary legislation

323 Jones, art. cit., p. 163.
324 See the summary in *County Councils Gazette*, lxxvii (1984–5), pp. 255–6.
325 See e.g. the White Paper on Organic Change in Local Government, 1978–9 (vol. x), Cmnd. 7457, ch. 1.
326 KCA (1983), p. 32200A (32205); Streamlining the Cities: Government Proposals for Reorganising Local Government in Greater London and the Metropolitan Counties, 1983–4, Cmnd. 9063. For a summary of the Conservative case, see 'Abolition of the GLC and Metropolitan Counties', *Politics Today* (CRD no. 15; 10 September 1984).

received the royal assent in July 1985. So the functions of the GLC and the metropolitan counties are being transferred to the respective London boroughs and metropolitan district councils or to joint authorities established to provide certain services such as police (outside London), fire brigades, civil defence, and (again outside the capital) passenger transport. In London the ILEA is to be a directly elected authority (with a possible review by 1991). And there is special provision for certain miscellaneous issues, like responsibility for the arts complexes on the South Bank in London which will pass to the Arts Council. The transitional costs of the changes are not slight (being estimated at £400 millions) but the government hopes (optimistically perhaps) that some 7,000 posts will go as a result of the removal of an entire layer of local government and that in this way and through the avoidance of duplication of functions there will be annual savings of the order of £100 millions.[327]

How do all the changes which have occurred over the past fifteen or so years appear in the light of the difficulties revealed in the late nineteenth-century arrangements? Clearly the clash between town and county has been formally resolved in favour of the latter. Maitland observed, not long after the changes of 1888, that there was sometimes 'undue haste to cut the boroughs loose from their counties.'[328] They have now been restored.[329] The conurban problem has at least been recognized even if the precise arrangements necessary to deal with it have not been agreed. The distribution of functions between the tiers has achieved a new equilibrium though whether it will remain settled is still to be seen: there may be problems about shared or cognate responsibilities in particular. And there is still a disparity in respect of area, population, and resources between institutions of the same legal category despite a considerable reduction of their number and so an increase in their average size. However most do fall within the preferred population ranges and so, to a degree at least, there is a match between their 'capacity' (as it might be called) and their duties.[330] There has been some continuing loss of responsibility to agencies of the Public Concern. Thus at the same time as the local government changes took place, the personal health services

---

327 *KCA* (1985), p. 33801A (33803–5).
328 F. W. Maitland, *Township and Borough* (Cambridge, 1898), p. 38.
329 Somewhat surprisingly perhaps W. A. Robson seems to have favoured such a transfer: see his *Local Government in Crisis*, pp. 81, 138.
330 The shire counties vary in population from 110,000 (Powys) to $1\frac{1}{2}$ millions (Essex, Hampshire, and Kent) though, outside Wales, most have a population of over 500,000. The districts vary from 21,000 (Radnor, Powys) to 400,000 (Bristol, Avon) with a preferred population range of 75–100,000. With only a handful of exceptions, the metropolitan districts have populations in excess of 190,000 while all the London boroughs are over 150,000 except five, the smallest of which has 133,000.

were transferred to a reorganized NHS; water and sewerage functions were taken over by the new regional water authorities (on which, however, local government has majority representation); London transport has lately reverted to an appointed executive; and (as mentioned) the Arts Council now has charge of the South Bank theatres.[331] Taken together these are major losses though offset to a minor extent by the acquisition of some new duties as in the field of child care.

In itself the reorganization is unlikely to diminish the central control which often causes so much concern. One symptom of the prevailing unease in this regard was, for instance, a document jointly put to the government early in 1978 by the local authority associations. It complained of a steady erosion of local powers and argued that existing plans would speed up the process. It called on ministers to halt and indeed reverse this trend, to reduce the mass of unnecessary and unnecessarily specific controls, to stop sending out over-detailed advice and to cut demands for reports and statistics. 'The immediate aim', the paper urged, 'must be to seek ways of reversing the drift to centralism and to find ways of strengthening local autonomy'.[332] It was at least compatible with the professed policies of the Conservative government elected in 1979 that it expressed the intention of removing a substantial number of central controls over a wide range of local functions and of relaxing some others. The Environment Secretary announced at the same time (in September 1979) that he was reviewing some capital expenditure controls.[333] Yet over the following years that same government sought increasingly to subject local authorities to stringent restrictions in respect of their level of grant-related expenditure and even the exercise of their rating power. Support has been cut for authorities deemed to be overspending; and the Rates Act (1984) confirms the government's power to keep down the rates of authorities held to be thus delinquent and, further than this, to implement a wider scheme of general rate limitation.[334] The grip seems to be tightening rather than the reverse, though it is understandable perhaps given both the government's commitment to reduce public expenditure and the significant part played by local government in the overall national pattern of spending and borrowing.

Finance is indeed vital in this as in other contexts: in the end everything

---

331 For the plans to privatize some at least of the water authorities, see below pp. 426–8.
332 See the report in 'AMA News', *Municipal Review*, xlviii (1977–8), p. 357.
333 Central Government Controls over Local Authorities, 1979–80, Cmnd. 7634. Cf. KCA (1981), p. 30683A.
334 1984 c. 33. Cf. the summaries in KCA (1985), p. 33801A (33805–8); Byrne, op. cit., pp. 230–6; and G. Jones and J. Stewart, *The Case for Local Government* (London, 1983), Part III.

hinges on questions of money. And the expenditure of local authorities has grown enormously over the past century rising from just 4 per cent of the national income in 1890 to nearly 19 per cent today (see Table 3). Their revenue had to rise to meet this growing cost, and any reform of local government would be wholly incomplete without close attention being paid to this financial aspect for, as the Wheatley Commission observed, the basic problem is that the resources of authorities 'do not

Table 3 Local government expenditure in England and Wales, 1870–1984[a]

Year	Expenditure (£m in current prices) Current	Out of loans and on capital works	Total (i)	Net national income (£m in current prices) (ii)	(i) as a percentage of (ii)
1870	27.3	n.a.	n.a.	936	—
1890	48.2	7.1	55.3	1,385	4.0
1910	125.8	40.6	166.4	1,984	8.4
1930	423.7	108.9	532.6	3,957	13.5
1950	849.1	331.1	1,180.2	10,784	10.9
1969–70	5,405.3	1,707.9	7,113.2	39,599	18.0
1983–4	38,573.3	6,467.1	45,040.4	239,506	18.8

a Data up to 1950 are from tables in B. R. Mitchell and P. Deane, *Abstract of British Historical Statistics* (Cambridge, 1962), pp. 367–8, 416–21 and B. R. Mitchell and H. G. Jones, *Second Abstract of British Historical Statistics* (Cambridge, 1971), pp. 151, 164–6 (any discontinuities are explained in footnotes to the relevant tables). Figures for 1969–70 and 1983–4 are from the CSO's *Annual Abstract of Statistics*.

match their responsibilities.'[335] And it could reasonably be urged that the main defect of the 1974 arrangements was precisely that they failed to include any effective adjustment of this matter.[336] The key issue is simply that without sources of revenue under its own control local government is hardly as autonomous as it might be. As a *Times* leader once put it, if 'local authorities are to become more independent in some real sense – not like glorified French prefectures – they ought to have a broader and more buoyant revenue base of their own.'[337] Certainly, if the process towards centralization is to be, at the least, halted (let alone reversed), it is vital for structural reform to be complemented by changes that will

335 Local Government in Scotland, R. Com. Rep., 1968–9 (vol. xxxix), Cmnd. 4150, p. 1 §3.
336 e.g. N. P. Hepworth, 'Local Government and the Economic Situation', *National Westminster Bank Quarterly Review* (February 1976), p. 10; C. Warman, 'Reorganisation: Lessons of the First Five Years', *Municipal Review*, l (1979–80), p. 3.
337 *The Times* (16 September 1968), p. 23.

help diminish reliance on central funds which now contribute so significantly to the revenue of local authorities.[338] Moreover the existing system has intrinsic defects. It encourages overspending because authorities do not have to raise in taxes much of the money they disburse. There is no close link between rates and the local franchise in that half or more of the total rate bill is met by non-domestic ratepayers who have no vote. Bargaining and political manoeuvre are not insignificant factors. And the larger urban centres tend to benefit to the detriment of other, not less deserving, places. The existing procedures hardly conduce to a careful and rational allocation of resources.[339] Fortunately it is not necessary here to attempt an exploration of the Rate Support Grant, the needs element, regression analysis, the recent block grant changes, and similar mysteries.[340] The point at issue is more basic than these minutiae (important though they are), being whether local dependence on any kind of central grant can be reduced to a more acceptable level by increasing the proportion of revenue under council control. For, as the report of the Redcliffe-Maud Commission said, it must be recognized 'that a reasonable measure of financial independence is an essential element in local democracy'.[341] And some would add that 'reasonable' must mean a very considerable measure indeed.[342]

Over the years numerous possibilities have been canvassed by which local authorities could raise more money of their own. Rate levels could be raised and existing elements of derating eliminated. Yet the many intrinsic disadvantages of rates as a tax would remain: they are regressive (which is why rate rebates were introduced), are not levelled on all members of a household, may have a deleterious effect on the maintenance or improvement of property, are based on an artificial valuation, do not keep pace with inflation, and so on. Consequently other possible sources of local revenue to supplement or replace rate income have often been sought: more charges for services offered; additional assigned revenues (like those on motor vehicles, motor fuel, or

---

338 See Table 2, p. 72 above.
339 For one critical account, see 'Government Grant System under Fire from Audit Commission', *County Councils Gazette*, lxxii (1984–5), pp. 186–7; also J. A. Redwood, 'Local Government Finances', *National Westminster Bank Quarterly Review* (February 1977), esp. pp. 7, 9. Cf. G. W. Jones on the way the present system intensifies the tendency to central control, *Municipal Review*, l (1979–80), pp. 58–9.
340 On the RSG in particular, see R. J. Bennett, *Central Grants to Local Governments: the Political and Economic Impact of the Rate Support Grant in England and Wales* (Cambridge, 1982), esp. pp. 60ff.
341 Local Government in England, R. Com. Rep., 1968–9 (vol. xxxviii), Cmnd. 4040, p. 134 §532. For a similar, more recent comment, see M. Crawford and D. Dawson, 'Are Rates the Right Tax for Local Government?', *Lloyds Bank Review* (July 1982), pp. 18–19.
342 Cf. Rees, *Government by Community*, pp. 65–7, 71.

entertainment); transfer of a proportion of national taxation; a specific tax on income or wealth as whole, on pay-rolls, or on site values; a poll tax; and no doubt there are other exciting prospects. The list of possibilities is not small and the ingenuity displayed is a remarkable tribute to the reformers who take the cause of local government to heart.[343] At the same time none of the proposals is without disadvantages. For example they might cause local variations in price levels, affect central government's ability to regulate economic life in general or public spending in particular, would not necessarily help the poorer areas, might in some places constitute a major disincentive, and so forth. Even so the prospects raised are considerable: thus it was estimated in the mid-seventies that a slight local income tax (of a little less than 4p in the £) would yield almost as much as the domestic rate.[344] Obviously, however, even this would hardly be enough despite the effect it would perhaps have of bringing financial and electoral responsibility into closer relationship and of diminishing the anomalies of the grant formula. For, the psychological effect apart, so long as any margin of funds comes from the centre it is likely to be crucial; indeed control of some kind could continue even if all local revenue were independently raised (were this ever possible).[345]

The Layfield Committee looked into these matters, reporting in 1976. It started from the assumption of 'accountability', that is, that whoever incurs expenditure should also be responsible for raising the necessary revenue.[346] Those matters in respect of which local authorities are merely the agents of national policy should be financed by grants; other activities in respect to which those authorities have discretion should rest on local taxation.[347] And, as the report suggested the need for more local initiative, it went on also to propose an increase in the proportion of income derived from locally raised revenue. Various possibilities were considered but the key solution pressed was that of a local income tax

---

[343] For recent reviews of the options, see The Future Shape of Local Government Finance, 1970–1 (vol. xxxii), Cmnd. 4741; Local Government Finance, Committee of Inquiry Rep., 1975–6 (vol. xxi), Cmnd. 6453, ch. 11; Alternatives to Domestic Rates, 1981–2, Cmnd. 8449; Environment, Sel. Cttee 2nd Rep., 1981–2, HC 217; Rates: Proposals for Rate Limitation and Reform of the Rating System, 1983–4, Cmnd. 9008; also Bennett, op. cit., pp. 258–72.

[344] Local Government Finance, Cttee of Inquiry Rep., 1975–6, Cmnd. 6453, p. 191 §39.

[345] Cf. the discussion in The Constitution, R. Com. Rep., 1973–4 (vol. xi), Cmnd. 5460, pp. 200–2 §§659–62; also G. W. Jones, 'Central-Local Government Relations: Grants, Local Responsibility and Minimum Standards', in D. Butler and A. H. Halsey (eds), *Policy and Politics* (London, 1978), ch. 6.

[346] Local Government Finance, Cttee of Inquiry Rep., 1975–6, Cmnd. 6453, p. 62 §44, p. 283 §2. This is not, of course, a newly observed principle: see e.g. S. Amos, *The Science of Politics* (London, 1883), p. 293.

[347] Local Government Finance, Cttee of Inquiry Rep., 1975–6, Cmnd. 6453, p. 63 §48.

(which was not to replace but to supplement the rates) plus an increased system of charges.[348] This was seen indeed as 'a necessary condition of greater local responsibility' which must be implemented if the alternative prospect, the growth of the central role, is not to become inevitable.[349] These proposals have been widely discussed. There has been some criticism as with the suggestion that it is not more locally raised revenue which is required but an 'unhypothecated grant' or that the rating system itself is not so deficient as supposed.[350] The general response was, however, favourable; and the case made by the committee has subsequently been authoritatively reasserted.[351]

The Labour administration in office when the report came out did not commit itself on the major recommendations made; and it is easy to see why. In the first place the government's Parliamentary position was a difficult one and was unlikely to be strengthened by embarking on so radical a proposal as the introduction of a local income tax, especially as the Treasury was opposed to the idea. As well the financial aspects of the devolution policy (to which the ministry was committed) were based on a system of block grant; and, a provincial income tax having been rejected in that context, it would not be easy to offer it to local authorities.[352] But above all the role of central policy in the management of the economy, together with the general level of expectation about a high and uniform standard of public services, made it difficult for government to give greater flexibility to local bodies: it would be hard to control their levels of expenditure and its timing and direction and to prevent unacceptable variation in provision. Nor have similar considerations been uninfluential in determining the practice and changing the mind of subsequent Conservative administrations. In the seventies the party had committed itself to the abolition of the rating sytem. But by the end of 1981 the government had come to the view that, in the short-term at least, there was no alternative to the rates and all it did was issue a discussion paper on the possibilities of reform. And the Queen's speech after the 1983 election referred simply to tighter control of the rating system and to

---

348 ibid., p. 209 §109, p. 288 §17. The rating system itself should (it was recommended) be modified in various ways: the use of capital values, the re-rating of agriculture, the full assessment of Crown property, and the independent assessment of public utilities, ibid., pp. 290–1 §§27–8; on charges see p. 290 §26.
349 ibid., p. 298 §§58–9, pp. 299–301 §§63–7.
350 F. Cripps and W. Godley, *Local Government Finance and its Reform: a Critique of the Layfield Committee's Report* (Cambridge, 1976), p. 56; T. Travers, 'In Defence of the Friendless Rates', *Municipal Review*, lii (1981–2), pp. 96–7.
351 See e.g. A. H. Marshall, 'Layfield: Time to Fight for Local Power', *Municipal Review*, xlvii (1976–7), pp. 94–5; Sir J. Smart, ibid., liii (1982–3), p. 131; Environment, Sel. Cttee 2nd Rep., 1981–2, HC 217-I, pp. xxiii–xxvii §§41–53; Jones and Stewart, op. cit., esp. pp. 99–102.
352 Bennett, op. cit., p. 64.

measures to secure its improvement (as by putting rates on a capital instead of a rental valuation and by introducing some supplementary sources such as a sales or poll-tax).[353] Subsequently it appeared that the government decided (for the sort of reasons just indicated) that the rating system could not be satisfactorily replaced. Then in a notable U-turn it has lately committed itself to do just that substituting for the rates a form of poll-tax, a so-called 'community charge', though no change would take place until 1990 at the earliest.[354] There is indeed a certain paradox about the present Conservative position on these matters. As a party now formally committed to diminishing the role of the state, it ought perhaps to pursue a policy of reducing central control over local authorities and of creating greater opportunities for their independent action: the pluralistic dispersion of power and initiative is, after all, an important libertarian principle.[355] Yet the Thatcher administration has done nothing of the kind; rather it has taken an opposite course. The necessity for choice of this sort leads to the range of possible views about local government's future which constitutes the framework of current debate.

OPTIONS

... on his choice depends
The safety and the health of the whole state.
Hamlet, I. iii. 20–1

Seen overall the many structural and cognate changes reviewed in this chapter have constituted an important part of the local government response to the problems of a collectivist age, the issues and difficulties arising in the course of the Great Change. And, as indicated in an earlier section, there rumbled on for many years an often heated controversy about the role of local government in facing these burgeoning issues.[356] Those who favoured its extension won the day and it would be true to say that for much of the present century, the interventionist view was accepted. Perhaps the only real argument was about which local institutions should do the job and about the precise mix of local and central involvement. But latterly a new element has entered the debate – or rather an old viewpoint has been revived – one which questions as such the tendency to increasing action. The result is that, most interestingly, it is still possible clearly to discern those three types of attitude whose exponents once contended about the proper nature and office of local

---

353 *Alternatives to Domestic Rates*, 1981–2, Cmnd. 8449; *KCA* (1974), p. 26737A (26741); ibid. (1983), p. 32262A (32268).
354 *Paying for Local Government*, 1985–6, Cmnd. 9714.
355 Cf. *The Rise of Colletivism* (London, 1983) pp. 17–19; *The Ideological Heritage* (London, 1983) p. 330.
356 See above pp. 19–39.

government, those whom I called opponents, centralizers, and improvers. Naturally the precise form of the arguments deployed has altered somewhat; but the thrust of each case is recognizably the same as it was.

Thus there are those who disown much of the substantial local government provision that has been built up over the years. For instance one critic of the Layfield report questioned what he took to be its acceptance of this level and form of activity. Instead of taking the line it did, the committee should have

> dug deep into the nature of local government and asked how far the services it has accumulated willy-nilly for more than a century were really public goods that local government must supply and finance by taxes, and how far they yield separable personal benefits for which the appropriate method of financing is pricing.[357]

The committee itself had accepted that a radical change of this sort was feasible but 'could only be undertaken as part of a deliberate national policy'.[358] And of course such a direction has been congenial to the Thatcher administration since it took office in 1979. That government has objected in principle to the traditional high level of local activity and its cost, currently just under a fifth of the national income, and has deemed substantial economies desirable (not least perhaps because it has notably failed to reduce central government expenditure). Hence the attack on high-spending local authorities. The abolition of the GLC and the metropolitan counties was an important part of this policy: the GLC and ILEA alone accounted for 58 per cent of the 'overspend'.[359] The intention to limit and cut grants and to restrict local power independently to raise funds through the rates are equally part of the same programme. All this will inevitably – and deliberately – mean a cut in the level of locally provided services. The process is simple. The cash increase in expenditure allowed to local authorities is less than the anticipated rate of inflation.[360] If this 'target' is exceeded, grant is cut; and selective 'rate capping' is intended to take care of those authorities which attempt to make up the shortfall by an abnormally high rise in their rates. In such a situation a local authority – as Liverpool found – faces the choice of defying central government and perhaps going bankrupt or of cutting

---

357 A. Seldon, 'Layfield: Why Not Charge for Services?', *Municipal Review*, xlvii (1976–7), p. 98.
358 Local Government Finance, Cttee of Inquiry Rep., 1975–7 (vol. xxi), Cmnd. 6453, p. 290 §26.
359 J. Barton, 'Finance and General Statistics', *County Councils Gazette*, lxxvii (1984–5), pp. 93–4.
360 See e.g. the statement by J. Lovill, chairman of the Association of County Councils, reported ibid., lxxvi (1983–4), p. 322.

back its activities to keep within the financial limits imposed. In addition there is a series of proposals to privatize a number of the services, thus removing them from the sole sphere of local government. Clearly a high degree of central direction is involved in the achievement of all this as it was in the original development of local powers: but the purpose of the control is quite different. Its object is not to enhance the level of local interventionism but to reduce it and make the services that remain more efficient.

There are, secondly, the true modern centralizers, those who, so far as they would allow separate local authorities at all, see them and their powers as agencies of a collectivist central policy.[361] There is a sense in which such a view is required by the concept of popular democracy which (as Professor G. Langrod suggested in an interesting paper) necessarily demands 'administrative centralisation' and thus 'a breakaway from the fundamental idea of local government'.[362] The latter invites differentiation, individualization, separation, or even autonomy; certainly it entails 'the multiplicity of local representative régimes' and acceptance of the fact that they are likely to respond in diverse ways to their varying conception of local needs.[363] In contrast popular democracy

> is by definition an egalitarian, majority and unitarian system. It tends everywhere and at all times to create a social *whole*, a community which is uniform, levelled, and subject to rules. It avoids any splitting up of the governing (and at the same time governed) body, any atomisation, any appearance of intermediaries between the *whole* and the individual. It puts the latter face to face with the complete whole, directly and singly.[364]

And this is, of course, a view which may be traced back at least to Tocqueville's day.[365] In any case, if local government's deficiencies and

---

[361] For an examination of the centralizing doctrine developed in the past few years, see G. W. Jones and J. D. Stewart, 'The Treasury and Local Government', *Political Quarterly*, liv (1983), pp. 5–15. Cf. P. Bowness, 'There is a Price to be Paid for Our Freedom', *Municipal Review*, lii (1981–2), pp. 91–2.

[362] G. Langrod, 'Local Government and Democracy', *Public Administration*, xxxi (1953), p. 29.

[363] ibid., p. 28.

[364] ibid., p. 28 (italics in original). Cf. the discussion which followed Langrod's original article: K. Panter-Brick, 'Local Government and Democracy – a Rejoinder', ibid., pp. 344–8; L. Moulin, 'Local Self-Government as a Basis for Democracy: a Further Comment', ibid., xxxii (1954), pp. 433–7; K. Panter-Brick, 'Local Self-Government as a Basis for Democracy: a Rejoinder', ibid., pp. 438–40. See also the comments of G. W. Jones, 'Central–Local Government Relations: Grants, Local Responsibility and Minimum Standards', in D. Butler and A. H. Halsey (eds), *Policy and Politics* (London, 1978), p. 78.

[365] e.g. A. de Tocqueville, *Democracy in America* (1835–40; Fontana, 1968), vol. ii, Part IV, chs 2–5.

problems are not adequately addressed, new developments could lead, as *The Times* once pessimistically surmised, to a gradual reversion to an age when the shires were administered by agents of the Crown.[366] Certainly the belief in national minimum standards and in economic planning can be a highly centralist one, for in the context of that goal it might reasonably seem that only the government in London has the authority and resources required to achieve it.

Then thirdly there are the modern improvers: those who object alike to the views of the opponents and centralizers. These people wish to see a dispersal of political power and resources embodied in a system of local authorities genuinely – and that means financially – independent in their own sphere and thus free from the control of what one critic called 'the overgrown and overblown machinery of Whitehall'.[367] A certain divergence of view may emerge at this point. It is sometimes stressed that the community with which people can effectively identify is really quite small, even of parochial or neighbourhood size.[368] On the other hand there is the point that nowadays local units need to be reasonably large in order to handle services of importance and to have sufficient resources at their disposal. I suspect that even if Toulmin Smith were to Rip-van-Winkle onto the contemporary scene he might conclude that the parish has had its day and that, if local self-government is to survive at all, the main unit of administration must be on a fairly grand scale not least because nothing else will provide a bulwark against central encroachment. As one modern exponent of such a view put it: 'the real defence against the Centre is in powerful and not piffling local authorities. The parish council has no place in a local democratic system designed for the needs of our times.'[369] Of course provision for the small scale can be made within any scheme of local government organization. But there is a further dimension too. These modern improvers, wanting (through various reforms) to create free, vigorous, and diverse centres of local self-government, also envisage that such refurbished authorities would be very active within their allotted domain. And I fancy it is the assumption of many of those urging this view that an impressive and extending array of business thus locally conducted would be both usual and highly desirable. A most important statement of this sort of case was recently put by Professors Jones and Stewart who indicate a whole battery of changes – what they call a new settlement – which they think

---

366 'Exit the Town Hall?', *The Times* (10 November 1964), p. 11.
367 Professor Lord Beloff, intro. to I. B. Rees, *Government by Community* (London, 1971), p. xi. Conservatives themselves have often recognized this: e.g. P. Goldman, *Some Principles of Conservatism* (CPC no. 161; 1956, rev. edn, London, 1961), p. 10. Cf. J. H. Warren, *In Defence of Local Democracy* (CPC no. 170; London, 1957).
368 e.g. Rees, op. cit., ch. 4 esp. pp. 76–7, 97, 105.
369 Sir H. Page, 'Local Government in Decline', *Three Banks Review* (June 1971), p. 17.

are required to sustain a free and improving local government system.[370] Among these reforms are: the introduction of a local income tax and the reduction of central grant levels; the elimination of the non-domestic rate; the use of PR in local elections; payment of councillors; reorganization on the basis of the large district (with a population range of some 150–500,000) and, beyond this, joint action where necessary; promulgation of a local government charter to enshrine its rights; and much else. And the clear implication is that, on such a reformed basis, local administrations will be strong and realize new initiatives to deal with community problems. As well they ought to enhance their range of duties by being allowed to absorb responsibility for a number of tasks currently placed elsewhere: the National Health Service; the training and some other functions of the Manpower Services Commission; the probation service; and the distribution of gas and electricity. Local authorities should also be given a general competence to carry out any function not barred by law; and this would include the right to monitor the private sector within each area of jurisdiction. Jones and Stewart obviously envisage, therefore, authorities which, when refurbished, will be actively interventionist on a large scale.

* * *

Two of these attitudes at least might, to their proponents, seem to imply the need for the establishment of new institutions placed between the traditional local authorities and the national government. One manifestation of this possibility is the recent, though so far thwarted, movement towards some devolution of power in the United Kingdom: but this is not the only possible form of 'intermediate government'.

INTERMEDIATE GOVERNMENT

> To both our Houses, may they see
> Beyond the borough and the shire!
> TENNYSON, 'Hands All Round', *The Works*, 1894, p. 575

The term 'intermediate government' is quite helpful in the present context.[371] It is appropriately vague and may, therefore, adequately cover

---

370 See their *The Case for Local Government* (London, 1983), which brings together arguments they had previously expressed in various places.

371 The concept may be found e.g. in L. T. Hobhouse, *Liberalism* (1911; Galaxy, 1966), pp. 118–19 and in H. J. Laski, *A Grammar of Politics* (London, 1925), p. 309. For more recent use, see e.g. C. H. Wilson in the volume he edited, *Essays on Local Government* (Oxford, 1948), p. 11; W. Thornhill (ed.), *The Case for Regional Reform: Extracts from Essential Documents* (London, 1972), pp. 3, 6; The Constitution, R. Com. Rep., 1973–4 (vol. xi) Cmnd. 5460, p. 59 §188; ibid., Memorandum of Dissent, 1973–4 (vol. xi), Cmnd. 5460-I, p. xv §14 and *passim*.

the various institutions and political possibilities that lie between, on the one hand, the local authority as traditionally understood and, on the other, the national government at the centre. In the present section something will be said both of the intermediate bodies which actually exist and of those which have been proposed. But, first, consideration is due of the reasons why such agencies might be established.

Reasons

There are various factors and occasions involved in the emergence of intermediate institutions, considerations which are notionally distinct if in practice intermingled. The first is the recognition that the effective provision of certain services – such as main drainage, police, planning, some aspects of transportation – may demand an area of operation, pool of population, or fund of resources larger than that of the usual local authority. This was one reason leading to the creation of metropolitan government in London and other conurbations and the establishment of joint authorities; it was also an aspect of the many proposals which appeared from time to time for some form of provincial or regional government. A second factor was the concern that central government had become increasingly overloaded. The legislature and the administrative departments alike were, it was said, subject to so much pressure of work that they could not cope efficiently: hence the need to transfer elsewhere some at least of the responsibility. This is not a new feeling, having been part of the motive behind the reform of local government itself in the late ninteenth century and during the various discussions of devolution from that time to our own day. Of course the specific possibility in view varied: if the burden was held to weigh excessively on Parliament then the solution would entail some form of sublegislature; if on the executive departments then either a deconcentration of headquarters or a decentralization to regional (and local) offices would be needed. Perhaps both elements were required in that administrative arrangements ought ideally to be supervised by some form of elected assembly. There is thirdly a related (but different) point that government had become over-centralized, its power excessively strong and concentrated too much in one place, so that diversity and initiative alike were at a discount. This was a theme which could draw on the tradition of local self-government represented by Toulmin Smith. It was also sustained by the pluralist attack on the idea of monistic sovereignty and by the influence of the federal concept, the notion that 'the secret of liberty is the division of power.'[372] Freedom, the

---

372 H. J. Laski, 'The Problem of Administrative Areas' (1918), in *The Foundations of Sovereignty and Other Essays* (London, 1921), p. 86.

development of the creative impulse, and a desirable flexibility of social response all required that the centre be constrained or even weakened by the creation of countervailing seats of authority. This would have the added advantage of making possible a greater degree of popular participation in government. In this way 'federality' was frequently seen as the essential condition of a democratic future.[373] With all this there might be associated, fourthly, the search for (or the realization of) some provincial or national identity so that traditions and cultures regarded as distinct could be more easily preserved or renewed. Sentiment of the sort in question may obviously be a powerful force in its own right and be significant regardless of any merely technical or administrative consideration; while the purpose entailed may range from the desire for a merely token institutional recognition of a separate entity to the demand for separation from (and therefore the dissolution of) the United Kingdom itself. Finally there are the actual precedents to be cited as evidence to the possibility; for what we now call the United Kingdom has a long history of the dispersal of authority. Until 1707 Scotland had its own Parliament as did Ireland until 1800; and those constitutional curiosities, the Isle of Man and the Channel Islands, have existed in a kind of quasi-independence for many hundreds of years. There was also the separate Parliament and executive government which existed in Northern Ireland between 1921 and 1972. In addition there are the decentralized administrative arrangements of the Scottish, Welsh, and Northern Ireland offices.

This mélange of considerations has been explored by many publicists and others; and it was, of course, invoked with increasing frequency and intensity during the 1970s as the debate on devolution developed.

It remains briefly to describe the types of intermediate body which have been established or envisaged.

Existing forms

There are two existing kinds of intermediate organization: the joint local authority and the regional administrative office.

The joint authority

The joint authority is a rudimentary form of intermediate agency the need for which arises from the limitations of local government itself, either because the resources of an individual authority are insufficient for a given purpose or as a result of its area being too small for efficiency. In such a situation two or more authorities may be combined for the

---

373 The term 'federality' is Sidgwick's: see his *The Elements of Politics* (1891; 2nd edn, London, 1897), ch. xxvi.

purpose of providing a specific service. The creation of such a joint body may be deemed collectivist in the sense that it extends the ambit of public provision, creating a further element of local interventionism that would not perhaps otherwise be possible. At the same time it may nevertheless be preferable that a task (if it is to be done) should be carried out by the localities concerned than be assumed by some central body. Examples of such joint action may be found as far back as the late seventeenth and eighteenth centuries as in the various unions of parishes for Poor-Law purposes that were established during that period, a device also embodied in the Poor Law Amendment Act of 1834. Another instance was the Metropolitan Board of Works set up in 1855, in effect a sort of joint improvement commission to provide an array of drainage and highway services for the capital. The Metropolitan Asylums Board of 1867 was also a hybrid and included representatives of both central and local authorities. Not long after this the Public Health Act of 1875 gave general recognition to the principle and value of joint action by enabling local authorities to combine in a united district for a whole range of purposes. And this precedent was followed in many subsequent statutes notably the Local Government Act (1894) which empowered parochial and district authorities so to proceed in dealing with any task of mutual interest.[374]

Sometimes joint bodies set up were simply advisory; or common action might be agreed without any permanent machinery being created as with, say, sharing the services of a particular official such as a medical officer of health or an inspector of weights and measures or co-operating in the bulk purchase of supplies. But beyond this there were two types of joint arrangements which could be established. There was the joint committee which was subordinate to the authorities concerned so far as it depended on them for money and could (in most cases) be brought to an end by them too. On the other hand the joint board was a permanent entity with greater power and a legal status of its own which, once created, was little subject to its constitutors. Quite a number of these joint enterprises was brought into existence though fewer perhaps than might have been expected: in fact a considerable array of adoptive powers to this end was long unused.[375] However a large authority like the quondam Manchester County Borough, placed in a highly populated district governed by many local bodies, would necessarily be much involved in this form of co-operative activity. By the mid-1930s the City Council there was represented on something like twenty or more joint bodies dealing with a wide range of matters from assize courts, asylums,

---

374 56 & 57 Vic., c.73, §57.
375 W. A. Robson, *The Development of Local Government* (1931; 3rd rev. edn, London, 1954), pp. 180–1, 184.

and charities to regional town planning, war pensions, and upper Mersey navigation.[376] By the early 1940s there were in England and Wales more than 850 joint authorities of both types, the largest group (some 40 per cent) being in the public health field and for the provision of isolation hospitals in particular.[377] Of course many such functions were much affected by the creation of the National Health Service in 1948. The result was that, by the mid-1960s, the total number of joint authorities was lower: there were 30 burial boards or committees, 20 joint sewerage boards, 1 conservancy catchment board, 89 water boards, and 60 port health authorities.[378] Many of these have since disappeared, as through the reorganization of services entailed by the Water Act (1973); but others remain.[379] There were, in addition, some educational building consortia and housing groups; as well there have been the police amalgamations since the 1960s and the arrangements made for joint fire and ambulance services. Provision for joint action was retained in the local government reorganization statutes passed by Parliament in the early 1970s, and this possibility has been exploited in some cases not least since the pressures for economy began to increase. For example in 1974 the four Welsh counties of South, Mid, and West Glamorgan and Gwent established a purchasing consortium to obtain bulk discount on the whole range of supplies they themselves needed (together with such district councils as chose to deal with them). Since it began to operate this arrangement has cut costs by some £4½ millions, £1 million being saved in 1983 alone.[380] Joint committees were also recommended by the Bains report in 1972 to co-ordinate county and district functions and policies.[381]

The truth be told, however, many of these experiments in co-operative effort were never much of a success. Yet it is clear why they were attempted. And in the 1930s a radically-minded critic of the then local government system like W. A. Robson believed that effective joint action within the existing framework of authorities might to a degree be enough to overcome some of the obvious defects of structure and power.[382]

---

376 A. Redford, *The History of Local Government in Manchester* (London, 1939–40), iii. 290–1.
377 E. Howard, 'Joint Authorities', C. H. Wilson (ed.), *Essays on Local Government* (Oxford, 1948), Table I pp. 205–6.
378 P. W. Jackson, *Local Government*, 3rd edn (London, 1976), p. 185.
379 The regional water authorities, having a majority of local government representatives, might perhaps still be regarded as a kind of joint board; but as units of a national utility they are treated in the present volume as part of the Public Concern: see below pp. 426–8.
380 See the report in *County Councils Gazette*, lxxvi (1983–4), p. 346.
381 M. A. Bains *et al.*, *The New Local Authorities: Management and Structure* (London, 1972), ch. 8.
382 Robson, op. cit. (1st edn, 1931), pp. 110, 122–3. And cf. op. cit. (3rd edn, 1954), p. 62.

Clearly such arrangements could, in principle, achieve economy of cost combined with technically more appropriate areas of operation and, as well, duplication could be avoided.[383] In practice, though, the drawbacks became readily apparent, in particular the likelihood that the most hesitant participant in any such scheme might act as a drag on proposals for development for fear that its position as an independent entity would be increasingly compromised; and even where there was some achievement to record, it was doubtful whether political leadership or drive capable of countering local loyalties would develop.[384] In addition there was little sense of popular control. Thus when, in the mid-1930s, a royal commission was considering the economic and local government problems of the Tyneside area, it wondered whether a series of joint boards and authorities might not be the answer to these difficulties. But in the end it decided that not only was the *ad hoc* creation of bodies not directly representative undesirable in itself but also that the individual local authorities concerned would be reluctant thus to hazard their own rights and status, a feeling which would inhibit any possible advantage.[385] Similarly the Coalition government proposals for a National Health Service originally envisaged hospital organization through a form of joint authority.[386] But in the outcome another arrangement was preferred and for similar reasons. In fact the joint authority was largely overtaken both by the transfer of services to national bodies of a specialized kind, as in the case of hospitals and water resources; and, too, by the reform of the local government system itself to create larger units of administration and political control. On the other hand, with the abolition of the GLC and the metropolitan counties (as from April 1986), there is to be an increased range of joint action in the areas concerned as the boroughs and districts severally or together take over most of the responsibilities thus abdicated. Public transport is one of the major functions involved. After the 1968 Transport Act it was the responsibility of the joint boards then set up in the conurban areas (one of them, for instance, planned the Tyne and Wear metro). But with the local government reorganization the task was transferred to the passenger transport executives of the new metropolitan counties; and it will now revert once more to joint boards. In all, nineteen joint boards are to be established: three in each of the six metropolitan counties (fire services, police, and, as mentioned, passenger transport) and one in London (fire services). There will also be joint

---

383 Cf. Wilson, op. cit., pp. 221–5.
384 P. J. Madgwick, 'The Welsh Joint Education Committee after 21 Years', *Local Government Chronicle* (13 September 1969), p. 1703.
385 Local Government in the Tyneside Area, R. Com. Rep., 1936–7 (vol. xiii), Cmd. 5402, p. 40 §138.
386 A National Health Service, 1943–4 (vol. viii), Cmd. 6502, pp. 14–17, 48 §4(2), and Appendix C pp. 77–9.

arrangements for co-ordinating both waste regulation and disposal, and also for the collective funding of some voluntary organizations. But after these schemes have been operating for a reasonable time, the government intends that the boroughs and districts (or groups of them) may propose to withdraw from a joint board and provide a service direct.[387]

Regional administration
There is a substantial number of intermediate offices of an administrative or advisory kind most of which have been created since the 1930s, and in particular since the Second World War, as a result of an increasing and more complex array of responsibilities being assumed by central government.[388] Perhaps when state intervention was on a relatively small scale it did not matter that the conduct of affairs was concentrated in London. But since those days it has in many cases been found convenient, indeed necessary, to deploy the larger staffs involved outside the capital. Thus in 1944 the Machinery of Government Committee recognized that, so long as there was adequate departmental co-operation, the development of regional and local offices could make a significant contribution to dealing with the problems of reconstruction (even though much official thinking was conditioned by a centralizing view based on the doctrine of ministerial responsibility to Parliament).[389] And, more recently, the Crowther-Kilbrandon Commission reported (with respect to a recent phase of administrative development) that

> in the last decade or so decentralisation has been stimulated by the growth in the volume and complexity of government business, and by the grouping together in large departments of related functions hitherto dealt with in a number of separate departments. An important contribution to the smooth operation of these large departments has been made by parcelling out blocks of executive work to regional and local units, leaving the departmental headquarters to concentrate mainly on policy and planning.[390]

And by 1979 just over half of all non-industrial civil servants were employed in regional or local offices (mostly in the latter).[391]

387 Local Government Act, 1985 c. 51, esp. Part IV and, for membership of joint authorities, ibid., Schedule 10; *KCA* (1985), p. 33801A (33804–5).
388 For an historical survey, see B. C. Smith, *Regionalism in England* (London, 1964–5), vol. I ch. one and vol. II ch. two.
389 PRO, CAB 87/74, MG (44) 5, MGO 46 (20 March 1944), p. 2 §§6–7, 9, and Annex Part III; ibid., CAB 87/73, MG (44) 9 (18 May 1944), p. 1 §1; and J. M. Lee, *Reviewing the Machinery of Government, 1942–1952: an Essay on the Anderson Committee and its Successors* (n.p. [London], 1977), p. 114.
390 The Constitution, R. Com. Rep., 1973–4, Cmnd. 5460, p. 297 §980. On the giant department, see below p. 192 and in Part 2 pp. 656ff.
391 Civil Service Department, *The Civil Service: Introductory Factual Memorandum*

In 1951 the Treasury expounded the general principles underlying these developments as follows.[392] First the tasks of government were now so complex that a considerable degree of decentralization was essential to efficiency, for example so that work could be broken up into more manageable units and the pressure at the centre lifted. It is in this way often easier to perform appropriate executive functions or to supervise a network of local offices providing services to the public. Secondly, within the framework of general policy as centrally determined, there should be discretion swiftly responsive to special conditions and cases in the various regions and localities. Thirdly the decentralization should shorten a department's lines of communication with its 'clients' and enable them to participate in discussion of regional problems. In this way local authorities, industrial and commercial undertakings, and other interests could better convey to the department some understanding of particular conditions and needs. As a result the injection of regional considerations into policy-making would be facilitated. Finally regionalization may be pursued for strategic reasons, to take over in the event of war or extreme disorder should central government or its communications break down. To all of which must be added the further point that there may also be at work an historical factor or one associated with recognition of national identity as in the case of the many decentralized functions of the Scottish and Welsh Offices (or those relating to Northern Ireland).

Of course, a department may maintain a regional organization for more than one of these purposes; and clearly, the degree of decentralization will vary from one office to another. Where a department, like the Treasury, is mainly concerned with policy issues, regional decentralization is neither so easy nor so necessary as with offices having considerable executive functions like Trade and Industry or the Environment. But where the regional offices do exist they naturally increase the number of staff needed and also create problems of co-ordination. The region needs to know quite clearly what it can do on its own initiative without reference to London: the terms of reference have to be precise. It clearly helps, too, if these are uniform: much advantage will be lost, for instance, if one out of a number of departments in a region insists on certain problems being settled at national level while other departments concerned leave related matters to their regional

---

(London, 1980), p. 4 §1.6. Figure 1.2, ibid., p. 9, shows the numbers employed in each of eleven standard regions.

392 In *The Regional Boards for Industry* (1951) as cited by J. A. Cross, 'The Regional Decentralization of British Government Departments', *Public Administration*, xlviii (1970), p. 426, cf. The Constitution, R. Com. Rep., 1973–4, Cmnd. 5460, pp. 297–8 §§983–5; Sir R Clarke, *New Trends in Government* (Civil Service College Studies no. 1; London, 1971), p. 30.

offices. There has often been criticism about delay, rigidity, lack of effective responsibility and initiative, absence of co-ordination, and the like at regional level.[393] But the actual state of affairs worked out reasonably satisfactorily, difficulties being overcome, for instance, by the use of common offices.[394] And certainly W. J. M. Mackenzie suggested that the development of these decentralized departmental organizations was a vital 'new point of growth in English administrative history, as important in their generation as the invention of the Sheriff or of the Justice of the Peace.'[395]

A particularly important aspect of the development of decentralized administration was the idea of regional planning, a matter of obvious collectivist consequence. This notion emerged before the war with concern about the so-called special areas; and the Royal Commission on the Distribution of the Industrial Population suggested the value in this connexion of regional organization to help deal with the problem of depressed localities and questions concerning the balanced distribution and diversification of industry.[396] Subsequently Regional Boards were set up to help improve industrial production during the war and after 1945 these were transformed into advisory Regional Boards for Industry. There were also the various Industrial Development Councils created under post-war legislation. The regional organization of some departments tended to be wound down after the abandonment of many physical controls in the late 1940s and 1950s but the notion of regional planning took on a new lease of life early in the next decade. For this there were three sorts of reasons: a social concern about many of the consequences of the growth of industry and towns; a realization that the technical possibilities had considerably eased previous restrictions on the location of factories and so forth; and a stress on the importance of economic growth as a means of improving national standards. There were also subsidiary questions to do with avoiding any waste of resources or remedying regional imbalance of any kind.[397] And the whole

---

393 See e.g. Lee, op. cit., pp. 135–6 and the memoranda produced by the County Councils and Rural District Councils Associations in Estimates, Sel. Cttee 6th Rep., 1953–4 (vol. vi), HC 233, pp. 118–24, 133–5.

394 See the Treasury memorandum in Estimates, Sel. Cttee 6th Rep., 1953–4, HC 233, p. 153 §5.

395 Introduction to J. W. Grove, *English Regional Government: a Study of the North-West* (London, n.d. [1952]), p. 1. Cf. the evidence presented by government departments to the Commission on the Constitution, loc. cit., esp. ch. 21 and the memorandum of dissent, ch. V.

396 The Distribution of the Industrial Population, R. Com. Rep., 1939–40 (vol. iv), Cmd. 6153, pp. 181–4 §§379–86; A. W. Peterson, 'The Machinery for Economic Planning: III. Regional Economic Planning Councils and Boards', *Public Administration*, xliv (1966), pp. 30–1.

397 On all this, see e.g. E. Nevin, 'The Case for Regional Policy', *Three Banks Review*

impetus behind the idea was much, indeed crucially, reinforced by the establishment in 1964 of the Department of Economic Affairs and the following year of the Regional Economic Planning Councils and Boards in eight English regions and in Scotland and Wales. The boards consisted of the senior regional officers of the departments concerned with economic planning; the councils were advisory and representative of various interests including the local authorities and both sides of industry. Together the functions of the councils and boards were to assess the economic potential of their region and the measures necessary to realize it fully in the context of the National Plan and to see that full weight was given to the regional implications of national policies especially at their formative stage. They were also intended to aid greater intra-regional co-operation between departments.[398] G. Brown at least saw this machinery as the embryo of a new form of regional government.[399] However the problems that arose in the work of these bodies were substantial.[400] And the innovation, originally accompanied by euphoria at the prospects it revealed, was soon shrouded in disillusion attended by a series of local fracas and resignations.

Bodies other than central government departments have also established regional organizations to help carry out their functions. The NHS is so structured.[401] Similarly the various nationalized industries or services have, where appropriate, established regional or area organizations though (given the various technical or cognate considerations involved) these arrangements are naturally not uniform. There is indeed a notable array of regional authorities in this non-departmental category including, as well as those already mentioned, such bodies as regional sports councils, arts councils, tourist boards, and water authorities.[402] Also certain bodies have been established from time to time to operate enterprises of regional significance such as the Mersey

---

(December 1966), pp. 30–46; Peterson, art. cit., pp. 32–3 where there are references to the contemporary literature.

398 Smith, op. cit., vol. III ch. two; Peterson, art. cit., pp. 37–8. Cf. The Constitution, R. Com. Rep., 1973–4, Cmnd. 5460, pp. 64–5 §§205–7.

399 G. Brown, *In My Way: the Political Memoirs of Lord George-Brown* (1971; Penguin, 1972), p. 102.

400 Peterson, art. cit., pp. 39–40; J. Mackintosh, *The Devolution of Power: Local Democracy, Regionalism and Nationalism* (Penguin, 1968), pp. 101–2, 105, 107–9. For a particular study, see C. Painter, 'The Repercussions of Administrative Innovation: the West Midlands Economic Planning Council', *Public Administration*, l (1972), pp. 467–84.

401 See below pp. 421–3.

402 For a review of the regional organization of the *ad hoc* authorities, see The Constitution, R. Com., Memorandum of Dissent, 1973–4, Cmnd. 5460-I, pp. 72ff.

Docks and Harbour Board, the Port of London Authority, and the London Passenger Transport Board.[403]

Most of this complex array of administrative agencies has been created only over the past forty years. Nevertheless there is little system about it. It is all, as the Liberal Party evidence to the Crowther-Kilbrandon Commission said, 'a jumble of assorted bodies with varying functions, varying areas and varying compositions.' Moreover none of these bodies is elected and their work is too little co-ordinated. It is easy to see why it may be 'reminiscent of the chaos of local government in the nineteenth century' with its many boards, commissions, and so on, and why similarly, it may seem desirable or even necessary to bring all these bodies together 'into a coherent pattern' at regional level.[404] Yet even if the decentralized administrative arrangements were completely systematic and substantially extended this would nevertheless be unlikely to make the people in a given region feel that they had any real control over their affairs. For this an elective body is undoubtedly necessary. But that effective administrative decentralization may help create a consciousness of this possibility and of the need for it is also undoubtedly true.[405]

Devolution

A little while ago Professor Birch suggested it was becoming clear that the United Kingdom was 'entering a new phase in its history, in which the centralised system of government that has served for the past two centuries will have to be modified.'[406] It was a view then widely held and which had been gathering strength since the mid-sixties when, for instance, R. H. S. Crossman wrote in his diary (in the context of considering the idea of a Welsh Council or Parliament) that 'the great constitutional issue of the day' was 'decentralization' or 'nationalism'.[407] It culminated a decade later in the abortive movement for Scottish and Welsh devolution. Since then the pressure for such a policy has notably diminished; and Birch's anticipation now appears quite unrealistic (at least for the time being). We seem to be back in the days when it was

403 See below pp. 348, 357.
404 Liberal Party evidence to the Royal Commission on the Constitution, written evidence vol. 8 (London, 1972), pp. 89–90 §5. Cf. Liberal Party Regionalism Committee, *Power to the Provinces* (London, 1968); The Constitution, R. Com., Memorandum of Dissent, 1973–4, Cmnd. 5460-I, p. xiii §7, p. xv §15, p. 81 §202. For Goschen's famous remarks about the nineteenth-century chaos, see p. 48 above.
405 The Constitution, R. Com., Memorandum of Dissent, 1973–4, Cmnd. 5460-I, pp. 81–3 §§203–7.
406 A. H. Birch, *Political Integration and Disintegration in the British Isles* (London, 1977), p. 167.
407 R. H. S. Crossman, *The Diaries of a Cabinet Minister* (London, 1975–7), ii. 344, 536, 551, 594–5.

possible for an informed political commentator to say that support for such policies has never been very popular in Britain.[408] Yet of course the idea is by no means new; and it would be foolish to say it could never again erupt genie-like on to the political stage.

The possibilities raised by provincial or national devolution were explored from time to time as (to take a couple of random examples) by the Speaker's Conference which reported in 1920 or in the works of Professor R. Muir; while the Labour Party at least promised support for the idea in its 1929 election manifesto.[409] Yet the impetus had largely gone out of the idea and it is easy to see why. The Irish problem appeared to have been solved and slumbered on the sidelines so that one stimulus to sustained interest was removed. The difficulties being experienced by local government in many ways boded ill for the prospects of any larger authorities of a similar kind. As well the matter of legislative pressure was being met, without the upheaval devolution would require, by the delegation of legislative power to departments and other agencies. And, over all, the emerging crisis of the international order, world depression and the possibility of war, made questions like devolution seem not merely somewhat trivial by comparison but inappropriate as a response to situations which demanded not less but more control. Economic efficiency and the elimination of unemployment certainly seemed (to many observers) to demand the central assumption of greater powers of economic management. If an undertone of interest was sustained, by some nationalists or academics for instance, the issue was generally regarded as dead. But now, more recently, there occurrred a marked revival of interest to which a miscellaneous series of events contributed.

Perhaps the first straw in the wind was a number of exotic proposals which kept in public view the idea of federal union or something akin to it. One was the suggestion put forward in the mid-1950s that Malta should be integrated with the United Kingdom. Nothing came of this in the end despite the principle of such an association being accepted by the Conservative government of the day; but the policy did reflect a relationship of a quasi-federal kind and helped to bring such issues politically to the fore after a lapse of many decades.[410] The creation some

---

408 R. E. Dickinson, *City Region and Regionalism: a Geographical Contribution to Human Ecology* (London, 1947), p. 273.

409 Conference on Devolution, Letter from Mr. Speaker to the Prime Minister, 1920 (vol. xiii), Cmd. 692. For Muir, see his *National Self-Government* (London, 1918); 'The Machinery of Government', in Lord Robert Cecil *et al.*, *Essays in Liberalism* (London, 1922), pp. 141–2; *Politics and Progress: a Survey of the Problems of Today* (London, 1923), pp. 30, 72–3, 145–6; *How Britain is Governed: a Critical Analysis of Modern Developments in the British System of Government* (London, 1930), ch. viii. The manifesto referred to is in F. W. S. Craig (ed.), *British General Election Manifestos 1918–1966* (Chichester, 1970), p. 59.

410 See The Future of Malta, Round Table Conference, 1955–6 (vol. xxii), Cmd. 9657.

The Labyrinthine Maze 121

time later of the West Indies Associated States also involved a form of federal relationship with this country, as did proposals for federal union with Rhodesia which were considered during the talks of September 1966.[411] The introduction of federal constitutions in some colonial territories on their achievement of independence, as with Central Africa (1953), the Caribbean (1958), and Nigeria (1960) together with discussion about European federation also kept the theme of federality alive. Part of the then boom in academic political studies was reflected in the appearance of a number of prominent books and papers on federalism and its problems. The subject was in the air. Another such contemporary factor, and one of more immediate domestic significance, was the continuation of difficulties with the structure, power, and financing of local government. So long as these deficiencies continued and worsened, then radical concepts of reform flourished and often included a proposal to establish authorities either explicitly regional or at least of a conurban kind. A provincial level of organization was envisaged by the Redcliffe-Maud Commission in 1969 as well as by academic and other commentators. And, of course, the enlargement of the LCC, the creation of regional councils in Scotland, and of the metropolitan counties in England was a move in this direction.[412] Moreover, forms of regional administration have begun to develop, as through the establishment by central departments of regional and local offices. One implication was that this machinery should be made more directly responsible and open to popular pressure by making it accountable directly to an elected assembly. There was also a general worry about the growth of central power, of a form of rule which could seem remote, unapproachable, and secretive. One Welsh Labour MP, for instance, expressed alarm about the drift towards a society dominated by centralized authority and urged the need to disperse it and to ensure an effective role for citizens. In economic terms, he said, 'Public ownership under bureaucratic control can be as monstrous as unchecked private ownership.'[413] This concern is by no means necessarily the same as the feeling that there is too much government – though these sentiments may be linked – but rather a sense that decision-making is too much

---

There is a full account in *KCA*: see index *sub* 'Malta, U.K., relations with', in volumes for 1955–9. It is odd there is no detailed study of these rather interesting events and proposals: one should certainly be written now that the official papers are available.

411 The Constitution, R. Com. Rep., 1973–4, Cmnd. 5460, pp. 421–2 §§1395–7; *KCA* (1965–6), pp. 21234B, 21344B, 21441B; ibid. (1967–8), p. 21952B; H. Wilson, *The Labour Government 1964–1970: a Personal Record* (1971; Penguin, 1974), pp. 390, 410.
412 On the local government changes, see above pp. 91ff.
413 N. Edwards, *Is This the Road?* (Wrexham, n.d. [1955?]), pp. 5–6, 8–9.

concentrated in London where the conduct of business has become slow and inefficient and where decisions are made without due regard to the interests and special circumstances of those in the provinces. A factor of particular importance in this regard was the failure of centrally directed economic policy. People in Scotland and Wales (and some of the English regions too) often felt that their economic affairs had not been well managed or their interests adequately sustained by the decisions made in London. It may indeed have been this dissatisfaction with economic conditions that above all caused the nationalist resurgence in recent years.[414] Of course there is the intrinsic force of national feeling and cultural differences as well, in Wales for instance about the decline of the Welsh language and in Scotland located in a sense of historical separateness and sovereignty; but what were regarded as the great economic disadvantages of the Union have undoubtedly bulked large in the syndrome of factors involved. So long as the broad economic tendency could be thought of as upward or as having potential all was well: but the great depression of the 1930s began to shatter this assumption. The war provided both an interlude and a new hope, a belief in planning and management as a means to control and develop the economy, a situation from which Scotland and Wales like any other part of the UK could expect to benefit. Collectivist intervention from the centre was the answer to the country's problems. But it has (or so it might seem) proved a broken reed, the ineffective nature of which was symbolized by the complete failure of the National Plan of the 1960s and by the surge of inflation and unemployment occurring in the following decade. The ailing economy failed to revive. And not only had the grandiosity of London planning proved empty; there was, for Scotland, North Sea oil round the corner which, if pre-empted, would be a much more effective panacea. Hence the late spectacle of Scottish nationalism resurgent, a populism resentful of the unsuccessful features of the centralized state.[415] Nor has reaction in Wales always been different.

Moreover it is not necessary nowadays – or so it would seem – to be a part of a large state in order to achieve economic prosperity. This is because the advantages of a big market, financial aid, and so on can accrue to quite small units as members of such supranational organizations as the EEC and the IMF. As independent countries Scotland and Wales would have their own representatives in such bodies. There has undoubtedly been growing, too, a sense that centralization is

---

414 The Constitution R. Com. Rep., 1973–4, Cmnd. 5460, p. 3 §§2–3, pp. 25–7 §§80–5, pp. 37–8 §§122–5, p. 104 §336, p. 112 §363, pp. 137–8 §§442–4, etc.
415 The significance of the apparent economic disadvantages of union was brought out soon after the last war: see e.g. W. H. Marwick's pamphlet *Scottish Devolution* (Fabian Research Series no. 137; London, 1950), esp. pp. 9–11.

no longer necessary as perhaps it once was for imperial, diplomatic, or military reasons. No doubt to sustain control of a vast Empire and to play a major role on the international scene demanded national unity. But this role has now vanished and with it perhaps the feeling that the cohesion it required is any longer necessary or even feasible.[416] Smallness may even be a positive advantage in some diplomatic contexts nowadays. Equally military security is not today simply a function of size. As a member of NATO Luxemburg is as well or badly protected as the United Kingdom. There is also the point that the very development of supranational organizations tends to create scepticism about the traditional apparatus of the state and its self-sufficiency.[417]

Certainly during the 1960s and '70s there was a notable surge of support for the nationalist parties in Wales and Scotland, to such an extent indeed that the electoral position of the Labour Party seemed at one time to be seriously threatened. It had long taken a substantial majority of seats in Wales and at least half of those in Scotland so that the nationalist incursions seemed likely, if sustained, to undermine its very position as a potential party of government.[418] Its position in the Commons was affected; and the devolution proposals were part of the government's response to the situation. To this has to be added the effect of the revived troubles in Northern Ireland. If at first the latter circumstances might seem to raise doubts about the viability of experiments in provincial decentralization, nevertheless, after the period of direct rule, a new scheme of devolution was introduced in 1973 and, though this too was short-lived, it was widely accepted that something of the sort must ultimately be required for any political solution of the problems of the province.[419] Thus the proposals later enacted in 1982 were based on a programme of 'rolling devolution' to replace direct rule.[420] And, of course, what could be given to Ulster ought also to be available elsewhere: or so it might be urged. Out of the turmoil came two important developments. One was the appointment in 1969 of the Royal Commission on the Constitution; the other was the subsequent introduction of legislation to establish devolved institutions for Scotland and Wales. The commission was no doubt originally intended as a palliative or delaying device; the statutes reflected the later political assessment that (given the current Parliamentary situation) further

---

416 The Constitution, R. Com. Rep., 1973–4, Cmnd. 5460, p. 20 §64.
417 See the discussion of these and cognate matters in Birch, op. cit., pp. 172–5; V. Bogdanor, *Devolution* (Oxford, 1979), pp. 5–6.
418 See Table 7.1 in Birch, op. cit., p. 123.
419 See the description in the Commission's report, loc. cit., ch. 30; and the, on the whole, favourable review of the N. Ireland experiment since its inception, in Bogdanor, ch. 3, esp. pp. 72–3.
420 For details, see *KCA* (1982), p. 31749A.

inaction was impossible and that a substantial concession had to be made or at least be seen to be offered as part of the price of sustaining the political position of the Labour Party.

The royal commission issued two reports in 1973, one reflecting the opinion of a majority of its members, the other over the dissenting signatures of Lord Crowther-Hunt and Professor Alan Peacock. Both are extremely interesting documents in the context of this essay though there is also no doubt about the superior range and calibre of the minority report. Both reflect, too, an ambivalence about the role and office of government though the emphasis is different in each.

The majority report is, of course, much concerned with such questions as over-centralization, the need to provide substantial scope for regional autonomy and initiative as a means of strengthening democracy, and in particular to respond to undoubted national feeling in Scotland and Wales.[421] Perhaps inevitably, in view of the political context of the commission's appointment, its attention is largely concentrated on this last issue and within this scope it is, of course, extremely thorough. It considers a whole range of possibilities: separation, federalism, legislative devolution, executive devolution, regional councils, administrative devolution, and some form of regional organization in Parliament.[422] In the outcome the report was not uniform in its recommendations. Separatism and federalism were rejected it is true and it was agreed that some form of elected assembly was required in Scotland and Wales. Otherwise a series of different devolutionary schemes was put forward on the ground that it was not necessary for the same arrangements to be applied in each case.[423] Nevertheless, though the principle of some form of devolution was accepted, the majority of the commission did not envisage that this should necessarily entail any diminution of government activity. On the contrary the clear impression is created that devolution is seen in many respects as a means of making the interventionist role more effective. This basically collectivist emphasis appears in three main respects.

The first is the commission's curt and critical attitude to a federal solution (which had often been suggested in the past); and the reasons given are revealing. For federalism is seen as obsolescent in the age of the positive state and as incompatible with the creation of the kind of society 'the people really need.'[424] And in their pursuit of this 'general will' – a

---

[421] e.g. The Constitution, R. Com. Rep., 1973–4, Cmnd. 5460, p. 331 §1102.
[422] ibid., chs 17–22.
[423] ibid., pp. 332–4 §§1107–15, pp. 361–2 §§1216–18. The details are in chs 24–5; and the cases in N. Ireland, the Channel Islands, and the Isle of Man are discussed in chs. 28–33.
[424] The Constitution, R. Com. Rep., 1973–4, Cmnd. 5460, pp. 154–6 §§513–19, p. 157 §§522–3, pp. 237–8 §777.

concept of which the report seems rather fond – what might be called the libertarian issue is never at all raised let alone discussed: that is, the question whether it may not be precisely the so-called inefficiency or inconvenience derived from a federal structure which is needed deliberately to hamper government intervention and to restrict its growth. Instead the report accepts the 'tradition of unitary government based upon the complete sovereignty of Parliament' as an essential premiss of our political life if the present-day problems of the country are to be tackled.[425] The same sort of emphasis is revealed, secondly, in the commission's discussion of economic management and social provision. In many places the report stresses the need (whatever system of devolution may be created) for a strong central authority for purposes of economic control and long-term planning and to secure equality of treatment throughout.[426] Equally the possibility of substantial regional variation in (let alone secession from) the health and welfare structure is firmly rejected.[427] Of course the majority report stresses the importance in principle of substantial regional autonomy and initiative. But the language used belies this intent as is evidenced in the matter, thirdly, of the financial arrangements proposed. For instance on the crucial question of the revenue to be allocated to the regions, the report says: 'If the total volume of taxation taken out of central hands were *not too great*, and the regions' power of varying it were *not too extensive*, then the United Kingdom Government *might* well be able to tolerate some overall loss of control....'[428] This is evasive of crucial issues to say the least. But it is consistent with the general tenor of the diluted regionalism envisaged that it is proposed to retain a vital central control over levels of regional expenditure and of borrowing alike.[429] It is entirely compatible, too, with a collectivist emphasis that the commission adopts an 'expenditure' rather than a 'revenue' basis for its analysis of the financial questions: it assumes that no crucial degree of regional independence in this field should be tolerated and that the regional position should be rather like that of local authorities.[430] In truth the majority report is (for all its length) a very limited document for it is hedged in by its collectivist premisses which are strong, indeed crucial, albeit not overtly acknowledged. It is also constrained by its decision to concentrate on the question of devolution itself, a relative narrowness of attention that was not strictly required by its terms of reference but which arose from the

425 ibid., p. 158 §529, pp. 160–1 §§539.
426 e.g. ibid., pp. 174–5 §§573–6, p. 177 §583, p. 202 §663, pp. 259–60 §850, p. 264 §864, p. 362 §1220 etc.
427 ibid., pp. 216–17 §709, pp. 231–2 §§756–61, p. 248 §816.
428 ibid., p. 188 §621 (my italics).
429 ibid., p. 185 §612, pp. 195–6 §640.
430 ibid., pp. 198–200 §§652–6, p. 202 §663.

circumstances of its appointment. But this makes the majority report a markedly political document as well. It thus accepts the collectivist tendencies of the day and does not wish to hinder them; and it is basically concerned merely with mitigating a specific electoral difficulty. This is no doubt why, once the immediate occasion had passed, the report largely ceased to have any relevance to other contemporary issues despite its grandiloquent formal title and remit.

In its tone and style the minority report is more academic, deliberately more wide-ranging in its scope, and specifically critical of the majority for concentrating too narrowly on the question of devolution alone.[431] Consequently it reviews a series of possible reforms relating to the efficiency of government as a whole, an extensive range of political and constitutional issues dealing with questions of participation, protection against overcentralized bureaucracy, and the like. As well there is a broader frame of analysis given to the topic of devolution itself for it proposes the establishment of elected assemblies with important responsibilities in five English regions as well as in Wales and Scotland.[432] There are also, in the memorandum of dissent, a number of libertarian intimations though, in the end, these are perhaps blurred and overcome by other collectivist considerations. But at least the issues of this antithesis are explicitly raised. Thus Professor Peacock notes that part of the problem of contemporary government is that of the 'sheer size' of the public sector and the diversion of resources involved. 'I believe', he writes,

> that governments seriously interested in preserving democracy need to do much more to make it possible for its citizens to rely less on its support. It follows that the size and composition of the public in relation to the private sector needs to be kept under continuous review, and should not therefore be regarded as sacrosanct.[433]

At the same time there is no assumption that the scope of government could at present be substantially reduced. For instance, a major planning role is accepted for the intermediate level of government and the importance of central economic management is stressed (though not so strongly as in the majority report).[434] Yet, in a sense, this concession about the continuing size of the public sector is made with reluctance and it is recognized that so doing leaves a vital issue relatively unexplored.[435]

431 The Constitution, R. Com. Memorandum of Dissent, 1973–4, Cmnd. 5460-I, e.g. Preface.
432 ibid., ch. VI.
433 ibid., pp. x–xi §1(d).
434 ibid., p. xi §2, pp. 88–9 §218, p. 104 §262, p. 127 §332. Cf. ibid., Appendix A, pp. 137–8 §2(a)–(b).
435 ibid., p. xi §4.

The Labyrinthine Maze 127

And it is stressed that the 'basic cause' of the present discontents is a general feeling that traditional liberties are being eroded by a massive growth of state power and bureaucracy.[436] Hence the concern to increase the authority and effectiveness of representatives, to augment possibilities of popular participation, to provide better means of redressing individual grievances, and the like. If, for purposes of argument, the object is not drastically to reduce the scope of collectivist government – which in any case is admitted to be a very difficult thing to do – nor is it to increase it; and certainly its radical reform is required.[437]

The two main parties were split on the commission's proposals. But the electoral threat to Labour, revealed in particular by the SNP gains in the 1974 elections, determined the Labour government to press ahead with legislation with a view to mitigating nationalist demands in such a way that its own position was not threatened. It was all, as Professor Birch suggests, a 'crude gerrymander'.[438] In September 1974 the government announced its acceptance of the idea that some change was desirable and it undertook to establish elected assemblies in Wales and Scotland though what it had in mind differed crucially in some respects from the Crowther-Kilbrandon proposals – and indeed from its party's own previous position which has been notoriously hostile to devolution, describing it in one policy document as 'a serious error'.[439] The details of subsequent events are of no concern here: how the initial proposals were rejected, others later introduced, and finally passed into law in mid-1978; how, too, as a result of the referenda and the Tory victory in the 1979 election the legislation was repealed.[440] Yet important issues long dormant were thus raised. Nor need they in the future necessarily remain merely latent: at least one close observer of these matters has firmly asserted it is a mistake to suppose that the issue will go away, that (north of the Border at least) the urge to separation has declined.[441] And the question continues to be raised in Parliament if only as a series of legislative gestures.[442]

All sorts of issues of detail are involved in this matter, concerning the division of functions envisaged, the question of overriding legislation, the

436 ibid., p. 1 §2.
437 ibid., p. xiv §10, p. 79 §193.
438 Birch, op. cit., pp. 163–4. For a fuller account, see Bogdanor, op. cit., chs 6–7.
439 e.g. Labour Party, *Labour's Policy for Wales* (Cardiff, 1954), p. 3.
440 The formal course of events may be followed in *KCA*, consulting the indexes *sub* 'United Kingdom: constitution'.
441 Professor C. Harvie reviewing C. M. Clapperton (ed.), *Scotland: a New Study*, in *TLS* (26 August 1983), p. 908.
442 e.g. leave refused to bring in a Bill to establish a Scottish Parliament, 50 H.C. Deb. 6s., 14 December 1983, cols 1009–11; leave granted to introduce a Bill to set up regional assemblies in England, 51 H.C. Deb. 6s., 21 December 1983, cols 438–9.

128 A Much Governed Nation

problems of finance, and so forth: all the topics raised by the Commission on the Constitution and in subsequent discussion. But in the present context perhaps the most fundamental concern relates to what might be called the 'impact-potential' of devolved power: Will it lead to greater substantive intervention in the life of the individual or less? The strongly anti-centralist feeling involved (London being seen as too powerful and excessively interfering) might seem to imply the latter.[443] Yet, even after the establishment of some degree or other of provincial autonomy, the national government might (in its remaining sphere) legitimately act in a commanding way. And at the same time, the regional governments themselves might, within their own allotted ambit, seek to fasten on the citizens they rule a greater degree of control than before: did not Michels warn us that decentralization might well mean not more liberty but rather the creation of smaller oligarchies each no less powerful within its sphere than the centre which is feared and replaced?[444] This might very well be the case if the object of the exercise is simply to create more effective planning mechanisms or a more paternalist control of the local authorities.[445] And something of the general possibility was revealed long ago in the very detailed scheme of regional government worked out by G. D. H. Cole. His point of departure was the Guild Socialist attack on the centralized sovereign state; but equally his purpose was *inter alia* to assert the need for 'a vast expansion' of civic and economic services through the various organizations envisaged.[446] In this respect much would depend on the nature of the regional authorities established. In England they would be quite new and artificial, reflecting no existing regional consciousness, and it is hardly possible to say anything about the way they might operate save to suppose that they would feel the need to act positively in some fashion so as to justify their creation. In Scotland and Wales the nationalist ideologies, which are rather different in form and emphasis, would be important. No doubt either might seem oppressive. The Scots, with their emphasis on publicly induced industrial efficiency, would presumably press on down the interventionist path. This is anathema to at least some of the Welsh, those who view things in the mirror of Saunders Lewis. The future they envisage reveals fascinating prospects of a distributist kind, arousing recollections of the

---

443 See e.g. an American viewpoint in T. Hewes, *Decentralize for Liberty* (London, 1950); Committee of the Parliament for Wales Campaign, *Parliament for Wales* (Aberystwyth, 1953), pp. 4–6; also the references in *The Ideological Heritage* (London, 1983), index *sub* 'Decentralization'.
444 R. Michels, *Political Parties: a Sociological Study of the Oligarchical Tendencies of Modern Democracy* (1911; New York, 1968), Part Two ch. 7 esp. p. 202.
445 Cf. the fears expressed in G. Jones and J. Stewart, *The Case for Local Government* (London, 1983), pp. 86–8.
446 G. D. H. Cole, *The Future of Local Government* (London, n.d [1921]), pp. 8, 174–5.

guildsmen and some of the (perhaps less reputable) Catholic theorists of France. There is a primary emphasis, of course, on the language. But there is also a stress on the role of the small organic group; hostility to substantive economic and social control and the bureaucracy it entails; advocacy of de-industrialization; concern about the spiritual deprivation caused by mechanization and standardization which reduce individuals to mere units; a stabilized 'no growth' economy based on a redistribution of wealth; above all, belief in an omnipresent Law the moral values of which should suffuse everyday life and enhance respect for individuality. This doctrine addresses the major problems. Whether it could be realized even in Wales is another matter. But as one enthusiast believed, 'Wales is the ideal home for such an order to first emerge'; and if it is not done there, then 'there is little hope for the rest of the world.'[447] It may be so. Yet the political and social order in view might equally sustain the sort of narrow and intrusive atmosphere characteristic of the close medieval world that is its inspiration.

The point is simply that, while decentralization may have a liberating effect through improved participation and accountability, this will not necessarily be the case or the only consequence. It might simply create the conditions for a more effective form, another level, of public control. If the question is one of how the individual may be brought to recognize and accept his personal role and responsibilities, a new layer of merely representative bodies will not necessarily achieve this. The problem Toulmin Smith grasped all those years ago remains; and it may reasonably be wondered whether devolution or regionalism (as usually understood) will solve it. In any case this sort of development misses the real issue for libertarians which is one of diminishing the role of public authority wherever it may be located. So perhaps the root of the matter lies not at local or intermediate level at all but at the centre where the growth of the administrative machine has, ultimately, been of much greater consequence.

---

447 J. Osmond, *The Centralist Enemy* (Llandybie, 1974), p. 161.

3
IN DARK WONDER

> What these strange Entities in Downing Street intrinsically are; who made them, why they were made; how they do their function; and what their function, so huge in appearance, may in net-result amount to, – is probably known to no mortal. The unofficial mind passes by in dark wonder....
> T. CARLYLE, 'Latter-Day Pamphlets', 1850, in *The Works*, 1871–4, xx. 80

GROWTH AND ITS PHASES

> How in the end can anything but a chain of great departments govern, when all this mass of multifarious work is being thrown on the Government?
> A. HERBERT, *A Politician in Trouble about his Soul*, 1884, p. 290.

A PRIMARY feature of collectivist change is that central government assumes more and more responsibilities with the consequence that its departments grow in size and number and the body of its 'ministering officials' is thereby enlarged.[1] And if, as Baldwin once presumed, the machinery of government may be 'a subject distasteful or dull', it is without doubt also of the utmost significance: the creation of the modern Civil Service was perhaps the really great political invention of nineteenth-century Britain.[2] While the initial burden of dealing with the consequences of the Great Change fell on the various local authorities, in due time the central departments of state were also inevitably affected. And, as with the local bodies, the process at work was one of adapting, reforming, and supplementing a set of traditional institutions to enable them to cope with the pressing and multifarious tasks assumed, a pursuit of improvement that has continued to the present day.

1 The phrase cited is from Sir E. Barker, *The Development of Public Services in Western Europe 1660–1930* (London, 1944), p. 3.
2 Baldwin's remark comes from a lecture on the Civil Service given in 1933 and reprinted in *This Torch of Freedom* (1935; 4th edn, London, 1937), p. 61; the other suggestion is from G. Wallas, *Human Nature in Politics* (1908; 4th edn, London, 1948), p. 249.

In Dark Wonder 131

The traditional duties of the national government were concerned not so much with the regulation of everyday life as with a quite other dimension of public affairs, with foreign relations, defence, law and order, and of course the collection of revenue for such purposes. Consequently, save in the matter of tax gathering, they were without continuous significant impact on the ordinary life of the citizen. At the end of the eighteenth century there were fifty-three central offices (over seventy if Ireland is taken into account).[3] They included the departments for Home and Foreign Affairs and the Treasury; the numerous military and naval branches; the boards dealing with customs and excise; and an array of smaller agencies like the Post Office, the Mint, and the Aliens Office. Most employed less than a hundred people though customs and excise, by far the largest, had over 6,000 employees each. The staff supporting a great officer of state, though it might contain 'very important persons', was little more than a ministerial secretariat.[4] The total number of such officials and their ancillaries was probably less than 17,000; and they constituted not so much a single service as a collection of independent office-holders. To assess the relative scale of activity it is only necessary to recall that this was a time when some 40,000 or more people were responsible for (it is true largely unpaid) duties at local level.[5] As Leslie Stephen once wrote, there was a 'combination of an absolute centralisation of legislative power with an utter absence of administrative centralisation.'[6] But things were beginning to change and the 'new wants' of the 'new age' were responded to 'in a new manner'.[7] Half a century or so later, by the mid-1800s, the country was in the way of being ruled, not simply by the exercise of the Crown's prerogative or through the patchwork of local bodies which had survived or been called into existence, but increasingly by means of statutory powers conferred explicitly on the great officers or departments of state. From being in most cases little more than a private office attached to one of the sovereign's confidential advisers, and consisting largely of clerks doing copying and similar routine work and ancillaries such as porters, messengers, and 'necessary women', the departments were becoming administrative entities of increasing size and complexity with a growing range of duties. A large 'constitutional bureaucracy' of permanent

---

3 E. W. Cohen, *The Growth of the British Civil Service 1780–1939* (London, 1941), p. 23 and Appendix pp. 34–5 which lists each office and the number of people it employed.
4 The characterization cited is Maitland's: see *The Constitutional History of England* (1908; Cambridge, 1974), p. 416.
5 Sir N. Chester, *The English Administrative System 1780–1870* (Oxford, 1981), pp. 53–4.
6 Sir L. Stephen, *The English Utilitarians* (1900; London, 1950), i. 30.
7 Maitland, op. cit., p. 417.

132   A Much Governed Nation

officials was in process of creation.[8] Something of the expanding burden of public business that had to be dealt with is reflected in the larger number of registered papers. At the Treasury the annual average number of such papers in the 1760s was less than 1,000; during the period 1783–93 it was between 2,500 and 3,000; by 1800 it had reached over 4,800 and twenty years after that was nearly 22,300. In 1849 it was only just short of 30,000.[9] The longer-term trend to expansion (as indicated by the number of non-industrial civil servants employed) is shown in Table 4. Of course,

Table 4   The growth of the Civil Service since 1797[a]

Year	Number of civil servants (thousands)	Year	Number of civil servants (thousands)
1797	16.3	1911	172.4
1821	27.0	1921	366.9
1832	21.3	1931	315.1
1841	16.8	1941	566.1
1851	39.1	1951	675.4
1861	31.9	1961	650.2
1871	53.9	1971	498.4[b]
1881	50.9	1979	565.8
1891	79.2	1981	539.9
1901	116.4	1984	504.3

a The figures (which exclude industrial civil servants) are derived as follows: (i) 1797–1911 from a table in H. Finer, *The British Civil Service: an Introductory Essay* (London, 1927), p. 14; (ii) 1921–31 from 'Staffs Employed in Government Departments', 1921 (vol. xxiii), Cmd. 1290 and 1930–1 (vol. xxii), Cmd. 3898; and (iii) 1941–84 from the *Annual Abstract of Statistics*.
b The decline indicated by this figure was due to the exclusion of Post Office staff from the series after 1 October 1969 when the GPO ceased to be a government department and became a public corporation. The underlying trend was none the less still upwards as is shown if the Post Office staff is excluded throughout as in the historical table covering the period since 1902 in HM Treasury, *Civil Service Statistics* (London, 1985), p. 11. This table shows the downturn in the total of non-industrial civil servants to have begun in 1977–8. Cf. Table 7, pp. 266–7 below.

over such a long period as the table covers, the figures (not being standardized or even readily available) are often only approximate at least for the earlier years.[10] But even allowing for the statistical deficiencies they give a clear enough indication of the general tendency under way.[11]

8   Of course I take the phrase cited from the title of H. Parris's invaluable *Constitutional Bureaucracy: the Development of British Central Administration since the Eighteenth Century* (London, 1969).
9   For this and other instances, see ibid., p. 47 and Chester, op. cit., pp. 283–4.
10 See e.g. the comments in D. Butler and A. Sloman, *British Political Facts 1900–1979*, 5th edn (London, 1980), p. 263 and Chester, op. cit., pp. 166–8.
11 See also *The Rise of Collectivism* (London, 1983), pp. 35–9, 65.

The new functions being assumed by central government had obviously either to be added to the responsibilities of existing offices or placed with some specially created public agency whether a department, inspectorate, commission, or board.[12] Many of the new departments were in fact hived off from the three great traditional offices, the Privy Council, the Treasury, and the Secretaryship of State. A function or agency was initially nurtured within one of these established frameworks and then, as the duties concerned grew, was detached from the main stem to become a separate organization in its own right. For instance the present Department of Trade and Industry is the direct descendant of the old Board of Trade which began life as a committee of the Privy Council in 1696.[13] When it was first established the board was only advisory but, especially during the nineteenth century, it acquired an increasing array of administrative and supervisory tasks relating to the railways, merchant shipping, patents, bankruptcy, commercial intelligence, fisheries, gas and water supplies, the Companies Acts, and much else. Its growth represents, in effect, the steady extension of economic regulation by central government, a responsibility acknowledged in 1867 when the board became a full department. And if in 1786 it had a staff of six clerks, by 1840 there were thirty, a total which doubled in the following thirteen years; by the outbreak of the Great War there were over 3,000 while the present DTI has nearly five times that number. Moreover just as the board emerged from within the Privy Council so in turn it was the parent of a numerous administrative progeny, separate departments being later established to deal with functions it had once assumed, such as labour, overseas trade, food, and transport.

But this entire process of institutional fission and augmentation was, as Bagehot said in the 1860s, quite 'unsystematic and casual'. The 'English offices', he went on, 'have never, since they were made, been arranged with any reference to one another; or rather they were never made, but grew as each could.'[14] There was thus created what he nicely called 'a chronic contention of offices.' And, while their emergence might be explained historically as the result of continuous addition, adaptation, and development, it nevertheless lacked 'an administrative reason'.[15] In

---

12 For the emergence of the department as compared with other agencies, see e.g. F. M. G. Willson, 'Ministries and Boards: Some Aspects of Administrative Development since 1832', *Public Administration*, xxxiii (1955), pp. 43–58; B. B. Schaffer, 'The Idea of the Ministerial Department: Bentham, Mill and Bagehot', *Australian Journal of Politics and History*, iii (1957–8), pp. 60–78; Parris, op. cit., pp. 82–93; and Chester, op. cit., pp. 275–81.

13 For what follows I largely draw on Sir H. L. Smith, *The Board of Trade* (London, 1928).

14 W. Bagehot, *The English Constitution* (1867; Fontana, 1966), pp. 208, 210.

15 ibid., pp. 210, 211.

terms of the jargon lately fashionable, it reflected rather a 'disjointed incrementalism' than any sort of administrative planning. This is not to say, however, that (in Bagehot's own day and subsequently) there have not been attempts to reorganize this bureaucratic inheritance on the basis of comprehensive principles of reform regarded at the time as both rational and more appropriate to contemporary, and likely future, values, needs, and resources. Of course the motives and other factors involved in any specific changes proposed or undertaken will be diverse, but the desire for greater efficiency and the need to save money have usually been paramount. Looked at in the broadest context, the entire process may be seen as falling into three (or perhaps four) phases each of which confronts a specific *malaise* or related series of deficiencies and anticipates their effective treatment.

The first is concerned with the elimination of some long-standing defects and with the reorganization of traditional arrangements so as to constitute a more efficient and economical structure, though at this stage the goals of government are still relatively narrow and the tasks of the service largely secretarial. The themes appropriate to this initial transformation are those discerned in the Northcote-Trevelyan report of 1854. The second phase is one of continuing expansion in both responsibilities and agencies and so in the number of officials employed to carry out the increasing roster of duties. The crucial issue is the optimum allocation of functions between departments and the effective co-ordination of the administrative machine as a whole. The matter is brought to the fore by the extending role which executive government had assumed both before and during the Great War and by the assumption that the peacetime burden to follow would necessarily remain at a high and unprecedented level. The issues were primarily addressed in the report of the Haldane Committee on the machinery of government (1918), a document which also provided the starting point of similar consideration during the second war (even if, in the outcome, it was not viewed as a precedent slavishly to be followed in either form or prescription). The following period (or third aspect) is one of a more and more conscious collectivism actively pursued. In this context it is felt that in many respects the principles on which the service had been ordered since the middle of the previous century needed to be rethought, the better to tackle the tasks of professional management and technical administration so important in the large bureaucracy that had now come into being. This tendency is reflected in the pressures which led to the appointment of the Fulton Committee whose report appeared in 1968.

Three phases, then; three key documents to reflect the problems and remedies discerned at each stage; and three themes to characterize these concerns: recruitment and organization; rationalization and co-ordination; and efficiency in management. It is possible that we may currently be witnessing the emergence of a fourth phase, a further and maybe more radical change of climate, the main preoccupation of which will be retrenchment and the achievement, on the reduced scale intended, of greater administrative effectiveness. But this largely remains to be seen. Such however, are the cardinal aspects of our constitutional bureaucracy, as it has been formed in an increasingly collectivist age; and which are dealt with at large here. In addition there is also (in the next chapter) a specific study of the Treasury as a particularly useful and important focus of the problems created for the Civil Service by the emergence of the positive state and of the changes of function and role thereby entailed. The variations in the concept of Treasury control are, indeed, a kind of paradigm of the pattern assumed by these mutable affairs not least because they come to embrace that central notion of collectivist endeavour, economic planning and the machinery it requires together with some indication of the difficulties of this enterprise.

RECRUITMENT AND ORGANIZATION

... *the more efficient Administration of the Public Affairs of this Realm* ... is the subject of the age, so far as English politics are concerned....
DISRAELI to Derby, 18 December 1855, in W. F. Monypenny and G. E. Buckle, *The Life of Benjamin Disraeli*, 1929 edn, i. 1435–6
(italics in original)

The subject of administrative reform was indeed one of the major topics of discussion at mid-century. Carlyle's idiosyncratic but powerful voice spoke for many others when in the *Latter-Day Pamphlets* (1850) he wrote of an infinitely improved 'Governing Apparatus' as being the one great change in which 'some hope might lie': '"reform" in that Downing-Street department of affairs is precisely the reform which were worth all others' because 'those administrative establishments...are really the Government of this huge...Empire'. Equally Herbert Spencer inveighed against the red tape, waste, and inefficiency of government service.[16] These two great contemporaries, albeit from very different points of view, often agreed in the detail of their respective indictments of the official arrangements of their day. In fact a barrage of criticism developed, leading in the end to slow but radical improvement. The themes which infused the changes in the 'mysterious industry' of governance (Carlyle's phrase) were authoritatively explored in 1854 by the Northcote-Trevelyan report.[17] And as the principles relating to the recruitment and deployment of personnel there laid down have

---

16 T. Carlyle, *The Works* (People's edn, 1871–4), xx.78, 198; H. Spencer, *Social Statics*...(1851; Farnborough, Hants, 1970), Part III.
17 Carlyle, op. cit., xx.74.

subsequently guided Civil Service development right up to the present day, it is important to establish clearly the nature of the recommendations and their rationale. This can most appropriately be done after some reference to the state of departmental organization in the late eighteenth and early nineteenth centuries because this was an important part of the situation from which the inquiry and its proposals alike emerged.

The context of improvement

At the end of the eighteenth century a Civil Service in the present-day sense hardly existed. For one thing, there was no clear distinction between Parliamentary and official servants of the Crown. And, though some individuals enjoyed substantial security of tenure, there was no general idea (as there now is) of officials retaining a post during changes of government. In fact there was no 'body of full-time, salaried officers, systematically recruited, with clear lines of authority, and uniform rules on such questions as superannuation', of the sort that we now take for granted.[18] In matters of organization and procedure departments revealed every kind of heterogeneity.[19] However, confused and unsatisfactory as this state of affairs might seem to the modern eye, it was none the less accepted as normal; and powerful stimuli were required before it would be radically questioned. One such impulse was provided by Britain's failure in the war with the American colonies.[20] Another was the not unrelated attempt to curb the power of the Crown and its ministers, an important aspect of which was the 'economical reform' movement. Among its aims was a reduction of public expenditure and in the number of officials, to be achieved in particular by restricting opportunities for patronage. The need to have regard for 'the convenience of the State' was stressed, as in the numerous reports of the Commissioners of Accounts which appeared between 1781 and 1784.[21] Critical tendencies of this sort were naturally reinforced with the coming of the Great War with France and the burden of public expense it entailed: the Select Committee on Finance was particularly active to this end during the 1790s.[22] Even after peace returned in 1815, it appeared that

18 The sentence cited is from H. Parris, *Constitutional Bureaucracy: the Development of British Central Administration Since the Eighteenth Century* (London, 1969), p. 22.
19 For later, mid-nineteenth-century recognition of this diversity, see M. Wright, *Treasury Control of the Civil Service 1854–1874* (Oxford, 1969), pp. xxiii–xxiv, xxvi.
20 See *The Rise of Collectivism* (London, 1983), pp. 228–30.
21 H. Roseveare, *The Treasury: the Evolution of a British Institution* (London, 1969), pp. 118–23.
22 ibid., pp. 129–30; E. W. Cohen, *The Growth of the British Civil Service 1780–1939* (London, 1941), pp. 45–7. For the work of another such inquisition, see my 'The

the public offices and their cost were set to expand inexorably (as Table 4, page 132, suggests). Increasingly there were calls for this growing expense to be contained or diminished, for some guarantee that able men would be appointed to public posts, that the work would be conducted efficiently and without waste. Such contemporary concern was reflected in the activity of the so-called 'economists' like Joseph Hume and Richard Cobden.

Of course changes were occurring all the time. One transformation of special importance was the gradual emergence of the vital distinction between political and official responsibilities.[23] For one thing the number of posts compatible with a seat in Parliament was reduced and the political activities of minor office-holders limited. The growing mass of business fell more and more on the officials while the political heads concentrated on the Parliamentary aspects of departmental duties; and, as one consequence of this, for instance, the junior minister was clearly distinguished from the permanent secretary.[24] The Civil Service was thus slowly emerging as a distinct entity, a body of 'stationary' clerks employed by the Crown and ready to work at the behest of successive governments and less and less appointed as the result of political calculation. 'As the monarchy rose above party, so the civil service settled below party. Constitutional bureaucracy was the counterpart of constitutional monarchy.'[25] But it had as yet no unity of structure, no regularity of recruitment, no uniformity in conditions of work, no common principle of supervision: and it continued to increase in size and cost. Consequently the call for efficiency and economy in the public service resounded ever more clearly. The two aspects of the established arrangements that reformers particularly criticized were the role of patronage in recruitment and the still fragmentary nature of the organization.

Appointment

Before the era of reform appointment to a public office was achieved in one of two ways. As a post was regarded not so much as a position of trust but as a kind of freehold tenure – what Blackstone called an 'incorporeal hereditament' – openly disposable on the property market, a sale was not unusual. But this sort of transaction was increasingly seen as

---

Commission of Military Enquiry, 1805–1812', *Journal of the Society for Army Historical Research*, xli (1963), pp. 171–81.

23 A. L. Lowell, *The Government of England* (1908; New York, 1910), i. 145ff.; G. E. Aylmer, 'From Office-Holding to Civil Service: the Genesis of Modern Bureaucracy', *Trans. R. Hist. S.*, 5s., xxx (1980), pp. 91–108.

24 Roseveare, op. cit., pp. 154–5; Wright, op. cit., pp. 21–2. Parris, op. cit., pp. 106–21, 147–51 discusses the development of separate political and administrative hierarchies.

25 Parris, op. cit., p. 49.

open to abuse and in 1809 formally abolished though, in practice, it was not at once wholly discontinued.[26] Much more widespread and certainly more persistent was that mode of civil appointment known as patronage. By this procedure nomination to a post, whether initially or as subsequent promotion, was in the hands of either the political or official head of a department or the functionary in charge of a particular branch. The Parliamentary Secretary to the Treasury (known as the Patronage Secretary) played a central part because he not only controlled appointments to the Treasury itself and places subordinate to it but also kept an eye on the way in which positions were filled in all government offices. The system meant that a place was obtained on the basis, not so much or at all, of ability as of connexion and political usefulness. Thus patronage was often exercised in behalf of relatives or dependants: the way in which each of three clerks in Trollope's story entered the public service was to secure a nomination through some family relation as the author of their being had done himself.[27] Similarly another literary figure, Matthew Arnold, benefited from the practice whereby the private secretary of a prominent politician might be translated to an official post secured by the influence of his patron: in 1851, at the age of nineteen, Arnold went from being the assistant of the Marquess of Lansdowne to become an inspector of schools.[28] And of course political purposes of one kind or another were much involved: nominations were made to ensure electoral support, to gratify an important local figure or constituency stalwart, and to maintain party loyalty and Parliamentary backing.[29] A common pattern of hereditary appointment even grew up on this basis.[30]

While the effects of patronage might be deplored, it was at first unusual to question its legitimacy.[31] The reason was simply that the system helped to guarantee stability and collaboration in government. In 1823 Lord

26 Cohen, op. cit., pp. 41, 65. See the instances cited in J. Hart, 'Sir Charles Trevelyan at the Treasury', *English Historical Review*, lxxv (1960), p. 109. Of course commissions in the infantry and cavalry (though not in other branches of the army, or in the navy) were bought and sold until 1870, an arrangement which was economical and also ensured that officers were persons of substance, though it had notable disadvantages too: for a full account, see A. Bruce, *The Purchase System in the British Army, 1660–1871* (London, 1980).
27 A. Trollope, *The Three Clerks* (1858; World's Classics, 1952), pp. 3, 9, 12, 202; idem, *An Autobiography* (1883; World's Classics, 1928), p. 27. Cf. *The Three Clerks*, p. 431.
28 *DNB*, ii. 2364.
29 Numerous cases showing the different forms and motives involved are given in Parris, op. cit., ch. II. See also P. G. Richards, *Patronage in British Government* (London, 1963), ch. 2; Roseveare, op. cit., pp. 103, 115, 164–5.
30 J. R. Torrance, 'Sir George Harrison and the Growth of Bureaucracy in the Early Nineteenth Century', *English Historical Review*, lxxxiii (1968), pp. 77–8.
31 See the opinion of Sir George Harrison, Assistant Secretary to the Treasury, cited ibid., p. 68.

John Russell described how it worked. When a place falls vacant, he said, 'the treasury write to the member for the county or borough voting with the government, and ask for his recommendation.' In turn he could offer the nomination to a supporter or kinsman; and so it might be passed on. As Sir Charles Trevelyan observed, there was thus 'a tacit agreement to share the public Patronage'.[32] Obviously it was in the government's interest to keep as tight a hold as possible on these affairs simply because the more offices it had at its disposal the greater would be its influence on MPs and others. Yet, as a mode of official appointment and of Parliamentary control alike, the system went into a gradual decline. It has never, of course, come to an end even at the present day: consider, for instance, the 'jobs for the boys' that are still available in the sphere of the Public Concern.[33] But it ceased to play the vital role it once did; and this was a major change indeed. Professor E. Hughes (who studied these matters very closely) once expressed the view that, in the long run, the abolition of patronage was a more fundamental political revolution than the reform of Parliament.[34] In truth other forms of political persuasion and influence (or corruption) developed in its place, as through the growth of party and its discipline. But, as patronage came increasingly to seem unnecessary, disadvantageous, or unacceptable, the creation of a politically neutral and more effective Civil Service was thereby rendered possible.

The reasons for this sea-change were diverse, critics pressing various weaknesses as occasion offered. First of all there were the two great watchwords of the day – efficiency and economy – which were winning acceptance in many quarters as desirable, even essential, characteristics of the public service. With the growth of affairs, ministers became more and more dependent on their officials for the proper conduct of business. In the circumstances it was difficult to ignore the untoward effects jobbery might have on standards of administration; in addition to which the appointment of able staff was always, of course, more defensible in Parliament and elsewhere.[35] Similarly as the cost of running government offices rose so did the desire to cut expenditure and to secure less waste. Patronage was hardly compatible with this objective as the activities of

---

32 Lord J. Russell, *An Essay on the History of the English Government and Constitution from the Reign of Henry VII. to the Present Time* (1821; 2nd edn, London, 1823), p. 403; Sir C. Trevelyan, 'Thoughts on Patronage' (an unpublished paper dated 17 January 1854) in E. Hughes, 'Sir Charles Trevelyan and Civil Service Reform, 1853–5', *English Historical Review*, lxiv (1949), pp. 69–70.
33 See generally Richards, op. cit.; and, for the Public Concern, below pp. 466–70.
34 E. Hughes, 'Civil Service Reform 1853–5', *History*, xxvii (1942), p. 59.
35 Cf. Trevelyan to Gladstone (28 November 1853), cited in Hughes, 'Sir Charles Trevelyan and Civil Service Reform, 1853–5', loc. cit., pp. 68–9.

the financial reform movement in the 1840s emphasized.[36] Another major consideration was the often very troublesome burden involved: in many ways the power to nominate became an intolerable nuisance.[37] There were invariably more deserving, or importunate, claimants than there were vacancies; and, as Derby told Disraeli on one occasion, the person appointed was not necessarily grateful while those who were not successful became upset and discontented.[38] Jealousy, embarrassment, and other difficulties were commonplace and, together with all the correspondence that might be entailed, made jobbing an unpleasant and time-consuming business full of petty irritations that many of those concerned would be glad to be rid of. There were also political difficulties of one sort or another. It sometimes proved impossible to prevent patronage falling into the hands of those who were not supporters of the government.[39] And after 1832 certain political problems emerged. The increase in the number of voters was relatively slight but enough to make the operation of the patronage system more problematic. For many of the smaller constituencies in which the offer of appointments might have a crucial effect had disappeared; while the larger ones received few favours because they could not have a decisive impact there. Attention tended to concentrate on certain areas only, so there appeared an uneven distribution of advantages which was naturally not well regarded by those who received little or nothing.[40] Moreover appointments satisfactory on electoral or party grounds might otherwise be dubious leading perhaps to a lack of trust between a minister and the officials concerned. Along with many others Sir Charles Trevelyan, a major figure in the changes afoot, came to see patronage as a blight on the constitution, describing it as 'the great abuse and scandal' of the age demanding 'serious attention':

> From the broken down spendthrift who is sent to repair his fortune in a Colonial Government...to the idle, useless young man who is provided for in a Public Office because he is unfit to earn a livelihood in any of the open professions, the efficiency of the Public Establishments is habitually sacrificed to this system.

But, Trevelyan believed, its days were numbered.[41] The time was past, he

---

36 J. Hart, 'The Genesis of the Northcote-Trevelyan Report', in G. Sutherland (ed.), *Studies in the Growth of Nineteenth Century Government* (London, 1972), pp. 68–72.
37 Cf. Trollope, *An Autobiography*, pp. 35–6.
38 Derby to Disraeli (13 June 1859), cited Parris, op. cit., p. 72.
39 See e.g. Wellington to Peel (1829), cited in C. S. Parker, *Sir Robert Peel from his Private Papers* (2nd edn, London, 1899), ii. 140.
40 Cf. Trevelyan's letter to Delane (6 February 1854), cited in Hughes, 'Sir Charles Trevelyan and Civil Service Reform, 1853–5', loc. cit., p. 85.
41 Trevelyan, 'Thoughts on Patronage', ibid., pp. 69–70.

In Dark Wonder 141

wrote to the editor of *The Times* newspaper, when a state of affairs could be complacently accepted in which

> our high Aristocracy have been accustomed to employ the Civil Establishments as a means of providing for the Waifs and Strays of their Families – as a sort of Foundling Hospital where those who had not energy to make their way in the open professions, or whom it was not convenient to purchase one in the Army, might receive a nominal office, but real Pension, for life, at the expense of the Public.

The Dukes of Norfolk (who had, over the generations, thus provided for their illegitimate children) ought, he said, to be made to look elsewhere.[42]

Of course, as Professor Finer has warned us, it is a mistake to lay every deficiency of administration at the door of the patronage system; and it did after all permit the emergence of many able public servants.[43] Trevelyan, Stephen, Kay-Shuttleworth, Chadwick, Trollope, and their like were manifestly outstanding men all of whom had been appointed under the old arrangements. But it is clear that, for all the varied reasons indicated, an increasing interest was being shown in means by which the manifestly unfit might not be appointed to the public service in the first place or retained there. And already, in the 1830s and after, certain changes to this end had been introduced on a partial or piecemeal basis. Some departments had initiated a system of probation whereby clerks that proved unsuitable could be dismissed; the Treasury advocated its extension and by the early 1850s most offices made new appointees serve a trial period.[44] More than this, a number of departments had experimented tentatively and in various ways with examination (either individual or competitive) as a means of testing the ability of nominees. But all too often the requirements proved either inadequately stringent or merely temporary in operation; and in any case there was no common standard required.[45] One instance may be given. A Treasury minute of 7 May 1841, noting that candidates for clerkships in the Commissariat were often below standard, required that in future those nominated should be competent in arithmetic and double-entry bookkeeping, be

---

42 Trevelyan to Delane (6 February 1854), ibid., p. 85. Cf. his letter to Gladstone (27 February 1854), ibid., p. 210.
43 S. E. Finer, 'Patronage and the Public Service: Jeffersonian Bureaucracy and the British Tradition', *Public Administration*, xxx (1952), pp. 329, 333, 337–42, 344.
44 Cohen, op. cit., pp. 67, 95; Hughes, 'Civil Service Reform 1853–5', loc. cit., p. 53.
45 Cohen, op. cit., pp. 75–7; Hughes, 'Sir Charles Trevelyan and Civil Service Reform, 1853–5', loc. cit., p. 79. There is a list of offices already using some kind of examination in the Report on the Organisation of the Permanent Civil Service (1854) repr. in The Civil Service, Cttee Rep., 1967–8 (vol. xviii), Cmnd. 3638, Appendix B p. 111. For early examinations (and probation) in the Treasury itself, see Roseveare, op. cit., pp. 171–2. Cf. Trollope's account in *An Autobiography*, pp. 32–4 and *The Three Clerks*, pp. 4–5, 6, 12–15.

able to write in a good hand, and to compose English correctly. Similar conditions were laid down for subsequent advancement. But it seems that such instructions were not effectively observed in the departments as a whole.[46] Apart from anything else there were still many defenders of patronage in high places who continued to see it as an essential means of political manipulation. As late as 1858, for example, Disraeli wrote that the whole spirit of the Conservative Party depended greatly on the distribution of government posts.[47] And even those most ardent for reform necessarily participated in the system to obtain appointments for their own relations.[48] But the conditions in which patronage was useful, even crucial, to politicians were passing away; the climate of opinion was changing.[49] The practical problem was to find an acceptable alternative; and open competitive examination was the effective remedy to hand.

Nowadays this device may seem an obvious means to use for the purpose of selecting people of ability but this was not so in the early part of the last century. In many respects the idea was then new and untried. It was not until that time that an effective system of tests for the award of degrees, dependent on merit and not influence, was introduced at Oxford and Cambridge (until 1832 the only universities south of the Tweed).[50] But by 1852 a royal commission could report that examinations were well established as the chief instrument both for determining the proficiency of students and stimulating study. And once thus well founded as a basis of academic life the examination idea acquired considerable prestige.[51] There were other factors making the same way as well. The contemporary concepts of the open labour market, free trade, and self-help made the notion of competitive testing congenial: its ethos was clearly compatible with the theme that the fittest should survive. In

---

46 For the instructions, see The Army before Sebastopol, Sel. Cttee 3rd Rep., 1854–5 (vol. ix), Appendix 3 pp. 357–8; and for the doubtful efficacy of these attempts at improvement, see Trevelyan's comment cited in The Civil Service, R. Com. 4th Rep., 1914 (vol. xvi), Cd. 7338, p. 5 §4.
47 Disraeli to Sir J. Pakington (19 December 1858) in W. F. Monypenny and G. E. Buckle, *The Life of Benjamin Disraeli, Earl of Beaconsfield* (1910–20; new edn rev., London, 1929), i. 1658. There is an interesting discussion of the political role of patronage in R. Blake, *Disraeli* (London, 1966), pp. 682ff. Cf. Sir Thomas Fremantle's opinion (he had been Peel's Patronage Secretary) that the whipper-in had to rely on something more than his whip to maintain party support: see the letter of 1854 cited in Hughes 'Sir Charles Trevelyan and Civil Service Reform, 1853–5', loc. cit., p. 67.
48 On Trevelyan's disposal of patronage in his own family interest, see Hart, 'Sir Charles Trevelyan at the Treasury', loc. cit., pp. 97–9. For similar instances concerning Sir Stafford Northcote and Sir George Kekewich, see Wright, op. cit., pp. 74–5.
49 Parris, op. cit., p. 78.
50 See e.g. J. P. C. Roach, 'Victorian Universities and the National Intelligentsia', *Victorian Studies*, iii (1959–60), esp. pp. 133, 135.
51 Cohen, op. cit., pp. 82–3.

addition, influential foreign precedents existed. The earlier wave of chinoiserie had familiarized cultured circles with a much-admired political system in which definite and exacting educational qualifications, tested by examination, were required for admission to the public service.[52] The similar practice of France and Germany provided nearer witness of the same sort.[53] There were also, of course, the domestic, if often perfunctory, experiments already attempted by various departments and to which reference has already been made.[54] In the 1830s one public servant of some experience, Sir Henry Taylor, commended this practice of selecting on the basis of examination and probation and recommended its extension.[55] It was important, too, that considerable experience in the holding of examinations had been acquired under the aegis of the Privy Council Committee for Education in connexion with appointment to pupil teacherships and the like. In one year alone (1853) over 10,000 such tests were conducted. If examination was a practical proposition on this scale it was not unreasonable to suggest its use as a preliminary to public employment at large.[56] There were other reasons also advanced in favour of this: for example the stimulating effect it would in turn have on the educational system.[57] What gave specific impetus to the scheme to choose public servants by open competitive examination instead of patronage was the example of the East India Company. Its service had been reformed in various ways and, in particular, attention given to the need to train those going out to join the Indian administration, as by the founding in 1806 of the institution which later became Haileybury College. And when the company's charter came up for renewal in 1833, Macaulay (who was then Secretary to the Board of Control) sponsored a scheme to restrict the patronage of the directors by establishing a form of limited competition among nominees. The proposal was blocked for nearly two decades, however: but in 1853 the directors were deprived of their patronage altogether and it was ordered that, for the future, Indian civil servants should be selected by open competitive examination.[58] The first such examination was held in

52 A. O. Lovejoy, 'The Chinese Origin of a Romanticism', *Essays in the History of Ideas* (1948; Capricorn, 1960), p. 104; A. J. Toynbee, *Acquaintances* (London, 1967), pp. 164–5: both with references to the contemporary literature.
53 Hughes, 'Civil Service Reform 1853–5', loc. cit., pp. 76–7; Wright, op. cit., pp. 56 n. 1, 60.
54 See above pp. 141–2.
55 Sir H. Taylor, *The Statesman* (1836; Cambridge, 1957), pp. 88–9. Ch. XXIII of Taylor's essay is a review of executive reform remarkably similar to that of the Northcote-Trevelyan report nearly twenty years after.
56 Hughes, 'Sir Charles Trevelyan and Civil Service Reform, 1853–5', loc. cit., pp. 73–5.
57 Report on the Organisation of the Permanent Civil Service (1854), loc. cit., pp. 113–14. Cf. Hughes, 'Civil Service Reform 1853–5', loc. cit., pp. 63–5.
58 The President of the Board of Control was Sir Charles Wood who had been greatly

1855.[59] Two years before this *The Civil Service Gazette* had commented in a leading article that the 'end of the wedge has been inserted' and that the 'introduction of competition, as a test of appointment to the Civil Service of India, has forced on the discussion of its application to the Civil Service at home.'[60] If this could be done, a further advantage would be that the Indian responsibility could be transferred to the Crown – as it was after the Mutiny – without creating a mass of new patronage.

The case was strongly and often urged by a small group of men particularly influential in these matters. Two were public servants who had met in India: Charles Trevelyan who served there for fourteen years and who later became Assistant Secretary (that is, senior permanent official) to the Treasury; and T. B. Macaulay, subsequently an MP, Secretary to the Board of Control, and (as his biographer says) a warm and consistent advocate of appointment by competitive examination.[61] They were related by marriage and also close friends: knowing Trevelyan this well, Macaulay called him 'a most stormy reformer' whose mind was full of schemes of improvement.[62] Both were convinced of the need to introduce recruitment by competitive examination in Britain as well as in the eastern sub-continent. Robert Lowe, the Liberal politician, who also served at the Board of Control, was much interested in the process of university reform and convinced that the Indian precedent was crucial. So was Benjamin Jowett, the Master of Balliol, who was in touch with Lowe about all these matters. Sir Stafford Northcote was associated with Trevelyan in the early stages of Civil Service reform. Northcote's political master, Gladstone (whose private secretary he had been) summed up these Liberal views in a letter to Sir James Graham:

> In the case of Haileybury we have struck an undisguised and deadly blow at patronage; in the case of Oxford we are likely to propose measures which I think are strong, but which I hope will be salutary for the purpose of setting up competition as against restriction or

---

influenced by Trevelyan at the time of the Irish famine: see Wright, op. cit., pp. 54–5.
59 See the Report on the Indian Civil Service (signed by Macaulay and Jowett among others) and the subsequent regulations, repr. in The Civil Service, Cttee Rep., 1967–8, Cmnd. 3638, Appendix B pp. 119–31.
60 *The Civil Service Gazette* (2 July 1853) cited Wright, op. cit. p. 58.
61 Sir G. O. Trevelyan, *The Life and Letters of Lord Macaulay* (1876; 2nd edn, London, 1889), p. 294.
62 ibid., pp. 278–9. Cf. ibid., pp. 587–92, 609–12. Cf. Trollope's portrait of Sir Gregory Hardlines: 'Great ideas opened themselves to his mind as he walked to and from his office daily. What if he could become the parent of a totally different order of things! What if the Civil Service, through his instrumentality, should become the nucleus of the best intellectual diligence in the country, instead of being a byword for sloth and ignorance! ... It was his destiny that he should remodel the Civil Service', *The Three Clerks*, pp. 59–60.

private favour; I am convinced that we have it in our power to render an immense service to the country by a circumspect but energetic endeavour to apply a like principle to the Civil Service and the great administrative departments.[63]

Thus there existed 'a small but influential group of resolute and experienced men eager to apply to the Civil Service the fruits of experiments which had been carried out successfully in other fields.'[64] This was true not only in respect of the matter of recruitment but also that of organization.

Organization
The critical attention of reformers was also drawn to the point that administrative practice and structure were in many respects wholly antiquated, dating to later medieval times and even beyond. For, over many centuries, though functions had often disappeared few offices had been abolished. 'We inherit', wrote Blackstone in the 1760s,

> an old Gothic castle, erected in the days of chivalry, but fitted up for a modern inhabitant. The moated ramparts, the embattled towers, and the trophied halls, are magnificent and venerable, but useless. The inferior compartments, now converted into rooms of convenience, are chearful and commodious, tho' their approaches are winding and difficult.[65]

As Finer expressively put it (in a most interesting commentary on these matters), so long as the living organs of administration 'had to operate within a carapace of obsolete forms', the 'best personnel in the world could not have operated the system…more efficiently'.[66] The Exchequer, a crucial department, was in particular noted for following an 'ancient course'.[67] The 'general clumsiness and disjointed character' of much of the machinery of government was both inevitable and apparent.[68] And the need for change to secure efficiency and economy was increasingly recognized.[69] Above all, this meant more uniformity and less waste, objectives the case for which may be illustrated in respect to specific issues.

63 Gladstone to Graham (3 January 1854), in Parker, op. cit., ii.210.
64 Cohen, op. cit., p.86.
65 Sir W. Blackstone, *Commentaries on the Laws of England* (1765–9; 6th edn, Dublin, 1775), iii.268.
66 Finer, art. cit., pp.333, 336–7.
67 H. Roseveare, *The Treasury 1660–1870: the Foundations of Control* (London, 1973), pp.48–51, 150.
68 G. K. Clark, '"Statesmen in Disguise": Reflexions on the History of the Neutrality of the Civil Service', *Historical Journal*, ii (1959), p.22. Cf. Cohen, op. cit., pp.30, 34.
69 See above pp.134, 135ff.

One important area of concern was the income and superannuation of civil servants. As to the former the traditional practice was for a varying miscellany of payments to be made to officials: not only salaries in some cases but also fees, bonuses, gratuities, franking privileges, allowances for special duty, perquisites such as provision in kind – a house, candles, fodder – and so forth. For instance one senior clerk in the Home Department estimated his total income as £533 10s.10d. made up as follows: salary £175; East India Company new year gift £5 5s; from Post Office revenue £280; and from franking newspapers £73 5s. 10d.[70] Such arrangements were of long standing and justified (in respect of fees and gratuities for instance) by the view that those who benefited from a service should pay the person undertaking it. In addition, if the duties of an office grew, so would the receipts and this greater return made possible the appointment of more clerks or other assistance.[71] But there were obvious disadvantages too: an adequate response in terms of increased help of the sort just mentioned could not be guaranteed; an official tended to concentrate on work that yielded the highest return; and naturally he felt more beholden to the clients he served than to the public service. The Treasury showed the way to reform when it set up a fee fund from which its officials were paid on a settled scale, an example followed by some other offices; and a general system of salaries (which had been proposed by the Commissioners of Public Accounts in the 1780s) was introduced by Acts of 1810 and 1816 which helped to make the conventional forms of supplementation seem unnecessary and improper. There was still no complete uniformity, however, in respect of rates and modes of remuneration; and it became apparent that, as compared with private establishments, a good deal of the routine work in government offices was over-paid. Nevertheless a process had been set in train by which a civil servant's wages were regularized and on the way to becoming, not a matter of variable departmental concern simply, but by degrees more methodically scaled and related to responsibility. It was part of the transformation by which he turned from being the assistant of a minister or department and a person with rights in his office, to being a servant of the Crown paid under general Parliamentary authority.[72] As for superannuation, this followed the same pattern. Such pension provision as there was had been of diverse kinds. Obviously the sale of an

---

70 Cohen, op. cit., p. 28. There is a particularly complex example cited in Chester, op. cit., p. 136. For some other instances, see Sir T. Heath, *The Treasury* (London, 1927), pp. 37–8; Sir A. Strutt, 'The Home Office: an Introduction to its Early History', *Public Administration*, xxxix (1961), p. 121; and Roseveare, *The Treasury 1660–1870*, pp. 84 n. 28, 86.
71 Cf. Chester, op. cit., pp. 14–16, 61–2.
72 ibid., pp. 142–55 for details of the movement from fees and allowances to salaries in the case of both political and permanent office-holders.

office might be seen as a means of providing an income for retirement and at no cost to the state (the capital sum obtained being used to buy an annuity for instance). So to reform the manner of appointment also required a regular system of superannuation. Following various committee recommendations and departmental initiatives, this was gradually achieved, at first piecemeal, and then by general legislation from 1810 on.[73]

Then there was the related matter of sinecures, deputyships, and pluralism. These were obviously barriers to efficiency and the reduction of expenditure: posts were held (sometimes more than one) to which few or no duties were attached; and often the responsibilities were actually met by someone other than the formal office-holder and at a lower level of remuneration. A couple of examples will illustrate the situation. In 1808 one official held the three posts of Treasurer of the Navy, Clerk of the Parliaments, and Keeper of Records in Receipt of the Exchequer: none of them was effective but together they carried an annual income of £11,600. Again the official head of the Home Department was also appointed to the post of Engrossing Clerk in the Office of Alienations (which dealt with transfers of property) at £81 13s. a year, but he employed a deputy for £50 and kept the difference; in addition he himself deputized for a clerk in the Signet Office for which he received £230.[74] As to the general position, it improved by a slow process of suppression but (in 1810) 242 sinecure posts still remained attracting an income of nearly £300,000 per annum.[75] Naturally this situation aroused criticism. To abolish sinecures and related practices was part of the process of ending patronage; it could save money; and it would conduce to greater efficiency. For, as one official report had urged as early as the 1780s, their abolition would mean that every post would have useful duties annexed to it which were performed by the person appointed and this would make responsibility clearer; it would also make possible the removal of dead wood and a certain amount of consolidation.[76] There were difficulties in the way of implementing this radical programme however: questions of party advantage and personal deprivation were obviously involved; a good many cases affected the sovereign and the royal household; and there was also the barrier created by the fact that sinecures were regarded as a form of freehold property the rights of which were sacred so that abolition raised the question of compensation. But 'the Good of the

---

[73] For details, see ibid., pp. 129–30, 162–6.
[74] For these and other examples, see Cohen, op. cit., p. 55 and Roseveare, *The Treasury 1660–1870*, p. 84 n. 28. See also Chester, op. cit., pp. 123ff.
[75] Cohen, op. cit., p. 54; Roseveare, *The Treasury*, p. 130. Cf. Chester, op. cit., pp. 131–40 for a general account of the reform of all these contemporary practices.
[76] Public Accounts Commission, 14th Rep., cited Cohen, op. cit., p. 39; Roseveare, op. cit., p. 124.

Community' and 'the Advantage of the Public' needed consideration also and the reform was gradually effected.[77] Peel was one of those particularly insistent on the most rigorous economy in this respect.[78] In the outcome by 1834 the number of sinecure offices had fallen to 100 though these still carried total emoluments of nearly £98,000; many, however, were due to be abolished under existing legislation as they fell vacant. Over the years, therefore, much needless expenditure was avoided and a major obstacle to efficiency removed.[79]

The achievement of a stringent system of financial practice and audit was obviously another requirement of efficiency. It was regarded as perfectly proper for a minister or official to use monies to hand for private advantage and on leaving office to retain possession of substantial sums pending a final account. It was indeed often convenient for an official to have a balance to hand; and amounts earned were sometimes a legitimate part of his emoluments. But delays in dealing with balances were sometimes considerable, perhaps twenty years or more; and even then the authenticity of the figures produced was often doubtful.[80] In fact the system of public accounts needed complete reorganization so that all receipts and expenditures were brought together and subject to frequent independent audit.[81] Again much had been achieved by the early 1830s but a widespread concern about fraud and corruption remained.[82]

Equally there was the increasingly felt need for greater uniformity of conditions and for some more effective means of supervision. Thus there was a case for the standardization of hours of work, holidays, and similar matters as well as provision for any improvement in one department to be extended to others. Advantage and flexibility would result but at the cost of some departmental autonomy which was also clearly threatened by proposals (in the outcome not implemented) that the Treasury should have more effective powers of control.[83] There was in addition the related question of the internal organization of a department, in particular the chain of command and division of labour between officials. Of course when the number in a given office was small, little or no formal organization was necessary. But as the pressure of work grew and the staff increased, each department had to develop a more complex procedure for dealing with its business and this necessarily involved

---

77 The phrases cited are from the 11th Report of the Public Accounts Commission, as cited in Cohen, op. cit., pp. 38–9.
78 Hughes, 'Civil Service Reform, 1853–5', loc. cit., p. 57.
79 Cf. Cohen, op. cit., pp. 52–6.
80 Roseveare, op. cit., p. 125; Chester, op. cit., pp. 169–77.
81 Roseveare, op. cit., p. 125.
82 Hughes, 'Civil Service Reform 1853–5', loc. cit., p. 58.
83 Cohen, op. cit., p. 68 citing Public Expenditure, Sel. Cttee Rep. (1828).

various levels of authority.[84] A committee of inquiry into the Board of Trade (which had met the growing pressure by creating a number of sub-departments) urged the need for 'regular subordination'.[85] Questions were raised, too, about whether (given the existing hierarchy) the best use was made of the people employed. Trevelyan for one believed that, while the holders of higher posts were often overworked, the junior men were paid too much for the copying or other routine work they performed. In addition though this experience was supposed to prepare them for more responsible posts, by making them familiar with the duties of the office, it was often the cause of frustration among the more able of them not least because of the waiting period for promotion imposed by the seniority system coupled with the practice of appointing outsiders to higher posts. He put such points to a select committee in 1848 and went on to make radical proposals for the complete reorganization of the Treasury, his own department.[86] His suggestion was that the Treasury staff should be restructured into two separate grades to deal with the different kinds of work involved – 'intellectual' or 'mechanical' – and recruited and paid accordingly. It was not a new idea: for instance, it had been put forward in 1836 by Sir Henry Taylor; and had obvious Platonic affinities no doubt very persuasive in a classically imbued age.[87] At the time, however, the select committee did not pursue the prospect; but it was to be heard of again and considered in application, not just to the Treasury, but to all departments.[88]

Successive governments recognized that something had to be done about all these issues. But, as conditions varied from one department to another, it was thought impossible to draw up a satisfactory scheme of general reform without a detailed survey of existing circumstances. Consequently, in the years after 1848, various inquiries of different sorts were authorized to examine the organization of many (though not all) public offices.[89] These investigations (in which both Trevelyan and Northcote played a substantial part) indicated clearly enough the various

---

84 See the description of the way work was handled in the Treasury, Home Office, and Colonial Office in Chester, op. cit., pp. 300–4.
85 Parl. Papers, 1854 (vol. xxvii), pp. 129ff. cited Chester, op. cit., p. 305.
86 Some passages from Trevelyan's evidence are reprinted in Roseveare, *The Treasury 1660–1870*, pp. 201–4.
87 Taylor, *The Statesman*, pp. 85–6. G. M. Young suggested, too, the notion was of utilitarian provenance and reflected in the practice of the Poor Law Commission and of India House under James Mill: see his *Victorian England: Portrait of an Age* (1936; 2nd edn, London, 1966), pp. 40, 41 n. 1.
88 Cohen, op. cit., pp. 87–91, 102. On earlier intimations of this sort of specialization, see Torrance, art. cit., pp. 60–1, 67–8, and Wright, op. cit., ch. 5.
89 Details in Cohen, op. cit., p. 92 and n. 4; also Hart, 'Sir Charles Trevelyan at the Treasury', loc. cit., pp. 103–6.

difficulties concerning pay and staff, promotion and seniority, that existed not least because of the expansion of work that was taking place. It was also apparent that, difference of departmental circumstances notwithstanding, the public offices as a whole confronted similar problems especially those concerning a proper division of labour. The reports that appeared detailed many suggestions for reform, in fact all the essentials of the changes later introduced.[90]

In sum, then, a great many changes had been achieved or intimated and many economies had been made (between 1821 and 1832, for instance, over 5,700 posts and nearly £1 million had been saved).[91] Yet the forces for expansion were growing; greater efficiency had to be attained and costs restrained by 'practical executive improvements.'[92] This was the task which faced the Northcote-Trevelyan inquiry when it was instituted in 1853: it had to cap the many changes which had been introduced over the previous three-quarters of a century and show how to create a unified Civil Service. This would be recruited and organized on common principles, capable of dealing with the 'great and increasing accumulation of public business' and so of alleviating 'the consequent pressure upon the Government'.[93]

The Northcote-Trevelyan report

This climax of inquiry was initiated in 1853 when Gladstone, then Chancellor of the Exchequer and a fervent advocate of reform, set in train the general review conducted by Sir Charles Trevelyan and Sir Stafford Northcote.[94] Eight months later the famous report appeared. Mainly the work of Trevelyan it is entitled 'The Organisation of the Permanent Civil Service'. This document, much debated at the time and since, elaborated or generalized suggestions made during previous investigations. It thus represented not a set of completely unprecedented proposals but was rather the culmination of many years of thought and work on the part of Trevelyan and others.[95] The report involved a series of recommendations which have come to determine the form and

---

90 Cohen, op. cit., pp. 94–6; Hughes, 'Sir Charles Trevelyan and Civil Service Reform, 1853–5', loc. cit., pp. 60–1.
91 Cohen, op. cit., p. 70 citing the Return of Establishments (1833).
92 The phrase quoted in the text comes from Trevelyan's letter to Lord John Russell (16 December 1848) cited in Hart, 'Sir Charles Trevelyan at the Treasury', loc. cit., p. 106.
93 Report on the Organisation of the Permanent Civil Service (1854) in The Civil Service, Cttee Rep., 1967–8, Cmnd. 3638, Appendix B p. 108.
94 The Treasury minute appointing the committee may be found in the Return to the House of Commons, 1854–5 (vol. xxx), pp. 375–6.
95 See Trevelyan's letter books as cited in Hart, 'Sir Charles Trevelyan at the Treasury', loc. cit., pp. 106–7.

character of the Civil Service right down to the present day.[96] There is a certain paradox here however, Although the report enunciated the principles on the basis of which a modern bureaucracy was created to deal effectively with the demands of a collectivist age, this was not at all its prime purpose. The specific intent of the reforms proposed was to cut the cost of administration and to reduce the extent of state activity. The introduction of business methods would (it was thought) increase efficiency and make possible savings and better value for money spent; it would entail the consolidation and simplification of government functions and eliminate redundancy, waste, and overlapping. The document was infused with the notion, held by Gladstone, Trevelyan, and others, that state spending was essentially sterile and that money could only fructify in the pockets of the people. Collectivist intention was by no means involved, therefore: quite the contrary, in fact.[97] Yet, ironically perhaps, these same principles in the end prepared the basis on which the Civil Service was able to grow enormously in size and cost as a major instrument of the positive state.

The basic issue addressed by the committee was: What is the best method of providing the permanent Civil Service 'with a supply of good men, and of making the most of them after they have been admitted'?[98]

The first problem, therefore, was one of recruitment, how best to obtain proper men for the public service and in a manner which would avoid the deficiencies of the patronage system: for the existing arrangements tended to attract 'the unambitious, and the indolent or incapable'.[99] The report suggested it was best to consider young men at the beginning of their career rather than older men who had already started in another profession. It was not only cheaper but the recruits would be more eager and energetic, not already moulded into set ways. They would in addition obtain longer experience of official life.[100] But how to get these persons and to employ them on work suitable to their capacities and education? Here the report pursued intimations already present and developing. It drew on the growing examination idea, specifically on the fact that tests (albeit of varying types and efficacy) were even then in use in a number of departments and in respect of Indian

---

96 Cf. Sir E. Bridges, 'The Reforms of 1854 in Retrospect', *Political Quarterly*, xxv (1954), pp. 316, 323.
97 O. MacDonagh, 'Delegated Legislation and Administrative Discretions in the 1850's: a Particular Study', *Victorian Studies*, ii (1958–9), p. 30; idem, 'The Nineteenth-Century Revolution in Government: a Reappraisal', *Historical Journal*, i (1958), pp. 64–5; Hughes, 'Civil Service Reform 1853–5', loc. cit., pp. 54, 61–2.
98 Report on the Organisation of the Permanent Civil Service, in The Civil Service, Cttee Rep., 1967–8, Cmnd. 3638, Appendix B p. 111.
99 ibid., p. 108.
100 ibid., p. 111.

appointments. In the actual report the recommendation is firm and unqualified. It seems, however, that in an earlier draft much less emphasis was given to the value of open competition as a means of reducing the abuses of patronage. But Gladstone, in his pursuit of a pure ethic of public life, urged that the principle should not be diluted for this would leave too much power in the hands of the Treasury.[101] The examination as finally proposed was to apply to all those candidates 'whom it may be thought right to subject to such a test' and it was to be carried out and supervised by an independent and impartial 'central Board'. Save in those cases where some special talent or expertise was required, its form was to be that of 'a competing literary examination' so conducted as to test the intelligence as well as the scholastic knowledge and attainment of the candidates and to offer the widest possible range of subjects. As well there was to be adequate inquiry into 'the age, health, and moral fitness of the candidates.' We can, the authors of the report concluded, 'see no other mode by which (in the case of inferior no less than of superior offices) the double object can be attained of selecting the fittest person, and of avoiding the evils of patronage.'[102] Anyone was to be eligible to enter for the examination, but naturally only those who had received a good education could hope for success in the competition for senior posts: that is, it was expected that the system would recruit 'the youth of the upper and middle classes' with either a liberal education at a university or who had been the recipients of expensive private tutoring. It was specifically intended, therefore, to draw for the superior appointments on the higher levels of society. This would, of course, help provide employment for the increasing number of graduates, giving them places to go to other than the army, the church, or the bar. But the report is adamant in its attachment above all to the point that these measures 'for ascertaining the fitness of each person before his appointment' will produce 'the most marked and important improvement' in the public service.[103]

The second matter, in respect to the use to which the recruits thus selected were to be put, concerned questions about how the work of departments was to be organized. Clearly the object had to be to make use of the best abilities of those appointed. Specifically the aim was to ensure that those employed felt their promotion and prospects depended on their diligence and ability.[104] And here the report had two main recommendations to make. First of all, following the idea earlier put

---

101 Gladstone to Northcote (3 December 1853), cited Hart, 'The Genesis of the Northcote-Trevelyan Report', loc. cit., pp. 74–7.
102 Report on the Organisation of the Permanent Civil Service, loc. cit., p. 112.
103 ibid., pp. 112, 114.
104 ibid., p. 111.

forward by Trevelyan, it urged the separation of what was called 'intellectual' from 'mechanical' labour: 'This principle of the division of labour' was, Trevelyan thought, 'the key to the improvement of many Public Offices. Without it they cannot be efficiently or economically conducted.'[105] Trevelyan further believed the distinction between the proposed grades should be confirmed by one of salary. At present, he said in one place, 'those who *do the business*' are paid the same as 'those who merely register & copy the letters, keep the accounts, etc.'. The result is that 'there is small encouragement to well educated young men to enter the offices or to exert themselves when they have entered'. Moreover 'they are obliged to drudge for so many years at work which is less intellectual than that of most artisans, that when they do rise to the discharge of responsible functions, the exercised mind & matured judgement are entirely wanting.'[106] The main object of all this was to prevent the waste of superior talent which it was felt should not be used for routine duties as was then often the case. It was also thought that this separation would provide, on the one hand, a body of senior officials capable of leading their department, helping or even relieving the minister of some of his duties, and of dealing with general ideas and policy; and, on the other, of clerks to handle the copying and such-like ordinary tasks and who might, for this sort of purpose, be easily transferred from one office to another as the pressure of work demanded. On this basis, then, the Civil Service as a whole was seen in the report as consisting of two distinct classes, separately recruited from two different types of candidate and with different sorts of job.[107] This is the beginning of the hierarchical structure subsequently established. Promotion was to be by merit with adequate safeguards against abuse; and superannuation to be on a 'uniform and consistent system'.[108] The second recommendation concerning organization was described as a principle of unification. The Civil Service ought in some way to be consolidated so as to overcome both 'its fragmentary character' and also the 'evils' to which

---

105 ibid., p.115; Papers on the Re-organisation of the Civil Service, 1854–5 (vol. xx), p.426. It has recently been pointed out that the Trevelyan 'model' was not always appropriate to the kind of work undertaken in some at least of the government offices of the day: see A. P. Donajgrodzki, 'New Roles for Old: the Northcote-Trevelyan Report and the Clerks of the Home Office 1822–48', in Sutherland (ed.), *Studies in the Growth of Nineteenth Century Government*, pp.86–93, 102. Nor, given the nature of the 'work goals', was the sort of person recruited by patronage particularly unsuitable, ibid., pp. 93–102. On this last point, especially as it applies to the period after 1839, see also R. Johnson, 'Administrators in Education before 1870: Patronage, Social Position and Role', ibid., p.115.
106 Marginal comment on letter from J. Ball, MP (24 February 1854), cited Hughes, 'Sir Charles Trevelyan and Civil Service Reform, 1853–5', loc. cit., p.213.
107 Papers on the Re-organisation of the Civil Service, loc. cit., pp. 426–8.
108 Report on the Organisation of the Permanent Civil Service, loc. cit., pp. 116–18.

this led (such as the growth of narrow views and prejudices, excessive departmentalism, and inter-office friction).[109] And this was to be achieved through the introduction of 'some elements of unity' of the sort already indicated: the establishment of a uniform system of examination and appointment throughout the service; similarly by the setting up of general rules about salary, superannuation, and promotion. The committee also looked to the possibility of inter-departmental transfer. But in addition Trevelyan himself hoped much in this regard of the proposal that his own department, the Treasury, should be recognized as 'eminently a superintending office', a department of departments fulfilling the role of overseer to achieve all the other objectives. He thus referred to its 'high function of exercising a controlling and revising influence over the great establishments employed in the receipt and expenditure of the revenue, and over all other departments in their relation to finance.'[110]

Debating points

Prompted by Trevelyan *The Times* welcomed the recommendations of the report which it saw as promising another increment of reform in the popular movement against privilege. It described the proposals as 'so obviously just and beneficial that decency will demand acquiescence and even approval'. The paper went on:

> It is proposed to throw open upwards of 16,000 salaried places to the general competition of the country..., to sweep away for ever the entire system of patronage, which has hitherto been considered essential to party Government – to put an end to the barter of places for support, and to all that network of solicitation and intrigue which involves even high-minded men....
>
> The plan advocated by the Government is one the importance of which all classes ought to feel.... Nothing less is purposed than the creation of a new liberal profession, as freely open to all as the church, the bar, or the hospital.

The public service will thus become the birthright of the people, 'according to the talent, education, and industry of each', without (*The Times* added) 'any hindrance from those sinister influences which have hitherto, as a general rule, made access dependent on a powerful

---

[109] ibid., pp. 110, 118.
[110] Papers on the Re-organisation of the Civil Service, loc. cit., p. 427. See also Trevelyan's letter to Gladstone (9 February 1954), cited in Hughes, 'Sir Charles Trevelyan and Civil Service Reform, 1853–5', loc. cit., p. 207. For the Treasury's role in these respects, see below ch. 4.

connexion or a seared conscience.'[111] In fact the response to the report was in some ways not what the reformers had hoped and the subsequent changes were more limited and took longer to achieve than they had expected. Reflecting on the comments in the London clubs, Macaulay said Trevelyan had been too sanguine: 'The pear is not ripe.... The time will come, but it is not come yet.'[112]

The publication of the report sparked off a notable debate. Criticism of the recommendations was often searching and sometimes harsh; and undoubtedly the issues raised had a considerable significance being matters of fundamental principle concerning the organization of the public service. There were three major areas of controversy centring on the main pillars of the report's case: recruitment by open competitive examination; the division between 'intellectual' and 'mechanical' labour; and the unification of the service under the Treasury.

Recruitment
This was perhaps the most contentious issue. There was still support for the patronage system which was (in the picturesque phrase) a gnarled tree, no sapling growth to be disposed of by a single stroke of the woodman's axe.[113] There was also considerable doubt about the proposed alternative, selection by open competitive examination, 'that much loathed scheme' as Trollope called it.[114] Partly the idea was seen as a schoolmasters' ramp because of the stimulus it would give to educational establishments.[115] Naturally many existing officials did not like it because it impugned the system by which they themselves had been chosen. There were obvious worries of a political sort to be raised, too, altogether apart from the supposed effects of the loss of patronage. Ministers, actual or potential, might be dubious on the ground that it would be difficult to accept responsibility for the actions of officials unless they had the choosing of them; so that the ethos and efficiency of departments might alike be impaired.[116] Furthermore if the new mode of recruitment produced senior clerks of considerable calibre they might

111 *The Times* (9 February 1854), p. 6.
112 G. O. Trevelyan, *The Life and Letters of Macaulay*, p. 612.
113 Hughes, 'Sir Charles Trevelyan and Civil Service Reform, 1853–5', loc. cit., pp. 66–7.
114 A. Trollope, *An Autobiography*, p. 102. Trollope's view of reform was not always so hostile: see R. A. W. Rhodes, 'Wilting in Limbo: Anthony Trollope and the Nineteenth Century Civil Service', *Public Administration*, li (1973), esp. pp. 208–10, 216. Cf. also the critical attitude of *The Civil Service Gazette* as reported in Wright, op. cit., pp. 61–2, 63.
115 For the effect on the teaching and syllabuses of one new public school, see R. Blumenau, *A History of Malvern College 1865–1965* (London, 1965), pp. 5–6.
116 Sir E. Bridges, *Portrait of a Profession: the Civil Service Tradition* (Cambridge, 1953), p. 10.

well possess qualities hardly compatible with those of a docile, if efficient, subordinate. They would want influence on the determination of policy and initiative in decision-making, entirely regardless perhaps of merely party considerations. The felt need was not, in Sir James Stephens' famous phrase, for such 'statesmen in disguise' but for 'intelligent, steady, methodical men of business' and these could be obtained under the existing arrangements.[117] Beyond all this the main criticisms of recruitment by examination fell into three categories: academic, social, and (what might be called) logical.

The academic consideration rested on the feeling that examination is too narrow a test for the purpose involved. It only determines who can answer most quickly a string of questions put up by the examiners, in a word who has been best crammed.[118] And this has nothing to do with real education or ability nor does it test for the qualities most desirable in a public servant such as discretion, trustworthiness, impartiality, honesty, and so forth.[119] As one critic said, 'the best scholars' do not 'necessarily make the best clerks.'[120] Moreover 'mere college men' are likely to be narrow-minded and, coming (so to say) straight from the schools, will have little or none of that experience of the world so needed for administrative competence. A reasoned rejoinder was to hand, of course. Defenders of the report's proposal admitted that a lot depended on the type of examination used. Not only literary but scientific subjects should be permitted and the test ought to be not merely of factual knowledge but rather of the ability to argue, analyse, and collate. It should be of a form to discern what Jowett called 'general intelligence and power of thought and language'.[121] Moreover the testimonials which were to be required would give a supplementary indication of a candidate's broader qualities, just as suitability in the working environment would be assessed by a period of probation after initial appointment. And it might certainly be urged that the moral character itself was put to the test by the process of examination. 'University experience abundantly shows', wrote Jowett, that in nearly all cases 'men of attainments are also men of character. The perseverance and self-discipline necessary for the acquirement of any considerable amount of knowledge are a great security that a young man has not led a dissolute life.'[122] Macaulay believed, too, that experience sustained the view that 'the men who were

---

117 Papers on the Re-organisation of the Civil Service, loc. cit., p. 76.
118 Trollope, *An Autobiography*, pp. 34–5.
119 ibid., pp. 37–8; Papers on the Re-organisation of the Civil Service, loc. cit., p. 116 (Sir G. C. Lewis); pp. 131–2 (J. Booth); and p. 364 (Sir B. Hawes).
120 Papers on the Re-organisation of the Civil Service, loc. cit., p. 230 (Sir T. Redington).
121 Jowett to Trevelyan (January 1854), ibid., Appendix 2 (Report), p. 25.
122 ibid., Appendix 2 (Report), p. 24. Cf. J. S. Mill, ibid., p. 95.

first in the competition of the schools have been first in the competition of the world.'[123]

The second category of criticisms pressed home the charge that socially undesirable persons – 'low people, without the breeding or the feelings of gentlemen', as J. S. Mill described them in discussing the point – might be successful in an examination, whereas the public service was one of those spheres of life that can only properly be filled by those with superior social qualities.[124] Any unsuitable person who might thus be recruited to the senior ranks of the service would be out of his element, frustrated and ineffective, and, too, an embarrassment to his colleagues. Trollope urged this consideration in his *Autobiography* and elsewhere, as on the occasion when he writes that 'Since competitive examinations had come into vogue, there was no knowing who might be introduced'.[125] The point was one echoed in the papers of debate which were published with the report. 'Would competition recruit gentlemen?' was a question frequently asked.[126] Thus James Booth, then Secretary to the Board of Trade, was afraid that if social outsiders got into the Civil Service then it would be diminished in attraction as a career to men of acceptable standing. If, he said, 'picked clever young men of the lower ranks of society' were recruited then 'a lower tone of feeling would prevail'. Moreover, while the reservoir of intellectual talent might possibly be enlarged, other qualities would be lacking as would a sense of cohesion in the service as a whole. The result would be a 'painful anomaly'; and the business of the departments would not necessarily be better done.[127] Another critic insisted that, while the existing Civil Service was remarkable for its 'fidelity and trustworthiness', this 'high sense of honour' could 'be ensured only by selecting' officials 'from the class of society where it exists.' He went on: 'I would have Gentlemen in the public offices and I believe they can be obtained only by being selected as at present.'[128] The response of the reformers to this fear was simply to

---

[123] G. O. Trevelyan, op. cit., p. 391. Cf. Macaulay's eloquent justification (in 1833) of the proposal to use competitive examination for appointments in the East India Company's service, in *The Miscellaneous Writings and Speeches* (Popular edn, 1889), pp. 565–6.

[124] For Mill's remarks, see Papers on the Re-organisation of the Civil Service, loc. cit., p. 94. On the general point, cf. the opinion cited in J. Morley, *The Life of William Ewart Gladstone* (London, 1903), i. 511.

[125] Trollope, *An Autobiography*, pp. 36–7; idem, *The Last Chronicle of Barset* (1867; Everyman, 1974), i. 124.

[126] e.g. Papers on the Re-organisation of the Civil Service, loc. cit., p. 55 (R. M. Bromley); p. 289 (E. Romilly).

[127] ibid., p. 133. For other, earlier and later, instances of this sort of concern, see those cited in Roseveare, *The Treasury*, p. 178 and Wright, op. cit., p. 353.

[128] Cited in Hughes, 'Sir Charles Trevelyan and Civil Service Reform, 1853–5', loc. cit., pp. 72–3.

point out that the concern was groundless. This sort of criticism, Trevelyan said, 'assumes that the young men selected by open competition will be less gentlemen than those who are appointed by close patronage, but the real case will, as I believe, be exactly the reverse.'[129] The reason was simple: it was that only the most expensively educated young men could hope to succeed in the competition for staff positions; and the academic opportunities were clearly limited to the privileged classes. Only those (like the young gentleman in one of Trollope's novels) on whose education money could be spent pretty freely would in practice be eligible.[130] Northcote's view was that 'there is no kind of education, so likely to make a man a gentleman, to fit him to play his part among other gentlemen & to furnish him forth for the world, as that of an English university.' Trevelyan indeed urged that the consequence of the reforms would be 'decidedly *aristocratic*' and (as he told Gladstone) would positively strengthen 'our aristocratical institutions'.[131] The Prime Minister himself believed this.[132] J. S. Mill was perhaps more sceptical in some respects about this possibility but, as he observed in his comments on the report, 'the sons of gentlemen', if they have superior qualities, ought surely be able to demonstrate them in competition; if they do not have them, their social monopoly must in any case be unwarrantable. Certainly he believed in examination, thinking it 'one of those great public improvements the adoption of which would form an era in history.'[133]

The third kind of argument levelled at the report's recommendations was of a logical kind, in the sense that it rested on an accusation of inconsistency. For if there are virtues in open competitive examination, should it not be applied to all public and semi-public positions 'from the Lord Chief Justice downwards'? And if it is so advantageous, why do not private institutions and individuals use it in their choice of servants?[134] Of course if has to be remembered that Northcote and Trevelyan were dealing with a specific question, how to eliminate patronage and favouritism and to regularize recruitment by reference to an objective standard; and in so doing they were primarily concerned with young men straight from school or university with no professional or cognate experience. For these purposes examination is hardly inappropriate; and it seems unlikely in the extreme that the proposal was intended to apply

129 Trevelyan's remarks on the comments of the critic cited ibid., p. 73.
130 Papers on the Re-organisation of the Civil Service, loc. cit., pp. 22–3 (Rev. Charles Graves); A. Trollope, *Framley Parsonage* (1861; Everyman, 1973), p. 93.
131 Cited in Hughes, 'Sir Charles Trevelyan and Civil Service Reform, 1853–5', loc. cit., pp. 72–3 (italics in original); Hart, art. cit., p. 110.
132 See the letter to Russell cited at p. 160 below.
133 Papers on the Re-organisation of the Civil Service, loc. cit., pp. 92, 94.
134 ibid., p. 117 (Sir G. C. Lewis).

In Dark Wonder 159

to all appointments of whatever kind or seniority. As the MacDonnell Commission said later, the Northcote-Trevelyan report 'recognised that not every situation in the public service should be recruited by means of competitive examination' for it would be 'unreasonable to impose the examination test upon persons selected to fill appointments on account of their acknowledged eminence in the liberal professions, or their position in public life.'[135] Thus to its defenders the report was not inconsistent, just discriminating. As to private institutions, they did learn to use selection by examination in many cases; though they left it to the universities or professional bodies to conduct the tests for them. At the time some proponents of the examination system expected commercial concerns to come to rely on the examination principle to make sure of 'getting the best services they can for their money.'[136]

Division of labour
The second major area of debate concerned the proposal to divide the Civil Service into two distinct grades each with its characteristic tasks. Thus it was said that if this change were brought about senior officials doing 'intellectual' work would be deprived of any acquaintance with the routine of departmental work; and this would be undesirable because familiarity with 'mechanical' details was an essential preparation for situations of command.[137] It was also feared that the proposed division of labour would prevent the promotion of able and widely experienced men from the lower ranks of the service or who had not received the kind of education required by a competing literary examination. Edwin Chadwick was one who had a lot to say on this point; and it certainly was the case that many of the most valued officials of the time had risen from low in the hierarchy as one of them, Sir Alexander Spearman, a little immodestly pointed out.[138] Anthony Trollope was another who by his own merits achieved a position of some importance but who had never been to university.[139] It was not difficult to respond to these doubts. For one thing the clerk of higher status could easily be made familiar with 'mechanical' work and its importance as part of his official education. What was vital was that he should not be bogged down with routine and

135 The Civil Service, R.Com. 4th Rep., 1914 (vol. xvi), Cd. 7338, p. 7 §7.
136 The Dean of Hereford's letter (30 January 1854), cited Hughes, 'Sir Charles Trevelyan and Civil Service Reform, 1853–5', loc. cit., p. 83.
137 Papers on the Re-organisation of the Civil Service, loc. cit., pp. 411–13 (G. Arbuthnot).
138 ibid., pp. 163–6 (Chadwick); pp. 399–400 (Spearman). The latter was generally hostile to Trevelyan's proposals: for his career and opinions, see Sir J. Winnifreth, 'The Rt. Hon. Sir Alexander Spearman, Bart. (1793–1874): Gladstone's Invaluable Public Servant', *Public Administration*, xxxviii (1960), pp. 311–20.
139 For his education, or lack of it, see his *Autobiography*, ch. I and pp. 37–8.

that from the beginning of his career he should be engaged on 'intellectual' tasks and so not stultified by the absence of challenge appropriate to his potential.[140] As well the reformers never envisaged a rigid separation between the two divisions and had no intention of completely stopping the promotion of deserving men from the lower grade. And this distinction could be regarded with further favour because it was calculated to reinforce the superiority of gentlemen. As Gladstone wrote to Lord John Russell in 1854 about this social *raison d'être*:

> ... I do not hesitate to say that one of the great recommendations of the change in my eyes would be its tendency to strengthen and multiply the ties between the higher classes and the possession of administrative power.... I have a strong impression that the aristocracy of this country are even superior in natural gifts, on the average, to the mass: but it is plain that with their acquired advantages, their *insensible education*, irrespective of book-learning, they have an immense superiority. This applies in its degree to all those who may be called gentlemen by birth and training; and it must be remembered that an essential part of any such plan as is now under discussion is the separation of *work*, wherever it can be made, into mechanical and intellectual, a separation which will open to the highly educated class a career, and give them a command over all the higher parts of the civil service, which up to this time they have never enjoyed....[141]

Unification

The third crucial focus of controversy was the report's premiss that the Civil Service as a whole should be more of a single entity and its fragmentary character overcome by the Treasury acting as a superintending department, the establishment of common conditions of work, and so forth. Many observers doubted whether this was either feasible or desirable. For instance Sir G. C. Lewis claimed that the business of each office was so different that it would, to say the least, be very difficult indeed to find 'a common measure for appointments' or to reduce the essentials of their working to a common rule.[142] The argument was, in effect, that officials have duties which are intrinsically specialist in nature and so require particular knowledge. Consequently to think of moving 'an experienced clerk from one office to another would in general

---

140 Papers on the Re-organisation of the Civil Service, loc. cit., pp. 423–4 (Sir S. Northcote).
141 Gladstone to Russell (20 January 1854), in Morley, op. cit., i. 649 (italics in original). For further comment of this sort, see Northcote's memorandum (1860) and the remarks thereon reprinted as 'Document A' in E. Hughes, 'Postscript to the Civil Service Reforms of 1855', *Public Administration*, xxxiii (1955), pp. 299–301.
142 Papers on the Re-organisation of the Civil Service, loc. cit., pp. 110–11.

be like transferring a skilful naval officer to the army, or appointing a military engineer officer to command a ship of war.'[143] Departmental divisions were thus inevitable; and a single, unified Civil Service of the sort envisaged impossible.[144] This is, of course, an early manifestation of the debate about specialists and generalists (of which more anon).[145] It must be sufficient to say here that while, of course, there are differences between departments and their work, the modern service in Britain has largely been built on assumptions contrary to those of Lewis and to the effect that, in respect both of broad conditions of service and of the type of administrative task involved, there are substantial common elements. However whether, even to this day, sufficient progress along the road to unification has been made is another matter.

Catalyst and precedent

The debate about the report's proposals, fought out over such ground as that described, was often remarkably bitter. A few days after Macaulay had recorded his doubt whether the recommendations were timely, he also wrote: 'The news is worse... about Trevelyan. There is a set made at him by men who will not scruple to do their utmost.' And while he expected Trevelyan's principles to triumph in the end, their progress (Macaulay believed) would not be easy.[146] The opposition had a plausible case. Of course it had to acknowledge the existence of deficiencies in the existing arrangements but held at the same time, and most strongly, that the traditional service on the whole 'worked well' and had produced some outstanding public servants.[147] And the vested interests were powerful. The Cabinet was divided on the matter but decided to proceed though its proposals still retained an important element of selection. Even so this limited scheme had itself to be withdrawn such was the strength of the opposition.[148] Trevelyan himself reckoned that a broadly based appeal would be necessary for success: 'The classes interested in the maintenance of Patronage', he wrote to Gladstone, 'are so powerful that unless we can get our Plan read and understood by the rest of the Community I shall begin to fear for its success.'[149]

At this point a factor of catalytic significance supervened – the

143 ibid., p. 111.
144 Cf. the arguments of G. Arbuthnot, ibid., pp. 411–12, and of H. H. Addington, pp. 347–8.
145 See below pp. 199ff.
146 G. O. Trevelyan, op. cit., p. 612.
147 Papers on the Re-organisation of the Civil Service, loc. cit., p. 133 (J. Booth), pp. 348–9 (H. U. Addington), and pp. 383–5 (H. Waddington).
148 Hughes, 'Sir Charles Trevelyan and Civil Service Reform, 1853–5', loc. cit., pp. 63–4, 66; Wright, op. cit., pp. 62–3.
149 Trevelyan to Gladstone (1 March 1854), cited Wright, op. cit., p. 60.

162 A Much Governed Nation

Crimean War which provoked a furious outburst of bitterness and impatience with established institutions.[150] During the relatively brief period of campaigning a great deal of confusion and inefficiency was revealed in the departments concerned with the organization and supply of the army (the Commissariat being, as it happened, Trevelyan's own responsibility). Distressing stories of mismanagement and its consequences were widely retailed. And while often exaggerated or even untrue (and certainly not revealing new deficiencies) their effect was considerable.[151] A very hostile body of opinion was aroused which disparaged the state of the public service. The frame of mind was reflected in a *Punch* cartoon which showed one critical MP, A. H. Layard, remembered for his discovery of Nineveh, excavating John Bull (in the appropriate form of an Assyrian winged bovine) from a mass of rubble labelled 'routine', 'jobbery', 'muddle', 'incompetency', 'patronage', and 'red tape'.[152] The Aberdeen government itself fell early in 1855 after unsuccessfully resisting Roebuck's motion demanding a select committee to inquire into the state of the army before Sebastopol. A few months later a pressure group calling itself the Administrative Reform Association was formed 'to put an end to those influences which at present burden every department of Government with incapable officers' and to bring the level of public up to that of private management.[153] Its propaganda, in which it had the support of *The Times* (prompted again by Trevelyan), involved the usual meetings and pamphlets. But it also published past reports of inquiries into the public offices including that of Northcote and Trevelyan. Its supporters in Parliament attacked 'a blind adherence to routine' and the malign role in making appointments of 'party and family influences'.[154] There was some diversity in the specific demands the association made but its brief 'meteoric' career reflected and articulated a major body of dissatisfaction with the *status quo*. And undoubtedly the brunt of the attack fell on the Civil Service.[155]

---

150 See O. Anderson, *A Liberal State at War: English Politics and Economics during the Crimean War* (London, 1967), p. 97. Cf. ibid., ch. 3 *passim*; also Wright, op. cit., p. 64.
151 For the care that is necessary, even nowadays, in assessing these matters, see e.g. my 'Biography and the "Amateur" Historian: Mrs Woodham-Smith's "Florence Nightingale"', *Victorian Studies*, iii (1959–60), pp. 190–202. For a recent account of the contemporary system, see J. Sweetman, *War and Administration: the Significance of the Crimean War for the British Army* (Edinburgh, 1984).
152 *Punch*, xxviii (7 April 1855), p. 135. This illustration has frequently been reprinted: see e.g. Anderson, op. cit., p. 113.
153 Administrative Reform Association, *Official Papers*, cited Cohen, op. cit., p. 110 and Anderson, op. cit., p. 114.
154 See Layard's motion at 138 Parl. Deb. 3s., 15 June 1855, cols 2040–1.
155 For an account of the wider purposes of this group, see O. Anderson, 'The Janus

Palmerston, who succeeded Aberdeen as Prime Minister, was not himself really interested in (or was undecided about) administrative reform. But as some placatory gesture had to be made, to appease the public outcry and to meet the critics' demands, it was decided in May 1855 to establish a Civil Service Commission on the lines of the 'central Board' which the Northcote-Trevelyan report had envisaged as a means of regulating and improving appointments. As so often with changes which ultimately and in hindsight achieve a redoubtable significance, this step was extremely confined in its immediate form and impact; in fact it fell far short of the mark the radical reformers had envisaged.[156] And although it confirmed a tendency it hardly introduced a new principle.[157] The Order in Council which set up the Civil Service Commission endowed it in effect with only a limited function of authentification. General examination for all posts was not required. To the commission was transferred simply the duty of arranging such examinations and cognate inquiries (like those about age, health, and character) which some departments already conducted in respect of 'junior situations in the Civil establishments'. To this extent nominees might be impartially scrutinized and the tests co-ordinated. But the standards involved were low, a most flimsy obstacle to favouritism, and actual appointment was still a political or personal gift in that responsibility for nomination remained with heads of department. Competition and examination were simply permissible and not compulsory requirements.[158] Nevertheless the commission's first annual report showed how well-founded had been the reformers' criticisms of the traditional system. Out of just over 1,000 nominees examined, nearly a third were rejected on grounds of gross ignorance; some, it was found, could hardly spell the simplest words. It was clear, the commission deduced, that patrons who made the nominations did so in order to satisfy a personal or political obligation rather than to make proper provision for the public service.[159]

Face of Mid-Nineteenth-Century English Radicalism: the Administrative Reform Association of 1855', *Victorian Studies*, viii (1964–5), pp. 231–42; and idem, *A Liberal State at War*, ch. 3.

156 The Civil Service, R. Com. 4th Rep., 1914, Cd. 7338, p. 8 §1.
157 Cf. Gladstone's speech cited in Hughes, 'Civil Service Reform 1853–5', loc. cit., p. 79; also Trevelyan's letter to Gladstone (17 January 1855) cited idem, 'Sir Charles Trevelyan and Civil Service Reform, 1853–5', loc. cit., pp. 228–9.
158 Cohen, op. cit., pp. 116–17; Roseveare, *The Treasury 1660–1870*, p. 101 and n. 81. Cf. the quotation from J. Boulger, *The Master-Key to Public Offices...* (London, 1860) cited H. J. Hanham, *The Nineteenth-Century Constitution 1815–1914: Documents and Commentary* (Cambridge, 1969), pp. 329–31; and the experience of A. J. Munby as described in D. Hudson, *Munby: Man of Two Worlds. The Life and Diaries of Arthur J. Munby 1826–1910* (1972; Abacus, 1974), p. 61.
159 Civil Service Commissioners, 1st Rep., 1856 (vol. xxii), esp. Appendices. One of the

Yet some advance had been made for the power of nomination was no longer untrammelled. As the MacDonnell report noted at the beginning of the present century, a check had been placed upon the misuse of patronage in some cases and the principle of examination had been accepted. Moreover this step was powerfully reinforced by the Superannuation Act of 1859 which, 'with certain special exceptions', made the possession of a CSC certificate necessary for purposes of pension qualification thus ensuring that uncertificated appointments were increasingly unlikely from then on.[160] In all this the Treasury seems to have helped a great deal as an example to other departments: it accepted and supported CSC recommendations and refused to interfere with decisions or to act on behalf of other offices as a court of appeal; it also enforced the new superannuation requirements which considerably strengthened the CSC's hand.[161] None the less, as Northcote himself had warned the House, so long as the commission was confined to the imposition of a merely qualifying test, it would only be a 'Board for stereotyping mediocrity or concealing bad appointments.'[162] Even so, 1855 must be seen as the year that marked the beginning of the end of the old system of departmental autonomy in respect of recruitment.[163] The establishment of the commission created a basis on which to build further reform: it was, as it turned out, a powerful precedent.

Slow speed ahead

The last half of the nineteenth century saw the real commencement of the collectivist state so far as the Civil Service was concerned. New functions like education, factory inspection, poor relief, public health, and transport supervision were emerging or expanding in importance; existing departments were enlarged and new ones (like the Local Government Board and the Board of Agriculture) created; and the number of officials more than trebled.[164] The cost of the public service rose in proportion. Those who wanted to ensure that this growth was restrained or at least achieved with efficiency and economy invariably wished to secure the more sustained application of the Northcote-Trevelyan principles; though there were equally those (like R. R. W. Lingen) who feared that reform of the Civil Service would create a ground for the extension of its functions beyond what was absolutely

---

candidates rejected by the commission was a nominee of the Prime Minister, Wright, op. cit., p. 65.
160 The Civil Service, R. Com. 4th Rep., 1914, Cd. 7338, p. 8 §11.
161 Wright, op. cit., p. 66.
162 Cited in The Civil Service, R. Com. 4th Rep., 1914, Cd. 7338, p. 8 §12.
163 Cf. Wright, op. cit., p. 66.
164 See Table 4, p. 132 above.

necessary.[165] In the outcome resistance to the changes envisaged in the report of 1854 continued strongly though, in the end, with diminishing effect.

This was clearly the case with respect to the principle of open recruitment. Progress was slow and opposition considerable: during the 1860s the element of competition even began to diminish and was certainly not present in the great majority of appointments made. At the end of the decade less than one in 200 posts was filled after open competitive examination; nearly 95 per cent were filled without competition of any kind; and party and family considerations still dominated the scene.[166] When at this time it was proposed to abolish some of the remaining elements of nomination, the then Patronage Secretary protested most strongly, a sure indication that its political role and purpose were still seen as considerable.[167] And when a further attempt at improvement came in 1870 it was certainly not because there was general political or public pressure as there had been in 1855.[168] Critical concern about the service there was, but it largely focused on the growing number of officials and their cost and on the consequential need to achieve (what a Treasury minute called) 'a substantial reduction in the number of permanent civil employments'.[169] In this context the crucial factor at work was the influence exerted by Gladstone and Lowe from within the Cabinet. Both were determined that the increasing expense of the public service should be held in check; and they were convinced that efficiency and economy achieved by further reform were essential to this end. Gladstone, who as Chancellor of the Exchequer had commissioned the Northcote-Trevelyan inquiry, became Prime Minister in December 1868 and Lowe went to the Treasury. Not without opposition from their colleagues in government, a Cabinet committee was appointed and its recommendations embodied in an Order in Council promulgated in 1870.[170] This marked a definite, though again limited, advance. In future the Civil Service Commission would no longer examine only those candidates nominated by departments but would hold an open competition in respect of vacancies for all permanent posts in those departments whose ministers agreed (this recognition of the need for

165 Papers on the Re-organisation of the Civil Service, loc. cit., p. 100. Lingen was then secretary of the Privy Council committee for education.
166 Wright, op. cit., pp. 74–5.
167 See G. C. Glynn's letter in Hughes, 'Postscript to the Civil Service Reforms of 1855', loc. cit., pp. 305–6.
168 Cf. Wright, op. cit., pp. 76–7, 79.
169 ibid., pp. 77–8, 80–2.
170 The recommendations of the Cabinet committee are reprinted in Hughes, 'Postscript to the Civil Service Reforms of 1855', loc. cit., pp. 304–5. Cf. Wright, op. cit., pp. 80–1; and, for the opposition to the changes, ibid., p. 85.

ministerial concurrence being the key to the compromise which had been struck by the Cabinet). A further important step was taken in 1876 when a uniform lower division of clerks was created for it was required that recruitment should be by open competitive examination. In this way the Civil Service Commission, which up to 1870 had led 'a sort of twilight existence', was able to establish itself more effectively as a central recruiting agency.[171] Even so its writ did not run throughout the service and for quite a while notable elements of patronage remained.[172] Some of the major departments resisted the new order of things. For instance the Home Office did not give way until Lowe himself became Secretary of State in 1873, while the Foreign Office did not fall into line until the end of the Great War.[173] As well there was still no competition for professional posts (doctors, veterinary surgeons, museum specialists, solicitors, and the like) which continued normally to be filled without public notification. Many places in the inspectorates were in the gift of the Home Secretary.[174] The inspectors and examiners appointed by the Education Department of the Privy Council (or Board of Education as it became in 1900) were recruited by patronage until as late as 1924. Also higher administrative places – what were called 'staff' appointments – were not necessarily filled by promoted civil servants, lucrative posts often being given, for instance, to the private secretaries of ministers, whether they had previously been officials or not. In 1885 the Patronage Secretary still had more than 20,000 places in his gift, the majority of them in the Post Office.[175] None the less by 1912 most patronage posts had been given up and shortly afterwards the MacDonnell Commission recommended that they should be abolished completely: the end of an era was in sight.[176] Even so the position was still chequered. The day of patronage might be over but it did not follow that the Northcote-Trevelyan principle was universally applied in its stead:

> ...it has come to pass that while Open Competition regulates appointment to the administrative and clerical classes of the Civil

171 The phrase cited is from Bridges, *Portrait of a Profession*, p. 10.
172 For details, see H. J. Hanham, 'Political Patronage at the Treasury, 1870–1912', *Historical Journal*, iii (1960), pp. 75–84; also the summary in Wright, op. cit., pp. 92–3 n. 3.
173 The arguments used for staying outside the scheme of open competition are reviewed, Wright, op. cit., pp. 82–4. Cf. ibid., pp. 88–97; and, on the development of Treasury influence in support of the CSC, ibid., pp. 105–9.
174 For these and the following details, see Cohen, op. cit., p. 137; and G. Sutherland, 'Administrators in Education after 1870: Patronage, Professionalism and Expertise', in G. Sutherland (ed.), *Studies in the Growth of Nineteenth Century Government*, p. 263.
175 Hanham, art. cit., p. 80.
176 Roseveare, *The Treasury*, p. 228; The Civil Service, R. Com. 4th Rep., 1914, Cd. 7338, p. 64 §10 and p. 68 §28.

Service, and also to large and important groups of departmental situations, limited competition controls recruitment for certain other classes of such situations important in character though not numerous, and qualifying examination, into which the competitive principle does not enter, gives access to a very large number of subordinate situations; while even uncontrolled Patronage continues to fill some of the highest Departmental offices, as well as the lowest situations.[177]

Another aspect of the recruitment problem concerned the social and educational background of candidates for senior posts. The proposal to introduce open competitive examination for these places had (as already noted) sparked off a lively debate in that many officials in, and observers of, the public service believed the change would lower the social standing and ability level of those appointed.[178] In fact the issue emerged again half a century later (as it has done on many occasions since) but with a rather different emphasis, the suggestion being that (drawing as the system of senior appointment did only on the 'classes') it could be doubted whether open competition did provide access to the best reservoir of talent available. The MacDonnell Commission addressed itself to the question and found that, between 1906 and 1910, over 80 per cent of successful candidates for First Division posts were Oxbridge graduates a substantial proportion of whom had been to public schools; and over half of them were classicists. The majority report accepted the need to enable 'the clever sons of poor parents to benefit by University training, and thereby enter the Civil Service' so that 'the interests of democracy and of the public service' may be reconciled.[179] Not for the last time, other universities were invited to assert a claim to a share of these appointments.[180] It was the MacDonnell report which also recommended the use of a *viva voce* examination as a supplement to the written tests 'with the object of ascertaining the candidate's general mental calibre, and the possession of those qualities of common sense, sound judgment, resourcefulness and resolution, upon which the written paper rarely gives assurance.'[181] It was an issue on which the Northcote-Trevelyan proposals had also dwelt; and it pointed the way to a form of test that assumed greater and greater significance as the years passed. It was

177 The Civil Service, R. Com. 4th Rep., 1914, Cd. 7338, p. 24 §54.
178 See above pp. 155–8.
179 The Civil Service, R. Com. 4th Rep., 1914, Cd. 7338, p. 39 §42, p. 42 §48. Cf. the remarks of Lord Haldane cited ibid., p. 40 §43 and the report's general comments on the Oxbridge bias, ibid., pp. 41–3. It is at least interesting, however, that the student returns from the universities as a whole showed a not inconsiderable proportion (up to a quarter) to have a lower-class background.
180 ibid., p. 42 §47.
181 ibid., p. 41 §44.

suggested, too, that syllabuses be improved and the permitted range of subjects widened: matters taken up again during the war by the Leathes Committee.[182] But there was no suggestion that the subjects examined, let alone the recruitment procedure itself, should be closely related to the duties which would be faced in a department. Nor was there any departure from the, by then, conventional assumption that it was general qualities rather than specialized knowledge and ability that should be sought and tested.[183]

The matter of recruitment was thus largely dealt with, in the sense that the principle of open competitive examination had (after some travail) been widely applied. The division of labour – between 'intellectual' and 'mechanical' work – was accepted more easily though, as the Civil Service increased in size and complexity of task, the distinction in some respects necessarily assumed a more elaborate form. Some departments had been persuaded quite early on to accept the Northcote-Trevelyan division; but others had not done so. Additionally there was the fact that departments had dealt differently with the recruitment of clerks to deal with copying work. Some uniformity of conditions was introduced in 1870 but much was still organized on a departmental basis. For example rates of pay and hours of work varied from office to office; and there were no arrangements for inter-departmental transfer. One reason why the Treasury was loath to commit itself to uniform rules in all this was that, if it were done, expenditure would be likely to rise.[184] An inquiry into all these matters was set afoot in 1874 under the chairmanship of Lyon Playfair (a scientist with considerable administrative and political experience) and, for the rest, composed almost entirely of senior civil servants. Its object was, in effect, to take stock of the central departments twenty years after the Northcote-Trevelyan statement of the principles on which the Civil Service should be organized. Its report was an uncompromising reassertion of those principles and strengthened the foundations of the system in a notable way.[185] Open competitive examination was broadly approved as the best method of recruitment so long as it could be coupled with a fair process of departmental selection. And it was proposed that the service should be uniformly structured by the creation of two major grades: a Higher Division (later, after 1890, called the First Division) recruited from young men who had had a public school or university education; and a Lower Division comprising those with a tested knowledge of the Three R's, clerks who might be moved

---

182 ibid., ch. III, pp. 42–3 §50; The Scheme of Examination for Class I of the Civil Service, Cttee Rep., 1917–18 (vol. viii), Cd. 8657.
183 G. K. Fry, *Statesmen in Disguise: the Changing Role of the Administrative Class of the British Home Civil Service 1853–1966* (London, 1969), pp. 78–9.
184 Wright, op. cit., pp. 333, 355.
185 Cf. The Civil Service, R. Com. 4th Rep., 1914, Cd. 7338, p. 153 §(12).

from one office to another because they enjoyed uniform conditions of work. By this means an important element of departmentalism was eliminated.[186] One commentator, writing in the *Quarterly Review*, noted the important advance which the Playfair report marked:

> It broke down the artificial barriers which separated one office from another, and which permitted each office to consider that its own traditional methods of transacting routine, of recording facts, of registering correspondence, of tabulating statistics, were matters of national importance, which required special training and long experience, and acquaintance with which rendered a man's services necessarily of value.[187]

A further commission of inquiry under the chairmanship of Sir Matthew Ridley, a politician, and with only one Civil Service member, was set up in 1886 with the task, in effect, of showing how the by now established principles of the service might be more widely applied. The recommendations were thus basically of detail, in particular how the First Division might be further regularized as by the elimination of the remaining non-competitive appointments, the establishment of uniform conditions of employment, and such-like changes, points equally stressed by the MacDonnell Commission some twenty years later. In fact the hours of work were not regulated until 1910; and a unified salary scale not imposed until after the Great War.

By the end of the last century, then, the Civil Service had undergone a slow but radical transformation. 'The servants of departmental or office heads had become the servants of the State. They held their posts during good behaviour, received salaries, and were pensioned at the end of their working life.' An efficient technique of organization based on division of labour had been introduced, as was a method of recruitment by open, competitive examination to secure 'efficient, upright and intelligent officers.' Uniform grades, with uniform pay and conditions of work were (or were soon to be) established. 'Much had been done, and more had been envisaged. The Service had acquired most of its characteristic features.'[188]

However the Northcote-Trevelyan report had also envisaged that the service should be superintended by the Treasury as a means of overall co-ordination. This subject is dealt with in some detail in the next chapter. Here it must suffice to note that this aspect of the report has probably never been implemented as originally intended. The Playfair inquiry

---

186 Civil Service, Inquiry Commission 1st Rep., 1875 (vol. xxiii), pp. 10–18.
187 [H. Craik], 'The Civil Service: its Organization and Competitive Examinations', *Quarterly Review*, clxviii (1889), p. 465.
188 This and the preceding citations are from Cohen, op. cit., pp. 153–4.

believed the Treasury's position should be strengthened in this regard; while the Ridley Commission recommended machinery to achieve more effective central control over establishments.[189] And in 1914 the fourth report of the MacDonnell Commission likewise expressed the view that, because of a (quite proper) concentration hitherto on questions of recruitment and the like, the matter of the co-ordination and control of the service as a whole had been neglected. Hence the commission stressed the importance of securing the unification of the Civil Service under the Treasury. This, it believed, might be done by enhancing the possibilities of interdepartmental transfer, making the conditions of the various grades more uniform, and by strengthening Treasury control through the creation of a special branch in that department to supervise general conditions of service, to conduct investigations into problems of staffing and organization, to facilitate inter-departmental transfers of staff, and the like.[190] This was the basis of the establishments branch of the Treasury set up after the Great War.

As it happened the final report of the MacDonnell Commission did not appear until the spring of 1914. It was thus overtaken by the outbreak of hostilities and shelved for their duration. One effect of the long and traumatic war was a notable increase in the size and cost of the Civil Service. And it seemed highly likely, to many people desirable as well, that a considerable increment of these extended facilities and frictions should be continued, and even enlarged, in the peacetime period ahead. This brought to the fore further questions about the overall co-ordination of departments and their rapidly growing responsibilities.

RATIONALIZATION AND CO-ORDINATION

> ... should offices be divided according to the subjects with which they deal, or according to the persons with whom they deal: I mean to say, should one person see to good order in general, or one look after the boys, another after the women, and so on?
> ARISTOTLE, *Politics*, 1299[b]

The questions about the Civil Service to which attention had hitherto largely been addressed concerned recruitment, that is, the replacement of patronage by open competition and selection by examination, and the supersession of a varied array of places, offices, and conditions of work therein by a more regular structure of official grades and terms of service. But if a satisfactory classification of persons and their work had to some extent been achieved, the matter of the organization of the service as a

---

189 Cf. The Civil Establishments, R. Com. 2nd Rep., 1888 (vol. xxvii), C. 5545, p. x §6.
  The recommendations of the Playfair inquiry are summarized, ibid., pp. 570–2.
190 The Civil Service, R. Com. 4th Rep., 1914, Cd. 7338, pp. 84–7.

whole had received much less attention. However, as an enormous growth was taking place in public administration with departments becoming larger and new ones being created, it was increasingly difficult to ignore such issues as the proper allocation of functions and the optimum span of ministerial control in addition to the continuing questions. Part of the clamour about national efficiency in the early years of the present century had concerned the need for a better way of organizing and running government offices: one critical analysis had, for instance, stressed the need to establish a Board of Administrative Control continuously to review the entire public service in all such respects.[191] This general worry had indeed been one of the factors which prompted the appointment of the MacDonnell Commission in the years before the Great War. It noted the impact of the recent burst of legislative activity on the operations of government 'especially in connection with problems arising out of the conditions of social and industrial life', matters which were often of 'extreme complexity'. A minority report equally spoke of the issues arising from 'the formation of new departments for the transaction of novel forms of public business.'[192] Then, of course, the war itself proliferated agencies and activities on an unprecedented scale; and it was generally assumed that the difficulties of a subsequent period of reconstruction would be extensive and pressing. A separate ministry was established in 1917 to review these impending issues and to propose how to deal with them. As part of this process a committee was established with Lord Haldane in the chair to consider such questions as they affected the structure and work of the central government and its executive departments.

The Haldane Committee

In October 1917 Mrs Sidney Webb, one of those who had been appointed to serve on the inquiry, wrote to H. L. Samuel about the work of 'my' committee (as she proprietorially called it) saying she was quite sure that as, in the future, the country would come to rely more and more on 'Government machinery . . . for the performance of one service after another', it was absolutely necessary to 'overhaul' the offices of state. In the past, she added, 'we have put too little thought into the construction of Government Departments and have hardly been aware of certain . . . diseases which affect the bureaucrat'.[193] The committee's report appeared

---

191 P. L. Gell, 'Administrative Reform in the Public Service', *The Nineteenth Century*, xlviii (1900), pp. 48–51. For the national efficiency movement, see *The Rise of Collectivism* (London, 1983), pp. 105–7.
192 The Civil Service, R. Com. 4th Rep., 1914 (vol. xvi), Cd. 7338, p. 28 §4, p. 122 §3.
193 B. Webb to H. L. Samuel (27 October 1917), HLRO, Samuel Papers, A/54(3).

in 1918 and is still the only full-scale official document ever published in this country to deal with these matters. And, as Professor Mackenzie once remarked, it is a paper which 'for a generation of administrative reformers assumed the status almost of holy writ.'[194]

The point was, of course, not simply that the Civil Service was growing in size or complexity and likely to continue to do so. It was also that, despite the advances which had been made in respect both to recruitment and structure, the forms of civil administration were still excessively 'particularist'.[195] It was the Haldane Committee's task to show *inter alia* how the many and varied aspects of departmental activity might be seen consistently and as a whole in terms of some overall, rational principle the application of which would enhance national efficiency.

The origin of the inquiry may be traced to a specific official response to the strains and stresses of the Great War: a memorandum produced in 1916 by the Treasury and handed to the Financial Secretary, E. S. Montagu, who was also in the Cabinet (as Chancellor of the Duchy of Lancaster) and later to become a member of the Haldane Committee. This paper was concerned with the waste resulting from the overlapping of departments and went on to suggest a rearrangement of their duties.[196] There was no immediate reaction however; and new posts and offices continued to be created not least after the formation of the George government in December that same year. But, as one aspect of these changes, the Prime Minister created a Reconstruction Committee with himself as chairman though, in practice, this role was filled by Montagu who arranged for the establishment of the sub-committee which in due time produced the Haldane report. The occasion was a document on the 'Organization of Government' which Montagu composed at the end of April 1917.[197] It was concerned with the growth of the administration and urged that some systematic review was essential:

> For a long time past the haphazard growth of Government Departments without careful enquiry, the way in which their functions depended entirely upon the energy or lack of energy of particular incumbents of Ministerial Offices, had resulted in tremendous overlap, and at the same time fearful expanses of No-

---

194 W. J. M. Mackenzie, 'The Structure of Central Administration', in Lord Campion *et al.*, *British Government since 1918* (1950; London, 1951), p. 57.
195 The Civil Service, R. Com. 4th Rep., 1914, Cd. 7338, p. 124 §§8–9, p. 149 §70 I(a).
196 Lord Bridges, 'Haldane and the Machinery of Government', *Public Administration*, xxxv (1957), p. 260; H. Daalder, 'The Haldane Committee and the Cabinet', ibid., xli (1963), p. 119 which describes the events leading up to the appointment of the committee.
197 The memorandum is cited in Daalder, art. cit., pp. 119–20 on which the following account is based.

Man's Land. A government that wanted things done had no choice but to fabricate against time new machinery. It is expedient, it seems to me, in the highest degree, that we should look round over the whole territory before scrapping the new Departments or rehabilitating the old.[198]

Montagu then went on to review these matters in the context of Cabinet reorganization, considering the subject in terms of seven divisions or fields of responsibility.[199] Something, therefore, of the line taken in the report later issued was already established before the committee itself was set up in July 1917. It had seven members: Haldane as chairman; three MPs as representatives of the political parties (Montagu a Liberal, Sir Alan Sykes a Conservative, and J. H. Thomas for Labour); two senior civil servants (Sir George Murray, a former Permanent Secretary to the Treasury, and Sir Robert Morant who had been Permanent Secretary to the Board of Education and Chairman of the National Insurance Commission); and Beatrice Webb. The remit of the committee was 'To enquire into the responsibilities of the various Departments of the central executive Government, and to advise in what manner the exercise and distribution by the Government of its functions should be improved.'[200]

The discussions of the committee were, it seems, largely dominated by Haldane, Mrs Webb, and the two officials.[201] So the line taken by the report is hardly surprising: it is one which envisaged efficient and extending administrative control. Haldane himself was (in Sir Arthur Salter's phrase) 'essentially a planner' and had long been concerned with the establishment of systematic organization based on first principles.[202] The Webbs' point of view was similar; moreover they had long worked closely with Haldane.[203] Of the two civil servants Morant at least believed drastic change was necessary in the allocation and co-ordination of functions. He wrote of the need immediately to inaugurate the sort of reforms envisaged and did so in recognition of a context of growing collectivism:

> The problems of social economy in our modern democratic state, complicated as they are by the still existing results of centuries of many

---

198 ibid., p. 120.
199 ibid., p. 120–1.
200 Machinery of Government, Ministry of Reconstruction Cttee Rep., 1918 (vol. xii), Cd. 9230, p. [2].
201 Daalder, art. cit., p. 123.
202 Sir A. Salter, *Personality in Politics: Studies of Contemporary Statesmen* (London, 1947), pp. 114, 118–19; Bridges, art. cit., pp. 254ff.; Viscount Waverley, 'Haldane the Man', *Public Administration*, xxxv (1957), p. 220.
203 Bridges, art. cit., pp. 259–60. On the Webbs' attitudes, see *The Ideological Heritage* (London, 1983), pp. 381–411.

successive varying methods of seeking after the general good, are now so complex, the pace with which so many of them are simultaneously flinging themselves upon us for immediate action is so exacting that it must be realized as amongst the most seriously urgent duties of all of us, at the present moment, to put our administrative house in order, without a moment's delay, without a trace of timidity, and without a shadow of lingering prejudice.[204]

Certainly the fragmentation of administrative responsibility must have seemed a major and frustrating hurdle to those reformers who (like these members of the committee) wished to see a centralized and concentrated power at work.

The report was drafted by Haldane himself and attempted to define 'the general principles which should govern the distribution' of responsibilities between departments and, on this basis, 'to illustrate the application of these principles in sufficient outline.' It brought out very definitely the view that there was a great deal of 'overlapping and consequent obscurity and confusion in the functions of the Departments of executive Government.' The committee was also clear that the two main reasons why this undesirable situation had grown up were, first, that in response to current needs many departments had over the years acquired, on a pragmatic or *ad hoc* basis, a range of functions not all of which were easily compatible; and secondly that offices had been hastily established without due preliminary thought being given to 'definition of function and precise assignment of responsibility.'[205] For example, the Home Department, a long established prerogative office and traditionally a residuary legatee, had acquired many varied responsibilities in respect of the public peace and good order ranging from prisons and aliens to factory inspection and the control of burial grounds. One specific topic especially dear to Mrs Webb and Morant was public health the central administration of which was conducted by a number of offices. Indeed the situation in this area of public policy and concern is a good illustration of the state of affairs the reformers wanted to improve. In the mid-nineteenth century at least four major departments had been involved.[206] By the time of the Great War the position had grown even more complex for there were by then twice as many agencies concerned with questions affecting the physical well-

---

204 Cited Daalder, art. cit., p. 124. Cf. ibid., pp. 131–3.
205 Machinery of Government, Ministry of Reconstruction Cttee Rep., 1918, Cd. 9230, p. 4 §§3–4.
206 See e.g. the excellent summary of the position at that time in R. Lambert, *Sir John Simon, 1816–1904, and English Social Administration* (London, 1963), ch. 14 esp. pp. 304–7; also the general survey in P. R. Wilding, 'The Genesis of the Ministry of Health', *Public Administration*, xlv (1967), pp. 149–68.

being of the community. The Privy Council supervised the professional qualifications and conduct of midwives, doctors, dentists, and pharmacists; the Home Office had powers relating to the protection of children, the administration of the Lunacy Acts, and safeguarding the health of industrial workers; while the Board of Trade had responsibilities for the health of merchant seamen. As the department primarily responsible for the supervision of town and county authorities, the Local Government Board had a wide range of functions concerning public health and including such matters as tuberculosis, venereal disease, and maternity and child welfare; and the last matter was also one in which the Board of Education was interested. The Board of Agriculture and Fisheries inspected milk and food for impurities. And two new agencies with health responsibilities had recently sprung up: the Insurance Commission (1911) which supervised the health insurance scheme, and the Ministry of Pensions (1916) which was concerned with the health of disabled officers and men of the armed forces. In the report's summary:

> The present position is that no single Department is charged with the superintendence of ... these activities, which rests in the hands of a number of separate Departments, each exercising jurisdiction over a portion of the province of health.... We are satisfied that the exercise of the functions of the central Government in this sphere could be improved by the further concentration of health services under a Minister of Health, who should be charged with the general surveillance of all matters relating to health of which the Government from time to time takes cognisance.[207]

A similar case for centralization was suggested in respect of other public tasks especially the fields of research, justice, and employment which were equally major concerns of the active members of the committee.[208] But the general approach had to be sustained on the basis of a rational principle which could be used to overhaul and reorganize the entire central administration. The analysis adopted in the report had, in fact, been outlined in a detailed memorandum and a series of notes drawn up by Mrs Webb before the committee met. It was, she urged, a conflict of the two possible categories of division and a failure properly to discriminate between them which led to 'the present multiplication of Ministries and the overlapping and confusion of their functions.'[209]

The first formula was to distribute responsibilities between

---

207 Machinery of Government, Ministry of Reconstruction Cttee Rep., 1918, Cd. 9230, p. 58 §§2–3.
208 Mackenzie, loc. cit., p. 58.
209 Cited in Daalder, art. cit., p. 123.

departments according to the persons or classes to be dealt with. That is, each office would deal with certain sections of the population so that there might, for example, be a Ministry for Paupers, a Ministry for Children, or one for Insured Persons, or for the Unemployed. The committee considered this proposition and rejected it as unsatisfactory. This was because its application would inevitably lead to fragmentation, to 'Lilliputian administration', a large number of departments dealing with relatively small classes of people. And such agencies would necessarily be narrow and fail to achieve an adequate standard of efficiency.[210] The committee turned, therefore, to the alternative principle. This was that the functions of government should be distributed between departments according not to the people served but to the services rendered to the community as a whole.[211] For example a Ministry of Education would deal with the provision of all educational services whatever their nature and for all classes of persons. Similarly there would be (as already indicated) a Ministry of Health to provide all (or most) public health services, something that Morant and Mrs Webb were very keen to accomplish. Naturally there would be minor overlaps or conflicts of official interest as, for instance, with the two fields mentioned in respect of the health of school children. But these matters could be settled by departmental co-operation and agreement. And this was the principle that the Haldane Committee wished to see applied to the entire public service so as to do away with the existing confusion and put everything on a straightforward and rational footing. Apart from major gains in terms of efficiency and economy, it was thought that a lot of incidental advantages would accrue as well if this principle were applied. For example it would be easier for officials to acquire specialized knowledge and capacity in respect of their delimited field of work; and it would be simpler to allocate any new function to the right department.[212]

The principle of dividing up public functions in this manner, into various classes of service rendered by government to the community as a whole, might, of course, be interpreted in a variety of ways. The Haldane Committee itself suggested a particular scheme by way of illustration though it was not in any way 'cut and dried' or intended to be 'a complete

---

210 Machinery of Government, Ministry of Reconstruction Cttee Rep., 1918, Cd. 9230, pp. 7–8 §18.
211 ibid., p. 8 §19. Interestingly Sidney Webb had once written persuasively about the importance of recognizing that social well-being was increasingly coming to depend on 'the specialised scientific treatment of minorities – often of quite small minorities', *The Necessary Basis of Society* (London, 1908), pp. 3, 7: a reflection no doubt of the contemporary interest in the role of social groups but not compatible with the principle accepted by the Haldane Committee.
212 Machinery of Government, Ministry of Reconstruction Cttee Rep., 1918, Cd. 9230, p. 8 §§19–20, p. 9 §25.

or final solution' to the problem to which all sorts of practical considerations would be relevant.[213] This specific suggestion led to the following broad areas of responsibility: Production (including Agriculture, Forestry, and Fisheries, Transport, and Commerce); Health; Research and Information (because rational decisions on public issues can only be made on the basis of adequate data); Employment; External Affairs; Justice (an interest of Haldane's); Finance; Education; National Defence; and Supplies (i.e. to all government departments – not the type of Ministry of Supply that grew up during and after the Hitler war and which dealt primarily with *matériel* for the armed forces).[214] A good part of the Haldane report is then taken up with a detailed examination of the various services which fall under these ten headings.[215] Of course this kind of division was not new. Something of the sort had been proposed long before, for instance by Bentham in his *Constitutional Code* and was also presupposed by the various ideas about restricting the size of the Cabinet that were put forward from time to time, as with Disraeli's suggestion of the 1850s.[216] But the questions that arise are two: Is the analysis valid? and, Has it been influential in subsequent administrative reorganization?

Certainly it is not difficult to suggest aspects of the recommendations which are open to criticism. For one thing the committee was fundamentally in error to suppose that the two alternative principles it considered were necessarily exclusive. There are at least two other standards of classification which might be invoked: according to geographical area covered or the work-process employed. There is, in addition, a simpler categorization of a traditional kind that the committee simply ignored: the three classic functions of government (law and order, defence, and external affairs); finance (including not only ways and means but also questions of economic policy, employment, production, trade, and so forth); and a miscellaneous sphere of social services for individual consumption.[217] Secondly, the report was

---

213 Ministry of Reconstruction, *The Business of Government II: the Work of the Departments* (Reconstruction Problems no. 38; London, 1919), pp. 2–3. Cf. the first part of this double pamphlet, *The Business of Government I: the Central Machinery*, p. 4.
214 Machinery of Government, Ministry of Reconstruction Cttee Rep., 1918, Cd. 9230, p. 16 §55.
215 For the question of the number of *departments* envisaged, see the letter of E. N. Gladden in *Public Administration*, xlvii (1969), p. 249; also below pp. 187–90.
216 J. Bentham, 'Constitutional Code', in J. Bowring (ed.), *The Works of Jeremy Bentham* (1838–43; New York, 1962), Book II ch. xi.
217 Mackenzie, loc. cit., p. 79. I have here drawn much on Professor Mackenzie's invaluable analysis.

mistaken in believing that whichever principle it chose could be applied to make a permanent or definitive division of public functions. Politics is simply too volatile for this. The range of government activity has been expanding fast and with a varying emphasis. No detailed allocation of official tasks made a hundred, or fifty, years ago could necessarily be expected to be appropriate now. Departments are always altering or being tinkered with as the by-product of political and ministerial demand, social need, legislative addition, and their own momentum. It would be restrictive to try to confine this process of constant adaptation within the limits laid down by an abstract principle of the Haldane kind. And this is so not least because what constitutes a field or function – such as 'Production' or 'Health' – is itself continually changing in its nature or concrete content, scope, and importance and so cannot be tied down to a formula. Some of the Haldane categories are no longer so significant as they may once have seemed (as with Justice), others have been subsumed under other heads (Research and Information or Supplies), while new ones have emerged ('the Environment' for instance). Thirdly the committee was concerned primarily with administrative efficiency and convenience and paid much too little attention to those considerations which are so crucial at the highest levels of public work and organization.[218] In this context policy questions ramify far and wide and cannot be confined to a particular category: as economic affairs would be bound to cover the fields of finance, production, and employment alike. Fourthly while the allocation of functions according to services rendered to the whole community may make for economical organization and clear lines of administrative responsibility, it is not necessarily advantageous to the public for whom it is more convenient to be dealt with as groups or classes of persons.[219] The rejected principle might, that is, be better from the point of view of the consumer of public services; which suggests that the two principles may not be (as the committee thought) alternatives but rather in some way complementary to one another. Then there is the point that the chosen criterion may in another way be deficient. From a practical point of view it is necessary to consider whether any given service which may be rendered to the community as a whole provides enough, or too much, work for any minister. It seems indeed highly likely that considerations such as this must have been at the back of the minds of the Haldane Committee members because, in effect, they did take account of them. For example, they lumped together responsibilities (such as all those listed under the heading of Production) that, in terms of the given standard, might have stood separately, for each

218 Cf. the comments in Part 2 pp. 754–9.
219 Cf. Mackenzie, loc. cit., p. 81. For instance the Department of Employment and the DHSS deal with matters that may be related and a customer must often be shuttling from one to the other (not to mention the MSC Job Centres).

could be regarded as a distinct service rendered to the whole community. That is, the committee's suggestions were not solely based on the principle they enunciated; and they could not or did not admit this because to do so would have destroyed its cogency. Further, to stress considerations of administrative economy and efficiency is all very well, but again, in practical political life, frictional factors may be more important, matters such as personality, vested interest, tradition, and historical inheritance.[220] These may indeed produce consequences which, though unintended, are nevertheless acceptable or desirable. And it may, therefore, not be a good thing to meddle radically with such a situation in the name of 'scientific' principle. For example, it was one of the major recommendations of the committee – and one in which Haldane himself was especially interested – that the administration of justice and the responsibility for maintaining law and order should be brought under one control. Yet, however attractive in theory, doubts born of observation of what a centralized and efficient Ministry of Justice (or of the Interior) can do with its command of the courts, police, and elections may undermine the appeal of the Haldane proposal. In this country such supervision is diffused in an apparently wasteful way. For example control of the police is shared by the Home Office, the Scottish Office, the Northern Ireland Office, and a number of local bodies. In the same way the administration of justice is divided between the Lord Chancellor, the Home Office, the Lord Chief Justice, the law officers of the Crown, the Director of Public Prosecutions, together with the two organizations of the legal profession, the Inns of Court and the Law Society. In each case, therefore, there is a set of interlocking and countervailing institutions that may look administratively untidy but which is more congenial than an abstractly rational centralization that might have untoward consequences so far as political interference in the judicial and police processes is concerned. The established and traditional may have virtues over the apparently more logical. Government and administration are not simply matters of theoretical reasoning; and inefficiency, which is to be deplored in theory, is 'sometimes to be treasured in practice'.[221] Finally a last point of a similar kind. Departments are going concerns, they exist in their own right, have established ideas and procedures which, collectively, individuals in them probably treasure. When planning a reorganization of administration it is fatal to disregard this, to overlook the perhaps illogical prejudices about alteration which the people concerned may possess. A branch or department may be terribly badly

---

220 For the importance of tradition and experience as embodied in the 'practical philosophy' of a department, cf. Sir E. Bridges, *Portrait of a Profession: the Civil Service Tradition* (Cambridge, 1953), pp. 15–17.
221 Mackenzie, loc. cit., pp. 66–7, 77–8.

organized (or appear to be) yet it may nevertheless have a drive or life of its own which make it quite efficient. To change it may be to upset it so that it may not go as well as before. The general lesson is that dislocation caused by rationalization is not necessarily an improvement or worthwhile for its own sake.

In sum the major defect of the committee's proposal about the allocation of functions was that it was too rigid and over-simple To apply to it the contrast invoked by Professor Finer, it concentrated on 'the rational considerations of business efficiency' and overlooked 'the distorting influences of time, place and circumstance.'[222] In effect it was too intellectual and (in the Oakeshottian sense) rationalist. There is a classic example of the kind of frictional factor that in the practice of administration is so important and which the Haldane Committee tended to dismiss or overlook. The Factory Inspectorate was set up in 1833 and for what were then thought to be good reasons responsibility for it was placed with the Home Office. However, once the Ministry of Labour was set up in 1916, it might have seemed only appropriate to transfer the inspectorate and its functions to the new ministry and attempts were made to do this. But there was considerable opposition, again not without foundation; and the head of the Home Office Industrial Division, Sir Malcolm Delevingne, said in 1918 that 'he was prepared to die on the steps of the Home Office rather than yield one iota of its prerogatives to any upstart department.' And Finer comments: 'It took the dominant personality of Mr. Bevin, the demands of the Second World War, and a row in the Cabinet to wrench the function from the place where history had deposited it.'[223] The balance of ministerial and departmental pressures at any given time is clearly crucial. Similarly the influence of important individuals is always a significant element in the practical determination of these matters. For instance it was not until Lord Bridges retired in 1956 that a (theoretically) desirable division of the office of Permanent Secretary to the Treasury, to allow for specialization and a more manageable burden of work, could take place.[224] Then there is the effect of sectional interest and pressure as with the fight of the British Legion against the abolition of the Ministry of Pensions which was a major reason for the survival of a separate department until 1953. This was in the end an unsuccessful battle but it delayed the change. Another example is the struggle of the road interests to hold up the establishment of a separate Ministry of Transport in 1919 as merely a

---

222 S. E. Finer, 'Central Government Organization', *Political Studies*, v (1957), p. 310.
223 D. N. Chester and F. M. G. Willson, *The Organization of British Central Government 1914–1964* (1957; 2nd edn, London, 1968), p. 82 citing Sir Harold Butler, *Confident Morning* (London, 1950), p. 158; Finer, art. cit., pp. 310–11.
224 Cf. the mid-nineteenth-century example cited in Finer, art. cit., p. 311.

railway ramp. A further, more recent case would be the retention of the Commonwealth and Colonial Offices as separate entities for some time perhaps after their autonomous existence could really be justified. There is, as a result of such factors as these, a sort of vital 'indeterminacy' about administrative organization which is, therefore, to a degree impervious to the promptings of rationalization.[225] In 1946 Lord Bridges said (in somewhat Hegelian terms),

> I think the re-allocation of functions between departments is apt to be made *ad hoc* on particular occasions rather than as a result of a single comprehensive scheme. *Looked at in retrospect I think you can see a pattern in these re-allocations*; I do not think you will get them all worked out and applied at the same time.[226]

The history of the Civil Service since the committee reported would seem to bear out this view. Administrative development has been a series of *ad hoc* adaptations rather than actions in conformity with an independently premeditated principle. There seems to be little evidence that the recommendations were ever observed when administrative change was in view: 'it is surprising' (this is Bridges again) 'how often in the ensuing years the machinery of government has developed on lines different from those proposed'.[227] Of course the report's great virtue was that it inspired people to think in general terms about these matters. And certainly it was not without specific effect. It had some impact on the campaign for a Ministry of Health.[228] And its proposals in respect of research and information were one factor in the establishment in 1925 of the Committee for Civil Research; just as some of its suggestions about the work of the Lord Chancellor have been implemented. There are specific instances of influence even today. For example, appearing before the Expenditure Committee in 1977, E. Heath said that, when he became Prime Minister in 1970, he set out to rationalize the machinery of government and, faced with the two Haldane principles, chose that which based departmental division of labour on general function.[229] And there is the point that the broad division of departmental responsibilities which now obtains does bear a family resemblance to the sort of

---

225 ibid., p. 311; Chester and Willson, op. cit., pp. 390–1.
226 Cited Finer, art. cit., p. 311 (italics in original).
227 Bridges, 'Haldane and the Machinery of Government', loc. cit., p. 262. Cf. Mackenzie's remark that administrative development has proceeded 'largely in defiance of the only theoretical principle we possess, that of the Haldane Committee', loc. cit., p. 79.
228 Wilding, art. cit., pp. 163–4.
229 Expenditure, Sel. Cttee 11th Rep., 1976–7 (vol. xxxi), HC 535-II, p. 760, q. 1868. Cf. the comment of Dr J. Bray, MP, in Treasury and Civil Service, Sel. Cttee Minutes of Evidence, 1979–80, HC 333-iv, p. 81 q. 381.

arrangement proposed by the Haldane Committee. But to observe the similarity is not to suggest that contemporary arrangements have been explicitly based on that model.

Fifty years' march

The Great War inevitably brought in its train pressures for an augmented and strengthened bureaucracy. One instance of this perceived demand (and what it meant for Civil Service organization and purpose) must suffice. In February 1919 Sir Eric Geddes submitted to the Cabinet a memorandum on a proposed Ministry of Ways and Communications. He justified the suggestion in this way:

> One of the changes brought about in our national life by the War is the altered conception of the duties of government. The events of the past four years have shown that a national emergency demands more from Government Departments than the regulatory and restrictive functions which have hitherto been the main feautre [*sic* – feature] of their activities.

Consequently there was a need for 'drastic changes in the methods and functions of Government Departments. The war against Germany is over: the war against the obsolete and inefficient industrial and social conditions is just commencing.' The country expected a positive policy in this regard, a feeling which had, he believed, informed the proceedings and recommendations of the Haldane Committee.[230] And it was his considered opinion that, to meet the wider range of responsibilities in view, a number of new departments and agencies would be needed to deal with such matters as transport, housing, health, electricity supply, and much more.[231] The number of peacetime offices did indeed increase. Such wartime creations as Ministries of Pensions and Labour were continued; a health department was fashioned out of the old Local Government Board in 1919 and, during the same reconstruction period, a transport department and also one to deal with mines were set up. Existing offices grew in size so that by 1930 the number of non-industrial civil servants was nearly double that prevailing before the war.[232] The Civil Service was adapted to deal with these changed circumstances in a number of ways though criticism of its organization and procedures and, above all perhaps, its ethos, was often intense.

In 1919 the National Whitley Council was set up representing all grades of the service which thus acquired an official voice in the

---

230 PRO, CAB 1/28, file 13, pp. 1–2.
231 ibid., pp. 2ff. for details.
232 See Table 4, p. 132 above.

discussion of general questions. The following year the council issued a report on reorganization which accepted the broad division (originally suggested by the Northcote-Trevelyan inquiry) between mechanical and policy work, though it recommended (and the government accepted) that to carry this principle into practice in modern circumstances it would be necessary to employ not less than four categories of official recruited at the appropriate level of the educational ladder and with some provision for inter-grade promotion. These so-called 'Reorganisation Classes' were the writing assistant, clerical, executive, and administrative grades; and each was associated respectively with an elementary or central schooling; the possession of a school certificate (roughly O level); of a higher school certificate (A level); and of a university degree. There should also be a couple of ancillary shorthand typist grades. This proposed structure was introduced by an Order in Council of 1920 and remained the core of the general service hierarchy for half a century.[233] But of course this could not be all. For, as the work of the Civil Service extended, so did its need for specialists of one kind or another with the result that professional, scientific, and technical classes proliferated. As one mark of this increase, in 1921 a service-wide class of scientists and scientific assistants was set up. There were also the numerous departmental classes: many performed clerical duties but there were also large groups of customs and excise officers, tax officials, post-office workers, and the like. In addition there were the minor, messengerial, and industrial classes, numerically a by no means insignificant group. The Home Civil Service had become a large and complex organization indeed.[234] But it was now, more than ever before, a unified organization. This was symbolized by the formal confirmation in 1919 of the then Permanent Secretary to the Treasury, Sir Warren Fisher, as Head of the Civil Service: as he himself said, the necessities of efficient administration compelled departments to think of themselves as 'units of a complete and correlated whole.'[235] Treasury control was also strengthened by the creation there (and in other departments) of an establishments branch which, as it were, complemented the traditional means of supervision on the financial side.[236]

After the post-war arrangements had been in force for a few years, it was thought desirable to see how they had enabled the Civil Service to cope with post-war problems. So in 1929 a royal commission was

---

233 Cf. the summary in The Civil Service, R. Com. Rep., 1930–1 (vol. x), Cmd. 3909, pp. 12–13 §§36–9. The type of work envisaged for each grade is concisely described in J. Garrett, *Managing the Civil Service* (London, 1980), p. 7.
234 Cf. Table 6 pp. 216–17 below.
235 Cited H. J. Laski, *Parliamentary Government in England: a Commentary* (1938; London, 1952), p. 313.
236 The Civil Service, R. Com. Rep., 1930–1, Cmd. 3909, pp. 6–7 §§18–20.

appointed, under the chairmanship of a judge, Lord Tomlin, to review the structure and organization of the service (including methods of recruitment) and to examine as well such specific matters as pay, staff relations, conditions of retirement, and the position of women.[237] The general tone of the report was one of approval for the main principles of structure and the working of the service. It was indeed often, even generally, regarded as a paragon among bureaucracies. H. Finer wrote in 1937 that Britain had, 'taken all in all, the best Civil Service in the world'.[238] Notwithstanding such praise, critical views were frequently expressed. One such line of attack related to the great authority the service had acquired, the impact of which spread widely as government responsibilities were enlarged. Of course it had long been recognized that the political head of a department was bound to be much influenced by his senior advisers and, as well, would have to leave a great deal to them: as Harcourt had put it many years before, the function of the minister is simply to tell his civil servants what the public will not stand.[239] But hostile questions were increasingly asked about a role sometimes deemed malign; and accusations of 'bureaucracy triumphant' and of the emergence of a 'new despotism' were freely levelled in the public arena.[240] This was the characteristic charge of libertarians opposed to the extension of government functions and the bureaucratic intrusion it entailed. From the other side of the ideological spectrum a different sort of detraction was heard which questioned the suitability of the service, in particular its senior officials, to deal with the problems of the positive state. The relatively narrow social and educational background of the people recruited to the administrative class necessarily meant (it was often said) the dominance in the higher reaches of the service of attitudes which were politically partial and inconsistent with the forward-looking policies required by the problems of the day: these officials were incapable even of grasping, let alone dealing with, the technical and managerial difficulties involved. In 1937 Professor W. A. Robson pleaded that the Civil Service Commission should reform its selection procedures and 'devise a series of examination tests which would distinguish the cautious, negative, obstructive type of individual' from the 'positive, constructive, problem-solving, planning type' for the latter was needed much more than ever before.[241] Robson believed, too, that the 'traditional

237 ibid., pp. iii–iv.
238 H. Finer, *The British Civil Service* (London, 1937), p. 196.
239 The notion that ministers had not the capacity to control their growing departments was emerging as early as the mid-nineteenth century: see Sir N. Chester, *The English Administrative System 1780–1870* (Oxford, 1981), p. 366.
240 On these matters, see Part 2, ch. 6.
241 W. A. Robson, 'The Public Service', in his symposium, *The British Civil Servant* (London, 1937), p. 21.

distinction between "administrative" and "professional" work is irrelevant and obsolete in the most important spheres of the public service today.' Neither 'the pure technician' ignorant of the political, economic, and social aspects of his work nor the administrator who has to rely on others to advise him about elementary technical matters is likely to be as effective as necessary 'for the formulation of policy and far-sighted planning'.[242] The collectivist basis of such remarks is obvious. Laski's critical analysis of the character and habits of the service is in similar vein.[243] But the gravamen of the charge against the type of senior civil servant is perhaps best expressed in a pamphlet by Sir Michael Sadler, himself a renowned educational administrator. Most of those occupying the higher positions had, he wrote, come from the old universities, been drilled there in the humanities especially the classics, and had thus been bred in an attitude characterized by what he pejoratively called a 'dessicated humanism', 'Humanism with the sap dried out of it.' The mind of senior officialdom was always negative, critical, and barren, never warm, constructive, or imaginatively adventurous:

> If you read an official file, especially a file on a new project, you will find as a rule that the experienced official is better at telling a subordinate what NOT to do than at interesting him in ways of doing better what is already passably well done, or in encouraging him to conceive bold innovations in existing methods of administration.[244]

There was thus likely to be too little sympathy for the needs of the ordinary citizen; an attitude unfavourable to things technical; and a tendency to oppose planning and state regulation, the redistribution of wealth, and all the other programmes required both by the difficulties of the day and the implications of radical doctrine. Of course many senior officials were inclined to oppose interventionist policies; but equally some were not: in any case opinions and circumstances alike were much affected by economic depression and the Hitler war.[245] Nevertheless few of the criticisms were completely allayed by the experience and were even

242 idem, 'The Public Service Board: General Conclusions', in W. A. Robson (ed.), *Public Enterprise: Developments in Social Ownership and Control in Great Britain* (London, 1937), pp. 375–6.
243 Laski, op. cit., ch. 6. Cf. his introduction to J. P. W. Mallalieu, *'Passed to You, Please': Britain's Red-Tape Machine at War* (London, 1942).
244 Sir M. Sadler, *Modern Art and Revolution* (Day to Day Pamphlets no. 13; London, 1932), Appendix pp. 28–9 (capitals in original). I still recall the critical fervour, even glee, with which Harold Laski waxed eloquent about the defects of the Civil Service mind on the occasion (over forty years ago now) when he lent me his copy of this booklet.
245 For an actual instance of the variety of opinions held about the role of the state by senior officials in the Ministry of Labour, see R. Lowe, 'Bureaucracy Triumphant or

intensified and extended in the days which followed, and with important effect.[246]

During these times the service inevitably continued to expand especially, of course, during the war itself. And as hostilities wore on there was a flurry of detailed inquiries, both official and unofficial, into the problems the public administration would be likely to face during the reconstruction period: recruitment, the numbers required, and the methods to be used; training; reform of the higher echelons and of the Foreign Service; the question of equal pay; departmental structure; and so forth. Obviously no full-scale review by a royal commission was possible in wartime circumstances; nor was there any equivalent of a published Haldane report. A number of official documents did appear, however, dealing with some of the issues involved.[247] Equally the Select Committee on National Expenditure had drawn attention to the need, as it believed, to overhaul the entire machinery of government and on a systematic basis.[248] And in fact during the middle and later stages of the war there was a notable amount of investigation of the problems likely to be faced in the post-war period as with the detailed study of the difficulties of recruitment at a time of both extending official responsibility and a shortage of manpower.[249] But this was simply part of an intensive general review under way behind the scenes.

In April 1942 there was turn-over article in *The Times* on the Haldane report and its lessons.[250] A couple of months later Sir Stafford Cripps (then Lord Privy Seal in the War Cabinet) sent a memorandum to the Prime Minister urging that in view of

> the great extension of the field of Government action and the wide range of difficult problems which will call for solution through the agency of Government during the ten years which follow the conclusion of hostilities it seems most desirable to institute an enquiry into the adequacy of our existing Government machine to deal with the tasks ahead.

Denied? The Expansion of the British Civil Service, 1919–1939', *Public Administration*, lxii (1984), pp. 291–310 esp. pp. 298, 307.
246 See below pp. 197ff.
247 e.g. The Training of Civil Servants, Cttee Rep., 1943–4 (vol. iii), Cmd. 6525; Recruitment to Established Posts in the Civil Service during the Reconstruction Period, 1943–4 (vol. viii), Cmd. 6567; The Scientific Civil Service, 1945–6 (vol. xviii), Cmd. 6679.
248 National Expenditure, Sel. Cttee 16th Rep., 1941–2 (vol. iii), HC 120, pp. 26–7 §§81–2.
249 PRO, CAB 87/74, MG(43)4 (8 April 1943), pp. 1–6. The result was the White Paper mentioned in n. 247 above.
250 'The Administrative Machine: Need for a Concentration of Authority. Lessons of the Haldane Report', *The Times* (27 April 1942), p. 5.

The paper went on to say that the Haldane report, although a classical exposition of the problems with which it deals and of 'outstanding quality', was nearly a quarter of a century old and that, since it appeared,

> there has been an enormous expansion in the normal, as well as in the war-time, field of government activity. Many new problems have arisen. Many new Departments and public institutions have been created. And the range of executive and administrative decisions, especially those affecting economic and social policy, has widened greatly. The present war has in many ways acted as a forcing house of ideas and institutions the validity of which is unlikely to diminish with the end of hostilities. It seems important, therefore, that the principles of the Haldane Committee should be reviewed in the light of twenty-five years' experience and in the view of our anticipations of post-war demands upon the machinery of democracy.[251]

Cripps therefore proposed a new committee on the machinery of government to look into these matters and to be composed of ministers under his own chairmanship.[252] Churchill was at first somewhat diffident and suggested that 'Such academic and philosophical speculations ought, in these times, to be the province of persons of leisure.'[253] But other representations were made and the difficulties were overcome by a Cabinet decision taken in the Prime Minister's absence.[254] Churchill persisted, however, in recording his disapproval. In a minute of 19 October 1942 nominating members of the proposed committee, he insisted that certain principles be borne in mind: war-work must not suffer 'through speculative inquiries'; there must be no change for the sake of it or in the attempt to achieve 'unnatural symmetry'; the organic nature of departments must be remembered as must be the disadvantages of brand-new groupings; and he stressed above all that the inevitable constraints of peacetime politics must be kept in view.[255] So from late 1942 onwards a small group of ministers under Sir John Anderson was supervising an inquiry similar to that of the Haldane Committee during

---

251 PRO, PREM 4/63/2 (487), WP(42) 297 (15 July 1942), originally sent to the Prime Minister on 20 June 1942.
252 Varied suggestions about the membership and terms of reference of the proposed inquiry are to be found in PRO, T222/71.
253 PRO, PREM 4/63/2, C22/2 (27 August 1942), p. 523. Cf. Sir E. Bridges' suggestion of untoward speculative influence by such people as H. Laski and K. Martin, ibid. (26 August 1942), p. 524. Laski was indeed one of those who urged the appointment of a Haldane-type committee: see the correspondence with Churchill in October 1942, PRO, PREM 4/63/2, pp. 497, 501–4.
254 PRO, CAB 65/27, WM(42) 117 (24 August 1942), p. 112 §2.
255 Prime Minister to Bridges (19 October 1942), in PRO, PREM 4/63/2, C22/2, pp. 508–9.

188 A Much Governed Nation

the Great War whose example was thus specifically in view.[256] It was intended, therefore, to review such questions as the general distribution of government functions; the role of 'super' or directing ministers; the composition and size of the Cabinet; and the consequences of these issues for the principle of collective and ministerial responsibility.[257] At its first meeting the ministerial committee set up a parallel group of three senior officials to which it delegated for study and report detailed points such as the role of the Treasury; the functions of the Cabinet Secretariat; the place of scientific research; the collection of statistical and other information; the organization of and recruitment to the Civil Service; regional devolution of central government offices and relations with local authorities; government supplies after the war; and non-departmental organizations.[258] The terms of reference, agreed at the second meeting of the ministerial committee, were 'To consider the machinery of givernment [sic] and to report what changes in the organisation and functions of the Central Executive are desirable to promote efficiency under post-war conditions.'[259]

The two secretaries, T. Padmore and E. C. S. Wade, held a number of meetings to consider 'The Distribution of the Functions of Government' and produced a memorandum for discussion.[260] The Haldane report was taken as the point of departure but found in various respects to be unsatisfactory. The principle of allocating functions according to service rendered was, given a widening range of government responsibilities, thought likely to lead to the creation of more departments than was desirable, 'to dissipate, rather than to concentrate ... the functions of government.'[261] Moreover the Haldane Committee had 'expressly refrained' from exploring the implications of its principle for the membership and structure of the Cabinet, in particular the respective roles of supervising and departmental ministers.[262] However the memorandum accepted that it was in principle possible to apply the Haldane type of classification to the 'more extensive' range of government activity in existence or in prospect; and it gave an example of the sort of grouping that might emerge on this basis, though it departed

---

256 PRO, PREM 4/63/2 (484), extract from WM117(42) (24 August 1942); CAB 87/73, MG(42)1 (12 November 1942), p. 2 §2. The Haldane report was reprinted the following year presumably as an aid to public discussion. I was at the time a sixth-form pupil studying the British Constitution and made to gorge on this heaven-sent manna.
257 PRO, CAB 87/73, MG(42)1 (12 November 1942), p. 3 §4.
258 ibid., p. 2 §3, pp. 3–4 §4.
259 PRO, CAB 87/73, MG(42)2 (9 December 1942), p. 1 §1.
260 PRO, CAB 87/74, MG(42)2 (3 December 1942).
261 ibid., p. 1 §§1, 3.
262 ibid., pp. 1–2 §4.

Table 5 Haldane revised, 1942[a]

Group of Subjects	Minister	Departmental Units
1 Finance or central department	Chancellor of the Exchequer	Treasury
2 External Affairs	Foreign Secretary	Foreign Office Dominions Office Colonial Office India Office Burma Office
3 Defence	Minister of Defence	Admiralty War Office Air Ministry (Economic Warfare) (Information)
4 Home Affairs (Economic)	Minister of National Development	Ministry of Labour Ministry of Health Board of Education Ministry of Planning (separated from Ministry of Works) Ministry of Pensions
5 Home Affairs (Law and Order)	Home Secretary	Home Office Lord Chancellor's Department (administrative functions)
6 Production	President of the Board of Trade	Board of Trade Department of Overseas Trade Ministry of Agriculture and Fisheries Ministry of Fuel and Power
7 Communications		Ministry of Transport (road, rail, sea) Post Office
8 Supply		Ministry of Supply Ministry of Food Ministry of Works (Ministry of Aircraft Production)

a Source: PRO, CAB 87/74 MG(42)2 (3 December 1942), memorandum on 'The Distribution of the Functions of Government and the Role of the Supervising Minister', pp. 2–3.

from the actual headings used by the Haldane Committee and specifically excluded, as not being feasible, the category 'Research and Information' (which Haldane himself and Mrs Webb had regarded as so vital).[263] What was thus in view is indicated in Table 5. But the official paper recognized that the result was rather arbitrary and artificial: some offices had been omitted; the number of subject groups might be varied (as, for instance, by combining groups 6 and 8 or 4 and 5); and the allocation of departmental units among the various headings could be different.[264] The conclusion was that this sort of proposal is unworkable: 'no system which divided groups of Departments into watertight sections would correspond with actual needs.' Some more flexible arrangement was preferable which would enable differently constituted groups of departments to be associated for different purposes. A policy of physical planning, for instance, would cut across the revised Haldane *schema* because it would involve a range of agencies including the Board of Trade and the Ministries of Agriculture, Labour, Transport, and Health, and no doubt others. This suggests, the memorandum concluded, that any 'rigid classification' based on a revision of the Haldane principle should be rejected in favour specifically of the 'fluid grouping' made possible by a system of ministerial committees.[265]

When the ministers concerned reviewed these considerations they accepted the main point, that there were too many problems in adopting the Haldane principles.[266] Once this strategic decision was made, the question of departmental organization fell into place: functions would have to be allocated simply to ensure that a department constituted a reasonably sized unit of administration and that, beyond this, overlap or duplication was avoided.[267] So (as a later review of these matters said) with respect to departmental co-ordination there is a need for 'more effective arrangements . . . for keeping under systematic review the allocation of duties between Departments'.[268] And it was envisaged that the supervisory role in this regard would be played by the Cabinet Secretariat and the Treasury.[269] There was, in addition, provision for continuing ministerial and official scrutiny of the machinery of government to see whether any changes in organization and the

263 ibid., p. 2 §5, p. 3 §9.
264 ibid., p. 3 §§7, 8.
265 ibid., pp. 3–4 §9.
266 PRO, CAB 87/73 MG(42)2 (9 December 1942), p. 2 §3(a).
267 PRO, CAB 87/74 MG(43)3 (12 March 1943).
268 PRO, CAB 87/75 MG(45)16, MGO 74 (June 1945), 'The Centre of the Government Machine', a report by the official committee on the machinery of government, p. 6 §26(a).
269 ibid., pp. 6–7 §§26(a)–(b). Also ministerial consideration of this report, loc. cit., MG(45)10 (18 October 1945), pp. 1–2.

allocation of functions were necessary. In November 1946 the Prime Minister decided that the Machinery of Government Committee should be reconstituted as a standing committee of the Cabinet under the chairmanship of the Lord President of the Council, its terms of reference being 'To keep under review the executive machinery of Government and to deal with such machinery of Government questions as require consideration by Ministers.'[270]

The war ended with the prospect of a considerable permanent increase in the size and duties of the Civil Service. This was a possibility not uncongenial to most of the senior officials of the day who, as compared with their predecessors after the first war, were much more favourably inclined to the idea of interventionist government.[271] The issues of political and administrative organization likely to arise had (as already indicated) been reviewed closely and at a high level; and were also to receive Parliamentary emphasis and support.[272] The major developments in the first two decades after 1945 may be summed up under specific phases or heads of consideration.

First of all there were the various departmental alterations that occurred in order to tidy the organization and adapt it to changing needs. Where prerogative powers were involved, any transfer of duty could be arranged by administrative action simply (as with the removal in 1949 of responsibility for certain African territories from the War Office to the Foreign Office). But otherwise legislation might be required and to avoid the difficulties entailed at a time of considerable Parliamentary pressure, the Ministers of the Crown (Transfer of Functions) Act was passed in 1946 to simplify and facilitate the procedure for non-prerogative departments.[273] This statute made it possible by Order in Council to dissolve a department and transfer its functions elsewhere; also to

---

270 PRO, CAB 134/504 MG(46)15. H. Morrison was then Lord President. The other members were: Chancellor of the Exchequer (Dalton), President of the Board of Trade (Cripps), Minister without Portfolio (Alexander), Home Secretary (Ede), and Secretary of State for Dominion Affairs (Addison). Two files in the PRO are particularly useful guides to developments in the machinery of government in the immediate post-war period: (i) T222/26 covers the working parties set up (1946–8) to consider various aspects of post-war adaptation such as HQ accommodation, recruitment, training, business efficiency, and the like. (ii) PREM 8/1443 deals with proposals put forward from 1949 to 1951 for dealing with such questions as departmental overlap, transfer of functions, abolition, etc.
271 J. M. Lee, 'The British Civil Service and the War Economy. Bureaucratic Conceptions of the "Lessons of History" in 1918 and 1945', *Trans. R. Hist. S.*, xxx (1980), pp. 190, 195.
272 e.g. Estimates, Sel. Cttee 5th Rep., 1946–7 (vol. vi), HC 143, pp. cxliv, 684 q. 1500.
273 9 & 10 Geo. VI, c. 31. A list of all the orders made in the first thirty-eight years of this statute's use is given in the Cabinet Office, *Transfer of Functions Orders, 1946–84: Chronological Table and Index* (London, 1985).

transfer functions between departments or change a department's title. It did not, however, confer any power to create new ministries or functions or to modify any existing statutory duty. But obviously the procedure introduced a new flexibility in the reallocation of functions which was clearly important at a time when the pace of change was increasing. A good many of the modifications were necessary in order to adapt the inflated wartime organization to peacetime purposes. Thus certain offices were continued in some form like information (which is still with us) or food (which lasted only a few years as an independent department); others such as aircraft production or home security were abolished as separate entities and their functions transferred. Some areas of responsibility in particular underwent a prolonged transformation. For instance as a result of constitutional advance in the Commonwealth, the Dominions Office was transformed in 1947 into the Commonwealth Relations Office; and with the grant of independence to India, Pakistan, and Burma, the affairs of the India and Burma Offices were absorbed in the CRO (in respect to India and Pakistan) and the Foreign Office (in respect to Burma which left the Commonwealth). With the further alienations that occurred the Colonial Office declined in relative importance and its rump was merged with the CRO in 1966 which two years later was itself combined with the Foreign Office. The previously separate Foreign, Commonwealth, and Trade Commission Services were amalgamated to form one Diplomatic Service in 1965. The sphere of defence is another example. In 1955 the Ministry of Supply was broken up and its duties transferred, those concerning ordnance, for instance, going to the War Office. And, more significantly, there was the creation of the Ministry of Defence itself in 1946 and the subsequent subordination, albeit very gradual, of the service departments which were, too, increasingly reorganized on functional lines.[274] But there were also numerous changes in the social and economic field as when in 1951 the Ministry of Local Government and Planning was created by combining some of the functions of the Ministry of Health with those of Town and Country Planning; another such instance was the merger of the Ministry of Civil Aviation with Transport two years later. It was all a continuing process with no final or definitive arrangement in the achievement of which further adjustment would be unnecessary. As Lord Wilson reminded us recently, only one thing is certain in this matter and that is that 'whatever is decided will be wrong – it is a choice of evils.'[275]

---

274 Cf. Part 2, pp. 656, 657 below.
275 H. Wilson, *The Governance of Britain* (London, 1976), p. 102. Cf. ibid., pp. 103–4 for some major transfers of function and the considerations involved. For analysis of recent changes, see C. Hood *et al.*, 'Scale Economies and Iron Laws: Mergers and Demergers in Whitehall 1971–1984', *Public Administration*, lxiii (1985), pp. 61–78;

Secondly there was the growth of the many specialist, departmental, and professional classes of civil servant. Up to the beginning of this century, central government (given its relatively limited range of functions) did not need either large numbers or numerous varieties of specialists, most of them then being either lawyers or inspectors. Sir Warren Fisher told the Tomlin Commission in 1930 that the experts were still a relative innovation though, in their evidence, the professionals themselves stressed the range and variety of grades involved.[276] In any event the main changes really came after the last war when a major regrouping of the various specialist hierarchies took place. For example the Scientific Civil Service was created in 1945 by a reorganization of the numerous scientific officers then employed; and in fact central government and its various agencies became the largest employer of science graduates in the country. And it is undoubtedly the case that, in considerable contrast to the position a century ago, government nowadays uses the services, and on a very large scale, of such people as draughtsmen, veterinary surgeons, pharmacists, chemists, forestry officers, agronomists, those technically qualified to serve in the various inspectorates, economists and statisticians, and many more as well as traditional specialists such as doctors, architects, engineers, accountants, and solicitors. This development raises, in fact, a very important general issue: the proper place of the expert in the Civil Service and the problem of how the best technical advice may be obtained and channelled to those, almost certainly not themselves professionally knowledgeable or competent, who have to make the decisions. Traditionally two main devices have been tried to deal with this matter. There was the board system, as in the Post Office or Admiralty, by which the various technical branches of the department or service concerned were directly represented in the senior body. There was, too, the arrangement whereby a special committee was set up to proffer expert advice to the minister, as with the Chiefs of Staff Committee, the Economic Advisory Council, or the Prime Minister's 'Statistical Section' under Professor Lindemann during the last war. The broad issues involved were raised in the fascinating story told (not without a certain moulding of character and plot) by the late Lord Snow in his Godkin lectures on the relation between science and government. He dealt specifically with a couple of crucial wartime questions on which there were opposed technical opinions: the development and use of radiolocation as a defence against

---

also, very fully, C. Pollitt, *Manipulating the Machine: Changing the Pattern of Ministerial Departments, 1960–83* (London, 1984).

276 Cited from G. K. Fry, *Statesmen in Disguise. The Changing Role of the Administrative Class of the British Home Civil Service 1853–1966* (London, 1969), pp. 198–9.

hostile aircraft and the policy of mass area-bombing. Obviously these were vital matters and a great deal depended on the decisions reached, amid much else the allocation of scarce resources and the outcome of major military operations. Snow's recommendation about the lesson to be learned from these cases is that more than one channel of technical advice must be available to the deciding authority.[277] The question is still one of large importance and frequent occurrence in an age when government does so much and faces decisions with a vital technical element. What sort of nuclear reactor (if any) to use in power stations? Should the Concorde project be proceeded with; or the TSR2? Ought the Blue Streak missile to be cancelled; or Britain's strategic nuclear force be re-equipped with the US Trident system? Should all motorways be lit; and should they be constructed with two- or three-lane carriageways? Should the American airborne early-warning system be purchased or a British equivalent developed? These examples make clear that the question is especially important in the extremely expensive field of defence; but it is significant not only there. Of course in the last resort the decision is always political; but a rational determination requires the assessment of complex technical and financial problems. Not least is it telling in this regard that the traditional Civil Service was dominated by the 'cult' of the 'intelligent amateur', something which much exercised the Fulton Committee in the late sixties.[278]

Next there has been considerable development in the regional and local organization of central government departments. But I will say nothing more here as the matter has already been mentioned in another context.[279]

Fourthly there were changes in the field of recruitment. During the war the Barlow Committee had recommended some modification of the usual procedures not least because ex-service candidates would often have had their education interrupted so that the pre-war type of examination was unsuitable. It was decided (as after the Great War) to use a selection process involving a series of tests and interviews (rather like those employed to consider potential officers during the war).[280] Then, in 1948, it was decided to retain a modified version of this reconstruction system (Method II) alongside an improved form of the pre-war competition. Up to 1957 the latter method covered the majority of vacancies, but

---

277 C. P. Snow, *Science and Government* (London, 1961), pp. 66–8. See also idem, *A Postscript to Science and Government* (London, 1962), pp. 5–6, 35–6.
278 See below pp. 199–202, 207–8, 211, 216–17.
279 See above pp. 115–18.
280 Recruitment to Established Posts in the Civil Service during the Reconstruction Period, 1943–4, Cmd. 6567, pp. 8–9, 18–19; Civil Service Commissioners' Report for 1941–9 (Non-Parl.), 1950, pp. 11–12.

subsequently it rapidly became the less important avenue of entry; and in 1963 the two methods were brought closer together, as by a common qualifying examination and similar interviews.[281] None the less the ideal recruit continued to be the 'all-rounder' and the typical successful candidate was still an arts graduate from Oxbridge with a middle-class background.[282] As at the beginning of the century, in the early 1960s over 80 per cent of the successful administrative class candidates fell into this category.[283] This sort of bias led to some criticism; but it proved difficult to widen the area of recruitment.[284] Open competition was still the only rule, therefore; but a full-scale academic type of examination had ceased to be predominant. Even for the general classes, examination has (in the way described) given way to a qualifying test plus interview as a means to detect desirable personal qualities, or to interview alone, as in the case of many specialist posts.

Finally there was more recognition of the need for post-entry training. Between the wars (despite the growing range and complexity of duties involved) there was little attempt to deal with the question beyond (in a few departments) some arrangement for job rotation.[285] But in 1944 the Assheton Committee urged the need for a well-thought-out scheme to aid the induction of administrative grade recruits.[286] The practical response was varied and hardly compared, for instance, with the facilities provided at the Ecole Nationale d'Administration in France. But after further inquiry and exhortation, a Centre for Administrative Studies was set up in 1963 to give a highly intensive training (over four to five months) to young members of the Administrative Class in such subjects as public administration, economics, statistics, and so forth. Even so, this was often regarded as not going far enough.[287] By the mid-1960s, however, it was deemed necessary to review the effects of these developments not least because it was felt that the Civil Service must bear its part of the responsibility for the failures of economic management. How could it be improved and made more effective in this and other respects? The result was the Fulton inquiry of the mid-sixties and subsequent changes.

---

281 Fry, op. cit., p. 85 and n. 4.
282 ibid., pp. 88–9, 91–6, 98.
283 ibid., p. 90 n. 2.
284 For discussion and details, ibid., pp. 87–8 n. 2, 98–110.
285 ibid., pp. 111–12.
286 The Training of Civil Servants, Cttee Rep., 1943–4 (vol. iii), Cmd. 6525, p. 26 §91. Some such development had been suggested before this e.g., National Expenditure, Sel. Cttee, 16th Rep., 1941–2, p. 37 §121.
287 e.g. Fry, op. cit., pp. 147–50. For later developments, see below pp. 211–12, 222–4, 230.

MANAGERIAL EFFICIENCY

> ... the Service has now reached the end of an epoch – an epoch stretching back to the days of the Victorian Liberals, whose attitudes and outlook provided the foundations upon which the Service was built and upon which it still rests. The Committee's task ... is to draw up the outline for a new Service, designed for the very different functions of government in the late twentieth century, for the very different environment in which government now has to operate, and for the very different tools and techniques which it now has at its disposal.
>
> J. H. ROBERTSON, Memorandum no. 143, The Civil Service, Cttee Rep., 1968 (Non-Parl.), vol. 5(2), p. 1025 §4

In a lecture on the contemporary public service (which he gave a couple of years ago) Sir D. Wass, then Permanent Secretary to the Treasury and joint Head of the Civil Service, said that 'If there is a single theme which dominates current political and public interest in the civil service, it is that of efficiency.'[288] In one sense, of course, this is a concern which goes back to the very beginning of the modern service though the precise motives and context of consideration have naturally varied. Nevertheless it is indeed an issue which has moved to the fore over the past couple of decades.[289] And a crucial occasion in this regard was the appointment of the Fulton Committee in 1966, an inquiry intended to help make the Civil Service a more effective instrument for the modernization of Britain and whose report emphasized the need for greater professionalism in public administration. The impetus thus provided seemed to be reinforced by the changes introduced by the Heath government between 1970 and 1974: the new forms of departmental organization, the stress on business efficiency, and so forth, a so-called 'new style of government' which also entailed reform of the local authorities and the NHS. The House of Commons was also becoming more actively concerned in the scrutiny of the government machine as through the developing select committee system. Yet after a while it seemed that in important respects the Civil Service had not changed all that much and that the movement for reform was losing its drive. Then Mrs Thatcher's accession to power in 1979 provided a further impulse with the intention to reduce the scope of government and to make the service remaining more effective in its operation. And an interesting paradox lies here, a contrast not without relevance to the general theme of this book. For whereas the purpose of the Fulton report was to remould the bureaucracy and make it a more serviceable tool of the positive state, the changes latterly under way are of

---

288 Sir D. Wass, 'The Public Service in Modern Society', *Public Administration*, lxi (1983), p. 9.

289 For a fascinating analysis of what is involved in both the undoubted change of emphasis from 'administration' to 'management' and the basic continuities, see N. Johnson, 'Management in Government', in M. J. Earl (ed.), *Perspectives on Management: a Multidisciplinary Analysis* (Oxford, 1983), ch. 7.

rather different intent. These matters are reviewed in this section and the next.

The Fulton inquiry

The investigation undertaken by the Fulton Committee was essentially about the kind of professionalism, qualities, and expertise appropriate to the Civil Service, and especially its senior members, in an age of growing state activity. Its report was said to have created a 'ferment', to be 'an ice-breaker', 'a catalyst' which 'enabled all kinds of ideas to come through.'[290]

Background
The general context of concern was created by the considerable growth in the Civil Service which had occurred as the state extended its functions. In the early 1960s the number of non-industrial staff was over twice as large as it had been thirty years before.[291] During the same period a significant number of new departments had been established especially as a result of the war.[292] And one result of this was a more than proportionate increase in the senior ranks of the home service: in 1929 there were under 300 administrative class officials; by 1950 the total had more than trebled; and in 1968 (the year the Fulton report came out) there were about 2,300 – a more than sevenfold growth in only forty years and one which greatly exceeded the enlargement of the non-industrial Civil Service as a whole.[293] Naturally the expansion brought with it numerous problems which became the basis of an increasing volume of criticism of the capacity of civil servants, especially those in senior positions, and of the arrangements by which their business was conducted. Of course public servants were in general well regarded as being of high ability, zealous, and incorruptible. Labour Party leaders, who at one time were among those most suspicious of possible bias and deliberate hindrance, on the whole emerged from their wartime experience as ministers much impressed with the quality of advice and loyal service which could be expected.[294] In the late 1940s (according to one academic observer who had himself served as a temporary civil servant during the war) British administration 'stood at the peak of reputation.... [It] was easily top of

---

290 The phrases cited are from evidence in Expenditure, Sel. Cttee 11th Rep., 1976–7 (vol. xxxi), HC 535-II, p. 656 q. 1499 (Sir W. Armstrong) and Treasury and Civil Service, Sel. Cttee 1st Rep., 1980–1, HC 54, p. 7 q. 789 (Sir R. Armstrong).
291 See Table 4 p. 132 above.
292 See *The Rise of Collectivism* (London, 1983), Table 4 p. 38.
293 J. H. Robertson, memorandum no. 143, The Civil Service, Cttee Rep., 1968 (Non-Parl.), vol. 5(2), p. 1032 §28.
294 e.g. H. Morrison, *Government and Parliament: a Survey from the Inside* (London, 1954), pp. 334–6; C. R. Attlee, 'Civil Servants, Ministers, Parliament and the Public', *Political Quarterly*, xxv (1954), p. 308.

the league.'[295] And running through the literature of the 1950s there was also 'a thread of unquestioning assurance and self-confidence.'[296] But the mood was undoubtedly changing; scepticism increased and the previously dominant attitude came to seem complacent with the result that in the following decade the volume of critical comment began to grow. The depreciation comprised accusations of various sorts which have continued, indeed, to show a remarkable persistence to the present day. One inevitable concern reflected alarm at the growth of officialdom and about the untoward way its power was sometimes, or often, exercised. This sort of disquiet was obviously akin to the long-standing fear about functionarism and bureaucratic despotism represented by a long line of observers from Spencer and Toulmin Smith to Hewart and Ernest Benn. And in the post-war years any such unease would hardly be assuaged by experience of the many regulations then in existence or by such scandals as the Stanley and Crichel Down affairs, the ground-nuts fiasco or the chalk-pit case, which suggested waste, official tyranny, red tape, maladministration, or worse. The bureaucratic Leviathan might seem often to be beyond effective control, the doctrine of ministerial accountability being in most respects a merely formal façade of little practical moment and serving only to obscure an enlarging sphere of *de facto* official autonomy and influence. In an extreme version of this view Whitehall is even seen to be a kind of conspiracy, dominating the Constitution, overriding (to the frustration of democracy) the authority of ministers and Parliament alike.[297] Beyond this there were (or are) three specific lines of criticism which, though notionally distinct, are often linked with one another and with the general anti-bureaucratic tendency.

The first was a suggestion of social and educational bias in the senior ranks of the service. This view had not been uncommon in some radical circles before the war.[298] And while there had, of course, been important changes since then in both the distribution of wealth and in the school and university system, the argument did not die away being sustained by both independent sociological inquiry, such as R. K. Kelsall's *Higher Civil Servants in Britain* (1955), and official statistical data about candidates for, and recruits to, the administrative class. For the senior grades of the service had largely remained the preserve of the upper and middle ranks of society, those who had been to public school, and arts

295 W. J. M. Mackenzie, 'Does Our Administration Need Reform?', *The Listener* (21 February 1963), p. 320.
296 Wass, art. cit., p. 8.
297 e.g. Expenditure, Sel. Cttee 11th Rep., 1976–7, HC 535-I, draft chapter I, pp. lxxviii-lxxxiii; also ibid., HC 535-II, p. 757 q. 1858 (B. Sedgemore). Cf. A. N. W. Benn, 'Manifestos and Mandarins', in Royal Institute of Public Administration, *Policy and Practice: the Experience of Government* (London, 1980), pp. 66–77 for a review of the means whereby Whitehall gets its way.
298 See above pp. 184–5.

graduates from Oxbridge. The social survey commissioned by the Fulton Committee itself firmly confirmed these characteristics and elicited, in addition, a disquieting tendency for the quality of such candidates to fall (at least as measured by the class of their degree). There was, the survey concluded, 'reasonable ground for questioning the effectiveness of Civil Service recruitment'. Later on, in the mid-seventies, the Commons' Expenditure Committee found the situation unchanged.[299] The thrust of the criticism suggested by these data was twofold. One was that the process of recruitment did not tap the widest possible reservoir of ability, a point conceded (or so it would seem) by the frequent, if unavailing, attempts of the Civil Service Commission to attract a broader range of applicants. The other was that the wrong type of person was being selected for the senior grades of the service. In one respect this was simply (as in the 1930s) to suggest a tendency to political bias, unsympathetic to the needs and policies of the positive state. As one Labour MP later put it,

> the whole training, background and ethos of the Civil Service is such as to develop people who are conservative and who feel that their main responsibility is to make the existing institutions function with as little fuss as possible; and that therefore, in the result, at a very high level the Civil Service is always frustrating radicals....[300]

But altogether apart from this ideological point there were specific comments about the style and competence of the senior official that, in the circumstances of the day, were much more damaging.

One concerned the dominance of the 'generalist' which was discerned by many critics as 'the central fault in the system.'[301] Throughout the history of the modern Civil Service it had been accepted that the leading permanent officials in the departments, the staff primarily responsible (in Northcote-Trevelyan terms) for undertaking 'intellectual' tasks, should be those who had shown their ability in a competing, literary examination or in tests and interviews of a kind to elicit cognate qualities. The result was the creation of a caste of senior civil servants most of whom came from Oxford and Cambridge (mainly in fact from the former) and who had in most cases graduated in arts subjects (mainly in classics and history). The prevailing view was that senior officials should, above all, not be mere specialists or possessed of simply technical

---

299 The data on which these generalizations are based are conveniently summarized in J. Garrett, *Managing the Civil Service* (London, 1980), pp. 15, 29–33. For details see e.g. Expenditure, Sel. Cttee 11th Rep., 1976–7, HC 535-III, Appendix 14 pp. 890–905.
300 Expenditure, Sel. Cttee 11th Rep., 1976–7, HC 535-II, p. 63 q. 59 (B. Sedgemore). Cf. B. Sedgemore, *The Secret Constitution: an Analysis of the Political Establishment* (London, 1980), chs 4–6 and A. N. W. Benn, *Arguments for Democracy* (1981; Penguin, 1982), ch. 3.
301 Garrett, op. cit., p. 36.

skills. Of course experts and professional advisers were necessary but they properly worked in a subordinate capacity. Sir Warren Fisher had told the Tomlin Commission in 1930, 'Let us guard ourselves against the idea that the head of a department should be an expert; he should not be anything of the kind.'[302] The rationale of this view had been succinctly described a century and a half ago by the then Chief Clerk of the Revenue Branch in a memorandum on the qualifications to be sought in those appointed to the Treasury:

> It is easier for a mind of general information to acquire a branch of knowledge which is technical than for a mind which has been confined to one branch to extend itself to a multiplicity of objects. It is not therefore from any technical knowledge, high or low, that I should be desirous of selecting a Clerk for the Treasury, but from those usual general acquirements by which the mental powers are prepared for a more extensive range of information and judgment than is found in a counting house or within the limited circle of mathematical rules: and having in view the higher duties [involved], I should consider it as erroneous to select the Clerks for the Treasury upon the qualifications of mere manual or technical ability....[303]

The virtues of the generalists were invariably acknowledged to be considerable. They possessed (as any reader of official papers in the PRO can confirm) an admirable ability to summarize lucidly both complex chains of events and a complicated array of arguments. They knew how to be detached and objective. They were socially acceptable. Because of their career pattern they acquired a wide experience of policy-making and an acute awareness of ministerial responsibility. This sort of gumption constituted indeed their own particular specialism so that in this sense they are far from being amateurs but are rather highly professional operators in the political environment in which policy is determined and carried out. It is a crucial role. Moreover ministers, being themselves laymen, want to deal with people like themselves, with politically aware, lay minds that have been applied to specialist and technical difficulties. All this establishes a context the importance of which cannot easily be denied.[304] Of course, this is not to say that those with other expertise than theirs cannot, given the right experience, also learn the part concerned: but then they cease to be simply specialists in

---

302 Cited in G. K. Fry, *Statesmen in Disguise. The Changing Role of the Administrative Class of the British Home Civil Service 1853–1966* (London, 1969), p. 57.
303 PRO, T1/4306, T. C. Brooksbank, memorandum, 2 February 1831 cited H. Roseveare, *The Treasury 1660–1870: the Foundations of Control* (London, 1973), p. 199.
304 Cf. P. Self, *Administrative Theories and Politics: an Inquiry into the Structure and Processes of Modern Government* (London, 1972), p. 182; J. E. Powell in J. Grimond et al., *Whitehall and Beyond* (London, 1964), pp. 52–3.

their own fields. However, there was undoubtedly a considerable, and growing, feeling that the dominance of the generalist (for all his strengths) weakened the service in important respects and made it unable to cope with the demands imposed by a collectivist age, the pressures of administering a planned economy and the welfare society, the conduct of an often very technical policy.

In particular – and this was a major line of criticism in its own right – the generalist was not well suited to the managerial role which the demands of a vastly expanded public service increasingly required and tended indeed to place a low valuation on the technical skills involved. Though benevolent, he was, for instance, hardly competent in personnel matters in an age which attached increasing importance to industrial relations; and as a rule he was too little familiar with the ideas and techniques of modern management science. A senior cadre of general administrators was thus quite inappropriate when what was often needed was a more specialized skill than in the past.[305] The entire critical case in this respect was summarized in 1967 as follows:

> The main function of the Civil Service today is management. The administrative class is something of a hangover from the past: splendid men of high intellect, but exclusively recruited from Oxbridge, subject to promotion from the executive class as a secondary source, and devoid of any management training, who find themselves in charge of great machines which they do not know how to control. They are too inbred. Scientists and professionals in the Civil Service are overlooked when it comes to promotion to top jobs; outsiders are practically never let in.[306]

Or, in epigrammatic form: 'In the contemporary Civil Service there can only be players: the gentleman has had his day.'[307]

Efficiency was the main point.[308] The amateur tradition of the service might have been adequate in the days of merely regulatory government; but it was not producing or sufficiently open to the new themes and expertise appropriate to the positive state: specifically it was not achieving the degree of professional competence required to run what was really a series of very large businesses.[309] Ideas about the importance

---

305 Cf. T. A. Smith, memorandum no. 150, in The Civil Service, Cttee Rep., 1968 (Non-Parl.), vol. 5(2), p. 1138 §17, p. 1140 §22, and p. 1147 §48.
306 Sir E. Playfair, 'Improving the Top Echelon of the Civil Service', *The Times* (26 July 1967), p. 9. Playfair had been Permanent Secretary to the Ministry of Defence (1960–1).
307 N. Johnson, memorandum no. 133, The Civil Service, Cttee Rep., 1968 (Non-Parl.), vol. 5(2), p. 973 §100.
308 See the remarks of Lords Fulton and Crowther-Hunt in Expenditure, Sel. Cttee 11th Rep., 1976–7, HC 535-II, p. 466 q. 1046 and p. 472 q. 1050.
309 Cf. Sir J. Dunnett, 'The Civil Service Administrator and the Expert', *Public*

of the managerial role had of course long been creeping in. Courses on management techniques and services had been introduced in 1961: some senior civil servants were thus being inducted into the mysteries of the new administrative technology; and others were taking steps themselves to overcome any deficiency in this regard.[310] But the function of management was still not seen as an essential part of the role of senior officials who tended, therefore, to remain resistant to its lure. It was not so much that they discounted the value of 'the gospel of management ... and its trappings – productivity wall charts, office computers, work study processes, and similar activities', but rather that these things were regarded as being 'largely irrelevant to the tasks of the upper reaches of a government department.'[311]

And these supposed deficiencies were seen as having very serious consequences, as constituting in fact a major reason for Britain's failure to cope with the many difficulties facing it in the age of its decline, in particular those relating to the central management of the economy and to the numerous large and advanced technological projects with which modern government is so often involved. For it follows that if major decisions affecting all aspects of community life are to be taken by government then the role of senior officials must be crucial indeed. But in this fashion the service could be made 'a scapegoat for our real or imaginary ills.'[312] For instance one critic said that the Treasury 'had messed up everything over the past 25 years.'[313] Again P. Shore wrote in 1966 that

> No one can doubt that the poor quality of the official advice tendered to Ministers over the past decade has been one of the major causes of our dismal national record.... [Again] and again, in the post-war period, the wrong official advice has been supplied.... [The] advice tendered to successive Chancellors by the Treasury has been abysmally inept, as Britain's stop–go record so clearly illustrates.
>
> The record of the overseas departments – Colonial, Commonwealth and Foreign Office – has been even worse.[314]

A critical point of view, drawing on these various strands of concern,

---

Administration, xxxix (1961), p. 227. And see below pp. 300–13 for the specific example of O & M.
310 P. D. Nairne, 'Management and the Administrative Class', *Public Administration*, xlii (1964), p. 119; J. Delafons, 'Working in Whitehall: Changes in Public Administration 1952–1982', ibid., lx (1982), p. 261.
311 Nairne, art. cit., pp. 115. Cf. ibid., pp. 121–2.
312 W. A. Robson, 'The Fulton Report on the Civil Service', *Political Quarterly*, xxxix (1968), p. 399.
313 Expenditure, Sel. Cttee 11th Rep., 1976–7, HC 535-I, draft chapter I, p. lxxxi §5.
314 P. Shore, *Entitled to Know* (London, 1966), pp. 12, 153–4.

was frequently expressed in the post-war period. An early and very powerfully argued case was put in H. R. G. Greaves' *The Civil Service in the Changing State* (1947), still perhaps the definitive exposition of many of the issues involved. The problem was also recognized at the official level itself, as in a report produced by one of a series of official working parties set up in 1946 and intended to examine the various problems of adapting the Civil Service to post-war conditions, specifically 'Business Efficiency in Departments'. In the course of preliminary correspondence, O. Franks (then Permanent Secretary to the Ministry of Supply) had argued that the functions of the Civil Service had 'changed from being purely regulative (the functions for which the education and training of Civil Servants are ideally suited)' and had become 'more and more those of management.'[315] The report itself suggested that the pre-war Civil Service was not wholly without experience of direct management work as with that of the Inland Revenue, Customs, Excise, Pensions, and the Post Office, all of which had never been purely regulative in character. The working party continued:

> We agree, however, that Departments are likely to be called upon in future to take a more positive rôle and to show greater initiative than was required of them before the war. Even though actual management may be left to other bodies, Departments may be increasingly responsible for the allocation and distribution of resources. Some large Departments, *e.g.*, the Ministries of Supply, Food and Works, are already discharging functions similar to those of a large business organisation. And, even when the nature of the work remains essentially regulative, Departments now have to undertake positive responsibilities for forecasting, planning and initiating which they were not required to assume before the war. The proportion of Civil Servants engaged in this type of work is much greater than ever before; and the Civil Service must adapt itself to handle the increased volume of this class of business.[316]

The report went on:

> Good management calls for qualities of speed and decision. It is a long standing criticism of the Civil Servant, repeated in the evidence given to us, that he is reluctant to take risks; that there is in every Department, especially at middle levels, a pervading atmosphere of caution and a stifling of initiative. While admitting the arguments for a more deliberate method of working in the public service, our witnesses suggested that the price paid to avoid mistakes was too high. As

315 PRO, T222/26, Organisation of the Civil Service: Working Party no. 4, 'Business Efficiency in Departments', final report (July 1947), p. 3 §7.
316 ibid., p. 3 §8.

Government intervenes increasingly in the day-to-day life of the citizen, the public demand more speed in administration; and our witnesses argued that the Civil Service system is hindering the development of those qualities which would enable more expeditious and businesslike methods to be adopted.[317]

The report then referred to the difficulties entailed by Parliamentary control and ministerial responsibility. And it urged that there was no single cure for departmental deficiencies.[318] But a series of recommendations to improve efficiency – ranging from the selection of 'high flyers' to the enhancement of O & M work – followed.

Concern of the same sort was also expressed in the fifties and sixties in both moderate and intemperate terms, and in a wide range of contexts.[319] The impetus of criticism had, too, been notably reinforced by the report of the Plowden Committee published in 1961. Its primary concern was the control of public expenditure but, as its investigation proceeded, it 'became increasingly conscious of the importance of management' by which was meant such things as:

> the preparation of material on which decisions are taken; the technical efficiency with which large operations of administration are carried out; the cost-consciousness of staff at all levels; the provision of special skills and services (scientific, statistical, accountancy, O & M, etc.) for handling particular problems, and the awareness and effectiveness with which these are used; the training and selection of men and women for posts at each level of responsibility.

'These', it was added, 'are the real substance of management, and it is upon them that the effective control of expenditure and value for money must in the last resort depend.'[320] And the primary responsiblity for management efficiency in each department 'must rest with the Department itself.' And this includes:

---

317 ibid., p. 3 §9. Much of the evidence referred to came from business men who had had experience of the Civil Service during the war.
318 ibid., p. 4 §§10–11.
319 For a miscellaneous collection to hand, see: W. A. Robson (ed.), *The Civil Service in Britain and France* (London, 1956); H. S. Thomas (ed.), *The Establishment* (London, 1959); idem (ed.), *Crisis in the Civil Service* (London, 1968); Fabian Society, *The Administrators: the Reform of the Civil Service* (Fabian tract no. 355; London, 1964), a report which shared much common ground in assessment and recommendation with that of the Fulton Committee; D. Hurd, *An End to Promises: Sketch of a Government 1970–74* (London, 1979), pp. 117–18; M. Nicholson, *The System: the Misgovernment of Modern Britain* (London, 1967), pp. 464, 470. See also G. K. Fry, 'The Attack on the Civil Service and the Response of the Insiders', *Parliamentary Affairs*, xxxvii (1984), pp. 353–63.
320 Control of Public Expenditure, Cttee Rep., 1960–1 (vol. xxi), Cmnd. 1432, p. 16 §44.

the organisation of the work; the scrutiny of new departmental policies to ensure that the staff implications are fully taken into account when policy is decided; the detection and removal of deficiencies in management; the critical review of the Department's existing activities, particularly those which are static or declining; and so through the whole gamut of management.[321]

The staff involved should be of high quality; and it was important that the Permanent Secretary should devote a considerable amount of personal time and attention to problems of management as well as to policy advice and finance. 'His responsibilities to ensure that approved policies are carried out economically and that his Department is staffed as efficiently as possible for this purpose seem to us no less important than his responsibility for advising his Minister on major issues of policy.'[322] The very establishment of the Plowden inquiry and the nature of its recommendations (which were widely reported) were, if only by implication, critical of existing procedures. Four years later the Select Committee on Estimates expressed concern that the Civil Service's recruitment arrangements had not been adapted to the changes which had occurred in the country's educational system such as the great increase in the supply of graduates; and it recommended a full inquiry.[323] Criticism often achieved quite substantial penetration, as with the series of radio interviews subsequently published under the title *Whitehall and Beyond* (1964). Add to this a change in the political climate. In 1964 the Labour Party had returned to office after long years in opposition and was in a more than usually intense crusading mood. Wilson had campaigned on a programme offering a white-hot technological revolution: modernization, it was said, had become 'the national theme of the 1960s.'[324] The impetus was still strong two years later when the Labour manifesto stressed the need to undertake a thorough reorganization of 'obsolescent institutions', including 'the whole machinery of the state'.[325] The Augean stables of the Civil Service were clearly to be swept clean by this reforming flood; and the initiation of the Fulton inquiry early in 1966 was a vital part of the operation.

The committee
The Fulton Committee was given the task of examining 'the structure,

321 ibid., p. 16 §46.
322 ibid., p. 16 §47.
323 Estimates, Sel. Cttee 6th Rep., 1964–5 (vol. vi), HC 308, pp. xxxii–xxxiii §§101–9.
324 N. Hunt, 'Foreword', J. Grimond *et al.*, *Whitehall and Beyond*, p. 9. Dr Hunt (later Lord Crowther-Hunt) became a member of the Fulton Committee and subsequently a Labour minister.
325 F. W. S. Craig (ed.), *British General Election Manifestos 1918–1966* (Chichester, 1970), p. 267.

recruitment and management, including training, of the Home Civil Service, and to make recommendations.'[326] These terms of reference deliberately excluded machinery of government questions about the number and size of departments and so forth.[327] When announcing the decision to set up the committee the Prime Minister said it had been reached because there 'have been so many changes both in the demands placed on the Civil Service and in the educational organization of the country that the Government believe that the time has come to ensure that the Service is properly equipped for its rôle in the modern State.'[328] The committee itself re-affirmed the context of its deliberations at the very beginning of its report. 'The Home Civil Service today', it said, 'is still fundamentally the product of the nineteenth-century philosophy of the Northcote-Trevelyan Report. The tasks it faces are those of the second half of the twentieth century. This is what we have found; it is what we seek to remedy.'[329] As the Civil Service developed on the old basis, there had emerged the tradition of the 'all-rounder' in the senior grades supported by non-graduates to do executive and clerical work and by specialists of various kinds in some departments.[330] And although the service had become much larger, more complex, and sophisticated in many ways, nevertheless the basic principles and attitudes of a hundred years ago still prevailed and the essential features of a century-old structure remained intact.[331] Yet circumstances have altered radically as the report indicates in a classic summary of collectivist growth:

> the role of government has greatly changed. Its traditional regulatory functions have multiplied in size and greatly broadened in scope. It has taken on vast new responsibilities. It is expected to achieve such general economic aims as full employment, a satisfactory rate of growth, stable prices and a healthy balance of payments. Through these and other policies ... it profoundly influences the output, costs and profitability of industry generally in both the home and overseas markets. Through nationalisation it more directly controls a number of basic industries. It has responsibilities for the location of industry and for town and country planning. It engages in research and development both for civil and military purposes. It provides

---

[326] The Civil Service, Cttee Rep., 1967–8 (vol. xviii), Cmnd. 3638, vol. i, p. 2. (In the rest of this section all unattributed references are to this volume of the Fulton report.)
[327] Appendix A p. 107 §6. However the committee did touch, rather obscurely, on Haldane-type matters such as the principles which should govern the grouping of departments, pp. 18–20 §§42–8.
[328] 724 H. C. Deb. 5s., 8 February 1966, col. 209.
[329] p. 9 §1.
[330] p. 9 §§3–4.
[331] pp. 9–10 §§5–6.

comprehensive social services and is now expected to promote the fullest possible development of individual human potential. All these changes have made for a massive growth in public expenditure. Public spending means public control. A century ago the tasks of government were mainly passive and regulatory. Now they amount to a much more active and positive engagement in our affairs.[332]

And there are numerous aspects of this change which, in addition to the sheer size of the responsibility involved, have made the tasks of officials more complicated and difficult. Technological advance has lengthened the time-scale required to reach a decision and carry it out, as with the introduction of a weapons system in defence, a choice between different sources of fuel in respect of energy policy, or a decision about forms of transport. And it is not simply that Parliament and the public expect greater initiative, foresight, and control in these matters, it is also that this sort of problems compels 'civil servants to use new techniques of analysis, management and co-ordination which are beyond those not specially trained in them.' In addition it is necessary to bear in mind the involvement of government in the notable range of 'para-state organisations' that has grown up and, as well, in the activities of local authorities.[333] The assessment of the committee is bluntly frank:

> In our view the structure and practices of the Service have not kept up with the changing tasks. The defects we have found can nearly all be attributed to this. We have found no instance where reform has run ahead too rapidly. So, today, the Service is in need of fundamental change.

In particular the committee discerned six main respects in which the Civil Service was 'inadequate . . . for the most efficient discharge of the present and prospective responsibilities of government.'[334]

The first is the emphasis on the philosophy of the amateur or all-rounder on which the service was still essentially based, a concept most evident in the administrative class but also to be observed in the executive and even some of the specialist classes.

---

332 p. 10 §7.
333 p. 10 §§8–10, 12.
334 p. 11 §14. Professor Lord Simey expressed reservation about these views because he felt they were unfair to the Civil Service and failed fully to recognize its many achievements, qualities, and adaptability, in particular that its contemporary characteristics were the result of modern (rather than nineteenth-century) developments. He rejected, therefore, the notion that revolutionary change was required while conceding that many improvements were possible and desirable. The task is not one of 'the total reconstruction of an obsolete institution' but of reform which is 'discriminating', pp. 101–3.

The ideal administrator is still too often seen as the gifted layman who, moving frequently from job to job within the Service, can take a practical view of any problem, irrespective of its subject-matter, in the light of his knowledge and experience of the government machine. Today . . . this concept has most damaging consequences. It cannot make for the efficient despatch of public business when key men rarely stay in one job longer that two or three years before being moved to some other post, often in a very different area of government activity.

This 'cult of the generalist' was 'obsolete at all levels and in all parts of the Service.'[335] Secondly the existing system of classes 'seriously impedes' the work of the service. It was divided horizontally (between higher and lower grades in the same broad area of work) and vertically (between different skills or professions). The non-industrial staff (and excluding the Post Office) comprised 47 general classes and over 1,400 departmental classes. As each civil servant was recruited to a particular class with its own pay scales, career structure, and range of jobs, there had grown up a 'prolific compartmentalism' that, despite some movement between classes, was excessively rigid. This arrangement was cumbersome in that it 'seriously hampers the Service in adapting itself to new tasks, prevents the best use of individual talent, contributes to the inequality of promotion prospects, causes frustration and resentment, and impedes the entry into wider management of those well fitted for it.'[336] Thirdly many scientists and others in the specialist classes, being organized in a separate parallel hierarchy, found 'their access to higher management and policy-making' was restricted even though they might have the necessary qualities for such tasks. In 'the new Civil Service' which the committee had in view, 'a wider and more important role must be opened up for specialists trained and equipped for it' as with the French *polytechnicien*.[337] Related to this was the next point of criticism (which applied in particular to the administrative class) that 'too few civil servants are skilled managers' recognizing a responsibility for such things as 'organisation, directing staff, planning the progress of work, setting standards of attainment and measuring results, reviewing procedures and quantifying different courses of action.' One major reason for this deficiency was that there was no adequate training in these matters; another was the tendency to think in terms not of managing the administrative machine but rather of giving advice on policy to

---

335 p. 11 §15. Cf. the similar comments of Lord Crowther-Hunt in his memorandum to the Commons Select Committee on Expenditure, 11th Rep., 1976–7, HC 535-III, Appendix 48 esp. pp. 1096–9; also in Treasury and Civil Service, Sel. Cttee 1st Rep., 1980–1, HC 54, p. 47 q. 987.
336 pp. 11–12 §16.
337 p. 12 §17.

In Dark Wonder 209

ministers.[338] A specific aspect of this kind of shortcoming to which the committee made particular reference was the failure to tackle questions of personnel management. There was too little of it in the service and what there was was 'not sufficiently purposive or properly conceived'. Civil servants were moved too frequently between unrelated jobs often with scant regard to personal aptitude or preference; in addition there was not enough encouragement and reward for individual initiative and achievement and (especially in the lower grades) promotion depended too much on seniority.[339] Finally the committee held that there was 'not enough contact between the Service and the rest of the community' leading to inadequate awareness of how 'the world outside Whitehall' works and how government will affect it, of the new ideas and methods afoot in business, the universities, and so forth. This was the reflection of two factors. One was the isolation of the civil servant who usually spent his entire life in a service career; the other was 'the social and educational composition' of the service which, especially in the administrative class, had been too exclusive.[340] For all such imperfections the committee believed the Treasury must accept a notable responsibility; though it conceded that the urgent need for fundamental reform was to some extent obscured 'by the Service's very considerable strengths'.[341] Undoubtedly much could be learned in this regard from the virtues of foreign systems of administration.[342] In concluding this critical analysis the committee urged the need for basic change resting on a single guiding principle, one which in fact 'applies to any organisation and is simple to the point of banality': though a great deal of the trouble derived from its not being observed.

> The principle is: look at the job first. The Civil Service must continuously review the tasks it is called upon to perform and the possible ways in which it might perform them; it should then think out what new skills and kinds of men are needed, and how those men can be found, trained and deployed.[343]

It was without doubt a powerfully presented indictment and provided a firm foundation on which to build detailed recommendations for reform. The parallel with the Northcote-Trevelyan report a century before is striking and, one assumes, deliberately contrived. Both documents are brief and crisp in style and analysis. Both concentrate on the aspects of the service open to criticism and overlook (or notably

338 p. 12 §18.
339 p. 13 §20.
340 pp. 12–13 §19.
341 p. 13 §§21–2.
342 p. 13 §23; Appendix C pp. 132–49.
343 p. 13 §24.

underplay) the virtues of the existing arrangements. Just as the mid-nineteenth-century reformers singled out for attack the corruption and inefficiency of the day and tended to ignore the very high calibre of many officials, so did their successors concentrate their criticism on 'the cult of the generalist' and related matters and pass over lightly the achievements of the recent past. And, in respect of reform, just as the earlier document stressed the need for open competitive examination, promotion by merit, and the division into 'intellectual' and 'mechanical' labour, so the new proposals emphasize the need, above all, for job evaluation and managerial professionalism. And each ignores the degree to which what they want was already being attained. There are even quite detailed similarities as with the mutual concern over officials confined to routine work below their capacity or the adulation of what are taken to be the key and forward-looking aspects of contemporary business or other outside practice whether this be in terms of open recruitment or efficient management. And if the proposals of the Northcote-Trevelyan report (stressing competition, open choice, and self-help in the context of a less expensive public service) were manifestly compatible with the libertarian ethos of its own time, it is equally apparent that the Fulton report reflected the collectivist attitude of the present day (by emphasizing the necessity for the professional skills of management and control on the assumption that there would be a very wide and costly range of government functions indeed to be carried out and large departments to administer them).[344]

In the context of this critical framework the Fulton Committee urged that what was needed today was a genuinely professional Civil Service fully equipped to tackle all the problems of our time.[345] The terms 'professional' and 'professionalism' are indeed watchwords reflective of the key principles and proposals the committee had in view.[346] There was first of all professionalism in the sense of an acquired specialist or technical skill, as with doctors, architects, engineers, draughtsmen, statisticians, and so forth (for some obscure reason the committee put economists on a par with these experts). Of course the Civil Service has long employed large numbers of such specialists, though it has not always recognized the need for them quickly enough or for high quality: this is particularly true, for instance, of the failure to enlarge the scope for modern management accounting. Nor has the service allowed its specialists to carry the higher responsibilities of administration, to the public disadvantage, leaving the top financial and policy aspects of a department's work to the generalist. But secondly there is another kind of

344 See e.g., p. 15 §28, pp. 21–22 §§51–2.
345 p. 16 §31.
346 p. 16 §§31–2.

professionalism the committee had in mind. This is the skill appropriate to the senior administrator himself.[347] Too often he moves so frequently from job to job that he never acquires 'adequate knowledge in depth' of any one aspect of a department's work or even of its general area of responsibility; and he will often be faced with subjects he does not fully grasp. This can only lead to inefficiency, or worse. Consequently the committee believed it was necessary to ensure that the administrator was so selected, trained, and deployed that he did have or could acquire the appropriate expertise.[348] Thus it should be ensured that the general skills of an administrator are complemented by specialist training, experience, and knowledge in one of the two broad areas in which departmental work falls: economic, industrial, and financial; or social.[349] The principle is 'that those engaged in administration and management must not only be skilled in running the government machine, but must also have the basic concepts and knowledge relevant to their area of administration.'[350] This, broadly, is the 'pattern of professionalism' the committee proposed for the future.[351]

> From all these professionals, administrators and specialists alike, will come the future top management of the Service. They will be men and women experienced in running the government machine; they will have a basic expertise in one or more aspects of a department's work; and they will have been broadened by increasing responsibilities and experience to become the fully professional advisers of Ministers and managers of their policies.[352]

It is the cameralist dream of the Webbs stalking the land again.[353]

It followed, given this sort of objective, that new and appropriate methods of recruiting, training, and career management would have to be devised. In future, the report said, persons

> should not be recruited for employment as 'generalist' administrators and intelligent all-rounders – to do any of, and a succession of, the widely differing jobs covered by the 'generalist' concept. Instead, they should be recruited to do a specified range of jobs in a particular area of work, at any rate during their early years.

The service should thus aim to recruit people with 'the best qualifications, aptitudes and qualities' relevant to one of the two broad

---

347 pp. 16–18 §§35–8.
348 p. 18 §§39–41.
349 pp. 19–23 §§45–58.
350 p. 22 §55.
351 p. 23 §58.
352 p. 23 §57.
353 See *The Ideological Heritage* (London, 1983), ch. 11 esp. pp. 359–64, 381ff.

categories of administration.[354] (In this context a majority of the committee believed that preference should be given to those with a 'relevant' academic background while a minority argued a different view.)[355] What was, it was thought, clear was that the practical, managerial qualities required in the higher levels of the service 'are not necessarily identified with success in a written degree examination taken many years before or, indeed, by any selection method for testing young people in the late 'teens or early twenties.'[356] It followed, therefore, that training had to be much enhanced and a Civil Service College created to this end.[357] Job allocation and promotion procedures had similarly to be refined.[358] Equally movement in and out of the service should be facilitated by temporary secondments, regular interchanges of staff, short-term appointments from outside, late entry, and other such devices.[359]

Another major plank in the committee's programme of reform was the improvement of the work and structure of departments so as to increase efficiency, and a number of recommendations was made to this end. It was proposed, for instance, that executive activities should be organized in such a way that 'the principles of accountable management' can be applied which involves measuring, so far as possible, the performance of individuals and units and holding them responsible for the results achieved.[360] Again the service was urged 'to devise the right machinery for ensuring that each department keeps its organisation up to date, conducts a regular audit of its efficiency, and constantly applies the best available methods and techniques to its tasks.'[361] Partly this might be done by the use of outside consultants but also through the development of 'central management services'. However the main spur must come from the individual department itself as by an upgrading and

---

[354] p. 27 §74. Specifically it was proposed that the departments should take a much more active and important part in the recruitment process; and that the Civil Service Commission should be absorbed within the suggested Civil Service Department, pp. 24–5 §§63–7, p. 27 §73.
[355] The two points of view are stated at pp. 28–30 §§76–80.
[356] p. 66 §206.
[357] pp. 35–40 §§97–114.
[358] pp. 40–2 §§115–22.
[359] pp. 43–6 §§124–33. The plea that there should be more 'regular infusions, temporary and permanent, of highly motivated people of proven ability into the higher Civil Service' continues to be made: see Treasury and Civil Service, Sel. Cttee 7th Rep., 1985–6, HC 92-I, p. xxii §§5.16–5.18. The government response was sympathetic (not least, no doubt, because of its critical attitude towards the existing service): see Civil Servants and Ministers: Duties and Responsibilities, 1985–6, Cmnd. 9841, p. 7 §§26–8.
[360] pp. 51–4 §§149–62.
[361] p. 54 §163.

enhancement of its O & M work and through the establishment of 'a management services unit' to promote the use of the best techniques.[362] The committee also proposed that the machinery for policy planning and research in departments should be improved so that, in the press of immediate business, long-term needs and problems were not overlooked.[363] For this sort of purpose one or more 'planning units', not too detached from the everyday work, should be set up in each department. Such a unit's task 'should be to identify and study the problems and needs of the future and the possible means to meet them; it should also ... see that day-to-day policy decisions are taken with as full a recognition as possible of their likely implications for the future.'[364] The committee also thought there was room for change in the top departmental structure so that overall control could be improved. It accepted that, as at present, there should be one person, the permanent secretary, who is responsible to the minister for the smooth working of the departmental machine. But as head of the office he has a very considerable burden of work ranging from policy advice and ultimate responsibility (as accounting officer) for all departmental expenditure, to managing day-to-day operations and questions of staff and organization; and no official head of department could be equally skilled at all aspects of his job.[365] The committee therefore suggested that the permanent secretary should be supported by a senior policy adviser, as head of the planning unit, who would have 'direct and unrestricted access' to the minister to advise on longer-term policy and its implications for everyday business.[366] In some departments there might also be need for another top post to direct technical work and act as professional head of the specialist staff, a chief scientist or engineer for instance.[367] It was not intended that these senior officers should constitute a formal board; the working arrangements should be informal and vary from one department to another (as appropriate, for instance, to the minister's way of working).[368]

There was one other, most crucial aspect to the committee's proposals to improve the organization and working of the Civil Service. This concerned the grading structure, changes in which were seen as necessary to make the other reforms effective.[369] The existing arrangements,

362 pp. 54–7 §§163–70. For the story of O & M in the Civil Service, see below pp. 300–13.
363 p. 57 §172.
364 p. 57 §173.
365 pp. 58–9 §§178–80, pp. 60–1 §187.
366 pp. 59–60 §§182–4.
367 p. 60 §185.
368 p. 60 §186.
369 p. 63 §192.

basically the product of the Northcote-Trevelyan report, had become most complex as a result of the expansion of the public service and the extension of its tasks.[370] And they presented serious obstacles to the most flexible use of staff; led to the inefficient organization of work; prevented the most efficient matching of people to jobs; and impeded application of the principles of accountable management.[371] The problem was particularly acute where there was little or no discernible difference in content between work done at the lower level of one class and the upper levels of the one below. The existing structure stood, indeed, 'in the way of... the only efficient method of matching men to jobs' and should be abolished.[372] It was held, therefore, that all classes should be replaced by a single, unified grading structure covering all non-industrial civil servants with an appropriate number of pay levels matching different degrees of skill and responsibility and with the correct grading for each post determined by job evaluation.[373] This would promote more effective management of work; it would ease the creation of 'an open road to the top of the Service for all kinds of talent' making it possible, too, for suitable specialists to take part in policy-making and management.[374] The distinction between higher and lower classes should go, therefore, as should the traditional arrangement that certain posts are the preserve of a particular group.

There were also crucial recommendations concerning the 'central management' of the Service, and hinging on the creation of a new Civil Service Department. Because of their significance, these matters are reviewed separately in a later part of this section.[375]

Of course there was criticism of these proposals, the main thrust of which was nicely exemplified by the comments of N. Johnson.[376] He accepted that the report's 'breezy radicalism' and its 'abrasive and rather undiscriminating' view of the Service well reflected much contemporary opinion, as did the confident optimism it displayed about the likely success of the reforms in view. Some of the committee's diagnosis rested on merely fashionable depreciation the limitations of which would soon be recognized: this was, for instance, surely the case with much of the attack on the generalist and the alleged neglect of managerial techniques.

370 See above p. 193; also Fulton report, pp. 64–6 §§199–205.
371 Ch. 6 *passim* esp. pp. 66–9 §§206–13.
372 p. 63 §§192–3.
373 p. 63 §192, pp. 104–5 §6.
374 p. 64 §§197–8. In fact in 1939 20 per cent of the administrative class had been promoted from below, a proportion that had doubled by 1965; see Fry, *Statesmen in Disguise*, pp. 166, 171.
375 See below pp. 225–36.
376 For what follows, see N. Johnson, 'Editorial: Reforming the Bureaucracy', *Public Administration*, xlvi (1968), pp. 367–74.

As well some of the recommendations (like those concerning the better use of specialist staff, integrated administrative units, or quicker recruitment procedures) simply confirmed developments already under way. 'The hard core of innovation proposed is really quite small.'[377] And even in regard to this there should be doubts: about the likely effectiveness of the proposed Civil Service Department, for instance, or whether the unified grading structure envisaged might not prove in some respects too rigid. Basically the inquiry had proceeded in too piecemeal a fashion, had too little appreciated the complexities and subtleties of the service, and had not related its specific points of emphasis – such as job analysis, professionalism, and accountable management, each of which was undoubtedly important – into a general framework for the scrutiny of public administration. So far as there was an overall philosophy it was that provided by a 'managerial model'; yet this could never be exclusive and must often be inadequate.[378] It might be added that the committee seems simply to have assumed that society should continue to be as dominated by public regulation as it currently was or even that this control should be, or was likely to be, intensified.

And for all the furore the committee aroused, now that its work and proposals can be looked at in a reasonable perspective, it seems appropriate to say (some two decades later) that its long-term effect has been, or will prove to be, rather less than its supporters hoped for. It achieved only what one commentator, himself an official, called a 'pseudo-revolution'.[379]

Flow and ebb

The anticipations aroused by the committee's report were not slight or few. As one, admittedly unsympathetic, observer put it (somewhat sarcastically), the feeling was in the air that

> here was a chance to drag this stuffy Victorian civil service ... into the twentieth century. Surely, it was argued, many of our difficulties and failures must be attributable to this antiquated bureaucracy of ours, insensitive to the changing demands of our much-governed society and led by dilettante mandarins with a taste for Greek verse or Baroque music. How much better we shall be governed by thrustful managers such as are said to abound in the business-oriented Federal

---

377 ibid., pp. 367–8.
378 ibid., pp. 371–3.
379 C. H. Sisson, 'The Civil Service – 1: After Fulton, the Pseudo-Revolution', *The Spectator* (20 February 1971), p. 250. Cf. N. Johnson, 'Management in Government', loc. cit., p. 175.

Table 6 The structure of the non-industrial Civil Service, 1912–85[a]

class 1912[b]	number (000s)	class 1936	number (000s)	class 1966	number (000s)	class/group 1985	number (000s)
administrative and clerical		administrative	1.9	administrative	3.6	open structure	6.24
higher administrative and class I	0.6	executive	17.6	executive	80.6	general category[c]	224.73
intermediate	1.3	clerical and sub-clerical	87.4	clerical and clerical assistant	205.6	secretarial category	24.81
second division	3.9	typing	11.3	typing	25.5	science category	13.52
assistant clerks	2.7	inspectorate	2.9	inspectorate	2.8	professional and technology category and related grades	34.34
boy clerks	2.8	professional, scientific, and technical	8.3	professional, scientific, and technical	79.2		
women and girl clerks	0.5	ancillary technical, etc.	14.5	ancillary technical, etc.	52.3	social security category	48.94
typists	0.6	minor and manipulative	143.3	minor and manipulative	210.4	general service classes[d]	25.31
departmental customs and excise	6.0	messengers, porters, etc.	15.2	messengers, porters, etc.	28.4	departmental classes[e]	65.75
patent office	0.3					other categories[f]	19.43
labour exchanges, and national and health insurance	2.9						
inland revenue	n.a.						
post office	n.a.						

professional and technical engineers, surveyors, chemists, etc.	n.a.			
temporary and unestablished mainly messengers, doorkeepers, porters, charwomen, etc.	25.0			
Total	—[g]	302.4	688.4	463.07[h]

[a] Sources: for 1912, 1st, 2nd, and 4th Reports (and Appendices) of the MacDonnell Commission on the Civil Service, 1912–14; for 1936 and 1966, CSO, *Annual Abstract of Statistics*; and for 1985, HM Treasury, *Civil Service Statistics 1985* (London, 1985), pp. 20–5.

[b] The information available is scanty and incomplete and some of the figures cited are only approximations; as well, the existing official nomenclature was often 'wanting in precision', The Civil Service, R. Com. 4th Rep., 1914 (vol. xvi), Cd. 7338, p. 126 §14.

[c] Includes the following groups: administration, economist, information officer, librarian, and statistician.

[d] The most numerous of these classes (comprising some 60 per cent of the whole) are the messengers, photoprinters, and draughtsmen. The remainder range from actuaries and cleaners to psychologists and telephonists.

[e] Mainly various inland revenue grades (constituting 63 per cent of all these classes) and prison officers (27 per cent). The remaining 10 per cent include, among others, customs and excise officers, driving and traffic examiners, factory inspectors, and court bailiffs.

[f] Under this miscellaneous heading (which is not an official classification) I include the following categories/groups: security officers, data processors, training and instructional officers, legal staff, museums staff, police, and research officers.

[g] The total for 1911, as given in an official return, is 135,721: see 1911 (vol. l), HC 210. The inland revenue staff is there given as 2,669 and that of the post office as 99,355.

[h] The total for all non-industrial grades is given in the official table as 496.78, the discrepancy being due to timing differences and to the fact that the grade coverage is not comprehensive: see HM Treasury, op. cit., pp. 20–1 and n. 3. The fall since 1966 is due both to reductions and to the deletion of the Post Office staff when it became a public corporation in 1969.

218 A Much Governed Nation

bureaucracy of the U.S.A., or by the intellectual supermen from the E.N.A. and the Ecole Polytechnique.[380]

When the report appeared its main recommendations were formally accepted by the government the day it was published.[381] There had been some controversy among ministers however: the Chancellor of the Exchequer (R. Jenkins) was one who, naturally perhaps, opposed complete endorsement; while R. H. S. Crossman, the Secretary of State for Social Services, thought the report was 'second-rate', being 'written in a very poor style by Norman Hunt.' Hunt and the Prime Minister (Crossman went on to record in his diary) 'are tremendous buddies who live in the same world of uninspired commonsense. The Report is perfectly sensible but, oh dear, it lacks distinction.' But the press and much of the political public would like it; the Prime Minister needed a success and wanted to improve 'his image as a great modernizer'; so the Cabinet authorized his statement to the House of Commons.[382] And, as he put it later, in consultation with the staff associations 'the successive reforms went through smoothly and rapidly.'[383] However the report itself was a short and somewhat general document being content, in large part, with a rather bald statement of principles and objectives. So a preliminary stage of extensive exploration, fact-finding, and pre-planning was necessary.[384] By the spring of 1970 these investigative preliminaries – undertaken by a National Whitley Council Joint Committee – were over; but obviously the task of completing in detail the comprehensive job analysis required by Fulton would be a long one.[385] What happened in the aftermath of the report may be exemplified in respect of various of the proposals made.[386]

The first relates to the position of the generalist civil servant whom the

380 Johnson, 'Editorial: Reforming the Bureaucracy', loc. cit., p. 367.
381 767 H.C. Deb. 5s, 26 June 1968, col. 455.
382 R. H. S. Crossman, *The Diaries of a Cabinet Minister* (London, 1975–7), iii. 98, 101–2, 103, 107.
383 H. Wilson, *The Labour Government 1964–70: a Personal Record* (1971; Penguin, 1974), p. 683.
384 R. W. L. Wilding, 'The Post-Fulton Programme: Strategy and Tactics', *Public Administration*, xlviii (1970), pp. 399–401.
385 ibid., p. 402; Sir W. Armstrong, 'The Fulton Report 1. The Tasks of the Civil Service', ibid., xlvii (1969), pp. 2, 3, 9. The first report of the National Whitley Council Joint Committee (the Armstrong Committee as it was called) appeared in February 1969. Other reports were produced on various aspects of the post-Fulton changes until the committee was wound up in 1973.
386 For a detailed review of the changes introduced, see the CSD paper on 'The Response to the Fulton Report' in Expenditure, Sel. Cttee 11th Rep., 1976–7 (vol. xxxi), HC 535-II, pp. 1–49.

Fulton Committee had described as 'obsolete'.[387] Yet as one recently retired senior official put it 'in 1982, the generalist is still alive and flourishing.'[388] And the reason is simple: it is that the general administrator is useful to the political system within which he operates; essentially he assists his minister to serve Parliament and reflects the qualities that are necessary to do this.[389] But it may still be that administrators should have a more specialized experience or some of them at least be drawn from other forms of employment. It may also be the case that professional staff are given too subordinate a role. One critic noted that 'it is extraordinarily unusual for an accountant, or an engineer, or a scientist to get into top general management.'[390] Here the committee's recommendations about the reorganization of structure were seen as a crucial step to unify the service, make it more flexible, and specifically open up senior administrative posts to able and experienced officials with a professional or technical background (as well as to raise their grading and status). But in some respects this goal is still a long way from achievement. From 1971 onwards a series of mergers took place to reduce formal barriers between the different classes of official and to facilitate promotion by merit within the larger groups created. Something of the changes so far wrought is shown in Table 6 (which also gives an indication of the increase in the size and variety of the major classes that has occurred since the Great War). Clearly, however, what has in this way been achieved is far from the unified grading system envisaged in the Fulton report. This has only been approached in the so-called Open Structure embracing the highest ranks of the service (down to the old senior principal grade or its equivalent).[391] The name derived from the intention that promotion within this select band should be open to eligible persons from all groups regardless of their background, discipline, profession, or previous duties. It was hoped that by means of this arrangement the problem of blending, at top level, a variety of people with different skills and experience would be well on the way to solution.[392] By January 1985 the Open Structure comprised 6,243 posts at

---

387 See above p. 203.
388 Sir K. Clucas, 'Parliament and the Civil Service', in RIPA, *Parliament and the Executive* (London, 1982), p. 28.
389 ibid., pp. 27–9.
390 J. Garrett, memorandum, in Treasury and Civil Service, Sel. Cttee 3rd Rep., 1981–2, HC 236-III, Appendix 4 p. 46 §9. Cf. ibid., p. 47 §14.
391 Cf. Sir G. Wardale et al., *Chain of Command Review: the Open Structure* (CSD; London, 1981), p. 4 §2.1–2.3; HM Treasury, *Civil Service Statistics 1985*, p. 10.
392 Sir R. Clarke, *New Trends in Government* (Civil Service College Studies no. 1; London, 1971), pp. 26–7. For some later doubts about the rate of change, see e.g. Expenditure, Sel. Cttee 11th Rep., 1976–7, HC 535-II, p. 468 q. 1046 (Lord Fulton); and cf. ibid., p. 21 §111, p. 327 q. 847. See also Treasury and Civil Service, Sel. Cttee 3rd Rep., 1981–2, HC 236-I, p. xxxvi §89; HC 236-II, p. 75 qq. 321–4.

the summit of the Civil Service hierarchy (some 1.3 per cent of its total non-industrial manpower) though many of these positions are of a senior professional nature and not necessarily concerned with policy or management.[393] However, one specific instance of the implementation of the intended new principle was the appointment in 1976 as permanent head of the Department of Education and Science of a scientist and engineer who had previously served at the Royal Aircraft Establishment, Farnborough. A single swallow never makes a summer of course; but on the other hand it has lately been claimed that nowadays problems are always handled by a mixed team of generalists and specialists. 'I know of no case in recent years', one senior official wrote, 'in which the specialist has been denied access to Ministers or where he has not played a full part in the formulation of advice on policy.'[394] Certainly Sir James Dunnett (himself a former permanent secretary at the Ministry of Defence and a member of the Fulton Committee) believed that this integration at the top of the service was 'the best thing' the report achieved.[395] Yet while the Fulton goal has been approached at this senior level, albeit partially, otherwise there is still only a series of separate parallel hierarchies, simplified it is true but still a good way from the unity the committee had in mind. Even if there are some opportunities for 'lateral transfer' between the new groups and categories, the very concept of such movement (together with the existence of special 'opportunity posts') tends rather to imply a continuing division of the service. As the Institution of Professional Civil Servants once complained, 'The fact of the matter is that there has been very little change since Fulton reported.... There are still parallel hierarchies instead of integrated hierarchies.'[396] Moreover the dominance of an élite of the more or less traditional type continues as the matter of recruitment indicates.

This was one of the questions explored by the Commons' Expenditure Committee in its post-Fulton inquest. The data it obtained seemed to sustain the usual strictures about the dominance in the fast-stream entry of persons from the two older universities and who had been to independent or grammar schools (though this sort of partiality apparently did not appear in the appointment of executive officers or their departmental equivalents).[397] For instance in 1982 about three-

---

393 Cf. Wardale, *et al.*, op. cit., p. 4 §§2.1–2.2 and Garrett, *Managing the Civil Service*, pp. 45, 47.
394 Clucas, loc. cit., p. 33.
395 Sir J. Dunnett, 'The Civil Service: Seven Years after Fulton', *Public Administration*, liv (1976), pp. 374–5.
396 Expenditure, Sel. Cttee 11th Rep., 1976–7, HC 535-II, p. 327 qq. 846–7. Cf. ibid., p. 331 q. 866 and p. 335 q. 891.
397 For the relevant data, see Expenditure, Sel. Cttee 11th Rep., 1976–7 (vol. xxxi), HC 535-I, pp. xviii–xx; and the detailed Tables 1–11 in the Civil Service Commission

quarters of the candidates successful at the final selection board for administration trainee were Oxbridge arts graduates.[398] The continuing nature of the bias is pretty clear though it might be at least partially mitigated if seen in the appropriate context. Thus a preponderance of successful candidates from Oxbridge may in part be accounted for by the fact that all schools (including the comprehensives) tend to encourage their brighter pupils in that direction so that if the Civil Service is to select the ablest people it will inevitably tend to favour recruits from those two universities. There is also the point that those who incline to government service as a career will, if they can, go there for their higher education simply because of the tradition of Civil Service entry and the encouragement they receive. The two tendencies reinforce one another. Moreover many of those who go to Oxbridge will have the advantage of having taken an extra year in the sixth form or after leaving school before going up to university and so will have one more year of development behind them at every stage up to competing for admission as administrative trainees.[399] As to the subject bias, although efforts had been made to increase the flow of recruits from those with scientific and technological qualifications, relatively little success was achieved; and undoubtedly a major difficulty here is that, for instance, good engineers simply want to stay in the practical field to which they are dedicated and not to become administrative civil servants: only the not-so-good ones apply.[400] Of course, none of this mitigates the preponderance of public school success, though perhaps too little weight is given to the way that nowadays many of these institutions draw on a wider clientele than used to be the case not so long ago. The committee made a series of proposals: that extensive statistical data should be kept and published about the educational background of applicants so that there might be greater understanding of any bias at work and so the possibility of overcoming it;

---

memorandum, ibid., HC 535-II, pp. 230–40. See also the note on the 'Educational Background of Administration Trainees', HC 535-III, Appendix 14 pp. 890–905. There is a trenchant analysis of these matters by Lord Crowther-Hunt in HC 535-III, pp. 1090–5. For the difference between administration trainees and executive officers, see Tables 13–19, HC 535-II, pp. 242–5 and p. 474 q. 1058.

398 Sir A. Atkinson, *Selection of Fast-Stream Graduate Entrants*... (MPO; London, 1983), p. 42 §94.

399 Cf. Sir L. Pliatzky, 'Mandarins, Ministers and the Management of Britain', *Political Quarterly*, lv (1984), p. 24.

400 On this specific point, see Expenditure, Sel. Cttee 12th Rep., 1977–8 (vol. xxxiv), HC 576, pp. 23–4 q. 97; Sir J. Dunnett, 'The Civil Service Administrator and the Expert', *Public Administration*, xxxix (1961), p. 230. Cf. K. Gillender and R. Mair, 'Generalist Administrators and Professional Engineers: Some Developments since the Fulton Report', *Public Administration*, lviii (1980), pp. 333–56 which suggests the picture concerning the position of specialists may not be so bad as the Fulton report suggested.

that the Civil Service Commission and its selection boards should be widened to include more outsiders and a wider variety of them; also that the method of selection be reassessed and changed.[401] In the outcome the government accepted most of these suggestions though it was still accused of wanting to perpetuate 'the mandarin caste' so strongly criticized by Fulton.[402] Critics continue to stress the need to improve the efficiency of the service by ensuring it is headed by a cadre of 'technically qualified, numerate managers'.[403] One way would be to improve the field of recruitment by attracting a wider range of candidates, a matter which (we are assured) is still of great official concern.[404] Another means, more radical, would be to recruit from outside, as with Sir John Hoskyns' proposal, though this idea is not without difficulties and might seem to entail the re-introduction of an element of patronage.[405] Alternatively it is simply important to emphasize the need for relevant training and experience if the generalists, who still dominate the higher echelons of the service, are to be managerially competent and if specialists of outstanding ability are to be prepared for administrative tasks of greater responsibility.

The main proposal made in this regard by the Fulton Committee was for the establishment of a Civil Service College which was seen as a vital means of introducing a higher level of managerial professionalism into the service.[406] This institution was created in 1970 to take over, develop, and complement the considerable amount of in-service training which was already provided by the Treasury Centre for Administrative Studies (which dated from 1963) and other agencies which existed.[407] The college had in practice to provide for a variety of forms of training: initial courses

401 Expenditure, Sel. Cttee 11th Rep., 1976–7, HC 535-I, pp. xx–xxi §§13–15. The system of selection which has now replaced the older type of examination is described in Atkinson, op. cit., esp. Annex 2.
402 See the government observations on the report, 1977–8 (vol. xxxvii), Cmnd. 7117, pp. 4–5. For the criticism mentioned, see Expenditure, Sel. Cttee 12th Rep., 1977–8, HC 576, p. 3 q. 4.
403 J. Garrett, memorandum, in Treasury and Civil Service, Sel. Cttee 3rd Rep., 1981–2, HC 236-III, Appendix 4 p. 46 §9.
404 Atkinson, op. cit., pp. 7–10 §§21–8, pp. 41–3 §§90–6.
405 See e.g. Sir J. Hoskyns, 'Conservatism Is Not Enough', *Political Quarterly*, lv (1984), p. 15. For the difficulties, see Sir D. Wass, 'The Public Service in Modern Society', *Public Administration*, lxi (1983), p. 13, and Pliatzky, art. cit., p. 25. On this question of outside recruitment, see also Treasury and Civil Service, Sel. Cttee 1st Rep., 1980–1, HC 54, p. 40 q. 953, pp. 41–2 q. 958, p. 95 q. 1157.
406 pp. 36–40 §§99–114. The idea was not new and had, for instance, been suggested during the war by Attlee: see PRO, CAB 87/74, MG(42)6 (31 December 1942), pp. 1–2 §1. But in late 1945, as Prime Minister, he seemed not especially interested in having the topic pursued: see PRO, PREM 8/17. It had also been proposed in 1967 by a Treasury Working Party on Management Training in the Civil Service: see Fry, op. cit., p. 152.
407 On the pre-Fulton arrangements, see B. C. Smith, 'The Development of Central

In Dark Wonder 223

for graduate entrants, both generalist and specialist, and for executive officers; in-service training for experienced officials (assistant secretaries and above); instruction in specific administrative skills at middle management level; and, as well, the many courses and seminars of a 'staff college' sort provided for senior civil servants.[408] It was also intended to have a research function. It constituted, no doubt, an increase in the overall level of training activity. But there was a lot of criticism about, for example, the often poor quality of the teaching, the over-academic nature of some of the courses, a lack of coherence in the various programmes, coupled with an insufficiently clear definition of its role and objectives. In addition there were difficulties in recruiting the academic staff, confusion about the line of responsibility between the administrators and the teachers, untoward effects from expenditure cuts, a lack of involvement in the life and work of the service, and (on the other hand) too little support from the departments which, even after the college was well established, still provided for themselves most of the training their staff needed.[409] It was doubtful, in particular, whether the arrangements to afford training and experience in administration for promising scientific and professional officers were satisfactory.[410] The college's poor record was probably due at least in part to the fact that it was (as it were) wished on the service by the government as an element of its response to the Fulton report; and there was little belief in its long-term aims or value.[411] Certainly the broader Fulton purposes were not achieved: in no way did the college become the power-house of a reformed service, teaching the new style of management, carrying out relevant research, and spreading fresh ideas broadcast.[412] Instead it came to be seen as a failure; the Expenditure Committee, for instance, regarded it as a 'major disappointment' and proposed that its work be cut back to allow concentration on training senior administrators in higher

---

Training in the Civil Service', in R. A. W. Rhodes (ed.), *Training in the Civil Service* (London, 1977), p. 30; D. Keeling, 'The Development of Central Training in the Civil Service 1963–70', *Public Administration*, xlix (1971), pp. 51–71; also E. Grebenik, 'The Civil Service College: the First Year', ibid., l (1972), pp. 127–8.

408 Grebenik, art. cit., pp. 130, 138. See also detailed survey and evaluation in Smith, loc. cit., pp. 31–9 and in E. J. Razzell, 'Recent Changes at the Civil Service College', in Rhodes, op. cit., pp. 50–61.

409 Treasury and Civil Service, Sel. Cttee 1st Rep., 1980–1, HC 54, p. 19 q. 851; Fry, op. cit., p. 152.

410 For this litany of defects, see Garrett, op. cit., pp. 37–8; C. Painter, 'The Civil Service: Post-Fulton Malaise', *Public Administration*, liii (1975), p. 433; and R. N. Heaton and Sir L. Williams, *Report on Civil Service Training* (CSD, 1974).

411 Garrett, op. cit., p. 40. Cf. the interesting essay by Professor Self, 'The Purposes of Civil Service Training', in Rhodes, op. cit., esp. pp. 19–23.

412 e.g. Garrett, op. cit., p. 37; Expenditure, Sel. Cttee 11th Rep., 1976–7, HC 535-II, pp. 750–1 qq. 1827–8.

management. Certainly recent trends at the college involve more such courses, and more to train 'technological generalists' and to develop skills in financial management.[413]

Above all perhaps there loomed the question of management on which the achievement of economy and efficiency alike were said to depend. It involved a whole range of tasks and issues such as

> the preparation of the material on which decisions are taken; the technical efficiency with which large administrative operations are carried out; the cost-consciousness of staff at all levels; the provision of special skills and services (scientific, statistical, accountancy, O & M, etc.) for handling particular problems; and the training and selection of staff.[414]

Part of the Fulton diatribe was (as recapitulated by J. Garrett, a Labour MP who was on the Expenditure Committee) that 'too few Civil Servants were skilled managers' and that not enough senior members of the administrative group saw themselves in this role for which, in any case, they received no training.[415] Sir K. Clucas agreed that the 'areas in which ... the service has most failed to develop specialist skills are to be found in ... managerial and service functions', of which dealing with personnel is a major instance.[416] This was not only a major deficiency in itself; it was also bound to hinder a number of the Fulton recommendations among them the introduction of 'accountable units' over a wide range of departmental duties. The idea was that this work should be organized in separate 'commands' the manager of each being given clear-cut responsibility for its operation and adequate authority for the task. He would be held accountable for the results achieved by his unit within the framework of the overall objectives laid down. Of course there were numerous difficulties in this prospect not least that arising from the convention of ministerial responsibility and the danger of politicizing the officials in charge who might find themselves publicly called to account.[417] But obviously a great deal would depend on the managerial capacity which could be tapped for the purpose of establishing successful

---

413 Expenditure, Sel. Cttee 11th Rep., 1976–7, HC 535-I, ch. III esp. §§20–1; N. Johnson, memorandum, HC 535-III, Appendix 18 pp. 932–4. For later reaction to this prospect of concentrating on mid-career training, see Cmnd. 7117, loc. cit., ch. III; Expenditure, Sel. Cttee 12th Rep., 1977–8, HC 576, pp. 3–5 qq. 5–9; and Treasury and Civil Service, Sel. Cttee 3rd Rep., 1981–2, HC 236-II, p. 491 q. 1329, p. 494 q. 1349, and p. 495 qq. 1354–5.
414 Treasury note on 'The Responsibilities of an Accounting Officer', Expenditure, Sel. Cttee 12th Rep., 1977–8, HC 576, p. 36.
415 J. Garrett, memorandum, Expenditure, Sel. Cttee 11th Rep., 1976–7, HC 535-III, Appendix 1 p. 841 §1(iv).
416 Clucas, loc. cit., p. 33.
417 Cf. Wass, art. cit., pp. 10, 12.

accountable units. In any event the Expenditure Committee believed there had been too little determined effort to implement the Fulton recommendations in this regard not least in the failure to train the professional personnel necessary to operate the units.[418]

Parallel with this sort of criticism was another about long-term policy planning within the general framework of which any accountable units would have to operate. In many respects the whole theme is an interesting confirmation of the collectivist tendencies involved. Fulton had emphasized the importance of such planning and of the need to have responsibility for it clearly defined and allocated to special planning units each mainly staffed by experts and headed by a senior policy adviser to take the lead in forward thinking. There was also the need for some means of central direction and co-ordination which was partly met by the establishment of the CPRS.[419] Yet there seems to have been no move to create departmental units of the kind envisaged, largely (it might be inferred) because it would create a source of ministerial advice not under the control of the permanent secretary.[420] Lord Crowther-Hunt in particular stressed that 'the underlying assumption' in Fulton was 'a much more positive concept of planning', one that did not react simply to existing trends and demands.[421]

But the failure of the Fulton proposals is best reflected in the story of the central innovation proposed: the establishment of a Civil Service Department to oversee the process by which the Service was to be made professionally competent in a collectivist age which was placing more and more demands on it.

The rise and demise of the CSD

Traditionally the Treasury and its ministers (including the Prime Minister) were responsible for the central management of the Civil Service as well as for financial and economic affairs: for all such matters were obviously closely related.[422] But the Fulton report urged that the former role should be detached from the Treasury and enhanced.[423] This

---

418 Expenditure, Sel. Cttee 11th Rep., 1976–7, HC 535-I, pp. xlvi–xlvii §§93–4. Cf. ibid., HC 535-II, pp. 828–30 qq. 2073–80, p. 834 qq. 2104–7; also its response to the government observations (Cmnd. 7117, p. 14 §§48–9) in its 12th Rep., 1977–8, HC 576, pp. 11–12 qq. 35–8.
419 Cf. the review of these points by Lord Crowther-Hunt, Expenditure, Sel. Cttee 11th Rep., 1976–7, HC 535-III, pp. 1100–2.
420 ibid., pp. 1102–3, 1111. For detailed criticism of the existing planning machinery in the DES, see ibid., pp. 1116–23.
421 ibid., p. 1119.
422 The development and functions of the Treasury are reviewed in ch. 4 below.
423 The Civil Service, Cttee Rep., 1967–8, Cmnd. 3638, ch. 7. Cf. the review of the arguments for and against in 'Central Management of the Civil Service',

separation was seen as a means of improving the effectiveness of this function (by a focusing of attention and appropriate special recruitment of staff) and of removing it from a context of financial 'meanness' (Sir Douglas Allen's word). The move would also, it was thought, prevent the concentration of too much power in one department the size and scope of which prevented sufficient ministerial attention being given to Civil Service matters.[424]

The idea was by no means a new one.[425] The possibility of a separate department to deal with questions of establishments and organization had frequently been considered as by the Bradbury Committee, the Tomlin Commission, and (during the last war) the Select Committee on National Expenditure.[426] And the proposal was certainly not incompatible with the distinction, increasingly clearly recognized in the organization of the Treasury itself, between work relating to establishments on the one hand and to supply on the other.[427] It would be only one more step, though a radical one, to create two separate departments for these discrete purposes. But any such proposal was usually rejected on the ground that it would entail discord and duplication, and consequently waste, and because the achievement of efficiency was deemed in the last resort to be closely bound up with questions of financial control and economy.[428] When Lord Bridges came to write his 'New Whitehall' volume on the Treasury he expressed the conventional view:

> to take the management side out of the Treasury and to make it into a separate department... would have been a false step and would have greatly weakened the effectiveness of both the management and the financial functions. After all, the Treasury is the central department of government. You cannot have two centres.... To have hived off management into a separate department would have been inconsistent with the essential feature of British organization whereby in every Department of State the responsibility for advice to the Minister on policy, finance and administration rests in the same pair of hands.

---

memorandum no. 14, The Civil Service, Cttee Rep., 1968 (Non-Parl.), vol. 5(1), pp. 97–102.
424 Expenditure, Sel. Cttee 11th Rep., 1976–7, HC 535-II, p. 56 q. 33, p. 746 q. 1817.
425 Cf. M. V. Hawtin and J. K. Moore, *The Integration of HM Treasury and the Civil Service Department: a Report of the Study Team* (CSD; London, 1980), Annex 1.
426 The Organisation and Staffing of Government Offices, Cttee Final Rep., 1919 (vol. xi), Cmd. 62, p. 5 §18; The Civil Service, R. Com. Rep., 1930–1 (vol. x), Cmd. 3909, p. 170 §588, p. 171 §590; National Expenditure, Sel. Cttee 16th Rep., 1941–2 (vol. iii), HC 120, p. 22 §68, pp. 31–2 §§98–102.
427 Cf. Hawtin and Moore, op. cit., Annex 1 p. 15 §40.
428 Though for one favourable consideration (by a PEP study group), see J. M. Lee, *Reviewing the Machinery of Government: 1942–1952. An Essay on the Anderson Committee and its Successors* (n.p. [London], 1977), p. 17.

Moreover, it would inevitably have led to administration being treated as something different from, and less important than, finance.[429]

Nevertheless one of Bridges' successors at the head of the Treasury was prepared to concede that radical change of this kind was not necessarily unthinkable.[430] It was certainly urged in other quarters.[431] Then, as the pressure for reform mounted, in November 1966 the Head of the Home Civil Service presented to the Fulton Committee a memorandum expressing the collective official view about the central management of the Civil Service, the paper having been prepared in consultation with the permanent secretaries of all departments. The existing range of Treasury responsibilities was described and its dual relationship to the Prime Minister and Chancellor of the Exchequer. The arguments for and against the idea of a separate Civil Service Department were reviewed and the conclusion reached that it could be done if it was so decided. But, the paper added, it might look a bigger change than it really was and give rise to expectations that, in the outcome, would not be met.[432] These were prescient words. However the Fulton report proposed that the Treasury should be split and the government decided to accept the recommendation. It did so for three reasons.[433] One was the wish to enhance central management without enlarging the Treasury which was already overburdened. The second was that the expertise to deal with management questions was quite different from that required to cope with financial and economic problems. The last rested on the view that the officials concerned with improving standards of management and training should be able to take an independent line and indeed 'to fight the Treasury' itself. Basically it was felt (with the Fulton Committee) that the Treasury 'had not given sufficient emphasis to the development of management techniques'; and there was generally a lack of 'confidence in the Treasury's willingness to undertake the management of the government's direct employees with the enthusiasm and single mindedness that was considered necessary to induce departments to participate in the overall pursuit of efficiency.'[434]

---

429 Lord Bridges, *The Treasury* (1964; 2nd edn, London, 1966), pp. 203–4. For a similar view, see Sir R. Clarke, *New Trends in Government*, pp. 57ff.
430 See the evidence of Sir L. Helsby in Estimates, Sel. Cttee 6th Rep., 1964–5 (vol. vi), HC 308, p. 167 q. 837.
431 e.g. Fabian Society, *The Administrators* (Fabian tract no. 355; London, 1964), pp. 9, 32–6.
432 'Central Management of the Civil Service', memorandum no. 14, The Civil Service, Cttee Rep., 1968, loc. cit., p. 102 §28.
433 For this explanation, see the evidence of Sir D. Allen (at the time Permanent Secretary to the CSD and Head of the Home Civil Service) in Expenditure, Sel. Cttee 11th Rep., 1976–7 (vol. xxxi), HC 535-II, p. 822 q. 2040.
434 Hawtin and Moore, op. cit., Annex 1 p. 18 §45.

The new Civil Service Department was set up on 1 November 1968. The pay and management divisions of the Treasury were removed from their parent office to form the new department, to which the Civil Service Commission was also attached. The ministerial arrangement was that, under the Prime Minister, the Paymaster-General would have day-to-day responsibility.[435] The first permanent secretary was Sir W. Armstrong who was already Head of the Civil Service, a conjuncture which helped give the CSD a status it might otherwise have lacked.[436] The initial purpose of the CSD was to implement a detailed programme of reform based, though not slavishly, on the Fulton proposals: to manage officials and organize their work in such a way as to make the service 'a more effective, economical and humane instrument of Government.'[437] The key responsibility was for Civil Service manpower and its effective use, its recruitment, training, and deployment. Once appointed an official is the employee of a department, so the CSD's role was to see that the departments handled their staff in the best way and to provide advice to this end about management services, specialized equipment, and so forth. It was also involved (with the Treasury) in organizational reviews.[438] One token of the department's earnest intentions and its wish to get out of the conventional service mould, was the appointment of a team of business men headed by Sir R. Meyjes to examine possible developments in the field of management; and in mid-1970 it was reported that numerous investigations were under way among them being studies of procurement policy, computer utilization, the use of manpower resources, and management research.[439] As time wore on various new tasks added to the size and complexity of the department, the burden being augmented by such factors as the growth of a more active trade unionism in the Civil Service, advances in recruitment and training techniques, the development of computers, and the pressure for more purposeful and effectively monitored reviews of departmental operations.[440]

Sir J. Dunnett has recorded that more than one civil servant said to him that, whatever else the Fulton Committee had suggested, it justified itself

---

435 *KCA* (1967–8), p. 22988A.
436 Cf. J. M. Lee, 'Editorial: Epitaph for the CSD', *Public Administration*, lx (1982), p. 4; Garrett, op. cit., p. 18. But cf. ibid., pp. 44–5.
437 Wilding, art. cit., p. 391.
438 Treasury and Civil Service, Sel. Cttee 3rd Rep., 1981–2, HC 236-II, pp. 29–30 q. 157 (Lord Croham). For a comprehensive statement of the role and functions of the CSD shortly before its abolition, see Sir I. Bancroft's memorandum, ibid., pp. 174–85; also Hawtin and Moore, op. cit., Working Paper 1 and Annex 2.
439 R. Jones, 'Towards a Businesslike Government', *The Times* (3 August 1970), p. 19.
440 Details are given in Expenditure, Sel. Cttee 11th Rep., 1976–7, HC 535-III, Appendix 38 p. 1021 §3. Cf. ibid., Appendix 8 pp. 869–70; and HC 535-II, pp. 2, 49–50. See also Treasury and Civil Service, Sel. Cttee 1st Rep., 1980–1, HC 54, Appendix 1 p. 109 §5.

by this one recommendation to establish a Civil Service Department.[441] But, inevitably perhaps, the high expectations born of the zeal of the early days were frustrated and the impetus tailed off or was deliberately curtailed.[442] There was disappointment in some quarters; for many observers – Lord Crowther-Hunt was one – the vexation was considerable. In his view the department had been set up 'as a sort of battering ram of change, to make the Civil Service as a whole more professional and more efficient'; and it clearly failed to have any lasting effect of this kind. The staff (though almost entirely from the Treasury) never really matched the Fulton specification in numbers, experience, rank, or professional expertise. Nor did they have sufficiently powerful or interested political masters. In addition to lacking weight – there was nothing like the old 'mystery' of the Treasury working in its behalf – the department had too limited a conception of its role, failing to see its duty to act as 'the spearhead of the Whitehall drive for departmental efficiency.' It failed to set about rigorously reviewing the whole organization, structure, and staffing of the departments and to ensure that its own organization was adequate for this purpose.[443] Indeed in place of the integrated service originally envisaged there seemed to emerge 'a drift towards a less unified and more agency-oriented civil service'.[444] As well the CSD was not popular with departments being perhaps associated with delay, caution, and weakness in co-ordination.[445] Nor did they depend on it even for training facilities which they largely provided for themselves. Of course the practical restraints were considerable. What was attempted had to be acceptable politically and to public (or interested) opinion; and it had to be negotiated with staff associations and other departments. The resources available were limited and the CSD could not anticipate that demands for extra manpower or money would necessarily be met in order to achieve any changes in view.[446] One opinion of it all was that the Fulton recommendation to establish the CSD was a mistake, a 'particularly

---

441 Dunnett, art. cit., p. 373.
442 Cf. Expenditure, Sel. Cttee 11th Rep., 1976–7, HC 535-II, p. 788 q. 1931 (H. Wilson); Treasury and Civil Service, Sel. Cttee 1st Rep., 1980–1, HC 54, pp. viii–ix §§7–9, p. 1 q. 770, p. 21 qq. 867–9, pp. 91–2 q. 1152, p. 94 q. 1153. On the diversion of the permanent secretary's attention to other matters and the lack of ministerial weight, see Lee, art. cit., pp. 5–6.
443 Expenditure, Sel. Cttee 11th Rep., 1976–7, HC 535-III, pp. 1104–6, 1107; ibid., HC 535-II, pp. 56–7 qq. 34–5, p. 805 q. 1978; Treasury and Civil Service, Sel. Cttee 1st Rep., 1980–1, HC 54, pp. 37–9 qq. 950–1, p. 44 q. 968. For the vital importance of political leverage as a means of sustaining central control, cf. Treasury and Civil Service, Sel. Cttee 3rd Rep., 1981–2, HC 236-II, pp. 188–9 q. 604.
444 Johnson, art. cit., pp. 368–9.
445 Lee, art. cit., p. 7.
446 Wilding, art. cit., pp. 396–9.

unfortunate' one, and that even allowing for the problems, little was achieved: the innovation was a victory of the principle of change for its own sake.[447] When the department was about to be abolished one Conservative MP tartly referred to its 'net negative contribution to the efficiency of the Whitehall machine'.[448]

The 'doubtful practical value', the ineffectiveness even, of the CSD appeared in a number of contexts.[449] These issues were thoroughly canvassed not least by the Expenditure Committee in 1976–7 and the Treasury and Civil Service Committee four years later.[450] In 1980 there was also a special review, undertaken at the instance of the Prime Minister, of the possible reintegration of the CSD and the Treasury.[451]

There were numerous particular grounds of criticism of the way the CSD worked. For instance one such point related to the way in which the Fulton recommendation to combine staff inspection and management services work into a unified efficiency audit had been ignored resulting in some duplication of effort, waste of resources, and lack of effectiveness.[452] It was also said that the CSD had failed to develop a proper training strategy or to give the Civil Service College effective support.[453] But the central issue of concern was that the CSD seemed to have insufficient authority to impress its recommendations on the other departments and so was proving ineffective.[454] It was a point not unrelated to the consequences of the division of responsibility between the Treasury and the CSD which was deemed to weaken the position of the centre.[455]

So far as manpower cash limits were concerned CSD rulings were in theory 'mandatory' and imposed on the departments, potentially an extremely powerful weapon. But this was not the case with reviews of management or organizational efficiency which were 'collaborative' or

---

447 Treasury and Civil Service, Sel. Cttee 1st Rep., 1980–1, HC 54, memorandum by Sir D. Rayner, p. 50 §20; Fry, op. cit., pp. 147–8.
448 12 H.C. Deb. 6s., 12 November 1981, col. 662 (R. Whitney). Cf. ibid., col. 663 (N. Forman).
449 For the phrase cited, see Fry, op. cit., p. 146.
450 Expenditure, Sel. Cttee 11th Rep., 1976–7, HC 535-I, chs VIII–IX; Treasury and Civil Service, Sel. Cttee 1st Rep., 1980–1, HC 54. The latter report dealt wholly with the future of the CSD. The government's observations are in Cmnd. 8170, 1980–1; and there are earlier minutes of evidence in HC 333-ii to 333-viii, 1979–80 (also in HC 712).
451 Hawtin and Moore, op. cit., Foreword.
452 Expenditure, Sel. Cttee 11th Rep., 1976–7, HC 535-I, pp. lv–lvii §§116–18, p. lix §122; ibid., HC 535-II, p. 479 q. 1076, pp. 826–7 q. 2064. The committee re-emphasized the point on a later occasion, see its 12th Rep., 1977–8 (vol. xxxiv), HC 576, p. xii §14.
453 See above pp. 222–4.
454 Expenditure, Sel. Cttee 11th Rep., 1976–7, HC 535-I, pp. liv–lix §§112–22. Cf. J. Garrett, memorandum, in Treasury and Civil Service, Sel. Cttee 3rd Rep., 1981–2, HC 236-III, Appendix 4 pp. 46–7 §§10, 12.
455 Expenditure, Sel. Cttee 11th Rep., 1976–7, HC 535-I, pp. xxxviii–xxxix §§72–4.

'optional'.[456] A great deal depended on the co-operation and participation of departments and on the amount of influence the CSD could exercise.[457] There was almost a sense that the CSD did not intervene unless invited to give advice or undertake a management study.[458] The Wardale review team which examined the Open Structure in 1981 noted that the CSD was 'largely dependent on departments to bring to its attention posts the functions of which have diminished or which for other reasons should be abolished or downgraded.'[459] And as a matter of course departmental involvement in any management review was considerable. And while this might induce departmental co-operation in any recommendations made, the conclusions could equally be ignored; and in that sense there seemed to be inadequate central power of enforcement as well as insufficient 'drive for efficiency'.[460] The CSD's own attitude was that its role was not to command or be dictatorial (which was impossible) but to offer advice and specialist services, to ask questions, to persuade and instruct, and to see that the departments themselves – where the prime responsibility was deemed to lie – had made adequate arrangements to secure efficiency in organization and economy in the deployment of staff resources.[461] The CSD position thus rested on a principle of partnership in which there was no substitute for departmental self-discipline and which accepted (so to say) a kind of federal situation.[462] Of course this was a state of affairs not unlike that which had come to prevail in regard to Treasury control of finance.[463] It

456 Treasury and Civil Service, Sel. Cttee, Minutes of Evidence, 1979–80, HC 333-iii, p. 30 qq. 149–51; Expenditure, Sel. Cttee 11th Rep., 1976–7, HC 535-II, p. 51 q. 11, p. 71 §6.
457 Treasury and Civil Service, Sel. Cttee 1st Rep., 1980–1, HC 54, pp. 4–5 qq. 773–7.
458 Expenditure, Sel. Cttee 11th Rep., 1976–7, HC 535-II, p. 82 q. 132, p. 89 q. 165, pp. 751–2 q. 1831, p. 805 q. 1979, pp. 826–7 q. 2064.
459 Wardale et al., op. cit., pp. 8 §3.3.
460 Expenditure, Sel. Cttee 11th Rep., 1976–7, HC 535-II, p. 76 q. 100, p. 82 q. 133, p. 777 q. 1909, p. 784 q. 1921, pp. 821–2 qq. 2035, 2038. See also ibid., HC 535-III, pp. 1105–6 §64(b)–(d). The phrase cited is E. du Cann's: see Treasury and Civil Service, Sel. Cttee, Minutes of Evidence, 1979–80, HC 333-viii, p. 159 q. 718; also the admission of Sir I. Bancroft (then Head of the Civil Service), Treasury and Civil Service, Sel. Cttee 3rd Rep., 1981–2, HC 236-II, p. 78 q. 352 and the related suggestion by a member of the committee that the heads of departments were too much like independent Chinese warlords, ibid., pp. 78–9 q. 353; also ibid. p. 474 qq. 1220–1.
461 Expenditure, Sel. Cttee 11th Rep., 1976–7, HC 535-II, pp. 49–50 q. 1, p. 75 q. 97, pp. 76–7 q. 102, p. 78 q. 111, p. 87 q. 156, pp. 94–5 q. 182, pp. 99 q. 205, p. 101 qq. 214–15.
462 ibid., p. 3 §14, p. 653 q. 1485, p. 831 q. 2089. See also ibid., HC 535-III, Appendix 3 esp. pp. 851–2 §§4–9.
463 ibid., HC 535-II, p. 805 q. 1979; Treasury and Civil Service, Sel. Cttee 1st Rep., 1980–1, HC 54, p. 14 q. 822, p. 18 q. 848, p. 45 q. 975, pp. 83–4 q. 1123. And see below ch. 4 on the question of the effectiveness or otherwise of Treasury control.

was no more perhaps than a recognition of the political realities and of the necessary implications of constitutional principle: the significance of the individual responsibility of ministers, and also of accounting officers, for their departments was crucial; and the sheer size of the modern service was a not unimportant practical factor.[464] Even so the Expenditure Committee and others felt that, as compared with the Treasury, the CSD was inadequate in this sort of departmental surveillance and that it lacked what was often expressively but vulgarly called 'clout'. In sum the CSD's relationship to other departments had not been satisfactorily defined, its work in securing efficiency had been hindered by departmental 'sovereignty', its powers to implement proposals were inadequate, and the support of ministers (and even senior civil servants) which was vital to the success of the enterprise had been diverted or diluted.[465] It seemed only logical (to some critics) to propose that the CSD's authority needed to be strengthened and that it should be given specific powers of compulsory entry and enforcement.[466] Of course it was also possible to draw the conclusion that the experiment had failed and that other arrangements were necessary.[467] This last consideration was particularly pertinent given the CSD's ambivalent relationship with the Treasury and the often suggested disadvantages of the division of responsibility involved.

Sir John Hunt, then Secretary to the Cabinet, put the point to the Expenditure Committee in these words:

> I think that the case for setting up the CSD at the time that it was set up was absolutely overwhelming. There was a feeling, whether rightly or wrongly, that the Treasury had done the Civil Service on the cheap, ... that there had been insufficient attention paid to personnel management and to training, ... that the load on the Chancellor was far too great for him really to give a lot of personal attention to the problems of the Civil Service and, perhaps above all, there was a

---

[464] Expenditure, Sel. Cttee 11th Rep., 1976–7, HC 535-II, p. 653 q. 1485, p. 805 q. 1979, p. 819 q. 2028, pp. 821–2 q. 2033; Treasury and Civil Service, Sel. Cttee 1st Rep., 1980–1, HC 54, p. 5 q. 777, p. 6 q. 783, p. 8 q. 798, p. 18 q. 848, p. 109 §9.

[465] Expenditure, Sel. Cttee 11th Rep., 1976–7, HC 535-I, p. lv §§113–15; ibid., HC 535-III, memorandum by N. Johnson, p. 1047 §6; Treasury and Civil Service, Sel. Cttee 4th Rep., 1979–80, HC 712, p. 92 qq. 436–9. The vital role of ministerial leadership and support and the effect of changes of policy were continually stressed by official and other witnesses: see Treasury and Civil Service, Sel. Cttee 1st Rep., 1980–1, HC 54, p. 14 qq. 820, 822, pp. 24–5 qq. 893–4, p. 29 qq. 919–20, pp. 32–3 qq. 936, 938, p. 45, q. 978, p. 48 §§2–3, p. 56 q. 1010, p. 64 §5, p. 92 §5. See also the government's observations on this report, 1980–1, Cmnd. 8170, p. 3 §9.

[466] e.g. Expenditure, Sel. Cttee 11th Rep., 1976–7, HC 535-I, pp. lvi–lviii §§117–18, 120, p. lix §122.

[467] Cf. ibid., p. xxxix §74.

feeling that a separate Cabinet Minister and a separate department were needed to push through a programme of change and reform in the light of Fulton. I do not think that what the CSD has achieved ought to be underrated.

But (he went on) having said that, he thought that the separation of supply from establishment expenditure between the Treasury and the CSD 'was always a little illogical.' Moreover in respect of matters concerning manpower and efficiency 'there is a risk under the present separation, of some aspects falling down the middle between the two departments.' The division probably worked well at first because of post-Fulton dynamism and because of the close personal contacts remaining between the officials in the newly-sundered departments: but this was a wasting asset and the inherent difficulties of a somewhat 'artificial' arrangement had been emerging to confirm 'a slight divorce between manpower and expenditure control that is really rather undesirable.'[468] The select committee itself put the point much more strongly referring to the separation of control of expenditure from responsibility for efficiency as 'indefensible'.[469] Of course there was also evidence of co-operation and a close working relationship between the Treasury and the CSD.[470] Nevertheless the Expenditure Committee report felt it necessary to look closely at the possibility of improving the state of affairs revealed. In the outcome the matter was deliberately put off until after the 1979 election.[471] Attention was then given to the question by the special study team in 1980 and shortly afterwards by the Treasury and Civil Service Select Committee. Various options emerged though interestingly it was the one least canvassed which at the end of 1981 was put into effect.

The obvious course perhaps was to retain the *status quo* while improving both the effectiveness of the CSD and the closeness of its co-operation with the Treasury (as by co-location and the sharing of common services, for instance). A second possibility was often called the bureau of the budget solution. It entailed putting the Treasury public expenditure divisions into the CSD, creating thereby an office of combined expenditure and manpower control, leaving the Treasury simply as a ministry of finance. The third option required the manpower

---

468 Expenditure, Sel. Cttee 11th Rep., 1976–7, HC 535-II, pp. 746–7 q. 1817, p. 749 q. 1822. Cf. the view of his successor in office, Sir Robert Armstrong, in Treasury and Civil Service, Sel. Cttee 1st Rep., 1980–1, HC 54, pp. 1–2 q. 770.
469 Expenditure, Sel. Cttee 11th Rep., 1976–7, HC 535-I, p. xxxix §75.
470 ibid., HC 535-II, pp. 128–9 qq. 329, 331, p. 822 q. 3029. Cf. Expenditure, Sel. Cttee 12th Rep., 1977–8, HC 576, p. 8 q. 22; Treasury and Civil Service, Sel. Cttee 1st Rep., 1980–1, HC 54, p. 32 q. 937.
471 Treasury and Civil Service, Sel. Cttee, Minutes of Evidence, 1979–80, HC 333-ii, p. 27 q. 131.

control and management functions of the CSD to be returned to the Treasury, leaving the rump of the former as a sort of public service commission to look after such remaining responsibilities as recruitment. The fourth possibility was quite simply to merge the two departments: the re-integration solution as Sir R. Armstrong called it. Each of these prospects had its advantages and deficiencies.[472] And each had its supporters. The Expenditure Committee, for instance, was quite firm in its view that the dichotomy created by following the Fulton recommendation had to be overcome and responsibility for efficiency and staff inspection returned to the Treasury.[473] Sir R. Clarke clearly agreed. The virtue, he said, of 'handling men and management and money together is that the knowledge and contact with departments' performance can come through the "money" channel.' He believed that a firm impression of how a department was performing could be derived from the Treasury's dialogue with it.[474] There was also the worry expressed by Lord Diamond that it was almost irresponsible for the Chief Secretary to have to sign estimates when he could not take responsibility for one of the major elements involved, that is, manpower and its cost. He believed, therefore, that the two should go together and be reunited in the Treasury.[475] And though he feared the upheaval of yet another rearrangement, Sir S. Goldman also thought it was illogical to separate expenditure programmes from departmental organization and the use of manpower.[476] On the other hand the Treasury and Civil Service Committee came out against re-integration and believed it would be most helpful to retain and strengthen the CSD.[477] Likewise E. Heath said he would not be in favour of putting the greater part of the CSD back into the Treasury.[478] Of course other issues dominated the political scene, culminating in the general election of 1979. The new government temporized, and waited until the select committee reported, and did not announce its intention until early in 1981, a Parliamentary statement

---

[472] Consideration of these four main possibilities (and sub-variations) is scattered throughout the official papers mentioned; but there is a succinct review of the pros and cons of each in Sir R. Armstrong's evidence to the Treasury and Civil Service Select Committee: see its 1st Rep., 1980–1, HC 54, pp. 2–3 q. 770. See also the joint Treasury–CSD memorandum, ibid., pp. 35–6.
[473] Expenditure, Sel. Cttee 11th Rep., 1976–7, HC 535-I, p. lix §122.
[474] Sir R. Clarke, *Public Expenditure Management and Control: the Development of the Public Expenditure Survey Committee (PESC)* (London, 1978), pp. 36–7.
[475] Expenditure, Sel. Cttee 11th Rep., 1976–7, HC 535-II, p. 798 q. 1960.
[476] ibid., pp. 802–3 q. 1969. Cf. ibid., p. 804 q. 1974; also his *The Developing System of Public Expenditure Management and Control* (Civil Service College Studies no. 2; London, 1973), pp. 30–2.
[477] Treasury and Civil Service, Sel. Cttee 1st Rep., 1980–1, HC 54, pp. xvi–xx §§27–39.
[478] Expenditure, Sel. Cttee 11th Rep., 1976–7, HC 535-II, pp. 760–1 q. 1868.

being followed by a White Paper on the select committee proposals.[479] In effect things were to be left alone and only very limited changes envisaged in order to improve the existing organization. However the CSD, already perhaps under a cloud, did not commend itself by its pusillanimous attitude and the compromise it advocated during the Civil Service strikes that took place during the spring and early summer of the same year. The minister in charge of the CSD was dismissed in a Cabinet reshuffle.[480] And there was obviously continuing concern about the role of the office. This was barely mentioned in a further White Paper on Civil Service efficiency which came out in July 1981 and which reported progress in the pursuit of less waste and better methods of administration.[481] But Sir Derek Rayner, the Prime Minister's adviser on efficiency (who had, significantly, been placed not in the CSD but in the Cabinet Office) left no doubt about his own view: he thought it was 'crazy' to have an organization 'with two headquarters at opposite ends of the street.'[482] Then towards the end of 1981 the Prime Minister announced her decision (the Leader of the Opposition called it 'a volte-face' – he said he would not use the offensive term 'U-turn').[483] The government now intended to abolish the CSD by splitting its functions between the Treasury and the Cabinet Office.

This idea did not come completely out of the blue, something like it having been canvassed, cursorily and not always favourably, during the Treasury Select Committee's recent investigation.[484] Presumably there was a considered review of all the options before a decision was made but it is not clear how this was done.[485] However Mrs Thatcher told the House of Commons that, whatever advantages there may once have been in having a separate CSD, there was one consequence the deficiencies of

---

479 997 H.C. Deb. 5s., 29 January 1981, col. 1072; The Future of the Civil Service Department, 1980–1, Cmnd. 8170.
480 See G. K. Fry, 'The Development of the Thatcher Government's "Grand Strategy" for the Civil Service: a Public Policy Perspective', *Public Administration*, lxii (1984), p. 330.
481 Efficiency in the Civil Service, 1980–1, Cmnd. 8293, p. 4 §18.
482 *Sunday Telegraph* (1 February 1981), cited Fry, art. cit., p. 330.
483 For the statement and the questions which followed, see 12 H.C. Deb. 6s., 12 November 1981, cols 658–66.
484 Treasury and Civil Service, Sel. Cttee 1st Rep., 1980–1, HC 54, p. 41 q. 957, p. 57 q. 1014, p. 58 qq. 1018–23, p. 89 q. 1147, p. 97 qq. 1164–5, and p. 98 q. 1170. Interestingly in 1942 Attlee had considered the possibility that the responsibility for establishment and personnel matters in the Civil Service should be allocated to a new Permanent Secretary in the Cabinet Office who would be 'something equivalent to a chef de cabinet' to the First Lord of the Treasury: see PRO, CAB 87/74 MG(42)6 (31 December 1942), memorandum from C. R. Attlee, p. 4 §4.
485 Treasury and Civil Service, Sel. Cttee 3rd Rep., 1981–2, HC 236-II, pp. 440–2 qq. 1125–39; ibid., pp. 482–3 q. 1270–1.

which had become increasingly apparent: it divorced central responsibility for the control of expenditure on manpower from responsibility for the control of Government expenditure as a whole. She went on: 'I judge that the balance of advantage now lies in favour of consolidating the CSD's manpower control responsibilities with the central control of resources.' The Treasury would thus resume control over Civil Service manpower, pay, superannuation, allowances, and the Central Computer and Telecommunications Agency. The CSD staff concerned were to be transferred to the Treasury where a minister of state would be responsible.[486] However it was not desirable totally to merge the CSD with the Treasury: questions relating to the organization, management, and overall efficiency of the Civil Service (including policy on recruitment, training, and other personnel matters) – which are as important as the control of public expenditure – would remain separate as issues in which 'any Prime Minister is bound to take a close personal interest.' They would be the charge of the Prime Minister as Minister for the Civil Service though the day-to-day responsibility was to be that of another colleague (for most of the time since, this has been the Chancellor of the Duchy of Lancaster). The staff was to constitute a new Management and Personnel Office and work alongside the Cabinet Office where, of course, the Rayner efficiency unit already existed. The Secretary to the Cabinet would be the head of this new office but he was to be assisted in its business by a second permanent secretary.[487] After the 1983 election the MPO was reconstituted as an integral part of the Cabinet Office (i.e. not simply 'alongside' it as it was before).[488] There the position now rests: though whether it will last into the next century is another matter.[489]

This review of the rise and fall of the Civil Service Department has already carried the narrative forward into the period of Conservative rule which began in 1979. A new emphasis of reform was then introduced.

---

486 For the passages cited, see 12 H.C. Deb. 6s., 12 November 1981, col. 658. The Treasury probably did not want to get back more that the package of functions it received: see Lee, art. cit., p. 6.
487 12 H.C. Deb. 6s., 12 November 1981, cols 658–9. For details about the allocation of responsibilities, see *KCA* (1981), p. 31260A.
488 *KCA* (1983), p. 32341A. The MPO is, however, physically separate from the Secretariat.
489 Cf. Treasury and Civil Service, Sel. Cttee 3rd Rep., 1981–2, HC 236-II, p. 442 q. 1135. The same committee has lately stressed the need for control of the Civil Service to be focused on a single minister and not split as at present: see its 7th Rep., 1985–6, HC 92-I, pp. xxvii–xxviii. The government's response to this suggestion was simply to say that the current arrangements remain valid while accepting that the question must be treated flexibly according to the circumstances: see Civil Servants and Ministers: Duties and Responsibilities, 1985–6, Cmnd. 9841, p. 10 §§36–9.

RETRENCHMENT AND EFFECTIVENESS

> The Government's objectives have been to review the functions of government, to eliminate those that are unnecessary or are no longer required [and] to make sure that those that are retained are performed as efficiently and effectively as possible....
> Efficiency and Effectiveness in the Civil Service, 1981–2, Cmnd. 8616, p.2 §5

By the time the Conservatives took power the failure of the Fulton initiative was apparent. Writing a few years after the appearance of the report, one of the committee's members claimed that its main achievement was to make people think about the Civil Service in a critical and appraising way.[490] This may be so on a generous view; but in the end much less came of the furore than had been anticipated. This was reflected in the proceedings of the Commons' Expenditure Committee, the eleventh report of which, published in July 1977, constituted an attempt to review developments in the Civil Service in the wake of the Fulton report and the changes it had initiated. It was a kind of inquest therefore; and perhaps the term is not inappropriate for, although the select committee eschewed any general verdict, its overall conclusion was undoubtedly that in many respects the Fulton recommendations had fallen dead-born from the press. Of course there had been changes, some of which seemed quite radical, like the creation of the Civil Service Department, the reclassification of grades, the introduction of the Open Structure, and the establishment of the Civil Service College. And new ideas swam to the fore: accountable management, efficiency audits, programme analysis, policy planning units, and so on and so forth. Yet the tide seemed to ebb and close examination revealed that the changes were, in the outcome, more limited than had been envisaged by Fulton, were merely superficial or even cosmetic, creating the appearance of reform in a service that remained basically the same. Above all the new breed of managers had not appeared; the service was still dominated by generalist arts graduates from public schools and Oxbridge; and its ethos had hardly been transformed in the way intended. The exasperated, almost despairing, tone of the evidence presented by Lord Crowther-Hunt (the main author of the Fulton report) witnessed this most clearly.[491] It was the cry of a disappointed and frustrated man who had seen the report he did so much to sustain fail of the significant effect anticipated, and even be ignored. One close academic student of these

---

[490] Sir J. Dunnett, 'The Civil Service: Seven Years after Fulton', *Public Administration*, liv (1976), p. 373.

[491] Expenditure, Sel. Cttee 11th Rep., 1976–7 (vol. xxxi), HC 535-II, pp. 471–86 qq. 1049–98; memorandum on 'Civil Service Reform', 1976–7 (vol. xxxii), HC 535-III, Appendix 48 pp. 1090–1123. Lord Fulton's bland monologue was, one imagines, of little help, HC 535-II, pp. 466–71 qq. 1046–8.

questions summed up the matter in the dismissive sentence: 'The Fulton legacy was a meagre one in terms of worthwhile change.' And the general climate had so altered from the original euphoria that *The Times* could say in 1977 that the report itself was 'one of the poorest pieces of analysis to emerge from a major government inquiry since 1945 and an opportunity for valuable reform sadly missed.'[492]

Thus in 1979 the Conservatives inherited a failed revolution. But equally they had the intention of initiating one of their own.

The Conservative revolution

From the late 1960s onwards a libertarian renewal occurred in the Conservative Party.[493] This did not necessarily mean a move in the direction of less and less government on every single front; but it did entail a firm attempt to halt the expansion of bureaucracy which had been under way for so long and to begin the withdrawal of the state from those areas of activity where, in terms of the doctrine now prevailing in the party, its intervention was seen as either inappropriate or excessive. The Heath government of 1970–4 had been committed to the contraction of the Civil Service and to improving its efficiency.[494] And it was recognized that the kind of reform required would be (in some respects at least) different from that appropriate to the expanding positive state.[495] But, like so much else in connexion with the purpose of that administration, the effort ran into the sands and the impetus was lost well before the electoral defeat of 1974. There was some fall in Civil Service numbers during the rest of the decade but this was the result rather of the implications of IMF requirements than of deliberate government intent. It was not until the advent of the new Conservative ministry in 1979 that the nettle was grasped at all firmly and directly.[496] The broad purpose of the Thatcher government was to stimulate the economy, not by substantive intervention and control, but by creating the conditions in which industry and trade can flourish through their own efforts. This meant bringing down inflation, reducing direct taxation, and limiting the

---

492 G. K. Fry, *The Administrative 'Revolution' in Whitehall: a Study of the Politics of Administrative Change in British Central Government since the 1950s* (London, 1981), p. 156; 'Educating our Masters', *The Times* (18 January 1977), p. 15.
493 See *The Ideological Heritage* (London, 1983), ch. 9 esp. pp. 326ff. Also *The Rise of Collectivism* (London, 1983), pp. 153–63 on 'The monetarist counter-revolution'.
494 For the 1970 Conservative manifesto, see KCA (1969–70), p.24008A (24010); The Reorganisation of Central Government, 1970–1 (vol. xx), Cmnd. 4506, pp. 3–4 §§[1]-5.
495 D. Howell, *A New Style of Government* (CPC no. 463; London, 1970), p. 8.
496 Cf. the view that it was not until 1979 that 'a real break-through' was made: J. Delafons, 'Working in Whitehall: Changes in Public Administration 1952–1982', *Public Administrations*, lx (1982), pp. 263–4.

claims of the public sector on national resources. The Prime Minister explained what this objective involved for the Civil Service in the following terms:

> In the past, Governments have progressively increased the number of tasks that the Civil Service is asked to do without paying sufficient attention to the need for economy and efficiency. Consequently, staff numbers have grown over the years. The present Government are committed both to a reduction in tasks and to better management. We believe that we should now concentrate on simplifying the work and doing it more efficiently. The studies that Departments have already carried out, including those in conjunction with Sir Derek Rayner, have demonstrated clearly the scope for this.
>
> All Ministers in charge of Departments will work out detailed plans for concentrating on essential functions and making operations simpler and more efficient in their Departments.[497]

There were thus two major aspects of the policy to be pursued: retrenchment, that is, reducing the functions and so the size and cost of the Civil Service; and the achievement of greater effectiveness of operation in the still considerable organization which would remain.

Retrenchment
A recent publication of the Conservative Research Department has described the reduction of the Civil Service as a fundamental part of the government's strategy, for 'Excessive manpower is one of the most obvious obstacles to achieving maximum efficiency.'[498] On coming into office in May 1979 the new government carried out a review of the service's manpower requirements and decided its performance would be improved if it were slimmed. In the announcement already cited the Prime Minister went on to say it had been decided to cut the number of officials by 100,000 by April 1984. This would leave a total in all civil and defence departments of about 630,000, a fall of some 14 per cent.[499] In fact the rate of reduction achieved was slightly faster than that originally envisaged, the target figure being reached by the new year of 1984. The

---

497 984 H.C. Deb. 5s., 13 May 1980, col. 1050. Cf. the remarks of Baroness Young (then the minister responsible for the newly created MPO) about the different world which had emerged over recent years with a changed view emerging both of government functions and of the appropriate size of the Civil Service: in Treasury and Civil Service, Sel. Cttee 3rd Rep., 1981–2, HC 236-II, p. 445, q. 1155.
498 Conservative Research Department, 'The Machinery of Government', *Politics Today* (no. 4; 12 March 1984), p. 61.
499 ibid., p. 61; 984 H.C. Deb. 5s., 13 May 1980, col. 1050. The figures cited include both industrial and non-industrial civil servants. The total on 1 July 1979 for the latter category only (on which Table 4 p. 132 above is based) was 565,800.

240   A Much Governed Nation

Minister of State at the Treasury deals with Civil Service affairs and in October 1983 the then incumbent, B. Hayhoe, had described the process of contraction as follows:

> It has meant a significant reduction in the Civil Service pay bill of well over £500 million a year. This substantial reduction has been achieved without massive redundancies. The processes of natural wastage, retirement, and resignation have been sufficient to cover the reduced numbers.... During the four years from 1979–80 to 1982–3 over half the reduction in manpower has been achieved by improving efficiency; about 20 per cent. by dropping or materially curtailing functions; about 10 per cent. by privatisation, including contracting out; and some 2 per cent. by hiving off to new or existing private sector bodies.[500]

Subsequently further reductions have been announced and each department has been given a target to show by how much its manpower must be cut.[501] The latest proposal is that the total (for industrial and non-industrial staff combined) will, by April 1988, fall to 590,400. This is a fall from the 1983 figure of more than 10 per cent and of nearly 20 per cent from the 1979 total.[502] If the goals are attained, then over the whole period (1979–88) most departments will show a decline in numbers. In some cases this will be substantial: for instance the staff of the DOE will go down by almost 50 per cent and the Ministry of Defence by over 25 per cent. On the other hand some ministries will show an increase, for instance the Department of Employment, the Home Office, and the Department of Transport. But overall the substantial reduction in view is undoubted.

Obviously this enforced decline in the number of official posts will have reduced severely the career prospects of civil servants: there may be fewer opportunities for job experience and, above all, there will certainly be less chance of promotion. The abolition of the CSD was also widely seen in the service as a blow to its prestige; for that department had, rightly or wrongly, come to be looked on as much more likely than the Treasury to be sympathetic to the interests of officials and their trade unions. There was indeed said to be a deliberate policy on the part of the Thatcher government to 'de-privilege' the Civil Service.[503] This must all have contributed to a sense of frustration intensified by opposition in many cases to Thatcherite ideology and policy. Civil Service impartiality

500   47 H.C. Deb. 6s., 28 October 1983, col. 547.
501   See e.g. 48 H.C. Deb. 6s., 17 November 1983, cols 555–6.
502   The Government's Expenditure Plans 1986–87 to 1988–89, 1985–6, Cmnd. 9702-II, p. 28 Table 2.22.
503   The term is G. K. Fry's: see his 'The Development of the Thatcher Government's "Grand Strategy" for the Civil Service: a Public Policy Perspective', *Public Administration*, lxii (1984), p. 325.

and willingness to serve the party in office seems (in curious reversal of traditional radical fears) to be limited when the preferred politics of 'consensus' are foregone in favour of specific libertarian intent.[504]

As well the government has taken a hard line on public sector pay and pensions as another aspect of the policy of diminishing the size and cost of the service. With this in mind it was determined to undermine the favourable position civil servants had enjoyed as a result of the Priestley Commission report in 1955. Under the formula then proposed and accepted Civil Service pay was to be based – though this was not a completely new principle – on 'fair comparison' as determined by inquiry into rates prevailing in the private sector, appropriate internal relativities, an allowance for inflation, and special machinery for determining the salaries of higher officials.[505] But this arrangement had rarely worked to the satisfaction of all concerned. If most officials had (in comparative terms) done well out of the arrangement, many had not.[506] For its part government found it most inconvenient to be excluded from the process of settlement – which was supposed to be 'outside politics' – until the very last stage. In fact administrations of both parties had often then intervened to secure adherence to the current incomes policy. As well the pay research undertaken (and by which a large part of public expenditure was determined) was frequently deemed inadequate and committed the government too firmly. Finally in October 1980 the Thatcher government repudiated the Priestley system because of the unacceptable cost it entailed and because a commitment to pay officials what 'fair comparison' might deem they were entitled to was incompatible with limiting public expenditure. The prevailing cash limits were imposed; and this led to the unsuccessful Civil Service strikes of March–July 1981. While this was going on a committee had been set up to examine the question of Civil Service pay, reporting in July 1982.[507] The majority report rested on a compromise between the principle of fair comparison and reference to market forces. Recognition of the importance of the latter was enough to persuade the government to accept the report's broad approach which seemed to give ministers more opportunity to control salary awards and keep them within acceptable

---

504 Cf. the curious remarks in C. Ponting, *The Right to Know: the Inside Story of the Belgrano Affair* (London, 1985), pp. 7–8.
505 The Civil Service, R. Com. Rep., 1955–6 (vol. xi), Cmd. 9613, pp. 23–7. Cf. CSD, *The Civil Service: Introductory Factual Memorandum* (London, 1980), ch. 4 which gives details of the pay negotiating system.
506 For an account of the working of the system, see G. K. Fry, 'Civil Service Salaries in the Post-Priestley Era 1956–1972', *Public Administration*, lii (1974), pp. 319–33.
507 idem, 'Compromise with the Market: the Megaw Report on Civil Service Pay 1982', ibid., lxi (1983), pp. 90–6; Sir H. Phelps Brown, 'How Should Civil Servants Pay Be Fixed? The Megaw Proposals', *Three Banks Review* (September 1983), pp. 19–31.

limits.[508] The government also seems determined, if it can, to place Civil Service pensions on a more realistic contributory basis.[509]

Effectiveness

Cutting down the size and cost of the Civil Service might reduce its morale. Equally it could act as a spur to better administration. The minister of state told the Treasury and Civil Service Committee in January 1980 that, while cuts were 'an essential feature of the Government's policy', the 'promotion of more efficient work' was at least as, if not more, important.[510] 'Effectiveness' is simply a general term or slogan – one of a number currently on offer – used to label such a goal. It entails various considerations or objectives such as economy in the use of resources (including manpower), securing better value for money, controlling costs, improving the quality of Civil Service management, programme evaluation, ensuring the availability of data adequate to decision-making, and so forth. In a sense these are, of course, permanent bureaucratic objectives though in recent years there has been a tendency to highlight them through the medium of some fashionable technique or other: organization and methods, the public expenditure survey, programme analysis and review, cost-benefit studies, and the like. In the pursuit of its so-called 'efficiency strategy', the Thatcher government has introduced three particular devices through which it hopes to achieve a more effective public service. These are the departmental scrutiny programme (the 'Rayner projects'), a management information system for ministers (MINIS), and the financial management initiative (FMI).

Within days of the new government being formed in May 1979, a unit was established in the Cabinet Office to advise on how to improve efficiency and eliminate waste in the public service.[511] Its head was Sir Derek (now Lord) Rayner, then joint managing director of Marks and Spencer. He had (unpaid) responsibility for the inquiries which bore his name until December 1982 when increasing company commitments led to his resignation. However the programme of scrutinizing government departments has continued under his successor Sir Robin Ibbs, a director of ICI and former head of the Central Policy Review Staff, who is assisted by eight management specialists. The projects undertaken have primarily been concerned with the efficient use of resources and are of two kinds.

---

508 On the need for a right of resort to arbitration, see Phelps Brown, art. cit., pp. 29–31.
509 The superannuation arrangements (as at 1980) are described in *The Civil Service: Introductory Factual Memorandum*, ch. 5.
510 Treasury and Civil Service, Sel. Cttee, Minutes of Evidence, 1979–80, HC 333-ii, p. 23 q. 102. Cf. 3rd Rep., 1981–2, HC 236-II, p. 70 q. 288.
511 Sir D. Rayner, memorandum (12 February 1980), in Treasury and Civil Service, Sel. Cttee, Minutes of Evidence, 1979–80, HC 333-iv, p. 46 §1; ibid., 3rd Rep., 1981–2, HC 236-II, pp. 77–8 qq. 344–7.

While a few of them have been multi-departmental reviews of service-wide topics, most concentrate on the examination of a specific activity in a single department.[512] Departmental co-operation was from the outset crucial, the scrutinies relying heavily on self-examination.[513] And the purpose was preparation for action, never merely inquiry for its own sake.[514] The main features of a typical investigation have been described by a member of the unit:

> First, it shows what is actually being done, what results come from doing it, how this generates costs and how these costs are changing. Secondly, it challenges the value of the activities; it looks at the need for them as well as at the scope for substantial improvements in efficiency and effectiveness. Thirdly, it goes deeper...to tackle the underlying causes of problems, including issues about managerial authority, accountability, and incentives or impediments to efficiency. Finally, it makes constructive and practicable recommendations which are firmly based on analysis.[515]

The projects are selected by departmental ministers and the work is largely done by one or two officials (usually of principal grade) from the department concerned over a period of about three months, though they receive general guidance in the form of ground rules from the Rayner unit which also helps co-ordinate the wider reviews.[516] It was made clear from the outset that the responsibility for the scrutinies lay with the minister as

---

[512] The initial twenty-nine projects in the scrutiny programme for 1979 are listed in Treasury and Civil Service, Sel. Cttee, Minutes of Evidence, 1979–80, HC 333-iv, p. 48 Annex 1; most of the thirty-seven projects for 1980, ibid., pp. 61–2 Annex 3; and the thirty-seven proposed for 1981 in Treasury and Civil Service, Sel. Cttee 3rd Rep., 1981–2, HC 236-II, pp. 90–1. There are clear parallels with O & M and PAR, on which see pp. 286–9, 300–15 below.

[513] Treasury and Civil Service, Sel. Cttee, Minutes of Evidence, 1979–80, HC 333-iv, p. 51 §3.1; though cf. ibid., 3rd Rep., 1981–2, HC 236-II, p. 106 qq. 478–80.

[514] Treasury and Civil Service, Sel. Cttee, Minutes of Evidence, 1979–80, HC 333-iv, p. 51 §3.2(c).

[515] I. Beesley, 'The Rayner Scrutinies', in A. G. Gray and W. I. Jenkins (eds.), *Policy Analysis and Evaluation in British Government* (London, 1983), pp. 33–4. See also N. Warner, 'Raynerism in Practice: Anatomy of a Rayner Scrutiny', *Public Administration*, lxii (1984), pp. 7–22, an account (by one of the officials involved) of the 1979 inquiry into DHSS benefit payments and of the political and other problems which arose over the implementation of the team's proposals.

[516] The original note of guidance by Sir D. Rayner is reprinted as Annex 2 in Treasury and Civil Service, Sel. Cttee, Minutes of Evidence, 1979–80, HC 333-iv, pp. 49–60. For Rayner's own role during the initiation and preparation of projects, ibid., p. 46 §§4–6, p. 52 §3.3(b), p. 57 §4.12. A detailed account of the scrutiny process is given in an Efficiency Unit study by K. Jenkins et al., *Making Things Happen: a Report on the Implementation of Government Efficiency Scrutinies* (London, 1985), esp. the enclosed folders.

did the decision about implementation, though Sir D. Rayner could add his own advice.[517] The results are incorporated in reports which are monitored at six-monthly intervals by the unit to ensure that the scope for improvement is fully exploited. The main conclusions are referred directly to the Prime Minister whose interest and support have undoubtedly given the programme a good deal of its strength.[518]

The immediate and lasting impact of all this has no doubt been considerable in itself, possibly greater than that of all the techniques paraded during the 1960s and later discarded.[519] During the years 1979–84 there were 266 scrutinies which identified opportunities to save £600 millions a year leading to cumulative economies so far realized of about £750 millions. For instance it is claimed that £2 millions were saved by the abolition of 3,600 forms and the radical revision of 2,700 others; £26 millions by savings in the administration of unemployment and supplementary benefits; and £15 millions in the support services provided for scientists engaged in research and development work.[520] And there is evidence that an independently stimulated inquiry of the Rayner kind does achieve a speedier introduction of worthwhile change than would any internal review: it acts as an 'organizational catalyst'.[521] All the same there are also indications of notable slowness in making decisions on and implementing recommendations; to such an extent indeed that a special investigation of the reasons for this sort of delay was lately undertaken.[522] Nevertheless the main changes which have been thus effected include

> the principle of charging for the use of common services, the establishment and development of cost centres, the introduction of latest technologies for processing work, the development of appropriate experience through more systematic career planning and training, and an incentive to be more efficient through a system of merit payments, promotions (and honours?).

517 CSD, *The Civil Service: Introductory Factual Memorandum*, p. 41 §8.2. Cf. Treasury and Civil Service, Sel. Cttee, Minutes of Evidence, 1979–80, HC 333-ii, pp. 21–2 q. 86; ibid., HC 333-iv, p. 46 §§5–6, p. 62 q. 275; and Warner, art. cit., p. 8. The report on DHSS payments went to Cabinet before being finalized, Warner, art. cit., p. 13.
518 Treasury and Civil Service, Sel. Cttee, Minutes of Evidence, 1979–80, HC 333-iv, pp. 76–7 qq. 348–53; ibid., 1st Rep., 1980–1, HC 54, p. 22 qq. 874–6; ibid., 3rd Rep., 1981–2, HC 236-II, p. 93 q. 399; Beesley, loc. cit., p. 33; L. Metcalfe and S. Richards, 'The Impact of the Efficiency Strategy: Political Clout or Cultural Change?', *Public Administration*, lxii (1984), pp. 441–2, 452.
519 See e.g. the editorial comment in 'The Banners of Bureaucracy', *The Times* (10 October 1983), p. 15; also Delafons, art. cit., p. 269.
520 Jenkins *et al.*, op. cit., p. 1; CRD, 'Machinery of Government', *Politics Today* (no. 4, 12 March 1984), p. 65.
521 Warner, art. cit., pp. 18–19.
522 Jenkins *et al.*, op. cit., esp. Annexes 1, 4.

But the real object was not so much to achieve such savings as were thereby induced as to secure lasting reforms and changed attitudes, to develop not only 'an awareness of inefficiency' but also to make 'self-evaluation' part of ordinary administration in Whitehall.[523] And by employing fast-stream administrators on reviews of management matters, the scrutiny programme has also perhaps helped overcome the distinction between policy formation and executive management.[524]

Rayner himself has suggested there are five lessons to learn for the future.[525] First, because of the diversity of government activities, it is not possible to deal with efficiency at large. Consequently improvement has to come about through specific scrutinies so as to inhibit the things that prevent the service giving of its best. And clearly reviews of the sort his unit had been undertaking 'should be a permanent part of the apparatus for promoting effective administration.' Secondly it was necessary to see that rule books and procedures laid down 'in clear, simple and common-sense terms what people are expected to do.' Thirdly it has to be accepted that the process of reform must be continuous. There is always room for improvement not least because a policy and its administration, once satisfactory, get amended piecemeal and supplemented and 'the result can be a jungle of procedures and inefficiencies.' Simple things are often needed like costing as accurately as possible or getting clear exactly who is the client. The next point stresses the importance of decentralization of responsibility:

> we must push responsibility down the line to where the costs are incurred; define more clearly the framework of accountability, so that, where possible, individual managers have the authority to run their establishments or divisions. This will avoid complex bureaucratic procedures and give financial incentives to those who commit expenditure.

As to the role of the central departments (then the Treasury and the CSD),

> I have no time for a centre which second-guesses the experts down the line on decisions they should take on their own responsibility: but I appreciate a centre, in individual Departments as well as in the Whitehall public expenditure system, which exercises a controlling role through making the intelligent effort to define delegated authority

---

523 A. G. Gray and W. I. Jenkins, 'Lasting Reforms in Civil Service Management?', *Political Quarterly*, lv (1984), p. 422.
524 Warner, art. cit., pp. 19–20. Cf. Rayner's purpose as expressed at Treasury and Civil Service, Sel. Cttee, Minutes of Evidence, 1979–80, HC 333-iv, p. 81 qq. 378–80.
525 For what follows, see Treasury and Civil Service, Sel. Cttee 3rd Rep., 1981–2, HC 236-II, pp. 91–2 q. 392, pp. 92–3 q. 394, and p. 95 q. 406.

and to ensure that departments are operating systems which are adequate for financial management.

Finally ministers must feel responsible for the efficiency of the departments though much necessarily falls to the senior officials. Thus there is need for continuing political pressure – 'unmistakable instructions to run policies for good management' – while, for its part, the higher civil service must acquire the relevant skills and experience. There must be monitoring of performance; a framework of finanical management to get good value for money; a succession policy for key posts and accelerated promotion for those who show they can manage: all in an attempt to create a new Civil Service state of mind.[526] One specific suggestion Rayner had: every permanent secretary should be asked, as part of his annual account, 'what he has saved, what he has done this year to simplify and update his part of the show, just as indeed anybody else would do outside.'[527]

Certainly it may be said the Rayner influence has extended beyond the individual scrutinies to help secure the development of the two other aspects of the government's policy for achieving greater efficiency and effectiveness in the Civil Service, a policy reflected in the three White Papers of 1981–3.[528] These others aspects are the introduction in each department of a management information system for ministers (MINIS) and of the so-called financial management initiative (FMI), the latter really being a generalized development of the former and intended to relate the pursuit of effectiveness in administration both as a whole and in particular to the government's overall economic policy. There had been preliminary work elsewhere, but MINIS was effectively pioneered by M. Heseltine in 1980 and after when he was successively Secretary of State for the Environment and for Defence.[529] The FMI was formally launched

---

526 See also ibid., pp. 93–4 qq. 401–2, p. 100 q. 439, p. 101 qq. 443–5.
527 ibid., p. 101 q. 443. And cf. the floundering response of Sir I. (now Lord) Bancroft, then Head of the Civil Service no less, when faced with this sort of question, ibid., pp. 79–82.
528 Efficiency in the Civil Service, 1980–1, Cmnd. 8293; Efficiency and Effectiveness in the Civil Service, 1981–2, Cmnd. 8616; and Financial Management in Government Departments, 1983–4, Cmnd. 9058.
529 Efficiency and Effectiveness in the Civil Service, 1981–2, Cmnd. 8616, p. 8 §27; Treasury and Civil Service, Sel. Cttee 3rd Rep., 1981–2, HC 236-I, p. xvi §26; ibid., HC 236-II, p. 158 q. 490; G. K. Fry, 'The Development of the Thatcher Government's "Grand Strategy" for the Civil Service ...', loc. cit., p. 332; Financial Management in Government Departments, 1983–4, Cmnd. 9058, p. 5 §14. The main features of the system are summarized and analysed in A. Likierman, 'Management Information for Ministers: the MINIS System in the Department of the Environment', *Public Administration*, lx (1982), pp. 127–42. See also his memorandum in Treasury and Civil Service, Sel. Cttee 3rd Rep., 1981–2, HC 236-III,

In Dark Wonder 247

in May 1982.[530] In each case the objects were similar and may be described as: to provide ministers and Civil Service managers at all levels with a clear view of their objectives and means to assess performance in attaining them; to define clearly the responsibility for the best use of the resources of manpower and money allocated; and to see there is available the information (especially about costs), the training, and the advice needed to discharge this managerial task.[531] The White Paper on Financial Management described in detail the plans of thirty-one departments and offices, showing how they intended to establish the information systems necessary to manage their objectives and expenditure and what policies for staff management and training they had elaborated. The document also reviewed the progress so far made. It was explained that the

> plans are generally directed towards dividing departments' work into appropriate blocks, and into 'cost centres' within each block; making their managers accountable for the management of the costs within their control and for the results they achieve; and establishing procedures, information systems and measures for setting the targets and budgets against which performance will be judged.[532]

Clearly all this represents a move towards delegation and decentralization (as with the Fulton report's earlier stress on accountable units).[533] More than this perhaps, it constitutes yet another attempt to achieve a highly significant alteration in the entire ethos or 'culture' of the Civil Service. For to be implemented fully attitudes will have to change and recruitment, training, promotion prospects, and practice must all be transformed.[534] In this regard three specific priorities were announced: the introduction of incentives as by 'performance related pay' (that is, merit awards); the improvement of career development for managers as by accelerated advancement; and the extension of the unified grading system.[535]

Appendix 5 pp. 49–61. There is a brief account of the first three 'rounds' of the DOE system, ibid., HC 236-II, DOE memorandum Annex 2 pp. 125–8.
530 See the Treasury and MPO document reproduced in Efficiency and Effectiveness in the Civil Service, 1981–2, Cmnd. 8616, Appendix 3 pp. 21–36.
531 Efficiency and Effectiveness in the Civil Service, 1981–2, Cmnd. 8616, p. 5 §13.
532 Financial Management in Government Departments, 1983–4, Cmnd. 9058, p. 8 §18. Cf. Fry, art. cit., p. 332; and the Earl of Gowrie's speech to the Institute of Personnel Management in October 1983 cited in CRD, 'The Machinery of Government', loc. cit., p. 67.
533 Cf. Treasury and Civil Service, Sel. Cttee 3rd Rep., 1981–2, HC 236-I, pp. xxix §§65–6; Efficiency and Effectiveness in the Civil Service, 1981–2, Cmnd. 8616, p. 6, §17.
534 38 H.C. Deb. 6s., 9 March 1982, col. 918 (B. Hayhoe).
535 Financial Management in Government Departments, 1983–4, Cmnd. 9058,

A Conservative Research Department publication has claimed that 'the years since 1979 have marked a watershed in the history of the Civil Service'; and it went on to cite the opinion of Lord Bancroft (once Head of the Civil Service) to similar effect.[536] Certainly there have been considerable changes (as indicated in this section). But of course it remains to be seen whether these initiatives will be any more successful than earlier attempts to rationalize and improve the government machine.[537] Many questions remain unanswered; and traditional views and practices always show a notable resistance to anything more than superficial or cosmetic reform. The sheer size and diversity of the modern government machine makes it difficult to ensure a uniform and effective change of direction as does the constitutional autonomy of departments (which rests after all on the independent status of ministers and their responsibility to Parliament). Moreover there is (as so often) a paradox or seeming contradiction at the heart of the reforms recently and currently pursued. For if worthwhile accountable units are developed this can only be to the degree that detailed central control is diminished. Yet equally the power of the centre has often been criticized for being too negative and cautious.[538] The major responsibility now lies with the MPO though the Treasury is necessarily involved because of its duties in respect to public expenditure and Civil Service manpower and pay. The same dilemma of control has long been revealed at large in the story of the Treasury's role as it has developed over the years. This is the subject of the chapter which follows.

Appendix 1 pp. 17–18 §4. Cf. Sir D. Rayner's memorandum in Treasury and Civil Service, Sel. Cttee 3rd Rep., 1981–2, HC 236-II, pp. 88–9 §§32–4.
536 CRD, 'The Machinery of Government', loc. cit., p. 67.
537 Likierman, art. cit., p. 129; Fry, 'The Development of the Thatcher Government's "Grand Strategy" for the Civil Service...', loc. cit., pp. 333–4.
538 Cf. Treasury and Civil Service, Sel. Cttee 3rd Rep., 1981–2, HC 236-I, p. xxxi §§73–4; and Sir I. Bancroft's memorandum (October 1981), ibid., HC 236-II, pp. 174–5 §§4–6.

4
THE DEPARTMENT OF DEPARTMENTS

> Over all public departments the department of finance is supreme. Erected upon the vital springs of national prosperity, wielding the mysterious power of the purse, the final arbiter in the disputes of every other office,...the Treasury occupies in the polity of the United Kingdom a central and superior position.
> W. CHURCHILL, *Lord Randolph Churchill*, 1905, repr. 1952, p.533

THE TRADITIONAL centre of the Civil Service is HM Treasury, a department whose importance is formally indicated in a number of ways. There is the modern convention that the office of First Lord is normally held by the Prime Minister (a practice now recognized or assumed by the law).[1] The Chancellor of the Exchequer is Second Lord and, in peacetime at least, always one of the most senior and influential members of the government. The Treasury was the first department in recent times to have two ministers in the Cabinet and is the only one in respect to which this practice has latterly been usual. It has a bigger ministerial team than any other office. The Parliamentary Secretary to the Treasury is the government Chief Whip and among his assistants are the junior Lords. When the post of Head of the Civil Service emerged after 1867 it was the Permanent Secretary to the Treasury by whom it was naturally assumed. And, as classes of official common to the whole Civil Service developed, it was the Treasury which was charged with securing uniformity of treatment and the regulation of conditions of work, a position confirmed by the creation of its Establishment division in 1919 and the Order in Council of 1920. Above all it wields the power of the purse, an authority from which its influence and prestige alike derive, giving it, as it were, a right of eminent domain in matters of finance and administration. Apart from the Cabinet Office, a relatively recent creation, it is the only major department dealing with the entire range of government responsibility, the others being concerned simply with particular aspects of that duty. Because of its paramount position it was not unreasonably called 'the

---

[1] As e.g. by the Ministers of the Crown Act (1937), 1 Edw. VIII & 1 Geo. VI, c. 38, §4.

department of departments'. Clearly in a review of central administration it is necessary to give some specific attention to this ubiquitous bureaucratic focus, 'the heart of our whole administrative system'.[2]

Richard Greaves once wrote that the Treasury is 'one of those curiosities of the British system of government which defy simple analysis.'[3] Yet without too much oversimplification, its role (as it has emerged over the past century and a half) may be seen as a threefold one. It is basically a ministry of finance dealing with the collection of revenue and supervising its expenditure by departments and other state agencies. As a result it is concerned with both 'regularity' and economy in the conduct of the public service. Because of this preoccupation it also became, secondly, the office with a responsibility for the efficiency of the government machine as a whole and for its effective operation and co-ordination. Finally in more recent times the Treasury assumed as well the task of advising on the regulation and direction of the nation's economic affairs. Of course the pattern of development revealed has, aptly perhaps, not been unchequered but its broad outline is clear enough. And, most significantly in the present context of exposition, the changes which have occurred in the Treasury's various areas of function, and so in the part it plays at the very centre of the modern Civil Service, exemplify just that transition from an age of limited government to the positive state which it is the purpose of this study to describe. Thus the story of the Treasury reveals the rise of collectivism in significant administrative microcosm, all aspects of its work having been crucially affected by the growth of public intervention.

COLLECTIVISM AND THE CRISIS OF PUBLIC EXPENDITURE

> The central problem is that of how to bring the growth of public expenditure under better control, and how to contain it within such limits as the Government may think desirable.
> Control of Public Expenditure, Cttee Rep., 1960–61 (vol. xxi), Cmnd. 1432, p. 5 §6

Whatever else it may have become the Treasury is basically and in origin a ministry of finance. Its functions in this respect are numerous and were classically described by the Haldane Committee.[4] First of all the Treasury

---

2 The phrase cited comes from a letter written in 1869 by G. A. Hamilton, first Permanent Secretary to the Treasury: see M. Wright, *Treasury Control of the Civil Service 1854–1874* (Oxford, 1969), p. 1.

3 H. R. G. Greaves, *The Civil Service in the Changing State: a Survey of Civil Service Reform and the Implications of a Planned Economy on Public Administration in England* (London, 1947), p. 136.

4 Machinery of Government, Ministry of Reconstruction Cttee Rep., 1918 (vol. xii), Cd. 9230, p. 17 §2.

is, subject to Parliament, responsible for the imposition and regulation of taxation and the collection of the revenue. In this task it has the assistance of the Boards of Inland Revenue and of Customs and Excise. Secondly the Treasury controls public expenditure in various degrees and ways but especially through supervision of the Estimates which have to be laid before Parliament. Thirdly it arranges for the provision of funds required from day to day by the public service and has considerable borrowing powers for this purpose as by the issue of Treasury Bills. Again it is the department with the responsibility for initiating and carrying out measures affecting the public debt, currency, and banking. For example, in conjunction with the Bank of England the Treasury is concerned with the determination of Bank (or Minimum Lending) Rate and for managing the exchange rate of sterling. Finally, it is the Treasury which prescribes the form in which the public accounts should be kept. It is the second of these functions which is the most important here, not least in the context of rapidly rising government expenditure. As the Haldane report said, experience seems to show on the whole that

> the interests of the tax-payer cannot be left to the spending Departments; that those interests require the careful consideration of each item of public expenditure in its relation to other items and to the available resources of the State, as well as the vigilant supervision of some authority not directly concerned in the expenditure itself; and that such supervision can be most naturally and effectively exercised by the Department which is responsible for raising the revenue required.[5]

Yet in this regard the influence or authority of the Treasury has never been as clear and complete as sometimes supposed or claimed. Moreover the formal character of Treasury surveillance has itself changed quite radically over the years: specifically it may be deemed to have passed through three phases. The first is dominated by the traditional view of detailed and severe Treasury control; the second by the clear acknowledgement that, because the task is so great, responsibility has to be divided between the Treasury and the spending departments; while the third reflects the contemporary crisis of government expenditure and the apparently insuperable difficulties of holding it in check. Each is associated with a stage in the growth of public sector spending; and together they suggest the paradox that as this expenditure has increased (indeed because of this tendency) the grip of the Treasury has loosened and this during a time when, it might rather be supposed, a tighter

---

5 ibid., pp. 18–19 §12. Lord Bridges attributed this passage to Sir George Murray, an ex-Permanent Secretary to the Treasury and a member of the committee, 'Haldane and the Machinery of Government', *Public Administration*, xxxv (1957), p. 261.

supervision was required. The implication is that the conventional image of Treasury control has long been misleading, a myth even, its credibility dependent on an environment which sustains only a limited range of government functions and relatively low expenditure. Once these conditions no longer obtain, the ineffectiveness of that control becomes apparent. And it is manifest, what was always in fact crucial, that it is political will alone that can determine the level of public expenditure and restrain its growth.

The paradigm and its limitations

The traditional view of Treasury control derives from or is associated with the budgetary attitudes appropriate to a period dominated by libertarian views. One object of policy was the attainment and preservation of free trade which implied that the interference of public authorities, and so their cost, should be sustained at the lowest possible level. Another goal was the reduction, even the elimination, of the National Debt which meant the pursuit of a balance of income over expenditure so that the surplus could be devoted to this end. Again a compatible stress on the moral virtues of thrift and probity, coupled with the belief that public spending was an unfruitful as well as a demoralizing substitute for private initiative, suggested that money should be allowed to fructify in the pockets of the people rather than be used to sustain an excessive functionarism. Purposes and values of this kind invited the strictest possible public parsimony. Operating within such a framework of ideas Treasury officials would properly be negative and destructive, firm in their conception of a due economy, prone to make difficulties over all expense however slight, to oppose any increase of cost, to niggle over details, to demur, and to delay. The concept of Treasury control will thus be one which highlights the office's omnipresent power, attributes to it a searching authority relentlessly pursuing savings however small, at all costs preventing unnecessary or undesirable public expenditure and bitterly hostile to its increase. However it is apparent that, even in its supposed prime, such control was never unalloyed and, in various ways, likely to be hindered. What has to be described, therefore, is both the paradigm itself, the concept of severe Treasury control and the procedures associated with it, and as well the reasons why this attitude was never fully effective.

The appropriate rules and procedures were a long time developing as many difficulties had to be overcome and ancient practices reformed and replaced. For instance it was not until the 1820s that the use of the English language and of Arabic numerals in accounting was generally introduced or the custom of keeping old tallies finally abolished. The various national revenues were not completely amalgamated into one

Consolidated Fund until 1854; and a single Board of Inland Revenue had not appeared until the late 1840s. It was later still that government offices were persuaded to adopt a uniform financial year and to relate all their income and expenditure in a system of double-entry bookkeeping. The obligation to present fully audited appropriation accounts was slow to spread even after Sir J. Graham's initiative at the Admiralty in 1832. And it was not until all salaries were fully charged on central funds that there was any hope of controlling the number and cost of officials.[6] Clearly the process of introducing a standard and properly controlled financial administration was a very slow one. What was crucial in the end was the development of collaboration between the House of Commons and the Treasury to secure an effective means of Parliamentary accountability. The reason was simply that, in the last resort, the matter was one depending on the balance of political pressures; and the Commons could lend an important effective sanction to Treasury views.[7] Departments were important official entities in their own right and headed by ministers with their special authority and responsibility to Parliament. Against this twin array the Treasury could not ultimately stand alone and needed Cabinet support and Parliamentary follow-up. Its influence depended first and last on political insistence that it should make its formal responsibilities effective. None the less, even though MPs might urge the need for economy or reorganization and the Treasury reacted positively to such suggestion, there could be no question of its view being imposed: it had to lead by example and recommendation, its weapons being persuasion and advice rather than command.[8]

The circle of control was completed by the reforms of the 1860s. The Public Accounts Committee of the House of Commons was established on a regular sessional basis in 1861 and, five years later, the office of Comptroller and Auditor General was created. Together with the Treasury these institutions completed a strong framework of financial supervision. It had three salient features. The first was the requirement of prior approval for all expenditure. As the ordinary expenses of government were withdrawn from the Crown's civil list it was established that departmental estimates of spending should be placed before Parliament annually and in an intelligible and regular form so that they might be considered by the House of Commons and, if deemed reasonable, accepted. And as a necessary preliminary the Treasury was

---

[6] For the examples cited, see H. Roseveare, *The Treasury: the Evolution of a British Institution* (London, 1969), pp. 134, 137–9; Sir T. Heath, *The Treasury* (London, 1927), pp. 35, 55–6; and Sir N. Chester, *The English Administrative System 1780–1870* (Oxford, 1981), pp. 180–3.

[7] Cf. H. Roseveare, *The Treasury 1660–1870: the Foundations of Control* (London, 1973), p. 160.

[8] idem, *The Treasury: the Evolution of a British Institution*, p. 132.

involved in the preparation of these proposals. Indeed it bore the formal responsibility for their fitness and accuracy and so was entitled to be satisfied in advance that they were defensible in Parliament. Consequently the Treasury could call for them in draft to inspect them and, if necessary, suggest their revision. By this means Treasury supervision of expenditure was put on a more methodical and consistent basis than before. An instance of the way the principle was laid down is provided by a ministerial ruling of 1869 which stressed the importance of previous consultation with the Treasury in regard to proposed legislation or public announcements of policy:

> The Cabinet desire notice to be taken by all members of the Government or others who may either have to take proceedings in Parliament, or prepare bills on the part of the Government that whenever it is proposed to repeal, or alter, or to grant exemption from any tax or duty... or to impose any charge upon the Exchequer, much inconvenience will be avoided if the person or persons concerned communicate with the Treasury before making any declaration, or taking any public proceedings, of a nature to commit themselves and the Government, so that the matter may be considered, and a common conclusion arrived at. And the Cabinet accordingly, direct that such communication shall be made in all cases without fail....[9]

The second important aspect of the system was the arrangement whereby the funds voted by Parliament were strictly appropriated to specific needs and clearly defined purposes. Any variation of the approved spending pattern – say an overrun which had to be dealt with by virement, excess vote, or supplementary estimate – required Parliamentary or Treasury authority; and sums not spent had to be surrendered. Thirdly an independent, non-political agency, the reformed Exchequer, was set up to issue appropriated monies and also to audit the annual accounts as required by the Treasury. Moreover the Comptroller and Auditor General and his staff were authorized to penetrate the internal workings of a department in order to sustain established canons of financial regularity, in particular to see that the Executive received no money except for purposes already approved and subject to later audit. The C & AG presented reports on these matters to the Public Accounts Committee of the House of Commons which thus became a powerful ally of the Treasury by carrying the threat of public exposure if any irregularity was revealed. The Treasury assisted with this inquest and had to deal with any criticisms made by the committee of the process of financial regulation. Over the years a considerable body of case-law in these

---

9 Cited J. P. Mackintosh, *The British Cabinet* (1962; 3rd edn, London, 1981), p. 270. Cf. Heath, op. cit., p. 58 for the later confirmation of this rule.

matters grew up constituting a set of guiding rules and principles for the control of public expenditure and for the conduct of departmental officials in this regard.[10]

It was widely accepted that the Treasury should enforce stringent economy and so help to limit the extent of government action. Already, by the very beginning of the nineteenth century, it was possible for a high view to be taken of the Treasury's status as 'a *superintending*, and *directing*' office with a more or less absolute discretion as to the propriety and expediency of expenditure.[11] And this notion of the suzerainty of the Treasury, as the centre of a single system of public finance, was not unechoed in the decades which followed.[12] Gladstone, for instance, was always opposed to what he called 'construction', that is, 'taking into the hands of the state the business of the individual man.'[13] Not least this was because it leads to increased spending and this, in turn, creates 'a spirit of expenditure' which had somehow to be 'exorcised'. Economy, he wrote in 1859, was 'the first and great article' in his financial creed.[14] He never wavered in this belief and, in a speech made some twenty years later, said that

> The chancellor of the exchequer should boldly uphold economy in detail; and it is the mark of a chicken-hearted chancellor when... because it is a question of only two or three thousand pounds, he says that is no matter. He is ridiculed, no doubt, for what is called candle-ends and cheese-parings, but he is not worth his salt if he is not ready to save what are meant by candle-ends and cheese-parings in the cause of the country.[15]

Sir C. Trevelyan was one who shared this position. He believed that Chadwick and reformers like him were reckless spendthrifts with a view of public money that ought to disqualify them from office; he also held that the roving eye of the Treasury official ought always to be searching out practices that might be abolished or improved so as to secure some

---

10 These rulings are embodied in the Epitomes of Reports from the Committee of Public Accounts: (i) 1857–1937, HC 154, 1937–8 (vol. xxii); (ii) 1938–1969, HC 187, 1969–70 (vol. xx).
11 J. R. Torrance, 'Sir George Harrison and the Growth of Bureaucracy in the Early Nineteenth Century', *English Historical Review*, lxxxiii (1968), pp. 64–5 (italics in original).
12 See also the examples cited in Roseveare, *The Treasury 1660–1870*, pp. 65–6, 94–5, 158–60, 196.
13 Gladstone to Lord Acton (11 February 1885), in J. Morley, *The Life of William Ewart Gladstone* (London, 1903), iii. 173. Cf. *The Ideological Heritage* (London, 1983), pp. 145, 226.
14 Cited from Morley, op. cit., ii. 62.
15 ibid., ii. 63.

saving.[16] He claimed in 1855 that the Treasury was 'the chief office of the Government' and that the 'whole Public Service is ... either directly or indirectly subjected' to its economizing influence.[17] Sir S. Northcote (Trevelyan's colleague in producing the famous report) explained the situation as he saw it in 1859 on an occasion when the War Office wanted to spend more money on staff:

> If the Treasury are to be responsible for the financial results of any arrangement, they must be allowed to inquire into the details of the arrangement, in order to ascertain whether its advantages are worth the cost it will entail, whether those advantages can be attained at a cheaper rate, and whether the arrangement which is proposed is likely to affect the arrangements already in existence.[18]

Another such was Lord Lingen, one of Trevelyan's successors in the chief official post at the Treasury (which he held from 1870 to 1885), who quite early in his career had shown a notable 'ability to negative claims' on public funds. He was (as one account puts it) 'well qualified' to carry aggressively into practice the 'doctrine of economy', proving himself 'an enemy of growing expenditure and a vigilant guardian of the public purse'.[19] In an obituary notice, *The Times* said he was 'resolutely determined that the expenditure of public money should be severely checked' and that he looked 'with a suspicious and grudging eye upon every claim involving an increase of outlay.'[20] Again it was firmly asserted in the mid-1860s that the 'right of the Treasury to determine what the several departments may spend...is incontestable.... [The] decision of the Treasury as to what expenditure is or is not sufficiently authorised, is final and without appeal.'[21]

A more extended illustration may be provided by the relationship between the Local Government Board and the Treasury during the period 1871-1905 as revealed in R. M. Macleod's fascinating study of ideology and administration. This has as its theme the way in which Treasury control stood athwart the path of collectivist advance on social matters: 'the L.G.B. exemplifies a classic case of a Victorian department which found itself forced by circumstances and repressive Treasury control to oppose the innovation of fresh policy and the acquisition of

---

16 J. Hart, 'Sir Charles Trevelyan at the Treasury', *English Historical Review*, lxxv (1960), p. 95.
17 Memorandum in Treasury Library cited in Chester, op. cit., p. 208.
18 Northcote to Sir B. Hawes (20 May 1859) cited M. Wright, *Treasury Control of the Civil Service 1856–1874* (Oxford, 1969), p. 144.
19 DNB, ii. 2754.
20 *The Times* (24 July 1905), p. 8.
21 Public Accounts, Sel. Cttee Rep., 1865 (vol. x), Appendix 1 pp. 145–6 §70.

new duties.'[22] More generally this control was a 'critical factor which must enter into any interpretation or explanation of the internal workings' of a government agency at that time.[23] The LGB's functions continued to grow inexorably leading to requests for increased staff which met 'inflexible Treasury resistance' embodied above all in the person of the aforementioned Sir R. Lingen.[24] Equally, in a Treasury minute of December 1886, the Chancellor, Lord Randolph Churchill, stressed the need for increased watchfulness and the limitation of plans for extensions of function and increases of staff or pay.[25] And although the pressures for the growth of LGB expenditure proved very powerful, the Treasury was often able to frustrate departmental proposals.[26] Macleod (who is clearly unsympathetic to the Treasury point of view) summarizes the results of his investigation as follows:

> It is clear that over-cautious control by a handful of Treasury officials, who justified their policies on grounds of 'sound finance' and the presumed need to guard against the capricious waste of public money by Government departments, both underlay and aggravated the unsuccessful attempts of the Board to generate an efficient, contented and productive staff. The Treasury frustrated such attempts by construing requests for reorganisation as occasion...for 'periodical purgations'.... The factor of fiscal frustration intensified the factor of administrative exhaustion.[27]

The stern conventional view of Treasury responsibility and the libertarian dislike of increased public expenditure with which it was often associated was authoritatively reflected, too, in the account of the office written in 1927 for the old Whitehall series by Sir Thomas Heath. He was a mandarin cast in traditional intellectual mould and says, right at the outset of his book, that the Treasury

> is generally looked upon as a kind of bugbear or bogey, especially by those who advocate proposals for the extension of Government activities in connexion with, say, social, educational, or industrial services, the inevitable effect of such extension being almost always some increase in expenditure out of taxation, which it is the primary duty of the Treasury to control.

---

22 R. M. Macleod, *Treasury Control and Social Administration: a Study of Establishment Growth at the Local Government Board 1871–1905* (London, 1968), p. 8.
23 ibid., p. 9.
24 ibid., p. 13 nn. 16–17, pp. 18–19.
25 Cited ibid., p. 25.
26 ibid., p. 32.
27 ibid., p. 52.

258 A Much Governed Nation

This very reputation itself had a useful consequence from this point of view:

> The administrative staff of the Treasury, by means of their specialised knowledge and experience, acquired as a rule by long training, are often able to offer advice to the Chancellor of the Exchequer which secures the rejection of a proposal for increased expenditure...; but it is safe to say that there is a still greater number of proposals which the mere existence of the Treasury prevents from coming forward at all.[28]

Heath goes on to sustain the established legend of Treasury control that, in Gladstone's day, 'the Treasury could almost refuse applications from Departments without giving reasons; the *onus* was rightly considered as being on the Department to justify the proposal.'[29] This position of authority had been formally confirmed in 1919 – partly as a reaction against wartime waste, partly to strengthen the Cabinet in deciding priorities – when it was determined that proposals involving expenditure should not be discussed by the Cabinet or its Home Affairs Committee unless Treasury approval had been given or, if the Treasury opposed, the spending department concerned had notified the Treasury that an appeal to the Cabinet was pending.[30] And, of course, Sir W. Fisher, who had been designated Head of the Civil Service in 1920, had a vision of the Treasury as a 'general staff' which would form 'independent and constructive views' on policy and not indulge in merely negative criticism. It would not supplant other departments but 'should not hesitate to concern itself with policy as necessary in exercising the power of the purse.'[31] Nor did the traditional view of the Treasury diminish easily. Lord Chatfield's experience during the inter-war period as Controller of the Navy (concerned with *matériel* development and supply) and later as First Sea Lord led him to write that 'Overpowering everything, was the immense power given to the Treasury. That power was to be found everywhere. Its proper function of avoiding waste and extravagance, was extended until it ruled as an autocrat in Whitehall, a veritable tyrant.'[32] An interesting restatement of the traditional view about the influence of the Treasury is to be found in the pages of R. H. S. Crossman's diary. His experience as a Cabinet minister led him to believe it was impossible to overestimate the Treasury's role in controlling expenditure:

28 Heath, op. cit., pp. 1–2.
29 ibid., p. 64 (italics in original).
30 G. C. Peden, 'The Treasury as the Central Department of Government, 1919–1939', *Public Administration*, lxi (1983), p. 375.
31 Cited ibid., p. 376.
32 Lord Chatfield, *It Might Happen Again* (London, 1947), p. 198.

All the civil servants I worked with were imbued with a prior loyalty to the Treasury and felt it necessary to spy on me and report all my doings to the Treasury, whether I wanted them kept private or not. There was nothing I could do, no order I could give, which wasn't at once known to the Treasury, because my staff were all trained to check with the Treasury and let it know in advance exactly what each of them was doing. When this Treasury system is reinforced by PESC, you get a staggering centralized control....[33]

Of course there was always complaint about the 'dead hand' of the Treasury as a restraint on desirable state activity. This was recognized, for instance, in a Treasury memorandum written at the end of the late war:

... if any agency of government is to centralise demands upon the public resources, to attempt to make some judgment between their relative merits and to secure the establishment of priorities between them – in brief to ensure that limited means are used to the best effect – it will incur hostility. Not only is it certain that its assessment of priorities will displease many, but it will frequently be accused of under-estimating the resources available to meet all the demands that are made.[34]

And there can be no doubt that in important respects or on frequent occasions Treasury control of expenditure was as firm and meticulous as the conventional view implied. But the interesting thing is that, even during its supposed hey-day, it was never so complete or severe in practice as this view suggested or as the paramount libertarian doctrine required. The truth be told, given that for so long the general object of policy was to keep public spending down, the system of financial regulation intended to achieve this was never very successful; and the Treasury itself was aware of the weakness of its position.[35] Public expenditure continued to rise inexorably and the Treasury seemed unable to stem the tide. In the particular case of the Local Government Board described above, it could in the end only delay or create obstacles; ultimately the forces arrayed against it proved too great and it was unable to prevent the growth of the department, the extension of its duties, and

---

33 R. H. S. Crossman, *The Diaries of a Cabinet Minister* (London, 1975–7), i. 615–16. Cf. ibid., i. 343; ii. 200; also the references to the 'uninspired' slashing of the Treasury, ii. 407–8. See also B. Castle, *The Castle Diaries 1974–76* (London, 1980) where the need to submit statements to the Treasury is often noted, pp. 43, 44, 49, 58, etc. On PESC, see pp. 277–86 below.
34 PRO, CAB 87/75 MG(45) 16, MGO 74 (June 1945), Appendix I p. 12 §15.
35 Wright, op. cit., p. 330; Roseveare, *The Treasury: the Evolution of a British Institution*, p. 10.

so the cost that this involved.[36] As Alpheus Todd said, in summary of contemporary experience, while in formal terms Treasury sanction was necessary and getting it might involve trouble and delay, it 'invariably' gave way 'in the end.'[37] In a not dissimilar tone G. J. Goschen (who succeeded Lord R. Churchill as Chancellor) held that departments must be made to be careful in their demands and compelled to give good reasons for any proposal requiring increased expenditure. Consequently the Treasury had to intervene in a ubiquitous, unflagging, and detailed way. Often, too, it would have to decline its sanction. Yet he did not believe it was possible to lay down 'precise principles as to the control to be exercised' and he was sure that a certain 'large-mindedness' and flexibility were often appropriate.[38] In fact, during the entire second half of the last century, the Treasury rejected relatively few applications from the spending departments for increased funds: 'few enough', says M. Wright in his admirable commentary on these matters, 'to cast serious doubt' upon the adequacy or reliability of usual ideas about Treasury control. The Treasury might have 'the necessary constitutional authority' to act with autocratic caprice but 'it exercised it relatively rarely'. Even more limited was its ability to enforce an actual reduction in expenditure.[39]

The reasons for this practical limitation of Treasury control were largely, though not entirely, political. And they have a continuing relevance up to the present day.[40]

The basic factor was a strong sense of the traditional power and dignity of the great offices of state, involving almost an assertion of autonomy: in 1873 Lingen told a select committee that each department was 'almost a little kingdom in itself'.[41] Constitutionally the position rested on the personal responsibility of a minister of Parliament for the policy and conduct of his department. In attempting to regulate or reduce spending, the Treasury (led in these matters by the relatively junior Financial Secretary) was in effect impinging on the authority and

36 Macleod, op. cit., pp. 19–23, 29–32, 49.
37 A. Todd, *On Parliamentary Government in England: its Origin, Development, and Practical Operation* (London, 1867–9), i. 563.
38 See the exchange of minutes recorded in Sir H. Hamilton, 'Treasury Control in the Eighties', *Public Administration*, xxxiii (1955), pp. 14–15. For Goschen's libertarian views, see *The Rise of Collectivism* (London, 1983), pp. 29–30, 102, 214–15, 226 and *The Ideological Heritage*, pp. 84, 144–6, 275–6.
39 Wright, op. cit., pp. 165–6; cf. ibid., pp. 168–9, 176–8, 184 and Heath, op. cit., pp. 64, 135.
40 Cf. the summary in Lord Bridges, *The Treasury* (1964; 2nd edn, London, 1966), pp. 40–1; and the interesting echo of many of the crucial points in H. Young and A. Sloman, *But, Chancellor* (London, 1984), *passim* but esp. ch. 2, 'The Language of Priorities'.
41 Cited Wright, op. cit., p. 340.

freedom of action of a Cabinet minister and leading member of the governing party who had to answer, for what his officials had (or had not) done, to his colleagues in the government and to Parliament as well as to constituency and other interests not to mention the public at large. Secretaries of State were accorded a particular deference in this regard. They were, Trevelyan said in 1848, 'held in a degree of respect by the Treasury' so that however trivial an issue – it might be merely the quality of paper used in a department – 'we have not felt that we had precisely the same control over them ... as over the other offices'.[42] In consequence if an adverse Treasury decision seemed important enough or was deemed an undesirable precedent, a minister might get in touch with the Chancellor himself.[43] This recourse failing, he could then appeal to the Prime Minister (who was also normally First Lord of the Treasury) or to the Cabinet as a whole. The Treasury's case would be put, no doubt strongly, by the Chancellor who might, or might not, have the backing of the Prime Minister on any particular issue. But equally the department's view was represented by a minister politically powerful in his own right and who might receive substantial support from colleagues either on grounds intrinsic to the issue in question and the policy it reflected or because they could easily envisage a situation in which the claims of their own department might be under similar Treasury scrutiny. The ultimate decision in crucial cases was bound to be a collective one for the main role of the Cabinet is to act as a final court of appeal in respect of issues it has not been possible to determine elsewhere.[44] The Treasury might hope to be influential in any such discussion but it could not of itself determine the outcome: though it would certainly have to cope with the financial consequences.[45] In the last resort, therefore, a conflict over spending between the Treasury and another office could depend on the political position of the Chancellor and the head of the department *vis-à-vis* one another and their colleagues in government. It was a matter of bargaining and ultimately of political will.[46] And such a question might, if pressed, and depending on the circumstances, arouse difficulties best left undisturbed. In the face of an actual or possible political appeal of this kind a Chancellor might often, even usually, decide it was expedient to give way or agree to some compromise. And that this was the usual practice is shown by the general lack of serious conflict between

---

42 Cited Roseveare, *The Treasury: the Evolution of a British Institution*, p. 149.
43 Public Monies, Sel. Cttee Rep., 1856 (vol. xv), q. 2198 cited Roseveare, *The Treasury 1660–1870*, p. 169.
44 Cf. W. S. Churchill, *Lord Randolph Churchill* (1906; new edn, London [1952]), p. 537; and Part 2 pp. 645, 758–9 below.
45 Roseveare, *The Treasury 1660–1870*, pp. 27–8, 37.
46 Cf. Peden, art. cit., p. 385.

departments and the Treasury.[47] And if it did come to the crunch Chancellors did not always get their way as the case of Lord R. Churchill – or much later that of P. Thorneycroft – showed. In time this ability to withstand Treasury pressure was reinforced at official level by the position of the departmental accounting officer who, since 1872, has been separately answerable to the Public Accounts Committee for the regularity and economy of the spending of his department and so for its efficiency. Given that such a formal responsibility exists it must to a degree inhibit Treasury influence.[48] Moreover the autonomy of departments was shown by the fact that there were several sorts of question on which the Treasury was not normally consulted at all: such matters as special allowances, office hours, leave, or discipline which could all have cost aspects. These were seen as subject to the discretion of the minister concerned.[49] And, although estimates from all departments were submitted to the Treasury before they went to Parliament, not all were minutely investigated.[50] As well there was little or no control over the general extent of naval and military expenditure, the force levels being settled by the Cabinet; and it was not until 1870 that the Admiralty and the War Office accepted even formally the Treasury's authority to regulate their spending on establishments.[51] And in practice the Treasury's intervention was usually restricted to cases of new or increased expenditure. The Treasury itself stated the position in a minute promulgated in April 1868:

> It appears to my Lords that it would be beyond the functions of this Board to control the ordinary expenditure placed under the charge of the several departments, within the limits of the sums set forth under the sub-heads of the several grants of Parliament, and that it is only in exceptional cases that the special sanction of the Treasury should be held to be necessary.
>
> My Lords consider that such sanction should be required for any increase of establishment, of salary, or of cost of a service, or for any additional works or new services which have not been specially provided for in the grants of Parliament.[52]

47 Cf. Wright, op. cit., pp. 168–70, 334–5, 338–43.
48 Cf. Sir E. Bridges, *Treasury Control* (London, 1950), p. 11. Up to 1925 the accounting officer was usually the principal finance officer; since then it has normally been the permanent secretary.
49 Wright, op. cit., pp. 272, 295–303, 306, 324–5. Cf. ibid., pp. 331, 335–6 with a slightly different emphasis but to the same general effect.
50 Roseveare, *The Treasury 1660–1870*, pp. 167–8.
51 ibid., p. 167; Wright, op. cit., pp. 344–5. At one time defence spending constituted more than a quarter of all public spending though this proportion has now substantially diminished: see *The Rise of Collectivism*, Table 2 p. 34.
52 Public Accounts, Sel. Cttee Rep., 1867–8 (vol. xiii), Appendix 1 no. 4 p. 55 (repr. in

The point was reiterated during the inquiries of the Ridley Commission a couple of decades later. The then Permanent Secretary to the Treasury was asked whether it could be assumed that there was 'virtually no Treasury control' unless there was a demand for increased expenditure. He replied that in the main he thought that was so, the effective control being applied 'when an increase is asked for.'[53] Thus the Treasury's power to secure cuts in existing levels of cost was always far slighter than its ability to refuse or reduce proposed increases.[54] It is a mistake, therefore, to suppose that a department was without resource when faced with Treasury pressure. There was even positive hostility to the Treasury, and sometimes it was expressed in the highest quarters. Lord Salisbury, three times Prime Minister, was very censorious about the way the Treasury carried out its supervisory task. In the House of Lords in 1900 he publicly accused it of doing so in a way that caused delay, difficulty, and disadvantage to the public.[55] At the time, and in the context of the disasters suffered in the early stages of the second Anglo-Boer War, these remarks had especial reference to the supposedly malign influence of Treasury parsimony on the national defences. But Salisbury had expressed before this his concern about the Treasury and its role. For instance he had on one occasion written to the Chancellor of the Exchequer, 'I am bound to say that as a result of my experience during some fifteen years of cabinet office that I think in small matters the Treasury interferes too much. In large questions its resisting power in frequently inadequate.'[56] Dr Roseveare puts in appropriate context this flurry of criticism of the so-called 'Treasury ring'. Salisbury's outburst, he writes,

> was the remarkable climax to at least half a century of tension between the Treasury and the great spending departments. It marked also the collision of rival social, political and foreign policies. The issue at stake was essentially the survival of the Gladstonian tradition of rigid economy against the mounting demands of a nearly democratic state. It was an issue of minimal, balanced Budgets against large, continuous programmes of social and military expenditure. It was therefore, an

---

Public Accounts, Sel. Cttee, Epitome of the Reports 1857 to 1937, 1937–8 [vol. xxii], HC 154, pp. 20–1).

53 Civil Establishments, R. Com. 1st Rep., 1887 (vol. xix), C. 5226, Minutes of Evidence, p. 2 q. 8.

54 Roseveare, *The Treasury 1660–1870*, p. 161.

55 78 Parl. Deb. 4s., 30 January 1900, col. 32. On these matters, see Roseveare, *The Treasury: the Evolution of a British Institution*, pp. 183–4 and Sir H. Hamilton, 'Treasury Control in the Eighties', *Public Administration*, xxxiii (1955), pp. 16–17 on both on which I draw here. Cf. the adjournment debate on the control of the Treasury over other government departments at 80 Parl. Deb. 4s., 20 March 1900, cols 1354–60.

56 Cited Roseveare, *The Treasury: the Evolution of a British Institution*, p. 184.

issue of free trade against preferential tariffs, of 'Little England-ism' against expansionist Imperialism. These conflicts cut across party lines.

He adds that the very fact that the Treasury 'was so thoroughly permeated by the old Gladstonian tradition' tended to increase its isolation. By the end of the nineteenth century, the evolution of British politics had made it 'very nearly' a matter of 'the Treasury *versus* The Rest.'[57] Further there is the point that, however much MPs and peers (or the political public as a whole) might feel the need for stringent economy in government expenditure, they were increasingly subject to contrary pressures to deal with the needs created by the new towns, the growth of population, the poorer classes, and to spend money on education, public health, and so forth. And these demands were, of course, reinforced alike by the extension of the electorate and the growing pace of administrative momentum. There was in addition the increasing cost of modern war and of preparation for it.[58] It all constituted a tendency the Treasury could hardly withstand not least because it meant it could not always look to Parliament or ministers for steady support in any fight against increased expenditure or to achieve reductions.[59] Lord Welby, who had been Permanent Secretary to the Treasury from 1885 to 1894 and who was himself a great believer in rigid economy and a strong Treasury, told the new Select Committee on National Expenditure in 1902 that the turning point had come in the 1880s, since when 'the wind was in the sails of the spending Departments'. Once, when Welby had urged economy on Lord Salisbury, the latter had replied, 'Who are we that we should try to swim against the tide?'[60] In the inter-war period, too, financial policy (although it could have some effect in reducing expenditure) was not proof against what Sir R. Hopkins called in 1932 'the onward march (even under a severe economic policy) of the cost of Education, Widows Pensions, Housing and other things'.[61] And in due time the attitude hostile to increased state expenditure gave way to one which had a different, and much wider, view of the proper objects of public concern and which accepted, too, the positive economic value of government spending as a stimulus, for instance, to production and the employment of resources including labour.[62] Sir T. Heath signalled the transformation

---

57 ibid., p. 186.
58 See *The Rise of Collectivism*, chs 2–4.
59 Cf. S. Baldwin's comment as cited in A. T. Peacock and J. Wiseman, *The Growth of Public Expenditure in the United Kingdom* (1961; new edn, London, 1967), p. 69.
60 Roseveare, op. cit., p. 199; *DNB*, ii. 2956.
61 Cited Peden, art. cit., p. 381.
62 Bridges, *Treasury Control*, pp. 7, 9. Cf. *The Rise of Collectivism*, pp. 127–36 esp. p. 133.

or switch of emphasis involved when he noted the tendency to suppose that, instead of a department having to make an unassailable case for a proposal, it was rather up to the Treasury 'to justify the refusal'.[63] Moreover as public expenditure continued to rise, it became more and more difficult to control with the result that Treasury supervision became increasingly inadequate. In time even the attempt to review these burgeoning sums in detail was given up and the Treasury began rather to leave such review to the individual departments, contenting itself with broad totals only coupled with whatever specific inquiries seemed possible or prudent: the test audit of a particular policy or activity; calling for periodical reports (say, to spot management deficiencies or falling standards); or, most important of all, simply the inspection of the department's own arrangements for financial self-regulation.[64] Given the vast sums involved, nothing more was possible perhaps. Certainly as Sir E. Bridges told the Public Accounts Committee in the early 1950s, 'to say that every conceivable type of day to day administration must be checked in detail by the Treasury I really think leads you ultimately to an extremely cumbrous system which I believe would break down under its own weight.'[65] Of course a lot depended on the type of expenditure concerned. Where it arose from administrative routine the Treasury and the department acted on reasonably well-defined rules which both accepted. Where it arose from a new departure in policy (implemented by the minister or approved by the Cabinet) the control of the Treasury was likely to be more limited.

Again it has always to be remembered, as another aspect of this same problem, that as a superintending and not an executive department the staff of the Treasury was not at all large. As public spending grew, the limited number of senior officials there could inevitably supervise less detail; indeed a smaller proportion of the steadily increasing cost of state activity could come under central review. There was necessarily a diminution in the effectiveness of the Treasury supervision of finance and establishments as indicated, no doubt very crudely, by the enlarging Treasury 'control quotient' measured in Table 7.

Related to this was the fact that increasingly much of the new expenditure was on projects the assessment of which required technical knowledge or expertise which in the nature of things the Treasury officials did not possess. Nor did (or does) the Treasury have at its disposal any alternative reservoir of specialist information apart from that provided by or available in the spending department itself.

63 Heath, op. cit., p. 64.
64 Cf. B. Chubb, *The Control of Public Expenditure: Financial Committees of the House of Commons* (Oxford, 1952), pp. 178–9.
65 Public Accounts, Sel. Cttee 4th Rep., 1950–1 (vol. iv), HC 241-I, p. 568 q. 7205.

Table 7 *Treasury work and staff, 1805–1985*[a]

Year	Total supply services expenditure (£ millions) (i)	Total Civil Service staff (non-industrial) (000s) (ii)	Treasury staff total	Treasury staff senior[b] (iii)	'Control quotient' (1) (i) ÷ (iii)	'Control quotient' (2) (ii) ÷ (iii)
1805	42.1	n.a.	65	21	2.01	—
1834	20.3	21.3[c]	79	27	0.75	0.79
1856	64.9	39.2[d]	82	32	2.03	1.23
1871	41.0	53.9	68	25	1.64	2.16
1881	51.4	50.9	110	26	1.98	1.96
1891	69.5	79.2	109	29	2.40	2.73
1901	173.5	116.4	113	27	6.43	4.31
1911	147.5	172.4	119	31	4.76	5.56
1921	845.8	343.4	374	110	7.69	3.12
1931	521.0	318.9	299	69	7.55	4.62
1941	3,723.5	566.1	560	169	22.03	3.35
1951	2,883.8	675.4	1,385	436	6.61	1.55
1961	5,398.6	650.2	1,342	411	13.14	1.58
1971	14,817.8[f]	498.4[e]	1,014[j]	230	64.43	—[j]
1981	74,090.8[g]	539.9	1,006[j]	172	430.76	—[j]
1985	93,412.1[h]	498.0	2,533[k]	282	331.25	1.77

a *Sources*: Total supply services expenditure: (1) 1805–1931 from B. R. Mitchell and P. Deane, *Abstract of British Historical Statistics* (Cambridge, 1962), pp. 396–9 (total gross expenditure less debt charges); (2) 1941–61 from B. R. Mitchell and H. G. Jones, *Second Abstract of British Historical Statistics* (Cambridge, 1971), p. 161; (3) 1971–85 from CSO, *Annual Abstract of Statistics*.
Civil Service staff: (1) 1832–1911 from H. Finer, *The British Civil Service: an Introductory Essay* (London, 1927), p. 14; (2) 1921–31 from Staffs Employed in Government Departments, 1922 (vol.xv), Cmd. 1567 and 1931–2 (vol.xviii), Cmd. 3984; (3) 1941–85 from CSO, *Annual Abstract of Statistics*.
Treasury staff: (1) 1805–56 from J. C. Sainty, *Office Holders in Modern Britain I: Treasury Officials 1660–1870* (London, 1972), pp. 104–8 (some names appear more than once in these lists, but, in such cases, only one post has been counted in the totals given); (2) 1871–1985 from Civil Estimates, British Imperial Calendar and Civil Service List, Civil Service Yearbook, and Civil Service Statistics.
b 'Senior staff', although it has since the Estimates of the early 1960s received an official definition, is here an arbitrary and impressionistic category which includes broadly the top four grades and equivalent posts at the various dates. I have tried to make the count in each year uniform but clearly the totals are liable to minor variation and useful only for a rough relative indication of the size of the senior group of Treasury officials. But it was obviously no good using the total Treasury staff as a criterion as this includes everyone from the permanent secretary to the newest messenger.
c 1832.
d 1851.
e The main factor in the decline from 1961's higher figure was that in 1969 the Post Office became a public corporation and its staff were therefore excluded from the Civil Service total.
f 1971–2.
g 1981–2.
h 1984–5.
j Between 1968 and 1981 the Civil Service Department was responsible for pay and management.
k The increase in the 1985 figure is due to return of certain functions to the Treasury when the CSD was abolished at the end of 1981. Other duties were, however, then transferred not to the Treasury but to the new Management and Personnel Office so that the Treasury's subsequent (and current) role is not strictly comparable to that before 1968.

268   A Much Governed Nation

Inevitably the Treasury found it difficult in such cases to rebut claims for more money or staff; and equally it came to rely more and more on departmental advice and recommendation. Nor is it a new problem except in scale, as an example from the last century shows; for Sir John Simon, head of the Medical Department of the Privy Council, was often successful in blinding the mere administrators with science. Lingen at the Treasury was the last person to give money away without careful scrutiny. Yet he confessed in reference to one of Simon's demands: 'I do not know who is to check the assertions of experts when the government has once undertaken a class of duties which none but such persons understand.'[66] The most the Treasury could do was try to establish an informed opinion about the soundness of any proposals by reference to past experience of similar projects (if any) and by consultation with, or cross-examination of, the departmental officials concerned. But clearly to an important extent an independent financial check ceased to exist in such cases; and the problem remains in respect to, say, expenditure on a weapons system.[67] Or to take another instance relating to welfare expenditure (and which also bears on the matter previously mentioned), there were in 1982 ten Treasury staff (including 'clerical support') dealing with all the spending on the staff and benefit side of the DHSS. The assistant secretary in charge said:

> Now it stands to reason that there's quite a lot of what the department does that we don't actually see and we don't know about. Overall the system should ensure that public expenditure is planned according to faintly [sic] rational principles – whether it does, that's another matter, that's what it's designed to do. But there are quite large areas of departmental spending on which the Treasury is not expert, cannot by nature of what it is and how many we are, be expert on everything that's done. I think it's amazing that we are expert, in the superficial sense that we are [sic], on all the main areas.[68]

There are other points too. So much expenditure (like pensions and other social service payments) came to be fixed and automatic; was authorized by statute; or represented a long-term commitment difficult to renege. In such cases discussion could really only concentrate on the margins. With more new schemes, especially those concerned with welfare or with modern weapons, or where a policy had to be introduced

---

66 Lingen minute of 1 June 1871, cited R. J. Lambert, 'A Victorian National Health Service: State Vaccination 1855–71', *Historical Journal*, v (1962), p. 16. For more recent comment on Treasury control in respect of technical programmes, see Public Accounts, Sel. Cttee 4th Rep., 1950–1, HC 241-I, p. 584 q. 7343, pp. 585–6 qq. 7350–1, pp. 586–7 qq. 7361–8.
67 Young and Sloman, op. cit., pp. 46–7.
68 ibid., p. 49.

very quickly thus precluding a full review, it was impossible to say whether estimates of cost were adequate. All too often they proved to be imprecise or drastically low, as with the assumptions about the NHS which proved wildly at variance with what actually happened. But the Treasury could do little once the policy decisions had been made or until the expenditure ran so completely out of hand that it became a political issue (not to say scandal) in itself. The same sort of difficulty could arise with respect to unforeseen events, contingencies such as the unexpected need to mount a military expedition or an increase in the world price of some essential commodity such as cotton or oil. As well there were the dangers of waste which could arise from expenditure continued because of political unwillingness to induce necessary change or where the need no longer existed.[69] Further the development of a whole range of non-departmental organizations was often deliberately pursued as a means of avoiding the usual trammels of ministerial and Treasury responsibility.[70]

For all such reasons, then, Treasury control has always been limited and has become increasingly so. In practice, and even when public expenditure was at much lower levels than later became usual, the control was never as severe, complete, or uniform as the formal picture might have suggested. Even Gladstone admitted that, had the regulatory ideal been the reality, Treasury authority would have been widely regarded as tyrannous.[71] And Professor Wright cites the case of Acton Ayrton, a Liberal politician, who in 1869 was removed after a few months from his post as a junior Treasury minister because his brusque zeal for economy did not match the temper of the office.[72] The truth is that the great spending departments always enjoyed a certain discretion in financial matters in so far as they could resist Treasury attempts to cut or restrict their expenditure. In this sense the system of financial control was limited for it relied to an important extent on their restraint or self-regulation, on their 'willingness' to accept changes proposed by the Treasury.[73] True the Treasury's prior approval was formally required; it could resist a proposal for more expenditure; call for more information; or impose delay, as by insisting on an unofficial committee of inquiry to explore the issues.[74] And, of course, the possibility of such a review or cross-examination might lead a department to withhold some

---

69 Cf. Control of Public Expenditure, Rep., 1960–1 (vol. xxi), Cmnd. 1432, p. 31 §§101–2.
70 For this development, see below ch. 5, pp. 345–6.
71 Wright op. cit., p. 348.
72 ibid., pp. 336–7. Cf. *DNB*, ii. 2366.
73 See the evidence of the then Permanent Secretary to the Treasury to the MacDonnell Commission: The Civil Service, R. Com. 4th Rep., 1914 (vol. xvi), Cd. 7338, pp. 85–6 §96 citing qq. 1903–4.
74 Wright attributes some importance to these committees as a means of Treasury supervision, op. cit., pp. 339–40, 349.

applications and to submit only those it considered really necessary. Goschen told the committee on War Office organization in 1901:

> The first object of the Treasury must be to throw departments on their defence, and to compel them to give strong reasons for any increased expenditure, and to explain how they have come to have to demand it. This control also contributes to make the departments careful in what they put forward.[75]

Yet such 'moral' or indirect control was also restricted in its effect, could be challenged, and (in the outcome) certainly did not serve to check the tide of expenditure which was rising all the time.

In the circumstances it was a system of dual supervision which grew up; and this formed the basis of the second concept or phase of Treasury control.

A divided responsibility

As already explained, it was always open to departments and their ministerial heads to resist Treasury pressure for economy. Of course the degree of success would vary according to the persons and circumstances involved. But the possibility of compromise of this sort implied the notion of a divided financial responsibility shared by the Treasury and the spending departments themselves. And in due time this potential for difference and adjustment (together with the other limitations on Treasury authority) became the basis of a new orthodoxy, a doctrine more appropriate to an age of rising expenditure in which it was all too apparent that the traditional view of severe Treasury control was manifestly quite impracticable.

Naturally the reality of a divided responsibility had often been recognized. As early as 1856 the Principal Clerk of the Treasury's Finance Division explained to the Select Committee on Public Monies that the 'great departments charged with the execution of the public business are the departments that really control the expenditure. The control of the Treasury is of a general character, to see that these departments keep within the limits of the sums appropriated by Parliament'.[76] Over half a century later the Haldane Committee stressed again how vital it was to recognize this state of affairs:

> The superiority of the spending Departments in knowing what is required for the execution of their several services, in accordance with the policy with regard to them which has been determined by

---

75 Cited ibid., p. 346.
76 Cited Roseveare, *The Treasury 1660–1870*, p. 169.

Parliament or the Government, must necessarily limit the scope of any useful exercise of the restrictive authority of the Chancellor of the Exchequer.

At the same time, of course, the experience and knowledge of the Treasury will enable it 'usefully to criticise the methods of other Departments' or 'to make suggestions for amending their proposals' with a view either to reducing the cost or to securing a greater return for the outlay. 'It is none the less true', that report concluded, 'that the execution of any scheme will necessarily depend on the goodwill and co-operation of the spending Departments concerned.'[77] It was perhaps the second war, together with the higher level of public expenditure that appeared in its train, which finally laid to rest the original myth of Gladstonian Treasury control. The reality had always been rather different; the circumstances of the day now made a formal paradigm shift inevitable. In 1942 Attlee stressed that Treasury attempts to impose excessively detailed financial supervision should be avoided and that departments ought to develop their own checks.[78] Similarly in 1945 an official memorandum stressed both the financial responsibilities and controls of the spending departments themselves and the high degree of co-operation which had grown up between the Treasury and other offices. It went on to say that this delegation of authority plus the close contacts maintained created a 'mutual confidence which makes close scrutiny of financial proposals unnecessary over a wider field'. The Treasury was sure, too, that the stock comments about 'cheeseparing' would not (in respect of recent times at least) be endorsed by the departments.[79] Of course this observation was made at the end of a long war during which financial restraints were necessarily relaxed but its tone was a portent for the future. A few years later Sir E. Bridges, then Permanent Secretary to the Treasury, referred (in a lecture devoted to the question of financial supervision) to the contemporary trend away from the 'meticulous control of detail' in favour of 'greater delegation to Departments' with his own office needing simply 'to satisfy itself that the standards of prudent housekeeping' were being observed.[80] Similarly a few years on, Professor Beer's study of the subject made clear that the Treasury had no overriding power of command and that greater responsibility had fallen

---

77 Machinery of Government, Ministry of Reconstruction Cttee Rep., 1918, Cd. 9230, p. 19 §14. Cf. ibid., p. 10 §29, p. 19 §13.
78 Memorandum for the Machinery of Government Committee in PRO, CAB 87/74 MG(42)6 (31 December 1942), p. 3 §(3).
79 PRO, CAB 87/75 MG(45)16, MGO 74 (June 1945), Appendix I pp. 12–13 §§17–18. The Machinery of Government Committee itself strongly endorsed the Treasury's general approach, ibid., MG(45)10 (18 October 1945), p. 2 §5.
80 Bridges, *Treasury Control*, p. 27. Cf. idem, *The Treasury*, pp. 40, 205–6.

to departments.[81] Nor was other recognition of the transformation lacking at this time.[82] This stress on partnership and negotiation with the departments rather than the imposition of detailed Treasury control is still the paramount orthodoxy today.[83] One permanent secretary said very recently, 'Far from it being an adversarial relationship, I see it as a continuing, constructive dialogue.' Another confirmed that over the last quarter-century 'there has been a very decided swing towards greater delegation to departments and disengagement of the Treasury from the detail of expenditure.'[84] Or, as it was described in another image, the Treasury is traditionally 'the hub of the system of public expenditure control with lines radiating to all departments which are inalienably responsible for their own spending programmes.'[85]

Thus the high ground of control was perforce formally surrendered because of the sheer weight of public expenditure and the impossibility of sustaining the traditional position. Of course there was a great deal of concern about the looser degree of financial supervision now officially accepted as adequate especially as it depended for its operation on departments which had become accustomed to high spending. As one exasperated observer pointedly said to a very senior Treasury official, 'I ... do not see how you can claim that you are exercising a closer and more effective control by relaxing control.'[86] Parliamentary concern was aroused, the Public Accounts Committee expressing the whole range of disquiet. In a series of reports it reflected the by now usual worry that current expenditure was ineffectively supervised, that too little disciplinary action was taken against officials responsible for waste or loss, that Treasury influence was insufficient, and so forth.[87] The Select Committee on Estimates had also turned its attention to the matter in an important and very critical report on 'Treasury Control of Expenditure' which appeared in 1958. This stressed the absence of anything like a coherent system of Treasury control, or even of a systematic view of public expenditure as a whole. And it emphasized the fact that what supervision there was tended to be *ad hoc* or piecemeal and varied from one department to another depending on historic circumstances rather

---

81 S. H. Beer, *Treasury Control: the Co-ordination of Financial and Economic Policy in Great Britain* (Oxford, 1956), pp. 10–11.
82 See e.g. the statement in Estimates, Sel. Cttee 7th Special Rep., 1958–9 (vol. iv), HC 227, p. 6 §14.
83 Young and Sloman, op. cit., pp. 44–7, 52–5, 61, 64; G. C. Beard, *Government Finance and Accounts: Background Notes* (MPO; n.p. [London], 1982), p. 20.
84 Both cited from Young and Sloman, op. cit., pp. 50, 52.
85 Sir S. Goldman, *The Developing System of Public Expenditure Management and Control* (Civil Service College Studies no. 2; London, 1973), p. viii.
86 Public Accounts, Sel. Cttee 4th Rep., 1950–1 (vol. iv), HC 241-I, p. 344 q. 4243.
87 ibid., pp. xlvi–l; 2nd Rep., 1959–60 (vol. iv), HC 256, p. 17 §45.

The Department of Departments 273

than actual necessity.[88] As well, officials and very senior politicians expressed disquiet. One retired permanent secretary acknowledged in 1956 that the increase in government spending which had occurred had by no means been matched by a sufficient adaptation or strengthening of the rules governing Treasury control.[89] And in the early sixties, an MP (soon to become First Lord) said that perhaps the Treasury had too much to do and so was paying too little attention to the traditional task of securing due economy and the prevention or elimination of waste.[90] Certainly the bargaining process could be extensive but one Labour minister described how it was possible 'to beat those Treasury officials at their own game.'[91]

A specific example dating from the immediate post-war period may indicate the sort of practical difficulties involved and the kinds of issue which worried critics. It concerns the proposal to build an airfield at Changi on Singapore Island.[92] In and after 1946 a development scheme of this sort was urged but was treated diffidently because of the cost, thought likely to exceed £4 millions. A major reason for this high level of anticipated expenditure was that the site in question was largely mangrove swamp. The Japanese had started filling in and so forth during the war but the standard of work was not regarded as adequate. The structure of the subsoil to a depth of ten feet was then tested by trial bores; and on this basis the site was pronounced suitable. However when preliminary construction work began, some instability was revealed. Further test boring to the much greater depth of sixty or more feet was then undertaken and these experiments showed that the original scheme could only be carried out at a quite prohibitive cost. Consideration was given to these matters; a revised scheme for lighter aircraft only was put into effect with the subsequent abandonment of the original project which had involved nugatory expenditure of £400,000. It is clear, looking back, that this was caused through the lack of proper preliminary enquiry. Why were not adequate tests, calculations, or forecasts made in the first instance? Who was responsible for the failure and loss: the Treasury, the department, or some other public body? The department was supposed to see its scheme had a sound technical base and the Treasury had somehow to satisfy itself that this was done. Yet clearly in this case the arrangements were not able to prevent the waste that

---

[88] Estimates, Sel. Cttee 6th Rep., 1957–8 (vol. v), HC 254-I, esp. pp. xxxvi–xxxvii §§94–5.
[89] Sir J. Woods, 'Treasury Control', in W. A. Robson (ed.), *The Civil Service in Britain and France* (London, 1956), p. 118.
[90] H. Wilson, in J. Grimond *et al.*, *Whitehall and Beyond* (London, 1964), pp. 16–17.
[91] Castle, op. cit., p. 173. For some other instances of departmental bargaining with the Treasury, see ibid., pp. 54, 65–6, 75, 140–1, 171–2, 175–6, 199–200, etc.
[92] Public Accounts, Sel. Cttee 4th Rep., 1950–1, HC 124-I, pp. xxxi–xxxii.

occurred. Inevitably, at a time when there was a vast and growing expenditure much of it undertaken on the basis of technical or scientific advice, it was feared that a relaxed or divided financial control must often lead to losses of this kind. Over the years a critic would be able to refer to such cases as the groundnut scheme, the Gambia egg project, the profits made by Ferranti on the Blue Streak rocket, and the escalating costs of such aircraft projects as the TSR2 and Concorde.[93] Of course these are collective policy decisions taken on many grounds: but it was worrying that the financial aspects seemed to be so little regarded and that the continuing cost controls were inadequate. There was a concern that too loose an attitude to public spending had grown up and that the process of supervision was insufficient. There seemed to be neither the political will nor the administrative machinery to secure really effective control of expenditure. Crucially the climate of opinion had been transformed: the traditional, received idea of limitation or retrenchment which was once the norm had, over the years, given way to the seemingly bottomless reservoir of taxable capacity. Neither Parliament nor ministers were prepared (or wanted) to stem the collectivist tide; and in the face of its onrush the Treasury seemed, inevitably perhaps, to be abdicating even the pretence of detailed control and was leaving more and more responsibility to the spending departments themselves. The only limits in practice were the greater taxation entailed and the possible economic effects of that and of the expenditure in view. Moreover a new dimension had been added to the traditional problem of expenditure control: the idea of macro-economic management or planning made it vital to secure an overall view of public expenditure of all kinds and a rational allocation of the resources it represented. The aim of Treasury control was thus widened and deepened. It had to help determine the aggregate of public spending and its role in the general economic context as well as to see that there was an efficient management of funds and resources within that public sector.[94] Yet there was no confidence that the, by now, accepted system of bilateral bargaining between the Treasury and individual departments was any longer adequate to restrain expenditure or keep it within the scope of prospective sources available.[95] Certainly few actual economies ever seemed to be achieved. Reconstruction was necessary to deal with nothing less than a crisis of public expenditure.

---

93 Cf. D. Wood, *Project Cancelled: a Searching Criticism of the Abandonment of Britain's Advanced Aircraft Projects* (London, 1975), esp. chs 9–10 on the rise and fall of the TSR2.

94 Cf. C. Pollitt, 'The Public Expenditure Survey 1961–72', *Public Administration*, lv (1977), pp. 127–8.

95 Sir R. Clarke, *Public Expenditure Management and Control: the Development of the Public Expenditure Survey Committee (PESC)* (London, 1978), p. 25 §67.

The crisis of control

There was, then, a growing suspicion that the essentially collaborative character of contemporary financial supervision was not so effective as it should be in respect both of the total of government and public spending and of specific policies or areas of expenditure. The Estimates Committee had urged the need for an independent review of the whole matter. Instead a confidential inquiry under the chairmanship of Lord Plowden was set in train in the summer of 1959 aided by a group of senior officials and persons from outside the government service. It took two years to complete the series of reports involved though these were not published. However a consolidated account was drawn up and appeared in July 1961.[96] It had an immediate impact and a continuing authority leading to what has been called the 'Plowden Revolution'.[97] But, as one academic commentator put it, 'What did not follow was that public expenditure was brought under effective control.'[98]

By and large the Plowden report was a monument to collectivism. Inevitably perhaps, given its provenance and authorship, it assumed that a rising public expenditure extending over wide areas and sustained by Keynesian policies (as well, more generally, by Parliamentary and public opinion) was an aspect of affairs that would continue.[99] However it was acknowledged that the existing system of financial control needed to be reorganized for not only had it been created when different attitudes to the public service – an 'austere discipline' – prevailed, in addition it was difficult even to sustain the piecemeal methods that had become usual (so hard had it become to get to grips with the problem).[100] What was needed was a more rational and efficient means of planning the use of public money and other wealth. The four elements of reconstruction proposed were: regular long-term surveys of the entire range of public expenditure and prospective resources in the context of which decisions about future spending could be taken; more stability of expenditure policy (that is, no more 'stop–go'); more tools of control (as by the reform of the Estimates and the greater use of quantitative methods); and more effective machinery for ministers to take collective decisions.[101] Something of these

---

96 For this background, see Control of Public Expenditure, Rep., 1960–1, Cmnd. 1432, p. 1.
97 For the factors involved in the report's influence in both official and political circles, see Pollitt, art. cit., pp. 130–1. Cf. the papers of comment in *Public Administration*, xli (1963). The phrase cited comes from G. K. Fry, *The Administrative 'Revolution' in Whitehall: a Study of the Politics of Administrative Change in British Central Government since the 1950s* (London, 1981), p. 77.
98 Fry, op. cit., p. 77.
99 Control of Public Expenditure, Rep., 1960–1, Cmnd. 1432, p. 6 §§10–11, p. 12 §31.
100 ibid., pp. 5–6 §§8–9, 11; p. 29 §91.
101 ibid., pp. 6–12.

changes was already under way as with the reviews of spending on defence and nuclear power which had been initiated and the public sector programme first drawn up in 1957.[102] But in the Plowden group's view the tendency needed to be intensified. Thus was intimated the era of 'forward-looks', PESC, PAR, cost-benefit analysis, the greater use of computers, and all the rest of it.

On the specific question of the Treasury control of supply expenditure the report accepted the usual division of responsibility. It stressed, therefore, the idea of co-operation, of the Treasury and a department jointly 'working together in a common enterprise'; and it suggested, too, that 'the scope for delegation' of responsibility to departments should gradually widen. The safeguard suggested was that the Treasury should 'have submitted to it a sufficient number of proposals relating to individual items of expenditure' to enable it to know how a department conducts its business and to make an informed assessment of its financial needs. But the Treasury should primarily concern itself with the adequacy of the department's own machinery of control rather than with the individual submissions.[103] Changes in the Treasury's own structure and working were also introduced to try to strengthen its effectiveness.[104] Some adjustments had already been made at the most senior level when Bridges retired in 1956. Because of the very considerable burden, he was replaced by two joint permanent secretaries, one to be concerned with the financial and economic side, the other (who would be official Head of the Home Civil Service) to deal with the remaining aspects of the Treasury's work (and also to continue as Secretary to the Cabinet).[105] The further, post-Plowden changes were more radical affecting more than the top of the Treasury and, though not entirely unprecedented, constituted a major break with tradition.[106] There continued to be two Joint Permanent Secretaries but the Secretaryship of the Cabinet was now to be held separately as a post of similar status. Beyond this the Treasury's organization was completely remodelled on a more functional basis. Hitherto a government department had dealt with one of the Treasury's 'mixed' divisions so-called because they handled both supply and personnel matters. These divisions were now abolished and the Treasury organized into two 'sides', one dealing with pay and management, the other covering economic and financial questions

102 Clarke, op. cit., pp. 18–20.
103 Control of Public Expenditure, Rep., 1960–1, Cmnd. 1432, pp. 13–14 §§34, 39.
104 ibid., p. 20 §59.
105 KCA (1955–6), p. 15011A.
106 On these changes, see D. N. Chester and F. M. G. Willson, *The Organization of British Central Government 1914–1964* (1957; 2nd edn, London, 1968), pp. 352–3; and D. N. Chester, 'The Treasury, 1962', *Public Administration*, xl (1962), pp. 419–26.

including the control of public expenditure on which more resources than before were concentrated.[107] At ministerial level, too, a new Cabinet post – that of Chief Secretary – was created in 1961 to assist the control of public expenditure.[108] His job, as one incumbent later said, was 'to be the abominable "No-man" and once he becomes less than that, he is failing in his job.'[109]

However the major change after Plowden was the introduction of the Public Expenditure Survey, known generally as PESC after the official PES Committee established to oversee the whole range of public spending and to co-ordinate the advice tendered to the Chancellor and to ministers collectively.[110] Obviously it needed to be supplemented by machinery to monitor the detailed control now largely in the hands of the departments. This was provided by later arrangements for what was called Programme Analysis and Review.

From PESC to cash planning

The basic point of departure was the growth of public sector spending, a tendency the forces behind which were so strong it was felt that responsibility for controlling them could not be left to the Chancellor alone. Rather there ought to be a systematic review of 'the whole body of public expenditure' undertaken by ministers collectively.[111] And their judgements ought to be reached after a more informed consideration than was hitherto possible, relative priorities being established with regard not only to total public spending but also to the diverse and competing claims of individual policies. Moreover this should be done in a way which enabled resources and costs to be matched to the objectives sought with due recognition being given to government's responsibility for managing the level of demand and productivity in the economy at large. All this meant in turn a reform of the Estimates. Traditionally these reflected proposed central government expenditure only, and solely for one year ahead. But there were two major defects in this arrangement. The first was that the time-scale was too short and needed to be replaced by a planned cycle of spending over, say, three to five years. For instance a building programme would typically involve relatively little expenditure

---

107 Pollitt, art. cit., pp. 132–3; Bridges, *The Treasury*, pp. 141–3, ch. XV, and Appendix I pp. [210–11].
108 Clarke, op. cit., pp. 27–8; Bridges, *The Treasury*, pp. 162–3.
109 Expenditure, Sel. Cttee 11th Rep., 1976–7 (vol. xxxi), HC 535-II, p. 801 q. 1967 (Lord Diamond). Cf. L. Brittan's summary in Young and Sloman, op. cit., p. 59; also ibid., p. 62.
110 HM Treasury, *Public Expenditure White Papers: Handbook on Methodology* (London, 1972), p. 6 §18. Cf. Goldman, op. cit., pp. 35–6.
111 Sir A. Cairncross, 'Foreword', in Clarke, op. cit., p. xii; Sir R. Clarke, 'Parliament and Public Expenditure', *Political Quarterly*, xliv (1973), p. 138.

in its first twelve months but much more in the following years as construction got fully under way; and then when completed it would entail a given level of costs in making use of the buildings. This future pattern of activity and spending ought to be presented at the outset as part of a planned review of the future use of money and resources. The second deficiency in the conventional form of the Estimates was that they covered only the spending of the central departments. It was clearly necessary, however, to take account of all public sector expenditure and to include that of local government, the nationalized industries, and other state agencies.[112] Following the Plowden inquiries, steps were taken to create a statistical apparatus for the new system, to educate departments in its working and implications, and to persuade ministers to accept it. In 1960 the newly appointed Chancellor, S. Lloyd, aided by a small ministerial group, prepared the ground for the introduction of the Public Expenditure Survey system which, initiated the following year, became the recognized basis for the overall planning of public expenditure.[113] The Treasury handbook summarized its purpose as follows:

> The system provides Ministers with a regular means of seeing where their existing policies will lead in public expenditure terms, and for considering this against the economic prospects and their own social and political priorities. In this way they can decide whether the demands upon resources likely to be made by the public sector need to be altered, or left unchanged, and whether the allocation of these resources between the various programmes of expenditure should be varied. In short, the system is designed to facilitate the Government's decision-taking by providing a better perspective.[114]

The story since then falls into three phases.[115]

The first covers the establishment of PESC as, in effect, a replacement of the traditional Estimates.[116] PESC was initially seen as a means of planning, allocating, and controlling public expenditure in the medium term during which it was supposed that fairly stable conditions would show steady economic growth achieved by Keynesian management of the economy. It involved an annual exercise whereby the allocation of

---

112 HM Treasury, op. cit., pp. 3–4; Pollitt, art. cit., pp. 129–30; Sir L. Pliatzky, 'Have Volumes Gone Underground? An Interim Report on Cash Planning', *Public Administration*, lxi (1983), p. 323.
113 Clarke, *Public Expenditure Management and Control*, pp. 50–1; HM Treasury, op. cit., pp. 1–4, 7.
114 HM Treasury, op. cit., p. 7 §19.
115 Pliatzky, art. cit., pp. 323–6.
116 Sir R. Clarke, *New Trends in Government* (Civil Service College Studies no. 1; London, 1971), pp. 42–3.

resources for the whole public sector, calculated in terms of existing policies and constant prices, was indicated in respect of six groupings of twenty or so functional programmes. The latter included such areas as defence, health, education, social security, roads, law and order, and so forth and each usually involved more than one department. Further division was possible into sub-programmes and also into quite other categories such as type of expenditure (capital or current) or spending authority (central or local government or public corporation). The forward look involved the current year and four years beyond (or, in a few cases, more). And the entire costing operation was revised and updated annually.[117] As compared with the previous Estimates system, therefore, the range of data was more comprehensive, covered a longer time-scale, and was expressed in a functional form. And a report about the proposed allocation of resources and the cost of existing policies went to ministers for a collective decision in late summer or autumn.[118] PESC was the basis of public expenditure review during the '60s and '70s and often regarded with pride as the best control system in the world.[119]

However, serious practical deficiencies emerged which (in the view of one careful observer) revealed that PESC's claim to economic rationality was somewhat spurious.[120] The Cabinet's consideration of the PESC proposals was, by all accounts, rushed and scanty. As well individual ministers still exercised their right to take an expenditure question affecting their department to this final court of appeal, often over quite small sums. To this extent the whole intention of the exercise was thwarted (though the situation was hardly unprecedented).[121] Moreover the Treasury's role was not enhanced and it still acted simply as arbiter to competing departmental claims for resources: thus 'Whitehall's essential federalism was preserved'.[122] Professor Wright commented that it was 'difficult for the Treasury to resist the individual and collective pressure of ministers to maintain and improve the level of service-provision in their programmes.' In contrast there are, he added, few pressures

---

117 HM Treasury, op. cit., pp. 4–5, 8, 11–16.
118 ibid., p. 6. For the first ministerial PESC exercise, see Clarke, *Public Expenditure Management and Control*, pp. 113–25; Crossman, *The Diaries of a Cabinet Minister*, i. 256, 266–8.
119 See the claims cited by A. Likierman, 'Planning and Control – Developments in Central Government', in A. Hopwood and C. Tomkins (eds), *Issues in Public Sector Accounting* (London, 1984), p. 148.
120 M. Wright, 'From Planning to Control: PESC in the 1970s', in idem (ed.), *Public Spending Decisions: Growth and Restraint in the 1970s* (London, 1980), pp. 91–4.
121 For comment on PESC as it was dealt with by ministers, see Crossman, op. cit., ii. 434; iii. 231–2; Castle, op. cit., pp. 360, 548. See also A. Sampson, *The Changing Anatomy of Britain* (London, 1982), p. 187.
122 Pollitt, art. cit., pp. 140–1.

motivated by a concern for economy.[123] That is to say, the traditional bargaining between the Treasury and the spending departments continued, little affected by the new language and arrangements of PESC.[124] Indeed the introduction of PESC might be seen to have loosened Treasury control over expenditure in important respects.[125] Because the time horizon was lengthened it became more difficult to ensure on an annual basis that what was financially entailed by departmental activity during a twelve-month period corresponded to the approved expenditure for that year. And because public expenditure was defined more comprehensively, a more diverse array of spending authorities was involved over whom there was often little control. There were also certain other intrinsic problems. For instance the data produced were inadequate for some purposes and did not include costed options so that organized discussion leading to effective choice was difficult. Also some of the figures, like those for the final years of the cycle, proved too uncertain and were politically remote as well. In some open-ended schemes – where, say, a grant or benefit was payable at a fixed rate to all those eligible – the future cost was bound to be hard to estimate because it depended on the number of applicants coming forward. Nor was the precise timing of expenditure always easy to predict – for instance a capital project would be affected by the speed with which a contractor did his work and this, in turn, by such incalculable factors as the weather; and a variation in the, often long, construction period required by a major enterprise could have a significant effect on expenditure projections. Indeed all sorts of factors might be important in determining the level and distribution of resources in the public sector: the changing economic and financial situation; the attitudes of ministers, officials, and party supporters; the pressure of interest groups; public opinion; the IMF: that is to say, not just a rational economic appraisal of the claims made for various programmes. Moreover many such programmes proved resistant to short-term change except at the margin.[126]

More than this, the PESC programmes themselves appeared to get out of control.[127] The official PES committee had initially accepted that public expenditure would be of the order of 42 per cent of GNP; but it quickly became apparent that, without a fundamental change in social

---

123 M. Wright, 'Public Expenditure in Britain: the Crisis of Control', *Public Administration*, lv (1977), pp. 153, 154. Cf. Clarke, *Public Expenditure Management and Control*, pp. 99–100.
124 Wright, 'From Planning to Control: PESC in the 1970s', loc. cit., pp. 94–5.
125 For this case, see idem, 'Looking Back at "Looking Forward"', in B. Chapman and A. Potter (eds), *W.J.M.M. Political Questions* (Manchester, 1974), pp. 281–3.
126 Wright, 'From Planning to Control: PESC in the 1970s', loc. cit., pp. 92–4.
127 Sir A. Cairncross, 'Foreword', in Clarke, *Public Expenditure Management and Control*, p. xvii.

policy (which was politically unacceptable), even this limit could not be sustained.[128] For planning purposes an annual rate of expansion was built into the main block of public expenditure on the supposition that a 4 per cent growth rate in the economy would occur. But, as Clarke himself later admitted, this was a political calculation rather than a statistical appraisal. It was *assumed* that resources would grow to allow for the proposed expansion of spending: and they did not.[129] Moreover the way PESC came to work, the agreed 'volumes' (so many miles of road-building for example) were regarded as 'sacrosanct'. They were, in effect, entitlements protected against rising costs for four years ahead, and money was guaranteed to meet, say, pay or contract requirements whatever these turned out to be. The original plan was based on constant prices; the actual bills turned out to be very different and always bigger. The effect of high and variable rates of inflation caused the system to come under increasing strain: in itself this factor made the planning of public expenditure more and more difficult.[130] In addition departments tended to under-estimate the cost of their programmes; and, through the 'bidding' procedure that developed, what should have been a means of control was turned into a series of competitive claims on the anticipated increment of growth. The emphasis was on objectives rather than resources or costs.[131] In sum the Treasury badly under-estimated the intrinsic growth of public expenditure implicit in the policies being developed during PESC's early years; it proved impossible to restrain expenditure on a programme once it had been decided on even if costs increased. So there was little control of detailed spending and increases began to run ahead of prospective economic growth.[132] Clearly PESC was hardly proving an effective instrument of even medium-term control of public spending and it had to be faced that, instead, it 'had become a vehicle for escalation of public expenditure' in both real and cash terms.[133] Attempts were made at improvement and Goldman held that by 1970 a 'fully functioning' system had been established.[134] It proved a rash claim. His account was published in 1973, yet it was soon to be apparent

---

128 ibid., pp. 52, 55.
129 ibid., pp. 67, 72–3. Cf. Goldman, op. cit., pp. 8–9; Fry, op. cit., p. 181.
130 Cf. Pliatzky, art. cit., p. 324; Likierman, loc. cit., p. 149.
131 Clarke, *Public Expenditure Management and Control*, pp. 89–90; J. D. Stewart, 'From Growth to Standstill', in M. Wright (ed.), *Public Spending Decisions*, pp. 15–16.
132 Clarke, *Public Expenditure Management and Control*, p. 79. And cf. the remarks of the Expenditure, Sel. Cttee 1st Rep., 1975–6 (vol. xxviii), HC 69-I, pp. vi–vii §§2–3, p. ix §§11–12.
133 Pliatzky, art. cit., p. 325.
134 Goldman, op. cit., p. 12. Crossman thought the new arrangements an enormous improvement, op. cit., iii. 394, 686.

that expenditure was once more out of hand. This was manifest in the embarrassing and sometimes very large divergences which appeared between expenditure targets as originally planned and actual spending. In 1974-5, for instance, the out-turn exceeded the forecast which had been made in the 1971 survey by £6,500 millions.[135] Discrepancies of this order were taken to signal the breakdown of PESC for it was thus permitting the spending of money on a scale not contemplated when policies were determined. Nor was the wrath of critics assuaged by the Treasury's claim to be able to account for the 'missing billions': to explain an overspend after it had occurred was definitely not the same as being able to control or prevent it.[136]

It was obvious too that economic circumstances had changed and that controlling public expenditure 'in an era of persistent and high rates of inflation and unemployment, low productivity and stagnant industrial production' was bound to be 'an exercise of a different order' from that appropriate to the more stable economic conditions of the early 1960s. In this regard the turning-point was 1972-3 when the energy crisis not only stimulated inflationary pressure but generated a wide debate about the use of resources and the limits of economic growth. The mood changed; and the problem became one not so much of planning public expenditure (in the earlier sense) but of restraining it or cutting it back.[137] In sum: PESC was not designed to prevent ministers from increasing expenditure but to show them the consequences of so doing in terms of the estimated costs and of the resources available. Its major defect as it turned out was that it was not able to secure that what was spent was that planned and no more, an inadequacy very clearly revealed when inflation got under way.[138]

Obviously in the new circumstances certain things needed to be done. One was to achieve a more rigorous restriction of local authority spending for this amounted to a third or so of all public sector expenditure: a Consultative Committee on Local Government Finance was set up for this purpose in 1975.[139] Another was to secure better and more up to-date financial information to enable the flow of expenditure to be more effectively monitored.[140] But the most important was the

---

135 M. Wright, 'Public Expenditure in Britain: the Crisis of Control', loc. cit., p. 150 (see also Table 2, ibid., p. 148).
136 ibid., p. 149.
137 M. Wright, 'From Planning to Control: PESC in the 1970s', in idem (ed.), *Public Spending Decisions*, pp. 88, 97.
138 ibid., p. 113.
139 Wright, 'Public Expenditure in Britain: the Crisis of Control', loc. cit., pp. 162-4; idem, 'From Planning to Control: PESC in the 1970s', loc. cit., p. 101.
140 For the financial information system (FIS), idem, 'Public Expenditure in Britain: the Crisis of Control', loc. cit., pp. 160-2.

imposition from April 1976 of cash limits on given blocks of expenditure to prevent overruns: the medium-term planning of volume programmes continued but it was now subject to a short-term cash control.[141] This saved the PESC system from collapse and marked the second phase of development constituting an attempt to limit the effect of inflation (and thus to sustain the 'voluntary' incomes policy then in favour). If the amount of money for a given programme was limited there was obviously an incentive to economize and secure good housekeeping practices (one remembers the not unsalutary effects the cash limits policy achieved in the universities) and also to keep wage increases down. But there were two difficulties.[142] One was that cash limits could not be applied to open-ended or demand-response programmes such as social security without affecting the standard of service. The other was that any pay increases over the norm laid down would have to be financed either by job losses, a reduction of capital expenditure, or cuts in service. Because of such consequences, actual or implied, the PESC system as modified was still the subject of much criticism. Indeed by the end of the 1970s confidence in PESC had evaporated and the Treasury was once more under fire for its failure to deal with the crisis of public expenditure.[143] And the allocation of resources, as ever, still depended on the results of bilateral negotiations with departments. One summary of the situation put it this way: 'In the strict sense of ensuring a close match between outturn and planned expenditure, it is difficult to claim that the Treasury was controlling public expenditure more effectively at the end of the 1970s than at the beginning, despite the changes made to PESC.'[144]

There was, of course, a change of government at this time; and this, though the basic problem of control continues, indicates the advent of the third phase of post-PESC development, one associated with the system of so-called cash-planning of programmes first fully introduced for the financial year 1982–3. In fact this is simply an extension of short-term cash limits beyond a single year ahead. Pliatzky observed that there is not in this sense much 'planning' about it.[145] But, then, all that had already failed. The cycle has been reduced to three years; the impact of inflation and extra costs has been limited by building in a given – and low – rate of increase only; and at least ministers discuss the cash that will actually be spent instead of talking in terms of (what was called) 'funny money', the constant price volumes which usually turned out to be 'misleadingly different from the resultant cash spent'.[146] Again uncertain

---

141 Pliatzky, art. cit., p. 324.
142 ibid., p. 324.
143 Wright, 'Public Expenditure in Britain: the Crisis of Control', loc. cit., pp. 166–7.
144 idem, 'From Planning to Control: PESC in the 1970s', loc. cit., p. 116.
145 Pliatzky, art. cit., p. 326.
146 HM Treasury, *Public Expenditure; Planning in Cash* (Economic Progress Report

levels of service have resulted, a matter which has caused some commentators considerable concern.[147] And there has been a certain suspicion that cash limits have been used as a means simply of controlling public sector pay.[148] Monitoring techniques have been improved in particular by the use of the Treasury's computer-based Financial Information System.[149] There is also more effective restriction on the use of the contingency reserve.[150] On the other hand the relationship of forecast to out-turn has still been inexact: there has been overspending of some limits and a significant number of revisions.[151] Indeed the present government had less success in keeping its total expenditure within the aggregate envisaged than its Labour predecessor under Callaghan.[152]

Whatever the next step is, it seems problematic whether the PESC system in anything like its original form is likely to survive, and this despite Clarke's hope that it would stand alongside the changes of 1866 as one of 'the great historical reforms in the control and management of public expenditure', the point at which effective supervision was established for the second half of the twentieth century.[153] None the less Clarke's summary of the main conclusions to be drawn from the first decade and a half's experience of PESC acknowledge *inter alia* both the power of the collectivist tendency and the divided (or partnership) nature of financial control.[154] He accepts in the first place that 'the strength of the forces and interests in our society which favour increase of public expenditure...are much greater than diagnosed by the Plowden Committee' even. Secondly he believes that the basic PESC innovations are 'likely to survive as the permanent foundation of public expenditure planning and policy' though there will inevitably be modifications and improvements, as with the introduction of cash limits. Thirdly the responsibility is necessarily divided: it is the spending departments' job to create the programmes and control their rate of progress while the centre

---

no. 139 [1981]), cited Likierman, loc. cit., p. 149. For a recent account of the PES system, see Beard, *Government Finance and Accounts: Background Notes*, pp. 41–5.
147 e.g. P. K. Else and G. P. Marshall, 'The Unplanning of Public Expenditure: Recent Problems in Expenditure Planning and the Consequences of Cash Limits', *Public Administration*, lix (1981), pp. 274–6; T. Ward, 'Cash Planning', ibid., lxi (1983), pp. 85–90.
148 Likierman, loc. cit., p. 152.
149 See the description in Beard, op. cit., pp. 48–50. And on the APEX system, ibid., pp. 27–9.
150 Else and Marshall, art. cit., pp. 253–4.
151 Likierman, loc. cit., p. 154.
152 Else and Marshall, art. cit., p. 267.
153 Clarke, *Public Expenditure Management and Control*, p. 147; Ward, art. cit., p. 90. Cf. the doubts expressed by N. Johnson in *Public Administration*, lviii (1980), pp. 360–1.
154 Clarke, *Public Expenditure Management and Control*, pp. 163–4.

has to satisfy itself that they are properly organized and equipped for their task; and they should work jointly together in this common enterprise. And fourthly while, of course, PESC could not alter the essentially political nature of the final judgement made by the Cabinet, with PESC ministers were at least '"talking and bargaining about the right questions, and... making real choices.... I think this is the real gain, and... an important one."'[155] Or, as Cairncross suggested, PESC 'made an immense difference if only because it furnished... a map of total public spending.' On the other hand it is less clear what it 'contributed to the relationship between the Treasury and spending departments, to the grasp within the Treasury of the policy options open to departments, and to the making of wise choices between these options.'[156]

Whether a system of cash limits remains or is used in conjunction with the planning of 'volumes', and whatever the level of public expenditure envisaged, it is the political realities which will prevail. Despite all the talk about the rational control of expenditure, matching it to resources, and so forth, decisions depend on push-and-pull. Sir W. Armstrong once told the Procedure Committee that there is no 'economic calculus that will enable one to say what precisely the right amount of public expenditure is, or that it precisely should be *this* on defence, *that* on education and *that* on roads. These are basically political decisions'.[157] Of course the calculus may help those decisions to be good ones; but it cannot take their place. And the nature of political decision-making is characteristically different. When M. Kogan was writing about the politics of educational change he asked C. A. R. Crosland how a minister obtained from the public funds enough resources to implement his policies. Crosland (who had held various Cabinet posts including the Education and Science portfolio) replied:

> By persuading, arguing, cajoling, exploiting his political position, being a bloody nuisance in Cabinet. Above all by being persistent. Obviously success depends on a whole mixture of factors, a lot of them a matter of luck – your relations with the Chancellor; your standing in the Cabinet; the way the rest of the Cabinet feels towards the education service; whether you can exhaust your colleagues before they exhaust you. It is an endless tactical battle which requires determination, cunning and occasional unscrupulousness. In an ideal world it would all no doubt be settled by some omniscient central unit, but this is the way it happens in our crude democratic world.[158]

---

155 Cited in Sir A. Cairncross's 'Foreword', ibid., p. xviii n. 4.
156 ibid., p. xvii.
157 Procedure, Sel. Cttee 1st Rep., 1968–9 (vol. xv), HC 410, p. 30 q. 47 (italics in original).
158 M. Kogan (ed.), *The Politics of Education* (Penguin, 1971), p. 167.

Not much room here for the planned rationalities of PESC or for searching control by the Treasury as a surrogate for thirty million taxpayers.[159]

Reinventing the wheel

If PESC constituted an attempt to provide a more rational view of public spending as a whole, it was also more or less loosely associated with a range of specific techniques intended to enhance financial control and improve efficiency: accountable management, linear programming, cost-benefit analysis, and output budgeting for example. The stress is on economic rationality based on the collection of adequate information and the examination of alternative choices so as to minimize cost and achieve an optimal allocation of resources. Such developments depend, of course, on modern forms of data processing and the use of the computer. Perhaps the technique most associated in recent British administration with the new style of review and supervision was that called Programme Analysis and Review (PAR), intended to help ensure 'the regular re-appraisal of policies across the whole field of Government.'[160] It was supposed to complement PESC through the explicit examination of alternative means to a given end, there being little time for this during the PESC cycle itself.[161] The potential cost implications of this sort of exercise were obviously considerable. Of course what was involved was not completely new: it was in principle the sort of procedure the Treasury and other departments had often used. As Sir R. Clarke tartly put it, in 1970 the Heath government reinvented the wheel and called it PAR.[162] But it was now to be applied in the context of a much higher level of public expenditure; to be based on more sophisticated techniques; and the exercise was to be more regularly and systematically undertaken. Clearly it reflected dissatisfaction with whatever existing arrangements for programme review there were and reflected an attempt to improve and systematize them at a time of dramatically rising costs. Thus 'PAR was an important part of a wider movement, both in the UK and elsewhere, to develop "rational management" in government.'[163]

The need for this had been expressed for some time, as by the Select Committee on Estimates as far back as 1958.[164] The immediate impetus,

---

159 I steal this latter image from a remark cited in Young and Sloman, op. cit., p. 43.
160 HM Treasury, op. cit., p. 2 §4.
161 Pollitt, art. cit., p. 139; Goldman, op. cit., pp. 45, 48.
162 Clarke, *Public Expenditure Management and Control*, p. 100.
163 A. Gray and W. Jenkins, 'Policy Analysis in British Central Government: the Experience of PAR', *Public Administration*, lx (1982), p. 430. This is a most useful account on which I have relied for much of what follows.
164 Estimates, Sel. Cttee 6th Rep., 1957–8 (vol. v), HC 254, e.g. pp. xxxvi–xxxvii.

however, was derived partly from the Conservative wish to find means of controlling or reducing state functions, partly from the concern of the Cabinet Office and the Treasury to see established an effective system of programme evaluation.[165] The intention to establish machinery for the analysis of existing programmes and of policy options was announced in the White Paper on 'The Reorganisation of Central Government' where it was made clear that it was seen as an important reinforcement of PESC.[166] Two other main aims were involved: 'to increase the co-ordinative and controlling capacity of the centre of government, i.e. to enhance strategic management'; and 'to increase ministerial control over departmental activities'.[167] The intention, never fully realized, was thus to review 'departmental and interdepartmental programmes on a regular basis and in a fundamental way' with a rolling cycle of inquiries integrated with PESC.[168] Or, as a contemporary Conservative tract put it, it was supposed to be 'a routine pressure' on the major departments 'to ask themselves exactly what they are trying to achieve, what it costs, whether this is the best way of doing it, whether it is worth doing at all.'[169] Heath himself told the Expenditure Committee in 1977 that what he had wanted

> was to have a piece of machinery which could say, in effect: 'These things have been going on perhaps for 10 years, 20 years, 30 years or more. Are they still necessary?' The second question is that even if they are necessary, have they got as high a priority as the other things which we are trying to do today? And have they got a higher priority than the new things which people are asking us to do? This piece of organisation was set up, therefore, to examine systematically every aspect of a department's activities and to report in terms of priorities.[170]

A joint memorandum from the Civil Service Department and the Treasury stated that the object of each investigation would be to examine the goals of a programme, the amount and use of the resources allocated to it (that is, its cost), and any alternative ways of achieving the objectives in view.[171] It was originally intended to locate the central responsibility

---

165 Gray and Jenkins, art. cit., pp. 432–4. For the background, see also Goldman, op. cit., pp. 45–7.
166 1970–1 (vol. xx), Cmnd. 4506, p. 4 §7, p. 14 §§49–52.
167 Gray and Jenkins, art. cit., p. 434.
168 ibid., pp. 429; cf. ibid., 435, 436.
169 J. Bruce-Gardyne, *Whatever Happened to the Quiet Revolution?: the Story of a Brave Experiment in Government* (London, 1974), p. 118 (citing D. Howell). Cf. the detailed account given by Treasury witnesses to the Select Committee on Expenditure in January 1972, cited ibid., pp. 118–19.
170 Expenditure, Sel. Cttee 11th Rep., 1976–7 (vol. xxxi), HC 535-II, p. 765 q. 1877.
171 Gray and Jenkins, art. cit., p. 435.

for overseeing the PARs in the Civil Service Department but in the outcome this task fell to the Treasury and the Central Policy Review Staff which had also been set up as part of the new governmental look, ministerial responsibility for the PAR programme being given to the Chief Secretary.[172] Individual departments differed considerably in their response to, and organization for, the PAR process.[173] The Ministry of Defence (which had an embryo PAR system of its own) seems to have been enthusiastic; but others had resisted the idea. Among other things it meant that they, and their ministers too, had to be prepared to submit aspects of departmental policy and procedure to another process of outside scrutiny. And clearly ministerial readiness to do this was a main condition of the effectiveness of PAR.[174] Topics for review were selected as a result of bargaining between the Treasury and the department concerned; most of the detailed work was done by departmental working parties or individual officials; and the reports were formally submitted, with any CPRS comments, to the relevant Cabinet committee.[175] According to Goldman they were of two kinds: 'instrumental' PARs which examined the efficiency with which given activities and organization pursued certain ends; and 'objective' PARs which embraced the alternative options open to government.[176] The reports were not published but it is known that topics covered included: farm structure policies; rural depopulation; services for the elderly; higher education; schools expenditure; projecting Britain overseas; animal health policy; police manpower; preparing adolescents for work; tourism; horticultural improvement schemes; and policy for overseas development after entry to the EEC.[177]

The first two cycles of reviews, carried out from 1971 to 1973 and comprising twenty or so inquiries, were strongly supported politically. At this stage Goldman believed that with careful development (which meant recognition of PAR's limitations) its potential value was considerable, and that recognition would follow.[178] Certainly it was 'the only institution' that central government then had 'for regularly reviewing departmental programmes in relation to their objectives and saying "Is it worth doing it, and if so, how can we do it better."'[179] Subsequently the impetus was lost; and the reports remain 'as fossilized

172 On the Treasury's role, see Goldman, op. cit., pp. 49–50.
173 Gray and Jenkins, art. cit., pp. 435–8; Bruce-Gardyne, op. cit., p. 120.
174 Cf. Goldman, op. cit., p. 49.
175 Gray and Jenkins, art. cit., pp. 435–42.
176 Goldman, op. cit., p. 48.
177 ibid., p. 48; Gray and Jenkins, art. cit., pp. 430, 437, 441–2, 444.
178 Goldman, op. cit., pp. 50–1, 55–6.
179 Treasury and Civil Service, Sel. Cttee 1st Rep., 1980–1, HC 54, p. 99 q. 1175 (W. Plowden).

memories of a dead species', shelved 'like rows of completed dissertations in a university library.'[180] The suggestion of excessive academic abstraction, leading to practical ineffectiveness, is deliberate and prompts the question why this failure occurred. Partly it was because unsuitable topics were chosen, cumbersomely investigated, and productive of no specific and implementable conclusions: the reports were too often merely 'essays' and not sufficiently 'action oriented'. Nor were the persons employed on the task always of the highest calibre.[181] The reports were limited to two a year in each department and took a year or more to complete.[182] And they were not always (even usually) on topics of immediate political moment.[183] Clearly at this rate of production the idea of a regular and complete appraisal of departmental activities was hardly a short-term prospect. Central direction was insufficient, too, with the result that departments were left too much to go their own way.[184] Most important of all the political conditions for success were not present. There is little evidence of continuing ministerial support.[185] The Labour administration which came to office in 1974 was suspicious of its predecessor's innovations. Moreover the PAR reports seem to have been found unhelpful in making political judgements on matters which interested ministers. It simply became an 'irrelevance'. So it was hardly surprising that in November 1979 the Thatcher government finally ended 'Whitehall's major and perhaps only effort at institutionalizing rational policy analysis.' Thus PAR ran into the sand. After that 'sights were lowered' and (as with the CPRS and Rayner exercises) pragmatism reigned.[186] Lord Croham said in 1981 'it was a good idea which was rather disappointing; it did not get off the ground'; or (as another senior official put it) when it died the death it was not fulfilling any very useful function.[187] But at least it had some effect in instilling a sense of economy and efficiency (the Rayner scrutinies later being intended to achieve the same end).[188]

In sum, then, the Treasury is still the hub of the system of public

---

180 Gray and Jenkins, art. cit., pp. 429, 442.
181 ibid., pp. 442, 443–5. For the similar, earlier story of O & M, see below pp. 300–13.
182 Cf. Heath's evidence to the Expenditure Committee, 11th Rep., 1976–7, HC 535-II, p. 765 q. 1877.
183 See the topics listed on p. 288 above.
184 Gray and Jenkins, art. cit., pp. 445–6.
185 ibid., pp. 446–7; W. Plowden memorandum in Treasury and Civil Service, Sel. Cttee 1st Rep., 1980–1, HC 54, p. 93 §6. Cf. ibid., p. 96 q. 1160.
186 Gray and Jenkins, art. cit., pp. 429–30, 442, 446–9; Treasury and Civil Service, Sel. Cttee 1st Rep., 1980–1, HC 54, p. 22 q. 875 (Sir I. Bancroft).
187 Treasury and Civil Service, Sel. Cttee 3rd Rep., 1981–2, HC 236-II, p. 32 q. 166, p. 71 q. 297. Cf. HC 236-I, p. xxiv §47.
188 See above pp. 242–6.

expenditure management.[189] It has to maintain a dialogue with individual departments and also to conduct collective discussion with all of them on the size, composition, objectives, and management of their expenditure programmes and the policies which underlie them. It has as well to relate these specific activities and their outcome to the general position and prospects for the economy of which public expenditure is an important aspect. All these matters have to be co-ordinated and advice presented to ministers about the level and course of public spending for varying periods ahead. Moreover a wide spectrum of relationships is involved given that much of this expenditure (that of local government for instance) may not be fully under central control. In some cases, too, a continual watch may have to be kept on the development of policy and its implementation to see, say, whether expectations are being fulfilled, whether circumstances have changed and what this may require in the way of alteration of what is intended. Because of this continuity of involvement it is not possible simply to allocate funds and let departments or other agencies then run their own affairs. The Treasury must be concerned, therefore, to see that departments have an appropriate system for producing meaningful figures so that progress can be monitored and that a department's own supervisory system is adequate. In this regard it also has a vital responsibility to develop techniques of measurement and analysis appropriate, both in total and in detail, to the vast public expenditures of modern times. This is an essential part of the background to its dialogue with the departments and of the basis of programme control in the various offices. The Treasury also has the responsibility for drawing up the annual White Paper on public expenditure for ministerial approval, the document which sets out the government's strategy for the public sector in the short and medium term. And the Treasury is above all the department which has to liaise with the Parliamentary committees especially those on Public Accounts and the Civil Service.

This, then, is the Treasury's role. But what sort of verdict must be reached about the effectiveness of its control of public expenditure in the light of the above review? The truth seems to be that the Treasury is not and has never been in a position tightly to control or reduce expenditure especially where the pressures of the day are to contrary effect and, above all, where the political will is absent. Even if it had wanted to it could not have restrained or diminished the enormous growth of public spending which we have witnessed over the years. Nor has it been able to develop any new, effective machinery to monitor spending at the high levels to which we have seemingly become accustomed: rather its supervision

189 Goldman, op. cit., pp. 25-6.

seems, inevitably perhaps, to have weakened.[190] There is a sense that it has welcomed, or at least got used to, the situation that prevails. How far, therefore, it can be an effective instrument of libertarian purpose and the dramatic reduction in public sector spending which that end requires is a question still in the balance. One fears that the hostile spirit encountered by L. Chapman in his pursuit of economies might still prevail.[191]

But, of course, in addition to its role in respect to public expenditure the Treasury has functions concerning the organization of the Civil Service and the management of the economy. These are reviewed in the next two sections of this chapter.

EFFICIENCY AND ORGANIZATION

> ... it is the duty of the Treasury to see that this extensive and complicated machinery is neither redundant nor deficient, and that it is maintained in good working order by the adoption of every well ascertained improvement and the application of the requisite motive power.
> SIR C. TREVELYAN in Civil Service, Inquiry Com. 2nd Rep., 1875 (vol. xxiii), C. 1226, Appendix F p. 110 q. 79.

If traditionally the basic role of the Treasury is to act as a Ministry of Finance, securing a proper care and restraint in the use of public monies, it is also true that its tasks and interests cannot simply be restricted to the financial sphere alone. For due economy in administration depends, at least in part, on efficient organization so that the Treasury has, as well, always been (at least until quite recently) the one department responsible for the management and operation of the Civil Service as a whole and of its constituent offices. As an official review of the Treasury's functions put it during the last war, 'the general oversight of the Civil Service by the Treasury derives historically from the control of expenditure vested in the Treasury.'[192] The position is reflected in the special relationship that has traditionally prevailed between the Treasury and the Prime Minister, normally its First Lord, who as head of the government has a supervisory responsibility for the entire machinery of administration and its effectiveness. And it is the case that the Treasury has, within its domain, what were, for a long time (the Post Office apart) by far the largest government agencies, that is, the Boards of Inland Revenue and of Customs and Excise. Of course this managerial duty has also to be seen in the context of a public service which has been continually growing in

---

190 Cf. the comments of A. Robinson, 'The House of Commons and Public Expenditure', in S. A. Walkland and M. Ryle (eds), *The Commons Today* (Fontana, 1981), pp. 162–3.
191 L. Chapman, *Your Disobedient Servant* (1978; Penguin, 1979).
192 PRO, CAB 87/75 MG(45)16, MGO 74 (June 1945), Appendix 1 p. 13 §20.

size, function, and complexity. The array of departments has increased; and not only has the number of civil servants grown enormously, but also more grades and classes of officials have been created, involving a great variety of qualifications and duties of a professional, scientific, and technical, as well as of a general administrative, kind. Staff questions of all sorts, issues relating to conditions of work, training, and much else more and more engaged the Treasury's attention. Organizational changes were made to help cope with these matters, for instance the creation of posts (in the Treasury and individual departments alike) especially to deal with establishment issues; and over the years there was an increasing concern with managerial efficiency.

As with Treasury control of expenditure, questions have arisen about, first of all, the nature and extent of this supervisory responsibility and how well it has been carried out; and secondly over the Treasury's relationship with the departments and the degree of their autonomy. There was general agreement that the task of promoting efficiency existed and was one for which the Treasury should be responsible. Equally the 'constant reiteration of the point' testified for long to 'the Treasury's failure to find a successful mode of operation.'[193] The subject will be broached through a brief review of the development of the Treasury's central position in this regard and then of an exemplary theme.

The idea

Sir Charles Trevelyan always saw the Treasury as 'eminently a superintending office' and as 'the proper supervising and controlling body in all matters which relate to the public establishments.'[194] And he wrote to Gladstone that the office could be the means of introducing 'a powerful principle of unity' into the public service, one which 'would give a very beneficial stimulus to exertion in every other Department.'[195] Naturally the Northcote-Trevelyan report itself stressed the need to overcome the fragmentary nature of the contemporary administration, to make it less a collection of semi-autonomous public offices each with its different procedures and more a uniform and unified system under

---

[193] M. V. Hawtin and J. K. Moore, *The Integration of HM Treasury and the Civil Service Department: Report of the Study Team* (CSD; London, 1980), Annex 1 p. 3 §3.

[194] Papers Relating to the Re-organisation of the Civil Service, 1854–5, (vol. xx), p. 427; Civil Service, Inquiry Com. 2nd Rep., 1875 (vol. xxiii), C. 1226, Appendix F p. 109 q. 78.

[195] Trevelyan to Gladstone (9 February 1854) cited E. Hughes, 'Sir Charles Trevelyan and Civil Service Reform, 1853–5', *English Historical Review*, lxiv (1949), p. 207.

The Department of Departments 293

Treasury supervision.[196] And, together with Northcote, Trevelyan had perfected the procedure of unofficial inquiry and report, which, beginning with the subordinate revenue departments, came to be more widely applied as the Treasury's most successful device for controlling establishments.[197] It was, in fact, the forerunner of the modern management review. Trevelyan commended the use of these inquiries as follows:

> The established mode of transacting the business of each Department should from time to time be investigated and revised by the Treasury ... with a view to adapt the number and remuneration of the Persons employed to the actual state of the business, to recast obsolete modes of proceeding, and to establish uniformity or harmony of system throughout the Public Service.[198]

In the twelve years following the Northcote-Trevelyan report, over forty different departments and sub-departments were investigated by this means, a number of them more than once.[199] Because of the widely-held view that each department's problems were peculiar to it, an inquiry was usually concerned only with one office or one of its parts. But the Treasury did increasingly find that a solution to an administrative difficulty in one department could often be applied to others as well; and so there began to emerge groups of offices with a similar organization or pattern of establishment. There was thus a period in the years following the Northcote-Trevelyan report constituting a kind of transition between dealing with each department separately as an autonomous unit and dealing with the whole Civil Service on a uniform basis.[200] And a crucial point about these inquiries is that, although most of them were set up on Treasury initiative, they were essentially collaborative projects. Nothing was done without the concurrence of the departmental minister concerned; and mutual agreement determined membership (often with the Treasury in a minority) and the terms of reference.[201] As the inquiries thus depended on departmental co-operation, there was usually no radical disagreement about any recommendations made and so about effecting them.[202] But, as M. Wright pointed out in his study of these investigations, the manner in which the Treasury thus exercised supervision 'adds a new dimension to the concept of Treasury control in

---

196 See above pp. 153–4, 160–1.
197 M. Wright, *Treasury Control of the Civil Service 1854–1874* (Oxford, 1969), pp. 24, 141, and ch. 8 *passim*. Also see below pp. 295–7.
198 Trevelyan to J. Wilson (13 September 1853), cited ibid., p. 194.
199 ibid., p. 195. Cf. Table I, ibid., p. 196, giving a list of such inquiries 1854–65.
200 ibid., p. 197.
201 ibid., pp. 198, 201, 205.
202 But for one difficult case concerning the Home Office, see ibid., pp. 214ff.

the nineteenth century' for it was not a matter of command and obedience but (in the terms later used by Plowden) a 'joint working together in a common enterprise'. And with the 'continuous growth in the area and volume of government activity' this collaborative ethos constituted a vital factor in Treasury supervision of the Civil Service in the period after 1854.[203]

And, when the reforming current slowed, the Treasury's dependence on departmental co-operation was (as in the field of public expenditure) revealed as a weakness in its authority, for it had only limited powers of initiative at its disposal and little means of compulsion. The result was that during the late nineteenth century the Treasury found it very difficult to control departmental staffing and organization.[204] The Order in Council of June 1870, as well as clarifying the position in respect of examination for entry to the service, formally extended Treasury control 'somewhat beyond the region of finance into the domain of departmental administration.'[205] But, only three years later, the then Chancellor of the Exchequer, R. Lowe, told the Select Committee on Civil Service Expenditure, 'I do not apprehend that we have at any time any power to re-organise a department without the consent of the head of that department.' He also stated that the Treasury thus possessed very limited authority and what influence it had always depended on 'moral suasion and pointing out things' and on the indirect impact of its formal power to refuse any increased expenditure asked for.[206] The state of affairs revealed must have worried the committee, or some members of it, because an attempt was made to insert in its draft report comments to the effect that 'this impotency, or lack of administrative power in the Treasury deserves ... the serious attention of the Legislature.'[207] A couple of years later, the Playfair Commission expressed a similar concern about the Treasury's position in relation to other departments. This, it said, 'should be made as strong as possible', with the Treasury keeping itself informed about 'the wants and conditions' of other offices and 'acquiring their confidence' but also 'able to exercise an efficient and intelligent control.'[208] During the following decade, however, the Ridley

203 ibid., pp. 223–4. For the phrase from the Plowden report, see Control of Public Expenditure, Rep., 1960–1 (vol. xxi), Cmnd. 1432, p. 13 §34.
204 H. Roseveare, *The Treasury: the Evolution of a British Institution* (London, 1969), p. 203.
205 The Civil Service, R. Com. 4th Rep. 1914 (vol. xvi), Cd. 7338, p. 10 §15.
206 Civil Service Expenditure, Sel. Cttee 3rd Rep., 1873 (vol. vii), p. 234 q. 4494, p. 236 q. 4520.
207 ibid., pp. xvi–xvii. This passage was not, in fact included in the final report, ibid.
208 Civil Service, Inquiry Com., 1st Rep., 1875 (vol. xxiii), p. 23. Similar views were not infrequently expressed at that time: see the references cited in G. K. Fry, *Statesmen in Disguise: the Changing Role of the Administrative Class of the British Home Civil Service 1853–1966* (London, 1969), p. 49 n. 5.

Commission found that little had been done to this effect and its report revealed a vivid picture of weakness and conflict, observing that the Treasury was unable to promote uniformity or organization without a great deal of friction. In evidence the Permanent Secretary to the Treasury admitted there was no direct control over such matters as staffing, leave of absence, office organization, and the like and so no effective examination of a department's efficiency.[209] But the commissioners were insistent that some central machinery of supervision and co-ordination was vital and that existing arrangements should, therefore, be strengthened. To this end it was urged that general regulations should be sustained by the authority of Order in Council. The commissioners also revived a proposal originally suggested by Trevelyan and the Playfair inquiry that there should be set up a 'Permanent Consultative Committee' of permanent heads of department to superintend conformity to these rules and to examine all questions concerning establishment matters and requests for increased expenditure. Periodical reviews of all offices should also be undertaken to see whether staff reductions or other economies could be secured. 'Such a body', the commission said, 'would be of great value in securing uniformity of regulations, in suggesting reforms, in facilitating transfers, and, not least, in bringing about harmonious action between the Treasury and the other departments.'[210] The committee was established in 1890 but after only three or four years was acknowledged to have failed to tackle the problems of departmental organization. After 1894 it lapsed and the Treasury, on its own initiative, made greater use of *ad hoc* inter-departmental committees to solve problems of supply and organization.[211] In giving evidence to the new Select Committee on National Expenditure in 1902, Treasury witnesses expressed satisfaction at the effectiveness of the bilateral arrangements as means of checking even the defence departments. None the less in its report the select committee urged the need for periodical reviews, perhaps every five years, of departmental staffing and organization, though it was not until 1910 that this was prescribed by Order in Council.[212] Then, shortly before the Great War, the MacDonnell Commission once more indicated the view that the Treasury did not in fact exercise a sufficient control over departmental staffing and organization so that there was no real central control over what should be a homogeneous service. However successful

---

209 Civil Establishments, R. Com. 1st Rep., 1887 (vol. xix), C. 5226, Appendix, Minutes of Evidence, e.g., p. 4.
210 ibid., 2nd Rep., 1888 (vol. xxvii), C. 5545, p. xii §§18–22.
211 The Civil Service, R. Com. 4th Rep., 1914, Cd. 7338, p. 85 §95; Roseveare, *The Treasury: the Evolution of a British Institution*, p. 242.
212 National Expenditure, Sel. Cttee Rep., 1903 (vol. vii), HC 242, p. iv; Order in Council cited Roseveare op. cit., p. 242.

the *ad hoc* committees of inquiry on which the Treasury placed great reliance, they could 'never supply the place of a properly constituted and permanent organisation'. For one thing the inquiries usually originated with the department, not with the Treasury, in the sense that occasion for such investigation only arose when a department itself wanted some change and, by agreement, the opportunity was taken to have an inquiry.[213] But, the signatories of the majority report said, such

> committees originating with the departments themselves are not what we contemplate. Such occasional committees, sitting no matter how frequently, are probably differently constituted each time they sit. They deal at each sitting with different matters, not with the same matter in different phases; they can never accumulate and transmit to their successors that knowledge of men, of official practice, and of Service capacities, feelings, and aspirations which it is essential that the controlling authorities should be enabled to draw upon if Service administration is to be equable and prescient.[214]

The majority report expressed concern that, while there was a considerable amount of knowledge and experience available in the Treasury about organization and office methods, this was not effectively applied to the improvement of the service. Whatever its indirect influence on such matters, the report believed that, because it was loath to intervene and would never act without departmental agreement, 'the Treasury does not, in practice, exercise a sufficiently effective control over the organisation of departments unless a question of finance is involved.'[215] Once more, therefore, it was proposed that the Treasury should be strengthened for this purpose, the suggestion being this time that there should be created within it a 'special Section for the general supervision and control of the Civil Service' and which would 'of its own initiative' undertake any necessary inquiry into all 'matters connected with Departmental administration or methods of working.'[216] However this and the other recommendations of the commission fell dead-born from the press because of the onset of war.

But the same theme was later taken up and elaborated by the Haldane Committee which would naturally be concerned with any means to achieve optimum efficiency in the machinery of administration.[217] The

---

213 The Civil Service, R. Com. 4th Rep., loc. cit., p. 85 §95.
214 ibid.
215 ibid., pp. 85–6 §96.
216 ibid., pp. 86–7 §§99, 101. The minority report preferred the idea of a Consultative Committee but also urged that whatever permanent machinery of supervision was established should previously have been explored in detail, ibid., p. 142 §52(i).
217 Cf. the remarks in The Ministry of Reconstruction, *The Business of Government:III The Civil Service* (Reconstruction Problems no. 38; London, 1919), pp. 31–5.

role of the Treasury in achieving this end was necessarily crucial, covering recruitment, salaries, hours of work, and, indeed, any such matters requiring uniformity of treatment.[218] The report went on to say that 'Some of these functions arise directly from the control exercised by the Treasury over expenditure; others from its preponderant authority as the Department of the Prime Minister, or from the comprehensive relations which it necessarily maintains with all the other Departments of State.'[219] But Treasury officials needed to be strengthened in this regard: the adequacy of financial control itself depended on effective departmental arrangements; and, to this end, the Treasury should undertake 'more frequent enquiries ... into the general administration of Departments'; and, echoing again an earlier suggestion, an advisory committee (of some six or seven people, permanent heads of departments as well as outside persons with business experience) should be set up to consider 'general questions affecting the public service at large' or 'specific proposals from Departments.'[220] There was a further important reinforcement of the MacDonnell proposals for the adequate supervision of departmental work in an age of growing government intervention, especially that of a routine kind:

> In every Department there is a considerable amount of business of a routine character to be transacted..., in general terms, work performed by officers of ranks below the first division. The proportion of this work to the whole work of a Department has probably increased of late years, and is likely to increase still further in the future.
>
> The manipulation of this work involves consideration both of personnel and matériel. Attention has to be paid to the selection of the staff, their classification, their assignment to appropriate duties, their hours of work, promotion, increments, leave and sick leave. In addition ... there are various mechanical arrangements to be considered, such as the registering and custody of papers, the use of forms and statistical returns, copying, stationery, printing, office furniture and equipment, and labour-saving appliances.
>
> We think that in all such matters progressive efficiency can only be secured by constant expert attention, and that more systematic arrangements that at present exist should be made for this purpose.[221]

The report then made three specific suggestions to meet this need.[222] First,

---

218 Machinery of Government, Ministry of Reconstruction Cttee Rep., 1918 (vol. xii), Cd. 9230, p. 17 §3.
219 ibid., pp. 17–18 §3.
220 ibid., p. 20 §§16–17.
221 ibid., pp. 20–1 §19.
222 ibid., p. 21 §20.

in all departments where the staff was large enough, there should be an officer charged with studying all such questions as they arise in his department as well as with controlling the staff engaged on routine duties. Secondly, and again in all departments where the amount of business was sufficient, 'an attempt should be made to keep continuous records of the amount of work done, the time occupied in doing it, and the cost incurred' with a view to seeing how, over the years, the department's procedures have altered or improved. Thirdly, there should be, in the Treasury itself, a separate branch specializing in the study of 'all questions of staff, recruitment, classification, etc., and routine business generally.' This branch would maintain close contact with officials similarly engaged in the other departments and also with 'what was being done in business circles outside, and perhaps in foreign countries.' Here is the effective beginning of that concern with 'establishments' and 'organization and methods' that have inevitably come to bulk so large as the public service has increased in size, complexity, and scope.

Not long afterwards these ideas were expanded in the form of detailed proposals by the Bradbury Committee on the staffing and organization of government offices. Its final report concerned itself not only with the general limitations of Treasury control and such matters as organizational inadequacies (deriving, for instance, from overlapping of functions, disparities of salary, and the like) but also with how the situation might be improved. It suggested the now usual array of establishment appointments and included the recommendation that the Treasury officers should themselves, in co-operation with their departmental counterparts, personally investigate 'the actual working' of departments. The specially selected staff concerned should also have had experience of 'staff management' and be given opportunities to study 'the scientific organisation of staff both in the Government service and in the commercial world' at home and abroad.[223] And in 1919 a Treasury minute and a subsequent circular were promulgated which followed these recommendations closely. An Establishments Branch was set up in the Treasury in February and, later in the year as part of a major reorganization, placed under one of the three Controllers (the other two being concerned with Finance and Supply) – all of permanent secretary rank – with the duty of watching over the general conditions and work of the service as a whole, making inquiries into its operation, and drawing the attention of the Heads of Departments concerned to their outcome. Also an Establishments Officer was appointed in each large department to be responsible (in collaboration with the Treasury) for the supervision

---

223 Organisation and Staffing of Government Offices, Cttee Final Rep., 1919 (vol. xi), Cmd. 62, p. 4 §15, p. 5 §18.

The Department of Departments

and organization of personnel: and as well a standing committee of such officers was created under the chairmanship of the Controller of Establishments. This committee was to advise the Treasury on all general questions affecting staffing and organization and to secure cooperation between the Treasury and the departmenal Establishment branches. The National Whitley Council, set up at the same time, also would be concerned *inter alia* with general questions of work and conditions in the entire Civil Service. As part of the same general package of changes, intended to provide a basis on which the Civil Service could cope more effectively with the problems of the post-war era, there was a fundamental reclassification of the career structure. Instead of the old, rather confused, hierarchy of grades there were to be three main kinds of post – administrative, executive, and clerical – and within these comprehensive categories uniform scales of pay and so forth helped to consolidate a new degree of homogeneity, transcending the old departmental variations. Also the Permanent Secretary to the Treasury was formally elevated to a new status by the conferment of the title of official Head of the Civil Service. In March 1920 a Treasury circular affirmed that the Prime Minister's consent was required for the appointment or removal of permanent heads of departments or their deputies and of Principal Finance and Establishment officers. A few months later, in July 1920, the authority of an Order in Council was used to consolidate the Treasury position: 'the Treasury may make regulations for controlling the conduct of His Majesty's Civil Establishments, and providing for the classification, remuneration, and other conditions of service of all persons employed therein'.[224] Although these many changes were separately promulgated they constituted in fact an interlocking whole intended considerably to reinforce the Treasury's position, making clear that its traditional power of the purse and concern with economy extended to the sphere of administrative organization and the achievement of efficiency. By 1930 it was possible for the Tomlin Commission to report that the system of Treasury control in staff matters at least was 'satisfactory'; though it added that this was no justification for any relaxation on the part of the Treasury (or for any proposal to remove control over such matters to some other department).[225] And later still Lord Bridges wrote that the work and influence of Sir Warren Fisher 'set going the changes which have led us today to think of the Treasury as the department with responsibility for *management* of the Civil Service, and of the central processes of government, rather than a department

---

[224] Order in Council no. 1976 (22 July 1920), §6 cited National Expenditure, Sel. Cttee 16th Rep., 1941–2 (vol. iii), HC 120, p. 24 §75.
[225] The Civil Service, R. Com. Rep., 1930–1 (vol. x), Cmd. 3909, p. 171 §590.

endowed simply with powers of financial control.'[226] Yet whereas Establishments work in the Treasury had since 1919 become broadly comparable with that on Supply, after 1945 the former concern took rather a back seat not least because of the substantial new burden imposed by the problems of economic co-ordination.[227] And this at a time when management problems were intensifying. Personnel management is a case in point. This task was bound to increase greatly owing to: the growth in the total numbers of staff; the increasingly complex structure of professional, scientific, and technical grades; the greater difficulty of pay negotiations; and the considerable rise in the staff interchanging between ministries. Attempts were made to rationalize the structure of grades and classes throughout the service and the Treasury was necessarily much more closely involved in career planning and so forth.[228] But was the effort adequate?

What happened subsequently (at least until the last couple of decades) may conveniently be indicated by reference to the specific theme of organization and methods.

Organization and methods

The purpose of O & M (what is nowadays often called 'management services' or some such name) was once defined in a report by the Estimates Committee as 'to secure maximum efficiency in the operation of the Government's executive machinery; and, by the expert application of scientific methods to organisation, to achieve economy in cost and labour.'[229] The potential scope of the work is considerable. 'Organization' could mean anything from a 'planned review' of the general structure of a department (including such questions as the decentralization of authority to local and regional offices) to detailed analysis of the work of a single official. 'Methods' could embrace a wide range of administrative and clerical procedures from the way in which correspondence was dealt with to the system of arranging files and records, from the use of office machines to the design of forms. Both existing procedures and the conduct of new tasks could be examined. A Treasury booklet on *The Practice of O. & M.* said assignments involved the examination of 'objectives, activities, organization, staffing,

---

226 Lord Bridges, *The Treasury* (1964; 2nd edn, London, 1966), p. 198 (italics in original).
227 Hawtin and Moore, op. cit., Annex 1 pp. 12–13 §35.
228 J. H. Robertson, Memorandum no. 143, in The Civil Service, Cttee Rep., 1968 (Non-Parl.), vol. 5(2), p. 1034 §33.
229 Estimates, Sel. Cttee 5th Rep., 1946–7 (vol. vi), HC 143, p. vii §9. Cf. The Civil Service, Cttee, Report of the Management Consultancy Group, 1968 (Non-Parl.), vol. 2, p. 77 §280.

procedures and methods' as well as consideration of 'various other aspects of management such as planning, direction, control, standards, costs, equipment and working conditions.'[230] Responsibility for these matters now rests with the Management and Personnel Office which is part of the Cabinet Office. But it once fell to the Treasury; and the story of O & M's introduction into the Civil Service is the exemplary theme examined here to indicate the extent, adequate or otherwise, to which the managerial role of the Treasury was developed to cope with the expanding bureaucracy of collectivism and deal with its problems.[231] And if the verdict about what was achieved in this respect is often summed up in the phrase 'too little and too late', this may have been due as much to the usual dichotomy of responsibility between the Treasury and the other departments of state as to the diffidence of the Treasury's own officials. Yet it is the case that the Treasury was frequently far from forward in pressing innovation in this field.

Even what might be called the pre-history of O & M shows something of the Treasury's failure: it was slow to see the possibilities of the copying press and, later on, of shorthand and the typewriter.[232] And the MacDonnell inquiry revealed before the Great War that, though the Treasury had by then acquired quite a lot of information and experience about the problems of office procedure and the like and often conducted inquiries into such matters, it lacked the authority and perhaps the will to impose improvements in other departments. This was why the commission recommended that the Treasury should have a special section for the general supervision and control of the Civil Service, including the duty to 'carry out inquiries and investigations into any matters connected with Departmental administration or methods of working.'[233] The proposal was reinforced by the recommendations of both the Haldane and Bradbury Committees.[234] Action followed with the inauguration of Establishments branches in the Treasury and all major departments in 1919. As part of this post-war reorganization, and following, in particular, a suggestion by the Bradbury Committee, a

---

230 HM Treasury, *The Practice of O. & M.* (London, 1954), §51.
231 The earlier phases of this history are well described in R. A. Ablondi, *The Development and Functioning of 'Organisation and Methods' in British Central Government* (unpublished PhD thesis, Unversity of London, 1955), a pioneering study to which I am greatly indebted.
232 E. W. Cohen, *The Growth of the British Civil Service 1780–1938* (London, 1941), pp. 125, 144, 151–2. Cf. H. Martindale, *Women Servants of the State 1870–1939: a History of Women in the Civil Service* (London, 1938), pp. 65–9 on the early days of the 'typewriting women'.
233 The Civil Service, R. Com., Appendix to 1st Rep., Minutes of Evidence, 1912–13 (vol. xv), Cd. 6210, p. 44 q. 958, p. 47 qq. 989–91, p. 95 qq. 1902–4; 4th Rep., 1914 (vol. xvi), Cd. 7338, pp. 85–6 §96, p. 87 §101.
234 See above pp. 297–8.

small Treasury Investigating Section was established 'To advise the Establishments Department generally on office machinery, the keeping of registers, records and statistics, the employment of labour-saving machines, etc., in the Public Service, and to conduct special investigations as required into methods, output, etc.'[235] The three officials appointed to form this section constituted the effective beginnings of O & M in the British Civil Service.[236]

Given this basis, what was achieved by such means in the inter-war period as a means of making the growing and increasingly costly government organization more efficient? First of all the TIS did have an effect on improving routine office methods by the use of machines. The May Committee on National Expenditure said in 1931 that the method of overall control and specific advances of this kind in the Civil Service compared favourably with the best arrangements in British industry and were 'well calculated to maintain a high standard of administration'; and in the previous five years nearly half a million pounds had been saved by the introduction of labour-saving machines. Impressed by this the Select Committee on Estimates shortly afterwards urged that further economies of this kind should be sought.[237] Also some other departments had established small sections to deal with these questions. For instance the GPO explored this field in 1922 with a report on 'Labour-Saving Appliances for Clerical Work'; two years later it set up a 'Forms and Office Methods Committee' which examined such topics as the postal and money order systems and the sorting and storing of old-age pension orders. In 1928 a small section of two investigating officers was formally created to carry on this type of work and with authority to visit post offices all over the country as a kind of inspectors. It was perhaps a mundane enterprise but it was of a notable potential importance in improving the efficiency with which routine work of a substantially increasing kind was carried out. Rationalization and mechanization of this sort were also being tackled in other large departments which had a lot of routine business such as the Ministry of Labour, the National

235 Treasury office notice (3 January 1920), cited Ablondi, op. cit., p. 11. The Bradbury Committee recommendation is at Organisation and Staffing of Government Offices, Cttee Final Rep., 1919 (vol. xi), Cmd. 62, p. 6 §23.
236 There was a slightly earlier precedent in the small standing committee of the Stationery Office during the Great War which had some success in scrutinizing departmental demands for office machines of various sorts and whose work was continued by the Treasury Office Machinery Committee set up in February 1920. This committee of four, two of whom were members of the TIS, had the duty of considering all requests for office machines and investigating all new types coming on to the market. It was disbanded in 1926 and its function transferred to the TIS: see Ablondi, op. cit., pp. 12–13.
237 National Expenditure, Cttee Rep., 1930–1 (vol. xvi), Cmd. 3920, pp. 22–3 §§44, 46; Estimates, Sel. Cttee 2nd Rep., 1931–2 (vol. iv), HC 90, p. xv §16.

Assistance Board, and the Inland Revenue.[238] Of course all this was limited and relatively low-level. It was most definitely not anything like the systematic and periodical overhaul of the machinery of government as a whole that had been regarded as necessary by some observers ever since the Northcote-Trevelyan report. So it is not surprising that the Tomlin Commission in 1931 felt it necessary to assert that much remained to do and to reaffirm that 'provision should be made for the continuous overhaul of the machinery of Government by a small specially trained staff' so that the 'problems of departmental organisation' were studied as a means of promoting efficiency and economy and this whether any increased expenditure was in question or not. The report also pointed out that the Treasury was 'already regarded as a clearing house for questions concerning improved organisation, labour saving devices and the like' so that the recommendation was 'only a further development of the functions already in part performed by that Department.' The report was careful to add that this did not imply that anything should be done to detract from the authority and responsibility of individual ministers for the management and direction of their departments.[239] Yet this work (on which the Tomlin Commissioners believed something broader and even more useful might be built) was, it seems, itself little regarded by leaders of Civil Service opinion. Senior officials were often suspicious of technical expertise; their temperament was that of the 'amateur' generalist; and they believed that administration was an 'art' not amenable beyond certain limits to a merely fact-finding or theoretical approach. It is surely significant in this respect that, in his book on the Treasury which appeared in 1927, Sir Thomas Heath (a distinguished Joint Permanent Secretary during the Great War) hardly mentions the TIS at all: he pays tribute to the messengers but almost completely forgets the small group of Treasury Investigating Officers. There is a whole chapter on routine and office practice but only one brief reference to such matters as office machinery, investigation into methods of work, and so on.[240] There is naturally no reference to a general review of departmental organization as a whole the assumption being that this is a responsibility pertaining to the ministers and senior officials concerned. It is true that, in the late 1930s, the TIS had begun to undertake a few surveys of wider problems than those of mechanization and the rationalization of routine. It was involved, for instance, in working out for the GPO a plan to prevent the breakdown of

238 Ablondi, op. cit., pp. 22–3, 27–8.
239 The Civil Service, R. Com. Rep., 1930–1 (vol. x), Cmd. 3909, p. 172 §§594–7.
240 Sir T. L. Heath, *The Treasury* (London, 1927), ch. ix; the reference referred to in the text is at p. 122. Perhaps it ought to be said that Heath had himself left the Treasury before the TIS was set up; yet while he was Joint PST his concern had been with the administrative rather than the financial side of things: see *DNB*, ii. 2688.

pension and similar payments in the event of mass evacuation; and at the same time it helped organize a whole division in the new Ministry of Economic Warfare and to prevent overlap of functions there. This was indeed the section's first major excursion in the general organizational field.[241] Yet the section (which had never had more than four officers) had by 1939 dropped to two: it might seem a very meagre response to the demand that expert knowledge should be brought widely to bear on these problems of departmental organization and functioning.

There was some recognition of what was done in this regard, as with the report (already noted) of the May Committee which in 1931 commented favourably on the way the Civil Service had introduced mechanical devices to some routine work.[242] But reviewing the record in 1942 the Select Committee on National Expenditure was extremely severe in its structures. 'In the period between the two wars', it said, 'the response of the Treasury to the demand that expert knowledge and study should be brought to bear on the problems of departmental organization was meagre in the extreme.' And again: 'As far as the study and progress of administrative organization is concerned, the record of the period between the two wars is singularly disappointing. The recommendations of the Haldane and Bradbury Committees gave an unmistakeable lead' and 'a stimulating reminder' was later provided by the Tomlin report. But apart from the indispensable preliminaries – the creation of Establishment branches in 1919 – 'the results were negligible'. Even though the very small group of Treasury Investigating Officers was set up 'the scope of their activity was far below the level' contemplated by the inquiries mentioned.

> Even in the re-armament period from 1936 to 1939, when the threat of war was insistent, there was no overt sign that the Treasury or the Departments accepted the proposition that the organisation of administrative machinery was a subject requiring expert and specialised study or that any lessons in the art of management could be learned from industry and commerce either in this country or abroad.

Consequently, as a result of this 'twenty years' of neglect and of 'almost complete failure to foster the systematic study of organisation as applied to Government Departments', the outbreak of war in 1939 found the Treasury 'insufficiently equipped' to deal with the problems of administrative growth which were then forced upon it.[243]

---

241 Ablondi, op. cit., pp. 20–1.
242 See above p. 302.
243 National Expenditure, Sel. Cttee 16th Rep., 1941–2 (vol. iii), HC 120, p. 18 §56, p. 26 §§81–2. There had been earlier criticism in the press and in private letters to the Prime Minister: see the papers in PRO, PREM 4 8/7, e.g. pp. 825–7, 847–52, 855–6.

Of course the Hitler war brought a great upsurge of government activity. Existing departments were enlarged and new ones created, the personnel of the service doubling in size by 1942. There were many problems of organization and co-ordination as well as a pressing need for the most stringent economy in manpower. One result was a rapid increase in the TIS. In 1939 it had two officials, less than it had started with twenty years before, The National Expenditure Committee pressed for it to be strengthened and by July 1940 it numbered twenty-two. The committee also asked for departmental sections to be established.[244] A Treasury circular of May 1941 urged departments to take advantage of the facilities it could offer. There was, however, a varied response that included downright hostility: it is recorded that on 'one occasion a team of Treasury officers were "bundled out" of the Department in which they had started work.'[245] In 1941, too, J. Reid Young (a chartered accountant and director of Vickers Ltd) was asked to make an assessment of the results achieved to date. The main thrust of his report was that, while the work being done was useful, it needed to be increased so that all departments were undertaking a continuous scrutiny and overhaul of their administrative arrangements. Again the response was positive but limited.[246]

The position by mid-1942 was as follows. First the TIS had increased to forty-six and had been renamed the 'Organisation and Methods Division'; there were also thirty-six people engaged in this sort of work in the departments. Secondly most of these officials were not career civil servants. The necessary expertise and adequately trained staff did not exist in the service and had to be drawn from industrial consultancy firms, office appliance manufacturers, and so on. Thirdly most of the work handled was relatively low-level dealing with such matters as the design of forms, registry procedure, reviews of office machinery, the work of typing pools, and the like. In part at least this was the result of deliberate policy with the object of acquiring experience, building on the basis of sound results, and establishing a reputation for undramatic usefulness. Fourthly the assignments were undertaken *ad hoc* being dealt with as some particular exigency or possibility arose. There was little opportunity or inclination to attempt systematic reviews of departmental organization as a whole or large parts of it. Finally in an important sense the initiative for an investigation and responsibility for implementing its

---

244 National Expenditure, Sel. Cttee 4th Rep., 1939–40 (vol. iii), HC 121, pp. 12–13 §§13–14; 16th Rep., 1941–2, HC 120, p. 18 §57.
245 Treasury circular (22 May 1941) cited Ablondi, op. cit., p. 42; National Expenditure, Sel. Cttee 16th Rep., 1941–2, HC 120, pp. 18–19 §58.
246 On the report, see e.g. National Expenditure, Sel. Cttee 16th Rep., 1941–2, HC 120, p. 19 §59; Estimates, Sel. Cttee 5th Rep., 1946–7 (vol. vi), HC 143 p. vi §§5–6 and Minutes of Evidence, pp. 94–5 q. 1554.

recommendations lay with the department concerned; and there were still instances of refusal to co-operate. Clearly the scene had changed since before the war and there was an increased, if somewhat confused, realization of what was possible in this field.

This, then, was the position on the eve of the publication in October 1942 of the SCNE report on the 'Organisation and Control of the Civil Service'. This was a major catalyst in speeding up these developments. The work so far done was praised with the comment that, within the limits assigned to it, it had achieved 'valuable results in the direction of efficiency and economy'. The experience (the report continued) was 'sufficient to dispel any doubts...about the advantages of combining modern techniques with Civil Service procedure.' But it added that attention had so far been too much restricted to the lower levels of administration: 'concerned with some of the twigs rather than the branches and trunk of the departmental trees.'[247] What was needed, therefore, was to extend the scope of these investigations to include the general lay-out of departments and organization at the highest level. It was these areas that were most likely to lead to the overcoming of congestion, duplication, slowness, and the like. And to do this effectively required a notable increase in the status and scope of the work which should be given to officials of sufficient seniority such that their advice could not be ignored.[248] Detailed recommendations to these ends were made and the whole debated in the House early in 1943: a sufficient indication of the importance attached to the subject even at the height of a world war.[249] All this, together with the Treasury reply to the report, thus set out the foundation on which organization and methods work in British government was subsequently to be based.[250] The new order came into being during the summer months of 1943 and involved, for instance, a substantial upgrading of the Treasury O & M Division the new head of which was appointed at Principal Assistant Secretary level (the present-day equivalent to this rank is Under Secretary) whereas, before this, the Chief Organization Officer had been of the executive class. Previous functions were continued or extended and provision was made for the selection and training of staff. The Director, I. J. Pitman (who had been managing director of the famous publishing firm) acknowledged the widespread goodwill and support he received, especially from the Treasury.[251] And he recognized his main task was to 'sell' O & M to the

247 National Expenditure, Sel. Cttee 16th Rep., 1941–2, HC 120, p. 28 §84.
248 ibid., pp. 28–9 §§85–7, p. 30 §§92–4.
249 386 H.C. Deb. 5s., 28 January 1943, cols 639–716.
250 The Treasury reply dated 10 March 1943 is in National Expenditure, Sel. Cttee 7th Rep., 1942–3 (vol. iii), HC 79, Appendix 2.
251 Ablondi, op. cit., p. 67.

Civil Service, to persuade departments of its value, and so forth. In 1944 he set down a plan for all O & M branches to work to, a scheme which was, after discussion by all concerned, issued as a Treasury memorandum in January 1945.[252] This 'O. & M. Charter' constituted the basis on which the work would continue after the war. It postulated four major principles. First O & M was to continue to be an advisory service simply and the conventional division of responsibility was to be maintained, departments retaining untrammelled control of all such matters within their field. Given the importance of ministerial responsibility things could hardly be otherwise. Secondly a departmental O & M branch was to be a separate section within the Establishments Division and responsible to its head whose title should become Establishments and Organization Officer. Thirdly the functions should be twofold: to undertake planned reviews of all the divisions, branches, and sections of the department; and to advise on O & M problems in general and, in particular, the planning of new work. Fourthly the Treasury O & M Division itself should have three tasks: to provide staff for O & M investigations in departments with no O & M branch of their own; to assist departments which do have their own branches with particular assignments where required; and to administer the 'central services' such as training facilities, the provision of information, and examination of common problems. Clearly there was, as with financial matters, an acceptance of dual control and responsibility. It was assumed that, in pursuing efficiency as well as economy, the Treasury could not itself control in any complete sense. A great deal had to be left to the departments with the Treasury helping, guiding, and advising rather than imposing a solution to any organizational or procedural difficulty. None the less by the end of the war a considerable advance had been made as compared with 1939. Most large departments had their own O & M branches; the Treasury training courses were producing their first batches of Civil Servants with the necessary skills for this sort of work; and the planned reviews of departmental organization were getting under way. And the potential advantages were firmly grasped at least in some quarters. For example, late in 1944, one series of comments on a submission to the Machinery of Government Committee suggested that the Treasury could have saved a great deal of money in recent years had it been in a position effectively to conduct efficiency audits and otherwise review departmental procedures.[253]

Questions of business efficiency in the departments arose again when, after the war, a series of working parties examined various aspects of the

---

252 Repr. in Estimates, Sel. Cttee 5th Rep., 1946–7, HC 143, Appendix pp. 110–11.
253 PRO, T222/135, MGO 59 (12 November 1944), memorandum by Sir E. Gowers, Annex II, p. 13 §5.

adaptation of the Civil Service to peacetime conditions. In an interim report (1946) the importance of O & M was emphasized and detailed proposals made about such matters as office machinery, registry arrangements, messenger services, and the like. The following year a final report was produced. Machinery of government questions, that is, those concerning the allocation of functions betweeen departments were eschewed but there were various proposals relating to: the work and organization of the higher Civil Service (for instance the selection of 'high flyers' or the reduction of the burden on permanent secretaries); financial checks and accounting systems; the importance of O & M work; and much else.[254] The old idea was also reviewed of a standing committee of heads of departments and other senior officials, meeting under the chairmanship of the Permanent Secretary to the Treasury, to consider organizational and efficiency questions at the highest level. This led to the establishment of the Government Organization Committee for this purpose. The peacetime successor to the SCNE had also returned to the attack in 1947 with the suggestion that, whatever advances might have been made, O & M had still not been raised to its proper functioning level or made sufficiently high-powered given the great extension of government functions that had occurred. In addition to which there was in practice a considerable variation in the efficiency and influence of the departmental branches: some had tailed off or even not started well. There were other criticisms also: the higher ranks still took too little interest in this aspect of Civil Service responsibilities; the shortage of properly trained staff continued and O & M officials were so hard pressed in dealing with day-to-day and low-level problems that adequate and systematic review programmes of wider scope had been neglected.[255] A number of these critical comments was repeated in a report of mid-1947 sent to the PST by the Advisory Panel of Business Men.[256] This flurry of comment, criticism, and suggestion thus provided further evidence the O & M was there to stay but also that it would probably need continual sustaining if it were to be fully effective and developed as it should be.

254 PRO, T222/26, Organisation of the Civil Service, Working Party no. 4, 'Business Efficiency in Departments', interim report (October 1946), p. 3 §9; ibid., final report (July 1947), p. 2 §3; for the O & M recommendations, ibid., pp. 13–14 §§59–63.
255 Estimates, Sel. Cttee 5th Rep., 1946–7, HC 143, pp. xix–xxv. Cf. the Treasury reply in 4th Rep., 1947–8 (vol. vii), HC 100, Appendix II. A note to the Government Organization Committee from the Director of the Treasury O & M Division and which listed the reports produced or in progress between January and October 1947 clearly indicated the low-level nature of most of the studies undertaken. They dealt with such things as ready reckoners, suggestions schemes, photographic and reproduction services, addressing machines, and the control of forms. Relatively few topics of higher importance were reviewed. See PRO, T222/591 M.G., Government Organisation Committee, Correspondence, OM 383/1/09.
256 Ablondi, op. cit., pp. 81–2.

The Department of Departments 309

A crucial question, of course, was that of sanctions. Most of the officials involved in O & M work were of the executive class; and their conclusions were, formally speaking, simply advice to the Establishments Officer and to the Permanent Secretary of the department concerned. And the limits of Treasury pressure, even if it were exerted, were clear. The Treasury could set a standard by its own example in following O & M advice; and could have some effect through the direct and central service responsibilities of its own O & M Division. There was, too, the influence of its Permanent Secretary on his senior colleagues in other departments. The weight of this last factor was specifically raised by the SCE in 1947 when it directly asked, What happens if, in a particular department, O & M is not functioning well or at all or at too low a level, perhaps because the Permanent Secretary was not sufficiently interested or amenable? When questioned about this, Sir Edward Bridges, at the time Head of the Civil Service, replied:

> if we felt in the Treasury that O. and M. was languishing in a particular department, I certainly should not hesitate to get hold of the Permanent Secretary in that department and tell him that I thought so; in fact I have done so in certain instances.... [That] is the way in which the thing will, in fact, be handled.[257]

I. J. Pitman, the first Director of the Treasury O & M Division, has recorded that when, on being appointed, he asked about the sanctions available, he was told:

> 'In the final resort I will myself write to the Permanent Secretary of the Ministry. If he doesn't do what we want, I'll ask him round here for tea and a chat. If it's an obdurate case, I'll send out and get a small piece of cake with the tea.'

Pitman adds: 'though we kept our cakes in reserve, I received entirely satisfactory support in every case which I recommended for support.'[258] This may seem adequate; but it is none the less a reflection of the ultimately crucial division of responsibility involved in respect to efficiency in organization as in the control of expenditure.

In 1954 the Financial Secretary to the Treasury said in the Commons, 'We believe that the idea which organization and methods has established is a good one, and that some such organization is, and should be, a permanent and valuable part of the Government machine.'[259] Of

---

257 Estimates, Sel. Cttee 5th Rep., 1946–7, HC 143, p. 102 q. 1621. Cf. ibid., pp. 102–3, q. 1623.
258 I. J. Pitman, 'Organisation and Methods: an Important Select Committee Report', *Public Administration*, xxvi (1948), p. 4.
259 523 H.C. Deb. 5s., 12 February 1954, col. 1617 (J. Boyd-Carpenter).

course there are other aids to departmental efficiency (officials concerned with training, welfare, personnel, and so forth), but O & M itself may make a valuable and unique contribution, from payroll methods to the design of forms, from the need for small office machines to how the mail should be handled, or from the use of computers to the allocation of functions within and between departments. Yet clearly its progress has been chequered or sporadic. Very low key during the inter-war period there was then a sudden expansion; and in the ten years after 1942 the total number of O & M posts rose from 82 to a height of nearly 400 (in 1949) and then fell to just under 300 in 1954. It was thus assured of a place in the administrative world; but the attitude of senior Civil Servants could still be one of doubt; the Treasury had often seemed diffident and neglectful; and there was as a result trenchant criticism of the record both in public and private.

The history thus far recounted is a not unimportant part of the perspective in which later inquiries and developments have to be seen, notably the Plowden and Fulton reports with their concern about managerial efficiency and the need for the full development of new techniques and services.[260] In the present context the point to note is that the vital part which should be played by the Treasury is still being stressed. As the Plowden report said, the Treasury had the task of 'ensuring mangerial efficiency in the public service', though the theme of joint responsibility is, once again, firmly emphasized:

> the Treasury should have a definite and accepted responsibility for the development of management services in Whitehall. This should extend beyond providing Departments with assistance on questions of methods, and should include the provision of a service for Departments seeking to improve their organisation and tackling new problems of administration. The Treasury's success in carrying out this range of responsibilities will depend upon the co-operation which it receives from Departments; on their acceptance that Treasury participation is not an attempt to infringe their responsibilities but is intended to lead towards greater efficiency; and on having in the Treasury enough staff of sufficiently high quality and with enough experience of the working of other Departments, to enable them to make a constructive contribution to the problems with which Departments are faced. It is here of course that the concept of joint working in a common enterprise is of cardinal importance.[261]

The duty to develop management services covered many subjects, for example,

---

260 See ch. 3 esp. pp. 204ff.
261 Control of Public Expenditure, Cttee Rep., 1960–1, Cmnd. 1432, p. 17 §49.

The Department of Departments 311

the quantitative techniques of statistics, costing, accountancy, operational research and so on, as well as organisation and methods, and training;...taking the initiative in the introduction of new techniques; and...keeping an oversight over the practice of all the Departments, both to encourage and to help them in the improvement of efficiency and economy in management, and to ensure that Whitehall gets the full benefit of cross-fertilisation of ideas introduced by individual Departments.[262]

And while the committee felt that, in general, 'the scale and quality of effort directed towards the provision of management services in Whitehall' compared 'favourably' with outside standards, especially in those departments with 'large, nation-wide organizations', it also believed that there was often insufficient 'awareness' of the advantages to be gained by progress in this field. It urged, therefore, that greater emphasis should be laid on 'inculcating a better understanding of the capabilities of the various management services' among administrators and other senior officials. Clearly the committee felt that something was lacking here.[263] Similarly the committee accepted that good work was done, in the Treasury and departments alike, on O & M, automatic data processing, costing analysis, and so forth. But at the same time there was still room for improvement.[264] Some departments seemed insufficiently aware of the value of management techniques; not enough senior officials were being trained in their use and the proper attitude of mind was, therefore, not being inculcated as it should be; the wider application of quantitative methods to both policy and management was not being pursued as vigorously as possible; there is often too little systematic attempt to bring together the work done by departments in similar fields; the Civil Service does not sufficiently consider the aid it might give to other branches of the public service (such as the NHS and local government); opportunities are not always seized for the interchange of relevant information with commerce and industry.[265] Although there is recognition of the value of what had been achieved, these specific indictments taken together constitute a weighty accusation of neglect or, at least, lack of determination and purpose. It came as a warning shot across the Treasury's bows. It was being made plain that actual and impending developments in public administration would inevitably throw 'a heavy additional load of responsibility' on the Treasury 'in its work as the central Department exercising control over public expenditure and responsible for the overall management of the Civil

262 ibid., p. 17 §50.
263 ibid., p. 18 §§51–2.
264 ibid., pp. 18–19 §§53–4.
265 ibid., pp. 18–19 §§51–8.

Service.' The pattern and nature of the Treasury's work would be bound to change; and much would depend on its ability to adapt itself to the new situation and the responsibilities it entailed.[266]

In the Treasury reorganization of the early sixties 'management' as an area of concern was given a central place intendedly as a purposeful, creative enterprise.[267] But the strong feeling remained that the leopard had not changed its spots. And, seven years after Plowden, the Fulton clamour was unleashed following the report's harsh diatribe against the deficiencies of the generalist civil servant, in particular his failure effectively to respond to the managerial challenge.[268] In the aftermath the responsibility was transferred to the new Civil Service Department so that it might be more fully met.[269] Yet the concept of 'Management Services' at work there was, not surprisingly, little different from that which had prevailed at the Treasury. In particular it was still essentially 'collaborative' in nature, offering aid and advice with no attempt at command. Sir S. Goldman urged that (given the position of the Accounting Officer for instance) this was the only sensible approach.[270] All the same it was precisely the limited attitude for which the Treasury had been criticized; and the slow progress still being made in some respects was acknowledged.[271] The need to initiate the Rayner scrutinies was one reflection of the dissatisfaction felt with the existing situation.[272] And it did not last. The CSD was abolished in 1981; though the Treasury did not regain its quondam central responsibility for such services as O & M as these fell to the new Management and Personnel Office where they still remain.

In management matters, therefore, as in the fields of public expenditure and of policy, each department has an important degree of constitutional independence from the centre; and this is a vital factor of political and administrative life which complicates the question of how to achieve improvement. Realizing the significance of this range of departmental autonomy will affect what is expected of central control. Sir D. Wass described the position recently:

---

266 ibid., p. 20 §59.
267 Roseveare, *The Treasury: the Evolution of a British Institution*, p. 301.
268 For the report, see above pp. 205–15; and specifically The Civil Service, Cttee Rep., 1967–8 (vol. xviii), Cmnd. 3638, p. 13 §21, pp. 54–7 §§163–70. See also the report of a Management Consultancy Group, ibid., 1968 (Non-Parl.), vol. 2, pp. 78–9 §§286, 291–2.
269 Cf. Expenditure, Sel. Cttee 11th Rep., 1976–7 (vol. xxxi), HC 535-II, p. 805 q. 1978.
270 See e.g. ibid., p. 805 q. 1979; the CSD note on 'The Work of the CSD's Management Services Division' (1976), ibid., p. 71 §6; and generally the account in CSD, *The Civil Service: Introductory Factual Memorandum* (London, 1980), pp. 41–3.
271 CSD note, loc. cit., p. 73 §13.
272 e.g. Sir A. Part's memorandum in Treasury and Civil Service, Sel. Cttee 1st Rep., 1980–1, HC 54, Appendix 1, p. 109 §5.

The Department of Departments

The centre, that is the Treasury and the Management and Personnel Office, has only limited powers over departments. Some change can be enforced from the centre, though enforcement on an unwilling department is always a dubious course; but much change in the field of management, of behaviour and of custom can only be wrought by persuasion and example.[273]

STEERING THE ECONOMY

> The impact of the decade after 1940 was profound... because the sheer size of the task changed to the extent that it took on a qualitatively different character. That the War played a part is evident, but it was the Treasury's role in economic management that changed most dramatically.
> M. V. HAWTIN and J. K. MOORE, *The Integration of HM Treasury and the Civil Service Department*, 1980, Annex 1 p. 12 §35

It is perhaps hardly surprising that Sir Thomas Heath's volume on the Treasury, published in 1927 in the old Whitehall Series, has no reference to any role for the department in respect of economic management as this would nowadays be understood. What is more interesting is that an official paper on the functions of the Treasury produced in 1945 for the Machinery of Government Committee equally makes no mention of such a charge. However, five years later, the then Permanent Secretary did refer to the significance of 'the Treasury's newer responsibilities for general economic policy.'[274] Of course over the years there had indeed been much consideration of the need for economic planning and the machinery appropriate to it; yet such a development was not automatically seen even so late as 1944 as involving the Treasury itself. This is highlighted in a series of comments on a draft memorandum dealing with the Treasury and its duties: only one observer suggested that the development of 'the modern positive state' was bound to have 'profound consequences for the Treasury.' Specifically with 'the extension of Government activity in the economic sphere the responsibilities of the Treasury have grown enormously.' And he went on to wonder whether, in terms of the necessary ideas and techniques, the Treasury was equipping itself adequately to face the tasks ahead.[275] Of course it would be difficult to prevent the department which deals with

---

273 Sir D. Wass, 'The Public Service in Modern Society', *Public Administration*, lxi (1983), p. 9.
274 Sir T. L. Heath, *The Treasury* (London, 1927); PRO, CAB 87/75, MGO 74 (June 1945), Appendix I esp. pp. 8–9 §§2–4; Sir E. Bridges, *Treasury Control* (London, 1950), p. 5.
275 PRO, T222/135, MGO 59 (12 November 1944), memorandum by Sir E. Gowers, 'The Role of the Treasury', Annex II p. 13 §§4–5.

government expenditure, the revenue, and so forth being concerned with matters of broader economic moment. But the nature and extent of the involvement might vary substantially. Certainly it was frequently supposed that as the Treasury was basically a ministry of finance – moreover one with (as it was believed) a negative attitude to public spending – the administrative machinery to undertake the wider task might well have to be found or built up outside the Treasury itself.

Something of the Treasury's fluctuating significance in this regard will be reviewed in this section though, because the history is long and complex in its institutional detail, the account will inevitably be no more than a brief sketch. There are various phases of development involved.

Pre-history

During the era of Free Trade and the idea of limited government responsibility, there could naturally be little or no sense of an obligation on the part of the state to attempt a substantive control of economic life. Of course the law regulated banking, the operation of companies, factory conditions, and otherwise provided a framework within which commercial activity was carried on. And it was recognized that the management of public finance (as through changes in taxation or the level of government borrowing) would affect economic decision-making. But beyond this, public responsibility did not go. Then in diverse ways attitudes began to change: public works were undertaken to help mitigate unemployment; tariff reform came to seem an effective means of protecting domestic interests; official conciliation was adopted as a way to secure industrial peace; the labour market was regulated through a system of exchanges; and so forth. At first there was naturally a variety of *ad hoc* policies simply: it took a long time for the notion of overall economic planning to emerge.[276] The institutional response was similarly slow and diverse; nor was the Treasury seen as the body to whom the new tasks should naturally accrue.

War, of course, has been a major catalyst in these matters.[277] And 1914–18 saw a government largely unprepared to mobilize the nation's resources move a considerable way in that direction. Established departments (including the Treasury) expanded in size and responsibility; and new ministries were created to deal with such subjects as labour, food, shipping, and overseas trade. However most of these wartime innovations were short-lived for the return of peace in 1918 brought, in dominant political circles, a state of mind conducive rather to the dismantling than the continuance of the apparatus of wartime

---

276 For one account, see *The Rise of Collectivism* (London, 1983), ch. 3.
277 ibid., ch. 2.

The Department of Departments 315

control. There was a long-term shift in the collectivist direction – the so-called 'displacement effect' which occurs during war and its aftermath – but the economic orthodoxies were reasserted at least for the time being.[278] Financial policy meant balancing the budget, the restoration of the gold standard, and the need for public economy. So far as the Treasury was concerned, this required a stress on its traditional role as financial monitor; and although involved, for instance, in the contemporary programme of public works, it was rather dubious about the long-term efficacy of this sort of expenditure and so *a fortiori* about overall economic control.[279] In this climate of opinion the period up to 1939 was, so far as innovation in the field of economic management was concerned, one of tentative experiment only. The goal was not the establishment of machinery for peacetime planning so much as the creation of new sources of advice simply, a body (or bodies) which could keep a continuous eye on the various problems likely to affect national policy, especially concerning the development and competitiveness of industry, and make appropriate recommendations.

In 1918 the Haldane Committee had devoted some attention to the idea of a central service for economic intelligence stressing (in Webbian fashion) the need for investigation and thought prior to action. It recommended that a special office be established, on the lines of the Department of Scientific and Industrial Research (which had been set up in 1916), to carry out systematic inquiry in, among other areas, the economic field and to do this in close association with existing offices not least the General Economic Department established in 1917 in the Board of Trade.[280] However the recommendation was without immediate fruit. It was at this time, too, that the proposal was first canvassed for an Economic General Staff though, as on later occasions, when the suggestion was made, nothing came of it.[281] Arising from the discussions a new post of Chief Economic Adviser was created in 1919 and attached to the Board of Trade. The appointment was not made, however, with a view to domestic control (though the government did seek advice from time to time); rather its main purpose was to help with the burden of international economic negotiations expected to follow the setting up of the League of Nations and to represent the government at meetings of the Imperial Economic Committee.[282] In 1921 there was some investigation,

---

278 ibid., pp. 66ff.
279 ibid., p. 133; H. Roseveare, *The Treasury: the Evolution of a British Institution* (London, 1969), pp. 265–6.
280 Machinery of Government, Ministry of Reconstruction Cttee Rep., 1918 (vol. xii), Cd. 9230, pp. 6–7 §§14–15, ch. IV *passim*.
281 Cf. Sir J. Anderson, *The Organization of Economic Studies in Relation to the Problems of Government* (London, 1947), p. 7.
282 S. Howson and D. Winch, *The Economic Advisory Council 1930–1939: a Study in*

under the aegis of the Government Actuary, of the need to improve the collection and presentation of official statistics but the only result was the establishment of an inter-departmental consultative committee to advise on these matters.[283]

Meanwhile Haldane had changed his mind about the model appropriate to the establishment of the economic intelligence agency his committee had suggested: not the DSIR but the Committee of Imperial Defence was the precedent now in favour. The reason was the practical one that, whereas the former simply carried out investigations and formulated conclusions of general note, the CID was expected to carry its advice into the field of action under ministerial direction. The distinction was important from the point of view of likely political efficacy.[284] So when the Labour government of 1924, in which Haldane served as Lord Chancellor, considered the question it took up a proposal for the creation of a Standing Committee of Economic Enquiry on the lines suggested and which was to have the task of channelling the necessary political, departmental, and specialist expertise to ensure that economic policy was thought out in advance on a basis of fact and all its problems adequately explored. Nothing came of this at the time because of the fall of the government.[285] But during the following year the new Conservative administration adopted the suggestion and set up a body called the Committee of Civil Research 'analogous in principle' to the CID. It was advisory only with no administrative or executive functions; and it was not confined to economic matters, its remit charging it with the broader duty of 'giving connected forethought from a central standpoint to the development of economic, scientific and statistical research in relation to civil policy and administration'. In the outcome it reported on a variety of questions ranging from the iron and steel industry and industrial fatigue to locust control and the distribution of the tsetse fly in East Africa and in practice its concerns acquired a greater imperial and scientific bias than originally intended.[286] When Baldwin's government was replaced by

---

Economic Advice during Depression and Recovery (Cambridge, 1977), pp. 7–8; D. N. Chester and F. M. G. Willson, *The Organization of British Central Government 1914–1964* (1957; 2nd edn, London, 1968), p. 296; Anderson, op. cit., p. 7; PRO, CAB 87/74 MG(43)12, MGO 32 (15 November 1943), 'The Role of the Economist in the Machinery of Government', p. 2 §4(a).

283 PRO, CAB 21/2217, 'Outline History of the Central Organisation for Economic Policy, 1919–1947', §§2–4; Howson and Winch, op. cit., p. 8.
284 Anderson, op. cit., pp. 8–9.
285 PRO, CAB 21/2217, 'Outline History...', §5; Howson and Winch, op. cit., p. 10; Anderson, op. cit., pp. 9–10; S. S. Wilson, *The Cabinet Office to 1945* (PRO Handbook no. 17; London, 1975), p. 83 §701; and J. P. Mackintosh, *The British Cabinet* (1962; 3rd edn, London, 1981), p. 523.
286 Howson and Winch, op. cit., pp. 11–15; Anderson, op. cit., p. 10; S. S. Wilson, op. cit., p. 83 §§701–2, Annex 3 p. [154].

another Labour administration in 1929, some use continued to be made of the CCR's sub-committees to examine the state of certain industries. But more importantly an earlier proposal for the specific treatment of economic questions was revived and, after some modification, implemented (in lieu of the creation of either an economic general staff or a fully representative forum).[287]

This new body, the Economic Advisory Council, was established in January 1930 absorbing the CCR. It was a kind of standing committee reporting direct to the Cabinet and with the following terms of reference:

> To advise His Majesty's Government in economic matters. To make continuous study of developments in trade and industry and in the use of national and imperial resources, of the effect of legislation and fiscal policy at home and abroad, and of all aspects of national, imperial and international economy with a bearing on the prosperity of the country.

The council had instructions 'to keep in close touch with Departments affected by its work with a view to the concerted study of economic problems of national interest'; it was also enjoined not to interfere in any way 'with the functions or responsibilities of Ministers or of the Departments over which they preside'; and, with one minor exception, it had no administrative powers or executive functions and could only offer advice and institute inquiries. The membership had a permanent nucleus of the Premier and four other ministers (including the Chancellor of the Exchequer) to which from time to time others were added at the Prime Minister's discretion together with such other persons whom he might choose 'in virtue of their special knowledge and experience in industry and economics.'[288] Among the independent or outside members thus summoned were E. Bevin, W. Citrine, G. D. H. Cole, J. M. Keynes, J. Stamp, and R. H. Tawney.[289] The EAC was, in fact, the first attempt to call on a wide range of outside expertise and advice on a regular and formal basis.[290] However, as Anderson subsequently wrote, the 'Council cannot be said to have achieved much.'[291] Partly it was hampered by the other preoccupations of its members; partly, too, by important differences of view (though these were not perhaps so crucial as has often been suggested).[292] Undoubtedly, there were basic incompatibilities between the sorts of policy proposed by some members like Keynes and

---

287 S. S. Wilson, op. cit., p. 83 §703. Howson and Winch, op. cit., pp. 18–29, reviews in detail the process by which the EAC emerged and the role it was intended to have.
288 Treasury minute (27 January 1930) in S. S. Wilson, op. cit., pp. [152]–[153].
289 ibid., p. 84 §706.
290 Howson and Winch, op. cit., p. 1.
291 Anderson, op. cit., p. 11. Cf. Bridges, *Treasury Control*, pp. 13–14; idem, *The Treasury* (1964; 2nd edn, London, 1966), p. 90.
292 Howson and Winch, op. cit., pp. 156–7.

Cole and the ideas acceptable to the Chancellor, P. Snowden, who was an ardent free-trader, and to the business men. There was a confusion too, between the council's 'technocratic' and 'representative' roles which opened it to much criticism from both angles.[293] But, more fundamentally than this perhaps, its political failure arose from other factors. One was that, despite the injuction in its terms of reference, its work – often of intrinsic value – was not effectively integrated with that of the departments affected which tended in consequence to view its advice with diffidence; another was that there was no minister in charge to provide political weight to, and a channel for, its recommendations; and in addition the Prime Ministers of the day lost interest.[294] As Harold Laski said, in an interesting and perceptive review of these events, the council was, in fact, 'no more than a permanent Royal Commission, of highly miscellaneous membership' and so unlikely 'to agree upon any fundamental matters referred to it.' Moreover when it did report 'it could do no more than offer a body of advice which required to be dissected, from an administrative point of view, in the departments before it was ready for submission to the Cabinet.' In sum it 'never acquired an effective status in our administrative system.'[295] One lesson that could be learned from this experiment was, therefore, 'the necessity of ensuring that any central economic organization is effectively coupled up with the departments and of making some one Minister...responsible for its work.'[296] The practical inefficacy of the council was shown by the fact that when the unemployment problem was acute, the Prime Minister gave the task of examining possible solutions not to the EAC but to a 'panel' of senior civil servants under the chairmanship of the Permanent Under-Secretary to the Home Office and reporting to the Lord Privy Seal.[297] And by mid-1931, after the assumption of office by the national coalition, the EAC was virtually dead and most of its sub-committees on the verge of withering away. In fact it never met after 1932.[298] Its economic functions then passed to its Standing Committee on Economic

293 ibid., p. 154.
294 Anderson, op. cit., pp. 16–17; Bridges, *Treasury Control*, p. 14; S. S. Wilson, op. cit., p. 85 §711; Mackintosh, op. cit., p. 524. On the EAC, see also PRO, CAB 87/74 MG(43)12, MGO 32 (15 November 1943), 'The Role of the Economist in the Machinery of Government', p. 2 §4(b).
295 H. J. Laski, *Parliamentary Government in England: a Commentary* (1938; London, 1952), pp. 266–7. Laski later repeated this view to the Machinery of Government Committee during the war: see below p. 325 n. 327.
296 Anderson, op. cit., p. 17.
297 ibid., pp. 11–12. The chairman was Anderson himself.
298 Howson and Winch, op. cit., Appendix 1 pp. 354–70 provides a list of the meetings and reports of the EAC and its committees (other than those dealing with scientific matters). Cf. Sir P. Debenham, 'The Economic Advisory Council and the Great Depression', *Oxford Economic Papers*, n.s., v (1953), supplement, p. 29.

Information sitting under the chairmanship of Stamp. This met regularly until 1939 and every couple of months made periodic surveys of the economic situation.[299] It was never formally disbanded but gradually sank 'into complete oblivion'.[300]

In the present context, what is most interesting about these experiments is, firstly, that they are set up outside the usual departments, an indication that a specific and direct Civil Service responsibility is not yet recognized. The object is rather to get advice from ancillary institutions of the sort which have been described even though this raised problems about liaison with the Whitehall machine. Secondly so far as the Civil Service was concerned, the Treasury is no way especially involved.[301] The most pointed instance of this occurs perhaps in respect to the panel of civil servants set up to consider the unemployment issue which, as indicated above, was chaired by the permanent head, not of the Treasury but the Home Office, and reported not to the Chancellor but to the Lord Privy Seal. Yet the inter-war experience was important in two respects as Sir E. Bridges later observed. First it helped create a belief in the obligation of the state 'to do what it could to ensure that the conditions which made for good trade and high employment were as favourable as possible.' Secondly it suggested that since, in the Keynesian terms then coming into fashion, policy would 'require the use of the Budget to forward this end, this was a field in which the Treasury would in future be closely concerned.'[302] And it was the coming of the Second World War which effected a sea-change in this regard: it transformed the situation, the institutions, and the policies.

The Hitler war

As the war approached various suggestions were made about how to cope with the economic difficulties it would raise: a couple among them were (once more) the idea of an Economic General Staff and a special Department of Economic Planning.[303] Neither was taken up. But the story of what actually occurred is fairly straightforward. The main innovations made shortly before the beginning or after the outbreak of hostilities were four in number. First of all there was the so-called Stamp Survey instituted in July 1939 within the framework of the Cabinet Office

---

299 For the view that the work of the Committee on Economic Information has been seriously undervalued, see Howson and Winch, op. cit., ch. 5 esp. p. 109 regarding its influence on Treasury thinking.
300 S. S. Wilson, op. cit., p. 85 §710; Lord Robbins, *Autobiography of an Economist* (London, 1971), pp. 169–70.
301 Cf. the comments in Bridges, *Treasury Control*, pp. 14–15.
302 ibid., p. 15.
303 Anderson, op. cit., p. 12.

and on the basis of the previous EAC Committee on Economic Information. Its formal title was Survey of Economic and Financial Plans and the task of its three members (Stamp, Henderson, and Clay) was to examine, from the economic point of view, the arrangements which had been made by departments against the outbreak of war and to see whether there were any gaps or failures of co-ordination.[304] Secondly the Stamp Survey was aided by a staff of academic economists and statisticians who formed the Central Economic Information Service, constituting in fact the first entry of economists into government in a full-time advisory capacity.[305] Quite a number of useful studies was produced though (Anderson says) 'Whether full use was made of them is another matter.'[306] The CEIS also produced reports and data for ministerial committees, and its staff expanded accordingly so that it gradually put the Survey as such into the shade.[307] Thirdly there was the statistical branch under Professor Lindemann which Churchill set up when he went to the Admiralty in September 1939. Finally there was the ministerial committee on economic policy originally set up to give formal cover to the Stamp Survey and to provide a closer relationship to ministries and their departments. Its terms of reference were 'to keep under constant review the whole field of our economic war effort'. Its first chairman was the Chancellor of the Exchequer; and it was paralleled by an official committee of which Stamp was 'president'.[308] These arrangements were superseded or developed after the formation of the Churchill government in May 1940 in a series of changes completed by early the following year.

On the ministerial front there was no possible civilian counterpart to the degree of control of military affairs assumed by Churchill as Minister of Defence. But, after various permutations on a complex committee structure, the whole was tightened up by *inter alia* the abolition of the Economic Policy Committee and the emergence of the Lord President's Steering Committee (which had been first set up in June 1940) as 'the principal organ of the War Cabinet in co-ordinating the social and economic aspects of the war effort on the home front.'[309] Shortly after assuming office in May 1940, Churchill had minuted Bridges calling for

> a revision of the existing system of dealing with economic problems and placing it under the Lord President. I have it in mind that trade,

---

304 S. S. Wilson, op. cit., p. 85 §711, p. 109 §965.
305 Sir A. Cairncross, 'An Early Think-Tank: the Origins of the Economic Section', *Three Banks Review* (December 1984), p. 50.
306 Anderson, op. cit., pp. 13–14. For some of the studies, ibid., p. 14 n. 1.
307 S. S. Wilson, op. cit., p. 109 §966.
308 ibid., pp. 103–4 §949. There was also a ministerial Food Policy Committee (and its official counterpart) which overlapped a good deal with the EPC, ibid., p. 103 §948.
309 ibid., pp. 94–5 §§922–3. Details of the principal civil committees are given, ibid., pp. 103ff.

transport, shipping, MEW [Ministry of Economic Warfare], food and agriculture would all come into a general group, over which he would exercise a large measure of executive control.[310]

It was clearly the crucial committee on economic matters and achieved a pre-eminent position in respect of the home front generally. As Churchill said in February 1942 during a Commons debate: 'The Lord President of the Council presides over what is, in certain aspects, almost a parallel Cabinet concerned with home affairs. Of this body a number of Ministers of Cabinet rank are regular members, and others are invited as may be convenient.'[311] Its terms of reference were: to keep continuous watch on behalf of the War Cabinet over the general trend of economic development; to co-ordinate the work of the other economic committees; and to deal with any special economic questions. It was made clear that the Lord President's Committee would deal with price and wages policy, home consumption, financial policy, foreign trade, and export surpluses. And its work continued to grow.[312]

At the official level there were also major alterations. The Stamp Survey as such was discontinued. But the work of the Central Economic Information Service had considerably enlarged and, as part of these changes, its staff was divided into two parts both working within the Cabinet Office. At the end of 1940 the statisticians were hived off to form the Central Statistical Office so as to provide a common service for the government as a whole and that firm and coherent quantitative basis necessary for war planning. It circulated regular digests about such subjects as the war effort, the economic situation, munitions, and the like (such statistical data having been provided largely on a departmental basis and so liable to omissions and inconsistency).[313] The economists became the Economic Section working more and more to the Lord President and his committee and so at the centre of the machinery for economic co-ordination. It was recognized as 'an important experiment.'[314] The section was small, consisting then of a Director and eight assistants from the universities, each being allotted a particular area of review such as manpower, shipping, fuel, food, or national income and expenditure. Close contact was maintained with cognate departmental activities and with 'scientific' developments in analysis. The section's routine duties were dictated by the week-to-week business

---

310 PRO, CAB 71, 48/21 Part 4 cited ibid., p. 104 §950.
311 378 H.C. Deb. 5s., 24 February 1942, col. 38.
312 S. S. Wilson, op. cit., p. 104 §950, and Annex 9 pp. [176]–[177].
313 Bridges, *Treasury Control*, p. 17; S. S. Wilson, op. cit., pp. 110–11 §§968–9.
314 PRO, CAB 87/74 MG(43)12, MGO 32 (15 November 1943), 'The Role of the Economist in the Machinery of Government', p. 3 §5. The details which follow are based on this account.

of the Lord President's Committee, however: it briefed the Lord President on items on the agenda and gave technical assistance with the many special inquiries he was responsible for as general co-ordinator of the home front. The Economic Section issued a quarterly survey of the general economic position but preferred to embody its work in reports to the Lord President and his committee and in informal discussion. In this way it avoided friction with departments that might otherwise have developed. Lord Bridges later described the section's goal as being to produce an all-round, objective picture of the economic situation and of the economic aspects of projected government policies.[315] Finally Lindemann's section acquired a central position (and was housed in the Cabinet Office) as the Prime Minister's Statistical Branch to analyse and present to him all the statistical information he required and to warn him of any pending shortages or discordances in the war effort.[316]

This was the main central machinery for economic intelligence and co-ordination for most of the war period, though from time to time opinions were expressed in favour of the appointment of a minister with a specific responsibility for the oversight of economic affairs.[317] However the 'essential difficulty' about this proposal 'was always the conflict of responsibilities that would arise between the new Minister, the Chancellor of the Exchequer, the President of the Board of Trade and the Lord President of the Council.' Eventually it was decided that the sphere where direct ministerial direction was needed was that of war production, that is, 'the allocation of resources among the Supply Departments, the regular review of their programmes etc' and such a post was created early in 1942.[318] Wider economic issues continued to be dealt with by the Lord President's Committee and the Economic Section.

In the present context what is significant about all these arrangements is the fact that the Treasury's position was not a primary or central one. The CSO and the Economic Section were placed in the Cabinet Office and not in the Treasury. The Chancellor was simply one ministerial member of the Lord President's Committee. And the various bodies

---

315 Bridges, *The Treasury*, p. 91. Cairncross, art. cit., gives an interesting personal view of the section's work in its early days.
316 S. S. Wilson, op. cit., pp. 109–11 §§967–9.
317 The account which follows is based on PRO, CAB 21/2217, 'Outline History of the Central Organisation for Economic Policy, 1919–1947', §23.
318 Though not without difficulty. Churchill among others had intended the post to have complete overlord power on the economic front including labour matters and shipbuilding. But Bevin refused to accept the one, and the Admiralty the other. Beaverbrook, who had been appointed, resigned after only a few weeks in office, in which decision his position as Minister of Production was one factor. See A. J. P. Taylor, *Beaverbrook* (1972; Penguin, 1974), ch. 20; K. Harris, *Attlee* (London, 1982), p. 194.

concerned with production and the allocation of resources and manpower were operated under other auspices.[319] The core of the matter is that Churchill mistrusted the Treasury. He had had an unhappy experience as Chancellor in the 1920s; and the Permanent Secretary until 1942 was Sir Horace Wilson who had been one of Chamberlain's senior advisers and closely associated with the pre-war appeasement policy which Churchill had so strongly opposed. He tended, therefore, to remove Treasury influence to the sidelines wherever possible. At the time it was quite simply a politically unpopular office. And it was associated with the failure of economic orthodoxy in the great depression. In addition, of course, a ministry of finance necessarily had a more subordinate role to play in wartime conditions. Scarce resources like shipping and manpower rather than costs set the limits of action; and the traditional procedures of Treasury regulation were seen as unduly restrictive and inappropriate.[320] The main instruments of wartime economic policy were not financial but direct controls. And this policy operated not so much through public expenditure, taxation, monetary measures, and the exchange rate as through rationing, the allocation of materials, the direction of manpower, shipping programmes, and so forth. As one account put it, 'The units in which things were measured and controlled were men and tons, not money.'[321] A political indication of the Treasury's position was that the Chancellor was not always in the War Cabinet even: from February 1942 until September 1943 the post did not carry this status. However Anderson's appointment at the latter date and the reinclusion of the Treasury in the highest decision-making body (coupled with his own considerable personal prestige) is held to mark the renaissance of the wartime Treasury.[322] Of course it had always had a part to play in such matters as dollar diplomacy, the organization of the sterling area, and financing the war. In this regard, too, the budget of April 1941 and the historic White Paper on National Income and Expenditure which accompanied it have a crucial symbolic significance for they indicated a widening financial concern not simply for the government sector but for the balance of resources and demand in the economy as a whole. Thus was formally indicated the first acceptance of

---

319 Though when Anderson went to the Treasury in September 1943 he did take with him responsibility for preparing the manpower budget for consideration by the War Cabinet, S. S. Wilson, op. cit., p. 105 §950.
320 Cf. a leader in *The Times* (31 January 1940), p. 9.
321 D. MacDougall, 'The Machinery of Economic Government: Some Personal Reflections', in D. Butler and A. H. Halsey (eds), *Policy and Politics* (London, 1978), p. 174.
322 Chester and Willson, op. cit., p. 327n. When Anderson became Chancellor he retained ministerial responsibility for the Economic Section which was thus linked with the Treasury, Howson and Winch, op. cit., pp. 157–8.

Keynesian ideas in contrast to fiscal orthodoxy.[323] And it indicated the basis on which, in due course, the Treasury was to emerge to supremacy in the matter of economic management. The new kind of policy was further strengthened by the Coalition commitment in 1944 to the planned maintenance of full employment which would necessarily entail a greater degree of peacetime intervention in the economy than ever before: as Lord Bridges said, this commitment was 'perhaps the most important single landmark on the way to the post-war policy of managing the economy.'[324]

Thus the wartime developments may be crudely summarized as follows. From 1939 until May 1940, certain institutions were established in which the Treasury had a not inconsiderable part to play. For the rest of 1940, after Churchill's accession to power, a basically new committee structure was in process of development and the Treasury was not crucially involved. The remainder of the war period saw the confirmation of Treasury decline in this respect with the growing dominance in the management of economic affairs of the Lord President's Committee and the establishment in other places than the Treasury, of the CSO and the Economic Section. None the less the basis of future Treasury hegemony was already being laid though the pattern of development was not without interruption.

Treasury dominance

It was during 1943 that thought began to be given to the question whether, when hostilities were over, there would still be a need for some kind of central machinery of economic co-ordination and advice in addition to that provided by the departmental economists. Professor L. Robbins, who was then head of the Economic Section of the War Cabinet Secretariat, responded with 'an unhesitating affirmative'. His view was reported to the Machinery of Government Committee as follows:

> He feels no doubt that for years after the war we shall be confronted with a position of the utmost complexity and that, although opinions may differ concerning the extent to which economic planning by the State will eventually be necessary, it does not seem open to question that even in the most 'liberal' society of the future there will need to be a co-ordination of measures of economic policy much greater than has existed in the past.

And while that co-ordination must ultimately rest with the Cabinet of the

---

323 Roseveare, *The Treasury: the Evolution of a British Institution*, pp. 258, 274–6; Bridges, *Treasury Control*, pp. 17–18.
324 Bridges, *The Treasury*, p. 92.

day or a committee acting on its behalf, there was (Robbins believed) an obvious need, prior to the final decision, for issues to be properly sifted by a group of professionally expert people attached to the minister or group of ministers responsible for economic policy. This last proviso was important for otherwise the technical advice might well be ineffective. But the case for the continuance of an organization like the existing Economic Section was, Robbins thought, undoubted.[325] This view was not unchallenged for various reasons but in particular because of the friction that might arise between such a central body of economic advisers and the departments. It was to avoid a major difficulty of this sort, for instance, that it was suggested (among others by Sir Horace Wilson who had recently ceased to be PST), that any central economic section should be attached to the Treasury.[326] Keynes similarly accepted the need for comprehensive economic advice and also thought there was a case for placing such a service within the Treasury. The conclusion reached by the official Machinery of Government Committee was:

> There is thus a substantial measure of agreement that, while the main contribution to be made by economists to the work of Government should continue to be made in the Departments themselves, it will be desirable at the same time to have some central Government organisation conducting economic studies from a more general and synthetic point of view than is possible within the Departments; at the same time, it ... would be unwise to attempt to establish anything in the nature of a grandiose Economic General Staff.[327]

In the end it was decided to recommend the continuance of the Economic Section on an experimental basis in the first instance but within the Cabinet Office.[328] The White Paper on Full Employment (issued the following August) committed the government to a measure of economic planning and contained some reference to the organization which would be necessary for this purpose: a small central staff to measure and analyse economic trends.[329] The future of the CSO and the Economic Section was thus assured. A couple of years after the end of hostilities, Sir J.

---

325 PRO, CAB 87/74 MG(43)12, MGO 32 (15 November 1943), 'The Role of the Economist in the Machinery of Government', pp. 3–4 §§7–8. Cf. Keynes's view, ibid., p. 5 §12.
326 ibid., p. 5 §10. Cf. Sir Donald Fergusson's view at §9.
327 ibid., §18. The idea of an Economic General Staff was also rejected by both Laski and Beveridge, ibid., pp. 6–7 §§16–17.
328 ibid., pp. 8–9 §22. The detailed functions envisaged are listed at §22(b). The approval of the ministerial Machinery of Government Committee is at CAB 87/73 MG(43) 6th meeting (2 December 1943), pp. 1–2 §1 (1)–(2).
329 Employment Policy, 1943–4 (vol. viii), Cmd. 6527, pp. 26–8 §§80–7 esp. §81.

Anderson, who had himself played such a formative role in these matters, summarized the conclusions he drew from the experience of the war years:

(i) There should be included in the machinery of government a central economic organization in which each Department concerned with economic problems has an opportunity of collaborating effectively.

(ii) That organization should make use of statistical material and economic studies prepared by a specially selected technical staff maintaining constant touch with professional opinion outside.

(iii) The organization should report through its own departmental head to a Minister in Charge, specially designated by the Prime Minister, whose business it should be to see that the conclusions put forward receive prompt and effective Ministerial consideration.

(iv) Correlative to that organization, there should be an organization of commercial and industrial interests with which there should be continuous close consultation, with the twofold object of keeping all concerned with the execution of policy in line and ensuring unity of purpose throughout the economic field.

(v) Finally, special provision should be made for the widest possible dissemination of information to the public.[330]

Anderson simply sees the Treasury as one of the departments involved; and wartime thinking generally in these matters assumed that the general oversight of the economy and production would be in other hands.

It was hardly to be expected that the Labour government which took office at the end of July 1945 would make great changes at least initially. After all many of its senior members had helped to form the wartime arrangements: in particular Attlee himself had served as Lord President for nearly two years. Labour leaders had also been closely involved in the Coalition discussions about the regulation of the economy during reconstruction. As well all three political parties had agreed on the principles and machinery implied by their acceptance in 1944 of a policy of full employment. Hence the wartime institutions were continued and then supplemented and modified as seemed necessary: it was the easiest and most prudent course to follow. Thus the Lord President's Committee was still the main supervisory and co-ordinating body in respect of domestic economic policy. In a strange division of responsibility, overseas economic affairs were the concern of a separate ministerial committee under the chairmanship of the Prime Minister. The

---

330 Anderson, op. cit., pp. 23–4.

professional advice of the Economic Section continued to be available. And in September 1945 the organization was strengthened by the establishment of an official committee entitled 'The Official Steering Committee on Economic Development'. Its members were permanent secretaries from the main economic departments and the Permanent Secretary of the Treasury took the chair. In a way it was a sort of economic general staff.[331] Initially it reported to the Lord President's Committee and had very wide terms of reference: 'To advise Ministers on the use to be made of the nation's economic resources.' It operated through five working parties dealing with investment, the balance of payments, manpower, the economic survey, and statistics. An official account of its work says:

> Apart from dealing with questions of future economic policy which were referred to them, the main business of the Committee was to supervise the preparation of regular surveys of the economic situation in which the requirements of various kinds of national activity were balanced against national resources, and on the basis of these surveys to advise Ministers on the steps to be taken to control national economic development.[332]

In the early stages of the Labour government, then, the Treasury was not the office primarily concerned with supervising the economy as a whole. Of course it was represented on the main committees and had charge of fiscal policy. But the main co-ordinating responsibility lay with the Prime Minister's committee and Lord President's Committee as aided by the professional economists of the Economic Section of the Cabinet Secretariat and the senior officials of the Committee on Economic Development. In addition the main emphasis at this time was on the, somewhat *ad hoc*, use of physical controls (as over imports, manpower, and production) as a means of allocating scarce resources, so it followed that the main tasks fell to other departments than the Treasury.[333]

Difficulties were not slow to appear. One was the division of function between the two main ministerial committees dealing with domestic and with overseas economic policy. Another was the diffusion of responsibility that existed between the Lord President in charge of domestic economic co-ordination, the Chancellor concerned with fiscal policy, and the President of the Board of Trade occupied with the export drive. The ministers involved were respectively H. Morrison, H. Dalton,

---

331 H. Dalton, *High Tide and After: Memoirs 1945–1960* (London, 1962), p. 195.
332 PRO, CAB 21/2217, 'Outline History of the Central Organisation for Economic Policy', §26.
333 Lord Morrison, *Government and Parliament: a Survey from the Inside* (1954; 3rd edn, London, 1964), p. 308; Roseveare, *The Treasury: the Evolution of a British Institution*, p. 278.

and Sir S. Cripps and neither they nor their departments co-operated as ideally as they should have done.[334] As well the Steering Committee on Economic Development tended not to work effectively as a co-ordinating body because its members were so much pre-occupied by their departmental duties; and so in mid-1946 a new ministerial committee on economic planning was set up (with the Lord President as chairman) for the particular purpose of supervising and improving the official committee's work.[335]

The crunch came in 1947, a fateful year. The jarring effect of the fuel crisis ('that triumph of non-planning' as it has been called), a worsening balance of payments, and the impending disaster of sterling convertibility were dramatic events that led to basic questions being asked about the adequacy of existing machinery of economic control.[336] The outcome as the year wore on was 'a search for stronger central direction'.[337] In March, during a debate on the economic situation, the intention was announced to set up a Central Economic Planning Staff under a Chief Planning Officer, Sir E. Plowden, to work with the Lord President (again, be it noted, not with the Treasury). The CEPS, situated in the Cabinet Office, was to consist largely of departmental planning officers and would have the task of co-ordinating departmental programmes and thus of covering the whole field of 'forward planning' as well as of developing a long-term plan for the use of the country's manpower and other resources. In addition it was proposed to set up an Economic Planning Board to represent various interests in and out of government, to ensure their co-operation with economic policy, and to secure their advice on the best use of national resources. Finally in September 1947 a Minister of Economic Affairs was appointed, the choice falling on Sir S. Cripps. There was no department, only a small personal staff, though the assistance of the Paymaster-General was also available. The CEPS and the Economic Section were to work under the new minister's direction. The official announcement said that the Prime Minister would thus have the assistance of a senior colleague who could

---

334 S. H. Beer, *Treasury Control: the Co-ordination of Financial and Economic Policy in Great Britain* (1965; 2nd edn, Oxford, 1963), pp. 71–2; B. Donoughue and G. W. Jones, *Herbert Morrison: Portrait of a Politician* (London, 1973), ch. 26 esp. p. 354. Cf. ibid., p. 406.

335 Beer, op. cit., p. 72; PRO, CAB 21/2217, 'Outline History of the Central Organisation for Economic Policy', §26.

336 The phrase about the fuel crisis is cited from Roseveare, op. cit., p. 317.

337 For the following account of the 1947 changes I draw on: *KCA* (1946–8), pp. 8519A (8519, 8523), 8701A, and 8847A; PRO, CAB 21/1702, CP(47) 288 (18 October 1947), 'Cabinet Business and Procedure: Note by the Prime Minister' (including an appendix on the 'Inter-departmental Organisation for Economic Planning'); and Donoughue and Jones, op. cit., ch. 31.

give his undivided attention to economic problems both at home and abroad and frame, for submission to the Cabinet, 'a general economic plan for achieving the production required to meet the nation's needs'.[338] A new ministerial committee was set up to decide, subject to the Cabinet, major issues of economic policy whether arising at home or abroad. This provided a focus at which the two aspects of the economic problem (hitherto considered by separate committees) could be brought together. This Economic Policy Committee was very small: apart from the Prime Minister as chairman its only other members were Cripps, Morrison, and Dalton (who was then Chancellor). There was also to be a Production Committee under the chairmanship of the Minister for Economic Affairs and consisting mainly of departmental ministers directly responsible for such subjects as trade, agriculture, transport, and so forth. It was to be concerned with supervising the production programmes required to give effect to the approved economic plan. According to one member, this was the place where 'the main work was done'.[339] Its establishment meant that the Lord President's Committee lost its economic co-ordinating function (though retaining oversight of other domestic policy).

These expedients might or might not have lasted and proved fruitful. But there was, brooding omnipresently over it all, the question of the official and personal relationships concerned. The new minister was supposed to co-ordinate economic policy, both domestic and overseas; to frame an economic plan; and to supervise the execution of the requisite production programmes. He was also specifically enjoined together with the Chancellor to submit to the Cabinet proposals for achieving a favourable balance of payments. But it was not made clear what the precise division of responsibility was. The position entailed many potential difficulties and tensions, not least given the inevitable interest of the Treasury (especially under so strong-willed a Chancellor as Dalton) in broader economic matters. But the problem was then fortuitously resolved by Dalton's resignation after his Budget indiscretion and Cripps' appointment to the Treasury. The Ministry for Economic Affairs, after a brief and inconclusive life, was thus absorbed in the Treasury, as were the Chief Planning Officer, the CEPS, and the Economic Information Unit. Henceforth the Treasury assumed the task of economic co-ordination. Perhaps this was inevitable. As Sir D. MacDougall (who had seen much of the machinery of government in this respect both in war and peace) said, the instruments of economic policy in peacetime 'are likely to be mainly financial rather than physical – unless we are driven by misfortune or bad management into a siege economy or, heaven forbid, deliberately choose such a state of affairs – it

---

338 PRO, CAB 21/1702, CP(47) 228 (18 October 1947), Prime Minister's note, p. 1 §1.
339 D. Jay cited in K. O. Morgan, *Labour in Power 1945–1951* (Oxford, 1984), p. 367.

would seem natural that that Minister should be the Chancellor of the Exchequer.'[340] Thus the Treasury was now acquiring and for the first time the administrative and professional apparatus necessary for the supervision of national economic policy; and, until 1964, it remained the centre of official responsibility for the task of economic management, a role it had never had before and one which, since its assumption, has radically changed the role and character of the office. Morrison observed that the new developments 'imposed upon the Chancellor of the Exchequer heavy additional duties (and the duties of the Chancellor are very heavy anyway)'; but as well it broadened 'the work of the Treasury and merged economic policy and planning with financial and budgetary matters under the single control of the Chancellor of the Exchequer.'[341] Or, as another commentator put it, it is probably true to say that, when Cripps went to the Treasury, 'no minister before or since, even during the war years, had as great power to direct the economy'. And clearly it put the Treasury at the centre of economic management.[342] In 1957 Sir Roger Makins (then Joint Permanent Secretary to the Treasury) said in evidence to the Radcliffe Committee on the working of the monetary system:

> Since 1948, when Sir Stafford Cripps combined the functions of Chancellor of the Exchequer with that of Minister for the Co-ordination of Economic Affairs, the Chancellor and therefore the Treasury, has had, in addition to the normal exercise of Treasury control through supply, the final responsibility for general economic policy.[343]

Precisely in order to help the Chancellor with this heavy new range of duties, in December 1947 a new Treasury post, that of Economic Secretary, was created. His role was to deal with general economic policy and planning including oversight of the relevant aspects of Treasury supply work; overseas financial negotiation; and internal financial planning.[344] The Financial Secretary assisted as usual with the normal Treasury responsibilities. Clearly there was a more uniform and unified control than under the earlier, and abortive, arrangements.

And so there began a long period – nearly twenty years – of Treasury

---

340 D. MacDougall, in Butler and Halsey, op. cit., pp. 174–5. Though cf. the subsequent reflections on the need for 'some offsetting centre of power' so that all sides of a possible policy are effectively examined, i.e., no monopoly of advice on economic policy, ibid., pp. 175–6.
341 Morrison, op. cit., p. 309.
342 C. Dow, *The Management of the British Economy 1945–60* (1964; Cambridge, 1970), p. 33.
343 Cited Bridges, *The Treasury*, p. 94.
344 W. I. Jennings, *Cabinet Government* (1936; 3rd edn, Cambridge, 1959), p. 326. Abolished in 1964 the post was revived in 1981.

The Department of Departments

dominance, indeed near monopoly, in economic management. The position remained basically unchanged under the Conservative governments of 1951 to 1964 though, of course, some modifications were made from time to time both in ancillary posts and institutions and in the Treasury itself. For instance in 1953 the Economic Section was transferred to the Treasury from the Cabinet Office (it had since 1947 been working very closely with the Chancellor in any case). At the same time its chief was given the title of Economic Adviser to HM Government. The CEPS was also absorbed into the Treasury as the Home and Overseas Planning Staff.[345] Both these developments involved the absorption into the Treasury of previously separate parts of the economic planning arrangements. In 1956 and 1962 the reorganization of the Treasury itself recognized the new economic policy responsibilities more clearly and, in particular, the creation of 'National Economy' and 'Public Sector' groups seemed to provide more formidable agencies of economic control than before.[346] But the burden was considerable for, as well, financial policy and Civil Service management were Treasury matters. The increasing load was recognized by, for instance, the appointment of Joint Permanent Secretaries in 1956 when Bridges retired; and five years later of a new Cabinet post, the Chief Secretary to relieve the Chancellor of duties relating to control of supply. The Treasury certainly had a lot to do. The economic policy work fell under three heads.[347] First the necessary factual information had to be assembled; and the CSO (in the Cabinet Office) had the major role in this regard. Secondly general *ad hoc* studies of economic problems, both domestic and international, were undertaken, the work of the Economic Section being important here. Thirdly there was economic forecasting to be attempted and the co-ordination of general policies for economic growth.

A commitment to 'planning' continued throughout the 1950s, albeit of a more 'indicative' kind, resting less on direct controls over limited resources and more on government co-ordination and consultation. There was concern with such matters as incomes policy (how to combine full employment with price stability); regional balance and development as by the control of industrial location; planned investment for new technology such as atomic energy and computers; import substitution and export subsidy; provision of industrial capital; and so forth. One institutional development that proved to be of value was the establishment of the National Economic Development Council in 1961, representing government and both sides of industry, to act as a forum for

---

345 Bridges, *The Treasury*, p. 92.
346 Roseveare, op. cit., p. 332.
347 Cf. Bridges, *The Treasury*, p. 96.

the discussion of various economic strategies.[348] Although only advisory, much was hoped of its influence and the work of its industrial committees.[349] Another important innovation was the National Incomes Commission (which was later joined to the Prices Review Body to form the Prices and Incomes Board).

But as the fifties wore on there was, in some places at least, a growing sense that the Treasury (as the department primarily concerned) was not handling matters well enough, partly perhaps because of the range of responsibilities it had and the burden these involved. It failed to 'fine-tune' the economy adequately; there was too much 'stop–go', changing short-term measures of response, and too little attempt to achieve long-term growth; and an excessive concern with the stability of the pound and the balance of payments. As well too many vital questions (relating, for instance, to manpower and raw material acquisition) were outside the direct purview of the Treasury. And there were at this period numerous reports and inquiries that either directly or by implication were critical of the current situation in Britain: Beeching on the railways; Buchanan on traffic in towns; Robbins on higher education. They all drew attention to major problems of economic and social reconstruction that needed long-term attention. Many people, particularly on the Labour side, wondered increasingly whether co-ordination by the Treasury was of the right sort or sufficiently effective. Would all the problems besetting Britain be adequately tackled by a Treasury always preoccupied with short-term financial manoeuvres?[350] And would not some quite different arrangement secure a better level of economic management? The disenchantment was hardly new: in his resignation speech in 1951, A. Bevan had been characteristically blunt with his curt, 'Take economic planning away from the Treasury, they know nothing about it'.[351] It was in such a critical context of opinion that in 1964 a new

348 Bridges, *The Treasury*, Appendix III pp. 216–19. Earlier ideas of this kind are reviewed in T. A. Smith, *The Politics of the Corporate Economy* (London, 1979), p. 14–16, 20–1, 29–38, 45, etc. And cf. §(iv) in the citation from Anderson, op. cit., at p. 326 above.
349 Roseveare, op. cit., p. 331. Cf. MacDougall, loc. cit., pp. 176–8. The Economic Planning Board came to an end when NEDC was set up though Clarke, at least, thinks this was a mistake because the former was a superior forum being better informed and less political, Sir R. Clarke, *Public Expenditure Management and Control: the Development of the Public Expenditure Survey Committee (PESC)* (London, 1978), pp. 74–5.
350 e.g. G. Brown, *In My Way: the Political Memoirs of Lord George-Brown* (1971; Penguin, 1972), pp. 87, 104. Cf. M. Shanks, *The Stagnant Society: a Warning* (Penguin, 1961); N. Macrae, *Sunshades in October: an Analysis of the Main Mistakes in British Economic Policy since the Mid Nineteen Fifties* (London, 1963); B. Chapman, *British Government Observed: Some European Reflections* (London, 1963), and S. Brittan, *The Treasury under the Tories 1951–1964* (Penguin, 1964).
351 Cited M. Foot, *Aneurin Bevan: a Biography* (London, 1962–73), ii. 336.

Labour government took office and instituted other machinery to replace that which had existed for nearly two decades.

DEA: *the failed revolution*

When he became Leader of the Opposition in 1963, H. Wilson decided that, on assuming office, he would make a radical change in the machinery of government concerning economic affairs:

> The decision was that while the Chancellor of the Exchequer should be responsible for all action necessary in the monetary field, foreign exchange, internal monetary management, Government expenditure and taxation, Britain could hope to win economic security only by a fundamental reconstruction and modernization of industry under the direction of a department at least as powerful as the Treasury. This new department would be concerned with real resources, with economic planning, with strengthening our ability to export and to save imports, with increasing productivity, and our competitiveness in domestic and export markets.[352]

The idea of a separate ministry of economic planning was by no means new.[353] But apart from the Ministry of Economic Affairs of 1947 (which lasted only a few weeks and had little chance to grow beyond a small secretariat), no such department had hitherto been created. Now, however, there was a strongly influential body of opinion that it would be better to have a department which was superior to the Treasury in determining economic priorities and so free of the usual preoccupations and restraints.[354] Discussions with civil servants were actually held by Labour leaders well before they took office; and a series of overlapping study groups went to work. The establishment of such a ministry became a settled part of Labour Party policy.[355] The Department of Economic Affairs was set up in October 1964 with, at its head, G. Brown (for whom obviously an important post had to be found) appointed as First Secretary of State and Minister for Economic Affairs. He was (as the official announcement put it) to be 'responsible for framing and

---

[352] H. Wilson, *The Labour Government 1964–70: a Personal Record* (1971; Penguin, 1974), p. 24. Cf. J. Grimond *et al.*, *Whitehall and Beyond* (London, 1964), pp. 16–17.

[353] For some early suggestions, see those cited in T. A. Smith, op. cit., pp. 19–21, 28–30, 42–8. See also R. Marris, *The Machinery of Economic Policy* (Fabian Research Series no. 168; London, 1954), §5. A. Bevan had also wanted a Ministry for Economic Expansion, Foot, op. cit., ii. 376.

[354] Brown, op. cit., p. 88. Cf. C. Pollitt, *Manipulating the Machine: Changing the Pattern of Ministerial Departments, 1960–83* (London, 1984), pp. 51–2.

[355] ibid., pp. 88–9. For the Labour election manifesto, see F. W. S. Craig, *British General Election Manifestos 1918–1966* (Chichester, 1970), p. 233.

supervising the plan for economic development and for the general co-ordination of action to implement the plan, and of all economic policy related to industrial expansion, allocation of physical resources, and regional implications of the expansion programme.'[356] This National Plan, prepared in the fullest consultation with industry, took just under a year to prepare and was based on what quickly turned out to be false assumptions about growth in production and exports. Not long after it had failed, *The Times*, in a leader called 'Twilight of Planning', said it had largely been 'wishful thinking', a 'fantasy' which 'lasted barely ten months before the facts of economic life overtook it.'[357] Brown himself has written that the story of DEA is 'the record of a social revolution that failed.' It ought, he believed, have been a great contribution to 'the recasting of the machinery of government to meet the needs of the twentieth century.... It envisaged a wholly novel form of national social accountancy to replace the orthodox financial accountancy by which the Treasury has always dominated British life.'[358]

There were two major reasons why, within a mere two years, the experiment ran down and came effectively to an end. One was simply a diffusion of effort in the DEA and on the part of its minister. Dealing with prices and incomes policy resulted in heavy duties – came indeed to seem the department's major role – and which diverted attention from more fundamental but more long-term questions of industrial planning and productivity. A similar sort of division arose from coping with the endless problems of overseas economic policy.[359] In effect Brown interpreted the DEA mandate too widely and without a proper focus of attention on the essential issues: there was, in Wilson's phrase, too little 'quiet and orderly administration'.[360] No doubt the other reason was more important: the failure to get clearly established the superiority of the DEA amid all the inevitable personal, political, and departmental rivalries of the world of Whitehall. Of course the DEA's very existence posed a threat to half-a-dozen established departments which had a finger in the economic pie: the Board of Trade and the ministries of technology, power, transport, housing and local government, overseas development, and labour, not to mention the Treasury and even No. 10 itself.[361] But, of course, the Treasury and the Chancellor were the main

---

356 KCA (1963–4), p.20349A (20351–2). For something of the chaos and paucity of facilities that attended the establishment of the office, see S. Crosland, *Tony Crosland* (London, 1982), pp.129–30.
357 *The Times* (6 April 1967), p.15.
358 Brown, op. cit., p.87.
359 ibid., p.110. H. Wilson, op. cit., pp.26, 96, 544; R. H. S. Crossman, *The Diaries of a Cabinet Minister* (London, 1975–7), i.238.
360 H. Wilson, op. cit., pp.287–8, 352.
361 Brown, op. cit., pp.111–12; Pollitt, op. cit., p.56.

rivals. It was indeed realized that some sort of concordat would be needed to clarify the division of responsibilities between the two departments. And after discussion it was laid down that the basic distinction was to be between monetary policy (which was the Treasury's business) and the co-ordination of industrial requirements together with anything to do with the mobilization of real resources (which fell to the DEA).[362] But this agreement was never formally accepted and there were unending disputes at all levels. The result, in Brown's view, was that the Treasury was able either to filch things back or to make it difficult for the DEA to carry out a coherent and continuous policy in pursuit of its grand design. He admits, too, he did not realize the intensity of the battle that would have to be fought with the Treasury.[363] In this regard he felt let down by the Prime Minister who (he believed) was not prepared to declare the senior status of the DEA and probably hoped that 'a state of competitive existence' would keep everyone happy and on their toes.[364] The deficiencies of the position are commented on by others who were involved. Lady Falkender thought the DEA was bound to fail because, as a new department with relatively little bureaucratic backing, it had no chance against the Treasury so that its limited authority was bound to be eroded.[365] Crossman confirms this view. Writing in his diary in February 1965 about conflict between the Chancellor and the First Secretary of State over the housing programme, he said: 'It was very clear indeed that, despite all the efforts to ensure that D.E.A. was the real planning Ministry, the Chancellor of the Exchequer in Britain today, with all the authority of the Treasury behind him, still holds the power.'[366] And, in fact, Crossman believed that because of its concern with incomes policy the DEA left whatever planning there was to the Treasury.[367] In mid-1966 he noted that there was, on the home front, no effective planning machinery like that for defence; instead there were two ministries permanently at loggerheads, with the Prime Minister holding the balance between them and the Treasury gradually gaining ascendancy. Early the following year, Crossman observed that the DEA had been allowed to run down and was by then even less of a counterweight to the Treasury. Nor was the decline effectively halted.[368] And, as a result of his careful review of these matters, Dr Roseveare concluded that the real power of

---

362 H. Wilson, op. cit., p.26.
363 Brown, op. cit., pp.89–90, 92. For the similar difficulties Brown had with T. Balogh's advisory group in the Cabinet Office, Brown, op. cit., p.93.
364 Brown, op. cit., pp.104–5.
365 M. Williams, *Inside No 10* (1972; New English Library, 1975), p.202.
366 Crossman, op. cit., i.154. Cf. ibid., i.193, 203, 491–2, 495.
367 ibid., i.238.
368 ibid., i.582; ii.295; iii.675.

the Treasury was hardly touched by the creation of the DEA and this despite the undoubted desire that existed to limit the former's role and see it humbled.[369] The idea behind the DEA was that there should be a single minister with overriding responsibility for economic policy: but this involved a primacy that could hardly be achieved.[370]

The DEA effectively came to an end when Brown finally left for the Foreign Office in August 1966; and though it lingered on for a while in other hands it had only residual significance. Even the fact that the Prime Minister himself assumed direct charge in 1967, as part of a supposedly new style of economic management, hardly diminished the Treasury's role and influence.[371] 'So', Brown mused later, 'orthodox financial control won, and our basic social reformation failed.'[372] The department was given its quietus in the government reorganization of October 1969. In his memoir of these affairs Wilson himself says he does not regret the DEA experiment and claims – as Brown did – some positive achievement, as with the development of a policy for modernizing and restructuring British industry and the creation of regional planning machinery. The blame for failure is simply laid at the door of untoward circumstances and that convenient plaint, 'hostile speculative activity'.[373] Both Brown and Wilson still believed, however, that some department on the lines of DEA might in the future have a permanent and central role to play in the machinery of government, specifically (in Brown's view) to 'limit the outdated authority of the Treasury'.[374] The conviction survives that the Treasury is not the place to drive forward a Socialist industrial strategy. A. N. W. Benn said (a couple of years ago) that the Treasury has had a lot of influence and used it badly: 'the economic failure of Britain since the war could be attributed primarily to the Treasury because they've always been in power.'[375] Not surprisingly a joint Labour Party–TUC statement, published in 1982 and subsequently incorporated in the party's election manifesto the following year, included a provision to create a new Department of Economic and Industrial Planning.[376] There were other views, of course, and these tended to confirm the inevitable central authority of the Treasury in the supervision of economic affairs. Sir S. Goldman, for instance, believed that economic management required the

---

369 Roseveare, op. cit., pp. 345, 348. Cf. MacDougall, loc. cit., p. 179.
370 Cf. M. Shanks, 'DEA: Fact, Fiction and the Future', *The Times* (8 April 1968), p. 23.
371 Roseveare, op. cit., pp. 348–9 where details of the 1967 strategy are given.
372 Brown, op. cit., p. 111.
373 Wilson, op. cit., pp. 893–4.
374 ibid., p. 893; Brown, op. cit., p. 113. For trenchant analysis of the failure of Labour policy, see W. Beckerman (ed.), *The Labour Government's Economic Record: 1964–1970* (London, 1972).
375 Cited in H. Young and A. Sloman, *But, Chancellor* (London, 1984), p. 113.
376 ibid., pp. 112–13.

discriminating use of all the instruments available and that, as public expenditure is the major factor, the Chancellor and the Treasury must remain responsible for the conduct of economic policy. It was, therefore, most undesirable to split the functions of the centre.[377]

With the demise of the DEA, therefore, the *status quo ante* was more or less restored, and the Treasury formally resumed its central place in matters of economic management. And after a review in 1975 its internal organization was changed along functional lines the better to suit this purpose.[378] There have been some modifications since, not least in respect of the policies of the present government, but the arrangement broadly remains similar in kind. There is: a Public Services Sector which covers general expenditure policy and the supervision of the five major spending areas; an Overseas Finance Sector which deals *inter alia* with the European Community; a Chief Economic Adviser's Sector concerned with policy analysis and forecasting; and a division to handle public enterprises, taxation, and social security.[379] The nature of the Treasury's role in this regard has a number of important features. For one thing there is a greater stress on economic professionalism. The administrators themselves are generally a good deal more 'literate' in these matters; and certainly there are many more economists involved. In the Civil Service as a whole the number (in the two decades since 1964) has risen from 21 to 274; and 65 of the latter total are in the Treasury itself.[380] The existence of the Chief Economic Adviser's Sector is also a token of the significance attached to these matters. But as usual the ultimate emphasis must be political; and the Treasury's part is in this regard to be a kind of court of appeal before issues go to the Cabinet.[381]

THE EMPEROR'S CLOTHES

'But he has nothing on at all!' at last cried out all the people. The Emperor was vexed, for he felt that the people were right; but he thought the procession must go on now. And the lords of the bedchamber took greater pains than ever to appear holding up a train, although, in reality, there was no train to hold.
H. C. ANDERSEN, *Favourite Fairy Tales*, n.d., p. 113

'The Treasury stands out as one of the enduring landmarks of the

---

377 Sir S. Goldman, *The Developing System of Public Expenditure Management and Control* (Civil Service College Studies no. 2; London, 1973), p. 34.
378 J. M. Lee, 'The Context of Central Administration', in M. Wright (ed.), *Public Spending Decisions* (London, 1980), pp. 81–3.
379 I take these details from *Whitaker's Almanack 1986*, pp. 444–5.
380 Young and Sloman, op. cit., pp. 29, 34.
381 ibid., p. 50.

departmental machinery of government.'[382] Of course the degree of integration achieved in the fulfilment of its many functions has varied; and from time to time notable adjustments have been made of its responsibilities. But relative to other departments its load has always been considerable and, in the broad context of collectivist growth, has never diminished. At the present time its main tasks include: the management of the national economy and financial policy; oversight of the public sector including the allocation of resources between its competing areas; assisting government departments to maintain practices that have due regard to propriety, economy, and efficiency in the expenditure of public money and the numbers and deployment of staff; and the setting of common standards for the Civil Service and the negotiation and settlement of pay and conditions of service.[383] It is a very substantial burden indeed. But is the overlord concept of the Treasury perhaps misleading? Has its control over the government machine been so continuously effective as might be supposed? Even in the 'Gladstonian' era it had to rely on departmental co-operation and to acknowledge the limits to its power derived from the independent responsibility of ministers. And subsequently, as the size and cost of the Civil Service grew and the functions of government were enlarged, a relaxation of the level and a change in the form of control were inevitable. More and more of the detail was formally left to the spending departments themselves with the Treasury exercising a general supervision coupled with sporadic interventions and a concern that departmental mechanisms of control should be adequate. The essential paradox is that as expenditure has gone up, central supervision has not so much tightened as become more divided and attenuated. The pressures to maintain or increase spending have proved hard to resist; actually to curtail expenditure even more difficult. And in the attempt recent years have seen the system lurch from one unsuccessful expedient to another. Of course the problems are enormously complex and, in the last resort, can only be resolved by an exercise of political will reinforcing the position of the Chancellor and his officials. The same sort of pessimistic judgement is likely, too, of the efforts at supervising the tendencies of economic life or of managing government organization. The reputation of the Treasury is and has long been considerable. But after all the encomiums about the sophistication of its officials and the panoply of its powers, is it not proper for a small voice to wonder whether (in the light of the record) the skill or the authority is, or ever has been, real in the sense of being fully effective?

382 M. V. Hawtin and J. K. Moore, *The Integration of HM Treasury and the Civil Service Department: Report of the Study Team* (CSD; London, 1980), p. 2 §3.
383 Cf. ibid., p. 3 §4; G. C. Beard, *Government Finance and Accounts: Background Notes* (MPO; n.p. [London], 1982), pp. 20–4.

5
THE PUBLIC CONCERN
– AND BEYOND

> ...it will be impossible to notice all or nearly all the administrative Commissions which actually exist. They are disguised under very various names, and have gradually insinuated themselves into every branch of the public service. But the great stride which they have taken has been within the last few years.
> J. TOULMIN SMITH, *Government by Commissions Illegal and Pernicious*, 1849, p.257

A PARASTATAL WORLD

> **para-state** ... An institution or body which takes on some of the roles of civil government or political authority; an agency through which the state works indirectly.
> OEDS, iii.268

AS GOVERNMENT extends the range and depth of its intervention in the life of the community, existing institutions are reformed and new ones created to cope with the various pressures at work and the problems which arise. The first response was at local level though more and more associated with central aid, initiative, and supervision. Then in time the central departments themselves became the more important focus of provision and regulation. But there has also appeared a third institutional array of diverse form and purpose. This is the parastatal world embracing a multitude of bodies which are neither local nor central offices of state as normally understood. They thus stand outside the usual administrative (and judicial) structure though they are related to it in some way or degree. The groups of institutions concerned clearly constitute a most important category of public agency. The Pliatzky report showed that, shortly before it appeared in 1980, the nationalized industries (as there defined) had a turnover of nearly £24,000 millions and employed over 1.6 million people and that the National Health Service involved expenditure approaching £7,500 millions and had some 900,000 employees. Then there were the many non-departmental

340 A Much Governed Nation

organizations. Of these 489 had 'executive' functions and were the channel for expenditure on capital and current account of nearly £5,800 millions as well as having around 217,000 staff; in addition to which there were related departmental costs of some £24 millions. There were also over 1,500 advisory bodies entailing expenditure of about £13 millions by their sponsor departments. As well there were 67 'tribunal systems' with costs totalling £30 millions. This is by no means a complete tally of the bodies making up the Public Concern but it is enough to indicate its significance in terms of the amounts of money and labour involved at that time: over £37,000 millions spent a year and 2.72 million people employed.[1]

The total number of commissions, boards, committees, corporations, and so forth is considerable: as Sir A. Street once said, these bodies have grown profusely like flowers in the spring.[2] Recent estimates have ranged up to more than 3,000 depending on the definition in view. Nor is precise classification possible. An official report written in 1944 (and so before the considerable post-war expansion got under way) found the category problem 'bewildering' and 'intractable' even then; while a recent description of the way these bodies had proliferated was simply 'pragmatism run wild'.[3] They do indeed 'embrace a wide range of public functions, constitutions and relationships with government'; and they differ a lot in respect of legal status, method of establishment, source of revenue, level of staff and expenditure, type of organization, and much more.[4] It is hardly surprising that their Linnaeus is yet to come. I have no ambition in this regard and refer no further to the problem.[5] For present

1 Report on Non-Departmental Public Bodies, 1979–80, Cmnd. 7797, pp. 1–2 §§5–9. The most recent official list is in Cabinet Office (MPO), *Public Bodies 1985* (London, 1985) which also contains, ibid., pp. 4–8, annual summaries for the period 1979–85 of the number, cost, and staff of all executive, advisory, and tribunal bodies (but not nationalized industries).
2 Sir A. Street, 'Quasi-Government Bodies since 1918', in Lord Campion *et al.*, *British Government since 1918* (1950; London, 1951), p. 160.
3 PRO, T222/62, MGO (61) (3 January 1945), 'Non-Departmental Organisations', p. 2 §§4–5; N. Johnson, 'Accountability, Control and Complexity: Moving Beyond Ministerial Responsibility', in A. Barker (ed.), *Quangos in Britain: Government and the Networks of Public Policy-Making* (London, 1982), p. 209. The official report was compiled by B. D. (later Sir Bruce) Fraser. It is a key document in any study of these matters. So far as I know it has never been published; but copies are to be found at the PRO in T222/62, CAB 87/75, and no doubt elsewhere. Its origin is described in J. M. Lee, *Reviewing the Machinery of Government: 1942–1952. An Essay on the Anderson Committee and its Successors* (n.p. [London], 1977), p. 106.
4 The phrase cited is from Management and Personnel Office, *Non-Departmental Public Bodies: a Guide for Departments* (1981; London, 1982), Appendix 1 p. 35.
5 But see below pp. 344–51. One recent review of the classificatory issues is to be found in Barker, op. cit., esp. pp. 4–5, 34–8, 51–7, and 81–6. See also C. C. Hood and W. J. M. Mackenzie, 'The Problem of Classifying Institutions', in D. C. Hague *et al.*, *Public*

purposes I shall simply describe certain types of institution and forms of ownership that seem important in this context and hope this procedure will pass muster even if it does not wholly conform to current official usage.[6] The terminology is likewise unsettled. By now many names have been attached to the agencies involved, or at least to some of them (because the chosen title has not always been intended to cover the whole field). Among the terms or neologisms which have emerged are: administrative boards and commissions; *ad hoc* agencies; fringe bodies; independent regulatory agencies; quasi-public bodies; quasi-governmental offices; the wider public service; intermediate authorities; semi-autonomous bodies; para-state organizations; and several others. The latest to find popular favour is the acronym 'quango' while official circles tend to refer nowadays to 'non-departmental public bodies'.[7] In the circumstances perhaps there will be little harm in suggesting another name to describe this entire welter of institutions and connexions: I intend to use the expression 'the Public Concern' for this purpose. The term was used in the Liberal Yellow Book of 1928 to refer to trading enterprises of such great national importance that they must, in the general interest, be brought under a degree of governmental regulation or even operation.[8] Obviously this is, in the present context, only a part of what is intended. Yet the name has not subsequently been much used in this relatively narrow, or any other, sense; and today it has at least the advantage of novelty.[9]

Policy and Private Interests: the Institutions of Compromise (London, 1975), Appendix III pp. 409–23.

6 The latest official categorization of the many bodies listed is to be found in the Cabinet Office (MPO), *Public Bodies 1985* or, in some respects more fully, in the tables in The Government's Expenditure Plans 1986–87 to 1988–89, 1985–6, Cmnd. 9702-II: the official categorizations are not always compatible.

7 For the origins and use of the term 'quango', see the appendix in Barker, op. cit., pp. 219–25. For the official usage, see e.g. the Report on Non-Departmental Public Bodies, 1979–80, Cmnd. 7797. Even a simple term like 'board' covers different types of institution. There have been: (i) *ministerial boards* which never or rarely met, e.g. Board of Trade, Local Government Board, Board of Education, etc., and which constitute a merely fictitious façade to the effective authority of President or Chairman; (ii) *departmental boards* in which the responsible minister is chairman of a group of permanent Crown servants, e.g. Board of Admiralty and the Army or Air Councils; (iii) *administrative boards* on which the minister does not sit but for which he is responsible e.g. Inland Revenue, Customs and Excise. All these are, in effect, forms of departmental organization and to be distinguished from (iv) the considerable range of non-departmental public bodies in question here (some of which are specifically called boards).

8 *Britain's Industrial Future being the Report of the Liberal Industrial Inquiry* (London, 1928), ch. VI.

9 However, see the occasional usage in W. A. Robson (ed.), *Public Enterprise: Developments in Social Ownership and Control in Great Britain* (London, 1937), *passim* but esp. p. 107 and n. 1.

In any event the process at work is itself well recognized, as in the Fulton report of 1968:

> The increase in the positive activities of government has not been solely an extension of the powers and functions of the State in an era of technological change. There has also been a complex intermingling of the public and private sectors. This has led to a proliferation of para-state organisations: public corporations, nationalised industries, negotiating bodies with varying degrees of public and private participation, public participation in private enterprises, voluntary bodies financed from public funds. Between the operations of the public and the private sectors there is often no clear boundary.[10]

Certainly there were those in the mid-nineteenth century who inveighed passionately against the propensity to create at the centre appointed 'General Boards' or 'administrative Commissions' as being quite contrary to the fundamental laws of the kingdom and incompatible with the liberties of the people. Nor has this shrill note of critical protest disappeared.[11]

However the device is neither merely new nor without justification or at least reason why the fingers of government should in this way reach out and touch many aspects of the community's life.

RATIONALE

... in modern conditions their use is essential if our administrative system is to shoulder the burden placed upon it. There is likely to be increased scope for their use in future.
PRO, T222/62, MGO (61) (3 January 1945), 'Non-Departmental Organisations', Note by the Treasury, p. 1 §2(i)

The growth of the Public Concern has been hailed as perhaps the most significant development in the field of political institutions to have taken place this century.[12] Yet, while it is true that most of the bodies inhabiting

---

10 The Civil Service, Cttee Rep., 1967–8 (vol. xviii), Cmnd. 3638, p. 10 §9.
11 See e.g. J. T. Smith, *Government by Commissions Illegal and Pernicious...* (London, 1849) and the numerous polemics of Sir P. Holland the latest of which is *The Governance of Quangos* (London, 1981). The attitude is interestingly reflected in the remark of a Ministry of Health official in 1922 (concerning a proposed central water authority) that 'the Commission system is alien to the British constitution': cited by J. Sheail, 'Planning, Water Supplies and Ministerial Power in Inter-War Britain', *Public Administration*, lxi (1983), p. 388.
12 Cf. W. A. Robson, (ed.), *Public Enterprise: Developments in Social Ownership and Control in Great Britain* (London, 1937), pp. 9, 359–60 (part of this last passage is cited at pp. 379–80 below); W. I. Jennings, *Cabinet Government* (1936; 3rd edn, Cambridge, 1959), p. 95: idem, *The Law and the Constitution* (1933; 5th edn, London, 1964), pp. 195, 213–14.

this penumbral region are recent creations, the establishment of non-departmental agencies charged with specific duties is 'an administrative device of long-standing' going back at least to Tudor times.[13] They were set up by either government or Parliament or constituted by private initiative and then sustained or supervised by public authority. Among early examples are: Trinity House (1514); the Commissioners of Bankruptcy (1570); the East India Company (1600); the Bank of England (1694); Queen Anne's Bounty (1704); and the National Debt Commission (1786). They proliferated during the first half of the nineteenth century as with the Holyhead Road Commission (1801); the Public Works Loan Board (1835); the Poor Law Commission (1836); the Ecclesiastical Commission (1836); the Railway Commission (1846); the Patent Commission (1852); and the agency that so aroused Toulmin Smith's ire, the Board of Public Health (1848). Subsequently after electoral reform and the changes in the Civil Service got under way, there was a tendency, in England and Wales at least, to prefer the ministerial department: there was, that is, more willingness to entrust tasks to officials properly selected and responsible to a minister who was in turn answerable to a representative House of Commons.[14] So while *ad hoc* agencies were still established of course, it became usual to regard them with some diffidence, even 'apprehension', a feeling reflected in the Haldane Committee's judgement that it was highly undesirable to sustain or create administrative boards 'immune from ordinary Parliamentary criticism' and not subject to full ministerial control.[15] In practice, however, strictures of this sort were frequently disregarded especially after 1945. However there was no single sort of occasion or intent to account for their origin or proliferation.[16] There were numerous reasons (not always consistent with one another) why, over the years, the semi-independent agency should have been preferred, a factor which in turn helps to explain why the species reveals so little uniformity and standardization. Two general points may, however, be made at the outset of review. One is that the development of the Public Concern has

---

13 PRO, T222/62, MGO (61) (3 January 1945), 'Non-Departmental Organisations', p. 8 §33.
14 See e.g. H. Parris, *Constitutional Bureaucracy: the Development of British Central Administration since the Eighteenth Century* (London, 1969), pp. 82–93; B. B. Schaffer, 'The Idea of the Ministerial Department: Bentham, Mill and Bagehot', *Australian Journal of Politics and History*, iii (1957–8), pp. 60–78; and F. M. G. Willson, 'Ministries and Boards: Some Aspects of Administrative Development since 1832', *Public Administration*, xxxiii (1955), pp. 43–58.
15 The Civil Service, R. Com. 4th Rep., 1914 (vol. xvi), Cd. 7338, ch. IX; Machinery of Government, Ministry of Reconstruction Cttee Rep., 1918 (vol. xii), Cd. 9230, p. 11 §§31–3.
16 Cf. C. Hood, 'Keeping the Centre Small: Explanations of Agency Type', *Political Studies*, xxvi (1978), pp. 30, 45.

little or nothing to do with party or ideology and has proceeded for a long time under governments of all political colours.[17] The other is that the catalogue of motives and occasions involved is really little more than a list of advantages discerned or anticipated. These may for present purposes be categorized under half a dozen rough-and-ready headings.

The first is simply 'historical survival'. Sometimes it is easier just to let an established practice or institution continue than to replace it with a new arrangement. As the wartime report on 'Non-Departmental Organisations' put it, there are

> a few cases where functions which would appear to be more naturally performed directly by the Government are entrusted to a non-departmental organisation as a result of long-standing practice or privilege. For instance, few more obvious duties of the central Government can be imagined than the periodical verification of the standard coinage or the maintenance of lighthouses to increase the safety of navigation in coastal waters: yet the 'Trial of the Pyx' is still performed by the Worshipful Company of Goldsmiths, and the nation's lighthouses are in the main under the charge of Trinity House and the Commissioners of Northern Lighthouses, which are not Government Departments and are not under ordinary ministerial control.[18]

A couple of other instances may be discerned in the list with which this section began. The National Debt Commission and the Public Works Loan Board survived until 1980 when they were merged to create the National Investment and Loans Office; and Queen Anne's Bounty and the Ecclesiastical Commission have since 1948 been continued in amalgamated form as the Church Commission. In neither instance was the occasion for review taken as an opportunity to create a new departmental organization: the old quasi-public agency was simply continued in a new guise.

The second caption relates to what might be called 'loadshedding'. The creation of a fringe body, especially where the task in view does not fit easily into the existing pattern of functions, enables the direct responsibilities of a department and its minister to be reduced; or the activities of government may be extended without increasing its own administrative burden. Again the Fraser report, commenting on the period between the wars, noted the tendency concerned as follows:

> The activities of Government have expanded in a remarkable manner, particularly in the direction of control over, or assistance to, the

---

17 ibid., p. 33; Outer Circle Policy Unit, *What's Wrong with Quangos?* (n.p. [London], 1979), p. 3.
18 'Non-Departmental Organisations', loc. cit., pp. 17–18 §77.

commerce and industry of the country; and it has been essential, in order to avoid overloading the administrative machine, to assign the administration of much of the new legislation to organisations separate from the ordinary departmental routine. The difficulties of the agricultural industry have been a particularly prolific cause of such devices, but there is scarcely a single major Goverment Department which has not at least one non-departmental organisation attached to it in more or less close allegiance.[19]

Nowadays, of course, the number of sponsored bodies related to any given department can be considerable, but the general point may be taken: imagine the extra burden on a department if it had directly to run (say) a nationalized industry, the NHS, or the water supply. E. C. S. Wade (then a temporary civil servant) pointed out, too, that if fringe agencies were not used then two further undesirable consequences would follow: the number of ministers would probably have to increase, with consequential problems of Cabinet size; and, as the work of existing departments would be extended, perhaps considerably, ministerial control would be even more difficult than it is.[20] A related advantage is that costs are likely to be reduced in many cases by thus using people who are not officials and, it may be, working only part-time or even without pay. This will also be possible if an already existing private or voluntary organization (the advice and co-operation of which may be desirable anyway) can be used with some financial topping-up or similar low-cost aid and sponsorship. Considerations of this sort relating to the possibility of loadshedding as well as to the desirability of decentralization as such were part of what lay behind the later proposals for devolution and the Fulton Committee's support for the process of 'hiving off'.[21]

Thirdly there are diverse points relating to the unsuitability or undesirability of ministerial control, the need to carry out some function at arm's length from the central core of government.[22] For example the case for setting up an intermediate body may seem good where the task concerned might be more easily or efficiently carried out by a single-purpose institution than by a department with a wide range of functions (or by a number of departments where the job straddles the responsibilities of more than one). An aspect of this advantage was well recognized in the wartime report which suggested that, as a general rule, in

---

19 ibid., p. 17 §75.
20 PRO, T222/61, E. C. S. Wade's note (10 December 1942), §4.
21 For 'hiving off', see The Civil Service, Cttee Rep., 1967–8 (vol. xviii), Cmnd. 3638, pp. 61–2 §190; devolution is referred to at pp. 119–29 above.
22 Management and Personnel Office, *Non-Departmental Public Bodies: a Guide for Departments* (1981; London, 1982), p. 31 §138.

many comparatively restricted fields, lying outside the main spheres of public and parliamentary interest, [non-departmental organizations] enable concentration and continuity of administration to be achieved, and an intimate knowledge of the subject matter brought to bear, in a way which would not be possible if the matter were handled, as a minor part of their duties, by a branch of a busy Ministry, subject to all the distractions which arise from the ebb and flow of priorities in Whitehall and the personal predilections of successive Ministers.[23]

There may be an advantage, too, in being able to secure in this way some uniformity of administration through a nation-wide agency with an overall remit. It may also be deemed necessary to avoid allocating a task to a department so as to avoid a degree of political pressure or interference incompatible with sound administration or commercial requirement. Detailed Parliamentary inquisition (in the form, say, of a spate of questions about the details of operation) or continuous departmental intervention may be prevented if an enterprise or activity is wholly or partly outside the sphere of ministerial responsibility. This was an important consideration in determining the position of a nationalized industry or trading body. A factor of similar reference is the view that departmental organization is not well adapted, in organization, staffing, or methods of work to carry out certain tasks. More flexibility may be obtained by evading the rules and constraints which normally apply, for instance, in respect of salary scales, recruitment procedures, methods of working, financial accountability, the need always to consider consequences for a minister (or local council), and so forth. Sir Norman Chester suggests that the growth of fringe bodies is quite simply a reflection of the 'growing doubt about the adequacy or effectiveness' of the normal political and Civil Service procedures.[24] This may be especially significant where commercial competitiveness, a spirit of boldness or enterprise, or promotional activity is concerned (or required) and it is desirable to operate at arm's length from government. As W. A. Robson once put it, there is a 'desire to escape from the excessive caution and circumspection which day-to-day responsibility to Parliament necessitates'.[25] This was, of course, an important factor in the pre-war establishment of various government-sponsored finance corporations (intended to help particular industries or areas); it was also relevant to the creation of the public service board and in the conventional theory of nationalization. A fringe body may also seem particularly suitable where

23 'Non-Departmental Organisations', loc. cit., p. 36 §164.
24 Sir N. Chester, 'Fringe Bodies, Quangos and All That', *Public Administration*, lvii (1979), p. 53.
25 W. A. Robson, 'The Public Service Board: General Conclusions', in the symposium he edited, *Public Enterprise*, p. 363. Cf. ibid., pp. 377–8.

close departmental control or involvement is not deemed essential. This is likely to be the case where the work is of a more or less 'executive' character entailing no ministerial concern with day-to-day management and where there is perhaps little scope for political judgement. The more routine or relatively autonomous the work involved, the more it may easily, or with advantage, be hived off in this way. The avoidance of departmental responsibility is also desirable with respect to some negotiating, discretionary, or adjudicating functions in which a politically neutral stance and an independent source of judgement are appropriate. This is obviously the case with, for instance, the grant of loans or subsidies, the administration of a licensing system or grading scheme, or the very numerous quasi-judicial suits that arise in so many fields but especially in social security and other welfare matters. Placing a responsibility outside the political and departmental arena is similarly apt where regulatory functions of a technical or professional character are involved and where, too, matters are not publicly controversial.[26] This is clearly suitable for, say, the maintenance of standards in medicine, the law, dentistry, and the like. Again a quasi-independent institution may be created or used where special knowledge or experience is required – say, to deal with complex technological problems – which is not available in official circles.[27] Related to all this there is, finally, a point sometimes made concerning a change which (it is said) is taking place in the character of modern bureaucracy. If present-day government operates in the midst of a complex network of relationships (territorial, functional, hierarchical) then it may tend to become not so much executant itself as 'money-moving', that is, it may operate rather by the provision of grants or other financial aid to independent or quasi-autonomous bodies than by running things through the traditional ministerial department.[28] Of course this creates problems of accountability and central control but it may nevertheless be accepted as inevitable in contemporary circumstances.

'Consultation' is another significant reason for establishing an autonomous agency, many such being established simply to advise a department on policy whether the role be one of providing information

---

26 See 'Non-Departmental Organisations', loc. cit., p. 15 §65 for the case of the Public Works Loan Commissioners.
27 Though technical and specialist functions are often exercised direct: the Ordnance Survey comes under the Department of the Environment; the Patent Office is part of the Department of Trade; the Meteorological Office of the Ministry of Defence; and so on.
28 See e.g. E. Bardach, *The Implementation Game: What Happens After a Bill Becomes a Law* (Cambridge, Mass., 1977), pp. 70–6; H. H. Heclo, 'Issue Networks and the Executive Establishment', in A. King (ed.), *The New American Political System* (Washington, D.C., 1978), esp. pp. 92–3.

or of recommending a course of action merely or (as it may be) tantamount to decision-taking itself. A fringe body may be set up where it is desired to bring about closer contact with the particular interests, areas, industries, or professions concerned. Involving them in this way may get the job done better or at least secure their support, foster co-operation, and the like, when direct control by a government department might be regarded as 'intolerably irksome'.[29] Managerial functions of regional significance have often been treated in this light from the time of the Mersey Docks and Harbour Board on. In this general context there may even be a deliberate intention to create 'an independent point of influence and power' which will reflect, promote, and defend a particular interest, area, or attitude.[30]

And this also suggests the next aspect which is one of 'participation'. For all these *ad hoc* bodies may also be seen as a means of securing wider co-operation and involvement in government through association with the process of decision-making and administration. They 'harness to the national purpose', it is said, the services of persons of standing 'who are not attracted by a career of whole-time Government employment but are ready to devote part of their time to the service of the State by accepting membership' of a board, commission, or trust.[31] And this is related, of course, to the question of reconciling the people concerned to the degree of regulation required (to which reference has already been made).

Then there is a dimension best described as 'political tactics'. There may, for instance, be a wish to avoid direct responsibility for some sensitive task or for an anticipated 'under-supply' of a given service. The Unemployment Insurance Statutory Committee, set up in 1934, was designed to strengthen ministers' hands in resisting inconvenient political pressure; as was giving the Health Services Board the duty of phasing out pay beds.[32] Or creating an outside body gives a reason for government itself not to act in the matter concerned. It may be simply that it is desired to keep some area of policy or administration out of the hands of a particular minister or department thought unsuitable (one reason why in 1911 a commission was created to implement the National Insurance Act instead of the Local Government Board).[33] Or perhaps it is simply that the field is an innovatory or experimental one and the department

---

29 'Non-Departmental Organisations', loc. cit., p. 36 §164.
30 R. Wilding, 'A Triangular Affair: Quangos, Ministers, and MPs', in Barker (ed.), op. cit., p. 39.
31 'Non-Departmental Organisations', loc. cit., pp. 35–6 §164.
32 J. Winkler, 'Changing Role of the State and the Administration of Welfare' (SSRC seminar paper, 1979), cited Barker, op. cit., p. 109; 'Non-Departmental Organisations', loc. cit., p. 33 §156.
33 E. Halévy, *A History of the English People in the Nineteenth Century* (1913–46; 2nd trans. edn, London, 1961), vi. 360.

concerned prefers to keep a low profile and not to be fully or openly associated with it.[34] As the Fraser report had it, fringe bodies often act 'as a sort of tentative patrolling force over ground' which may 'before long have to be fully occupied by a regular Government Department.'[35] Or it may simply be that government wants to assist or stimulate an activity deemed to be worthwhile – say by a grant, provision of income from a levy, or some other form of financial aid – but without becoming further involved in a direct way. In particular it may not care to assume responsibility to Parliament for the money so spent. This may be the case in respect to, say, a subsidy given to a cultural activity or organization, or to financial aid extended to an industry or firm of national importance which has fallen on hard times. Nor may the patronage involved be unimportant, a modern form of jobbery to reward friends and supporters as well as to mobilize support or secure agreement. Accusations of 'jobs for the boys' have always been part of the Conservative post-war attack on state ownership and were certainly present in the recent campaign against the 'quango explosion'.[36] And Professor Finer has lately referred to the arrival of 'The New Nepotism'.[37] It appears that in 1978 seventeen ministers disposed of 8,411 paid appointments and nearly 25,000 unpaid ones (expenses only).[38] And these posts are often used to favour party supporters.[39]

Finally there is an element of 'self-generation' about the extension of the Public Concern. It becomes fashionable, or usual, to create a non-departmental agency as a response to a new administrative problem. There may even be a second-order level of fringe bodies, one being created to regulate or co-ordinate others.[40] Similarly one major organization may generate subsidiary bodies, perhaps of an advisory or consultative kind or to carry out specific tasks.[41]

Of course most of the Public Concern derives from the domestic responsibilities of central government. But aspects of it also relate to

---

34 See the examples cited by Hood, art. cit., p. 44.
35 'Non-Departmental Organisations', loc. cit., p. 16 §71.
36 See e.g. P. Holland, *Quango, Quango, Quango: the Full Dossier on Patronage in Britain* (London, n.d. [1981?]); idem, *Quelling the Quango* (CPC no. 691; London, 1982); P. Holland and M. Fallon, *The Quango Explosion: Public Bodies and Ministerial Patronage* (CPC no. 627; London, 1978).
37 S. E. Finer, *The Changing British Party System, 1945–1979* (Washington, D.C., 1980), p. 158.
38 Holland and Fallon, op. cit., p. 18. The information is derived from answers to Parliamentary questions.
39 See the examples given in Finer, op. cit., pp. 159–61. Cf. pp. 466–70 below.
40 e.g., see A. Doig, 'The Machinery of Government and the Growth of Governmental Bodies', *Public Administration*, lvii (1979), p. 312.
41 See the examples cited by C. C. Hood and W. J. M. Mackenzie, 'Appendix III: the Problem of Classifying Institutions', in Hague et al., op. cit., pp. 417–19.

local and international matters. Thus an *ad hoc* body may be created when it is desired to keep the function concerned out of the hands of the local authorities without burdening the central departments as was the case with the responsibility for the new towns, the national parks, many aspects of the health services, and the supply of water.[42] Similarly, because local authority areas were deemed unsuitable or technically inadequate, various trading services and utilities were ultimately removed from their control and placed in the hands of a public corporation: this was seen as the only way to secure uniformity and the necessary level of competence in administration or an appropriate area of operation (which is, of course, why local authorities themselves have often created joint boards or authorities).[43] A cognate consideration may also be an especially important dimension in Scotland, Wales, or Northern Ireland. By comparison with the national agencies, local fringe bodies are not so much explored; but it is clear they can be numerous. For instance, one recent study described a range of fifty-six such bodies associated with the London Borough of Bromley.[44] As to the international dimension, this sort of joint bodies is especially found in such fields as fisheries, quotas, telecommunications, and patents. The UK is involved in about a hundred organizations of this type.[45] There are also the numerous non-governmental organisations, both international and national, which may have 'consultative status' with one of the UN agencies. This is not unimportant as bodies so approved may, for instance, send representatives to UN advisory committees or be asked to undertake specific tasks on UN behalf. The UK government is involved in the process of selection.[46] There are also specifically Commonwealth bodies set up to secure the co-operation of the different governments concerned. Earlier examples are the Imperial Economic Committee, the Empire Marketing Board, the Imperial Institute, and the Imperial War Graves Commission. The last two bodies still continue in Commonwealth guise as do the old Agricultural Bureaux. More recently created such bodies include the Commonwealth Secretariat and the Commonwealth Fund for Technical Co-operation.

For all these sorts of reasons, then, it may be more economical, efficient, convenient, or even prudent to proceed with 'a unit of control and organisation' which lies somewhere between the individual and the

---

42 The Constitution, R. Com. Rep., 1973-4 (vol. xi), Cmnd. 5460, p. 95 §§305-6.
43 See above pp. 68-71, 111-15.
44 P. F. Cousins, 'Quasi-official Bodies in Local Government', in Barker (ed.), op. cit., ch. 9 esp. pp. 154-5.
45 Hood, art. cit., p. 39.
46 See the papers of the Steering Committee on International Organizations, PRO, CAB 134/422-4, IOC (NGO), (47)-(49).

state.[47] Often, too, government does not so much create a fringe body as simply use a private organization that already exists. And in this latter regard its involvement may be merely peripheral as through, say, making an appointment to the governing body, giving some financial assistance, or going through a process of consultation. In any event a widespread institutional pluralism has developed some aspects of which will be reviewed in what follows though it is but a cursory exemplification of the whole range revealed by the Public Concern and what lies beyond it, this vast and complex third arm of government.

However before embarking on this selective review I should mention a couple of important omissions. First of all there are some bodies often regarded as belonging to the fringe – the Charity Commission, the Forestry Commission, or the Public Trustee Office, for instance – but which are more appropriately seen as part of the departmental domain.[48] Secondly there is a miscellaneous collection of institutions of varying size and significance which are not, in the usual sense, government departments, though they may operate in close association with, or under the direction of, a minister and his officials. Yet nor are they obviously a part of the Public Concern (as I am here using the term). Undoubtedly, however, they – or some of them at least – perform functions of the utmost importance. I mean such organizations as: the armed forces of the Crown; the judicature; the police authorities; the Houses of Parliament and their offices; the royal households; and the Church of England. Naturally some aspects of this array do receive attention in this study.[49] But I am all too conscious that they all ought to receive more than this perhaps cursory and passing attention and that the omission is culpable: in any account that is really full the impact of collectivism on them should be examined. However, this confession made, let me turn to the various enterprises which are the first part of the Public Concern to receive detailed consideration here.

PUBLIC ENTERPRISES

The trend to state ownership ... continued almost without check until 1979.
T. EGGAR *et al.*, *Reversing Clause IV*, CPC no. 714, 1984, p. 7

Modern governments of all parties have taken steps to own, regulate, or participate in a considerable number of productive and trading activities.

---

47 Cf. J. M. Keynes, *The End of Laissez-Faire* (London, 1926), p. 41.
48 See e.g. Report on Non-Departmental Public Bodies, 1979–80, Cmnd. 7797, Appendix E pp. 185–6; or G. Bowen, *Survey of Fringe Bodies* (CSD; London, 1978), Annex III p. 21.
49 For Parliament, see below ch. 8 (Part 2), and for the police, see *The Rise of Collectivism* (London, 1983), pp. 178–83.

Thus the state has become involved in the operation of transport and communications facilities, the supply of fuel and energy, the production of basic industrial materials (like coal and steel) and of engineering goods (such as motor cars and aero-engines), the provision of services such as broadcasting, and indeed much else. These activities are organized in various ways. There are directly managed trading enterprises; the nationalized industries; other public corporations; various forms of major utility or service; and shareholding in, or granting loans or subsidies to, a wide range of companies. Each of these modes of state intervention or activity will be reviewed in this section.

Trading services

Over the years there have been numerous examples of government, at both central and local level, becoming directly involved in trading activities, that is, establishing or taking over facilities which are operated on a commercial basis and for the use of which a charge is made (though the purpose may be either service or profit).

Perhaps these enterprises should not strictly be regarded as part of the Public Concern quite simply because they were (or are) run by a local council or government department and ought, therefore, to be treated here in other contexts. Thus they might be seen as an aspect of local interventionism or of the growth of Civil Service activity. However it is convenient and not inappropriate to treat them both as public undertakings important in themselves and in some respects as a kind of forerunners to the development of the nationalized sector proper. And, as with social and economic regulation or involvement generally, it was the local authorities which showed the way.

The local precedent

The authorities thus active were mainly in or near the towns where, over the centuries, local bodies had supervised markets and been concerned with operating harbours, ferries, piers, canals, and docks.[50] Many erected public baths and washhouses, ran laundries, and built houses. Sheffield set up a municipal pawnshop; Bradford ran a conditioning house for wool products and a depot for sterilized milk; Brighton owned an aquarium and Bournemouth a municipal golf-links. Some authorities operated their own telephone system (though only the Hull corporation service still survives); and many opened municipal airports.[51] Other

---

50 A number of the examples here indicated are taken from M. Falkus, 'The Development of Municipal Trading in the Nineteenth Century', *Business History*, xix (1977), p. 135.
51 Cf. below p. 360 and n. 78.

occasional activities of a trading kind included mineral baths, winter gardens and entertainments, and cold stores. Much of this activity is still evident today. Anyone looking at his own and neighbouring authorities notices instances ranging from leisure centres and sports complexes to housing estates and car parks. Local authorities have long been involved with a considerable range of undertakings that might otherwise be provided by private entrepreneurs.

But, of course, the major developments in this regard related to the main utilities: water, gas, electricity, and forms of public transport.[52] In the first decade of the present century, of the 327 county and non-county boroughs in England and Wales, 207 owned water undertakings, 104 supplied gas, 144 electricity, and 70 controlled tramways while 35 others were involved in the joint management of such enterprises.[53] Similarly, in the same two countries between 1884 and 1914, local authority loans outstanding in respect of such undertakings rose from £45.3 to £223.8 millions, an increase of nearly 400 per cent. During the same period annual expenditure went up from about £8.5 to £42 millions, a similarly large percentage rise.[54] Though considerable in size, this development had occurred piecemeal and was never universal; and the private sector remained substantial. The growth of these utilities was haphazard, varying in form and from place to place, though it did occur more quickly and extensively in the north of England. Also it was largely ungoverned by principle in the sense that authorities were never obliged to acquire, or set up in rivalry to, private undertakings and there was little or no national political debate about the matter until the end of the last century. Nor, until after the Great War, was the movement supervised other than by the safeguards and limitations imposed by Parliament in the case of each local Act.[55] The major practical point was simply that competition between private enterprises seemed inappropriate in respect of these major services; while if there was to be a monopoly (or anything approaching it) it was deemed better it be in municipal hands. But this attitude was (as intimated) slow to emerge. During the first decades of the nineteenth century, Parliament adopted 'a generally passive attitude' and allowed improvement commissions or other local agencies to develop these facilities if they wished; but there was no pressure to do so with the

---

52 Standard accounts are W. A. Robson, 'The Public Utility Services', in H. J. Laski *et al.*, *A Century of Municipal Progress 1835–1935* (London, 1935), ch. xiv; and H. Finer, *Municipal Trading: a Study in Public Administration* (London, 1941).
53 D. Knoop, *Principles and Methods of Municipal Trading* (London, 1912), p. 101.
54 For these figures, see Falkus, art. cit., p. 135.
55 ibid., pp. 137–9. At the beginning of the present century there were two Parliamentary inquiries: Municipal Trading, Jt. Sel. Cttee Rep., 1900 (vol. vii), HC 305 and 1903 (vol. vii), HC 270; also the Return covering all aspects of the undertakings then in operation, 1909 (vol. xc), HC 171.

result, for instance, that in 1846 only 10 out of about 190 local authorities owned their own water supplies.[56]

The tendency afoot may be indicated in respect to the main utilities in question.

In Manchester the police commission had in 1817 developed the first municipally owned gas works in the country. By the next decade gas began to be widely used for lighting and other purposes. However, with the exception of Manchester and a handful of other towns, the supply was provided by private companies as on the whole this was not thought to be a matter suitable for public action. Indeed competition between different companies was often deliberately fostered: at one time, for instance, there were as many as fourteen separate companies operating in the metropolitan area. Yet dissatisfaction with this situation was always present and tended to grow for various reasons: the multiplication of works was thought to keep prices up; the rival companies were constantly digging up the streets to get at their mains; the quality of gas was not uniform; price-fixing agreements were made so that one of the supposed advantages of the market was nullified; and so on. Moreover there was a growing feeling that a service on which the public had come to depend so much should not be left in private hands and operated for profit.[57] By 1850, therefore, the general belief in competition in this field had been modified and there was from then on a tendency to stimulate either outright municipal ownership or some form of unification together with effective local regulation.[58] Thus in the seventy years after 1844 local authorities acquired many gas undertakings so that by the mid-1930s nearly 40 per cent of the whole industry had passed into municipal ownership.[59] It was, of course, nationalized in 1948.

The provision of water was one of the tasks with which local bodies had been involved for many centuries. Even so, by 1835 a piped supply was available in only a few towns and this usually from private companies. And in 1848 the Royal Commission on the Health of Towns revealed a state of affairs that demanded rather than invited change: the poor in particular often had great difficulty in getting any water at all; even when available its price was often high; it was frequently of bad quality or contaminated; its supply was invariably intermittent and its source inconvenient of access. The commission recommended that it should be the duty of the local authorities to ensure or actually to provide an adequate supply of water in towns and to secure its proper

56 Falkus, art. cit., p. 140.
57 See e.g. the passage from the *Manchester Times* (25 January 1834) cited in S. and B. Webb, *English Local Government from the Revolution to the Municipal Corporations Act* (London, 1906–29), iv. 270–1.
58 Cf. Falkus, art. cit., pp. 146–51.
59 Robson, loc. cit., p. 308 and n.

distribution. The local boards of health set up under the 1848 Public Health Act were authorized *inter alia* to supply water to their districts subject to safeguarding the interests of existing private water companies; and there was an increasing amount of private legislation to this end. But a generally effective provision had to wait until the Acts of 1872 and 1875 when for the first time a definite obligation in this respect was imposed on local government. Even so in 1879 the authorities provided piped drinking water only in 413 out of 944 urban sanitary districts; in another 290 the supply was received from private companies; but in the remaining 241 there was still no supply at all. However from that time on more steps were taken to ensure municipal ownership and operation of water undertakings and it is estimated that by 1915 two-thirds or more of the entire population were supplied with water by local authorities (including a number of joint committees). Subsequently central supervision of the various water undertakings gradually increased so that the creation in 1973 of a national organization seemed but a logical next step.[60]

The possibilities of electricity were transformed by the development around 1880 of the carbon filament lamp and, as with gas, the facility was initially used for street lighting purposes, the first Act authorizing this being passed in 1882. In this field, however, local authorities were permitted to enter from the outset or (following earlier precedents) given power to buy out after a given period any private undertaking established. A number of municipalities did embark on this enterprise not least if they had gas works and wanted to control a likely competitor.[61] There was, too, the point that the Act of 1882 by its stringent terms hampered the investment of private capital and thereby held the industry back; while, on the other hand, few municipalities were going ahead either. Hence the need for amending legislation of 1888. But it quickly became clear that electricity would be a major source of power as well as lighting and that, in the context of this great potential increase in demand, small areas and generating plants would not provide a service of optimum technical efficiency. Similar and more long-lasting difficulties existed on the distribution side of the industry. Hence a series of changes that led ultimately to nationalization.[62]

The development of street transport has broadly followed the pattern of initiation by private companies and capital, increasing municipal involvement and, recently, partial nationalization. Tramways were introduced after 1860 either by private Act or under the Tramways Act of

---

60 For the new water authorities, see below pp. 426–8.
61 On the competition in Manchester see A. Redford, *The History of Local Government in Manchester* (London, 1939–40), iii. 89, 94–5.
62 See pp. 365–7 below.

356 A Much Governed Nation

1870. Local authority interest was accepted in that there was always provision for the municipality to buy out the private companies and there was as well by this time a certain general prejudice against allowing the supply of public utilities by private enterprise: hence the provisions of the 1870 Act.[63] In practice a compromise developed by which even though the authority might own the tramway it was managed and operated by private hands. Manchester, for instance, although rather slow off the mark in developing a tramway system, matured its plans quickly, the track being laid by the city and operated under lease by a private company.[64] By the end of the century, however, the principle of municipal operation had been increasingly accepted and there was at that time (in terms of mileage) a roughly equal division between local authority and company tramways. But the advent of electrification (in place of horse and steam operation) altered the balance substantially. Its cost was more easily met by the municipalities which increasingly purchased the company rights: Manchester municipalized its extended and electrified service at the turn of the century. By 1925 some 80 per cent of the country's tramways were under local authority control and ownership.[65] In the 1930s the situation broadly was that the tramways were municipalized in the big towns and cities, while the companies operated the inter-urban services and those in the smaller towns. Motor buses developed rapidly after the Great War because of their great advantages over trams (mobility, comfort, lower capital outlay) for which, therefore, they were a powerful competitor. Because of this some local authorities restricted the development of rival bus services (which as the licensing bodies they were able to do). However the situation was altered by the Road Traffic Act of 1930 which *inter alia* authorized the localities to run a bus service where they already operated a tramway and subsequently the proportion of buses in municipal hands slowly increased. Of course, except at Blackpool and Llandudno, all the trams have now gone (as have the trolleybuses). The ownership and operation of motor buses and coaches has been greatly affected by the nationalization statutes of the post-war period but local authority undertakings (outside London) still own some 13 per cent of these vehicles, a proportion which will increase to a third when the conurban passenger transport executives are replaced shortly by local joint authorities.[66] London, as usual, is different. Private and municipal undertakings alike were taken over by the LPTB in 1933, then in 1968 by the new GLC, an interesting reversal of the general

63 Redford, op. cit., iii. 39.
64 ibid., iii. 41.
65 W. A. Robson, 'The Public Utility Services', in H. J. Laski *et al.*, *A Century of Municipal Progress 1835–1935*, p. 322.
66 See the data in *Britain 1986: an Official Handbook* (London, 1986), pp. 303–4.

The Public Concern – and Beyond

tendency. However in 1984 these transport responsibilities were again transferred to a regional board answerable to the Secretary of State.

All this local activity was of considerable importance. The many and varied enterprises concerned were often pioneering and innovative. At the same time there were difficulties and criticism deriving, for instance, from a reluctance to embark on new investment not least for fear of endangering that already undertaken; a tendency to use profits to hold or reduce rate levels rather than to develop the service itself; questions about efficiency of operation and inadequacy of area; and multiplicity (even chaotic variety) of provision. In respect to the last point, for instance, Greater London's electricity supply at one time depended on seventy generating stations, fifty different systems, ten frequencies, and twenty-four voltages. It was hardly surprising that the issue was raised that some wider scope of public operation might be more economical and efficient. Hence the more or less ready acceptance of nationalization in respect of the major services which had hitherto represented considerable business and technical enterprises reflecting a notable degree of local intervention. An important institutional precedent may also be discerned, that of the functional board. As described in an earlier chapter, local *ad hoc* bodies were often created for special purposes to deal with a particular problem or provide a given service whether this was to build a road or provide a watch.[67] All these improvement agencies constituted a precedent on which the idea of the LPTB was ultimately based. The specific line of descent was that derived from the management of harbours, ports, and similar facilities by municipal authorities or their close connexion with this provision by a port trust. In Liverpool in particular the town had been involved in running the port since the reign of King John and, since 1715, in operating the docks which the municipality itself had constructed. Over the years, however, various difficulties and differences of opinion ultimately led in 1857 to the establishment of a Mersey Docks and Harbour Board divorced from the corporation and elected largely by the shipowners and merchants who paid the dock rate.[68] This was the model used when reform of the London dock arrangements became necessary half a century later. In 1908 the creation of a Port of London Authority was authorized, a majority of its members to be elected by port users with others appointed by various public authorities. In turn this was the model in mind when the LPTB was set up in 1933. In this sense the local boards mentioned were among the precedents contributing to the general idea of the public corporation.

67 See above pp. 15–17, 41–9.
68 L. Gordon, 'The Port of London Authority', in W. A. Robson (ed.), *Public Enterprise: Developments in Social Ownership and Control in Great Britain* (London, 1937), pp. 13–16.

Central undertakings

Of course during a war the government trades in raw materials and foods on a large scale. But the concern here is rather with continuing enterprises of a more or less commercial or productive kind in which either central departments themselves own and manage the assets concerned, or the work is done on a department's behalf by some closely related subsidiary. Over the years there have been numerous examples of government departments being involved in trading activities. The leading instance was the Post Office which, in return for payment, provided postal, telegraph, telephone, banking, and other services. Of course this particular situation is now altered: the Post Office became a public corporation in 1969 and subsequently, in 1981, British Telecom was created by the separation of a large part of the non-postal business. The savings branch was also hived off to become a separate department in 1969. But for long the GPO was a large-scale trading concern run by a government department under a minister responsible to Parliament. Nor are other instances lacking. Some no longer exist, as with the state management districts through which, from 1916 (directly from 1921) until 1971, the government owned and operated public houses, other licensed premises, and breweries in a few northern areas and (for a brief period) in the new towns created after the last war.[69] But some trading bodies still remain as part of the central government sector and, as such, subject to more direct control and supervision than a public corporation or non-departmental organization.[70] Yet, as became apparent in the aftermath of the Fulton report, when at least the idea of hiving-off was all the rage, there remained relatively few 'truly commercial operations' of this kind, that is, where the production of goods and the sale of services was 'the central purpose of the activity, financed by Votes and staffed by civil servants.'[71] Some were largely concerned with the supply of goods and services to government departments and agencies, for instance HM Stationery Office, the Royal Dockyards, the Property Services Agency, and the Royal Ordnance Factories. Others such as the Royal Mint, the Ordnance Survey, and the Export Credits Guarantee Department have a more general role. International Military Services Ltd, the shares of which are now vested in the Defence Secretary, acts as the main contractors in the sale of defence equipment and supporting services to

---

69 KCA (1971–2), p. 24744A; Sir F. Newsam, *The Home Office* (London, 1954), pp. 86–8.
70 Cf. NEDO, *A Study of UK Nationalised Industries: their Role in the Economy and Control in the Future* (London, 1976), Appendix vol. p. 2.
71 Sir R. Clarke, *New Trends in Government* (Civil Service College Studies no. 1; London, 1971), p. 81. The Government Trading Funds Act (1973 c. 63) provided for the operation of certain services (like those next listed) to be conducted by means of a trading fund established with public money instead of by annual vote and appropriation.

overseas government; in 1984 it had a turnover of over £150 millions.[72] And there are other instances ranging from the NAAFI (of blessed memory) to the Public Trustee.[73]

Certain questions have always dogged these activities, such as whether departmental management is inconsistent with the accepted philosophy of public enterprise and whether profitable organizations have a place in the government sector.[74] This is perhaps one sort of reason why other forms of involvement have been developed not least the nationalized industries themselves.

The concept of nationalization

The conversion of assets from private ownership to public property is a transformation to which a number of descriptive terms has, from time to time, been attached: communalization, socialization, municipalization (where a town council is to take over), and – the now generally favoured word – nationalization.[75] One important initial point must be stressed. The endeavour is commonly associated with Socialism and, more particularly, with the policies of the Labour Party, nationalization being regarded as a means – perhaps the crucial means – of changing capitalism into a completely different and more acceptable economic system, one run for service and not for profit (as the jargon has it).[76] On the other hand a state take-over in certain important areas may be seen rather differently. It may be regarded as a device not to transform but to sustain the existing economic arrangements and system of property ownership as by securing an efficient infrastructure of basic industries and communications. In ideological terms, this is a contrasting context of consideration indeed.[77] There was obviously no Socialist doctrine at

---

72 Report on Non-Departmental Public Bodies, 1979–80, Cmnd. 7797, p. 59 §§9–10; Cabinet Office (MPO), *Public Bodies 1985* (London, 1985), p. 17.
73 The Navy, Army, and Air Force Institutes was incorporated in late 1920 as a trading company which does not operate for profit, 'a semi-official organisation, under Government supervision', National Expenditure, Sel. Cttee 5th Rep., 1941–2 (vol. iii), HC 58, p. 4 §§2, 3. This report gives an account of the origin, functions, and operation of the NAAFI. It conducts a considerable range of business from running canteens to insurance, from selling cars to putting on stage shows; in the early 1980s its total sales were in excess of £324 millions.
74 Cf. J. W. Grove, *Government and Industry in Britain* (London, 1962), pp. 410–12.
75 On 'socialization', see E. E. Barry, *Nationalisation in British Politics: the Historical Background* (London, 1965), pp. 302–3. The term was still commonly used in official papers as late as the last war and after; and it seems that Herbert Morrison preferred it: see Sir N. Chester, *The Nationalisation of British Industry 1945–51* (London, 1975), p. 64.
76 For the controversy in the Labour Party about the significance of nationalization, see *The Ideological Heritage* (London, 1983), pp. 466–87. Cf. ibid., pp. 494–5.
77 For some Liberal and Conservative attitudes favourable to nationalization, see ibid.,

work when, in the inter-war period, Conservative governments created state monopolies in electricity and the airways. Nor had there been when the Post Office was established in the seventeenth century; when in 1868–9 the private telegraph companies were bought out; or when, just before the Great War, the same policy was followed with respect to the telephone system.[78] Disraeli's Cabinet had in the 1870s considered a Bill to replace the eighteen water companies supplying the London area with a single public authority.[79] And in the ranks of Liberal supporters, radicals as different in their political style and belief as H. Spencer, J. S. Mill, and T. H. Green urged the nationalization of the land (or at least of its use).[80] Similarly so strong an individualist and opponent of Socialism as Patrick Dove had argued that all rents should belong to the nation.[81] The later approach to nationalization has over the years been equally chequered. Thus, seen in party or ideological terms, the impetus may derive from either left or right. As R. H. Tawney explained to an American audience not long after the last war:

> It is an illusion, to suppose...that the advocacy of an extension of public ownership is...confined in England to members of one party.... Authorities whose political sympathies...are not to be grouped under any single heading, have recommended it, on grounds of practical expediency, in the case of monopolies – a large category – agricultural land, transport, coal and power.[82]

In fact a number of pragmatic factors may be at work: the need to bring a monopoly under control; the advantages of obtaining economies of scale; securing industrial rationalization; ensuring adequate capital investment (perhaps where there is no prospect of immediate commercial return); protecting employment; sustaining a national interest; and so forth. None the less whatever the precise political provenance of the idea or the motives at work, the tendency of its application must obviously be to extend the ambit of the state and so intensify what is called in these volumes the rise of collectivism. Yet the trend is one of contrasts for

---

pp. 85, 113, 156, 172–9, 234, 236, 244, 250–1, 253, 255–7. And cf. pp. 363–5 below.
78 Of the five municipalities then running their own telephone systems, Hull alone refused the offer of purchase made by government and still retains its own service. For a general survey, see A. Hazlewood, 'The Origin of the State Telephone Service in Britain', *Oxford Economic Papers*, n.s., v (1953), pp. 13–25.
79 R. Blake, *Disraeli* (London, 1966), pp. 701, 704.
80 *The Ideological Heritage*, pp. 65, 112–13, 134–5, 373.
81 P. E. Dove, *The Elements of Political Science* (Edinburgh; 1854), p. 318.
82 R. H. Tawney, 'Social Democracy in Britain' (1949), in *The Radical Tradition: Twelve Essays on Politics, Education and Literature* (1964; Penguin, 1966), pp. 158–9. For another comment about the empirical rather than the ideological origins of nationalization in Britain, see A. E. Thompson, 'The Forestry Commission: a Reappraisal of its Functions', *Three Banks Review* (September, 1971), pp. 30–1.

nationalization itself has often been seen in libertarian terms, as a way of preparing the ground for a wide diffusion of political and economic power and the reduction of officialism as through an extension of co-operation or some form of industrial democracy. Any actual possibility of this sort may be slight and the hope naive; but that the purpose has been expressed there is no doubt. Like so many words in our political vocabulary, therefore, 'nationalization' may be of ambivalent implication.

However, as already intimated, the idea itself is hardly new, being well over a hundred years old.[83] The term seems first to have been employed by Bronterre O'Brien in the 1840s and subsequently at the Chartist convention of 1851.[84] In the early days the public ownership of such resources as land and coal or of facilities like the railways was often suggested on either economic or ethical grounds.[85] Numerous organizations sprang up during the latter part of the nineteenth century to urge some scheme of this sort, the English Land Registration League and the Land Nationalization Society for instance. Naturally the sort of case made varied but very often it rested on the old view, going back to the Diggers and beyond, that land (as an asset that was limited yet necessary to the sustenance of all) was intended by God to be held by the people and used for the common good: private ownership by a few was, therefore, immoral and contrary to divine intent.[86] The doctrine naturally proved very congenial at a time of agricultural depression; and Henry George's *Progress and Poverty*, first appearing in 1879, became a sort of Bible of the land reform movement. Nor was it difficult to extend the idea of common ownership from land to other wealth contained in it such as coal. For example in the early 1890s the Scottish miners urged the need for a royal commission on the nationalization of the whole industry, and this not simply on grounds of equity but also to improve safety, efficiency, and conditions of work generally. Shortly after this the TUC committed itself to establish a Parliamentary fund which should be used to support only candidates (outside the two main parties) who accepted a programme of widespread public ownership.[87]

[83] I draw here on E. E. Barry's most useful, if partisan, work cited at p. 359 n. 75 above; also on the admirably succinct analysis in L. Tivey, *Nationalization in British Industry* (1966; rev. edn, London, 1973), pp. 15–26.
[84] Barry, op. cit., pp. 31, 39, 44 n. 60. The OED gives 1869 as the date of first use; and, most oddly, the new supplementary volume (1976) has no reference to these earlier occurrences which are by now well documented.
[85] For an early phase of the idea, see T. M. Parsinnen, 'Thomas Spence and the Origins of English Land Nationalization', *Journal of the History of Ideas*, xxxiv (1973), pp. 135–41.
[86] See e.g. the trade union programme of 1848 cited in Barry, op. cit., pp. 33–4.
[87] E. Halévy, *A History of the English People in the Nineteenth Century* (1913–46; 2nd trans. edn, London, 1961), v. 225–6, 261. Cf. ibid., vi. 106; TUC Annual Report, 1893,

362   A Much Governed Nation

Of course land and coal were limited natural assets and might be regarded as completely different from industry which constituted a more obviously human creation. For some radicals this was an important distinction and suggested a crucial dividing line. However many men involved in public life were prepared to regard at least the railways as an appropriate object of state purchase. They were a vital means of public communication and so had a social character; and uniformity and efficiency of service were necessary to the commercial well-being of the nation as well as in its strategic interest. Yet as a result of the way in which the companies had developed there were many wastes: little or no standardization of fares and other charges, duplication of lines and services, variations in gauge, and generally too little co-ordination. As well there was a continuing problem of safety. Moreover the precedent of state interest had been created from the beginning with the requirement of initial statutory authority; and this was compounded by the early regulation of railway rates and the like. It was merely to pursue the intimations of the situation to envisage a wider degree of state supervision or even, eventually, outright ownership as in the report of the select committee of 1844 and, albeit in diluted form, in the subsequent legislation. The case interested such public figures as Gladstone and J. S. Mill and, of course, Socialist groups and various trade unions such as the railwaymen themselves. It had a precedent in the Post Office and received a boost with the nationalization of the telegraph in 1868–9 and, of course, the growing activities of local government respecting public utilities such as the supply of water and gas. Those who were generally in favour of *laissez faire* were indeed often prepared to make an exception of the railways. In some respects it is not a little surprising that the consummation, devoutly wished by many, took so long to achieve.[88]

Naturally committed Socialists found ideas such as these wholly congenial and extended them widely. For instance in 1879 E. B. Bax published an article on 'Modern Socialism' in which he stated a case, possibly the first made by an Englishman, for the popular ownership of all the 'productive wealth of the community whether land, raw material or instruments of production'.[89] The theme was also adopted by Hyndman and the Social Democratic Federation which was formed in 1884. Their policy was to urge political reform, on the old Chartist lines, in order to democratize the constitution so that the electoral power of the workers might then be used to prompt legislation for the national (or in

---

p. 48 cited A. M. McBriar, *Fabian Socialism and English Politics 1884–1918* (1962; Cambridge, 1966), pp. 286–7.
88 See the account of all this in Barry, op. cit., ch. 3 'The Railways and "State Purchase"'.
89 E. B. Bax, 'Modern Socialism', *Modern Thought* (August, 1879), cited ibid., p. 135.

The Public Concern – and Beyond 363

some cases municipal) control of major economic assets and services.[90] It was this sort of programmatic context that the Fabians inherited: Annie Besant, for instance, saw some form of public ownership as a solution to the problem of monopolistic heavy industry though this was to be combined, in Owenite fashion, with an array of county farms and municipal workshops.[91] Similarly the declared objective of the Independent Labour Party, founded in 1893, was a wide degree of collective ownership.[92] Many Socialist publicists followed this sort of line as in the influential tracts and articles published by Robert Blatchford. It is hardly surprising that commitments of this sort were taken over by the Labour Representation Committee and then the Labour Party itself. Thus, at the conference in 1900 at which the LRC was formed, an SDF delegate moved that 'the representatives of the working-class movement in the House of Commons shall form there a distinct party' based on recognition of the class war and having as its ultimate object 'the socialisation of the means of production, distribution, and exchange.'[93] This goal was, after some equivocation, accepted by the Labour Party itself at its Hull conference in 1908.[94] Yet while, in this way, large-scale nationalization became by 1914 a left-wing or radical orthodoxy, it is the case that neither the Labour Party nor the trade unions made very much of public ownership in their policy statements or propaganda in the period before the Great War. This did not mean that attempts were not made to give legislative effect to the idea in some form or other: thus one of the first Bills presented by the new groups of Labour MPs in 1906 encompassed proposals for widespread public ownership. It was simply that nationalization was not yet the crucial basis of Labour Party doctrine that it later became. Moreover the motives initially at work were often as much pragmatic as doctrinaire, a government take-over being seen not so much as a means of overthrowing capitalism as of, say, ensuring the better enforcement of safety standards in the pits.

The experience of the Great War had a notable impact in this as in other spheres. It saw a considerable expansion of state trading and control of industry; and meeting the demands of post-war reconstruction seemed likely to require its continuance or even extension.[95] This was

---

90 See e.g. the SDF programme and rules as adopted in 1889, cited S. Webb, *Socialism in England* (London, 1890), pp. 14–15.
91 A. Besant, 'Industry under Socialism', in G. B. Shaw *et al.*, *Fabian Essays* (1889; Jubilee edn, London, 1950), p. 146.
92 *The I.L.P. in War and Peace: a Short Account of the Party from its Foundation to the Present Day* (London, 1940), p. 7.
93 *The Labour Party Foundation Conference and Annual Conference Reports 1900–1905* (Hammersmith Reprints of Scarce Documents no. 3; Barnes, 1967), p. 17.
94 M. Beer, *A History of British Socialism* (1919; rev. edn, London, 1953), ii. 330–4.
95 Cf. *The Rise of Collectivism* (London, 1983), pp. 72–6.

364 A Much Governed Nation

accepted by politicians of varied party hue. For example in January 1917 the Liberal MP Sir Leo Chiozza Money (then Parliamentary Secretary at the Ministry of Shipping) stressed, in a paper to the War Cabinet, the need not simply to supervise the shipping industry for a limited period but, much more, to nationalize it.[96] During the election of 1918 Churchill, then still a Liberal, advocated the nationalization of the railways; while for the Conservatives J. L. Garvin wrote in *The Observer* that the public ownership of transport, electricity, and coal was inevitable.[97] A little later, too, another Liberal, Henry Clay, considering the possibility of his party's revival, reckoned it should support the transfer to the public (on the model of the PLA) of those economic functions that might require a monopolistic organization if they were to be efficiently run including railways, electricity supply, and banking.[98] An even more well-known Liberal publicist, Professor R. Muir, for long advocated national ownership of the coal-mines and railways and increased community control of other industries and assets vital to the country's prosperity.[99] These were views widely shared and climactically expressed, of course, in the Liberal Yellow Book of 1928.[100] Nor at this period were some Conservatives slow to accept the need for state intervention of this kind: Harold Macmillan among others was perfectly prepared to accept a notable advance in public control or ownership in order to deal with the problems of the day.[101] Certainly it was Conservative dominated governments which carried through Parliament early experiments in state regulation – electricity and broadcasting – and which later transferred to the public such assets as London transport, coal royalties, and the airways. At the same time it is the case that the grass-roots Conservative view was very different, at least if the rather crude propaganda leaflets issued are a good guide to opinion. In the early 1920s, for instance, opposition to nationalization and to the extension of municipal services was one of the main points urged against the policies of the Labour Party in NUA tracts and leaflets.[102]

[96] PRO, CAB 1/23, file 15 (26 January 1917), e.g. summary in §26.
[97] C. L. Mowat, *Britain between the Wars 1918–1940* (1955; London, 1968), pp. 16–17.
[98] H. Clay, 'Liberalism, Laissez Faire and Present Industrial Conditions', *Hibbert Journal*, xxiv (1925–6), p. 739. Cf. *The Ideological Heritage*, pp. 172–3.
[99] R. Muir, *Politics and Progress: a Survey of the Problems of Today* (London, 1923), ch. IV (x), 'The Management of National Assets and of Basic Industries'.
[100] See, for example, Lord Robert Cecil *et al.*, *Essays in Liberalism* (London, 1922); National Liberal Federation, *The Liberal Way* (London, 1934); and *Britain's Industrial Future being the Report of the Liberal Industrial Inquiry* (London, 1928), esp. ch. VI and Book 4. And generally on the collectivist tendency in modern Liberalism, see *The Ideological Heritage*, chs 4–5.
[101] *The Ideological Heritage*, pp. 250–1. Cf. Barry, op. cit., ch. 14, 'Conservatives and Nationalisation (1934–9)'.
[102] e.g. NUA, *Fighting Notes* (no. 2062; November 1922) §§22–4 and *Put Up the*

Thus the public ownership of certain nationally important assets or services was not a policy derived solely from the attempt to realize Socialist doctrine or confined to the Labour Party. There were numerous other grounds on which a scheme of public ownership might be urged. For instance it might be regarded as the sole means in prevailing circumstances of securing a necessary degree of industrial rationalization or some essential technical advance, that is, of attaining optimum efficiency.[103] There were, too, general economic arguments relating, say, to the ability of existing industries to obtain the capital needed for improvement; to the importance of government control of large-scale capital in the maintenance of a high level of employment; to the value of planning and co-ordination; and the like. Moreover, altogether apart from the actual condition of an industry, public regulation, assistance, or ownership may have already proceeded so far that the further step to more or less complete nationalization might seem relatively slight. The position may easily be exemplified. For instance, a substantial part of the transport system was brought under public control during the Second World War. But at its end the railways in particular were badly run down as a result of air-raid damage, inevitable lack of investment and maintenance, and intensive wartime use. By 1945 nationalization of the railways at least was almost a dead issue since some form of public ownership or control was inevitable whichever party came to power.[104] As well public bodies already owned a good part of road passenger transport. The LPTB had been created in 1933 (the Bill having been taken over from Labour by the National government); while outside London most of the tram and trolley-bus services were owned by local authorities as were a quarter of the bus and coach lines. There was also the licensing control exercised over these operations and, although to a much smaller degree, over the private road haulage industry.[105]

The electricity industry is also a case in point. It had developed very rapidly over not much more than a few decades though many of the large number of undertakings which grew up were very small and there were few or no arrangements for co-operation or the interchange of current. An extreme example of the difficulties created is that for a person to move from one place to another (even in the same town) might render all his appliances useless because the voltage was different. Hence a number of power companies was created by private Acts with the right to supply

---

Shutters, Shut Up the Shop (no. 2063; 1922), both in NUCA, Tracts and Leaflets 2035–2206 (1922–4), BM press-mark i. 8139. dd.
103 Cf. Chester, op. cit., pp. 19–21.
104 D. H. Aldcroft, British Railways in Transition (1968), pp. 105–6 cited ibid., p. 13. Similarly even the Mining Association was no longer opposed to the principle of coal nationalization, ibid., p. 55.
105 ibid., p. 14.

over large areas. Yet in 1919 the report of the Williamson Committee bluntly observed that the existing situation in respect of electric power supply was 'incompatible with anything that can now be accepted as a technically sound system'.[106] There was a manifest need for larger generating units. But in existing conditions there was, too, no possibility of adequate long-term investment. The logic of the policy necessary was quite clear and had nothing doctrinaire about it: it was simply a matter of the technical efficiency and development of a utility increasingly crucial to the country's ecomomic life.[107] The Electricity Commission, set up in 1919 to supervise the industry and to secure concentration in a smaller number of power-stations, had no compulsory powers and made slow progress. So a further step in the direction of central control was taken in 1926 with the establishment of the Central Electricity Board which had the task of further rationalizing the generation of power and its transmission through the creation of a national grid which was by then technically feasible. A national system on a standard frequency and voltage was complete by 1934. This would still leave distribution untouched of course; and overall, as the McGowan Committee found in the mid-thirties, there were still a great many small units differing too much in important essentials to secure optimum standards and a growing supply. On technical grounds and the economic importance of the industry alike, it was not unreasonable, to overcome its backward and uncoordinated state and to secure the uniformity as well as the expansion of supply, to suggest the need for a greater degree of public control or even ownership. As it was by the middle of the last war the position was as follows.[108] Some 60 per cent of the industry was already in public ownership, a sector that might easily be enlarged by the local authorities using statutory powers of purchase. The Central Electricity Board supplied current for the grid system for which purpose it bought supply from other generating undertakings. There was also the North of Scotland Hydro-Electric Board which had been set up in 1943 to be responsible for both generation and distribution (though it was not yet in effective operation). The whole industry (both generation and distribution) was under the general supervision of the Electricity Commissioners. During the second war itself the industry came under the wing of the new Ministry of Fuel and Power. And it was, in fact, in specific consideration of electricity's future that many of the general issues concerning nationalization and the public utility corporation were

106 Cd. 9602 cited T. H. O'Brien, *British Experiments in Public Ownership and Control* (London, 1937), p. 32.
107 Cf. ibid., p. 37.
108 This account is based on PRO, CAB 124/828, Report of the Official Committee, the Public Utility Corporations (November 1944), pp. 9–10 §§29–31.

raised at that time.[109] In fact the Coalition government provisionally decided that closer control and a greater degree of actual public ownership were desirable: all generation should be subject to a central generating board and all distribution to fourteen regional boards operating on a monopoly basis. So when nationalization finally came in 1947 it could, despite the undoubted changes involved, be seen in some respects simply as a further stage in a process that had, taking account of early municipal involvement, been under way for half a century and which had received quite intensive attention from all parties in immediately preceding years.[110]

This is not to say that, in either case – of transport or electricity – public ownership was inevitable. But it was certainly not *outré* or a merely theoretical or ideological response.

It was equally pragmatic considerations which, during the years between the wars, led Conservative dominated administrations to other ventures of a similar sort: the BBC founded in 1926; the passage in 1938 of a measure nationalizing mining royalties and establishing a Coal Commission to administer the funds created and to secure amalgamations; and the setting up in 1939 of the British Overseas Airways Corporation. This last case demonstrates very clearly a pattern of growing state involvement. In 1924 the government had sponsored the amalgamation of four operating companies into Imperial Airways to which it gave a subsidy. In the mid-thirties a second British company was formed which also received financial aid. In effect government was giving money to two rival enterprises. Their amalgamation into one organization would be both a means of economy and a sensible rationalization in the face of overseas competition and the need for substantial capital investment. But if a monopoly was thus to be created, it seemed only proper and prudent to ensure a degree of accountability and control through public ownership. After an inquiry this was effected by the Conservative government in 1939.[111]

In addition nationalization did clearly become a policy of increasing significance in the Labour Party. Its position and that of the trade unions had been enhanced during the Great War, a change reflected in the increased number of candidates it fielded: 42 in December 1910 but nearly 400 in 1918. It was natural for the party to seek a new image of its

---

109 In addition to the report on the public utility corporations already mentioned, there was also completed in January 1944 an official inquiry specifically on the future of the electricity industry: see Chester, op. cit., p. 44.
110 On the innovation that was necessary, cf. ibid., pp. 44–5; and the comment of the Parliamentary draftsman, ibid., p. 50.
111 Cf. Chester, op. cit., p. 19. It is interesting that in earlier Cabinet inquiries, in 1927 and 1933–4, there was no suggestion of nationalization though supervision and subsidy were regarded as inevitable: see PRO CAB 27/354 and 558.

own, and a vital phase of this process was the adoption at the end of hostilities of a new constitution and statement of policy; and nationalization of at least what Tawney called 'the foundation industries' was a crucial part of this programme.[112] Over the years this element of Labour policy became stronger though it was not always dominant in practice. Thus the brief minority government of 1924 initiated neither inquiry into particular industries nor any measure of state ownership and this quiescence led to much disquiet in the ILP and among left-wing critics generally such as Clifford Allen.[113] In fact there was at that time the possibility that the idea of nationalization might become a 'dead issue' or be pressed only in general terms.[114] The programme adopted in 1928 did promise the nationalization of coal, transport, life insurance, and power as well as the public control of the Bank of England but of these and similar proposals only those relating to the land and the mines were specifically mentioned in the election manifesto the following year.[115] However, there was one practical success arising from the next Labour administration in the Morrisonian initiative which led (albeit under later National government auspices) to the creation of the LPTB in 1933. From this time on, the principles of nationalization and their detailed working out began to receive more attention, as in the election of 1931 when the party (no doubt in response to a felt need, in the political and economic circumstances of the day, to present a more radical image) pledged itself to the general extension of public ownership and to particular nationalization projects.[116] Similarly the report of the TUC Economic Committee issued in 1932 and the programme *For Socialism and Peace* adopted by the Party Conference two years later were based on the idea of national economic planning and the public ownership of primary industries and services together with the reorganization of others. Nationalization was specifically proposed for a list of a kind later to become very familiar: the Bank of England and the joint-stock banks; railways; coal; iron and steel; electricity; and gas. The Labour Party was thus beginning to contemplate a public commitment to a much greater and more specific degree of state intervention than ever before. In this, of course, it was continuously stimulated by such organizations as the Socialist League and by numerous theorists and publicists. For example, in the *New Clarion* journal, G. D. H. Cole and H. N. Brailsford urged a strong frontal attack on the economic bastions

---

112 On 'Clause Four', see *The Ideological Heritage*, pp. 466–87. Tawney's phrase is to be found in *The British Labor Movement* (New Haven, Conn., 1925), p. 53.
113 Barry, op. cit., pp. 259ff.
114 ibid., ch. 12.
115 F. W. S. Craig (ed.), *British General Election Manifestos 1918–1966* (Chichester, 1970), pp. 57, 58.
116 ibid., pp. 69–71.

of capitalist society so that its key institutions should be brought into public hands and thus make possible effective government control and planning of the entire economy.[117] Again in 1935 *The Labour Party's Call to Power* urged a programme of 'Socialist Reconstruction' including several schemes of public ownership.[118] There was, therefore, a continuing formal reassertion of specific proposals for public ownership and by 1937 the detailed programme outlined needed little up-dating when the, much delayed, election finally came in 1945.[119]

Of course the climactic period of nationalization was 1945–51 during which the Labour government enacted, more or less, the programme developed over the years, worked out in a certain amount of detail by various NEC committees during the war, and especially by the inquiry set on foot by the TUC which has been described as 'a well-analysed contribution to thinking about some of the problems involved in nationalisation.'[120] There was also the impact of the wartime experience of planning and regulation. All this formed the basis of the nationalization proposals in *Let Us Face the Future* the election manifesto of 1945. This document was quite clear and explicit about nationalization policy as part of 'the national plan' proposed. First 'the Bank of England with its financial powers must be brought under public ownership'. Then there are 'basic industries ripe and over-ripe for public ownership and management in the direct service of the nation.' This was spelled out in the following 'industrial programme':

1 Public ownership of the fuel and power industries. For a quarter of a century the coal industry, producing Britain's most precious national raw material, has been floundering chaotically under the ownership of many hundreds of independent companies. Amalgamation under public ownership will bring great economies in operation and make it possible to modernise production methods and to raise safety standards.... Public ownership of gas and electricity undertakings will lower charges, prevent competitive waste, open the way for co-ordinated research and development, and lead to the reforming of uneconomic areas of distribution. Other industries will benefit.

2 Public ownership of inland transport. – Co-ordination of transport services by rail, road, air and canal cannot be achieved without unification. And unification without public ownership means a steady struggle with sectional interests or the

---

117 See e.g. Cole's articles in the *New Clarion* (18 June–17 September 1932) and those of Brailsford (3, 17 September and 29 October 1932).
118 Craig, op. cit., p. 82.
119 Cf. K. Harris, *Attlee* (London, 1982), p. 137.
120 Chester, op. cit., p. 43.

enthronement of a private monopoly, which would be a menace to the rest of industry.

3 Public ownership of iron and steel. – Private monopoly has maintained high prices and kept inefficient high-cost plants in existence. Only if public ownership replaces private monopoly can industry become efficient.

These socialised industries, taken over on a basis of fair compensation, to be conducted efficiently in the interests of consumers, coupled with proper status and conditions for the workers employed in them.

The list is, as it were, rounded off with the oldest plank of all: 'Labour believes in land nationalisation and will work towards it....'[121] And the large part of this proposed series of take-overs, and more, was achieved by 1951 when the Labour government was displaced. Up to 1949 there was little more than ritual political opposition, though the problems about the 'shopping list' for future nationalization, and over the iron and steel industry in particular, showed what could occur when it was proposed to take over vital and hitherto prosperous enterprises as opposed to those that were in severe difficulties of one kind or another.[122] There was in fact quite a wide range of prospects including the clearing banks, pharmaceuticals, the construction industry, insurance – or simply the top thirty (or one hundred) companies remaining in the private sector, such as Shell, Unilever, ICI, etc. Nor did the favoured lists diminish with the passing years.[123]

In this general context, therefore, it will be apparent that a wide variety of reasons might be used in favour of a broad policy of full or partial public ownership or of a particular proposal of this sort. There were, of course, the sort of arguments and motivations that ranged from the class envy of the unpropertied to the moral demands of equity in the distribution of divine gifts or scarce national resources. But there were also other considerations of more practical moment. Strategic factors might be involved as with the purchase of shares in the Suez Canal and Anglo-Iranian Companies. If (for one reason or another) a monopoly or

121 These citations from Craig op. cit., pp. 99, 100, 101, 103. By contrast the Conservative policy statement declared its opposition to state ownership and any form of monopoly public or otherwise though central direction was envisaged where necessary, ibid., pp. 93–5. For their part the Liberals declared their willingness to accept nationalization 'without hesitation' where it would be 'more economic', ibid., p. 109.
122 For some aspects of the wrangling in the Labour Party itself, see *The Ideological Heritage*, pp. 466–87.
123 For possibilities lately considered, see *KCA* (1974), p. 26373A (26376); ibid. (1975), pp. 27063A (27063, 27068); ibid. (1979), p. 29629A; and ibid. (1983), p. 32200A (32206).

near-monopoly existed, it might be not unreasonable to suggest that some degree of public accountability was needed especially if a subsidy from government funds was paid or envisaged. This was the case in respect of the airways companies in the 1930s, which led to the creation of BOAC in 1939. Technical improvement was another purpose as with electricity. So also was a simple confiscatory desire, as to secure that any profit should accrue to the public. Or the aim might be to abolish profit as a means of lower prices and increase investment. Again an aspect of these matters that can never be disregarded is the purely political. A government may adopt a policy of nationalization to enhance its position, to get credit (for instance) for a major reform intended to contribute to a process of economic reconstruction. Some element of this kind was involved in the decision to create the Central Electricity Board in 1926. The improvements to which this step could lead would (it was hoped) help the growth of British industry especially in the depressed areas as the board should be able to favour appropriate firms in the placing of contracts.[124] To increase productivity and so the standard of the economy was always a major goal (the market being seen as inefficient and wasteful) and became of increasing importance with the growth of foreign competition, the existence of unemployed resources, and the general decline in Britain's international position. There were two areas in which public ownership seemed significant in this regard. One was the improvement of the infrastructure of communications: road transport, ports and docks, railways, airways, and postal and cognate services. The other concerned the rationalization of basic industries or resources vital to national efficiency: land, electricity, coal, iron and steel, and so forth. The prevention of waste (as through unnecessary duplication of railway lines); achieving uniformity of charges; amalgamation to achieve economies of scale and lower costs; elimination of surplus capacity; the introduction of new technology: these were the sorts of economic gains in view. To some advocates of public ownership, control of the commanding heights was, too, a necessary prerequisite to the prevention of instability and the achievement of effective economic policy and national planning with the object, for instance, of securing full employment or controlling capital investment and the distribution of resources: one thinks of (say) Macmillan or Bevan in this connexion. And natural monopolies (where full exploitation seemed to require only one producer) demanded state ownership if the public was not to suffer. Finally what might be termed the social dimension was never far from consideration. The improvement of the status and condition of the worker would (it was assumed) somehow follow in the wake of public ownership leading perhaps to industrial democracy: even that, in

[124] O'Brien, op. cit., p. 37.

consequence, strikes and other unrest might be eliminated. Acceptable levels of service, price, and safety would be secured if necessary by subsidy; and, especially, socially necessary (but unprofitable) provision would more easily be made as with the supply of electricity in rural areas or the maintenance of uneconomic railway lines. Undesirable external effects would be eliminated or controlled and amenities more firmly considered, as during the building of the grid system or in the operation of open-cast mines.[125] Or it was supposed that cultural matters should not be left in private hands and subject to merely commercial considerations: hence the creation of the BBC.

For all sorts of reasons, then, nationalization appealed to reformers of all parties though it was not clear (even as late as 1947) whether a state-owned enterprise was to be accepted as another kind of industrial undertaking simply or regarded as a new type of government machinery.[126] Equally there was no necessary agreement as to priorities among the various objectives proposed, the desirable extent of public ownership, the pace of change, or the administrative form envisaged.[127] This last is a focal point of some importance.

The institutional form

The process of nationalization has come to be associated with administration through the public corporation. Yet this has never been the only possibility. If transfers to common ownership were to occur and on an increasing scale, there was no necessary institutional corollary to this process at all. The type of organization entailed might take several forms of which the semi-independent board was only one, a point often

---

125 I have never understood why this was supposed to be the inevitable result of state action: look at the enormities wrought in the countryside by the appalling planting policy of the Forestry Commission.

126 See the brief provided for Sir E. Bridges prior to a meeting of the Government Organization Committee (6 March 1947) in PRO, T222/591 M.G. (file no. 383/1/09).

127 For one recent exchange on these matters, compare the contrasting views adopted by J. Redwood – broadly libertarian and somewhat critical of nationalization – and Professor M. Lipton who is more favourably disposed to public ownership and intervention: J. Redwood, 'Government and the Nationalized Industries', *Lloyds Bank Review* (April 1976), pp. 33–46, and 'The Future of the Nationalized Industries', ibid. (October 1976), pp. 33–44; M. Lipton, 'What is Nationalization For?', ibid. (July 1976), pp. 33–8 and, in reply to a reader's comments, ibid. (October 1976), p. 50. Mr Redwood has, of course, later expounded his views at greater length in *Public Enterprise in Crisis: the Future of the Nationalised Industries* (Oxford, 1980) and, with J. Hatch, *Controlling Public Industries* (Oxford, 1982). The latest variation on the priorities of purpose is reviewed in the former work, ch. 11 on 'Pushing Back the Frontiers of Nationalisation'.

recognized by the pre-war commentators.[128] In fact the fashion in this respect has passed through four phases which may be rendered in mononymic series as reflecting a stress on accountability, representativeness, efficiency, and diversity. Naturally these emphases are not exclusive; though taken together they do represent the syndrome of purposes sought through the device of public ownership. And each sustains a characteristic institutional preference.

Accountability
So far as the early days are concerned, it would be true to say that in radical or Socialist circles there was little consideration of the administrative means through which publicly owned services would be operated. Consequently there was no settled or dominant view.[129] Experience with the public board form of organization had not been too happy as in connexion with the Poor Law and public health. Some form of co-operative enterprise had an appeal in certain quarters: no less an observer than J. S. Mill had seen this as a possibility of major significance to secure social and economic progress combined with the optimum degree of human liberty and spontaneity.[130] And proposals for workers' co-operatives, home colonies, and so forth appeared elsewhere from time to time as in the Social Democratic Federation programme of the 1880s which spoke of the 'organisation of agricultural and industrial armies under State Control on Co-operative principles.'[131] In addition there was the alternative view that the transfer of assets to the public domain might most effectually be achieved by augmenting the responsibilities of municipal or other local authorities. Not only were these bodies elected and increasingly experienced in the operation of various utilities, their assumption of further tasks of a cognate kind would bring numerous advantages relating to decentralization, flexibility of operation, participation, and so forth; and the general cause of local self-government would be much advanced. It is quite understandable why some radical reformers thought of public ownership almost entirely in

---

128 e.g. R. H. Tawney, *The Acquisitive Society* (1921; London, 1943), pp. 148–9; idem, *Equality* (1931; 4th edn, rev., London, 1964), pp. 181–8; M. E. Dimock, *British Public Utilities and National Development* (London, 1933), chs I, IX; L. Gordon, *The Public Corporation in Great Britain* (London, 1938), chs I, VI; and F. H. Lawley, *The Growth of Collective Economy* (London, 1938), i. 186–402 (where the various possibilities are discussed in great detail).
129 Cf. Sidney Webb's remarks in his introduction to the 1920 reprint of G. B. Shaw *et al.*, *Fabian Essays* (1889; Jubilee edn, London, 1950), p. xxi; and Beer, *A History of British Socialism*, ii. 373.
130 See *The Ideological Heritage*, pp. 120–1, 357–8.
131 Programme and Rules of the SDF as revised at the Annual Conference, 5 August 1889, cited S. Webb, *Socialism in England* (London, 1890), p. 14.

terms of the extension of municipal trading schemes.[132] Yet this course might invite a fragmentation of operation and control that was not always technically appropriate and might be commercially disastrous. It could be ludicrous, as well, to think of, say, the railways being run by local councils. Something of the diversity of possibilities was revealed in a Fabian report to the International Socialist Congress in 1896 which defined Socialism as 'the organisation and conduct of the necessary industries of the country... by the nation as a whole, through the most suitable public authorities, parochial, municipal, provincial, or central.'[133] An equally complex mosaic was implied in the new Labour Party constitution of 1918 which urged 'the common ownership of the means of production' through 'the best obtainable system of popular administration and control of each industry or service'.[134] Sometimes different strands of proposition naturally coalesced as in the proposal, embedded in the Booth survey, for the London docks to be run through a public trust or board on which the trader, consumer, and labourer were represented, this being seen as a kind of municipal Socialism.[135]

None the less, so far as any single administrative solution was widely accepted at this stage, it rested on the simple assumption that the nationalization of a major service or resource should proceed on normal centralized lines: that is, public control through a department of state with a minister responsible to Parliament, this accountability to the legislature being crucial. The relevant model was the Post Office: when, in the mid-nineteenth century, the telegraph companies were bought out they had been placed under that office; and this precedent was followed by the like disposition of the telephone system in 1911. And it was very widely assumed that if public ownership and management of the land, railways, or mines were likewise to come about, these assets would similarly be placed under an appropriate (or new) government department. Robert Blatchford was quite clear about this; and so, often, were the Fabians.[136] So that when, for instance, in 1893 Keir Hardie proposed the nationalization of the mines, he had in mind a mining department under the control of a minister responsible to Parliament.

---

132 e.g. J. A. Hobson, *The Crisis of Liberalism* (London, 1909), Part II ch. V.
133 Cited Beer, op. cit., ii. 374.
134 The Constitution of the Labour Party (1918), §3(d) cited G. H. L. Le May, *British Government 1914–1953: Select Documents* (London, 1955), p. 353.
135 Cited in B. Webb, *My Apprenticeship* (1926; Penguin, 1938), ii. 356 n. 1.
136 'Nunquam' (Robert Blatchford), *Merrie England* (1893; London, 1976), pp. 44–5; G. B. Shaw et al., *Fabian Essays*, pp. 135, 172–3; A. M. McBriar, *Fabian Socialism and English Politics 1884–1918* (1962; Cambridge, 1966), p. 114. This Fabian emphasis was not exclusive, of course, in that municipal control was also favoured, and sometimes administration by a series of boards. For the latter, see e.g. *Fabian Essays*, p. 146.

The same sort of provision appeared in the six coal nationalization measures submitted by the Labour Party to the legislature between 1906 and 1913.[137] And when towards the end of the Great War the Haldane Committee came to examine these prospects it, too, stressed the importance of 'placing the sole responsibility' for administration in the hands of 'a single Minister', thus securing 'those safeguards which Ministerial responsibility to Parliament alone provides.'[138] Nor, in thus preferring conventional departmental accountability to the presumed advantages of the administrative board, was the committee alone.[139]

Yet there was a tendency for the departmental solution to be eschewed in discussion after the Great War (though it still had its adherents). In theoretical terms this may have been due to the impact of pluralist, syndicalist, and guild ideas as (say) with the pre-war demands by the National Union of Railwaymen for a share in the management of a nationalized railway service.[140] But the practical experience of wartime bureaucracy was probably more significant. A little after the end of hostilities, one exponent of state ownership took some trouble to discuss criticisms of the idea and paid particular attention to the accusation that officialism, red tape, and delay will necessarily predominate. But he was careful, while admitting the force of the accusation, to attribute these deficiencies not to officialdom as such but to factors like large organizational size, the need for uniformity, a monopoly position, and, above all, the fact that the existing official class was drawn from a small ruling group. And these difficulties could surely be overcome?[141] But not everyone was so sanguine about the likelihood of this happening and the fear of officialism continued strong especially in respect of enterprises of a commercial type. There was a growing fear, too, that direct government control through a department would not in itself improve the position of the workers concerned, might mean no more than the continuation of capitalist control by other means. Thus in 1911 T. Mann asked, Who is to control industry? and himself replied:

---

137 Details in G. Ostergaard, 'Labour and the Development of the Public Corporation', *The Manchester School*, xxii (1954), p. 194; D. N. Chester, 'Management and Accountability in the Nationalised Industries', *Public Administration*, xxx (1952), pp. 28–9. For K. Hardie's proposal, see S. T. Glass, *The Responsible Society: the Ideas of the English Guild Socialist* (London, 1966), p. 11.
138 Machinery of Government, Ministry of Reconstruction Cttee Rep., 1918 (vol. xii), Cd. 9230, p. 11 §§31–3.
139 See e.g. The Civil Service, R. Com. 4th Rep., 1914 (vol. xvi), Cd. 7338, pp. 78–9 §§68–9, 72, pp. 82–3 §§84–9; A. E. Davies, *The Case for Nationalization* (London, 1920), ch. viii.
140 Barry, *Nationalisation in British Politics*, pp. 100–3. For a general review of these pluralist themes, see *The Ideological Heritage*, pp. 88–95, 417–39, 495–508.
141 Davies, op. cit., pp. 30–7.

376   A Much Governed Nation

> The industrial syndicalist declares that to run industry through Parliament, i.e. by state machinery, will be even more mischievous to the working class than the existing method, for it will assuredly mean that the capitalist class will, through government departments, exercise over the natural forces, and over the workers, a domination even more rigid than is the case today.[142]

From this point of view little was to be expected from the state as an employer. It was for this sort of reason, too, that H. J. Laski was at the time very dubious about Fabian proposals to transfer 'rent' or the control of industry to direct state management. He doubted whether the administration would be effective and it would as well have the great drawback of creating 'a bureaucracy more powerful than the world has ever seen' and so would 'apotheosise the potent vices of a government department.' The worker would thus be left 'face to face with government' and (his argument goes on) 'there is little reason to suppose that a civil service is more merciful or efficient than the present system'. So while the 'feudalism' involved might be benevolent and improve conditions, it was really 'the subtlest form of poison' to properly democratic society.[143] Direct departmental administration would, therefore, all too easily create Belloc's 'Servile State'.[144] Of course the problem might be avoided if a new type of civil servant were to be found, different from those recruited by the usual means from a restricted social class and capable of conducting departmental administration in a less conventional way.[145] But this could not be guaranteed. It was not unsymptomatic of these tendencies of opinion, that when R. H. Tawney (in *The Acquisitive Society*) discussed the several different types of management that might be appropriate for publicly owned industries and services, he noted that the 'chief characteristic of almost all recent programmes of nationalization' had been an insistence that, unless it was absolutely unavoidable, 'the ordinary machinery of the political state' should not be used. Some other administrative body unlike a government department must be employed.[146] H. N. Brailsford only a little later wrote that all Socialists at least agreed in rejecting the old GPO model because of the excessive extent and rigidity of departmental and

---

142 T. Mann, 'A Two-fold Warning', *Industrial Syndicalist* (April 1911) cited Barry, op. cit., p. 174.
143 H. J. Laski, *Authority in the Modern State* (New Haven, Conn., 1919), pp. 94–5; idem, *The Foundations of Sovereignty and Other Essays* (1921; London, 1931), pp. 82–4; idem, 'Democracy at the Crossroads', *Yale Review*, n.s., ix (19–20), p. 800.
144 On which, see *The Ideological Heritage*, pp. 91–3.
145 e.g. A. E. Davies, op. cit., pp. 34, 35–6, 151. Cf. idem, *The State in Business* (1914; 2nd edn, London, 1920), introduction to the 2nd edn, pp. xxxi–xxxii.
146 R. H. Tawney, *The Acquisitive Society*, p. 148.

The Public Concern – and Beyond

Treasury control.[147] So at about this time a second phase of consideration may be discerned which suggests avoidance of departmental organization and thrusts forward instead the idea of institutions which would reflect the interests of the workers and, perhaps, of others concerned.

Representativeness

A certain precedent might be invoked by referring to the way in which important regional bodies like the Mersey Docks and Harbour Board (1857) and the Port of London Authority (1908) had been constituted. But more important was the fear about the growth of monolithic government expressed at the time by Syndicalists and Guild Socialists.[148] They were worried that control by the ministerial department might mean no more than red tape and a 'centralized Capitalism of the State'. Instead labour itself must control both finance and administration.[149] It was not insignificant that guild ideas were adopted by the Union of Post Office Workers who might be assumed to be closely familiar with the disadvantage of that departmental paradigm, the GPO. Even those not enamoured of the prospect of complete workers' control in the nationalized sector nevertheless often repudiated the Post Office model in favour of national boards representative of employees and management alike as well as of the general interest, of consumers for instance.[150] A full and moderate statement of this position was provided by Harold Laski. In *A Grammar of Politics* (1925) he explored *inter alia* the detail of the economic institutions appropriate to the pluralist state. And while accepting that there need be no identical form of administration in each socialized industry, he none the less laid down certain principles which fully exemplify this 'representative' phase of discussion (as it might be called).[151] He explicitly rejected 'any purely syndicalist plan of industrial organisation' on the ground that there was no reason to suppose the labour interests concerned would be any more careful of the general public interest than the existing private owners. Such exclusive control would constitute a 'special privilege' which is bound to be 'morally vicious'. In any national plan of industry, therefore, self-government is impossible and the ownership of the means of production must be vested

---

147 H. N. Brailsford, *Socialism for Today* (1925; London, 1927), p. 88.
148 See *The Ideological Heritage*, pp. 417–39, 497–510.
149 M. B. Reckitt and C. E. Bechhofer, *The Meaning of National Guilds* (1918; 2nd rev. edn, London, 1920), pp. 250–4. The phrase cited is at p. 253.
150 e.g. S. and B. Webb, *A Constitution for the Socialist Commonwealth of Great Britain* (London, 1920), pp. 169–70, 173, 176–8, etc.; P. Snowden in the *Socialist Review* (1919), p. 122 cited Barry, op. cit., p. 301.
151 H. J. Laski, *A Grammar of Politics* (1925; 5th edn, London, 1948), ch. 9 esp. §II.

in the state itself.[152] But he at once goes on to reject as inadequate the 'classical method' of 'a system like that of the British Post Office' in which a minister is responsible to Parliament for the operations concerned.[153] Certainly there must be ultimate ministerial responsibility for general policy and co-ordination but the detailed administration of any nationalized enterprise must be by 'a governing board' representative of management and technicians, manual and clerical staff, and of those reflecting wider public or related industrial interests.[154] The functions of such a board and bodies subordinate to it in the running of the industry are then examined in some detail.[155] In fact this notion of a representative, administrative board separate from the central departments had been already accepted by the Labour Party in 1921 and was also reflected in the proposal put by the Miners Union to the Sankey Commission and in the plan for the coal industry put forward five years later.[156] Similarly during the mid-twenties H. N. Brailsford had, in an influential study, lauded the virtues of 'the semi-independent Industrial Corporation of the future' provided it represented both the work force and able, innovative management.[157] And the question continued to be discussed within the Labour movement: for instance, at the party conference in 1933 a resolution was passed declaring that wage-earners 'should have a right acknowledged by law to an effective share in the control and direction of socialised industries which their labour sustains'.[158] But the emphasis was changing. Guild or Syndicalist ideas seemed of diminishing cogency not least after the failure of the General Strike and a period of mass unemployment seriously weakened the position of the trade unions. There was the feeling that a nationalized industry or service should be run for the good of the community as a whole and not just on behalf of the workers directly involved, as in the question, Would the miners be fair to the consumers? (It is this type of concern indeed which led to a proliferation of proposals for consumers' councils and the like).[159] There was the realization, too, that the position of union representatives on the directing body of a public industry could be very difficult especially in matters concerning such things as wage negotiations or disputes of any kind. Moreover if unions could demand to be represented there why

152 ibid., pp. 439–40, 444.
153 ibid., p. 442.
154 ibid., p. 445.
155 ibid., pp. 445–62. Cf. Lawley, op. cit., i. 386–93.
156 Chester, *The Nationalisation of British Industry*, pp. 457–8; Ostergaard, art. cit., pp. 196–201, 204–5; Chester, art. cit., pp. 29–33.
157 Brailsford, op. cit., pp. 87–9. For the influence of this study, see Barry, op. cit., pp. 301–2.
158 Cited Chester, *The Nationalisation of British Industry*, p. 459.
159 Chester, art. cit., pp. 33–4.

should not other interests urge a similar claim (with the possible result that the union representatives might find themselves in a minority)? And there was, too, a growing realization of the need for special expertise at the top executive level and, generally, for the highest possible business efficiency. But the appeal of the representative or, more strictly the Syndicalist, principle did not entirely wane especially in those major industries where strong unions existed. It was still even applied elsewhere as in Snowden's scheme for the Bank of England.[160] But it was never so vital again until fairly recently when the idea of workers' control was revived, quite firmly in some quarters.[161]

Efficiency
But if departmental organization or some representative body were to be eschewed, what institutional form should the structure of a nationalized industry take so as to achieve maximum efficiency in operation? The answer increasingly urged was, of course, the 'public corporation'. The term itself (initially one of a number of synonyms) is first found in 1926 in the report of the Crawford Committee on broadcasting which recommended for the field in question 'a public corporation... to act as a Trustee for the national interest'; and it was also used in the preamble to the first charter of the BBC set up later the same year.[162] Somewhat paradoxically, therefore, the first public corporation – the BBC – was established specifically to insulate the activity concerned from commercial considerations rather than to secure that such factors could operate relatively untrammelled. But the Central Electricity Board, which began operation the following year, was intended to be managed independently precisely so that business methods would not be subjected to continual political interference. And this, of course, was the objective the new form of institution was later primarily intended to achieve in the case of the LPTB and the nationalized industries. In 1937 Professor Robson commented in a famous passage:

> The rise of the public service board as a new type of concern for operating, organizing, or regulating industrial activities is the most important innovation in political organization and constitutional practice which has taken place in this country during the past twenty years. These boards grew up in a typically British fashion. They were

160 Ostergaard, art. cit., pp. 208–9.
161 *The Ideological Heritage*, pp. 495–529.
162 Broadcasting, Cttee Rep., 1926 (vol. viii), Cmd. 2599, p. 5 §4(d); Wireless Broadcasting, 1926 (vol. xxiii), Cmd. 2756, draft Royal Charter for BBC, p. 2. Other similar terms often used included 'Public Service Board', 'Public Utility Board', and 'Independent State Authority'. For discussion of the early terminology, see D. N. Chester, 'Public Corporations and the Classification of Administrative Bodies', *Political Studies*, i (1953), pp. 34–5.

not based on any clearly defined principle; they evolved in a haphazard and empirical manner; and until quite recently very few people were aware of their importance or even of their existence. Now suddenly they have become all the rage. Politicians of every creed, when confronted by an industry or a social service which is giving trouble or failing to operate efficiently, almost invariably propose the establishment of an independent public board. The idea appeals equally to the Right and to the Left.[163]

Lord Reith (who had, of course, served both at the BBC and BOAC) confirmed the importance of the innovation. In the mid-fifties, after a decade which saw a considerable extension of the device in the post-war nationalization programme, he referred to the public corporation as 'a new fashion of government' which constituted 'a momentous change in technique and procedure'.[164] Yet oddly enough there has never been any occasion for the term 'public corporation' to be legally defined.[165] However a convenient (if partial) designation is that adopted by Sir Arthur Street during the early post-war phase of the institution's development: 'a financially autonomous non-profit making body created by an act of State to provide a monopoly of goods or services on a commercial basis, ultimately responsible through a Minister to Parliament and the public but free from full and continuous Ministerial control.'[166] The advantages of both worlds would thus be enjoyed: a degree of public accountability coupled with freedom and flexibility in operation leading to optimum efficiency.

As Robson's remarks suggested the concept evolved gradually and found favour in diverse political quarters as a solution to the problem of public ownership. Many Conservatives even were able to accept it: after all, in some respects it was little different from establishing a board of directors for a public company and secured as much as possible the virtues of private business management. Harold Macmillan for one acknowledged the growing acceptance after 1918 of the use of some semi-independent agency of this sort as a means of industrial reconstruction.[167]

---

163 W. A. Robson, 'The Public Service Board; General Conclusions', in idem (ed.), *Public Enterprise*, p. 359.
164 Lord Reith, 'Public Corporations: Need to Examine Control and Structure', *The Times* (3 July 1956), p. 11.
165 Report on Non-Departmental Public Bodies, 1979–80, Cmnd. 7797, p. 4 §21; J. F. Garner, 'Public Corporations in the United Kingdom', in W. Friedmann and J. F. Garner (eds), *Government Enterprise: a Comparative Study* (London, 1970), p. 4.
166 Sir A. Street, *The Public Corporation in British Experience* (Westminster, n.d. [1947?]), p. 3. Cf. the definition in NEDO, *A Study of UK Nationalised Industries*, Appendix vol., Appendix A p. 1.
167 H. Macmillan, *Reconstruction: a Plea for a National Policy* (London, 1933), pp. 28–9.

And, of course, it was Conservative (or Conservative-dominated) governments which initiated the first experiments in the form during the inter-war years. The effusions of Liberal publicists and the policies of the party alike reflected this acceptance even more positively. For example, Ramsay Muir suggested that when the coal and railway industries came under public ownership they should not be administered on departmental lines but each placed under the direction of a commission to be set up by statute and 'enjoying a good deal of freedom under the terms of the Act.' This would help too, he thought, to avoid further overloading Parliament with direct responsibilities. Similarly Keynes recommended the extension of 'semi-autonomous bodies' for the purposes of public ownership and management, a view repeated in the Liberal Yellow Book which regarded the *ad hoc* body as the correct line of evolution for many schemes of public economic management.[168] But, of course, the main impetus behind the use of this form of institution ultimately came from the Labour Party though its adoption there proceeded in a slow and somewhat haphazard way and was certainly not the result of any firm doctrinal commitment. As already indicated the labour movement had, when considering public ownership, hitherto accepted that either it ought to assume a departmental form and so be accountable to the legislature or be structured so as to represent, in particular, working-class interests. And there was some diffidence about accepting the public corporation instead. The Central Electricity Board, for instance, was sometimes regarded as reflecting a merely 'Conservative method' of administration appropriate only to a party of 'autocratic traditions'.[169] But such diffidence, though never completely eliminated, was at the time fairly quickly and firmly overcome. The authority of the Webbs was thrown behind the idea that, for the 'highest efficiency', each socialized industry or service should be run by 'a National Board'.[170] And in 1925 a Labour Party–TUC committee produced a comprehensive scheme for nationalization which adopted the idea of a National Coal Council to run the mines and of a Power and

---

168 R. Muir, *Politics and Progress*, pp. 173, 174; idem, 'The Machinery of Government' in Lord R. Cecil *et al.*, *Essays in Liberalism* (London, 1922), pp. 142–3; J. M. Keynes, *The End of Laissez Faire* (London, 1926), p. 41; Liberal Party, *Britain's Industrial Future*, pp. 77, 79, 80–1. See also H. Clay, 'Liberalism, Laissez Faire and Present Industrial Conditions', *Hibbert Journal*, xxiv (1925–6), p. 739. For Clay, see *The Ideological Heritage*, pp. 172–3.
169 Ostergaard, art. cit., pp. 205–6 where detailed references are given.
170 S. and B. Webb, *A Constitution for the Socialist Commonwealth of Great Britain*, pp. 176–8. Lawley, *The Growth of Collective Economy*, ii. 378–93 discusses the shift of Socialist thinking away from the idea of direct state operation to the notion of some form of autonomous body and indicates the reasons and factors involved.

Transport Commission to develop the industries concerned.[171] A couple of years later W. Graham (who had been a member of the Crawford Committee on the electricity industry) was writing in the *Encyclopedia of the Labour Movement* of those industries 'ripe for public corporation'.[172]

In fact a pretty full analysis of the concept was set out in an interesting memorandum produced in 1928 by two young Labour politicians, E. Shinwell and J. Strachey.[173] Their paper was a direct reaction to the Labour plan for coal and other industries which had been put to the Sankey Commission two years before and which had attempted to combine the 'representative' and 'efficiency' principles. This earlier suggestion had been strongly criticized on many counts not least the politically impossible position in which it would place the minister concerned. The memorandum accepted these strictures as a point of departure and went on to urge the need for a fresh consideration of the question as 'purely and simply' a 'business one'. For 'after all, ... the first essential for any scheme of nationalisation is that it should work efficiently. Unless it does that, it will have to be abandoned, and Socialism discredited for generations.' It was proposed to vest the legal ownership of a nationalized industry in 'a Public Utility Corporation of a special type', the directors being persons of 'proved industrial ability' who would, within given legal limits, be 'perfectly free to conduct the industry... as they pleased.' The minister would not be able in this respect to give them orders and would, therefore, have no Parliamentary responsibility for their actions. Not a great deal is said in the memorandum about the industry's internal organization – this would be a matter for the corporation – but, although collective consultation was regarded as essential, there would be no attempt to provide for workers' control as through direct union involvement:

> We do not propose that the present trade union structure ... should be used as an instrument for the conduct of the industry. The existing trade union structure has been designed to protect the interests of the men and is efficient for that purpose, but for that purpose alone. To attempt to use this machine for administering a great industry, a purpose for which it was never intended and is totally ill-designed, would, in our opinion, be nothing short of disastrous.

The memorandum was in a sense inopportune: union reaction to its

---

171 Barry, op. cit., pp. 248–50.
172 Cited ibid., p. 300. Cf. ibid., p. 308 n. 92. Attlee seems similarly to have regarded the CEB as a model to be followed, see Harris, *Attlee*, pp. 70–1.
173 The extracts from the memorandum cited in the text are taken from A. H. Hanson, 'Labour and the Public Corporation', *Public Administration*, xxxii (1954), pp. 203–9.

The Public Concern – and Beyond

advocacy of 'managerial socialism' was hardly favourable; and it was never, in fact, published. But it was clearly a straw in the wind and not at all unreflective of a growing body of opinion in the Labour Party. Thus at the 1928 party conference Snowden spoke of moving towards 'our Socialism' very largely through public corporations controlled 'by the best experts and business men whose brains and capacity can be commanded.'[174] This background makes quite understandable Morrison's adoption and advocacy of the public corporation at that time (although there is, I think, no evidence that he was affected by the Shinwell–Strachey memorandum itself). He was, however, certainly indebted to both the ideas of the Liberal Yellow Book and the Soviet experiments in planning.[175] And Morrison's influence was as it turned out a crucial factor in the later development of Labour policy.

His own interest arose out of the reorganization of London transport, a complex problem not unlike those which had earlier been handled by the creation of single authorities for the ports of Liverpool and London and for the electricity industry. The metropolis was expanding in size and population and its transport arrangements had proliferated accordingly. In 1930 there were still over eighty separate concerns running the capital's buses, trams, and railways and naturally many difficulties arose. To avoid duplication and waste (and so to increase the return on capital invested) it seemed only sensible to consolidate and co-ordinate these services under one body, a step which had often been proposed. As Minister of Transport in the second Labour government of 1929–31, Morrison had been authorized by the Cabinet to proceed with a Bill. However he had no detailed scheme worked out and wrote in his autobiography that, while there was plenty of theory for him to study, there were 'but few concrete facts as regards the legal, administrative and managerial problems involved.'[176] Being an ardent advocate of municipal enterprise his original inclination was to favour control by a Greater London authority but this would have entailed a major local government reform. He did not like the alternative of some joint authority scheme and was very much aware of the disadvantages of direct departmental administration.[177] So, not least as a result of discussions with his officials,

---

174 Labour Party, *Report of the 28th Annual Conference... 1928*, p. 232.
175 For the Yellow Book's influence on Morrison, see B. Donoughue and G. W. Jones, *Herbert Morrison: Portrait of a Politician* (London, 1973), pp. 146, 148; see also the references in Morrison's own *Socialisation and Transport: the Organisation of Socialised Industries with Particular Reference to the London Passenger Transport Bill* (London, 1933), pp. 116, 282. For the influence of Soviet planning, see *The Rise of Collectivism* (London, 1983), p. 146.
176 Lord Morrison of Lambeth, *Herbert Morrison: an Autobiography* (London, 1960), p. 119. Cf. his *Socialisation and Transport*, pp. 113–14.
177 Morrison, *Socialisation and Transport*, pp. 123–4, 139–46.

he moved towards the solution provided by the idea of a public corporation.[178] The detailed proposals were worked out by a Cabinet committee of which Morrison was chairman. The legislation was based on the assumption that the interests of efficiency would be best served by placing responsibility for London transport in the hands of 'a small Board consisting of persons of proved business capacity.'[179] The minister concerned was to have some supervisory power over large issues of policy and financial arrangement but, so far as possible, the board would function free of political interference in questions of management.[180] There was some objection from those, like E. Bevin, who wanted specific provision to be made for a workers' voice on the proposed board but this was overruled on the ground that business and administrative ability alone should be the criterion of appointment and not the representation of interests.[181] And Morrison was able to convince the party as a whole that his Bill was a vital step towards Socialism, was indeed (what he later described as) 'the first major experiment' in the nationalization of a complex industry, a blueprint for other developments of the same sort.[182] Though the Bill was lost by the fall of the Labour government in 1931 it was taken up as a sound way of coping with a pressing issue by the National coalition and became law two years later. Morrison himself (who had not been re-elected to the Commons) had had in view other schemes of a similar kind and explored these possibilities for the extension of public ownership in a rash of journalism and one quite influential book. He made clear that, while a number of administrative possibilities existed, the public corporation was the form appropriate to those industries or services which are commercial in character and require considerable flexibility in operation to deal with varying market conditions.[183] He was able, too, to influence the development of Labour policy in this direction. For example he was most active on the NEC subcommittee which, during the 1930s, worked out schemes to deal with transport, electricity supply, banking, agriculture, and coal; and he virtually wrote single-handed the first of the two policy statements which

---

178 ibid., pp. 27ff., 73ff., 108–9, 121 etc.; Donoughue and Jones, op. cit., p. 141.
179 Morrison, *Socialisation and Transport*, p. 124 citing the government statement of October 1930. Cf. ibid., ch. x 'The Nature of the Board'.
180 ibid., p. 125; Donoughue and Jones, op. cit., pp. 142–3. Attlee's experience at the Post Office in 1931, although brief, had convinced him too that administration by an independent board was preferable to departmental control because it would involve less ministerial intervention, see Harris, op. cit., pp. 90–1.
181 Morrison, *Socialisation and Transport*, chs xi, xiii; idem, *Herbert Morrison: an Autobiography*, pp. 120–2; Donoughue and Jones, op. cit., pp. 144–5. Attlee agreed with Morrison, Harris, op. cit., p. 326.
182 Morrison, *Herbert Morrison: an Autobiography*, p. 119. Cf. Donoughue and Jones, op. cit., p. 145.
183 See e.g. the summary of advantages in his *Socialisation and Transport*, p. 148.

The Public Concern – and Beyond

envisaged co-ordinated industries under national boards in preference to departmental management.[184] In fact, by the middle of the decade, the policy of both TUC and the Labour Party was wedded to the public corporation principle though (as already mentioned) there was still some division of opinion about the extent to which a board should be representative in character. The TUC had also accepted the principle of the public corporation in a report of 1932 on the *Public Control and Regulation of Industry and Trade*; and this was later confirmed in its interim report of 1944 on post-war reconstruction, a most influential document. As D. N. Chester said, it had by 1945 been accepted for a dozen or so years as the party's 'chosen instrument' for nationalization.[185] Certainly by the end of the thirties the view was increasingly held in all parties that the public interest required greater state involvement in, or even ownership of, major economic assets and that the semi-independent public board was the most efficient way of organizing this intervention.[186]

During the second war these matters were naturally reviewed in relation to the problems of reconstruction likely to ensue. In 1942 one permanent secretary had told the official Machinery of Government Committee that a department could not effectively conduct a state undertaking because of the continual 'hostile scrutiny' to which it would be subjected in Parliament, especially from the opposition. A remedy might, however, 'be found in the extended use of semi-independent Commissions'.[187] It was also realized that any great degree of ministerial control – as would be implied by the departmental arrangement – 'would throw a great and novel burden on the Civil Service and could hardly avoid acting as a clog.'[188] It was not surprising, therefore, that (after a thorough review of the possibilities) the official Committee on Public Utility Corporations came to the conclusion that the board system was to be preferred (though not to the exclusion of other arrangements in some circumstances).[189]

It is clear, therefore, that when the Labour government assumed office

---

184 Labour Party, *The Reorganization of the Electricity Supply Industry* (London, 1932), pp. 3, 15–17; idem, *The National Planning of Transport* (London, 1932), pp. 3, 11–13. See also Donoughue and Jones, op. cit., pp. 184–5.
185 Chester, *The Nationalisation of British Industry 1945–51*, p. 386.
186 Lawley, *The Growth of Collective Economy*, i.354. Cf. ibid., i.396 for a clear rejection of the form of direct departmental management in favour of the public board; also very similar comments in O'Brien, op. cit., pp. 13, 14, 292.
187 PRO, CAB 87/71, 4th meeting of official committee (11 December 1942), pp. 1–2.
188 PRO, CAB 124/828, J. A. Barlow to Chancellor of the Exchequer (9 December 1944), p. 1 §2.
189 ibid., Report of the Official Committee on Public Utility Corporations, p. 5 §§9–10. See also the papers in PRO, T222/119, file no. OM 299/4/01 (19 July–14 December 1944) mainly relating to this committee's work especially H. Henderson, 'First Thoughts on the Public Corporation Problem'.

in 1945 questions about both the socialization of industry and the appropriate constitutional and administrative institutions to adopt had long been considered. At the same time there was not a lot prepared in the way of detailed plans about how the state take-over should be accomplished. Unlikely as it may seem, E. Shinwell wrote that, as Minister of Fuel and Power, he found there was nothing available in the form of a practical blueprint for the nationalization of the coal industry.[190] The formal determination of these matters was reached late the same year. A meeting of ministers in November 1945 with Morrison in the chair agreed that 'socialised industries should normally be run by Boards.'[191] This decision confirmed previous expressions of ministerial opinion, for instance that of the Minister of Supply, J. Wilmot, on the future of the iron and steel industry: 'It would not be practicable to operate the industry as a Department of the Civil Service. A management Board or Corporation fully responsible for the management of the industry within general lines of policy laid down by the responsible Minister appears to be the best solution.'[192] Again the Minister of Fuel and Power (E. Shinwell) wrote:

> I presume there is agreement that the general form of organisation for nationalised industries should be the Public Corporation – a non-profit making self-supporting body, run by a Board appointed by the responsible Minister, subject to his directions on matters of general policy, but free from interference in the day-to-day conduct of the industry. Within this general framework, the organisation may vary from industry to industry.[193]

Thus the board form of organization came to be adopted.[194] And this assumption was the basis of the work of the Cabinet committee set up at

---

190 E. Shinwell, *Conflict without Malice* (London, 1955), pp. 172–3. Cf. the comment in Chester, op. cit., pp. 1008, 1025. But see H. Dalton, *High Tide and After: Memoirs 1945–1960* (London, 1962), p. 135 and n. 3 on the scheme worked out for the nationalization of iron and steel.

191 PRO, CAB 78/39 Gen 98 (1st meeting), 9 November 1945, p. 3 §14.

192 ibid., Gen 98/1, memorandum by Minister of Supply and of Aircraft Production (25 October 1945), p. 4 §19. These views were the result of a series of questions posed after a meeting of ministers on 10 September 1945 presided over by the Lord President, one of a series of such meetings of ministers responsible for industries 'likely to be socialised' held with the object of achieving a uniform policy: see PRO, PREM 8/293, memorandum from Morrison to Prime Minister (17 December 1945).

193 PRO, CAB 78/39 Gen 98/3, memorandum by Minister of Fuel and Power (31 October 1945), pp. 4–5 §13. Cf. the other ministerial responses: Minister of Civil Aviation, Gen 98/2 (revised), (9 November 1945), p. 2 §5; Minister of War Transport, Gen 98/5 (7 November 1945), p. 2 §5.

194 See e.g. PRO, T230/106, 'Problems and Principles of Socialisation', E. C.(S) (45)36 (25 October 1946), p. 3 §§22–6; also the note by the Economic Section attached to PRO, CAB 78/39 Gen 98/6.

the beginning of 1946 to co-ordinate the nationalization programme.[195] Nor were further claims made in behalf of workers' control allowed to override the needs of efficient management.[196]

As a kind of summary conclusion to this third phase of development, the advantages of the public corporation – or rather those it was hoped would ensue – may briefly be listed. Above all it was presumed the board would be free from continual and direct political pressure; for the minister would not interfere in day-to-day matters for which he was not responsible to Parliament. Thus the industry would be screened from what Sir A. Street described as 'a Gulliverian shower of pin-pricking inquiries' and so be able to operate more efficiently in business terms.[197] The minister would, of course, make general policy decisions in the national interest and be answerable for these but he and his officials would be saved from a great burden of work relating to the corporation's everyday affairs. The industry's administration would, therefore, be in the hands of those with specialized experience and skill (a crucial contrast with the 'generalist' control of the Civil Service) and less subject than otherwise to the consequences of frequent ministerial changes. Equally the corporation's activities would not be subject to the strict forms of Treasury control, although the minister would retain the power to approve the general lines of capital development, borrowing, the use of reserves, and the like. In fact the public corporation came widely to be equated with nationalization as such. It was assumed that, under this joint aegis, sound, indeed flourishing, enterprises would emerge providing (because of their size and importance) a firm basis for the growth of the economy as a whole and able at the same time to take account of the interests of their employees and of social need. In all respects there would be advance beyond what was possible within a system of merely private ownership and operation. There would be no need to pursue merely short-term profit at the expense of long-term gain; funds for capital investment would be more easily available; and the pricing system could be more flexible. The economies of scale and other advantages of monopoly organization could be attained without the fear that might arise if entire control were directly in private or political hands. A better state of industrial relations would ensue. Control over the commanding heights would make effective planning possible. A whole range of purposes was thus envisaged. Yet, after some decades' experience of the actual operation of numerous public corporations, it all began to sound incredibly optimistic. Consider the following passage

---

195 For the appointment of the committee, see PRO, PREM 8/293, Morrison to Prime Minister (17 December 1945); ibid., CP(46)1 (1 January 1946).
196 Harris, *Attlee*, pp. 325–6.
197 Street, *The Public Corporation in British Experience*, p. 17.

from a draft paper produced in the Economic Section of the Cabinet Secretariat late in 1946:

> The purpose of socialisation is to ensure that the industries concerned are operated as efficiently as possible. Broadly speaking this means that the industries must strive to increase their output per head; improve wages and conditions and lower prices to the consumer; and generally, so far as finance is concerned, stand on their own feet. They are not being converted into public charities or subsidised services, and would normally require no recourse to Treasury funds.[198]

As it happened almost all of this paragraph was deleted from the document as finally circulated, in recognition perhaps of the optimism or even *naïveté* of its judgements; yet the simple fact of its appearing at this level of consideration is significant. In any event the failure of such anticipations is the main reason why the post-public corporation phase of state ownership and control emerged as time went on and more diverse or flexible means were pursued.

Diversity
Of course it is easy to exaggerate the emphasis during the last half-century on the national board: it was in fact never exclusively recommended as the appropriate institutional form even though in practice it came to dominate the scene. It was often noted that one thing to be avoided in the process of achieving common ownership was (as H. Dalton once put it), 'the temptation to construct a doctrinaire and cast-iron pattern, and seek to make all socialised industries and services conform to it. There is no one best way of organising all socialised enterprises.' Still less, he went on, is there 'one permanent best model' which will remain unchanged in the future. 'We must experiment, adapt, learn from experience, and encourage variety of form to fit variety of conditions.'[199] Similarly C. R. Attlee, also writing before the last war, refused to lay down 'a hard and fast line' on how every publicly owned industry would be managed, accepting that a considerable diversity would be needed in accordance with the requirements of particular undertakings.[200] There was, too, the criticism of the public corporation that it would be irresponsible and give rise to the dangers of managerialism. A. Bevan, for instance, felt this sort of concern and seemed both to favour administration by government department and to

---

198 PRO, T230/106, 'Problems and Principles of Socialisation', E.C.(S) (45)36 (25 October 1946), p. 8 §23.
199 Dalton, *Practical Socialism for Britain*, p. 94.
200 C. R. Attlee, *The Labour Party in Perspective* (London, 1937), p. 153. Cf. the revised edn (1949), p. 116.

recognize the need for greater industrial democracy.[201] Then there was the revisionist disenchantment within the Labour Party about the exclusive emphasis on nationalization itself as the essential basis of Socialism. Some wanted to get away from an always extending programme of nationalization based on the public corporation; others wanted to continue the process and often supplement it with an emphasis on the need to achieve some form of industrial democracy or workers' control.[202] For their part Conservatives showed an increasing concern to avoid public ownership and management in any form if this were at all possible.[203] There was thus a notable degree of discord about the objectives and future of existing nationalized industries and services and whether (and, if so, how) their array should be extended. The literature of disenchantment was considerable and spread across the entire political spectrum.[204]

Criticism of the nationalized industries was levelled at various aspects of their position and activity. Two of the most important issues related to their accountability and efficiency.

In 1966 Lord Reith wrote an article in *The Times* suggesting that there was a great degree of disappointment with the existing public corporations in that they were not fulfilling the original intention behind their creation, that is, that they should provide service 'at maximum efficiency, normally untrammelled by any political interference [or] Civil Service procedures', and so on. In fact they had become a façade behind which the reality of ministerial control operated to full effect.[205] The original legislation gave the responsible minister important powers concerning appointments to the board (and dismissal), general policy directives, accounts, training, research policy, capital investment, and so on: a not inconsiderable formal authority in fact for the exercise of which he was accountable to Parliament. But ministerial influence – which is very considerable and continuous – has in practice been exercised, through so-called 'backstairs pressure' or 'arm twisting' which, because it is informal cannot be easily made a matter of public knowledge or

---

201 See e.g. A. Bevan, *In Place of Fear* (London, 1952), pp. 28–9, 97–9, 102–3; M. Foot, *Aneurin Bevan: A Biography* (London, 1962–73), ii. 372. In respect of the nationalization of water supply, proposed in 1950, Bevan preferred some form of 'Civil Service organisation', Chester, op. cit., pp. 1056–7.
202 On these Labour Party quarrels, see *The Ideological Heritage*, ch. 13.
203 ibid., ch. 9.
204 See e.g. R. Kelf-Cohen, *Nationalisation in Britain: the End of a Dogma* (1958; 2nd edn, London, 1969); idem, *Twenty Years of Nationalisation: the British Experience* (London, 1969); idem, *British Nationalisation 1945–1973* (London, 1973); G. and P. Polanyi, *Failing the Nation: the Record of the Nationalised Industries* (London, 1974); and M. Sloman, *Socialising Public Ownership* (London, 1978).
205 Lord Reith, 'Façade of Public Corporations', *The Times* (29 March 1966), p. 11.

responsibility. In this fashion government has become the dominant partner in this gigantic power complex with the boards ultimately mere emanations of its will.[206] In 1976 the National Economic Development Office summarized the formal changes which had occurred as follows:

> The present nationalised industries were established by statute as public corporations separated from government but subject to government influence through the exercise of 'arm's length' Ministerial powers, in particular, board appointments and provision of finance. This loose framework of control...has not changed substantially since the original statutes of 1946–49. There has, however, been a gradual development in the formal structure and systems of control in response to the problems and priorities which have emerged subsequently. During the 1950s the need for more accountability to Parliament resulted in the creation and development of the Select Committee on Nationalised Industries. In the 1960s attention was focused on the dangers of resource misallocation; as a result, guidelines on pricing policy, investment criteria and financial objectives were introduced by government and the industries' investment plans were integrated within government systems for review of public expenditure. In the late 1960s and during the 1970s government has become more interventionist, reflecting not only the increasing use of the public corporations as a means of implementing macro-economic policy, but also the pressures of higher social expectations and of particular sectional interests.[207]

The reality of the relationship between government and the nationalized concerns had become very different from what it was supposed to be with the result it was widely felt in the industries themselves that ministers and departments intervened 'excessively' in areas which the boards considered to be their proper managerial prerogative and by means not statutorily provided for.[208] And the strategic position of the nationalized sector in a low-growth economy and the increasing aspirations of major interest groups, not least the trade unions, ensured that during the sixties and seventies governments became more not less involved.[209] However

---

206 For comment of this sort see e.g. G. W. Keeton, *The Passing of Parliament* (London, 1952), ch. 11; Kelf-Cohen, *Nationalisation in Britain* (1958 edn), ch. IX esp. pp. 170–2, 176–7; also ibid., pp. 281–2, 283–4. The main phases or aspects of control are reviewed in NEDO, *A Study of UK Nationalised Industries*, Appendix vol., Appendices C–F.
207 NEDO, op. cit., p. 22. These issues are examined in detail, ibid., ch. 2, 'Problems of Control'; and in Appendices C and D in the accompanying 'Appendix Volume'. On the SCNI and its successors, see Part 2, pp. 834ff.
208 NEDO, op. cit., pp. 35, 38.
209 ibid., pp. 35, 36–7, 44.

justified this growing intervention might be, its effect on the industries was unfortunate. From the point of view of the boards, it

> delayed decisions, disrupted previously agreed plans, invalidated criteria for planning and assessing performance, resulted in financial deficits, and damaged the corporate morale of management and other employees. The level of decision making tends to be raised with resultant increased burden on senior management. The lack of prior consultation, the inconsistency with agreed procedures and guidelines and the apparent unwillingness of governments openly to carry the responsibility for their interventions give rise to particular resentment at board level.[210]

Clearly the original theory about these relationships and open accountability has not in practice worked as intended. And this is no doubt one factor contributing to the industries' disappointing performance.

Certainly the nationalized sector has frequently been seen as consisting of a number of 'ailing giants' which are failing the nation because of their inefficiency.[211] Most of them enjoyed a protected monopoly position with the almost inevitable result that there was little incentive to please the consumer or to achieve low prices. And because the normal pressures of the market do not exist, the nationalized industries generally show an inferior performance. Of course the very position they are in makes it difficult to assess this but, using where possible the usual indicators of efficiency (such as the return on capital; profit or loss made; subsidy received; productivity; borrowing and investment; and the like), it is arguable that they do not achieve (or at least are, through the supposed requirements of public interest, prevented from achieving) optimum output or service.[212] It follows that they lack effective financial discipline and so are often wasteful of capital and other resources. Nor have they even achieved the anticipated degree of employee loyalty and good labour relations. It is a far cry from the high hopes with which vesting day was greeted in the mines in 1947 – with Shinwell and Hyndley raising their hats to collieries to be managed by the NCB 'on behalf of the people' – and the appalling strike lately experienced.[213]

In fact most of the changes latterly introduced have been not so much

---

210 ibid., pp. 35–6. Cf. ibid., p. 44. The report went on to make proposals intended both to clarify the government's responsibilities and to insulate the executive management from *ad hoc* or excessive interference, ibid., pp. 45–51.
211 For the phrase cited, see G. and P. Polanyi, *Goodbye to Nationalisation* (London, 1971).
212 For one such critical assessment, see the summary in idem, *Failing the Nation*, pp. 5–6.
213 For the greeting cited, see the photograph in E. Shinwell, *Conflict without Malice*, facing p. 159.

within the by now conventional framework of state ownership through the public corporation – because it has been so much criticized – as attempts to find alternative methods of government intervention and control. It is notable that the Labour Party election manifesto in 1983 referred not simply to nationalization but as well to the encouragement of diversification in existing state enterprises and to the establishment of 'a significant public stake' in some industries by other means such as a new national investment bank.[214] Some of these possibilities are reviewed in later sections of this chapter, in particular those to do with government shareholding, financial aid, and the enormous range of non-departmental bodies. But recognition of the need for a diversity of institutional forms is not dissimilar in some ways to the initial flurry of varied ideas about public ownership. In a sense the wheel has turned full circle.

Nationalized industries: the high tide

The main period of growth in the nationalized field was between 1945 and 1951 but the following quarter-century saw further additions to this part of the public sector as with the establishment in 1977 of British Aerospace and British Shipbuilders. By the end of the 1970s there were eighteen nationalized industries which employed in total over 1.64 million people (over 6 per cent of the labour force in Great Britain) and which had a turnover of nearly £24,000 millions.[215] Obviously these enterprises constitute either key services essential to the running of the community's affairs such as railways, docks, or telecommunications; or are industries such as coal, steel, or electricity deemed to occupy a crucial place in the national economy and requiring a monopoly position to achieve 'rationalization or optimum efficiency'. Their significance is undoubted:

> By any standards the nationalised industries occupy a central role in our economy. Together they account for more than a tenth of the national product and nearly a fifth of total fixed investment. The four largest employers in the country (after central government) are nationalised industries. As suppliers they occupy a dominant position in energy, communications, steel and transport. They account for about a third of all the plant and equipment bought by British industry and for several sectors of industry they are the sole domestic customer.[216]

214 KCA (1983), p. 32200A (32207).
215 Report on Non-Departmental Public Bodies, 1979–80, Cmnd. 7797, Appendix B p. 182; *Annual Abstract of Statistics* (1981).
216 NEDO, *A Study of UK Nationalised Industries*, pp. 7–8.

Certain details of these organizations, as they were in 1979, are shown in Table 8. This date marked the high tide of the nationalized sector. The return of the Thatcher government and its confirmation in office in 1983 has meant the pursuit of a deliberate policy of denationalization; and in some respects the programme has bitten deep or is in the process of doing so.[217]

But before dealing with this there are other institutions which require brief attention if the full extent of the contribution of the national enterprises to collectivist growth is to be appreciated.

Other public corporations

In addition to the organizations nowadays usually classed as nationalized industries there are also six other traditional public corporations. These are listed with some related detail in Table 9. Clearly in the case of the three broadcasting agencies a national board was chosen as the form of administration so that (in the different circumstances) there was a degree of independence of both government and commercial pressures. The CGMA is, like the PLA and the old LPTB, a London authority in which perhaps a more than local or regional importance may be descried.

Mixed company

In 1972 Professor Robson introduced a brief review of mixed enterprise in the United Kingdom (and some other places) by saying that, in the past, we have had comparatively little of it. But, he added, 'the position has been changing and is likely to change still more in the future' – as indeed it did. He went on to define a mixed company as 'an undertaking in which public authorities and private interests participate substantially both as owners of the capital and as directors or managers.'[218] It is a form of state involvement that does not alter the legal status or basic administrative structure of the firm concerned; nor does it affect the fundamentally commercial nature of its operations; and it formally remains an example of private enterprise, though a less than rigorous adherence to the stricter demands of the market place is surely implied. The Expenditure Committee once referred to 'companies in the beneficial ownership of the Crown', giving British Leyland as an example.[219] The concept is certainly ambivalent: the CBI sees the device

---

217 See the section on 'Privatization' at pp. 428–52 below.
218 W. A. Robson, 'Mixed Enterprise', *National Westminster Bank Quarterly Review* (August 1972), p. 22.
219 Expenditure, Sel. Cttee 11th Rep., 1976–7 (vol. xxxi), HC 535-I, p. lxxvii §4.

Table 8 The nationalized industries in 1979[a]

Nationalized Industry	Foundation	Function	Current Cost Operating Profit 1979–80 (£ millions)	Turnover 1979–80 (£ millions)[b]	Expenditure on Fixed Assets 1979–80 (£ millions)	Government Subsidies and Capital Grants 1979–80 (£ millions)	Number of Employees (000s)[b]
British Aerospace	Formed in 1977 by merger of three aircraft construction companies	Design, development, production, and sale of military and civil aircraft, guided weapons and space systems, etc.	n.a.	894	42	—	70.2
British Airports Authority	1965	Management of Heathrow, Gatwick, and five other major airports	6	162	54	1	7.3
British Airways Board	Established in 1971 to control BOAC (1939), BEA (1946), and their subsidiaries	Airline operation and associated services	−9	1,640	289	—	57.7
British Gas Corporation	Replaced previous area boards and council (1948) in 1972	Exploration for, purchase, transmission, and supply of gas	466	2,972	402	—	102.9

British National Oil Corporation	1976	Exploration, development, and production of North Sea oil; trading in oil through right to purchase 51% of production on the UK continental shelf	175	432	218	—	1.0
British Railways Board	Took over in 1963 services previously carried on by the British Transport Commission (1947)	Provision of railway and various associated services (hotels, shipping, catering, etc.)	−725	1,979	381	687	182.2
British Shipbuilders	1977	Management of all publicly owned shipyards in England and Scotland	n.a.	810	18	31	84.0
British Steel Corporation	Industry originally taken over by the state in 1951 but denationalized two years later. Fourteen major steel companies renationalized in 1967	To supply iron and steel products (largest steel undertaking in Europe; made c. 80% of Britain's crude steel)	−561	3,288	289	—	186.0

Table 8 *The nationalized industries in 1979 (contd.)*[a]

Nationalized Industry	Foundation	Function	Current Cost Operating Profit 1979–80 (£ millions)	Turnover (£ millions)[b]	Expenditure on Fixed Assets 1979–80 (£ millions)	Government Subsidies and Capital Grants 1979–80 (£ millions)	Number of Employees (000s)[b]
British Transport Docks Board	Took over in 1962 facilities previously operated by the British Transport Commission (1947)	Ownership and operation of major dock undertakings (largest port authority in Britain)	15	120	13	—	11.6
British Waterways Board	Took over in 1963 services previously carried on by the British Transport Commission (1947)	Maintenance and operation of canal and river navigations, docks, warehouses, and terminals	−22	12	4	23	3.4

Electricity Council and 12 area boards	The industry was nationalized in 1947 and reorganized in 1954 and 1957	The council is the central co-ordinating body of the supply industry responsible for its efficiency and development. Current is generated and transmitted by the Central Electricity Generating Board and distributed by the area boards	514	5,116	834	5	159.8
National Bus Company	Established under the Transport Act 1968	Provision through subsidiary companies of stage carriage bus services in England and Wales and a network of long distance express coaches	−42	437	60	60	64.3
National Coal Board	Industry nationalized in 1946	Monopoly of coal production (distribution in private hands). Various ancillary activities also taken over (coke ovens, brickworks, etc.)	−327	271	665	244	234.9

Table 8 *The nationalized industries in 1979 (contd.)*[a]

Nationalized Industry	Foundation	Function	Current Cost Operating Profit 1979–80 (£ millions)	Turnover (£ millions)[b] 1979–80	Expenditure on Fixed Assets 1979–80 (£ millions)	Government Subsidies and Capital Grants 1979–80 (£ millions)	Number of Employees (000s)[b]
National Freight Corporation	Set up under Transport Act 1968 to inherit various assets from Transport Holding Company and British Railways Board	Provide integrated road and rail freight services in Great Britain	−2	394	35	11	36.9
North of Scotland Hydro-electric Board	Established in 1943	Generation, distribution, and sale of electricity in the Highlands (mainly hydro-electric power)	13	173	46	11	4.1

Post Office	Duties transferred from GPO in 1969	Responsible for postal, telecommunications, and giro and remittance services	755	4,619	1,284	—	411.0
Scottish Transport Group	1968	Operation of main bus services (outside major cities), ferries, and certain ancillary businesses	−9	106	16	14	13.8
South of Scotland Electricity Board	Replaced two previous electricity boards and made autonomous in 1954	Generation, distribution, and sale of electricity	−16	443	65	—	13.7
Total: 18[c]			—	23,868	4,715	1,087	1,644.8

a *Sources*: *Whitaker's Almanack* (1979); Central Office of Information, *Britain 1979: an Official Handbook* (London, 1979); Report on Non-Departmental Bodies, 1979–80, Cmnd. 7797 esp. Appendix B p. 182; *KCA* (various volumes); The Government's Expenditure Plans 1981–82 to 1983–84, 1980–1, Cmnd. 8175, p. 172 Table 3.3.

b Figures relate to 1978–9.

c Some of the bodies listed in the table have been, or are in the process of being, privatized (see Appendix 2 p. 512 below). On the other hand, there are four other bodies (or groups of them) now officially classified as 'nationalized industries' in MPO, *Public Bodies 1985*, namely the English and Welsh water authorities, British Nuclear Fuels Ltd, the Civil Aviation Authority, and London Regional Transport.

Table 9 *Other public corporations, 1984*[a]

Public corporation[b]	Foundation	Function	Total assets (£ millions)	Number of employees	Expenditure 1984–5 (£ millions)
Bank of England	Incorporated by royal charter in 1694	Central reserve bank. As government banker manages the note issue and the national debt	2,479.0[c]	5,750	184.8[d]
British Broadcasting Corporation	Incorporated by royal charter in 1926	Provision (on the basis of licence revenue received) of wireless and television programmes (also external radio services financed by government grant)	363.3	29,410	805.1
Cable Authority	Established by Cable and Broadcasting Act, 1984	Promotes the development of cable programme services and licences and regulates their provision	n.a.	n.a.	n.a.
Covent Garden Market Authority	Covent Garden Market Acts, 1961–77	Set up to build and administer a new fruit, vegetable, and flower market (which opened in 1974)	17.8	92	4.2

Independent Broadcasting Authority	Created by Act of Parliament in 1954 (as Independent Television Authority). Now operates under Broadcasting Act, 1981	Provision of local wireless and national television services by (i) owning and operating transmitters (ii) appointing the programme companies (iii) supervising programmes and schedules arranged by contractors, and (iv) controlling the advertising. The authority is financed by a rental paid by the 15 programme companies	86.5	1,480	56.6
Welsh Fourth Channel Authority	Set up in 1982 under the Broadcasting Act, 1981	Provision of t.v. programmes and schedules for S4C, a substantial proportion being in Welsh	7.1	63	27.2[e]

a *Sources*: Cabinet Office (MPO), *Public Bodies 1985* (London, 1985); *Whitaker's Almanack* (1986); The Government's Expenditure Plans 1986–87 to 1988–89, 1985–6, Cmnd. 7902-II, Part Six; annual reports and accounts of the bodies concerned.
b It should be noted that the official list of public corporations (other than nationalised industries) has recently been made more extensive than that presented here and includes various agencies normally categorized as 'executive' public bodies: for the new listing, see Cmnd. 7902-II, p. 377.
c Excluding assets of the Issue Department.
d Estimate based on data in the Bank's *Report and Accounts* (London, n.d. [1985]) being total income less retained profit. I am grateful to the Bank's Information Office for guidance in estimating this figure.
e Includes cost of programmes at £24.6 millions.

as nationalization by stealth, while left-wing opinion regards it as a means by which capitalism is underwritten. In fact the degree and nature of public involvement may vary considerably. For instance government may own the entire equity or only a small part of it; it may appoint directors to the board or it may not; it may hold a special veto or never interfere at all in the company's affairs. Equally the reasons for this form of engagement are diverse and may relate to strategic interests; to saving a firm of national significance from bankruptcy; or to securing a base for rationalization. It is an arrangement which is more flexible than outright nationalization and more easily permits of diversification or, say, participation by local authorities. Again there is variety in the size of the enterprises concerned for they may be an industrial giant or just a small local firm.

These industrial or commercial connexions, seen more widely, fall into three categories. There are those in which government itself is a shareholder; those in which the link is mediated through some third party, a device of which the National Enterprise Board was perhaps the most well-known instance; and those in which government is simply a source of aid and subsidy to private concerns. Each will be separately treated in this section for it is apparent that this general sphere, in which government keeps company with the non-public sector, is a major aspect of collectivist development.

Government as shareholder

There have been numerous reasons why governments have acquired shares in particular enterprises.

Three early examples show how this sort of commercial involvement occurred for reasons of national strategy or prestige: the Suez Finance Company (1875), the Cunard Steamship Company (1903), and the Anglo-Persian (now the British Petroleum) Company (1914).[220] The several purposes in these cases all related to what was seen as national and especially naval necessity: to secure some control over a major artery of oversea communications, specifically those of imperial significance; to prevent an important part of the mercantile marine from falling into foreign hands; and to ensure supplies of oil for the Royal Navy. Similar considerations played at least a part in some later transactions of the same sort as with Short Bros and Harland (1943), Power Jets Ltd (1944), and the take-over of part of Rolls Royce Ltd (1971). Shortages caused by

---

220 For the last-named case, see M. Jack, 'The Purchase of the British Government's Shares in the British Petroleum Company 1912–14', *Past and Present*, no. 39 (April 1968), pp. 139–68. On the relations between the minister and the BP chairman and board, see the interesting comments in R. Marsh, *Off the Rails: an Autobiography* (London, 1978), pp. 103–4.

war may also lead to government involvement of this kind. One example is the promotion during the Great War of British Dyes Ltd because the main supply of the products concerned had previously come from Germany. In 1918 this enterprise was amalgamated with the only substantial independent firm to form the British Dyestuffs Corporation; but eight years later the government sold its rights in the company to ICI.

However, as time wore on and as such connexions increased, the motivation became almost entirely economic and social. Again the reason varies. It might be to acquire control (or potentially to be able to do so) over a particular firm, product, or industry, as with the development of the jet aero engine. It may be that public money is invested as a *quid pro quo* for the rationalization of an industry, as with the production of computers. Perhaps the development of new resources or technology is the object, the risks or cost being too high for private enterprise to assume unaided. There was obviously an element of this in the examples already mentioned. But the intention has often been simply to inject money into an enterprise or industry to prevent its collapse. This was the case with the sugar-beet industry before the war; and more recently with the aero-engine production of Rolls Royce and such cases as Beagle Aircraft Ltd and the Fairfield Shipbuilding Company.[221] In 1968 the Industrial Expansion Act was passed with the intention *inter alia* of making the state acquisition of shares for this purpose a less *ad hoc* process than it had been. It thus provided for the purchase of an equity as a means of giving financial support to 'industrial projects calculated to improve efficiency, create, expand or sustain productive capacity, or promote or support technological improvements'. Before this statute was repealed in 1971 the government had invested many million pounds in enterprises which found themselves in difficulty.[222] British Leyland is another obvious example, being 'one of the largest public sector lame ducks of all time.'[223] The result of a long line of mergers in the car industry going back to the early 1950s, it had consistently failed to earn enough to reinvest in new products and facilities and so faced falling sales and revenue. As a result of the Ryder report (1975) it appeared that state funding on a considerable scale would be necessary if the industry was to survive and to be made efficient, with the result that the government became the main shareholder.[224] Obviously the equity acquired in such cases as these was not in a healthy condition. And, of course, government

---

221 For a detailed account of the shipbuilding case, see *KCA* (1965–6), p. 21733A; and for Rolls Royce, ibid. (1971–2), p. 24677A.
222 See the reports in *KCA* (1969–70), p. 23747A (23748); ibid. (1971–2), p. 24740A (24742).
223 Sir M. Edwardes, *Back from the Brink: an Apocalytic Experience* (1983; Pan, 1984), p. 14.
224 ibid., pp. 35–6.

shareholding is enlarged as a result of the process of privatization, at least for a period, as state concerns are transformed into private limited companies with the shares held by a Secretary of State until their sale either wholly or in part on the open market.

It should be noted, therefore, that the degree of government involvement in shareholding has increased considerably since the 1920s as Appendix 1 shows.

NEB and other intermediaries

A state shareholding is not necessarily held directly by a minister of the central government but may be held through some commercial legate. In fact the major part of the public interest in mixed enterprises is in this latter form.

The surrogate may be a nationalized industry. For instance the National Coal Board has a wide spread of investments and other financial interests in various enterprises engaged in the distribution and marketing of solid fuel, coal products, the manufacture and supply of bricks and other building materials, and much else.[225] Similarly the British Gas Corporation has a 50 per cent share in a number of subsidiary companies such as Methane Services Ltd.[226] The largest engagement of this sort is undertaken by the British Steel Corporation operating through two holding companies, the interests being inherited from the private steel-making concerns whose assets were transferred on nationalization. The extent of activity involved is considerable ranging from the manufacture and handling of chemicals and their by-products to the provision of low-cost housing for employees.[227] Obviously the motive for purchase or retention of these interests by a nationalized industry is 'to enter into partnership with firms engaged in ancillary activities likely to be profitable or helpful' to its main function: 'a reasonable method of escaping', suggests Professor Robson, 'from the straitjacket which legislation usually imposes on the nationalized industries in regard to the permitted scope of their activities.'[228]

The successor companies to previously nationalized concerns (in which the government usually retains a full or partial shareholding) may also keep such subsidiary interests. For instance British Airways p.l.c. has a minority interest in several airlines and investments in a number of hotel and tour companies.[229]

A state interest in commercial enterprise may also be sustained

---

[225] For details, see the National Coal Board, *Report and Accounts 1982/3*, pp. 65–88.
[226] British Gas, *Annual Report 1984–5* (London, 1985).
[227] See the details in British Steel Corporation, *Report & Accounts 1983–4* (London, n.d. [1984]), pp. 34–5.
[228] Robson, art. cit., p. 32.
[229] *British Airways: Review of the Year 1984–5* (n.p., n.d. [1986]), p. 24.

through a specially created institution. Equally there is the new municipal Socialism represented by the Greater London Enterprise Board and its imitators in many other Labour-controlled authorities; while another instance is the developments agencies set up in Scotland, Wales, and Northern Ireland. At a national level the now defunct Industrial Reorganisation Corporation is one such instance; the National Enterprise Board (now part of the British Technology Group) is another. Both are significant as examples of the way in which state intervention in economic life may be extended without recourse to outright nationalization. This device has been of great importance in the recent past and may well be used again in the future. So it merits some attention here.

The IRC was part of the crusade on which the Labour Party embarked to put Britain into good economic shape 'after years of Tory neglect'. It was an aspect of 'the New Thinking' that (in the rhetoric of the 1964 election manifesto) 'will end the chaos and sterility' and that was 'restless with positive remedies' for 'mobilising the resources of technology under a national plan'.[230] To make British industry more efficient, indeed profitable, in an increasingly competitive world it was necessary to inject new technology and achieve economies of scale. And the merger was the means whereby the appropriate structural changes, the rationalization and modernizing, were to be brought about.[231] To this end the IRC (similar in some respects to the Italian Institute for Industrial Reconstruction) was set up in January 1966 with capital of £150 millions at its disposal.[232] As one way of creating larger and more viable units and as one aspect of the financial arrangements or inducements involved, it sold or held securities though (unlike the later NEB) it was not intended to be a general holding company.[233] As it happened the IRC did not have a very long life – the Heath administration abolished it in April 1971 when its assets were transferred to the Secretary of State for Trade and Industry

---

230 Craig (ed.), *British General Election Manifestos 1918–1966*, p. 229. For a full account of the origins of the IRC, see D. Hague and G. Wilkinson, *The IRC – an Experiment in Industrial Intervention. A History of the Industrial Reorganisation Corporation* (London, 1983), ch. 1.

231 That the corporation's principal purpose, at least at the outset, was to act as a 'merger broker', see W. G. McClelland, 'The Industrial Reorganisation Corporation 1966/71: an Experimental Prod', *Three Banks Review* (June 1972), p. 23; and Hague and Wilkinson, op. cit., pp. 3–4, 8, 13–16, 24, 231–9.

232 For the White Paper and legislation, see Hague and Wilkinson, op. cit., ch. 1 Appendix 1.1 and ch. 2; also *KCA* (1965–6), p. 21446A (21448–9) and (1967–8), p. 21838A. On the importance of the Italian precedent, see S. Holland (ed.), *The State as Entrepreneur. New Dimensions for Public Enterprise: the IRI State Shareholding Formula* (London, 1972), esp. pp. 243–52.

233 McClelland, art. cit., pp. 31–7. For a general review of the IRC's work and the difficulties that arose, see Hague and Wilkinson, op. cit., ch. 3 and for assessment, ibid., ch. 14.

with a view to their disposal. But at the time of its dissolution (though most of its aid to industry had been in the form of loans) the corporation possessed a substantial portfolio of investments. Probably the most well-publicized instances of its involvement concerned: Rootes motors; the Cammell Laird shipbuilding group; the restructuring of the ball-bearing industry; and the battle for the control of Cambridge Instruments.[234] The total of the various payments made was nearly £25 millions.[235] Professor McClelland, a member of the IRC board throughout, noted that book losses were shown on the equity holdings in the IRC's final accounts but attributes this to the state of the market at that particular time. He also pointed out that the purpose for which the shares were acquired was not so much long-term profit as to give leverage in the firms concerned so as to improve their performance.[236] However both parties clearly felt the need for some such stimulus because, only a year after the IRC was abolished, the Conservative government set up what was then called the Industrial Development Advisory Board operating under a minister as part of the Department of Trade and Industry. It had less wide powers than the IRC but could take up company shares if this seemed a suitable way of doing its job.[237]

The IRC did, in fact, have power (at the request of the minister) to provide finance for a single company unconnected with any merger; but this provision of the Act was rarely invoked. Its essence was, however, the key to the role later assumed by the National Enterprise Board.[238] The idea of such a body was by no means new; and there were well-known continental precedents. After the IRC's demise S. Holland had suggested the creation of a state holding company to replace it.[239] The notion was considered by the Labour Party's industrial sub-committee, a discussion paper was published in 1973, and a commitment to set up 'a powerful National Enterprise Board' appeared in the party's election manifesto the following year.[240] The motivation was mixed: to some supporters of the scheme it was an indirect means of extending public ownership, an alternative perhaps to straightforward nationalization; to others it was one way of counteracting the growing power of the multinationals; or a

---

234 Hague and Wilkinson, op. cit. Parts 2 and 3 constitute a series of detailed case-studies of the more important of the IRC's activities in respect both to mergers and restructuring on the one hand and 'rescues and restorations' on the other. Appendix A, ibid., pp. 252–306 is a summary of all the projects in which the IRC was involved.
235 ibid., p. 306.
236 McClelland, art. cit., pp. 38–40.
237 Industry Act, 1972, c.63, §§7–9.
238 M. Parr, 'The National Enterprise Board', *National Westminster Bank Quarterly Review* (February 1979), p. 51. For the power concerned, see Industrial Reorganisation Corporation Act, 1966, c. 50 §2(1) (b).
239 Holland, op. cit., pp. 250–2.
240 KCA (1974), p. 26373A (26376).

means to make planning more effective; or of restricting the effects of private monopoly. The most ambitious view envisaged the take-over of a dozen or so top companies, mainly in manufacturing (but, on some versions, including banks and insurance companies) which would constitute the basic NEB portfolio.[241] Such extensive possibilities naturally had a strong Socialist appeal. Yet, after it was set up in 1975, this dimension of the NEB's activities and potential was notably diminished. The White Paper preceding the Industry Act (which authorized the establishment of the board) and the statute itself both referred to such matters as the extension of public ownership by the acquisition of individual firms and the development of industrial democracy. But rather more stress was given to such other functions as helping to develop the economy, promote industrial efficiency, or sustain productive employment.[242] Consequently the board came to see its main role as an investment bank, a source of finance for the expansion and modernization of manufacturing industry as a whole. Moreover as it happened this task was itself overshadowed and inhibited by a complementary duty which in practice assumed larger proportions than intended, that is, responsibility for British Leyland and Rolls Royce the government shareholdings in which were transferred to the NEB.[243] As Table 10 shows these two enterprises accounted for nearly 88 per cent by value of all its shareholdings and 93 per cent of all the loans made. This highly concentrated commitment coupled with the ceiling on funds available to the board meant that its other activities (either by acquiring equity or through loans) were very limited indeed and far from the potential originally envisaged. In fact its other interests were in a relatively few – some fifty – small and medium-sized companies only, in areas of high unemployment or where there were export possibilities. Yet, if its resources had not been so concentrated and given enough financial support, the board could have influenced performance and control over a wide range of industry, certainly much more extensively

---

241 Parr, art. cit., p. 52. Cf. the account of A. W. N. Benn's proposals in B. Castle, *The Castle Diaries 1974–6* (London, 1980), p. 103 and n. 1; and for his belief that NEB was an important means of carrying through Socialist policies, see Edwardes, op. cit., pp. 33, 35.
242 *KCA* (1975), p. 27063A (27063–5); NEB, *Annual Report and Accounts 1976* (London, n.d.), pp. 3, 5–6. (I am grateful to the Information Department, British Technology Group, for providing a complete set of NEB reports and other material.) When NEB was set up two other agencies were established, one for Scotland, the other for Wales, with the remit to further the development of the economy of the country concerned and to improve the environment: for details, see The Functioning of Financial Institutions, Cttee Rep., 1978 (Non-Parl.), vols 6 and 8.
243 Cf. the booklet *National Enterprise Board* (London, 1978) describing its aims and priorities; also The Functioning of Financial Institutions, Cttee Rep., vol. 4, NEB written evidence, pp. 1–2 §§4–6.

Table 10 NEB investments, 31 January 1979[a]

Industrial sector (number of companies)	Shares held	Loans made	Total
	(£ millions)		
automotive products (1: BL Ltd)	695.52	160.00	855.52
aero engines (1: RR Ltd)	203.00	62.00	265.00
computers and electronics (12)	35.90	4.10	40.00
machine tools (4)	36.73	6.59	43.32
scientific and medical instruments (2)	8.62	0.55	9.17
office equipment (1)	1.00	—	1.00
process control (2)	1.32	—	1.32
exports (1)	5.77	0.45	6.22
northern region (8)	1.54	0.20	1.74
north-western region (4)	0.93	0.35	1.28
miscellaneous and small companies (16)	32.54	5.57	38.11
Total	1,022.87	239.81	1,262.68

a *Source:* Department of Industry, *National Enterprise Board: Facts and Figures* (London, 1979), pp. 9–11 (I have corrected some errors in the totals there printed).

than any single nationalized business could.[244] In this prospect might lie a motive of a collectivist kind for its resuscitation in the future.

Like the nationalized sector itself, the NEB reached its peak in 1979 but since then has been run down and its remaining activities more firmly canalized. What happened after the Conservatives came to office reflects the basic ideological and policy differences involved for, committed as it was to restricting government intervention and reducing public expenditure, the new administration could only regard the NEB and the policy behind its establishment with considerable suspicion. This attitude was reflected very quickly in the statement made by the Industry Secretary, Sir K. Joseph, in July 1979.[245] The board was not to be abolished but he rejected the idea that there was any public benefit in its acting as a general merchant bank and intended to restrict its power to promote business and buy shares. In addition the greater part of its existing portfolio would be sold as circumstances permitted. In future its activities would be severely confined, its investment being concentrated in new high technology fields, in the north and north-west, and in small firms. The change of emphasis was starkly noted by the board's chairman:

Public ownership for the sake of public ownership is no longer a

244 Cf. NEB, *Annual Report and Accounts 1976*, p. 3.
245 KCA (1979), p. 29821A (29831–2).

function and, instead, the NEB is to [dispose] of assets in order to increase private sector involvement wherever possible. The notion that the NEB could be a major instrument of industrial reorganisation and rationalisation has also gone.[246]

Subsequently, in 1980–1, the assets of Rolls Royce and BL were transferred to the Secretary of State (with a view to their return in due course to the private sector). This brought to a head inevitable differences about the scope and purpose of the NEB's role and the entire board resigned.[247] Its successor (which, significantly, contained no trade union members) was subject to new guidelines requiring it to concentrate on the limited tasks now envisaged and with a view to transferring to private ownership as many as possible of the assets in its charge.[248] The new direction of policy was embodied in the Industry Act (1980). The previous statutory functions to extend public ownership, encourage industrial reorganization, and stimulate industrial democracy were revoked. Instead the NEB (and its Welsh and Scottish counterparts) were enjoined to promote 'the private ownership of interests in industrial undertakings by the disposal of securities and other property'.[249] Of course all these changes left a smaller range of business for the NEB to attend to than before; and because of this, and as well to emphasize the need for it to concern itself above all with assistance to the industrial application of new technology, the NEB was in the Autumn of 1981 joined with the National Research Development Corporation to form the British Technology Group, the NRDC chairman having some months previously already taken over as chairman of NEB. Each organization remains distinct under the umbrella of the BTG which is now the body through which the government acts in the private sector to support the development and commercial exploitation of British technical innovation.[250] Clearly, therefore, government prompting and assistance is accepted as necessary; but its scale, direction, and purpose imply a role for the NEB very different from that in view when it was founded only a decade ago.

This is a nice reflection of a key ideological contrast. But the NEB also

---

246 Chairman's statement in NEB, *Annual Report and Accounts 1979* (London, n.d.), p. 3.
247 *KCA* (1980), p. 30415A. Cf. Edwardes, op. cit., pp. 228–9.
248 NEB, *Annual Report and Accounts 1980* (London, n.d.), Appendix A, Secretary of State's direction (1 August 1980), p. 52 §8.
249 *KCA* (1980), p. 30415A (30418–9).
250 For the priority areas concerned, see BTG, *Annual Report and Accounts 1981: National Enterprise Board* (London, n.d.), pp. 4–5. There is now at the DTI a Minister of State for Information Technology whose task is to foster these developments. See also Public Accounts, Sel. Cttee 15th Rep., 1983–4, HC 144 and 144-i (on DTI monitoring of the BTG).

represents a possible new phase or means of public ownership and control. Often in recent years there were obvious political advantages to be obtained by proceeding through such an intermediary as compared with outright nationalization. For one thing the latter was no longer (outside the left) accepted in the way it had once been and an alternative of this kind avoided some of the obvious criticisms. And it was less open to direct anti-nationalization propaganda as well a being less likely to meet commercial opposition. It was indirect, more flexible, and simply more palatable in many ways; and the firms concerned were distanced from government controls or influence. On the other hand, of course, being more at arm's length, Parliamentary supervision seemed even less adequate than with the fully nationalized sector. And the process was seen by opponents of collectivism as a more hidden and subtle form of interference than what had preceded it. It might more easily cumulate and so undermine the whole system. A process of 'self-nationalization' might be involved even: when in financial trouble a firm could simply fall back on state aid and take-over. For when the assistance was given, there would necessarily be a *quid pro quo*: a proportion of the equity taken in exchange, probably a majority of it at least; a binding legal agreement giving the minister a veto power; and representatives on the board. On the other hand the left-wing fundamentalist would often be dubious or hostile about such developments because he believed that share purchase simply tied the state to the market system, indeed strengthened it, and commercial considerations remained paramount.

Loans and subsidies

Government involvement in the private sector has not only taken the form of participation as shareholder either directly or through some intermediary organization like the NEB. An important part has also been played by financial aid given in various forms: loans or grants; provision of insurance facilities; guaranteeing repayment of interest; underwriting losses; the purchase of goods and services; the imposition of levies; and so forth.[251] The purposes for which this aid has been tendered have varied: to assist the smaller or medium-sized business; to promote re-equipment, innovation and technological development; to ease the raising of capital, to provide it in kind (as with government-built factories and equipment); to undertake a rescue operation; to support profitability (as by cash subsidy); to induce action compatible with or useful to government policy concerning, for instance, the maintenance of employment, regional aid, the promotion of exports, or industrial reconstruction.[252] Curiously enough these matters have only rather infrequently been the

---

251 For the amount of loans channelled through NEB itself, see Table 10, p. 408 above.
252 These aspects are all reviewed with examples in Grove, op. cit., ch. 10.

subject of attention by academic and other researchers.[253] But a great deal of light was thrown on this and other related aspects of government activity by an Expenditure Committee report on 'Public Money in the Private Sector' which appeared in the early 1970s in the aftermath of the decision to abolish the IRC and which *inter alia* gave considerable detail of help offered to a range of industries and firms (as well as comparative material about similar state activities in other countries).[254] Something of the later extent of this sort of involvement is shown by the use made of the Industry Act (1972).[255] During the four-year period 1974–7, assistance was offered to a wide range of industrial sectors to a total of £307.2 millions (of which £177.4 millions was actually paid out); and £97 millions was made available under sectoral industry schemes (and £12.9 millions taken up). In addition in 1975–6 £108.52 millions was advanced under the accelerated projects and selective investment schemes, the actual payments made up to the end of April 1978 being £23.62 millions.

Major utilities and services

The organizations brought together under this head are, it is true, grouped somewhat arbitrarily in the sense that most might be classified in another way. But where this is so each case stands out in some significant respect from the category to which it might otherwise be allocated. Those that could alternatively be regarded as 'fringe bodies' are none the less so large or costly (or both) as to constitute major institutions of some national importance in their own right: it might in some ways appear odd to see, say, the Housing Corporation and the Great Britain China Centre as members of the same genus when (in a recent financial year) one spent nearly £1,360 millions of public money and the other a mere £84,000. Again, one set of the agencies considered here – the water authorities – is now officially held to be a nationalized industry though this formal allocation is new and, in fact, the bodies concerned have characteristics still strongly suggestive of their origin in local government. At least one

---

253 e.g. PEP, *Government and Industry – a Survey of the Relations between the Government and Privately-owned Industry* (London, 1952), and Grove, op. cit., esp. ch. 10. A full account has lately appeared of the first occasion (in 1931) on which the Treasury joined forces with the Bank of England to rescue the Royal Mail Shipping group: see E. Green and M. Moss, *A Business of National Importance: the Royal Mail Shipping Group 1902–1937* (London, 1982), chs 7–8. For recent inquiries, see B. L. R. Smith (ed.) *The New Political Economy: the Public Use of the Private Sector* (London, 1975); idem, 'Accountability and Independence in the Contract State', in B. L. R. Smith and D. C. Hague (eds), *The Dilemma of Accountability in Modern Government: Independence versus Control* (London, 1971).
254 Expenditure, Sel. Cttee 6th Rep., 1971–2 (vols. xxvii–xxviii), HC 347 and 347-I-II.
255 I take the following details from 951 H.C. Deb. 5s., 6 June 1978, cols 139–46.

Table 11 *Major utilities and services, 1985*[a]

Name	Foundation	Function		Gross Expenditure, 1984–5 (£ millions)	% funded by government	Staff (4/1/85)
Agricultural Marketing Boards	Various statutes 1931–49	See text				
(1) British Wool Marketing Board			(1)	47.1	20.2	110
(2) Milk Marketing Board			(2)	426.8[b]	—	12,610[c]
(3) Potato Marketing Board			(3)	8.7	20.8	454
		Total MBs		482.6	—	13,174
Arts Council of Great Britain[d]	Royal Charter, 1946	Major channel for public financial support of the arts e.g. funds major arts organizations, administers some galleries and, indirectly, the South Bank complex		101.9	98.1	408
British Council	1934	Promotes wider knowledge abroad of Britain and the English language, develops closer cultural relations with other countries, and administers educational programmes		203.78	77.0	4,165
Health and Safety Commission and Executive	Established by statute in 1974	(i) the Commission is responsible for supervising the application and enforcement of health and safety legislation	(i)	0.15	} 96.0	3
		(ii) the Executive is the Commission's operational arm and consists largely of government inspectorates	(ii)	93.72		3,726

Housing Corporation	1964	To promote, supervise, and fund housing association schemes intended to provide subsidized rented accommodation for old persons, handicapped people, one-parent families, etc.		854.02	100.0	678
Manpower Services Commission	1974	(i) Helps place people in jobs and promotes mobility and training (ii) operates *inter alia* through various subsidiary bodies such as the training boards, Remploy Ltd, etc.	(i) (ii)	2,065.8 282.72	69.5 46.1[e]	20,803 14,825
National Health Service	1948	See text		16,304.00[f]	100.00[f]	1,057,154[g]
New Town Development Corporations[h]	From 1946	Development of self-contained new towns to encourage dispersal of industry and population from congested areas (28 designated to date)		997.3	23.1	8,306
Research Councils	1920–65	To allocate and monitor the use of government funds made available for research in the fields of agriculture, science and engineering, medicine, social science, and the natural environment. The British Museum (Natural History) has a similar function		636.95	97.0	12,122
UGC and the universities	1919 (UGC)	See text		1,982.8[j]	61.8	85,103[k]

Table 11 *Major utilities and services, 1985 (contd.)*[a]

Name	Foundation	Function	Gross Expenditure, 1984–5 (£ millions)	% funded by government	Staff (4/1/85)
UK Atomic Energy Authority	1954	Provides research and development support for the UK nuclear power programme; also undertakes work on other civil applications of nuclear energy	399.7	49.1	14,000
Water Authorities in England and Wales	1974	See text	2,033.9[l]	—	51,785
		Total	26,439.34	—	1,286,252

a *Sources:* Report on Non-Departmental Public Bodies, 1979–80, Cmnd. 7797; Central Office of Information, *Britain 1986: an Official Handbook* (London, 1986); *Whitaker's Almanack* (1986); Cabinet Office (MPO), *Public Bodies 1985* (London, 1985); The Government's Expenditure Plans 1986–87 to 1988–89, 1985–6, Cmnd. 9702-II; CSO, *Annual Abstract of Statistics*; UGC, *University Statistics 1983–4* (Cheltenham 1985), vol. 3 Finance; Committee of Vice-Chancellors and Principals, *University Statistics* (no. 5, Spring 1986); annual reports of the British Wool, Milk and Potato Marketing Boards.
b The figure shown covers producer and commercial activities but excludes inter-divisional purchases.
c Average for producer and commercial activities.
d There is a separate Arts Council of N. Ireland for which see Cabinet Office, *Public Bodies* (1985), p. 51.
e Expenditure net of receipts from patients.
f Payments made by MSC.
g Figure for 1983.
h Includes the development corporations in England, Wales, and Scotland; the Commission for the New Towns; and the Development Board for Rural Wales. (N. Ireland is excluded).
j Total recurrent income (1983–4) of universities in Great Britain.
k UGC-funded staff (1984–5).
l 1983–4.

of these institutions, the National Health Service, is simply *sui generis*; while others, such as the universities, are not normally regarded as (in the usual sense) public bodies at all. It is admittedly a miscellany but hardly an unimportant one. Apart from the marketing boards (which are constitutionally interesting) only one of these organizations (or groups of them) spends less than £100 millions a year; and most spend much more. Salient details are indicated in Table 11 and some of the more notable agencies are separately reviewed.

Agricultural marketing boards
Agriculture, including fishing and forestry, always has been and remains among the country's major industries and, as such, a prime object of concern to the state. At various times and in diverse ways governments have sought especially to protect, sustain, and develop this vital branch of our national life. In the outcome a number of non-departmental public bodies has grown up in and around the agricultural industry and outside the Ministry of Agriculture itself, among them such executive institutions as training and wages boards and a seed development organization.[256] There are also the marketing boards set up at various times since the early 1930s and which deserve brief mention in their own right, for they fall in a special category being producer's organizations of guild type.[257] They are statutory in origin but they operate with a large degree of independence of government.[258] This type of organization seemed suitable because there was a large number of small producers unused to thinking in terms of the industry as a whole; and it was assumed that the restrictive measures necessary would be more acceptable if they were not imposed by a government department.[259] The Fraser report explained in general terms the basis on which the boards operated:

> The majority of each Board consists of representatives elected by the producers, but there are additional members appointed by the Minister from outside the industry. Producers have to pay a levy to the Board and sell their produce to [it] at standard prices: the Board then markets the produce at prices which – roughly speaking – are uniform for the whole country. The main purpose of the Boards was to protect

---

256 For details of the various agricultural fringe bodies, see Report on Non-Departmental Public Bodies, 1979–80, Cmnd. 7797, pp. 49–53, 134–5; and Cabinet Office (MPO), op. cit., pp. 9–12.
257 Other bodies of this sort established in the inter-war period included the Cotton Industry Board and the Wheat Commission; but these no longer exist.
258 MPO, *Non-Departmental Public Bodies: a Guide for Departments*, Appendix 1 p. 35 §2(b).
259 Cf. the remarks of A. Street about the farmer's 'ineradicable distrust' of anything which seemed like '"farming from Whitehall"', PRO, T222/61, MGO(43)32 (3 November 1943), p. 3.

our most important home industry from disastrous falls in prices and, more particularly, to even out the gross inequalities in price between different parts of the country which were caused by transport problems and the varying accessibility of markets to producing areas.

In general the report concluded that these aims were achieved without placing an 'unreasonable burden' on the consumer.[260] In fact some boards had been trading concerns while others were simply regulatory (controlling the quantity or quality of the product brought to market) though all are supposed to be self-financing. The boards have authority to coerce producers who do not pay the levy and can discipline, by a fine, those who break the rules laid down about the marketing of the product. This is indeed 'an impressive range' of powers. But if the approval of registered producers is withdrawn the board concerned is dissolved. This element of producer control or self-government operates, however, in a publicly controlled environment. Ministers and Parliament can veto the initiation and amendment of schemes; there is a small number of appointed members on each board; there are statutory committees to protect consumers and the public interest; and there are limited powers of ministerial direction.[261] Parliament has, of course, several opportunities to debate or otherwise raise the affairs of a board, though in principle the same broad division of responsibility applies as in the nationalized sector, that is, between long-term policy and day-to-day administration. At the same time if a minister is badgered enough he will respond if it seems politically necessary to do so and this despite the boards' formal autonomy and 'democratic' base. In that sense the division of responsibility – as with all public boards – is always likely to be unclear.[262]

There have been boards for a total of seven products but now only three remain: milk, wool, and potatoes.[263] Because of their guild basis these boards are to be distinguished from such other agricultural

[260] PRO, T222/62, MGO 61 (3 January 1945), 'Non-Departmental Organisations', p. 28 §131.
[261] For the points mentioned, see P. Giddings, 'Parliament, Boards and Autonomy: the Case of the Agricultural Marketing Boards', *Public Administration*, liii (1975), pp. 384–5; also the very full detail in idem, *Marketing Boards and Ministers: a Study of Agricultural Marketing Boards as Political and Administrative Instruments* (Farnborough, Hants., 1974).
[262] Giddings, art. cit., pp. 385, 387, 393, 394–7, 398, 399.
[263] *Britain 1986*, p. 290 where the variations between the boards are noted. The now defunct boards were for hops, eggs, tomatoes and cucumbers, and bacon pigs. Scotland has three separate milk marketing boards; and in Northern Ireland there are boards for milk, pigs, and seed potatoes. A useful recent study is W. Grant, 'Private Organizations as Agents of Public Policy: the Case of Milk Marketing in Britain', in W. Streeck and P. C. Schmitter (eds), *Private Interest Government: Beyond Market and State* (London, 1985), ch. 10.

institutions as the Eggs Authority, the Home Grown Cereals Authority, the Meat and Livestock Commission, the Sea Fish Industry Authority, and the Apple and Pear Development Council which, though they may represent producer interests, are regarded as ordinary fringe bodies of executive type, while the Forestry Commission is in effect a department for which a minister is directly responsible.[264] The path of the marketing boards has not always run smooth: witness the stormy history of the one-time Tomato and Cucumber Board and the fight against its regulatory powers by that eccentric village Hampden from East Yorkshire, H. Wright.*

The National Health Service
The NHS stands out as a giant among all the agencies comprising the Public Concern. Indeed only a few years ago it was described in an official document as 'the biggest organisation in the country, in terms of money spent and staff employed'; while a recent commentary even referred to it as 'one of the world's largest corporate organisations'.[265] This sort of judgement is clearly validated by the figures. A royal commission reporting in 1979, found that just over one million people were then employed by the NHS in the country as a whole ranging from porters and clerks to highly skilled medical consultants. And the previous year its total expenditure was almost £6,900 millions. This was some 5.6 per cent of the then GDP: a proportion which had risen from just under 4 per cent thirty years earlier.[266] (It is reported that in 1984–5 central government spending on the service was over £16,000 millions a year which means that getting on for 7 per cent of national resources are thus devoted.)[267] Eighty-four per cent of these costs was met from general taxation, 11 per cent from health insurance contributions, the rest from charges and miscellaneous sources.[268] Medical provision, largely free at the point of service, is thus made for some 95 per cent of the population.

Administratively this large and costly enterprise is of 'doubtful' status (the epithet was used a few years ago in the report of a House of

264 Report on Non-Departmental Public Bodies, 1979–80, Cmnd. 7797, pp. 51–2, 185; Cabinet Office (MPO), op. cit., p. 9.
265 Expenditure, Sel. Cttee 11th Rep., 1976–7 (vol. xxxi), HC 535-II, p. 405 §2.2.2; P. A. West, 'Private Health Insurance', in J. Le Grand and R. Robinson (eds), *Privatisation and the Welfare State* (London, 1984), p. 111.
266 National Health Service, R. Com. Rep., 1979–80, Cmnd. 7615, p. 178 Table 12.2 and p. 431 Table E6.
267 *Annual Abstract of Statistics* (1986), Table 3.3 p. 45 and Table 14.1 p. 243.
268 The Government's Expenditure Plans 1986–7 to 1988–9, 1985–6, Cmnd. 9702–II, Chart 3.14.4 p. 212.

* This episode deserves, but has not yet found, its chronicler (so far as I know). There is a brief summary of Mr Wright's sixteen-year battle against officialdom in the *Daily Mail* (2 January 1967), p. 1. I am grateful to Dr A. Harris of the University of Hull for this reference.

Commons committee when an attempt was being made to define what a 'civil servant' was).[269] For although the NHS is headed by a Secretary of State, who is responsible for providing health services through the field authorities, its remunerated staff are not civil servants constituting a department under him: they are technically the employees of a variety of bodies, while GPs, for instance, are in a contractual relationship with the Family Practitioner Committees. Nor are the NHS authorities merely the agents of the minister. They have important policy-making responsibilities in their own right and they interpret national guidelines to suit local circumstances. At the same time they have no independent political base (such as election would give) and they depend financially on central government. The observation was made (early in the proceedings of the committee already referred to) that the NHS, not being a part of the Civil Service or of local government, nor a public corporation, was 'neither fish, flesh nor fowl'. This elicited the not unreasonable response from the senior official then being cross-examined, that the health service was simply what government and Parliament had made it when it was first set up after the second war and what it was confirmed to be at the time of its reorganization in 1973–4.[270] The NHS is thus an especially large and outstanding instance of that constitutionally ambivalent array of bodies which make up the Public Concern and which have developed as a crucial part of collectivist growth. The form it took was simply the result of the difficulties presented by any alternative.

The array of health facilities available by 1945 was considerable and derived from an amalgam of philanthropic and commercial enterprise together with a notable and growing effort on the part of both central and local government. But the arrangements were deficient in many ways: coverage was by no means complete, standards varied considerably, resources were badly distributed, funds were not readily available for improvement, the insurance system was a notable administrative mess, and so on. As one commentator put it, 'For over a hundred years, the services had developed spontaneously, without any sort of general direction' with a result that was far from optimum efficiency.[271] The war, too, had highlighted many shortcomings in established practice and facilities and, by its end, it was increasingly acknowledged, in a variety of professional and political circles, that change had to come. The question was what form the new order for the comprehensive delivery of medical care should assume.

It was more or less taken as given that, in the mid-twentieth century, it

---

269 Expenditure, Sel. Cttee 11th Rep., 1976–7, HC 535-I, Appendix p. lxxvii §5.
270 ibid., HC 535-II, p. 355 qq. 904–5.
271 H. Eckstein, *The English Health Service: its Origins, Structure, and Achievements* (1958; Cambridge, Mass., 1964), p. 45.

was no longer feasible to think of a health service based largely or wholly on some form of private, voluntary, or commercial foundation. We might make a different judgement today, forty years on, but that was undoubtedly the case then. It was supposed that the structure of health services would – and should – be supervised and perhaps funded by public authority. There were four possibilities. The first was to throw the burden directly on one or more central departments. But this was not feasible for two reasons. One was the extra burden of detailed administration involved; the other was the hostility of the medical profession (or, at least, a vocal and major part of it) to anything that seemed to imply a whole-time, salaried medical service under bureaucratic control which would (it was said) treat doctors as 'regimented units'.[272] At one time the Ministry of Health did toy with such a scheme but this simply caused the BMA (the co-operation of which would obviously be crucial) to take extreme fright. The second possible course was management through the local authorities or joint bodies formed by them. This had frequently been suggested ever since the Dawson Plan of 1920 and was, for instance, favoured by the Socialist Medical Association in a scheme it put forward four years later. Similarly the Coalition White Paper of 1944 proposed that local responsibility should rest jointly on county and county borough councils.[273] And in 1945 when the Cabinet discussed Bevan's proposals, Morrison and some other ministers argued powerfully but unsuccessfully for the preservation of local control of hospitals.[274] Yet this local option was hardly practicable. There was, for instance, the history of variation and deficiency in the personal health services for which local councils had been responsible. And above all the contemporary state of the local government system did not warrant such a step: the main structure of a national health service could hardly be made to depend on a set of arrangements known itself to be in need of substantial improvement and without adequate financial resources of its own.[275] In addition the medical profession was reluctant to work within a local government framework for fear clinical freedom would be adversely affected given that doctors would be absent from the controlling bodies. As Lord Moran said in 1946, 'For a whole decade every professional discussion of the hospital service has been dominated by the dread that the hospitals will come under the control of the local authorities.'[276] The idea that the

272 See the report of the BMA annual meeting in 1942, KCA (1940–3), p. 5378B.
273 ibid. (1943–6), p. 6523A.
274 K. Morgan, *Labour in Power 1945–1951* (Oxford, 1984), pp. 154–6. And cf. the comment, ibid., p. 162.
275 Cf. A. Bevan's views as reported in M. Stewart, *Life and Labour* (London, 1980), p. 70.
276 Cited M. Ryan, 'The Tripartite Administrative Structure of the National Health

NHS should be wholly run by local government has often been considered since but, in practice, the tendency of affairs has been in a contrary direction and local authorities have themselves lost health responsibilities to the national service.[277] The case is still urged, however, on two main grounds. One is that health services should be the responsibility of elected bodies; the other that they should be set in the main fabric of community government.[278] The third prospect – that of placing responsibility for the health service in the hands of a public board or commission – had also often been considered. For instance in 1942 the BMA had sponsored an inquiry which *inter alia* explored just such a possibility.[279] The recent royal commission also considered it but decided it was in existing circumstances unlikely to lead to any improvement.[280] Sometimes the suggestion was applied to particular parts of the service and there were some precedents to draw on. Thus, although the experiment was short-lived, the voluntary hospitals had (in the period after the Great War) been aided by funds channelled through a Voluntary Hospitals Commission. And the Coalition White Paper of 1944 had envisaged placing general practice under the control of two Central Medical Boards.[281]

The fourth, and last, possibility is simply what actually happened as the outcome both of haphazard development in the past (of the insurance system, the hospital service, and so forth) and of the numerous pressures and compromises involved at the time the NHS was established. That is, a set of arrangements was created that fell into no clear-cut institutional category: a hybrid or sport which was a 'compromise between state direction and professional independence.'[282] As one observer has put it, it was the 'representation of what was possible rather than what might have been desirable.'[283] On the basis of the 1946 statute the NHS which

---

Service – its Genesis and Reform', *Social and Economic Administration*, vi (1972), p. 220. On the general point, see also J. M. Lee, *Reviewing the Machinery of Government 1942–1952: an Essay on the Anderson Committee and its Successors* (n.p. [London], 1977), p. 131.

277 Cf. National Health Service, R. Com. Rep., 1978–9, Cmnd. 7615, ch. 16 esp. pp. 263–5.
278 See e.g. G. Jones and J. Stewart, *The Case for Local Government* (London, 1983), ch. 14.
279 *KCA* (1940–3), p. 5378B.
280 National Health Service, R. Com. Rep., 1978–9, Cmnd. 7615, pp. 306–7.
281 *KCA* (1943–6), p. 6523A.
282 Morgan, op. cit., p. 162.
283 C. Ham, *Health Policy in Britain: the Politics and Organisation of the National Health Service* (London, 1982), p. 16. I am grateful to Dr M. Ryan of University College, Swansea, for directing my attention to this most useful survey. The role of the many interests involved in the genesis of the NHS is described in A. J. Willcocks, *Interest Groups and the National Health Service Act, 1946* (Ph.D., University of Birmingham, 1953) (which is rather fuller than his subsequent published account).

came into operation two years later had a tripartite structure under overall ministerial control. The three main sets of institutions concerned – Regional Hospital Boards (and Hospital Management Committees), Executive Councils, and local government – were basically differentiated according to the function or type of facility they supervised or administered. Respectively these were: hospital and specialist services; family doctor, dental, and cognate arrangements; and personal health care.[284] These tasks were obviously all interdependent yet they were, within this framework, separately financed and planned. And there was no single body in any given area with overall responsibility for providing an appropriate and integrated combination of comprehensive health cover. This was an especially important deficiency since disease patterns were altering and it was being increasingly recognized that some groups (such as the elderly) needed co-ordinated help involving all three branches of the service.[285] Difficulties in respect of co-ordination were also highlighted by such other factors as restrictions on capital investment or by medical attitudes (say to the development of health centres).[286] Over the years, therefore, and not least in a context of rising costs, there was much discussion about the possibility of bringing the functionally separate aspects of the service under some more integrated form of management.[287] Various increments of change ensued beginning with those introduced in 1974 which transferred responsibility for the personal health services from the local authorities to the NHS and placed the service's organization on a more geographical (rather than a functional) basis. The changes were intended to unify and co-ordinate the various services provided and to introduce better management arrangements.[288] However almost immediately the new structure became the object of criticism: about delays, the bad relationships between the different administrative tiers, and because of the widespread feeling that the system was too complex and had too many officials.[289] This sort of dissatisfaction coupled with the expense of the reorganization itself had

---

284 There were anomalies arising from the practical political considerations involved. For instance all English and Welsh teaching hospitals were excluded from the regional framework, being accountable not to the RHBs but, *via* the Boards of Governors, direct to central government. 'This can best be explained', says Dr Ryan, 'by reference to Bevan's need to win over for the Service these world-famous centres of excellence and the influential specialists who taught and practised in them', art. cit., p. 221.
285 Ham, op. cit., pp. 23–4.
286 Ryan, art. cit., pp. 222–3, 224, 225.
287 For details of the earlier phases of criticism, see M. Ryan, 'Reform of the Health Service Structure', *Public Administration*, xlvi (1968), pp. 315–30; also Ham, op. cit., pp. 17–27.
288 Ham, op. cit., pp. 25–7.
289 ibid., pp. 28–9.

an impact on staff morale. There was unrest for various reasons among different groups of health service workers including the consultants who were upset by the government's proposals to phase out private beds in NHS hospitals.[290] The result was the appointment of the royal commission already referred to and which reported at the end of the seventies. Among many other recommendations concerning the organization, financing, and policies of the NHS, it suggested the removal of one of the existing layers of administration. After discussion reforms were introduced between 1980 and 1983 to create the structure as it now is.

The health ministers – the four Secretaries of State concerned – are responsible for all aspects of the health services in their respective areas including strategic planning.[291] Under this overall control the task of operational management falls to District Health Authorities which are, in turn, required to arrange their facilities into units of management at hospital and community service level to which as much discretion as possible is delegated. In England and Wales there are 201 such DHAs; in Scotland their equivalent is the fifteen Health Boards; while Northern Ireland has four Health and Social Services Boards. These are the basic statutory agencies which run the NHS. But in England, because of its greater size and population, there is an additional tier of fourteen Regional Health Authorities responsible for the allocation of resources to the districts, regional health planning, and certain services best administered on a wider basis such as blood transfusion, research, and major capital building work. The RHA has the task of interpreting DHSS guidelines on service provision and, in turn, of passing on policy to the districts. But in so doing it may develop modified alternative policies more suited to local needs.[292] As intimated earlier the health authorities, though they are in one sense the agents of central government, are also 'semi-autonomous bodies who themselves engage in policy-making, and as such exercise a key influence over the implementation of central policies.'[293] The Secretary of State is fully accountable to Parliament, however, for the operation of the NHS and as well he decides a number of important matters: the appointment of the chairmen and members of the RHAs and the chairmen of DHAs; personnel questions such as salaries and conditions of service; regulations concerning payments to patients; and last but not least he can control NHS expenditure and its overall

290 For the legislation to secure this end, see *KCA* (1977), p. 28456A; and its subsequent repeal, ibid. (1981), p. 30648A.
291 For these details, see *Britain 1986*, pp. 129ff.; *Whitaker's Almanack* (1986), pp. 396, 1195; and the National Association of Health Authorities, *NHS Handbook* (Birmingham, 1980ff.).
292 Ham, op. cit., p. 110.
293 ibid., p. 113.

allocation to the regions as well as major capital building projects.[294] Beyond this it is a matter of departmental guidance in circulars, consultative documents, and similar means: but these then have to be interpreted at regional and district level. There is thus a certain ambivalence about NHS administration. Though constitutionally the regional and district bodies are agents of the minister it was always intended they should have a certain independence of view and a freedom of action so that to an important degree his responsibility is only formal. And they, and not the minister, are the employers of NHS staff.[295] Central–peripheral relations are, therefore, necessarily flexible; and there is considerable autonomy for the regions and districts though ultimately the minister has powers of direction and supersession.[296] There has been some criticism about the balance of power and initiative in the NHS, as by the Public Accounts Committee, and suggestions of the need to strengthen controls.[297] In fact the relationship between the tiers is not one of dependence so much as a negotiating process through which policy is jointly evolved and implemented.[298] The position is further complicated by the professional dimension, that is, the important role of the doctors and their colleagues in respect of clinical independence and resource control. This is reflected, for instance, in the arrangements for the family doctor, general dental, pharmaceutical, and opthalmic services which are arranged through Family Practitioner Committees of which there are ninety-eight in England and Wales and which are representative of local doctors, dentists, and so forth, local councils, and the district authorities concerned. These FPCs, unlike the district and regional authorities, are not management bodies but exist to administer the contracts of the GPs, dentists, pharmacists, and opticians concerned while leaving them free in the exercise of their professional judgement. Advisory machinery is also incorporated within this general structure as is public representation through the community health councils which consist of persons appointed by local authorities and interested voluntary bodies.

This organization provides a comprehensive range of hospital, specialist, general practitioner, ambulance, and community health services (with personal social services – for groups such as the handicapped and the elderly – being provided by the local authorities equally under the aegis of the Secretary of State). As well as the question of accountability for the operation of the service many other issues have

---

294 ibid., pp. 113–14.
295 Cf. Expenditure, Sel. Cttee 11th Rep., 1976–7, HC 535-II, p. 411 §2A.13.
296 Cf. *KCA* (1980), p. 30411B on the case of a London Area Health Authority in conflict with the minister.
297 Ham, op. cit., pp. 118–19.
298 ibid., p. 120.

arisen. There are the problems derived from the way in which, inevitably in a 'free' service, demand continually outstrips the resources and funds available. Issues of resource allocation and priorities are always to the fore. Variations of provision between areas and parts of the service alike are noted. And there are the vexed matters of pay-beds and private practice; and whether taxation as a source of funds needs to be supplemented more or to a degree replaced by charges and insurance schemes.[299]

The UGC and the universities

Universities are corporations usually established by royal charter. But the legal autonomy implied by this status has, in important practical respects, masked a growing subjection to public policy. Over the years these institutions have increased in number and become more and more expensive to run as the result of a rise in the number of students and the increasing costliness of scientific training and research in particular. *Pari passu* they have fallen into dependence on government. The amount currently spent by universities in the United Kingdom is about £2,000 millions a year, a little more than 62 per cent of this sum being derived from government grants.[300] Inevitably the piper who pays calls the tune; and nowadays individual universities and colleges are much constrained in respect of (say) the number and mix of students they may admit, the subjects they may teach (or, rather, not teach), the number and grade of staff for which they will receive support; and the amount they spend on buildings and equipment. Of course the state is spending taxpayers' money and must properly supervise its use; but the extent to which this process has necessarily gone, with its corollary of regulation and command, is hardly compatible with that notion of the university as a free and independent institution which once prevailed and which in theory is still cherished. We all went too happily down this slippery slope and long ago passed almost unnoticed the level of financial aid beyond which more and more detailed monitoring was inevitable.

The distribution of funds to, and so the regulation of, the universities is exercised through the University Grants Committee set up by Treasury minute in 1919. Its task was to make a case to the Treasury for funds to aid or operate the universities and to advise about the distribution of the money allocated. Government grants of this sort had first been given in the 1880s but, with the growth of the university system and its cost, some formal machinery of this sort was thought desirable.[301] The members of the UGC (only one of whom, the chairman, is full-time) are nowadays

---

299 See below pp. 449–50.
300 UGC, *University Statistics 1983–4* (Cheltenham, 1985), vol. 3 Finance, Table 3 p. 10.
301 Cf. H. V. Wiseman, 'Parliament and the University Grants Committee', *Public Administration*, xxxiv (1956), p. 76.

appointed by the Secretary of State for Education and Science and most of them are from academic life, each serving, however, in an individual and not a representative capacity. Strictly speaking its role was always advisory though conventionally the government accepted the UGC's confidential recommendations about the distribution of the global sum allocated. This seemed a convenient device, for it permitted the minimum degree of departmental interference with university activities and so secured a nice combination of public funding and academic freedom. It was a much admired mechanism for transferring government money to the universities without subjecting individual institutions to detailed political accountability.[302] But, after the 1950s and especially after the Robbins report, as the universities expanded and their cost rose considerably, the political issues became more urgent. Escalating university expenditure, national needs, and the pressure of other social requirements inevitably seemed to demand a greater government role. It was increasingly felt that Parliament was entitled to expect more clear and explicit assurances than hitherto that the money granted was being administered with efficiency and economy, that there was no extravagance or waste. There was increasing pressure, for instance, that university accounts should be open to the inspection of the Comptroller and Auditor General, a claim which had finally to be conceded. Again, responsibility for the UGC was transferred from the Treasury to the DES. These were steps of notable symbolic significance for they marked a great watershed in the relationship between the universities (on the one hand) and the UGC and government on the other. The universities are still 'independent' but their position is now very different from what it was. The UGC, from being a financial conduit and a protective buffer, has become an active and increasingly intrusive monitor. It used to offer advice; nowadays it gives, in effect, instructions. The first chairman of the UGC, Sir William McCormack, threatened to resign when the Treasury attempted to apply to the universities its normal powers of review over money: and it withdrew the claim. It is hard to imagine a contemporary successor taking such a stand; and would many people regard it as proper that he should? Nor is government pressure likely to diminish in the remainder of the century. Quite the contrary because the demographic trend indicates that the number of school-leavers will fall by as much as a third in the ten years following 1982–3; and so, unless there is a substantial change in the proportion of the population wishing to attend

302 Cf. the comment of the Select Committee on Estimates in 1952 as cited ibid., p. 78; Sir R. Clarke, *New Trends in Government* (Civil Service College Studies no. 1; London, 1971), p. 86; and G. Williams, 'Higher Education: Adaptation Without Growth', in C. Jones and J. Stevenson (eds), *The Year Book of Social Policy in Britain 1983* (London, 1984), p. 130.

university (whether school-leavers or not) there will be considerable excess capacity leading perhaps to the closure or reduction in size of some institutions. The need for economy and the efficient allocation of limited resources will manifestly strain the relations between government, UGC, and the universities and the convenient fictions on which these connexions were built in the past.[303] One wonders whether the UGC in its traditional form can survive: its role and functions are currently being reviewed by a committee under the chairmanship of Lord Croham. Certainly there will inevitably be a considerable degree of adaptation in the universities themselves (and in other institutions of higher education) despite the shrill cries from Vice-Chancellors, Principals, and the lesser creatures of the academic pack.

Water authorities
Water management concerns the conservation of resources, supply, sewerage, and reclamation. The last is a relatively new responsibility, the other three tasks being carried out before 1974 by numerous bodies of different kinds. Over the years some rationalization had occurred through central supervision and recognition of the need for a 'national water policy' formally recognized by legislation at the end of the war.[304] Even so, immediately prior to the 1973 Water Act there were some 200 separate undertakings supplying water (most operated by local authorities or joint boards, the remainder by private companies), while sewerage and sewage disposal was an entirely local government function carried out by over 1,300 county borough and district councils and a few joint bodies. The conservation of water was the duty of twenty-nine river authorities set up in 1963.[305] Since the reorganization in 1974 the position has varied according to the part of the United Kingdom concerned. In Scotland the water services largely remain the responsibility of local government, that is, the regional and island councils; while in Northern Ireland they are administered by the province's Department of the Environment. However in England and Wales this function was transferred to ten regional water authorities with areas which coincide with the major watersheds (though private companies and local councils may still act as their agents for certain functions). These new water

---

303 Cf. G. Williams, art. cit., pp. 130–2.
304 For an account of the problems, see J. Sheail, 'Planning, Water Supplies and Ministerial Power in Inter-War Britain', *Public Administration*, lxi (1983), pp. 386–95. On the preliminaries to and passage of the 1945 Water Bill, see *KCA* (1943–6), pp. 6493A, 7205C.
305 I take these figures from H. M. Purdue, 'The Implications of the Constitution and Functions of Regional Water Authorities', *Public Law*, xxiv (1979), pp. 119–20. For details of the 1963 and 1973 Acts, see *KCA* (1963–4), p. 20317A (20323); ibid. (1973), pp. 25807A, 26060A.

authorities are multi-purpose being responsible for the management of the complete water cycle, not only for conservation and supply but also for sewerage and sewage disposal, reclamation and re-use, prevention of river pollution, land drainage, as well as fisheries and recreational use. The changes were clearly innovative in two important respects: the water industry ceased largely to be a direct responsibility of local government; and integrated bodies were established in place of the previously separate agencies.[306] The achievement of operational efficiency was obviously deemed more important than popular participation and control.[307] In the context of a rising demand for water there was obviously considerable doubt whether the local authorities would be able to achieve the level of management required, sustain the large investment that would be necessary, or overcome the conflicts of interest that had previously arisen. The new water authorities in England and Wales currently employ some 52,000 people, have a current expenditure of £1,950 millions a year, and an annual investment budget of about £825 millions.[308] In 1983 the previous supervisory body, the National Water Council, was replaced by a Water Authorities Association set up by the water regions which provides a forum for the authorities to discuss among themselves, and with the government and other bodies, matters of common concern. The WAA also co-ordinates any necessary joint action and provides press and public relations services. The traditional contact with local authorities is maintained in that the county and district councils in the region concerned appoint a majority of the members of each authority (the others including the chairman being nominated by the minister); at the same time it is true the areas are very large and not all the councils concerned are able to have members.[309] Obviously the water industry has some of the features of a nationalized monopoly and is now so regarded in official lists.[310] But in other respects it is more in the nature of a trading service of the kind provided jointly by local authorities.[311] The hybrid nature of these bodies was reflected in the fact that while they were open to investigation by the select committee on nationalized

306 A. G. Jordan et al., 'The Origins of the Water Act of 1973', *Public Administration*, lv (1977), p. 318.
307 ibid., pp. 320–3, 325–9 for the various prospects considered and the factors involved in reaching a decision. Cf. C. Gray, 'The Regional Water Authorities', in B. W. Hogwood and M. Keating (eds), *Regional Government in England* (Oxford, 1982), ch. 7 esp. pp. 146–8.
308 These details are taken from *Whitaker's Almanack* (1986), p. 622.
309 Purdue, art. cit., pp. 123–4, 142.
310 See e.g. Cabinet Office (MPO), *Public Bodies 1985* (London, 1985), pp. 28, 75; The Government's Expenditure Plans 1986–87 to 1988–89, 1985–6, Cmnd. 9702-II, pp. 371–4.
311 Report on Non-Departmental Public Bodies, 1979–80, Cmnd. 7797, Annex B3 p. 31 §1.

industries (now, of course, wound up) they also came under the jurisdiction of the local ombudsmen (as they still do). The service is clearly of great economic and social importance though questions necessarily arise about its performance and the extent and effectiveness of its accountability to the public it serves.[312] Further radical change impended given the government's intention to privatize the water authorities but this prospect appears now to have receded for the immediate future.[313]

PRIVATIZATION

...State ownership and control should be displaced or supplemented, wherever sensibly possible, by the discipline and pressures of the market place and by some degree of private ownership.
SIR G. HOWE, *Conservatism in the Eighties*, CPC no. 693, 1982, p.20

The attitudes and policies adopted by Conservatives are, like all political creeds, essentially ambivalent and there is certainly no incompatibility between their doctrine (or certain aspects of it) and the extension of state ownership and control in its many forms.[314] Even when critical of the nationalized sector many Conservatives have wanted not so much to eliminate it as to improve it, make it more efficient and accountable.[315] But equally an ideological set against state intervention has often been strongly in evidence; and over the past few years an emphasis of this sort has once more come to the fore. Since the time when Eden, Macmillan, and Butler were in the ascendant there has generally grown up a chorus of support for a policy of denationalization. Some of the cries have been pretty constant as with the ideas and activities of MPs like J. E. Powell and I. Gow or the propaganda of the Selsdon Group and Aims for Freedom and Enterprise. A couple of instances of this sort of view must here stand for many. In 1968 the case for a private enterprise telephone service was put in a CPC pamphlet as an example of a general view that no industry need be in the public sector. Ten years later T. Renton wrote for the press an article under the heading, 'Shareholders Bite Better than Westminster Watchdogs Bark'. He urged it was fundamental to diminish the relative size of the public sector and, wherever possible, to give 'a direct interest in the ownership of the nationalised industries back to the employees and the tax-payers themselves.' In effect the goal should be a

---

312 ibid., pp. 31–3 §§5–11. Some of the important issues are discussed in Purdue, art. cit.
313 See below p. 445.
314 For the general point about ideology, see *The Ideological Heritage* (London, 1983), ch. 1; and on the different modes of Conservatism, ibid., Part Three. Cf. *The Rise of Collectivism* (London, 1983), p.28.
315 See e.g. the Bow Group pamphlet by A. Lines, *Concerns of State* (London, 1961), p.5.

form of co-ownership, with the government, workers, the small investor, and the financial institutions (such as the pension funds) each owning a portion of the equity.[316]

These were unusually explicit recommendations. For it would, I think, be true to say that there was little detailed consideration (at least in the form of publicly available documents) about what might be involved in this sort of policy.[317] Of course there had been some precedents: for example the mid-1950s' episodes of removing road haulage and steel from state ownership, and similarly the disposal, some twenty years later, of Thomas Cook Ltd, a few other transport subsidiaries, and the state management districts.[318] There was, too, the Fulton report's emphasis on 'hiving off' to add some impetus to the theme perhaps.[319] Yet there were subsequently few specific commitments, only general promises to disengage the state from the nationalized industries.[320] After Mrs Thatcher became leader there was a party committee, chaired by N. Ridley, which (without going into much detail) did propose some candidates for denationalization; however the report was not published.[321] But the matter was hardly prominent up to 1979. However since then elaborate schemes of privatization (as it is often now called) have been developed, albeit it would seem without any consistent plan.[322] Of course this is an important aspect of that libertarian emphasis on private property and freedom from state control which has latterly become dominant once more in the Conservative Party and with which is coupled the realization that it is not necessary for the state to own

316 D. Alexander, *Dial ENTerprise 1971* (CPC no. 425; London, 1968); *Daily Telegraph* (24 February 1978), p. 16.
317 See above p. 386 for an interesting parallel relating to the absence in 1945 of prepared schemes for nationalization.
318 For details, consult *KCA* (1952–4, 1955–6), index *sub* 'United Kingdom': see 'Road Haulage' and 'Steel'; ibid. (1971–2), loc. cit., see 'Transport' and 'Licensed Premises'.
319 For the limited application of the 'hiving-off' process in the early 1970s, see C. Pollitt, *Manipulating the Machine: Changing the Pattern of Ministerial Departments, 1960–83* (London, 1984), pp. 101–4.
320 Conservative Central Office, *A Better Tomorrow* (London, n.d. [1970]), pp. 7, 13–14. For some other early stirrings, see C. Tugendhat, 'Defining a Role for the State', *Financial Times* (22 December 1970); Conservative Central Office, *The Right Approach: a Statement of Conservative Aims* (PY 5119; London, 1976), p. 33; N. Fowler, *The Right Track* (CPC no. 612; London, 1977); and I. Gow, *A Practical Approach to Denationalization* (Aims for Freedom and Enterprise; London, n.d. [1977?]).
321 It was, however, leaked to *The Economist*, 'Appomatox or Civil War?', (27 May 1978), pp. 21–2.
322 'Denationalization' is the older term dating back to the 1920s; while 'privatization' seems first to have been used as recently as 1959: see *OEDS*, i. 770–1, iii. 802. The latter is now the more commonly employed of the two words not least, perhaps, because it has acquired a wider connotation: see below pp. 433–7.

particular assets in order to see that services are provided to all who need them.[323] But there are in addition two specific sets of factors which have been not unimportant in the creation of the considerable (but perhaps insufficiently radical) programme at present under way. One concerns the relative failure of the government's economic and social policy in general and the difficulty in particular in achieving any reduction in public expenditure. Production has failed to take off; unemployment has risen inexorably; expenditure on social security, law and order, and defence has increased considerably. But by comparison privatization turned out to be, in some respects at least, easier to implement and thus seemed to offer the prospect of quick and tangible results. For example, if one object is to cut the Public Sector Borrowing Requirement, the process can obviously be much advanced (at least in the short term) by the sale of nationalized assets.[324] Moreover if a privatization policy is successful it should help reduce claims on public resources; though at least one commentator has suggested that the obstacles in the way of thus transferring some of the burden to the private sector appear 'in reality to be more difficult than rhetoric would suggest.'[325] The other factors relate to actual experience of the nationalized industries and the welfare state which entailed in many respects a saddening failure of expectancy. Exponents of nationalization had always believed that state ownership would result in numerous improvements and advantages: productivity and output would increase; full employment be achieved; better labour relations fostered; a sense of participation on the part of the work-force encouraged; economies of scale secured; lower prices and higher investment alike attained; social priorities and not just profit recognized; wastes like those of advertising eliminated; monopoly regulated; effective national planning made possible by control of the commanding heights of the economy; and so on and so forth. But such hopes had, as one Conservative commentary put it, 'been sadly tarnished by almost forty years' hard experience of the realities of nationalisation.'[326] The industries which had been taken into public ownership were

323 Cf. CPC, *Denationalisation* (Contact Brief, n.s., no. 29; London, 1984), pp. 3–4; idem, *Focus on State Monopolies* (Contact Brief, n.s., no. 8; London, 1984).
324 Interestingly this device was used by the Labour government in 1976 when it was announced that, in order to reduce the current borrowing requirement, it was proposed to sell part of the government's holding in BP: see *KCA* (1977), p. 28181A (28182).
325 M. O'Higgins, 'Rolling Back the Welfare State: the Rhetoric and Reality of Public Expenditure and Social Policy under the Conservative Government', in *The Year Book of Social Policy in Britain 1982. Thought, Rhetoric and Reality* (London, 1983), p. 175. Cf. ibid., pp. 173, 175–6.
326 R. Ehrman, 'Privatisation of the Nationalised Industries', *Politics Today* (no. 19, 28 November 1983), p. 347. For an extensive statement of the view in question, see J. Redwood, *Public Enterprise in Crisis: the Future of the Nationalised Industries*

undoubtedly crucial to the health of the economy in general; and, as if in token of this significance, they had received enormous amounts of state aid whether in the form of subsidies or the writing off of capital debt. Despite this their record had, on the whole, been rather unimpressive than otherwise, not to say depressing.[327] As one Conservative publication later put it: 'By 1979 it was clear that, far from being an engine for change and progress, the nationalised industries had become a heavy burden on the rest of the economy, and that their reform must be central to any strategy for overall economy recovery.'[328] Or, in the words of one now much involved in these matters, 'On balance, since the war the experience of...nationalisation teaches us that a corollary of public monopolies can easily be a declining standard of service, a rising relative price, and a growing volume of dissatisfaction amongst the public for whom the service was nationalised.'[329] Basically it was a question of the attitudes engendered. Sir M. Edwardes has recorded how (at British Leyland) incentives were diluted by the feeling of protection that government support created:

> Reality is blunted, the pain is reduced, the consequences of actions do not come screaming through; the strike that would kill off a private-sector company hardly makes a dent on Her Majesty's Treasury. When the new BL Board took over at the end of 1977 this feeling of invulnerability, of sheer complacency about the present and the future, permeated the company. There was a conviction at middle manager, staff, and shop floor level, that the Government would see the company through its vicissitudes.... This is why one seldom comes across a well run state-owned business.[330]

So to many Conservatives a hands-off attitude to the public sector was no longer possible. And a policy of privatization seemed an obvious way to deal with the inefficiency of the state-owned industries and curb the financial drain they entailed. As one recent Conservative pamphlet puts it:

(Oxford, 1980), esp. ch. 1: the bulk of this perceptive study is an industry by industry review of the experience of nationalization.

327 See above pp. 387–8, 391.

328 Ehrman, loc. cit., p. 348. The Conservative case is also summarized in CPC, *Denationalisation*, pp. 1–2; and T. Eggar *et al.*, *Reversing Clause IV: a Policy for Denationalisation* (CPC no. 714; London, 1984), p. 6. See also J. R. Shackleton, 'Privatization: the Case Examined', *National Westminster Bank Quarterly Review* (May 1984), pp. 60–4.

329 J. Redwood, *Public Enterprise in Crisis*, p. 5. Cf. idem, 'Government and the Nationalized Industries', *Lloyds' Bank Review* (April 1976), p. 39 and 'The Future of the Nationalized Industries', ibid. (October 1976), p. 40.

330 M. Edwardes, *Back from the Brink: an Apocalyptic Experience* (1983; Pan, 1984), p. 32.

> For more than thirty years successive governments have tried to find a way of managing the nationalised industries that will increase their efficiency, satisfy their customers and yield a return on the taxpayers investment.... Some of the ablest businessmen in the country have been put in charge of nationalised industries and they have tried. There have been any number of White Papers, cash limits, financial targets, required rates of return and cost objectives.... None, however, have [sic] succeeded. The fundamental problems, those of finance, of accountability and of monopoly remain, and they are all problems of ownership. The only sure way to improve the performance of the nationalised industries is to expose them to the normal commercial disciplines of competition and the introduction of private capital. Nobody has ever succeeded in finding a method of stimulating these pressures in the public sector, and the simplest and most effective way of introducing them is to transfer the nationalised industries, wherever possible, to the private sector. This is the purpose of privatisation.[331]

An official paper expressed it this way: 'The basic argument for privatisation is that the Government should not be involved in activities which the private sector could undertake just as well.' There are also practical benefits such as the improved and more economical service which will result from the introduction of competition.[332]

The same attitude is also applied to the paraphernalia of the welfare state. This broadly comprises three elements.[333] There are benefits in kind as with the provision of schools, health care, and personal social services (from social workers to home helps and meals on wheels). Secondly there are price subsidies to reduce the cost of such things as rents, public transport, home ownership, and house improvements. Then there is social security itself based on a system of income transfer from taxpayers to benefit recipients in the form of cash payments in respect (for instance) to sickness, unemployment, pensions of various sorts, and supplementary benefit. The criticisms levelled at these arrangements are of various sorts.[334] Thus it is urged that they encourage a wasteful use of resources: for instance, being universal in scope they provide benefits to many people who do not really need them. Also they damage the productive power of the economy because they often affect incentives to work or save, as in those cases where someone receiving benefit is

---

331 CPC, *Denationalisation*, p. 2.
332 Treasury and Civil Service, Sel. Cttee 3rd Rep., 1981–2, HC 236-II, Note by H. M. Treasury, p. 459 §29. Cf. the ministerial speech cited in *KCA* (1984), p. 32867A (32880).
333 I take this summary from J. Le Grand and R. Robinson (eds), *Privatisation and the Welfare State* (London, 1984), p. 2.
334 ibid., pp. 7–10, 20, 29, 48.

disinclined to seek employment because of the taxes he would incur or where, living in subsidized council housing, he finds it difficult to move. Moreover there is no real accountability for the very considerable sums spent which are often not used in a cost-effective way. And there are the suggestions that the service provided is often of poor quality or insensitive, that management is bad, and that there is substantial over-manning and similar deficiencies. As well consumer choice is too limited. Generally, the experience of public provision is unhappy, with waiting-lists for council houses or operations, queues at offices, red tape, and the like. And it is just too heavy a burden on the productive sector. The welfare state is said, in addition, to be illiberal:

> Individual preferences for diverse services are overruled; the taxation necessary to fund the welfare state's activities is coercive; recipients of welfare benefits have to conform to specific regulations and conditions; the welfare state creates a psychological condition of 'dependence', thus reducing people's ability to make their own choices; producers' interests predominate at the expense of consumers' liberties.

And to this must be added the general concern about the growth of state power involved.[335]

But what exactly does a policy of privatization mean or entail when applied to such areas of state ownership or provision? In fact it is not one thing but covers a range of objectives and methods though these may in practice be mixed up.

The key purpose must be to benefit the consumer by liberalizing the economy through the promotion of competition, creating rivalry between different firms and units, and giving freedom to enter a previously protected market. For instance a statutory monopoly or licensing system may be relaxed; or private provision may be encouraged as in the field of medical services or hospitals so as to provide an alternative to the NHS. Other examples are the degree of competition which has already been allowed in respect of long-distance bus services and the provision of telephone equipment. In respect of the former, for instance, it has undoubtedly been the case that deregulation has generated substantial benefits in the form of improved services and the like (and this without any transfer of ownership or fundamental change in the position of National Express).[336] While, since the Local Government, Planning, and Land Act of 1980 (c. 65), local authorities

---

335 ibid., p. 12.
336 E. Davis, 'Express Coaching since 1980: Liberalisation in Practice', *Fiscal Studies*, v (no. 1, February 1984), esp. pp. 77–8, 83, 86. On the possibility of further deregulation, as by freeing access to terminals, ibid., pp. 84–5.

have been obliged to run their direct labour organizations as separate trading bodies in competition with private firms.[337] The exposure of the public sector to the discipline of market forces in these ways will, it is urged, improve the allocation of resources, lower costs and prices, increase the efficiency and quality of production or service, and enhance variety of choice for the consumer. The economy as a whole will benefit from improvement in the essential areas concerned. In such terms the Competition Act of 1980 strengthened the prospects of preventing and eliminating anti-competitive practices in either the public or the private sector.[338]

A related objective is that, where, for one reason or another, a nationalized monopoly remains, or where a transfer of assets leaves the private company created in a monopoly position, then restrictive practices have to be prevented, fair trading secured, and optimum efficiency achieved.[339] Prices should be controlled as by explicit tariff restrictions and a limit placed on profits earned (perhaps expressed as a rate of return on capital). If there is any cross-subsidy it ought clearly to be shown up and acknowledged so that true costs are revealed; similarly if a particular service or item is subsidized for social reasons this should be equally open and specific. If management is to be improved it must be possible to recruit and pay suitable chief executives. Strategic objectives need to be agreed with an incoming chairman: perhaps his remuneration might be judged by performance measured against these goals. And detailed targets need to be established and regularly monitored as by efficiency or value for money audits. Businesses which consider they suffer from unfair competition with a nationalized enterprise, as by price discrimination or refusal of supply, should be able to sue in the courts or complain as of right directly to the Office of Fair Trading. Stronger powers of regulation are needed; and there should be more opportunities to refer a complaint to the Monopolies and Mergers Commission wherever a *prima facie* case exists. As well the MMC should be required to examine every five years the extent of monopoly in the remaining nationalized industries and advise how it may be reduced.[340] It may also

---

337 For the latest proposals, see *KCA* (1985), p. 33672A (33677–8).
338 ibid., (1980), p. 30476A.
339 Many of these matters are critically discussed by M. Beesley and S. Littlechild, 'Privatisation: Principles, Problems and Priorities', *Lloyd's Bank Review* (July 1983), esp. pp. 6–7; see also Eggar *et al.*, op. cit., pp. 11–12, 14–15.
340 Eggar *et al.*, op. cit., p. 11. For a review of the position in the public sector after the 1980 Competition Act, see J. Redwood and J. Hatch, *Controlling Public Industries* (Oxford, 1982), pp. 140–52; also P. R. Ferguson, 'The Monopolies and Mergers Commission and Economic Theory', *National Westminster Branch Quarterly Review* (November 1985), pp. 39–40. And on the development of monopolies and restrictive practices policy since 1948, see the summary in J. A. Kay and Z. A.

be possible to take steps to improve the organization of a public industry or service. Decentralization may have advantages with greater autonomy being given to, say, regional units or some more manageable component part.[341] There would not perhaps be any direct competition arising but at least comparisons would be possible – of performance, costs, and manpower, for example – with, hopefully, a stimulating effect on the laggards or an indication where changed practices or new management should be sought. As has been suggested in the case of British Steel, the benefits of more autonomous management of this kind could well outweigh the loss of limited large-scale economies.[342] At the same time none of this can be a substitute for opening monopoly to genuine competition, for which in fact there may be more opportunities than sometimes supposed.[343]

A third objective – and the one which has so far bulked largest in the policy of the Thatcher governments – is the reduction of the public sector by the transfer of assets to private ownership. This involves one or more of three prospects. First, in the case of a nationalized industry, a successor company is created under the Companies Acts; though of course where the government holds an interest in an already existing limited company (as with BL or Rolls Royce) no such conversion is necessary. The intention then is to float some or all of the equity on the stock market, the main question being whether the firm is generating enough profit to be sold to the public on satisfactory terms. Secondly it is possible to sell off certain assets or subsidiaries only, as with Jaguar cars in the case of BL or the hotels and Sealink in the case of British Rail. Thirdly the introduction of private capital may be encouraged through joint ventures with one or more firms from the private sector as in the case of the Nissan involvement with BL. Of course, the sale of public assets as such will not necessarily increase competition: a monopoly may remain albeit in private hands. And many problems are involved concerning the timing of the sale, the structure of the successor enterprise, whether any public shareholding should be retained, how non-commercial obligations will

---

Silbertson, 'The New Industrial Policy – Privisation and Competition', *Midland Bank Review* (Spring 1984), pp. 11–14.

341 The advantages of decentralization and substantial regional autonomy were realized during the post-war discussions about the organization of the nationalized industries, as in a draft Economic Section paper at PRO, T230/106, 'Problems and Principles of Socialisation', E.C. (S)(45) 36 (25 October 1946), pp. 9–10 §§28–32.
342 Eggar *et al.*, op. cit., p. 23. For similar possibilities in the electricity supply industry, ibid., p. 21.
343 For some examples, see S. Brittan, 'The Politics and Economics of Privatisation', *Political Quarterly*, lv (1984), pp. 116–20; also R. Miller, 'Denationalising British Telecom: One Step in the Right Direction', *Journal of Economic Affairs*, iii (1982–3), pp. 56–8.

be met, what sort of supervision might be required, and so forth.[344] From the Conservative point of view some advance towards this third general objective may be thought desirable not least for ideological reasons to do with the superiority of private property and the diminishing of the state. As well there will no longer be such easy and privileged access to public money and, if new capital is required, the responsibility for raising it will fall, not on the government, but on the management and shareholders. The burden on the Exchequer will be lightened, too, and the taxpayer advantaged both by the receipt of the capital sum from the sale and from increased tax revenue if the business prospers; and inflationary pressure is relieved because the PSBR is reduced. Managers will be less open to government direction or influence, able to act more flexibly, to respond to demand rather than to short-term political pressure. Moreover the full-scale stockmarket flotation of a nationalized industry or service provides an opportunity to encourage the creation of a large number of small shareholders. Employees in particular could be given a preferential opportunity to acquire an interest.[345] This closer involvement of the work-force should also have a good effect on industrial relations. In this connexion one last (but certainly not the least) advantage to be anticipated is that the strength of the trade unions concerned would be reduced thus ameliorating the problem of public sector pay and, indirectly, reducing the inflationary pressure hitherto often released in this regard. Even if public assets are not immediately saleable (because they do not seem commercially profitable) it might be worthwhile to let the industry or service go bankbrupt so that, at a written-down value, they could attract a buyer. Or they could simply be given away in whole or in part, with a suitable dowry perhaps, to the existing work-force or the public at large.[346]

Fourthly there are a series of other possibilities. One is to shed work from the public sector by contracting out a given service to a private agent: as for instance with laundry work in hospitals, school cleaning, refuse disposal, or as with the Ministry of Defence's refitting ships in

---

[344] For discussion of the modes of disposal and the problems involved in share sales, see R. Buckland and E. W. Davis, 'Privatisation Techniques and the PSBR', *Fiscal Studies*, v (no. 3, August 1984), pp. 44–53. Sale of assets has invariably resulted in companies reflecting both public and private ownership: for a review of the issues arising in respect of the relationship between such a hybrid and the government, see D. Steel, 'Government and the New Hybrids: a Trail of Unanswered Questions', ibid. (no. 1, February 1984), pp. 87–97.

[345] Ehrman, loc. cit., p. 352 gives details of employee share ownership to 1983. Cf. the more critical view in Shackleton, art. cit., pp. 66–7.

[346] Brittan, art. cit., pp. 121–5. Cf. M. Friedman, *From Galbraith to Economic Freedom* (IEA Occasional Paper no. 49, 1977; London, 1978), p. 53.

commercial yards or moving army freight by commercial planes.[347] In effect government is buying a good or service in a market (the competitiveness of which varies according to the circumstances); and in fact public procurement of this sort is a widespread and long-standing practice.[348] Another device is to reduce the existing level of provision (as by cutting back school meals) or to abolish it altogether handing it over perhaps to private or voluntary organizations (as with certain training services). Financial arrangements may also be altered with a view to throwing more of the cost on to the consumer. This is done by the reduction or elimination of a subsidy; or by the introduction of a charge (as for prescriptions or dental treatment in the NHS). A further possibility is to encourage the investment of private capital as with proposals to build new roads in this way.[349]

Naturally in practice the emphasis of policy will vary between these purposes and methods, as is clearly shown by the Conservative record over the last six years. It has to be acknowledged that the government's first legislative achievement in this regard is quite considerable; though the implementation of some at least of its plans has been slower than intended: certain sales have been delayed because of the poor financial health of the enterprises concerned. Moreover the government has often acted so as to suggest that the transfer of assets to private hands is in itself enough, seeming to forget it should be just a first stage in the more fundamental process of economic liberalization: there is in this respect still a very long way to go. However, something of what has been achieved or is immediately in prospect will now be reviewed in regard to the major areas of public activity and interest concerned.[350]

The nationalized industries

In 1979 the Conservative election manifesto promised to oppose any further Labour proposals 'to nationalize yet more firms and industries such as building, banking, insurance, pharmaceuticals and road haulage'

---

347 For a detailed study of the practical issues involved, see J. T. Marlin, *Contracting Muncipal Services: a Guide for Purchase from the Private Sector* (New York, 1984). The process of contracting out is very highly developed in Japan where it even covers tax collection: see idem, *Privatisation of Local Government Activities: Lessons from Japan* (Aims of Industry; London, 1982).
348 Cf. K. Hartley, 'Policy Towards Contracting-Out: the Lessons of Experience', *Fiscal Studies*, v (no. 1, February 1984), pp. 98–105.
349 See e.g. two publications of the Adam Smith Institute: E. Butler (ed.), *Roads and the Private Sector* (London, 1982) and G. Roth and E. Butler, *Private Road Ahead* (London, 1982).
350 See the summary in Appendix 2, p. 512 below; also a statement of the proceeds of privatization between 1979 and 1985 in Appendix 3, pp. 526 below.

and to do this on the ground that 'More nationalization would further impoverish us and further undermine our freedom.' In fact the current Labour Party programme was notably free of such specific plans though these had undoubtedly been mooted and received substantial support. The Conservatives further promised to 'offer to sell back to private ownership the recently nationalized aerospace and shipbuilding concerns, giving their employees the opportunity to purchase shares.' The party also aimed to sell shares in the National Freight Corporation so as to secure substantial private investment in it. It was proposed, too, to make it easier for private operators in the development of bus and other services. There was also to be a complete review of all the activities of the British National Oil Corporation. For their part the Liberals agreed there was no case for further large-scale nationalization but believed that at present attempts to undo the existing arrangements would merely disrupt the industries affected: that is to say, the present frontier between the public and private sectors should largely remain intact.[351]

Once in office the Conservatives set about their task. The Queen's Speech on 15 May 1979 referred to proposals to 'reduce the extent of nationalized and state ownership' and to 'increase competition by providing offers of sale, including opportunities for employees to participate where appropriate.'[352] This was followed before the summer recess by announcements of detailed proposals affecting British Airways, British Aerospace, BNOC, and the National Freight Corporation.[353] And the intention to continue with the process of transferring state-owned businesses to independent ownership and to expose them to more competition was further clearly signalled in the subsequent election programme of 1983.[354] To help speed the programme and make it more effective a Minister of State at the Treasury was given a specific brief to oversee privatization and thus co-ordinate policy towards the nationalized industries.

It would be tedious to list in the text all the detail of these and subsequent developments so they indicated in Appendix 2.[355] Here some salient points and issues only will be charted.

The measures intended to promote competition in or with the public

351 For these manifestos, see *KCA* (1979), p. 29629A. For later signs from the Alliance of a more favourable view of privatization, see the sources cited in Ehrman, loc. cit., p. 351.
352 *KCA* (1979), p. 29705A.
353 ibid., p. 29821A (29832).
354 ibid. (1983), p. 32200A (32203). For the contrasting Labour emphasis, ibid., p. 32207; and for the Alliance view, p. 32213. For the subsequent Queen's Speech, see ibid., p. 32262A (32268).
355 See below, pp. 512–25.

sector constitute, inevitably perhaps, a rather miscellaneous collection of changes either actually implemented or intended. They range from allowing competition with express buses and in certain trial areas to opening up an important part of British Telecom's operations. In respect to the latter a Conservative Party account claimed that the

> very important market for equipment has been liberalised. A general licence has been issued for the provision of value-added network services, such as viewdata, telephone conferences and electronic mail, and a large number of companies now provide these. A rival network, Mercury, has been set up to provide services for business. Two new radio telephone systems are also being set up.

The assumption is that the pace of technological change in this field is now so swift that 'competition will develop much sooner than many critics seem to suppose.'[356] Other experiments of a similar kind have been introduced into the fields occupied by the Post Office, the Electricity Council and its area boards, civil aviation, and other public industries.[357]

So far as actual transfers of ownership have been concerned the problems have not been slight.[358] For instance there are many questions which have to be settled after a decision is made to proceed and which affect the sponsoring department, the Cabinet Office, the Bank of England, the merchant bankers, accountants, solicitors, and others involved as professional advisers, as well as the management of the nationalized industry concerned; while in all these preliminaries the Treasury has usually acted as co-ordinator.[359] The sort of issues that arise are obvious given that more than a change in legal form is involved. The business might have to be reorganized to bring its management system and accounts into the form required by commercial law and practice. Perhaps the regulatory, strategic, or public service functions have to be separated from those operations appropriate to a private company. In addition the obligations of the industry to its employees and pensioners, creditors, customers, and suppliers have to be sorted out. Beyond all this, of course, the details have to be settled of the manner and timing of the sale of stock on the open market or its disposal in some other way. Then there is the problem of Parliamentary time. The nationalized industries were established by statute and legislation is required to alter their status; and of course any Bill has to compete for a place in a crowded timetable.

---

356 Ehrman, loc. cit., p. 355.
357 For details, see Appendix 2 cols 3 and 10.
358 For much of what follows, see C. Pickering, 'The Mechanics of Disposal', in D. Steel and D. Heald (eds), *Privatizing Public Enterprises* (London, 1984), ch. 3; Redwood and Hatch, op. cit., ch. 7; also Ehrman, loc. cit., p. 353.
359 Pickering, loc. cit., pp. 45–50.

The actual process of denationalization has assumed a broadly common pattern. An Act of Parliament is passed to transfer the assets and liabilities of the public corporation to the appropriate Secretary of State who then sets up a successor company under the Companies Acts though a good deal is left to be settled administratively.[360] The intention is then to sell off a given percentage of the equity in one or more phases with the employees having the opportunity to acquire an interest on preferential terms.[361] The government secures its own position by divers means: retaining a part of the equity (usually just less than 50 per cent so that the enterprise can be excluded from PSBR calculations); appointing one or more directors; or holding a 'special rights' share entitling it to intervene in a decisive fashion if a pattern of shareholding incompatible with the public interest should appear as, for instance, if foreign stockholders threatened to gain control of an enterprise important on defence or security grounds. The same sort of consideration could also apply where an industry plays a significant part in the national economy. Various personnel and pension issues have also to be settled at some stage.[362]

The nationalized industries so far affected by the privatization policy fall into three categories.[363]

The first group consists of those enterprises which compete in the open market and which are (or may be made) profitable. They are the easiest to deal with both because they do not present the problems of the monopolies and because, as they make money, there is little difficulty in finding buyers. These are the enterprises deemed ripe for rapid denationalization. The assumption is that once in the private sector they should be able to diversify and expand. One example is the National Freight Corporation. This had been set up in 1968 and had interests ranging from road haulage to removals, cold storage to package holidays, waste disposal to parcel delivery. Among its fifty or so subsidiaries were British Road Services, National Carriers Ltd, Roadline, and Pickfords. The NFC accounted for about 8 per cent of road haulage traffic. It was abolished by the Transport Act (1980) and the successor company later sold to a consortium with major bank support and on which the employees and pensioners had a majority shareholding. The Secretary of State for Trade claimed that, with this sale,

> a major road haulage company is transferred in good running order to the private sector where it belongs. The managers and employees

---

360 For variations in the Acts, see Pickering, loc. cit., pp. 51–2.
361 On the financial issues involved, ibid., pp. 53–5.
362 ibid., pp. 56–7, 66–7. For the attitude of the public sector trade unions and the limited nature of their opposition to government policy, see D. Thomas, 'The Union Response to Denationalization', in Steel and Heald (eds), op. cit., ch. 4.
363 Cf. Ehrman, loc. cit., pp. 353–4.

acquire a business which they are confident they can run successfully and competitively, entirely free from government control and no longer dependent in any way on public finance.[364]

Other saleable enterprises which may be seen as belonging to this first group include British Aerospace, British Airways, BNOC, the British Transport Docks Board, Cable and Wireless, the National Bus Company, and various subsidiary undertakings.

The second group consists of those industries which compete in the open market but without making a profit. The very existence of such national enterprises would probably have surprised earlier proponents of nationalization who assumed that industries taken over by the state would become models of commercial and technical efficiency. The continual grant of subsidies to substantial loss-makers, the assumption indeed that these grants are a right and proper due, was far from envisaged. Herbert Morrison wrote of the LPTB that a state financial guarantee would have encouraged 'a dangerous frame of mind', 'a spirit of slackness, or even recklessness on the part of the Board in matters of management, on the part of the travelling public in demanding lower fares and uneconomic facilities, and on the part of the work people in asking for big concessions as to conditions of labour', notably (one should add) in respect of wages unjustified by market conditions. Neither the industry nor its workers nor its customers must 'be tempted to say "Well, after all, the Treasury is behind us."'[365] In this mood the nationalized industries created after 1945 were expected to cover their costs and break even over a reasonable period: 'taking one year with another' was a phrase often used in this context. In fact vast sums of public money have had to be poured into the industries for various reasons: because of compensation terms that proved onerous, the need for re-equipment, the desire to prevent job losses, to serve some social purpose deemed worthwhile, and so on. Not to put too fine a point on it, some of these businesses are in the public sector *because* they are not commercially viable. The significance of this in the present context is that a history of loss-making which is severe and continuous makes a normal sale difficult if not impossible. Of course, if it is simply a temporary feature of the enterprise's operation due, say, to the effects of recession, then it is necessary for the government to see that the management rationalize the business to make it viable again, and so saleable. Alternatively it may be sold as a loss-making concern and its new owners left to turn it round if they can. Mr Ehrman suggests that the root of the

---

364 KCA (1980), p. 30481A; ibid. (1982), pp. 31289A, 31490A.
365 H. Morrison, *Socialisation and Transport: the Organisation of Socialised Industries with Particular Reference to the London Passenger Transport Bill* (London, 1933), p. 272.

problem is that often, when an industry was nationalized, a conglomerate was formed out of a disparate collection of companies; or there may be fringe businesses not central to the main activity. He goes on to say – undoubtedly in echo of the official Conservative view – that, in any case, as an industry is restored to financial health, some of its operations will be bound to recover before others and these should be sold off if possible before they become unprofitable by being starved of new investment; or they could perhaps be sustained by a joint operation with a private company. He continues:

> In this way the viable parts of an industry are not forced to subsidise loss-making operations with which they may have only a tenuous connection. Instead, their profits can become the basis for investment and expansion in the private sector, and the urgency of improving the loss-making parts is no longer obscured by cross-subsidy. So far, subsidiaries of BL, British Steel, British Airways and British Rail have been moved to the private sector in this way, and the Conservatives made clear in their 1983 General Election Manifesto that they expect to be able to accelerate this process during their second term.[366]

The sale of British Shipbuilders' interests illustrates this latest phase as do proposals to dispose of Post Office Crown Offices or the National Coal Board's open-cast pits.[367] However in all such cases a rump of the business – perhaps a very large fragment indeed – would remain in public ownership after the saleable parts have gone. Dealing with this has features similar to those cases that fall in the third category of national enterprises.

This group consists of the industries or services which do not compete and which often have to be subsidized because of the crucial nature of their activity or the social consequences of their deterioration. Genuine competition would be a real protection for the consumer and must be the first objective. But its introduction is not always possible or easy and, where this is the case, the public must be protected by some form of regulation of the 'natural' monopolies which may remain. 'The Government has, therefore, concentrated on hastening the introduction of competition and finding ways of devising a regulatory framework which will be effective without being unduly complicated and restrictive.'[368] British Telecom is a test case which illustrates the application of these principles: 'the first attempt to return a major British public utility to the private sector.'[369] In 1981 the Post Office was divided into two separate corporations: one to run the postal services (which

---

366 Ehrman, loc. cit., p. 354.
367 Cf. Eggar *et al.*, op. cit., pp. 23–4, 26.
368 Ehrman, loc. cit., p. 354. Cf. Eggar *et al.*, op. cit., pp. 10–12.
369 R. Miller, 'Denationalising British Telecom', art. cit., p. 56.

The Public Concern – and Beyond

were to be open to a certain element of competition in the carriage of high-speed mail); the other to look after the telecommunications and data-processing business. Two years later legislation authorized the eventual transfer of BT to the private sector and a major sale of half the equity took place late in 1984.[370] Where BT retains a monopoly for the time being it is subject to regulation and a price régime – the Local Tariff Reduction Scheme – that (it is hoped) will ensure a fall in the real cost of most services. This framework is incorporated in the licence under which it operates. There is also an obligation to maintain the kiosk and emergency telephone services and the rural network, even though losses may be involved. There is a new authority, a non-ministerial department called the Office of Telecommunications, to supervise this regulatory framework and promote effective competition where possible. It also has statutory powers to enforce the remedies it decides for consumer complaints. Thus privatized British Telecom is more open to competition and more clearly and effectively regulated than any of the remaining public monopolies.[371] There are various areas where competition is already, or may be, feasible, such as terminal equipment and call connexion.[372]

None of the other monopolies (except British Gas) has yet been prepared for privatization though the present government (1986) is in principle pledged to increase competition in, and attract private capital into, these industries wherever feasible. More might be achieved than is often regarded as possible. So far as electricity is concerned, for instance, the production side or the sale of appliances might be opened to competition.[373] The Energy Act (1983) already provides *inter alia* for the encouragement of the private generation of electricty.[374] Nor is there any reason why the National Coal Board's present monopoly should or need continue.[375] The case put suggests that investment funds should not be

---

370 KCA (1984), p. 32867A (32879); ibid. (1985), p. 33672A. There is a detailed account in M. E. Beesley, 'The Liberalisation of British Telecom', *Journal of Economic Affairs*, ii (1981–2), pp. 19–27; and in J. Kay, 'The Privatization of British Telecommunications', in Steel and Heald (eds), *Privatizing Public Enterprises*, ch. 5. For criticism of the scheme, see Miller, art. cit., pp. 56–8.
371 Cf. Ehrman, loc. cit., p. 355; Eggar *et al.*, op. cit., pp. 12–13.
372 See Kay, loc. cit., pp. 80–1. For the conflict of considerations between liberalization and ownership transfer, ibid., pp. 81–4; and on the deficiencies of regulation and the need for extended and intensified competition, see C. England, 'Competition for Telephones', *Economic Affairs*, v (1984–5), no. 1, pp. 23–6.
373 Ehrman, loc. cit., p. 355; Eggar *et al.*, op. cit., p. 21.
374 KCA (1983), p. 32222A (32226).
375 Cf. Eggar *et al.*, op. cit., pp. 25–6; S. C. Littlechild, 'Ten Steps to Denationalisation', *Journal of Economic Affairs*, ii (1981–2), p. 17. For a range of suggestions by one Conservative MP, see P. Rost, 'Pits, Privatisation and Politics', *Economic Affairs*, v (1984–5), no. 4, pp. 39–40. However the Energy Secretary has stated that the

used to prolong the life of mines that cannot pay their way. Profit and performance targets should be established for each pit or mining area and failure to reach them lead to automatic review. Those that are uneconomic should be sold, being first offered to the miners on favourable terms; as in due course should the profitable pits also. So far as BR is concerned Professor Littlechild has interestingly suggested that, after all the non-rail enterprises have been sold, separate subsidiaries for parcels and freight should be formed with a view to selling majority shareholdings in each. Then the whole rail network should be divided into two, BR (Intercity) and the Social Railway. The intention would be that the former would be a purely commercial organization ultimately to be privately owned; the latter would be publicly owned and partly financed by subsidies for the provision of specified uneconomic services.[376] Franchising of some kind is another possibility. Thus the state might continue to manage the infrastructure of an industry, say the railway track, stations, and signalling, while licensing competitive services to operate on them (a considerable extension of the precedent provided by the use of non-BR freight trucks or the Victoria–Venice service for the luxury market).[377] Again certain services offered to rail passengers (such as station management or catering) could be more economical or efficient if hived off. In addition or alternatively the infrastructure itself could be leased on a franchise which would periodically have to be retendered. This might apply also to the electricity power lines and gas pipelines.[378] Again where competition is unlikely, monopolies could be encouraged to contract out services to the private sector.[379] Beyond this regulation is important and, as already indicated, steps could be taken to improve the degree and level of supervision.[380]

The position in respect of the nationalized industries (as well as other aspects of government involvement) as it has developed since 1979 is indicated in Appendix 2.

Other aspects

As state ownership extends beyond the nationalized industries, so privatization policy must be seen in a wider context than denation-

---

government is not seriously considering privatization of the coal industry, 54 H.C. Deb. 6s., 20 February 1984, col. 550.

376 Littlechild, art. cit., p. 17. For similar suggestions relating to other nationalized industries, ibid. Cf. Beesley and Littlechild, art. cit., pp. 9–17.

377 As suggested e.g. by D. Starkie, 'BR...Privatisation without Tears', *Economic Affairs*, v (1984–5), no. 1, pp. 16–19.

378 Ehrman, loc. cit., p. 356; Eggar *et al.*, op. cit., p. 21.

379 Eggar *et al.*, op. cit., p. 11.

380 See above pp. 434–5.

alization of various kinds so far described. It must, that is, also embrace selling off government shareholdings (whether the investment is direct or undertaken via a body like the NEB) as well as other assets like forestry land and exploration licences, and transferring central government trading bodies to the private sector as proposed with the Royal Ordnance Factories. The main items so far disposed of in this way are also shown in Appendix 2 together with some indication of future plans. There are certain other aspects of privatization policy which are also indicated in the Appendix but, in addition, deserve special mention here.

Regional and local services
A number of these utilities or services, from airports to leisure centres, have been considered for partial or full transfer from the public domain.

The water industry is one such case. There is no reason why certain aspects of the work should not be contracted out to the private sector; and none why a proper regulatory framework should not be established with regard, for instance, to investment and pricing policy, with reference to the Monopolies Commission as a final sanction. Similarly local wage negotiation needs to be encouraged to avoid the possibility of a national breakdown of service. However, although proposals for privatization were announced early in 1986, these were later rescinded and the issue has, in effect, been held over until after the next general election.[381] Another important example is the field of housing policy, a major aspect of which in the period since the Great War has been the activity of government, both central and local, in creating working-class housing estates.[382] The privatization of this vast public housing domain is, in one respect, simply part of the process of reducing the size of the state sector as such and its cost and, in another, an outcome of the realization that existing arrangements constitute a barrier to labour mobility.[383] The role of the state has latterly been shifted in favour of the private sector in two respects: the 'production' of houses and their 'consumption'.[384] So far as the former is concerned the object is to reduce the role of local authorities as by restricting their investment in new building and, through cutting subsidies and raising rents, to enhance the relative attractiveness of private accommodation. As well emphasis has been placed on restricting the role of local authority direct labour

---

381 For the original proposals, see *KCA* (1986), p. 34319A (34322).
382 See *The Rise of Collectivism* (London, 1983), pp. 99–100.
383 Cf. R. M. Kirwan, 'The Demise of Public Housing?', in Le Grand and Robinson (eds), op. cit., p. 134.
384 I take this distinction from J. Dale, 'Privatisation and Politics: a Case Study of Housing', in C. Jones and J. Stevenson (eds), *The Year Book of Social Policy in Britain 1983* (London, 1984), p. 77.

organizations both in the building and maintenance of council housing.[385] Under the latter head of 'consumption' the thrust of government policy has been to encourage owner-occupation in various ways.[386] The most widely publicized aspect of this intention is the sale of council houses. Since the passage of the Housing Act (1980) over half a million council houses and flats – something like 10 per cent of the total stock – have been sold to tenants raising over £6,000 millions for the local authorities concerned and increasing the owner-occupied share of the market from 54.6 to 60.2 per cent between December 1979 and December 1983.[387] The policy seems popular (especially with the better-off tenants) as the average discount from the level of market prices has been high and there is a right to a mortgage.[388] Beyond this the reasons for adopting the policy seem fairly clear.[389] It is almost certainly advantageous electorally; it helps reduce public expenditure; generally Conservatives favour owner-occupation; and it is easy because there is a clear unit of sale. As well housing has never been fully recognized as a public service in the way that, say, education has. Possibly the main problem to have arisen so far in pursuing this policy has been the resistance of certain local authorities resulting in a considerable variation in sales from one area to another; but there is also the problem of mortgage default which appears to be increasing and which may limit the prospects of continuing sales.[390] None the less at least one observer has wondered 'whether the conception of a directly subsidised supply of family housing, owned and managed by local authorities, is likely to survive to the end of the century.'[391]

A further important possibility is that of reducing the cost of local services by contracting them out on tender to private operators. Obvious examples are street and office cleaning, care of parks and gardens, catering, vehicle maintenance, and refuse collection: there is the famous case of Southend which introduced private contractors for the last mentioned service and cut its cost to the council dramatically in the first year of operation. However, as commentators have observed, there are

---

385 ibid., pp. 77–9.
386 ibid., p. 80, Cf. C. M. E. Whitehead, 'Privatisation and Housing', in Le Grand and Robinson (eds), op. cit., pp. 127–8, 130–2; and Kirwan, loc. cit., p. 134.
387 Shackleton, art. cit., pp. 68, 72; J. Doling et al., 'How Far Can Privatization Go? Owner-Occupation and Mortgage Default', *National Westminster Bank Quarterly Review* (August 1983), p. 42.
388 Dale, loc. cit., pp. 81–2.
389 See G. Boyne, 'The Privatisation of Public Housing', *Political Quarterly*, lv (1984), pp. 180–4.
390 Kirwan, loc. cit., pp. 134–5; Boyne, art. cit., pp. 185–6; Doling et al., art. cit., pp. 44–51.
391 Kirwan, loc. cit., p. 133. For the difficulties envisaged, ibid., pp. 136–9, 144–5.

risks and problems involved.[392] For one thing there is obviously some danger of corruption in the award of valuable contracts of this kind. But more basically there is the point that, though there may be competition in the tendering, what is thereby established is simply a private monopoly. And, while it may be more efficient or cheap than the previous publicly provided service, it is certainly not to be equated with the introduction of market forces in the continuing provision of the service. The facility is likely to be cast in the conventional mould of a blanket service with no flexibility or consumer choice about, say, the frequency or volume of collection. There will be little incentive to operate it in a responsive and optimum way, to take advantage of new technology for instance, or to introduce new features. In this sense 'Claims by privatisation advocates to be restoring consumer sovereignty are unfounded.'[393] What they want to do is simply take over a state service paid for out of taxation and to provide it more effectively. They do not seem to question whether the state should be involved so substantively in this sort of responsibility at all. Why should it not simply lay down a basic framework with rules, say, governing the safety of the vehicles concerned and, for the rest – price and frequency of service and so forth – leave it to the consumer to decide or negotiate? Another prospect is that of charging or of introducing a voucher system for a wider range of local government services.[394] The field of education has been particularly considered in this regard.[395] The replacement of 'free' schooling by some kind of voucher system is one possibility making feasible a greater choice of school, more parental involvement, and even the possibility of contracting out of the state system with the vouchers provided, so encouraging the private sector.[396] The Conservative government considered one such scheme in 1982 but then dropped the idea because of the many problems involved not least that public expenditure would have been increased.[397] However it now appears there may be a more specific and firm commitment to this policy.

392 Cf. Shackleton, art. cit., pp. 69–70; J. Blundell, 'Privatisation Is Not Enough', *Journal of Economic Affairs*, iii (1982–3), pp. 184–7.
393 Blundell, art. cit., p. 186.
394 For a, rather sceptical, review of the possibilities, see A. R. Prest, 'On Charging for Local Government Services', *Three Banks Review* (March 1982), pp. 3–23. But see also the more optimistic view of M. Spungin, 'Local Government Shirks Charging', *Economic Affairs*, v (1984–5), no. 3, pp. 25–8.
395 For the following proposals, see Howe, op. cit., p. 23.
396 An excellent recent discussion is M. Blaug, 'Education Vouchers – It All Depends on What You Mean', in Le Grand and Robinson (eds), op. cit., ch. 11. See also the two contrasting views presented in the *County Councils Gazette*, lxxv (1982–3), pp. 375–7.
397 Blaug, loc. cit., pp. 165, 175–6. Cf. the more optimistic discussion in A. Peacock, 'Educational Voucher Schemes – Strong or Weak', *Journal of Economic Affairs*, iii (1982–3), pp. 113–16.

There might, too, be more encouragement of community participation in the financing and management of schools. Another aspect is the replacement of the system of student grants, a change surely long overdue?

Welfare provision
Over the years, and especially since the last war, there has been a considerable expansion in the social services and expenditure on them has grown steadily.[398] A comprehensive and universal welfare state has thus been created: a major aspect of collectivist development. But latterly there has been a certain reaction away from automatic acceptance of this tendency. As two teachers of social administration recently opined,

> Whatever one's political persuasion, it is difficult for any student of social policy in 1983 to avoid feeling disillusioned and disappointed with a [welfare] system of which so much was expected and from which so little of beneficial and permanent social achievement has apparently emerged. An atmosphere of gloom pervades the subject.[399]

This critical wave has not involved a denial of the community's duty to care for its poor and needy citizens as such but has questioned rather the means by which this purpose has been pursued: the idea of the 'welfare society' has perhaps challenged acceptance of the 'welfare state'. The whole issue has arisen partly as an aspect of trying to secure control of public expenditure during the recession of the 1980s; partly from a feeling that state provision was not always most effective or economical in its allocation of resources being universal and too little selective, and too arbitrary. Partly, too, there is the belief that the role of the state in this (as in other) respects ought to be diminished so as to make possible a greater role for voluntary action and self-help.[400] As well there ought to be more choice for the individual who should be, to a much lesser degree than he is, the passive recipient of state doles and services supposedly 'free' but for which in fact he pays heavily.[401] Nor are the implications of an ageing population for social service costs unimportant in this regard.

---

398 Cf. *The Rise of Collectivism* (London, 1983), p. 34 esp. Table 2.
399 C. Jones and J. Stevenson, 'Introduction', idem (eds), *The Year Book of Social Policy in Britain 1983*, p. 1. Several of the essays in this volume review the social policies of the Thatcher government.
400 Cf. T. E. Chester and M. G. M. van Oss, 'Economic Priorities and Social Expenditure: a Comparison of Dutch and British Health Service Policies', *National Westminster Bank Quarterly Review* (February 1984), p. 16.
401 For early stress on this point, see e.g. A. Seldon, 'The Humane Society: Some Thoughts on the Social Services in the Second Half of the 20th Century', *Swinton Journal*, vii (no. 1, March 1961), pp. 7–15; and the various opinion surveys published by the IEA, R. Harris and A. Seldon, *Choice in Welfare* (London, 1963ff.).

These various objects have been, or can be, sought in several ways.[402] One is to make greater use of the price mechanism, that is, charging, so as to secure, it is hoped, a more efficient distribution of resources.[403] Another is the rationing of the services available in some non-financial way, say, by 'benefit erosion', that is, either through the abolition of a benefit or a reduction in its real value (whether deliberate or through a failure to keep pace with inflation) or through restriction of eligibility. The effect is to reduce claimants' living standards and to force greater reliance on other sources of income and aid such as family, friends, or charity. This may be considered a form of, or alternative to, privatization in that it limits or cuts public expenditure, reduces the extent of government responsibility, and may lead people to make or increase their own arrangements for income security. Thirdly compulsory private provision could be extended on the analogy of motor insurance: cover is required by law but the individual is left to make his own arrangements with a private company. This system could be used for instance to provide income replacement benefits in respect of, say, sickness, unemployment, and retirement. If this were done the revival of the friendly society functions of the trade unions might perhaps be expected (as in Sweden). But in terms of both money saved and political difficulty involved, little is likely to be achieved by minor erosions. Hence the added importance of policies which explicitly transfer major welfare responsibilities from the state to other hands as with the idea that employers should provide sick pay for their workers or the plan to modify or phase out earnings-related pensions.[404]

The possibility of privatizing health care is obviously of major significance in this regard not least in the context of the reform and improvement of the NHS in respect of its efficiency, the allocation of resources, or its cost. The last-named problem emerged early of course: in February 1950 the then Chancellor of the Exchequer warned the Prime Minister about the way the cost of the service was already growing far beyond expectations. 'It is in fact out of control', he said.[405] And there is certainly much to be said for the view that the present arrangements for health care encourage people (as patients) to demand more services than they are (as citizens) prepared to pay for. A move in the direction of

---

402 For what follows I draw on M. O'Higgins, 'Privatisation and Social Security', *Political Quarterly*, lv (1984), pp. 129–39 esp. pp. 131–2; and K. Judge, 'Resource Allocation in the Welfare State: Bureaucrats or Prices?' *Journal of Social Policy*, viii (1979), pp. 371–82.
403 Judge, art. cit., pp. 372, 374–7 and the sources there cited. On the case against pricing, ibid., pp. 380–2.
404 O'Higgins, art. cit., pp. 133–5, 137–9. Cf. Adam Smith Institute, *Privatising Pensions* (London, 1982).
405 Cripps to Attlee (2 February 1950), in PRO, PREM 8/1443.

450 A Much Governed Nation

economic pricing by charging for services was an obvious recourse and it was first authorized, not without great opposition, in 1949 (not long in fact after the NHS was inaugurated). Since then the practice of charging has been extended; and might be more so. Also certain activities could be contracted out especially those like cleaning, catering, and laundering. Private health care (which has, of course, continued alongside the state system) could be further developed, as by tax concessions or the encouragement of investor-owned hospitals.[406] Or there might be joint financing of expensive medical equipment by private medical schemes and the NHS. And, in broader terms, general insurance-based provision is the obvious alternative which would also ensure more consumer choice.[407] Voluntary service might be encouraged also both as a support for, or alternative to, the NHS; though it is perhaps unlikely that much can be expected in this regard.[408] Of course given the crucial role of the doctors with their specialist knowledge and particular relation with patients, it is difficult to see how consumer sovereignty could be achieved.[409] And there are dangers of a greater geographical and social inequality of provision emerging. Nor does the market solution easily deal with the question of efficiency of provision.[410] None the less Conservative and other libertarians have frequently stressed the importance of moving towards the privatization of health care in particular and of social policy in general.[411] Equally the slow speed and minor results so far achieved indicate the difficulties. For apart from the practical functions there are very clear ideological issues and contrasts of value involved here.[412]

406 J. G. Larson, 'The Role of Private Enterprise in Providing Health Care: the Lessons of the American Experience', *National Westminster Bank Quarterly Review* (November 1980), esp. pp. 64–5.
407 For discussion of the possibilities and problems, see A. Maynard, 'Pricing, Insurance and the National Health Service', *Journal of Social Policy*, viii (1979), pp. 157–76; Judge, art. cit., p. 377.
408 Cf. the somewhat sceptical review of the possibilities in J. Morgan, 'The Voluntary Sector and the National Health Service', in Jones and Stevenson (eds), *The Year Book of Social Policy in Britain 1983*, pp. 107–21.
409 Cf. Shackleton, art. cit., p. 69.
410 For recent critical assessment of these matters, see e.g. Maynard, art. cit.; A. Maynard and A. Ludbrook, 'What's Wrong with the National Health Service?', *Lloyd's Bank Review* (October 1980), pp. 27–41; P. Seabright, 'Medicine, Monopoly and the Market Place', in C. Jones and J. Stevenson (eds), *The Year Book of Social Policy in Britain 1982: Thought, Rhetoric and Reality* (London, 1983), pp. 267–90 esp. pp. 270–1; G. McLachlan and A. Maynard, *The Public–Private Mix for Health* (London, 1982); and A. Maynard, 'Privatising the Health Service', *Lloyd's Bank Review* (April 1983), pp. 28–41.
411 e.g. Sir G. Howe, *Conservatism in the 80s* (CPC no. 693; London, 1982), pp. 21–3; A. Seldon, *Whither the Welfare State* (IEA Occasional Paper no. 60; London, 1981).
412 See the synopsis of contrasting themes in A. Maynard and A. Williams, 'Privatisation

Achievement and possibility

Privatization constitutes an attempt to dismantle the Public Concern (or major parts of it) and to achieve a new balance in favour of the private sector and the market on the assumption that state provision is often wasteful, otherwise inefficient and undesirable, and out-dated. As such the policy is perhaps the most vital aspect of the libertarian resurgence of recent years, a clear and explicit break with the bipartisan consensus prevailing since the second war with its favourable attitude to, or at least acceptance of, government intervention.[413] Yet given this, and the practical difficulties and doctrinal differences involved, it has to be said that in many ways there has been a curiously subdued response from those opposed to the policy.[414] In any event the programme continues to be pressed.[415]

None the less the question remains whether, on the experience so far, privatization will achieve its strategic goal and have more than a limited impact. For one thing the real core of national enterprises and services – electricity, railways, coal, the post office, steel, the NHS, education, and the social security system – has hardly been touched. And even if the government remains on target for its planned asset sales, it has been estimated that it will still have disposed of less than 10 per cent of the nationalized sector by the end of the present Parliament in 1988: and this is a still smaller proportion of total state assets.[416] Moreover there seems to have been a certain confusion between two different objectives: the transfer of ownership to private hands and the creation of genuine competition. The former, involving as it may simply the creation of private monopoly, is by no means a guarantee that greater efficiency will result. British Telecom is a case in point; another is the refusal to divest British Airways of its sole control over certain routes: this may improve its saleability but does nothing to open the service further to market forces, quite the contrary perhaps.[417] Equally the goal of wide share-owning has hardly been gained given that the smaller investor has often

---

and the National Health Service', in Le Grand and Robinson (eds), op. cit., ch. 6 esp. Tables 6.1–6.3.
413 Cf. Shackleton, art. cit., p. 60; Steel and Heald (eds), *Privatizing Public Enterprises*, pp. 13–15.
414 See e.g. D. Thomas, 'The Union Response to Denationalization', in Steel and Heald, op. cit., ch. 4; D. R. Steel and D. A. Heald, 'Privatising Public Enterprise: an Analysis of the Government's Case', *Political Quarterly*, liii (1982), p. 345. For the attitude of the Civil Service unions in particular, see Treasury and Civil Service, Sel. Cttee 3rd Rep., 1981–2, HC 236-II, pp. 337, 347–8, 378–82.
415 For a summary of the latest proposals to hand, see *KCA* (1985), pp. 33672A, 34073A.
416 Shackleton, art. cit., pp. 70–1.
417 Cf. ibid., pp. 66, 70. Cf. P. Forsyth, 'Airlines and Airports: Privatisation, Competition and Regulation', *Fiscal Studies*, v (no. 1, February 1984), esp. pp. 64–9.

sold his holding after a short period; and there is little reason to suppose that, despite the devices used in the British Telecom sale, the same will not be true in the end. It is the institutional investors who have largely gained.[418] There remains, too, the question of the regulation of the surviving public sector and of the array of 'hybrid enterprises' in which government retains a substantial shareholding (though ministers have often suggested that these 'mixed' institutions are simply an intermediate step on the way to full denationalization).[419] There are also general questions about access to any market created (a matter of income distribution) and of information about the possibilities.

Much of the reaction to the privatization programme as so far revealed has been merely rhetorical, an assertion of contrary values simply. I suspect however that when the dust finally settles, it will have been recognized that the reaction away from public provision depended for at least part of its impetus on the revealed deficiencies of the state sector as it had grown up: its wastes, the poor and often insensitive service, a lack of accountability, and so forth. The problem will be not so much one of restoring the *status quo ante* Thatcher as of considering how to overcome the defects of the public sector that remains and how to supervise it adequately. As well, perhaps, how improved and properly monitored experiments of a new type (rather than old-style nationalization) ought be pursued.[420] 'It would be churlish', Professor Donnison wrote recently, 'not to recognise that some of the questions about public services and the state posed by the present régime's actions badly needed to be asked.' And he pleads for 'people of goodwill in all parties' to formulate a civilized and sensible response.[421] Whether either ardent libertarians or collectivists will rest content with any new middle way is another matter.

FRINGE BODIES

> ...fringe bodies...are persisting elements in our governmental arrangements. They have a long pedigree and continue to be essential to the achievement of flexibility in the system of administration....
> G. BOWEN, *Survey of Fringe Bodies*, 1978, p. 1 §1.2

In addition to the enterprises, utilities, and services already reviewed, the

---

418 Pickering, loc. cit., p. 55.
419 See Heald, 'Will the Privatization of Public Enterprises Solve the Problem of Control?' *Public Administration*, lxiii (1985), esp. pp. 12–21; D. Steel, 'Government and the New Hybrids', in Steel and Heald (eds), *Privatizing Public Enterprises*, ch. 7.
420 For some suggestions, see e.g. D. Donnison, 'The Progressive Potential of Privatisation', in Le Grand and Robinson (eds), op. cit., ch. 3 esp. 49–57; N. Bosanquet, 'Is Privatisation Inevitable?', ibid., pp. 64–9.
421 ibid., pp. 56–7.

The Public Concern – and Beyond 453

Public Concern embraces a very extensive and varied array of other non-departmental organizations nowadays often called 'fringe bodies' or 'quangos'. The terminology of the subject is confusing. The (unpublished) Fraser report of 1945 used the name 'non-departmental organisations' to refer to the entire range of what is here called the Public Concern, whereas in 1980 Sir L. Pliatzky used the similar expression 'non-departmental public bodies' more narrowly to refer largely to what is here called the fringe. During the 1970s 'quango' became a popular acronym (originally from '*qua*si *n*on-*g*overnmental *o*rganization' later amended to '*qu*asi-*a*utonomous *n*ational *g*overnmental *o*rganization) though itself not without ambiguity in its meaning and scope. In a survey of these institutions undertaken, in 1975 and after, for the Civil Service Department, G. Bowen used the term 'fringe bodies'; and this seems to me the safest descriptive title to use. Its main defect is that it may imply agencies that are small, remote, and unimportant. But so long as it is clear that this is not necessarily what is intended, it is quite adequate to describe the variety of non-departmental institutions in this once hidden public sector.

Fringe bodies existed during the last century but most have been created since 1900 and especially over the past thirty or forty years.[422] It is this growth in numbers which gave rise to the expression 'the quango explosion'. My immediate concern is twofold: to give a reasonable impression of the diverse array presented by these institutions (without getting bogged down in mere lists or excessive detail); and then to describe the attack on the fringe bodies which has lately occurred.

The range of institutions

A considerable range of functions is covered by the many fringe bodies in existence. Although any categorization is bound to be arbitrary, Table 12 gives some indication of the many types of activity involved and a handful of examples of the agencies concerned. When the Pliatzky inquiry was instituted in 1979 there were in the United Kingdom some 2,000 of these institutions with executive or advisory functions together with 67 'tribunal systems'. The former involved annual expenditure of £2,115 millions (much of it funded by government) plus a further sum of nearly £29 millions disbursed on their behalf by the sponsoring departments. They had staffs numbering over 86,000.[423] By way of

---

[422] See the table in G. Bowen, *Survey of Fringe Bodies* (CSD; London, 1978), p. 1 §1.4.
[423] Report on Non-Departmental Public Bodies, 1979–80, Cmnd. 7797, pp. 1–2 §§5–7 and Appendix A. It should be noted that the figures cited in §§5–7 have had to be amended by detailed data taken from Appendix A because the former apply to a number of bodies here considered as national enterprises or major utilities and services, e.g. NEB, MSC, regional water authorities, etc.

Table 12 *Fringe bodies: functional areas*[a]

Function	Examples of the institutions involved
arbitration in disputes	Advisory, Conciliation, and Arbitration Service/rent tribunals
development of overseas resources	Commonwealth Development Corporation/Crown Agents
encouragement of science and the arts	British Film Institute/Council for Educational Technology
financing	General Practice Finance Corporation/Welsh Development Agency
government of professions	UK Central Council for Nursing, Midwifery, and Health Visiting/Hearing Aid Council
industrial research and development	National Research Development Corporation/industrial training boards
maintenance and improvement of standards of skill and quality	Design Council/Consumer Protection Advisory Committee
medical and social research	Public Health Laboratory Services Board/National Radiological Protection Board
prevention of discrimination	Commission for Racial Equality/Equal Opportunities Commission
protection of the environment	Countryside Commission/Royal Commission on Environmental Pollution
provision of nation-wide services	Trinity House/Development Commission
services of local concern	Edinburgh New Town Conservation Committee/Dartmoor Steering Group and Working Party
settling of wages	wages councils/Burnham Committees
trading	Horse-race Totalisator Board/Remploy Ltd

a Based on a memorandum (1952) by the Treasury Machinery of Government Branch in PRO, T222/274; but I have made numerous amendments. The examples cited are taken from Cabinet Office (MPO), *Public Bodies 1985* (London, 1985) and exclude those categorized under another heading in the present survey.

comparison it might be noted that at that time the NHS involved each year expenditure of nearly £7,500 millions and had some 900,000 employees while the nationalized industries had an annual turnover approaching £24,000 millions and a work-force of over 1.6 million.[424] While not on the scale of either, therefore, the total level of activity of the 2,000 fringe bodies, as here defined and as measured by the two variables of cost and labour, is by no means inconsiderable. Nowadays a complete list of public bodies is published annually by the Management and Personnel Office and includes *inter alia* details about executive and advisory fringe bodies as well as of some tribunals.[425]

The Pliatzky report employs the reasonable expository device of division into three main functional categories.

The first and most important group is comprised of those with executive, administrative, regulatory, or commercial-type responsibilities. In 1979 there were 449 of them and it was these which absorbed the greater part of total fringe body expenditure and staff.[426] They are concerned with a wide range of managerial, operational, or supervisory functions; various scientific and cultural tasks; and in some cases undertake activities of a trade promotional or commercial kind. All this might be done through departmental or local administration but is for various reasons carried on by these other means at arm's-length, as it were, from the normal institutions of government. Often this device is chosen because of the specialist or technical nature of the responsibility involved or as a result of its discretionary character.[427] However they do operate typically within broad policy guidelines set by ministers although they are to a varying extent independent in respect of their day-to-day activities. They depend for finance either on a direct grant or on a levy of fees and charges (or both) as approved by government. Because of this and of the powers vested in them, ministers carry a degree of ultimate responsibility. It is this group of fringe bodies which gives rise to most of the problems which occur.[428]

---

424 ibid., p. 1 §6.
425 For a summary of numbers, costs, and staff for 1979–85, see Cabinet Office (MPO), *Public Bodies 1985*, p. 4. There is also the 'quasi-autonomous local government organization' on which see D. Mason, *The Qualgo Complex* (ASI; London, 1984), 2–3.
426 The Cabinet Office list, p. 4, gives 492 for 1979 and 399 for 1985.
427 Cf. Sir A. Street, 'Quasi-Government Bodies since 1918', in Lord Campion *et al.*, *British Government since 1918* (1950; London, 1951), p. 162. There is a good account of some of the inter-war bodies of this regulatory type, ibid., pp. 162ff.
428 The following examples are chosen on a more or less random basis: Alcohol Education and Research Council; British Board of Agrément; British Library; Broadcasting Complaints Commission; Commonwealth Institute; Community Projects Foundation; Criminal Injuries Compensation Board; Development Board for Rural Wales; English Tourist Board; Enterprise Ulster; GB-USSR Association;

Next there is the large group of advisory bodies. Obviously as government does more and more it faces a greater range of problems, many of them involving specialized or technical issues. It needs information and assistance, to be kept in touch with professional expertise and opinion, as the basis for reasonable, practical decision and effective action.[429] As the Haldane Committee noted during the Great War, advisory bodies can be genuinely helpful to the process of administration affecting as it does, and on a continuous and increasing basis, 'the lives of large sections of the community.'[430] They are also in fact one way in which the pressure group acquires a place in the formal structure of government.[431] So the advisory councils, committees and boards have proliferated during this century.[432] By 1979 there were 1,560 of them of which over two-thirds fell into twenty-two main networks. Generally they do not employ staff or incur expenditure on their own account. But at the time of the Pliatzky report over £12 millions was spent on support of these bodies by the sponsoring departments.[433] Problems of accountability do not normally arise because the advisory groups have no separate corporate status and are simply the 'outriders' of a department through which alone they can normally have influence. Naturally, however, to the extent that their views carry weight or are invariably accepted they may, in effect, determine policy and so have something like an executive role, the minister finding it difficult perhaps to overrule their advice.[434] And while the need to consult them may slow

---

Health Education Council; National Consumer Council; National Dock Labour Board; National Youth Bureau; Pilotage Commission; Probation Board for Northern Ireland; Red Deer Commission; Royal Commission on Historical Manuscripts; Schools Curriculum Development Committee; Sports Council: and so they march on, 399 of them. I take these instances from the details in the Cabinet Office list for 1985.

429 R. V. Vernon, 'Introduction', in R. V. Vernon and N. Mansergh (eds), *Advisory Bodies: a Study of Their Uses in Relation to Central Government 1919–1939* (London, 1940), p. 22. Cf. PEP, *Advisory Committees in British Government* (London, 1960); and Sir R. Clarke, *New Trends in Government* (Civil Service Studies no. 1; London, 1971), p. 31.

430 Machinery of Government, Ministry of Reconstruction Cttee Rep., 1918 (vol. xii), Cd. 9230, pp. 11–12 §§34–7. For other early recognition of the value of advisory bodies, see e.g. H. J. Laski, *A Grammar of Politics* (London, 1925), pp. 376ff.

431 e.g. J. D. Stewart, *British Pressure Groups: their Role in Relation to the House of Commons* (Oxford, 1958), pp. 8–10.

432 The appendix in Vernon and Mansergh, op. cit., pp. 443–500 lists all the inter-war committees considered in the descriptive chapters of the survey, giving a total approaching 700; but there were many others not listed.

433 Report on Non-Departmental Public Bodies, 1979–80, Cmnd. 7797, pp. 1–2 §7.

434 PRO, T222/62 MGO (61) (3 January 1945), 'Non-Departmental Organisations', pp. 7–8 §§31–2.

down the taking of decisions, they may also be politically useful even if only as a window-dressing device or 'organ of propaganda'. As the official report of 1945 put it:

> Ministers can effectively discharge their duties only if they receive good 'advice'. This is normally provided by their permanent staff, but when a Minister is defending his decision in Parliament it is no sort of help to him to plead that it was taken on the advice of his officials. On the other hand, it is often useful for him...to be able to say that his decision accords with the advice of an advisory body of prominent outside persons whose names...command confidence among those most interested in the subject matter.

In addition a Bill conferring powers on a minister often secures an easier passage if it makes provision for an advisory council or committee.[435] In addition these bodies help secure continuing public involvement, however marginal, in the process of administration as was officially recognized at a very early stage of their development.[436] They may thus be seen as an important part of the democratic process in the age of the collectivist state.[437] Though whether such participation ought to be seen as the purpose of these bodies or whether they are a means simply to secure more efficient administration is another question. Again the range of subject-matter concerned is considerable.[438]

Thirdly there are many bodies with functions of an adjudicative kind and which are akin to courts of law: quasi-judicial tribunals with jurisdiction in a specialized field, licensing authorities, and appeal bodies with powers of decision. Most of these fall into sixty-seven main 'tribunal systems' which, in 1978–9, cost £30 millions to run.[439] As these

---

435 ibid., p. 6 §24. Cf. Vernon, loc. cit., pp. 25–7; and Sir A. Salter's Preface, ibid., pp. 8–9.
436 See Ministry of Reconstruction, *The Business of Government I: the Central Machinery* (Reconstruction Problems no. 38; London, 1919), p. 14.
437 Cf. Sir A. Salter, Preface, in Vernon and Mansergh, op. cit., pp. 7–8.
438 A few random examples: Advisory Committee on Advertising; Advisory Committee on Animal Experiments; Advisory Panel on the Importation of Sexually Explicit Films for Health Purposes; Black Country Limestone Advisory Panel; Historic Buildings Council; Joint Optoelectronics Research Scheme Assessment Committee; Law Commission; Legal Services Conference; Local Government Boundary Commission; Mobile Radio Committee; Nuclear Weapons Safety Committee; Poisons Board; Police Staff College Board of Governors; Political Honours Scrutiny Committee; Royal Fine Art Commission; Security Commission; Steering Group on Food Surveillance; Working Group on Trials of Early Detection of Breast Cancer; and many, many more to a total in 1985 of 1,069: see Cabinet Office, *Public Bodies 1985*, p. 4 (from which publication the bodies named are taken).
439 Report on Non-Departmental Bodies, 1979–80, Cmnd. 7797, p. 2 §9. In 1985 the number of tribunal systems was 64.

458   A Much Governed Nation

particular institutions are reviewed at length later on nothing more will be said of them here.[440]

The development and extent of these many executive and advisory agencies for long occasioned little comment or concern. But as the 1970s wore on they did emerge more clearly in the public gaze, becoming indeed the focus of intensive inquiry and criticism.

The great quango hunt[441]

There have, of course, always been expressions of disquiet about the development of the Public Concern as a whole.[442] Recently however one of the most vociferous manifestations of this unease has related to the so-called 'quango explosion'. And the declared policy of the Thatcher government to cut public expenditure and reduce the apparatus of the interventionist state has been applied to this aspect of the wider public service. The array of fringe bodies of various kinds seemed a desirable and easy target; though in the outcome less came of the assault than had been hoped. What followed was a cull rather than a hecatomb.

Obviously adequately to deal with this issue required, first of all, a complete statement of the facts about fringe bodies: how many there were, what they did, what they cost, and so on. Following a recommendation of the Fraser report it had been decided back in 1945 to keep an up-to-date register of all non-departmental organizations; but it would seem that this exercise was neither completed nor continued.[443] Moreover if there was to be effective reduction this information required publicity and to be generally discussed. The matter had received only limited academic attention. When the political role and importance of pressure groups became a subject of fashionable interest in the early fifties naturally some light was cast on the activity of fringe bodies.[444] There was other incidental scholarly reference; and Sir K. Wheare wrote an essay on the British Constitution in which fringe bodies were a central focus of attention.[445] But on the whole concern was lacking. I confess I do

---

440 See below ch. 6 in Part 2, esp. pp. 628–42.
441 This term is used in A. Barker (ed.), *Quangos in Britain: Government and the Networks of Public Policy-Making* (London, 1982), p. 225.
442 See the next sub-section on 'Issues and Remedies' esp. pp. 463–4.
443 For the original intention, see PRO, T222/62, 'Non-Departmental Organisations', p. 43 §196; the 'Note by the Treasury', ibid., pp. 1–2 §2 (iii); and the papers in T222/273–4. In 1952 the register contained only 180 entries which suggests it was far from comprehensive; see the report in T222/274 on 'Non-Ministerial Boards and Commissions', p. 1 §5. I infer the discontinuance from remarks in the CSD's introductory note to Bowen, op. cit., p. iii, about the need to collate scattered information on the subject.
444 On the emergence of an academic interest in these groups, see below pp. 489–91.
445 There is some reference to fringe bodies in e.g. W. J. M. Mackenzie and J. W. Grove,

not remember that, during my early teaching years when I was an assiduous student of all the academic journals (there were not too many to read in those days and what they contained was usually interesting), much was published on this topic or that it arose at all in professional conversation. Latterly it has become something of a minor industry.[446] The tribunals were, of course, a major focus of interest and for obvious reasons over many years before and after the inquiries of the Franks Committee.[447] The Fulton report on the Civil Service which appeared in 1968 stressed the importance of accountable management and of delegating (or 'hiving off') responsibilities to a wide variety of autonomous public bodies.[448] No doubt this helped direct official and other attention to the possibilities of the fringe (though the limitations were also clearly recognized).[449] Some official lists were occasionally published like those concerning members of public boards of a commercial character (first appearing in 1948) or paid public appointments made by ministers (1976 and after). And in 1970 a private research organization had produced a considerable survey of some 1,300 advisory, executive, and similar bodies active in British political life, though many of them were only remotely connected with the functions of government.[450] There was also the interest aroused by the colloquia sponsored by the Carnegie Foundation of New York and the publications which arose out of them and which largely focused on the issue of the public accountability of fringe bodies.[451] However the growth of these bodies – their large number, cost, and use of manpower, not to

---

Central Administration in Britain (London, 1957), esp. chs 15, 23–4; J. W. Grove, *Government and Industry in Britain* (London, 1962), *passim*; and W. I. Jennings, *Cabinet Government* (1936; 2nd edn Cambridge, 1951), ch. IV. Wheare's pioneering study is, of course, his *Government by Committee: an Essay on the British Constitution* (Oxford, 1955).

446 See e.g. the bibliographies in Barker, op. cit., pp. 232–41 and A. Davies, *What's Wrong with Quangos?* (London, 1979).

447 See Part 2, pp. 597–642.

448 The Civil Service, Cttee Rep., 1967–8 (vol. xviii), Cmnd. 3638, pp. 61–2 §§188–91.

449 See the draft report of 1 May 1952 (in PRO, T222/274), esp. pp. 8–9 §§32–5, which suggested very definitely that there was little prospect of relieving departments by hiving off; also the sceptical memorandum (26 October 1951) by Sir H. Emmerson, then Permanent Secretary to the Ministry of Works.

450 I. G. Anderson (ed.), *Councils, Committees, & Boards: a Handbook of Advisory, Consultative, Executive & Similar Bodies in British Public Life* (CBD Research Ltd, Beckenham, 1970).

451 Three volumes appeared in connexion with these conferences and research subsequently undertaken: B. L. R. Smith and D. C. Hague (eds), *The Dilemma of Accountability in Modern Government: Independence versus Control* (London, 1971); B. L. R. Smith (ed.), *The New Political Economy: the Public Use of the Private Sector* (London, 1975); and D. C. Hague et al., *Public Policy and Private Interests: the Institutions of Compromise* (London, 1975).

mention the possibilities of exploiting the patronage concerned – began to arouse disquiet for in 1975 the Civil Service Department, as a result of the feeling of unease in which it shared, commissioned a survey of these organizations as a preliminary to thinking what ought to be done. One of its senior officials later summarized the reasons why a problem was perceived: 'here are a lot of people disbursing public money and drawing their salaries from the public purse' but 'we are not sure that we know enough about what they are doing with this money to enable us to protect the taxpayer's interest...and to enable...Ministers to answer to Parliament for their ultimate responsibilities.' It was acknowledged at the same time that these bodies 'were expressly set up to enjoy a degree of independence'; also that the effort that would be needed to control them in detail was so great as to be quite beyond existing means (even if it were right to try).[452] The report (the need for which suggests again that the post-war lists were not kept up to date) was compiled by G. Bowen, a retired civil servant, and published in 1978. Perhaps its appearance was an example of official prescience for, of course, it was during this time that the libertarian emphasis of Conservative policy was reinforced by the appointment of M. Thatcher as leader. Consideration of fringe bodies began to increase and they emerged as a matter of some political importance. The great quango hunt was on.

There were numerous points at issue. The first was simply one of cost. The amount of money spent through fringe bodies (and the major utilities and services as well) was increasing notably and, on the more extreme versions of events, showed signs of getting out of control; and often the financial burden was seen as unnecessary. Secondly there was evidence of waste and extravagance as when the work of already existing private bodies was duplicated, when there was inadequate monitoring of expenditure, or when empire-building occurred as with the proliferation of related institutions. Thirdly the unregulated patronage involved worried many observers. The number of places was considerable, running into many thousands; pluralism was frequent; and there were fears of untoward political influence being exercised in making these appointments. Fourthly the creation of fringe bodies often crowded out purely private effort or voluntary service and this was undesirable and might be inefficient too. But finally, and above all, there was the matter of constitutional responsibility. The essence of the executive or regulating committee is that for all or some of its actions there may be no direct responsibility to an elected body; and this is incompatible with one of the central principles of Parliamentary government as it has emerged in the modern era. There is thus a lack of scrutiny of both spending and action;

---

452 R. Wilding, 'A Triangular Affair: Quangos, Ministers and MPs', in Barker, *Quangos in Britain*, pp. 37–8.

The Public Concern – and Beyond 461

and, in this sense, the establishment of these 'peripheral' but often large and significant institutions is an easy way out for the administrators and others concerned, a means of avoiding direct accountability. Quangos may thus be represented as a threat to Parliamentary democracy itself, as an extension of bureaucracy, and as an undesirable reflection of the march of collectivism.[453] What seemed to be required was a complete and continually up-dated listing of these bodies; a reduction in their number, size, and cost; a greater uniformity in crucial features such as status, finance, and powers; control over the patronage they represented; more standardized and effective legal supervision especially in respect of rights of redress – there might, for instance be an ombudsman appointed especially to deal with problems arising in respect to nationalized industries and cognate agencies (as the legal organization Justice suggested in 1976) or some equivalent to the Council on Tribunals created; and a greater degree of open accountability to Parliament especially on the part of those bodies the major part of whose funds are derived from public sources. As well there were questions to be posed whether government should be involved at all in the activity in question; and, if so, whether the job should really be done by a fringe body instead of by local or central government however hard pressed they might be.

The tally-ho was sounded and the chase began. Sir L. Pliatzky was given the task of producing a better and more comprehensive directory of fringe bodies and cognate agencies than had been provided in the Bowen report.[454] His review appeared in January 1980 and the information it contained has subsequently been up-dated.[455] In the outcome reductions were achieved resulting in substantial changes and the process continues.[456] A recent example is the abolition in 1985 of the National

---

453 One of the most persistent, even fanatic, quango hunters was the Conservative MP, P. Holland, and the nature of the case against fringe bodies and similar institutions may be gleaned from his numerous pamphlets on the subject, e.g.: with M. Fallon, *The Quango Explosion: Public Bodies and Ministerial Patronage* (CPC no. 627; London, 1978); *Quango, Quango, Quango: the Full Dossier on Patronage in Britain* (Adam Smith Institute; London, n.d. [1979?]); *Costing the Quangos* (ASI; London, 1980); *The Governance of Quangos* (ASI; London, 1981); *The Quango Death List* (ASI; London, n.d. [1980?]); and *Quelling the Quangos* (CPC no. 691; London, 1982). For a critical assessment of this output, see G. Drewry, 'Quelling the Quango', *Public Law*, xxvii (1982), pp. 384–9.

454 For all the value of the information it contained, the Bowen report had been regarded as inadequate in important respects: see e.g. the critical review in Sir N. Chester, 'Fringe Bodies, Quangos and All That', *Public Administration*, lvii (1979), pp. 51–4.

455 Report on Non-Departmental Public Bodies, 1979–80, Cmnd. 7797; the Cabinet Office (MPO) list of public bodies is updated annually. The need for a complete register was stressed e.g. by P. Holland, *The Governance of Quangos*, pp. 61–2 and Appendix 6.

456 For details up to 1980, see Report on Non-Departmental Public Bodies, 1979–80, Cmnd. 7797, pp. 6–11; and for a slightly later list, Holland, *The Governance of*

Film Finance Corporation, a reflection of the government's general strategy of forcing the arts to rely more heavily on private support (the corporation was replaced by a consortium made up of some of the commercial interests concerned). One bonus of the process of inquiry and reduction has been the greater publicity and the renewal of insistence on the regularity of procedures in relation to all these institutions, on their control and accountability, and the review of their work, as embodied for instance in the guide for departments promulgated in 1981.[457] This framework stressed the importance of a proper balance of independence and accountability, high standards of financial management, proper staffing arrangements, and how these objectives might be secured. If nothing else has been achieved by the brouhaha it will at least have awakened politicians, officials, and the public alike to the need for caution and vigilance in this regard.

But such matters and assessments are of more general significance and application, applying indeed to the sphere of the wider public service as a whole.

ISSUES AND REMEDIES

> ...I suggest that the Committee first needs to decide whether it is desirable to continue the process of setting up independent authorities at all.
> D. M. FOOT, memorandum on 'Mechanism of Government', 22 May 1943, PRO, T222/61

The growth of the Public Concern is clearly an important aspect of collectivist development. In 1945 a report presented to the Machinery of Government Committee said:

> ...of this...we are certain: the use of non-departmental organisations, already very extensive, has been of enormous assistance in enabling Government machinery to adapt itself to the ever-increasing demands which a steady expansion of Government activities has placed upon it, and there is every probability that still further use must be made of such bodies in future....[458]

At the same time this expansion of the wider public service has never been without its opponents or its difficulties.

Quangos, Appendices 3–5. The summary in the latest Cabinet Office tabulation shows a reduction between 1979 and 1985 of some 24 per cent: see *Public Bodies 1985*, p. 4. However the cost (at current prices) has gone up by slightly more, ibid.
457 Management and Personnel Office, *Non-Departmental Public Bodies: a Guide for Departments* (1981; London, 1982), the replacement of an earlier guide published in 1968.
458 PRO, T222/62, MGO 61 (3 January 1945), 'Non-Departmental Organisations', p. 43 §194.

The Public Concern – and Beyond 463

The antagonism is hardly new. Most of the issues ventilated during the late outburst over the 'quango explosion' or, more generally (in the period since the last war), about the development of public enterprises of various sorts arouse a certain sense of *déjà vu*. In the middle of the last century libertarians strongly attacked the propensity to establish 'General Boards' and 'administrative Commissions' as incompatible with the fundamental laws of the kingdom and the rights of the citizen. Such institutions, it was said, created opportunities for patronage and jobbery and led (or so one critic urged) to 'the arbitrary management and control of the properties and liberties of every Englishman' by 'exclusive cliques' which though paid from public funds, were self-appointed. This hostile observer – Joshua Toulmin Smith – went on to assert that the 'system is daily extending' and will continue to do so till either 'the public voice', alarmed at the extravagance and waste entailed, or the sheer practical difficulty of raising 'the millions of taxation' annually required, 'compels the entire and uncompromising abandonment of the whole.' Moreover, Smith argued, all these public agencies were incompatible with the basic constitutional principle of ministerial responsibility to an elected Parliament. It has been shown, he wrote, 'to have been the special object of our fundamental laws and institutions to secure' that '*one single person...alone*' is 'entrusted with authority in respect of each single object of executive attention' to be responsible to the common council elected by the nation. And so on and so forth.[459] The tone Smith adopts is shrill; but his arguments were representative of a wide and important body of opinion that has found expression in many quarters from that day to this. Even those who accepted that the Public Concern must grow if the increasing tasks of government were to be carried out invariably expressed a becoming diffidence. The report already cited as to the inevitability of the tendency urged that the creation of new non-departmental bodies should not be resorted to 'unthinkingly or uncritically or to an indefinite extent.'[460] In this the official committee no doubt deferred to the views of the Liberal MP, Dingle Foot, who chaired its proceedings when these particular matters were being discussed. He held a junior ministerial post in the Coalition administration and became formally involved with these machinery of government questions because it was deemed prudent to associate with their consideration someone of his party affiliation and known views (which are reflected, or

---

[459] The citations are taken from Toulmin Smith's *Government by Commissions Illegal and Pernicious* (London, 1849), pp. 250, 251, 253 (italics in original), and 257. For a closely similar modern sentiment, see P. Holland and M. Fallon, *The Quango Explosion: Public Bodies and Ministerial Patronage* (CPC no. 627; London, 1978), p. 4.

[460] 'Non-Departmental Organisations', loc. cit., p. 43 §194.

implied, in the citation used as epigraph to this section).[461] Even some of those who welcomed the positive state on ideological grounds expressed concern. In a popular account of British government published during the war years, W. I. Jennings wrote:

> We shall soon reach the stage where it can seriously be asked whether we have democracy when we are governed by a vast array of boards, commissions, corporations, companies, authorities, councils, and the rest whose relation to Parliament or to a local electorate is remote.[462]

Yet it is the case that in recent years the Public Concern has been one of the fastest growing areas of government in the country. Inevitably this unplanned and largely uncontrolled expansion – as in the 'quango explosion' – has generated further concern about the problems it has created.[463] For a substantial degree of expenditure is put into independent hands; and the concept of a unified public service is endangered.[464] Quite harsh opinions have been expressed. Among those recently noted are: 'With the best of intentions, we have created monsters'; 'pragmatism run wild'; and 'the proliferation of free-floating irresponsible agencies'.[465] The specific issues constituting this unease about the Public Concern range over matters relating to efficiency and economy in administration as well as to questions of constitutional propriety. They reflect the concern of those who are opposed to the extension of state intervention as such whatever form it may assume and of those who, while accepting its necessity are none the less worried about the absence of democratic accountability, especially given the patronage and money involved.[466] The central matters raised are reviewed seriatim in the rest of this section.

The absence of a legal framework

As compared with continental countries public law in Britain is much less well developed. One aspect of this state of affairs is that there are no

---

461 Foot was also opposed to the growth of the state as represented by the development of an extensive system of delegated legislation: see Part 2 pp. 566–7.
462 W. I. Jennings, *The British Constitution* (1941; Cambridge, 1945), p. 116. Cf. J. Grimond *et al.*, *Whitehall and Beyond* (London, 1964), pp. 37–8.
463 Cf. A. Doig, 'The Machinery of Government and the Growth of Governmental Bodies', *Public Administration*, lvii (1979), pp. 309–10.
464 Cf. Sir J. Dunnett, 'The Civil Service: Seven Years after Fulton', ibid., liv (1976), p. 376.
465 *Report of ... Annual TUC* (1983), p. 515 (W. Sirs); N. Johnson, 'Quangos and the Structure of Government', *Public Administration*, lvii (1979), p. 384; and M. Beloff, 'Examining the Working of Whitehall', *The Times* (19 June 1968), p. 9. Cf. the reference to 'opportunistic pragmatism' in A. Barker (ed.), *Quangos in Britain: Government and the Networks of Public Policy-Making* (London, 1982), p. 7.
466 N. Johnson, art. cit., pp. 380–2.

clearly defined legal categories of public body into which new tasks or institutions can be fitted.[467] As a result the development of the Public Concern has in many respects constituted a series of merely pragmatic innovations, bodies being established with little or no regard to their cumulative impact on one another or the structure of administration as a whole. And over the past half century, as the rate of creation has intensified, the patchwork nature of this aspect of the body politic has become ever more apparent. Of course there are always difficulties about historical parallels but (to chance a generalization of this sort) the position of the Public Concern in recent times has been not unlike the state of the central departments before the Northcote-Trevelyan report or of the local authorities prior to the reforms of the late nineteenth century. And just as much perhaps as these other institutions it needs to be systematized.

In a sense all of the issues to be reviewed here are the consequence of this deficiency. But there are difficulties specifically related to the institutional incoherence itself which inevitably gives rise to cases of duplication either between different public bodies or with the sponsoring departments. For instance, commenting on his time as Permanent Secretary at the Ministry of Technology, Sir R. Clarke said that firms would seek support from the Industrial Reorganization Corporation, the National Research Development Corporation, and the department itself: 'I don't think we ever went wrong, but the problem was always there.'[468] When this sort of thing happens lines of jurisdiction inevitably get blurred, divergences of practice occur and there is, too, waste of money and effort. The absence of proper frameworks may also lead to a failure to detect what is really an incompatibility of purposes allocated to a given institution: as with the Commission for Racial Equality which has both to champion the interests of minorities and at the same time determine whether particular practices constitute discrimination in law.

Various things might be or have been done in this regard. One is to establish clear definitional categories of bodies in the Public Concern and simply phase out any that do not fit. It might even be desirable to create a new fringe body, say a Standing Advisory Committee on Administrative Organizations, to carry out this task.[469] Another is to see that the fullest information is readily accessible about all the institutions making up the Public Concern. Of course many of them, like the nationalized

---

467 Cf. ibid., p. 393; Barker, op. cit., pp. 23, 51.
468 Sir R. Clarke, *New Trends in Government* (Civil Service College Studies no. 1; London, 1971), p. 88. See also the cases of duplication cited in P. Holland, *The Quango Death List* (ASI; London, n.d. [1980?]), pp. 5–6, 8–10; idem, *The Governance of Quangos* (ASI; London, 1981), pp. 37–41.
469 Johnson, art. cit., pp. 393–4.

enterprises and major utilities, publish reports and accounts and provide a lot of data about their operation. But there is still, across the whole gamut of them, too little information about such matters as their running costs, staffing levels, services provided, or tasks undertaken. It happens, too, that there are few studies appraising what they do, considering alternatives, and so forth.[470] However a list of public bodies giving basic, indeed the barest, information is now published each year by the Management and Personnel Office. And a formal framework of guidelines in respect of non-departmental public bodies has also now been promulgated dealing with such crucial matters as finance, recruitment and staff control, accountability, standards of conduct, and so forth.[471] It also stresses the importance of monitoring the performance of these bodies, and, from time to time, of undertaking an overall review of their activities to see they are still necessary and, if so, as economical and effective as possible.[472] A more effective dimension still in respect of fringe bodies in particular might be provided by the use of so-called 'sunset' legislation, a built-in time limit on the life of each agency beyond which its continued existence would require fresh justification.[473]

Patronage

A topic of particular sensitivity is the way in which persons are selected to hold the considerable range of appointments in the Public Concern. Many of the issues raised in this regard derive from the fact that 'Ministerial patronage is a dominant feature of the world of quasi-government' and that the number and scope of positions involved have expanded beyond ministerial capacity to cope with them adequately.[474] As Professor Finer put it, the new despotism has been replaced by the new nepotism.[475] It was stated in 1978 that seventeen ministers had in their gift over 8,000 paid appointments (either salaried or fee-paid) and some 25,000 others unpaid. Only about 250 of the paid posts were full-time most of these being in the nationalized industries. The total cost was over £5 millions a year.[476] It is clear, therefore, that the great majority of these

---

470 ibid., pp. 386–7. On the need for more public information, cf. A. Davies, *What's Wrong with Quangos?* (London, 1979), p. 59.
471 Management and Personnel Office, *Non-Departmental Public Bodies: a Guide for Departments* (1981; London, 1982).
472 ibid., pp. 25–6.
473 Cf. Clarke. op. cit., p. 88; Holland, *The Governance of Quangos*, pp. 57–60.
474 A. Davies, 'Patronage and Quasi-Government: Some Proposals for Reform', in Barker, op. cit., pp. 167, 171.
475 S. E. Finer, *The Changing British Party System, 1945–1979* (Washington, D.C., 1980), p. 158.
476 CCCXCVI H. L. Deb. 5s., 15 November 1978, col. 719. (Baroness Young). Cf. the similar estimates in Holland and Fallon, op. cit., p. 18. Details of over 5,600 paid

public positions are part-time and that about three-quarters of them are unpaid though their holders will be able to claim expenses. All the same the data were sufficient for quite a number of observers to suggest that a 'parasite state' had been created rather too closely reminiscent for comfort of the sort of situation that prevailed in the days before appointment to the central departments of government themselves was regularized.[477] The parallel is deliberately invoked as when Maurice Edelman urged that the whole question of ministerial patronage needed to be 'looked at with the insight and the probity of a Gladstone.'[478] Nor is the concern merely new, aroused by the late hubbub over fringe bodies, having been expressed earlier in relation specifically to the larger and arguably more important national enterprises of one kind or another.[479]

A number of specific grounds for disquiet has been expressed though they are of varied cogency. One is an allegation of political bias to the advantage in particular of organized labour. This assertion was a feature of some of the attacks made by P. Holland. For instance it was asserted that in 1977 the thirty-nine members of the TUC General Council held between them 180 state appointments; numerous trade union employees held others; and Labour ministers had (it was said) sometimes replaced existing appointees with their own supporters to ensure that the body concerned acted in conformity with Socialist policy.[480] It may be that similar accusations might be made against Conservative ministers also. I do not know; and I have not myself seen or assessed detailed evidence which could substantiate accusations in either regard. But, of course, a good part of the point is simply that no minister, of whatever political colour, should have in his gift a range of often very important appointments and be able to bestow them in an actually or apparently unregulated way so as to reward adherents or achieve an acceptable political emphasis in the bodies concerned. The system should not be such as to permit indictments of this sort to seem in any sense plausible. A related but different point is that a monopoly of patronage posts is held

---

posts appeared in Civil Service Department, *A Directory of Paid Public Appointments Made by Ministers* (1976; 2nd edn, London 1978); a table based on these data appears in Doig, art. cit., p. 313. D. Mason, *The Qualgo Complex* (ASI; London, 1984), pp. 2–3, estimates that there are also over 25,000 local fringe bodies involving a total of some 57,000 appointments. A list of some of these qualgos is given, ibid., pp. 27–37.

477 See above pp. 137–45, 151–2 on the reform of the old patronage system. For the phrase cited in the text (as used in relation to the trade unions), see P. Johnson, 'Towards the Parasite State', *New Statesman* (3 September 1976), p. 299.

478 See his letter to *The Times* (8 April 1971), p. 15.

479 See e.g. S. E. Finer, 'Patronage and the Public Service: Jeffersonian Bureaucracy and the British Tradition', *Public Administration*, xxx (1952), pp. 329–60; [L. Tivey], 'Government by Appointment' (PEP 1960), in W. J. Stankiewicz (ed.), *Crisis in British Government: the Need for Reform* (London, 1967), pp. 282–300.

480 Holland and Fallon, op. cit., pp. 18–20.

by privileged, élite groups, those already holding important positions in established circles of authority and influence. And the spectrum in some other respects also seems to be narrow: too few women perhaps or people from outside London. Another ground of criticism is simply that the process of appointment is so wrapped in secrecy. There is little or no public knowledge how selection occurs. A Public Appointments Unit (previously in the Civil Service Department but now in the Management and Personnel Office) keeps a central register of potential members for institutions of the Public Concern; and some departments have their own lists of people with special qualifications. Ministers may consult their colleagues in government or take the opinion of other departments. In respect to major appointments, like the chairmanship of an executive board, 'Departmental Ministers naturally seek the Prime Minister's concurrence.' They can also obtain names from outside sources and sometimes have to consult certain bodies or even accept their nominees.[481] But the criteria used in compiling these lists or the rules governing the process of selection are not made public; and what is known of them does not make the position clear. This in itself allows suggestions that appointments are made somewhat haphazardly and without any objective assessment of qualities. At the same time the task of selection is obviously a formidable one on any account; and is often perhaps simply a matter of finding people willing to serve, and with enough time and income otherwise secured to enable them to do so.[482]

Then there is the matter of pluralism, holding more than one post especially if fees or a salary are involved. Often, of course, this is simply a matter of using to the full the services of those who are available or who have special knowledge or skill. But equally this could be carried to excess. And the possibilities to be exploited in this way might not be inconsiderable. In 1966 one practitioner in the field claimed it was possible to make £5,000 a year (at current price levels the equivalent would be over £28,000) by getting one's name on the roster for miscellaneous commissions and employments.[483] On the other hand the average level of payment made to members of the boards of all these bodies in the Public Concern was usually quite modest: Sir L. Pliatzky found that in the case of one major sponsoring department he examined it was in the region of £200 a year and two-thirds of the persons concerned gave their services free.[484] Efficiency was another issue raised

---

481 Report on Non-Departmental Public Bodies, 1979–80, Cmnd. 7797, pp. 12–13 §§39, 41 (from which the passage cited comes); Davies, 'Patronage and Quasi-Government: Some Proposals for Reform', in Barker, op. cit., pp. 171–2, 176, 178.
482 Cf. Clarke, op. cit., p. 89; Davies, loc. cit., pp. 171, 173–4.
483 Anon., 'How Officialdom Spreads Itself Beyond the Civil Service', *The Times* (20 December 1966), p. 9.
484 Report on Non-Departmental Public Bodies, 1979–80, Cmnd. 7797, p. 12 §37.

by the critics who urged that the secret process of selection could not possibly produce boards operating effectively in the public interest. There was no guarantee that ministerial patronage would secure that the best available people were appointed especially if any political bias were at work. Alternatively it was likely that, whatever party was in power, safe and sound moderates would invariably be favoured: interests were balanced, the relevant professional and other groups included, Scotland and Wales represented, North and South, left and right, men and women. And this might merely mean deadlock, the dominance of the mediocre, or the service of some sectional concern rather than that of the broader public.[485] Incompetence or abuse must exist within so large a system but the power of dismissal has hardly ever been used. Nor are there any formal criteria for assessing performance.[486] Then there is the question of departmental influence. Because the appointments made are largely at the minister's discretion a committee's autonomy may be limited.[487] As the case of the NEB showed, if bodies will not come to heel their members resign and the minister simply appoints people who are more comfortable.

It is hardly surprising, therefore, that there have been proposals for reform to the system of ministerial patronage 'to reduce secrecy, encourage more open and fair competition, control the power of Ministers, introduce accountability for appointments made and provide some assessment of performance'.[488] Like the causes of concern the proposals for change have been various. One consideration was how to make the process of appointment more public, and a number of means has been suggested to this end including: open competition and nomination; inviting suggestions from the public; advertising at least full-time paid posts; and using the services of consultants. In 1978 a Cabinet committee looked at a bundle of such proposals and is said to have found them essentially sound; but nothing was done because of scepticism about the value of advertising and using consultancy services not least because of their cost and of concern about the increased administrative load the changes might entail (together with the need there would be to expand the Public Appointments Unit). There was also the fear that many suitable people might not be willing to apply and submit themselves to the selection process involved and, too, that admitting applicants would open the floodgates to cranks.[489] But one obvious suggestion is that appointments made solely on political grounds

---

[485] Davies, *What's Wrong with Quangos?*, pp. 52–3; idem, 'Patronage and Quasi-Government: Some Proposals for Reform', in Barker, op. cit., p. 178. Cf. ibid., p. 63.
[486] Davies, 'Patronage and Quasi-Government', loc. cit., pp. 175–6.
[487] Davies, *What's Wrong with Quangos?*, p. 55.
[488] ibid., pp. 64–5.
[489] ibid., p. 51; Report on Non-Departmental Public Bodies, 1979–80, Cmnd. 7797, p. 12

should formally be barred; and another is that there should be a limit on the number of places which can be held by a single individual.[490] The idea has also been advanced that Parliament ought to be involved in the appointing process at least in some supervisory role and especially in regard to posts on the boards of nationalized industries (and other major parts of the Public Concern). The select committees would be an obvious channel by which ministers might thus consult Parliamentary opinion. Any such procedure would certainly have the advantage of openness and lead to more publicly identifiable criteria for appointment. Yet there is, on the other hand, the likelihood that in itself the publicity might deter good candidates; and might, too, lead to even more pronounced political pressure being brought to bear.[491] Another device often suggested is the establishment of a Public Service Commission to parallel in this sphere the work of the Civil Service Commission and which would be responsible for bringing the Public Concern into line with procedures for departmental appointments.[492] But the cost would obviously be considerable.[493] Perhaps for the great majority of bodies, the present method of appointment is the most practicable though the procedures need to be more open and formalized. It is the absence of a stated policy on patronage which is disturbing rather than the thing itself?

Supervision and accountability

The arm's-length relationship which characterizes the position of the Public Concern is a recognition that, for various reasons, the institutions involved should enjoy a degree of independence from government and so be free from the sort of responsibility and control under which a central department or local authority office normally operates. Some people objected in principle to the idea of the non-departmental public body just because it thus escaped the bonds of full formal accountability.[494] It might be organizationally preferable from the point of view of better operation or management; but it entailed, what was constitutionally undesirable, less stringent Parliamentary or other monitoring.[495] The general perspective is described in the MPO guide in the following terms:

§40. In 1976 the appointment of the Director General of Fair Trading was made after public advertisement.

490 e.g. Holland and Fallon, op. cit., pp. 25–6.
491 ibid., pp. 25–6; Davies, *What's Wrong with Quangos?*, pp. 56, 65; Davies, 'Patronage and Quasi-Government: Some Proposals for Reform', in Barker, op. cit., p. 177.
492 M. Edelman, 'The Patronage Explosion', *New Statesman* (11 July 1975), p. 45–6.
493 Davies, 'Patronage and Quasi-Government: Some Proposals for Reform', in Barker, op. cit., pp. 178–9.
494 See e.g. Machinery of Government, Ministry of Reconstruction Cttee Rep., 1918 (vol. xii), Cd. 9230, pp. 11–12 §§31–7.
495 Sir A. Street, 'Quasi-Government Bodies since 1918', in Lord Campion *et al.*, *British*

The use of public bodies operating at arm's length from ministers has a long history, but their number has grown rapidly since 1945. In many cases the arrangements have worked well. But experience has been mixed. For example, the 'arm's length' approach can involve problems of control and accountability because it is not always easy for departments to strike the right balance between disengaging from detailed administration while exercising proper supervision. More generally, the scale, range and cost of the functions now carried out by non-departmental bodies means that they are the subject of close attention by ministers, Parliament and the public. This attention is directed not only to accountability but also to arrangements for control over the overall number of non-departmental bodies and over their expenditure.[496]

Naturally the practice varies from body to body according to its functions. In some cases an institution 'may essentially be an instrument of government policy' and so will 'operate under close ministerial supervision'; in others a greater degree of independence may be exercised.[497] In 1945 a Treasury note said it was 'by no means certain that either principles or practice have found their final expression.'[498] There was a great deal of attention devoted to this matter in the case of the nationalized industries created after the war; and it has recently come to the fore again in connexion with the 'quango explosion'. But the issue is hardly settled: it was recently said indeed that the present situation is 'a thorough mess' of *ad hoc* arrangements.[499] So, as the Expenditure Committee said a decade or so ago, it is still necessary to consider what are the 'proper control mechanisms for hived off bodies.'[500]

These matters are here reviewed seriatim as they relate to each channel of supervision and accountability. What is in general revealed is a dilution of control similar to that which has occurred in respect to the Civil Service and its relations to the Treasury and ministers alike.

Ministers
The growth of the Public Concern with its deliberate acknowledgement of autonomy on the part of the many institutions involved appears to weaken the application of the principle of ministerial responsibility which is indeed premised on the assumption that the government

---

Government since 1918 (1950; London, 1951), p. 179.
496 MPO, *Non-Departmental Public Bodies: a Guide for Departments*, p. 27 §118.
497 ibid., p. 4 §19.
498 PRO, T222/62, MGO 61 (3 January 1945), 'Note by the Treasury', p. 2 §2 (iv).
499 Barker, op. cit., p. 28.
500 Expenditure, Sel. Cttee 11th Rep., 1976–7 (vol. xxxi), HC 535-I, p. xlv §91 (words quoted are cited in bold in original).

department is the characteristic organ of central administration and that a minister will be responsible to Parliament for all aspects of its work. Yet this view of the constitutional position may not provide the right perspective. Of course it will if it is believed that all public offices of what form and provenance so-ever should be so subject in every detail. But for long – perhaps always – practice has been different, increasingly so with the growth of government activity. Departments nowadays do so much that it is quite impossible for a minister to know more than a fraction of what is done in his name. Of course he will answer publicly and in Parliament for all that is so undertaken in the sense of providing information about it, explaining policies and decisions, and dealing with any criticism. His political reputation may suffer if too much goes wrong and there is unfavourable publicity; in consequence he may be transferred in a reshuffle or dismissed from office by the Prime Minister; in a difficult or extreme case he may resign of his own volition though such instances are rare. But it is very clear today that there is no possibility of ministerial involvement in all the aspects of departmental work and no guarantee that he will supervise it. To that degree the classical doctrine of ministerial accountability is in truth no more than an ideal.[501] And the point relevant here is that, given some autonomy of action is essential to the work of the Public Concern, it would be inapposite to regard it in terms of a model of responsibility that does not in practice even apply to the central department itself.[502] To this extent, therefore, a certain looseness of accountability is inevitable. Even so there is an obvious political sense in which, while the bodies in the Public Concern are hived off to give them freedom of action and to avoid overloading the department, the supervisory or sponsoring minister cannot in the last resort avoid the final responsibility if a 'serious error is made and some really awful chicken comes home to roost'.[503]

The key point originally insisted on when the nationalized industries themselves were first created was a distinction between broad policy and day-to-day administration. The idea was that the minister concerned would be able to give general directions about the former (for which he would be responsible to Parliament) while leaving the board free, within this and any other limit established by the law, to run the industry in the way it thought best. But the two levels of decision were blurred and so, during the 1950s, there was a tendency to replace the distinction between

---

501 For a detailed review of these matters, see Part 2 pp. 811–16.
502 Cf. the remarks of N. Johnson, 'Accountability, Control and Complexity: Moving Beyond Ministerial Responsibility', in Barker, op. cit., p. 210.
503 R. Wilding, 'A Triangular Affair ...', in Barker, op. cit., p. 38. See also N. Johnson, 'The Public Corporation: an Ambiguous Species', in D. Butler and A. H. Halsey (eds), *Policy and Politics* (London, 1978), pp. 133–4 and the epigraph cited ibid., p. 122.

'policy' and 'administration' by one resting on a differentiation between 'the public interest' and 'purely commercial' considerations, the former being invoked to overrule the latter in any conflict where this was thought necessary as when, for instance, the purchase by the airlines of British rather than foreign aircraft was insisted on, uneconomic services kept in being, or a proposed rise in prices or charges interdicted. And it was gradually realized that the nationalized concerns were so important to the general economic life of the community that it was not feasible to allow them that substantial measure of independence once envisaged as the key to their successful operation. The most they could expect was a reasonable degree of managerial autonomy within a framework of detailed policy laid down by government (as in the economic White Papers). They became crucial instruments of economic policy so that control over them was necessarily more close (if not exercised in any uniform or steady way). Government interest in public sector wage settlements is a clear case in point.[504] In fact, however, ministerial directions of a formal kind have been very rare. Much more usual, and less easy to call to public account, are the informal means of influence and 'back-stage pressures' – the so-called 'implied powers' – which ministers and departments use to bring a corporation to heel.[505] The truth is – as the SCNE report on ministerial control and the later inquiry by the NEDO study group both recognized – that there is a basic confusion in the allocation of responsibilities between the nationalized industries and the government: the ideal of a substantially independent management is not compatible with ministers' views of their own right to determine the public interest in these matters.[506] In that sense the arm's-length theory has never really been effective.[507]

The position in respect to ministerial responsibility for, and supervision of, the major utilities and the fringe bodies was not given anything like the same degree of consideration as the nationalized industries have received. The situation varied but on the whole the claims of independence received priority save when a scandal occurred (as in the Crown Agents affair) or when the number and cost of the increasing array of institutions and activities brought the question to the fore (as

---

504 Cf. Clarke, op. cit., pp. 77–80; R. Marsh, *Off the Rails: an Autobiography* (London, 1978), p. 174.
505 For one minister's account of such 'interference', see Marsh, op. cit., p. 105. See also Johnson, 'The Public Corporation: an Ambiguous Species', loc. cit., p. 126; also A. Silberston, 'Nationalised Industries: Government Intervention and Industrial Efficiency', in Butler and Halsey, op. cit., ch. 10.
506 See the discussion in Johnson, 'The Public Corporation: an Ambiguous Species', loc. cit., pp. 128–37.
507 For some more or less radical alternatives, see 'The Battle of Britain's Dinosaurs', *The Economist* (6 March 1982), pp. 19–23 esp. p. 23.

recently during the great quango hunt).[508] The present régime is based on guide-lines published in 1981 in the aftermath of the Pliatzky report.[509] Though thus specifically related, the rules may be assumed to apply to all the relevant institutions of the Public Concern especially those with functions of an executive or commercial character. The general principle is stated as follows:

> Whatever the precise degree of independence, the minister is answerable to Parliament for whether the body is doing its work effectively, efficiently and with economy and that it continues to fulfil a useful purpose. The minister is also responsible for ensuring that the body establishes and maintains proper systems of financial management.

Consequently the legislation or other founding instrument should give the minister sufficient powers to discharge his overall responsibility and to exercise specific controls where necessary.[510] These powers will normally include those over the appointment and dismissal of the chairman and at least the majority of board members (if appropriate after consultation with specified organizations); the production of information; and suitable powers of direction 'to ensure compliance by the body with some essential aspect of government policy or to remedy some aspect of its performance.' The minister should also see that bodies conform to appropriate standards of conduct in respect, for instance, to appointments, hospitality, gifts, and so forth.[511] It is also the responsibility of the sponsoring minister to see that the rules about financial arrangements and control of costs are secured, scrutiny being especially detailed where over half a body's gross or administrative expenditure comes from government funds.[512] As in the parallel case of Treasury control, there is a recognized division of duty, a 'need for dual involvement in the development of policy and in the oversight of performance'.[513] Ministerial responsibility for the recruitment of staff and for the management of personnel is limited by the body's independent status as an employer and its need for operational

---

508 For the instance cited, see C. Hood, 'The Crown Agents Affair', *Public Administration*, lvi (1978), pp. 297–303 and G. Ganz, 'Parliamentary Accountability of the Crown Agents', *Public Law*, xxv (1980), pp. 454–80.
509 These rules were themselves based on an earlier review, the *Guide to Setting Up New Public Bodies*, issued by the Treasury in 1968. For the Pliatzky proposals which were closely followed, see Report on Non-Departmental Public Bodies, 1979–80, Cmnd. 7797, pp. 20–3.
510 MPO, *Non-Departmental Public Bodies: a Guide for Departments*, p. 4 §20.
511 ibid., p. 5–6 §§27–30A (citation from §30).
512 ibid., sections 3–5 and Appendices 2–3.
513 ibid., pp. 18–19 §83.

autonomy; but sponsoring departments must satisfy themselves that minimum standards (as expected in the public service) are maintained.[514] A minister has also to see that from time to time an overall review is undertaken of the work of any body which he sponsors to see, for instance, whether it is still needed, whether any savings are possible, whether it does its work effectively, and so on.[515] Ministers are also responsible for securing that new bodies are only set up 'if there is a copper-bottomed case for doing so.'[516]

In general, therefore, 'Ministers will ... look to the bodies they sponsor to be effective, efficient and economical in the conduct of their affairs so that the tax payer gets good value for money.'[517] And while intervention may not be continuous especially in the matter of routine work – there would be little point to having this sort of institution if it were – a minister could obviously lean very heavily on one of these institutions if he wished to as by laying down policy or financial ceilings and bringing pressure to bear on matters of a politically sensitive kind.[518] Sir L. Pliatzky believed that the sort of proposals he suggested and which were closely followed in the MPO guide-lines 'contain most of the ingredients indicated by experience for making up an alternative to a competitive market régime for those public bodies to which in their nature such a régime cannot apply.' Within a framework of this sort the function of securing efficiency and economy will depend on the organization itself but 'the main responsibility for oversight of its performance lies with its sponsoring Minister and Department' coupled with the further external scrutiny of the C & AG and the appropriate Parliamentary committees.[519]

One device often considered in this context is the idea of a Minister for the Nationalized Industries, a proposal that might be extended to envisage a minister to be responsible for the Public Concern as a whole. For after all there are common problems to be dealt with and there would be some advantage in an arrangement by which the relations with all these bodies were handled by a single minister, especially if the object were to reduce this aspect of the public sector and its expenditure. On the other hand the diversity of institutions and activities involved is considerable and the ambit of responsibility would be very wide, even incongruous. Moreover the creation of such a ministry, even for the restricted sphere of the socialized industries alone, would be

---

514 ibid., p. 22 §97.
515 ibid., section 7.
516 ibid., p. 27 §117.
517 ibid., p. 1 §4.
518 Cf. N. Johnson, in Barker, op. cit., p. 213.
519 Report on Non-Departmental Public Bodies, 1979–80, Cmnd. 7797, p. 22 §§81–3.

incompatible with the broadly functional distribution of departmental responsibilities. It would also tend to increase control in an area where a degree of independence and flexibility of operation has been deemed desirable. In addition co-ordination is perhaps as expeditiously to be achieved through the Cabinet committee structure.[520]

But ministerial supervision is not the only form of regulation or inquiry.

Parliament
Parliamentary procedure in this regard is traditionally attuned to the doctrine of ministerial responsibility and if this is attenuated by the emergence of the Public Concern, as to some extent it must be if the necessary autonomy is not to be compromised, then so will conventional opportunities of inquisition. Yet the extent and quality of supervision of the work of all these boards, councils, and committees, as well as of the expenditure of the considerable sums of public money they entail, depends greatly on Parliamentary attitudes and behaviour for this will condition the manner of ministers and departments towards these bodies. The basic questions are, How can power devolved in this way be systematically checked and scrutinized? and, How can Parliament play a constructive role in promoting administrative efficiency and financial regularity and economy?[521] The Royal Commission on the Constitution thought that in general it was 'probably true to say that Parliament either has or could obtain facilities for scrutinizing and debating the work of any government-appointed body' if, that is, there is 'sufficient demand'. The degree of control over *ad hoc* agencies may, therefore, be 'substantial'.[522] On the other hand the critic believes 'It is pertinent to ask what value for money we are getting in return for this vast expenditure of funds and alienation of Parliamentary authority.'[523]

Various opportunities for debate and inquiry exist, for example on the adjournment, the presentation of annual reports and accounts, an opposition day, the introduction of fresh primary or secondary legislation, raising borrowing powers, and so on. As well questions can be asked but only about the exercise of formal ministerial responsibilities. In practice shortage of Parliamentary time has meant

---

520 For consideration of a proposal from the Prime Minister for a single minister to deal with the socialized industries, see PRO, PREM 8/1443, Prime Minister's minute M. 268/49 (26 November 1949) and CAB 134/506, MG (49)1 (5 December 1949), p. 4.
521 D. Howell, 'Public Accountability: Trends and Parliamentary Implications', in B. L. R. Smith and D. C. Hague (eds), *The Dilemma of Accountability in Modern Government: Independence versus Control* (London, 1971), p. 243.
522 The Constitution, R. Com. Rep., 1973–4 (vol. xi), Cmnd. 5460, pp. 267–8 §§877–8.
523 P. Holland, *Quango, Quango, Quango: the Full Dossier on Patronage in Britain* (ASI; London, n.d. [1979?]), p. 4.

that normally the affairs of all these institutions, even of the major nationalized industries and utilities, receive relatively little discussion on the floor of either House. By far the most interesting development was the establishment in 1955 of a Select Committee on the Nationalized Industries which continued until 1979 when its work was absorbed in the wider framework of select committees then created.[524] These have authority to examine the work not only of departments but also of bodies associated with them. This is important in principle in that it makes feasible inquiry in a way that was not possible before; and the House of Commons Liaison Committee certainly intended this should be pressed.[525] But whether the committees have the time or the resources to be systematic and continuous in such inquiries may be doubtful, though certainly specific reviews can have an important impact: there have, for instance, been reports on university funding, the MSC's corporate plan, the Commission for Racial Equality, the Health and Safety Commission and Executive, the Post Office, Nationalized Industries Finances, BL, Rolls Royce, and others of relevance.[526] Perhaps what they can achieve is an insistence on and publicity for certain general principles of operation and, as well, the provision simply of more information than is presented in an annual report. But obviously the impact of select committees is at best random; though perhaps the new committee structure is an indication that Parliament is groping towards a greater interest in at least the nationalized industries and major utilities.[527] A more active role has been suggested as with the proposal that the appropriate select committee should have a power of approval of senior appointments in the Public Concern. Also that there might be a permanent monitoring committee of the Commons serviced by efficient auditors to oversee the work of these bodies.[528]

The need for financial supervision is obvious not least as a means to secure efficiency and effectiveness in operation.[529] The role of the C & AG is not unimportant. The then Head of the Civil Service told the Expenditure Committee in 1977 that in general the Civil Service Department did not, for lack of resources, examine fringe bodies in terms of efficiency and organization; and, when prompted, he said it should be

---

524 Examined in Part 2 ch. 8, esp. pp. 834ff.
525 Liaison, Sel. Cttee 1st Rep., 1982–3, HC 92, p. 13 §§26–7.
526 Lists of all the reports issued from 1979–84 are to be found in the annexes to Part II of G. Drewry (ed.), *The New Select Committees: a Study of the 1979 Reforms* (Oxford, 1985).
527 J. Redwood and J. Hatch, *Controlling Public Industries* (Oxford, 1982), p. 19.
528 Holland, *Quango, Quango, Quango*, p. 5; Redwood and Hatch, op. cit., p. 19 and ch. 2.
529 Cf. Treasury and Civil Service, Sel. Cttee 3rd Rep., 1981–2, HC 236-I, pp. xxxiii–iv; Efficiency and Effectiveness in the Civil Service, 1981–2, Cmnd. 8616, p. 13 §§45–6.

done by the Exchequer & Audit Department.[530] At that time the C & AG audited the operations of bodies in the Public Concern wherever this was statutorily provided and otherwise by agreement. This covered 'a large number of miscellaneous bodies'. He also had access to books and accounts to determine whether value was obtained for money spent even when he did not audit. The universities were an example of this.[531] And his involvement meant, of course, a report to the Public Accounts Committee.[532]

Other avenues
One of the most serious aspects of the haphazard development of the Public Concern has been the absence of any uniform rules or principles to determine the extent and conditions of the legal liability of the many institutions concerned. Yet, as N. Johnson reasonably argued, the citizen 'has a right to expect certain standards of procedural rectitude and fairness' not least given 'the inevitable weakness of traditional forms of political and administrative control'. Formally to establish such standards would, therefore, appear to be 'one of the more effective ways of bringing it home to those concerned ... that the duties laid upon them are of a public nature and must, therefore, be discharged in a manner which recognizes the importance of equity in administration.'[533] Of course there is then the question of how the standards might be sustained. Recourse to the courts might lie, or to a special tribunal; the remit of the PCA might be extended or a special commissioner appointed (as Justice suggested in 1976) to deal with national industries and agencies.[534] One variation is the proposal made from time to time that a standing advisory committee be created to survey, analyse, and report on the administrative structure of government and which would, therefore, embrace within its remit the task of reviewing the Public Concern.[535] There are also the consumer councils and similar bodies though it is generally acknowledged that they are rather ineffective: there should be more of them with more bite not least because of the absence of the commercial

---

530 Expenditure, Sel. Cttee 11th Rep., 1976–7, HC 535-II, p. 826 qq. 2057–8 (Sir D. Allen).
531 Expenditure, Sel. Cttee 12th Rep., 1977–8 (vol. xxxiv), HC 576, Appendix 1 pp. 33–5 §§6, 8, 12.
532 The auditing arrangements for all executive public bodies are given in Cabinet Office (MPO), *Public Bodies 1985* (London, 1985).
533 N. Johnson, in Barker, op. cit., pp. 215–16.
534 For these possibilities, see Davies, *What's Wrong with Quangos?*, pp. 66–8.
535 Barker, op. cit., p. 32; N. Johnson in *Public Administration*, lvii (1979), pp. 393–4; E. L. Normanton in Smith and Hague, op. cit., pp. 337–40. And for one early suggestion of this sort in connexion with *ad hoc* boards, see Procedure on Public Business, Sel. Cttee Special Rep., 1930–1 (vol. viii), HC 161, p. 207 q. 2194, p. 220 qq. 2352–3.

The Public Concern – and Beyond 479

or other pressures present in the private sector, their lack of independence and of effective power.[536] Some accounts stress the importance in this regard of self-policing through peer-group pressure and the influence of the professional ethic.[537] Nor is the role of the press insignificant.[538]

The real issue is whether the wider public service will continue to be allowed (as largely in the past) simply to grow haphazardly or whether some principles of order will be introduced to secure proper standards of performance, supervision, and accountability. But the nature of the Public Concern is such that ministerial responsibility will necessarily be more limited than it is even in respect of central departments, and other requirements will be vital: a clear specification of powers and duties; openness and an adequate flow of information; provision for effective audit and review; a clear statement of legal liabilities; Parliamentary and public scrutiny. All these things will be necessary if the Public Concern is to operate with a sense of its accountability to the nation.[539] It used to be thought that the whole range of institutions was so diverse that no hard and fast general rules could be laid down either for the whole field or even for parts of it. This was firmly stated as far back as 1945 when the array was notably smaller than it has since become.[540] But it is hardly now accepted, for certain themes that were outlined in the 1945 paper have since been developed, emerging most recently as the MPO guidelines.[541] It may be suggested, in conclusion, that there are four major aspects to this matter of supervision and accountability.[542] One is the need by appropriate audit to prevent the misappropriation of public funds; another is to assess performance so that value for money is secured and this, of course, requires access to adequate information; a third is to establish procedures whereby Parliament, in the search for improvement, is able to bring pressure to bear; the last is to supervise the operations of these bodies so that no citizen is treated unfairly or arbitrarily or without some avenue of redress.

---

536 L. Tivey, 'Quasi-Government for Consumers', in Barker, op. cit., pp. 148–9; M. Corina, 'Watchdogs Without Much Bite', *The Times* (21 August 1970), p. 21; Davies, *What's Wrong with Quangos?*, pp. 43–5.
537 D. C. Hague et al., *Public Policy and Private Interests: the Institutions of Compromise* (London, 1975), pp. 27–31, 357; P. Dunleavy, 'Quasi-governmental Sector Professionalism: Some Implications for Public Policy-making in Britain', in Barker, op. cit., ch. 11.
538 Hague et al., op. cit., p. 371.
539 Cf. N. Johnson, in Barker, op. cit., pp. 217–18.
540 PRO, T222/62, MGO 61 (3 January 1945), 'Note by the Treasury', p. 1 §2(i).
541 For these themes, ibid., p. 1 §2(ii) and MPO, *Non-Departmental Public Bodies: a Guide for Departments*, passim.
542 Cf. J. H. Robertson, memorandum no. 143, in The Civil Service, Cttee Rep. 1968 (Non-Parl.), vol. 5 (2), p. 1071 §147.

Effectiveness and doubts

It is without question difficult to make general judgements about the Public Concern as a whole because it embraces so many institutions of diverse size and status and covers such a variety of tasks. Of course the matter might be put in bluntly ideological form: the whole thing is anathema and, like other aspects of the public sector, should be cut back as quickly and as much as possible; or, alternatively, it represents a desirable and flexible advance which, though needing no doubt to be monitored, should be enhanced and strengthened as occasion offers in the name of the general good. These attitudes are real enough and either of them (or any intermediate view) constitutes an important motivation or ultimate purpose for politicians and their publics. But while they indicate a direction of travel of one sort or another the goals they have in view are in any event highly unlikely to be achieved in merely a few years. And for the practical future a sizeable Public Concern may be expected to remain as, inevitably, will doubts about its effectiveness and value.

There are obvious difficulties. One is the diversity of tasks and spheres of action: 'Whatever might be the criteria for assessing the performance of the Arts Council or the Sports Council, they cannot be the same as those appropriate to a Regional Water Authority, the National Coal Board or the Housing Corporation.'[543] Obviously only a few bodies can be made to work on a normal commercial basis; and this proves difficult enough even in respect of the nationalized industries. Certain criteria are available however: some measure of services provided; information about staffing levels and finances; or about how well or quickly the agency handles its business. A picture of trends in overall costs can be built up. At the same time outside the nationalized industries and major utilities and services little relevant information is available. Too little has been done (by official or other inquiry) in the shape of 'performance appraisal studies'.[544] Examples do exist, however, as with the recent investigation of the quondam Social Science Research Council and which led to its reform and transformation.[545] The whole issue raises, in any case, the question of alternatives: should (say) the UGC be abolished and the division of funds left to the DES? How is it possible to tell if this would be better?[546]

> ... on the issue of effectiveness in performance we have in our present state of knowledge to remain rather agnostic. No doubt some non-

---

543 N. Johnson, in *Public Administration*, lvii (1979), p. 386.
544 ibid., pp. 386–7.
545 See the account in *SSRC Newsletter*, nos. 45–7 (1982).
546 Johnson, loc. cit., p. 387.

departmental agencies represent a satisfactory bargain for the taxpayer: services are provided sympathetically, efficiently and cheaply, and there is a bonus in the shape of a voluntary lay commitment (which also contributes to cheapness). But then there are other bodies which probably have little in their favour: they perform ponderously, they assume the rigid form of vested interests and they provide but one more chance for responsibilities to be obscured and for the net of bureaucratic interference to be drawn tighter. However, before we can reliably distinguish the sheep from the goats we do need far more information on performance than is currently available.[547]

This was written in 1979 and, with only slight modification, is still very true today.

In any case there is need for caution in the sense that the development of the Public Concern may represent a drift that has gone too far. Interestingly diffidence about hiving off of this kind has always been strongly expressed in official circles. After the expansion of the war and immediate post-war years it became very apparent that 'non-ministerial boards and commissions' offered little scope for relieving the burden on ministers and their senior advisers. This was the conclusion of an inquiry into the matter undertaken in 1951-2.[548] The gist of the case is presented in a memorandum by Sir H. Emmerson who was then Permanent Secretary at the Ministry of Works. He pointed out that executive work could only be thus delegated once policy had been decided and only limited possibilities for this may exist in some areas of administration. Yet it is the policy responsibility which takes up the time of the minister and his advisers. In addition the division may actually add to the work involved because, for instance, of the greater difficulty in obtaining information, the absence of close control like that in a normal government office, and, possibly, the lack of sympathy between the agency and its sponsoring department. There may be some advantage in appointing a commission or similar body under strong leadership to develop a policy but equally this may have embarrassing results (as in the case of the Special Area authorities before the war). There are other problems also: there may be an untoward effect on the staff concerned (as by the creation of a blind alley for promotion); and an independent organization may be relatively expensive to run.[549] It is a view the like of which has been reiterated since then by those with official experience. For instance Sir R. Clarke wrote (in his survey of new trends in government which appeared in 1971 in the aftermath of the Fulton report) that he concluded

---

547 ibid., p. 387.
548 PRO, T222/274, final report (1 May 1952).
549 ibid., memorandum by Sir H. Emmerson (26 October 1951).

> the allocation of new tasks to public boards and agencies is not necessarily wise, and is positively dangerous if adopted for long-term tasks; and in my opinion we have to pay much more attention to our capability within the public service

– that is, the existing Civil Service –

> to carry out new current tasks. I think it is right to set up public corporations to do great permanent tasks.... But I think it is wrong both on the merits of the job and in the interests of the capability of the public service itself, to treat 'hiving off' as a desirable objective in itself, if one means by this the transfer from departmental management to a public corporation or other public board or agency.... I would myself favour being less eager than we have been in the last decade to set up outside agencies....[550]

Moreover if special expertise is required in the outside body the department is less likely to be able to monitor it effectively.[551] In any case, he points out, the more important the questions delegated the less likely it is that a minister and department can leave them alone so that the original purpose is likely to be frustrated. He takes as an example the Shipbuilding Industry Board, set up in 1967, which was to be the instrument for the rationalization of the industry. But the problems were considerable and politically sensitive so that the department itself was heavily involved. 'But, of course, if the government is going to be so implicated, the object in setting up the independent agency is destroyed; and if such a situation is foreseen it may be better to equip the department to do the job from the start.'[552] Sir James Dunnett (who had been a member of the Fulton Committee) also expressed concern about the process of hiving-off, but what he had to say in general terms may also be applied to the development of the Public Concern as a whole:

> I am nervous that if we are not careful we may be reversing the process of the last fifty years. During that period a substantial number of more or less independent boards were [sic] converted into ministries – and those ministries welded into a single civil service with the great advantage that staff could be freely moved between them. I suggest we should be careful not to dissipate the advantages of those measures.[553]

The Pliatzky report put the minimum consideration in this way:

---

550 Clarke, op. cit., p. 89.
551 ibid., p. 89.
552 ibid., p. 88. The SIB was set up with only a limited life and came to an end in 1971: see KCA (1967–8), p. 22593A and ibid. (1971–2), p. 25403A (25407).
553 Dunnett, 'The Civil Service: Seven Years after Fulton', loc. cit., p. 376.

Generally speaking the moral indicated is, not so much that we should set about turning the clock back, but that we should not think in terms of a further considerable extension of 'hiving off'... as an instrument for securing improved efficiency and economy across a wide range of public activities.[554]

There was also a sense that many at least of the bodies which make up the Public Concern are too remote from the public they are intended to serve.[555] This led to the fear that they might proliferate and flourish without effective democratic control over them; and this in turn to the suggestion that the drift towards nominated agencies, having gone too far, should be halted and replaced, wherever possible, by either the transfer of responsibility to an elected body or to seeing there was effective accountability decentralized to the local authorities (or to the regional and provincial assemblies proposed by the Royal Commission on the Constitution).[556]

As the Fulton Committee recognized, the 'creation of... autonomous bodies, and the drawing of the line between them and central government' raises 'parliamentary and constitutional issues'.[557] It is also an open question whether the use of non-departmental agencies on so wide a scale is administratively successful. Their existence raises a whole crop of such issues some of which have been briefly touched on here. One cannot help emerging from such a review of the Public Concern with the feeling that in some ways it presents a phenomenon like that facing Northcote and Trevelyan and that it may well be time to initiate an overall inquiry into its place and bona fides in the constitution of the next century: a Royal Commission on the Public Concern may be what we need?

BEYOND THE FRINGE

Our interest's on the dangerous edge of things.
R. BROWNING, *Bishop Blougram's Apology*, 1855, l.396

If the departments constitute the core of the administrative system, then this is surrounded by the institutions of the Public Concern which, in turn, is encompassed by a periphery of yet other connexions arising from the activity and interests of central government. This last area, lying as it were beyond the fringe, constitutes the other margin of our official and

---

554 Report on Non-Departmental Public Bodies, 1979–80, Cmnd. 7797, p. 19 §69. Cf. Doig, art. cit., p. 329.
555 See e.g. The Constitution, R. Com. Rep., 1973–4, Cmnd. 5460, p. 268 §878.
556 ibid., p. 96 §307, pp. 266–70 §§872–86; Hague *et al.*, op. cit., p. 378; Holland, *The Quango Death List*, pp. 4–5.
557 The Civil Service, Cttee Rep., 1967–8 (vol. xviii), Cmnd. 3638, p. 61 §190.

semi-official arrangements and to explore it is to voyage almost over the edge of the political world. Of course this image is in part misleading because the concentric domains suggested are not so much clear and separate as interlinked by complex lines of influence, aid, and other relationship which have become more numerous as governmental intervention has increased and the dividing line between the private and public spheres has become more blurred. There are two topics belonging to this outer realm which need to be considered here concerning what may respectively be called the mixed polity and the lobby.

The mixed polity

Instead of a clear disjunction between private and public sectors there is, in fact, a continuum, parts of which cover a substantial degree of mutual involvement. Some aspects of this relationship have already been noted: the way in which government has become, either directly or indirectly, a shareholder in nominally private firms or, if they seem crucial to the national or an important regional interest, aids them by loan or subsidy perhaps to assist during a period of difficulty or to encourage a scheme of rationalization.[558] But there are two other dimensions to the mixed polity to which reference must be made: the substantial contractual connexion that may exist between government and industry; and the way government makes use of private organizations for its own purposes.

We live in the age of the so-called 'contract state'. Though the term is recent the condition of things to which it refers is not.[559] Private firms or even whole industries have long been significantly dependent on government orders in both defence and civilian fields as in the case of the Admiralty shipbuilders, airline development between the wars, the provision of school buildings, or the production of telephone equipment for the GPO. Nowadays, of course, with the substantially greater demands of public agencies connexions of this sort are more considerable and diverse than they have ever been, from the drugs needed for the NHS to the purchase of computers for government establishments and universities. The social and economic impact of this patronage is clear from the significance attached to where an order for, say, a new aero-engine or destroyer is bestowed. Obviously the basic reason for this sort of development is that government can more readily obtain the product or service in view and the staff and facilities necessary to produce it by placing private enterprise under contract than by creating for the purpose

---

558 See above pp. 402–11; also *The Rise of Collectivism* (London, 1983), pp. 100–9.
559 The term is said first to have been used in 1966: see D. C. Hague, W. J. M. Mackenzie, and A. Barker (eds), *Public Policy and Private Interests: the Institutions of Compromise* (London, 1975), introduction, p. 32 n.2.

some new part of the Public Concern or adding to an existing agency or department.[560] And there are other specific advantages too. The response may well be quicker, cheaper, and more flexible than if government entered the field itself; an important industrial sector is stimulated perhaps and other business interests sustained through the placing of sub-contracts; wider social aims (such as those concerning the level and conditions of employment) can be furthered by manipulation of the contractual terms; and the enhancement of centralized bureaucracy is avoided.[561] Naturally there are also problems which arise from the creation of a government oriented sector of this sort especially those of a financial kind or concerning the avoidance of waste or loss. The full stringency of competitive tendering may not always operate; quality or cost controls may be inadequate; and there is the danger to the public that a firm may be able to make what are described as 'excessive' profits. A special fringe body, the Review Board for Government Contracts, was set up in 1969 (after a couple of cases of this sort) especially to keep under review the matters concerned.[562] A central feature of modern government is, therefore, this sharing of responsibility and operation by public and private institutions the latter becoming attached, completely or in part, to the pursuit of public purposes perhaps achieving thereby a sort of quasi-nationalized status. Government may also become dependent on this private capacity which is why, if an important firm or industry ails, it may be deemed necessary to give it extraordinary support as in the case of Rolls Royce. The problem then is, however, to prevent it becoming an unhealthy dependency merely.

Government also makes use of private or voluntary organizations in many other ways and for a similar variety of reasons: direct responsibility is avoided: the cost may be less; greater flexibility and experiment are possible; and participation is increased. The purposes served are also varied. Sometimes a private organization receives recognition or support as a means of regulating a particular activity or securing standards of operation in the field concerned. Government is thus able to see to the discharge of a certain duty but without direct involvement. There are numerous examples of this sort of body. One is the British Board of Film Classification set up on the initiative of the film industry which also finances it; a local authority is, however, entitled to vary its certificates. It is a curious arrangement but one accepted, and

---

560 Cf. B. L. R. Smith, 'Accountability and Independence in the Contract State', in B. L. R. Smith and D. C. Hague (eds), *The Dilemma of Accountability in Modern Government: Independence versus Control* (London, 1971), p. 3.
561 ibid., pp. 17–18.
562 See e.g. M. Edmonds, 'Government Contracting in Industry: Some Observations on the Ferranti and Bristol Siddeley Contracts', ibid., ch. 6; *KCA* (1967–8), p. 22332A; ibid. (1969–70), p. 23818A.

which works reasonably well, because the only alternative is a system of official censorship (which was at one time proposed and almost established.)[563] There are several such regulatory bodies in the field of housing, for instance the National Federation of Housing Societies, the British Standards Institution, and the National Housebuilders' Registration Council.[564] Again there is the Wine Standards Board of the Vintners' Company which was set up in 1973 by agreement between the company and the minister. It is the competent authority for the enforcement of EEC wine regulations. Technically it is regarded as a fringe body but clearly government has, for the purpose in question, found it useful to operate through an existing private organization with its special interest and expertise.[565] There are also regulatory bodies on which the government is represented as with the Joint Advisory Council on Building Society Mortgage Finance set up in 1973.[566] Sometimes government uses private bodies to administer schemes which it may have set afoot but in which for one reason or another it does not itself wish to be involved. The original National Health Insurance arrangements are an obvious case depending so much as they did in their working on the 'approved societies', that is, insurance companies and friendly societies.[567] Or again the Law Society is used to help administer the legal aid and advice schemes. Another example – which, it has been suggested, involves a specific kind of privatization – relates to the transfer of training responsibilities from statutory training boards to training organizations based on the appropriate employers' associations.[568] The role of private organizations in the provision of grant-aided social services is not inconsiderable and includes such bodies as housing associations, family service units, district nursing associations, tenants' associations, community centres, and so forth which often operate, of course, with the help of a local authority social service department.[569] A specific instance of a similar kind is the 'meals on wheels' service

563 For the origins of the Board of Film Censors (its title until recently), see J. Trevelyan, *What the Censor Saw* (1973; London, 1977), ch. 1.
564 On the work of the last-mentioned body, see A. Barker's detailed account in Hague *et al.*, op. cit., pp. 333–55.
565 Report on Non-Departmental Public Bodies, 1979–80, Cmnd. 7797, p. 52. For current details, see Cabinet Office (MPO), *Public Bodies 1985* (London, 1985), p. 9.
566 E. M. McLeay, 'Building Societies: a Question of Accountability?', *Public Administration*, lxii (1984), pp. 147–60 esp. p. 154.
567 See G. Carpenter, 'National Health Insurance: a Case-Study in the Use of Private Non-Profit Making Organizations in the Provision of Welfare Benefits', ibid., lxii (1984), pp. 71–89.
568 For details, see H. Rainbird and W. Grant, 'Non-statutory Training Organizations and the Privatization of Public Policy', ibid., lxiii (1985), pp. 91–5.
569 For a general review, cf. G. Rhodes, 'Accountability and Social Innovation: Some British Experience', in Hague *et al.*, op. cit., pp. 287–326.

operated by the WRVS (which also provides other facilities and advice of course). Often a private body is (or sometimes has by law to be) consulted in the formulation of policy and legislation. Thus when a statutory instrument was being drafted concerning (say) poisons or seeds, certain bodies had to be consulted and may thus be considered as part of the administrative or lawmaking process.[570] And where government wishes to encourage a particular activity it will often give assistance to the voluntary agencies concerned, perhaps in the form of a grant, subsidy, or tax concession. The field of sports is an obvious instance. The sports councils (themselves fringe bodies with substantial government support) make grants or loans to voluntary and commercial organizations and local authorities so they can improve facilities; they also aid the governing bodies of various sports (like the Jockey Club, the MCC, the Royal and Ancient, or the Football Association) for purposes of sport development, coaching, and administration.[571] State aid to private or voluntary organizations may take a number of forms: the tax exemption extended to charities is an obvious instance; so are the grants given to approved housing associations. Other examples of bodies given limited financial assistance are very numerous and range from (say) a homosexual rights group given some money each year by the GLC (which had latterly dispersed quite a lot of aid to small organizations of one kind or another) to the Royal Shakespeare Company which currently receives a subsidy of some £5.2 millions a year as part of the general policy of helping the arts. In the case of some bodies the role of the state is confined to making appointments, as with the established church, some public schools, and certain university positions: obviously in such cases the government is hardly 'making use' of the organizations concerned, its role being usually purely formal in the sense of being undertaken on advice. Then there are many voluntary bodies that have a 'special relationship' with government in that they have easy access to departments which will also as a matter of course seek their advice where this is deemed relevant: bodies such as the National Trust, the motoring organizations, the Howard League for Penal Reform, and many others. Among these is the Civic Trust which may be taken to indicate a number of aspects of the role of these mainly private bodies.[572] This institution was founded in 1957 and is a recognized charity supported by voluntary contributions. It encourages the protection and improvement of the

---

570 Sir C. Carr, *Delegated Legislation* (Cambridge, 1921), pp. 9, 16, 31ff. And cf. Part 2 pp. 589–91.
571 Central Office of Information, *Britain 1986: an Official Handbook* (London, 1986), p. 418.
572 For the details which follow I draw on *Whitaker's Almanack* (1986), p. 1114 and COI, *Britain 1986*, p. 187.

environment and high standards of architecture and planning. As such it makes awards for good developments of diverse kinds as with the initiation of co-operative street improvement schemes; coping with industrial dereliction and urban wasteland; problems of damage and disruption caused by heavy lorries; and promoting techniques for the transplanting of semi-mature trees. The Trust also encourages the formation of local amenity societies and gives advice and support to nearly a thousand such bodies now on its register and through which there is a general commitment to good planning and conservation.[573] It was closely associated with the drafting of the Civic Amenities Act (1967), which created the concept of the Conservation Area, and of the Town and Country Amenities Act (1974). It administers the Architectural Heritage Fund (financed by voluntary contributions and a matching government grant) which provides loans to local buildings preservation trusts. On behalf of the Department of the Environment it also administers the work of the Heritage Education Group. From 1973 to 1981 it also administered (on behalf of the Historic Buildings Councils) government grant-in-aid to conservation projects in non-outstanding conservation areas. Finally there is a kind of surrogate relationship that often exists. There may be a considerable public interest in the performance of certain tasks, say the provision of a service or the maintenance of standards, that government itself would have to undertake or for the conduct of which it would otherwise have to create some agency or other. But where an appropriate private body exists, government may be content entirely to leave the matter in its hands not specifically aiding it in any way. Thus the lifeboat service is operated entirely by the RNLI which depends on both voluntary contributions and labour; and professional standards in medicine, dentistry, and nursing are maintained by the general councils concerned which again are purely private bodies recognized but not aided by the state. If these institutions did not exist they would have to be created by government.

Governments may thus use such bodies as these in formulating policy, drawing up legislation, administering schemes, and making decisions; and their views will often be given weight or at least accorded respect. But here we are already on the frontiers of the 'anonymous empire' itself.

The lobby

This is the realm of the private or voluntary organization which, while not having a general programme or seeking office as a party does, may nevertheless have or try to acquire political connexions and influence of some kind or other. These are the so-called pressure or interest groups

---

[573] See A. Barker, *The Local Amenity Movement* (The Civic Trust; London, 1976).

The Public Concern – and Beyond 489

which, as Madison said, 'grow up of necessity in civilised nations'.[574] They abound in our society, and, in their collective political dimension (that is, as they seek to affect public policy) are often simply described as 'the lobby'.[575]

The story of the realization that these varied associations are politically important is an interesting one in itself. Naturally the role of interests and groups was always well understood by politicians, journalists, and people of that sort as well as by theoretical writers.[576] And a great deal about their activities has been fully documented in historical studies of, say, the movement to abolish slavery, the Anti-Corn Law League, the railway interest, the temperance alliance, sabbatarianism, the tariff reform campaign, and the like; an emphasis on the role of interests and 'connexions' was, of course, positively demanded by the so-called Namier school. Those authors who surveyed the story of things in the large might associate such a general theme as the decadence of Parliamentarism with the growing power of unofficial groups.[577] Nor was all this unfamiliar to sociologists with their focus of attention on sub-state activity and organization. Political scientists and other observers of the American scene had also paid great heed to these matters in explanation of the process of government in the USA: the motto was 'Look for the interest', and the terms 'lobby' and 'interest group' seem to have derived from that context.[578] In this country, too, entire theories of politics had been built up around some concept of the group, from pluralism to Guild Socialism though, by the end of the Great War, such doctrines were no longer so widely received as they had been; and there was some discussion of the role of groups in academic studies of British politics too.[579] However the significance of what Bentham had called 'sinister interests', especially those of an economic or class kind,

---

574 A. Hamilton *et al.*, *The Federalist or, the New Constitution* (1787–8; Everyman, 1942), p. 43.
575 S. E. Finer, *Anonymous Empire: a Study of the Lobby in Great Britain* (1958; 2nd edn, London, 1966), p. 4.
576 For the theorists, see e.g. Hobbes, *Leviathan*, II. xxii *ab init.*; Hegel, *Philosophy of Right*, §§250–6.
577 See e.g. O. Spengler, *The Decline of the West* (1918–22; trans. edn, London, 1926–8), ii. 415–16.
578 See *OED* and Supplement, *sub* 'interest', 'lobby', 'pressure', and 'pressure group'. There is an interesting review of the American and academic background of group theory in W. Y. Elliott, *The Pragmatic Revolt in Politics: Syndicalism, Freedom and the Constitutional State* (1928; New York, 1968), Appendix C; see also B. Crick, *The American Science of Politics: its Origins and Conditions* (London, 1959), esp. ch. VII.
579 e.g. C. Gill, *Government and People: an Introduction to the Study of Citizenship* (1921; 3rd edn rev., London, 1933), ch. XIX; R. Muir, *How Britain is Governed...* (London, 1930), pp. 295–309, 321; and in W. I. Jennings, *Parliament* (1939; 2nd edn, Cambridge, 1957), see the many index references *sub* 'Interests'.

was usually only stressed by writers of a left-wing or radical persuasion as, for instance, in *Tory M.P.* (1939) by 'Simon Haxey' or, in much more sophisticated form, Harold Laski's *Parliamentary Government in England* (1938).[580] Yet there was a sense in which the existence, political activity, and influence of pressure groups (the very term is depreciatory) was regarded by many students of politics as reprehensible and constitutionally improper, to be ignored or covered up like the chairlegs in a Victorian drawing-room. There was commonly a lack of realism in this respect masked by an excessive concentration on the formal machinery of government. The result was that, in the early and mid-1950s, the growing emphasis on the part played by such groups in British politics came with the shock of newness and revelation alike; there was the promise that the reality behind the constitutional façade was now to be made clear. I cannot recall that, when being taught about British government during the early 1940s, whether at school or university, any mention at all was made of this dimension of our affairs. Yet by the time I became a lecturer myself, some ten years later, it was simply not possible to overlook such matters which, indeed, rather seemed to demand a certain priority of attention. Pressure groups had by then become the fashion. And there are various reasons why this should have happened. There was the obvious part played by interest groups – like the BMA or the road haulage operators – in the passage of post-war legislation and the amusing propaganda of 'Mr. Cube'. Also the publicity accorded to the revelations of the Lynskey tribunal and the subsequent investigation into the operations of 'contact men'. It all advertised the considerable importance of the way various interests tried to influence government policy and decisions. And the republication in 1949 of A. F. Bentley's pioneering study of social and political pressures in the process of government both reflected and stimulated this academic interest and provided a theoretical framework for its development.

In any event it became almost a new orthodoxy that the more complex economic and social life becomes and the more the state intervenes in the affairs of the community, the more people will organize to resist or aid this intervention according to how it affects them or how they see it.[581] Academic attention was thus focused as never before on the lobby and its role in political life. Almost a 'new pluralism' was in the air, the community being seen as a collection not of individuals but of groups, and politics as the interplay between them. A considerable body of

---

580 A post-war instance of the same style of inquiry, much discussed at the time of its appearance, was the Universities and Left Review pamphlet, *The Insiders* (London, n.d., [1957]).
581 Cf. A. Toynbee, 'The Education of Co-operators' (1882), in T. S. Ashton (ed.), *Toynbee's Industrial Revolution*...(1884; Newton Abbot, 1969), p.223.

The Public Concern – and Beyond 491

literature began to emerge and the genre has never ceased to flourish since that time with the appearance both of general studies and of particular case-histories.[582] For instance one of the earliest studies to stress the importance of the role of pressure groups was Dr A. J. Willcocks' examination of their part in the emergence of the National Health Service. The relation, he says (in his original doctoral thesis), of the tentative plans of 1943 to the final Act of 1946

> is dependent in large measure on the views put forward by the interest or pressure groups most concerned with the health services, and... from the first 'official' plan the various Ministers of Health moved outwards in an attempt to reach some sort of compromise with the various groups.

The outcome was 'a piece of social legislation which, in its shape and context, is largely the result of the Government's assessment of the value and strength of [the views] of the many interest groups.'[583]

There was clear official recognition at this time also. The report of the Herbert Committee, published in 1949, described the 'large area within which Government Departments come into contact with the many organisations, firms and members of the public who nowadays have business to transact with them', and went on:

> It is evident that under modern conditions organised liaison between representatives of trade and industry and private individuals on the one hand and Government Departments on the other *is an essential and recognised part of the machinery of government*. This applies most obviously to the formulation and execution of general policy. ...We found that intermediary work was being carried out on a great scale by trade associations, trades unions and voluntary organisations....[584]

This is a view still echoed two decades later by Sir R. Clarke when he stressed that two-way contact, the closest possible liaison, between a government department and its 'public' – 'the organisations and interests and institutions within the department's field of responsibility' – was

---

582 See e.g. the bibliography in R. M. Punnett, *British Government and Politics* (1968; 4th edn, London, 1980), pp. 475–80 or in G. Alderman, *Pressure Groups and Government in Great Britain* (London, 1984), pp. 151–7.
583 A. J. Willcocks, *Interest Groups and the National Health Service Act, 1946* (Ph.D., University of Birmingham, 1953), pp. 5–6. Cf. ibid., pp. 355–6. The study later published in 1967 is based on this thesis but is not so full and detailed.
584 Intermediaries, Cttee Rep., 1950 (vol. xii), Cmd. 7904, p. 6 §§5–6 (my italics). For a contemporary academic recognition of the acceptance of groups as part of the constitution, see K. W. Wheare, *Government by Committee: an Essay on the British Constitution* (Oxford, 1955), pp. 30–5 and *passim*.

vital and 'overriding', 'one of its most important tasks.' Apart from anything else, he said, this relationship helps refute any charge of government 'remoteness'.[585] These connexions are frequently nurtured by the state because, in order to act effectively, it often needs specialized information and technical advice. Such a link, preferably with a unified and organized source, is often formalized through some advisory committee or by an automatic process of ministerial deliberation during the making (say) of primary and secondary legislation.[586] Consultation, as H. Morrison once put it, is 'a very blessed word in the administration of British democracy.'[587]

Naturally there are interests of all kinds, from the worlds of business and labour, the professions, the churches, education and culture, recreation and welfare, as well as an extensive range of minority and more specifically oriented organizations. Quasi-governmental public bodies may themselves be important souces of pressure.[588] And the number and size of all these groups have increased considerably during the course of this century. Overall totals are not easily come by but some indication of this expansion is available. For instance whereas there were in 1913 only some 500 manufacturers' trade associations, by the mid-sixties there were at least 1,300; and during roughly the same period the number of firms and organizations in the FBI rose from little more than fifty to nearly 9,000. Again the National Farmers' Union had only 20,000 members when it was formed in 1908 but nowadays it has more than nine times that number.[589] And all these groups tend to be more active and in ever more varied ways: agitation, publicity, 'education' through meetings and demonstrations, deputations, petitions, organized correspondence, circulating newsletters, publicity leaflets and other literature, advertising, use of the media – who among us has not been bored stiff by the smart or bumbling response of a representative of this union or that federation in the interviews which, to excess nowadays, follow a news bulletin on the wireless or television? Then there are the attempts to influence the political parties themselves; bringing pressure directly to bear on or through (or even threatening) departments,

---

585 Sir R. Clarke, *New Trends in Government* (Civil Service Studies no. 1; London, 1971), pp. 30–1.
586 See e.g. J. D. Stewart, *British Pressure Groups: their Role in Relation to the House of Commons* (Oxford, 1958), pp. 8–9, 15–20.
587 386 H.C. Deb. 5s., 18 February 1943, col. 2047. There were many references during this debate (on the Beveridge report) to the need to negotiate with the interests concerned.
588 For one recent case-study, of the National Consumer Council, see L. Tivey, 'Quasi-Government for Consumers', in A. Barker (ed.), *Quangos in Britain: Government and the Networks of Public Policy-Making* (London, 1982), pp. 138–44.
589 Finer, op. cit., p. 7.

ministers, MPs, and councillors; acting as a source of specialist knowledge and information; presenting evidence to royal commissions or select committees; sponsoring private members' Bills; and the like.[590] Two diverse aspects of the impact of groups may be mentioned to exemplify their significance. One is described by Professor S. E. Finer as follows:

> ...parties do not, on the whole, make their policies in a vacuum. Policies are usually framed in opposition, not when a party is in power; and in opposition, parties have no civil servants to advise them. Therefore they have to rely on working-parties of their supporters and on their research organisations; but these, in turn, tend to seek advice from those who are competent to give it; i.e. the various lobbies.

It does not follow, of course, that the party will accept everything thus suggested to it; but much of the detail of its programme may be traced to these sources.[591] The other instance relates to the consideration of Bills in Parliament much of which turns on detailed argument and information. One judgement is simply this: that the committee stage of a legislative proposal is 'rarely effective except when there is a discussion between one set of experts speaking through the Minister and other experts speaking through various back-bench MPs.'[592] However a student of national or local politics will not be interested in all of these many associations as such or all of the time. They become relevant or swim into his ken when they have some influence on or try to affect public policy. The Royal Shakespeare Company pursues its own affairs (as it were politically unperceived) until it presses its opinion about state support for the arts in general and itself in particular.[593] On the other hand some organizations are different, like CND which has existed since 1958 only to spread a particular attitude to nuclear weapons and their use. It has a central, indeed unique, purpose to influence national policy in this regard by arousing public opinion: there is no other overt goal or technique. And of course any of these groups may be active at the local as well as the central level of government.[594] In one sense, of course, all local councils are,

---

590 The Parliamentary activities of groups are fully reviewed in Stewart, op. cit., esp. chs V, VII–IX.
591 Finer, op. cit., p. 20.
592 W. J. M. Mackenzie, 'Pressure Groups in British Government' (1955), reprinted in idem, *Explorations in Government. Collected Papers: 1951–1968* (London, 1975), p. 279.
593 For this sort of activity, see S. Beauman, *The Royal Shakespeare Company: a History of Ten Decades* (Oxford, 1982), pp. 261, 263.
594 On local groups, see e.g. T. Byrne, *Local Government in Britain: Everyone's Guide to How It All Works* (Penguin, 1981), pp. 244–54 and the references there given. See

vis à vis the central and other political authorities, to be regarded as representative bodies; just as the smaller councils fulfil this role in relation to the larger ones.[595]

The classification of all these groups is, like that of the institutions of the Public Concern, a difficult matter only to be resolved by arbitrary authorial fiat. For present purposes it is good enough to invoke a simple and by now long-standing distinction between 'sectional' and 'cause' groups. It is not watertight and some activities obviously fall into both categories; but it will do to show the nature in principle of political activity 'beyond the fringe'.

Sectional groups are associations formed to forward the purposes and protect the interests of a particular section of the population – seamen, allotment-holders, directors, blind people, dentists, rotarians, farmers, tenants, civil servants, teachers, health visitors, property-owners, ex-servicemen, railwaymen, airline pilots, miners, journalists, bookmakers, religious or ethnic minorities, and so on and so forth. They may lobby, perhaps frequently and intensively, but this in itself is not usually the reason they were established and it normally remains incidental to their main or general objectives. Thus the BMA deals with a whole range of professional questions but only becomes significant in the direct political sense when it swings into action to influence, for instance, a government decision about pay-beds in NHS hospitals; the AA and RAC offer many services to motorists but may, as a means of protecting their interests, try in various ways to speed the motorway repair programme or to reduce the level of motor vehicle taxation; a hockey club may try to pressure local councillors to stop a proposal to build on the sports field it uses, or a parent-teacher association be spurred to action by a proposal to change a school's status. Another example has lately come to hand, apt for citation. The Consumers' Association is primarily concerned with testing products and services; but it also acts as a pressure group. One example is its campaign against the excessive disparity between the price of cars in the UK and on the continent and to sustain the right of a British buyer to import a vehicle from some other EEC country at the lower price obtaining there. Since 1981 CA representatives have

> sat on working parties of the EEC in Brussels debating the subject, lobbied Parliaments – both national and European, given evidence to

---

also Barker, *The Local Amenity Movement*; A. H. Birch, *Small Town Politics: a Study of Political Life in Glossop* (Oxford, 1959), chs 11–12; M. Stacey, *Tradition and Change: a Study of Banbury* (Oxford, 1960), chs 3–5; M. Stacey, *et al.*, *Power, Persistence and Change: a Second Study of Banbury* (London, 1975), esp. ch. 4.

595 Cf. W. A. Robson, *The Development of Local Government* (1931; 3rd rev. edn, London, 1954), pp. 222–4. The role of the local authority associations themselves is reviewed in B. Keith-Lucas and P. G. Richards, *A History of Local Government in the Twentieth Century* (London, 1978), ch. IX.

the House of Lords Select Committee on the European Communities, intervened at the European Court..., and engaged in numerous radio and television debates with the mandarins of the motor industry.[596]

The strike is, of course, one of the most extreme forms of pressure thus used nowadays by labour unions (not least in connexion with public sector pay settlements). Some of these groups are also associated more or less closely with a political party, a connexion which naturally tends to emphasize the degree of direct commitment involved; and they may have links with an MP who acts as spokesman or maintain a Parliamentary agent at Westminster. Where they are authoritative and representative (as by having a high percentage membership) or dispose of special information or technical expertise, they may be consulted by central or local departments (possibly a statutory obligation is involved) and so acquire privileged access to the policy-forming process or other activities of government.[597] Often they will provide members for advisory committees, tribunals, and other bodies of the Public Concern.

Cause groups are associations of people with only a single objective or cause to promote and one which is not related simply to the sectional interests of their members: to secure the introduction of proportional representation, abolish cruel sports, increase aid for the homeless, preserve rural England, promote Sunday observance, help needy foreigners, improve the legal position of women, prevent the fluoridation of water supplies, and the like. Very often the goal in view can only be achieved by political means so this may characterize the actions of the group in question. Such bodies are unlikely to be consulted or have privileged access: it is difficult to envisage even a Labour government consulting CND about defence policy though it might have been influenced by it. Consequently their main activity is to campaign which, in a sense, shows their relative ineffectiveness. Obviously some causes are more long-lasting than others. The need to prevent cruelty to children or to help the homeless is, alas, a seemingly permanent concern; while the battle against museum charges or the export of live animals for slaughter are (so to say) occasional issues that may come and go or that disappear when success is achieved.

There are plenty of well-documented examples of the success of pressure-group activity: the amendment of the NHS Bill in the 1940s (already mentioned) or of the Horserace Totalisator Bill in the early 1970s; the abolition of capital punishment; the establishment of commercial television; the introduction and passage of clean-air legislation; the proposal to have an Ombudsman; or the defeat of the

---

596 *Which?* (June 1985), p. 242.
597 For one instance showing the range of consultation that may be involved, see Part 2 p. 590.

Cublington Airport scheme – these are just a few instances. There are many more failures. And what is more significant than either is the process of continuous co-operation and interdependence between some outside bodies and governments which has led to suggestions about the development of 'quasi-corporatism'.[598]

One very full example of the way in which, and the extent to which, private organizations can influence the form of a major piece of legislation is that described in W. J. Braithwaite's account of the passage of the 1911 National Insurance Act. This work – ultimately a bitter and tragic commentary – was first published in 1957 and played a most important part in the renewal of interest in group activity then getting under way. Active preparation for the insurance scheme began in 1908. In that year the minister concerned, D. L. George, visited Germany to find out about the arrangements already in being there. On his return he was in close contact with the National Conference of Friendly Societies representing the most important groups involved. These bodies (such as the Ancient Order of Foresters, the Oddfellows, the National Deposit Friendly Society, and others) were voluntary organizations which already provided some form of insurance against sickness for their members. Other interests had also to be consulted at this preliminary stage later to be, where necessary, placated or bought off. These included the trade unions which had friendly society functions and gave sick pay; also the doctors and the BMA a majority of whom were opposed to a scheme for medical benefit being run by the friendly societies (which kept a select list of doctors only). By the threat of boycott they were able to get the Bill amended so that a free choice of doctor was secured and the benefit administered instead by special insurance committees on which they were represented. Another most important interest was the Industrial Insurance Companies, the collecting societies which conducted a large part of the life insurance business. Unlike the friendly societies and trade unions they were commercial concerns operating for profit and not controlled by their contributors. Because they did not deal in sickness insurance the government was opposed to their being part of the new scheme. But the influence they were able to exert was too great to resist and they were able to force their way in. As well there were various pressures brought to bear via the parties or specific MPs. The Irish were able successfully to insist on a separate system of administration for Ireland; one covey of MPs urged the case for the insurance of women; another respresented mercantile marine interests; and so on. There were personal pressures, too, as with the influence of the Webbs and their apostles who stressed the arguments of the minority Poor Law report in

---

[598] For an early instance, see S. H. Beer, 'Pressure Groups and Parties in Britain', *American Political Science Review*, l (1956), p.7.

favour of a non-contributory scheme run by the public health authorities. The Treasury consulted the Institute of Actuaries about the likely cost. Discussing one point of detail (whether death benefits should be included in the scheme or not) Braithwaite commented on the 'tremendous' political and social power of the collecting societies and industrial assurance companies:

> The Prudential destroyed Bottomley when he attacked it, and by a united attack the Societies could have ruined the Liberal Party. They had only to set the agents to work to spread... a whispering campaign from door to door; for the insurance agents in the course of business called at the vast majority of... homes in the country once a week regularly [and] knew the occupiers.... Such a machine could not be played with. And so a pledge had been given that nothing should be done to touch 'death insurance'....[599]

This is an excellent example how government policy may be determined by the desire to avoid the opposition of a powerful private interest. Braithwaite also describes *inter alia* the part played by groups in the process of formulating the details of the Bill: George has breakfast with representatives of the friendly societies to discuss the scheme with them; he receives deputations; Braithwaite cross-examines the chief secretary of one of the main societies, interviews the Registrar of Friendly Societies, the trade union representatives, medical officers of health, the BMA, and so on.[600] When a draft Bill was finally produced it was sent confidentially to a number of people for their comments: for instance, the 'Prudential people' were given copies of the clauses which especially affected them.[601] Even after the Bill is introduced into Parliament the same sort of process continues. One MP made himself the representative of the industrial insurance firms which were, said Braithwaite, by 'far the most formidable interest affected by the bill.' He went on to offer a general comment:

> Interests are very real forces in Parliament. They are alive and active. The public interest which should count before them is inert and dead compared with them, and has no spokesman or representative. I remember six weeks or so after the bill had been introduced saying to a friend that it was just as if we had poked a stick into a wasp's nest, or stirred up a lot of snakes – so many private interests were trying to sting the new proposals to death. The history of the bill is how they were bought off, conciliated, and in very few instances over-ruled.[602]

599 Sir H. N. Bunbury (ed.), *Lloyd George's Ambulance Wagon Being the Memoirs of William J. Braithwaite 1911–1912* (1957; Bath, 1970), p. 78.
600 ibid., pp. 92–7, 104, 106, 122–3, 140–1, etc.
601 ibid., p. 154.   602 ibid., p. 161.

The account of one day only will show the sort of process involved. The following extract is from Braithwaite's diary entry for 28 July 1911 when the Bill was in Committee of the Whole House. 'Here's a good day!', he said and later commented:

> Called down to No. 10 directly I got in. The Doctors there ... straight from the B.M.A. meeting at Birmingham....
>
> The Chancellor told them straight out that they could not have both [of their demands], and they were ready to drop the second.
>
> I took them up into the Treasury finally, to try to settle the wording.... Then to Board Room for Friendly Societies Conference. They seem relatively unimportant; then to my own room for people waiting for me; then 2.30 almost at a run to the House – temp. 89°! – to catch Liddell [First Parliamentary Counsel], then to the other end of the building for a deputation from the Midwives in the Attorney's room, then back to Chancellor's room for deputation from Ship-owners, then tea, and M.P.s to ask questions all round me for about ten minutes.

Then after attending a discussion between George and the Labour leaders – and the diary here briefly reviews the terms of the main opposition parties – Braithwaite records another 'conference for 1½ hours with the Ship-owners...to try and draw a scheme for the mercantile marine'. Later, after dinner, he 'wrote eight letters to the doctors and their representatives, telling them the alterations L. G. had made to meet their views.'[603] And so on. No doubt this was a particularly controversial piece of major legislation made more difficult because there had been no previous official inquiry to clear the ground. But certainly there is no better account or example of the practical art of politics. And it demonstrates very clearly the part likely to be played by affected interest groups in the process of passing a Bill into law as do the other detailed case-histories which have since appeared.[604]

Obviously there is much to be said for the lobbying activities of private organizations. They ensure that particular interests and attitudes secure a voice and even influence in the political process and thus provide for a form of popular participation in between elections and in addition to the formal constitutional approaches open to the individual. They also help secure the redress of grievances.[605] In addition they smooth the path of administration by providing advice and information, ensuring co-

---

603 ibid., pp. 195–6. The Labour Party finally agreed to give general support to the Bill if the Chancellor would introduce a proposal for the payment of MPs, ibid., p. 196 n. 2.
604 For detailed references, see the bibliographies mentioned at p. 491 n. 582 above.
605 Cf. Finer, *Anonymous Empire*, pp. 112–13.

operation, and the like as part of the process of consultation and negotiation. It could even be said that the vigour of groups constitutes a bulwark against centralized power and that without them we should all be helpless before the great Leviathan.[606]

On the other hand all this undoubtedly slows things up. And it is obvious that not all sections of the community or points of view can command an equal voice. A hierarchy of influence develops with some groups securing a privileged position of access to decision-making centres. Also there is too little openness, much of the influence being exerted informally and behind the scenes. In addition a group's leadership may not be at all representative of the general opinions of its members and its power may thus be misdirected or misused in their name. And it need not be employed constructively but in order to sabotage or obstruct government proposals. The general interest or that of other groups may simply be forgotten or ignored by a crucial association full bent in the pursuit of its own interests: this is a kind of violence by blackmail. And it involves a distortion of Parliamentary government, for the role of Parliament itself may be diminished by the process of group consultation. Once the negotiations over a Bill (say) have been concluded and a compromise reached with the various interests, it becomes very difficult if not impossible for the minister to accept further amendment.[607] This is a situation which may call for remedy by the action of the state as through a reduction of the great power of some organizations, regulation of the way in which they elect their leaders, a requirement of consultation before important action as by a referendum of the membership, and the recognition that entry and departure should be genuinely voluntary. Recent trade union legislation obviously had these points in mind; and there is no reason why they should not be more widely applied.

CORPORATISM

...the outriders of the corporate state.
P. HOLLAND, *The Governance of Quangos*, 1981, p. 27

In 1849 Toulmin Smith attacked the growth not only of government powers and officialism but also the emergence of irresponsible central boards. Nearly a century passes and the same phenomenon is still observed and concern expressed about it. S. Baldwin, in an address to an audience of civil servants, commented on the 'half-conscious, rule-of-

---

606 CLXVII H.L. Deb. 5s., 17 May 1950, col. 353 (Bishop of Southwell); 'Notes and Comments', *Political Quarterly*, xxix (1958), p. 4.
607 Cf. E. C. S. Wade in his introduction to A. V. Dicey, *Introduction to the Study of the Law of the Constitution* (1885; 10th edn, London, 1964), p. lxx.

thumb' creation of 'intermediate authorities' (as he called them). A few years later, just after the beginning of the second war, the regional commissioners were described as a clear and extreme example, indeed 'the apotheosis', of 'that dangerous trend in our political development which may be described as "Government by Commission"' – in fact Toulmin Smith's term – by which was meant 'some form of appointed board or officer exercising large administrative powers without direct responsibility to an elected body'. Agencies like the BBC and LPTB, the CEB, and the Coal Commission were cited as examples of the sort of institutions in mind.[608] Since then, of course, the parastatal world has expanded enormously. It has done so to such an extent and in such a way that the filaments of state interest, supervision, regulation, and aid reach deep into the body of civil society. And much of this activity seems itself to be little accountable in the traditional sense and is certainly very costly. Of course much is achieved and in various ways many people are drawn into the process of discussion and administration. Yet it can seem a danger, the creation, inadvertent or otherwise, of what is often nowadays called a 'corporate state'. A recent critic described the situation as one characterized by various features: the sheer scale of modern society; the limited influence of the electorate and of its representatives; the importance of major interest groups; and above all perhaps that major decisions are taken outside Parliament by the executive in conjunction with such bodies as economic planning boards, incomes commissions, public corporations, and so on and so forth and without any direct line of effective accountability.[609] Major economic decisions, for instance, are taken as the outcome of close collaboration or continuous contact between industrialists, trade unionists, ministers, and officials.[610] Usually the consultation is informal but it may be institutionalized as in the National Economic Development Council.[611] Or it may be embodied in a concord like the 'social contract' or a 'planning agreement'. The Thatcher governments have shown their revolutionary intent by setting their face against these tendencies. The post-war 'consensus' has been repudiated as has the Keynesianism on which it rested. Legislative attempts to trim trade union power have been

---

[608] J. T. Smith, *Government by Commissions Illegal and Pernicious* (London, 1849); S. Baldwin, *This Torch of Freedom* (1935; 4th edn, London, 1937), p. 77; 'Regionaliter', 'The Regional Commissioners', *Political Quarterly*, xii (1941), p. 152.

[609] E. Luard, *Socialism without the State* (London, 1979), pp. 88–93.

[610] For other analysis on these lines, see L. Hannah, *The Rise of the Corporate Economy* (1976; 2nd edn, London, 1983); K. Middlemas, *Politics in Industrial Society: the Experience of the British System since 1911* (London, 1979); and idem, *Industry, Unions and Government* (London, 1983).

[611] A recent assessment is J. S. Cassels, 'Can Tripartism Compete?', *Three Banks Review* (June 1985), pp. 3–19.

The Public Concern – and Beyond

launched.[612] And the first steps have been taken to dismantle the Public Concern, as by the policy of privatization and the abolition of quangos. It may seem overall that, after six years or so, precious little has been achieved. But the task is enormous: these bodies have grown up over several generations; it may take as long to undo them – if the will to do so persists and the opportunity remains.

---

[612] For one strong attack on trade unions, see P. Johnson, 'Towards the Parasite State', *New Statesman and Nation* (3 September 1976), pp. 299–304.

APPENDIX 1

HM Government as shareholder, 1928–85*

Description of holding	Department	1928–9 (£)	1948–9 (£)	1968–9 (£)	1978–9 (£)	1984–5 (£)
Various agricultural and other co-operative societies shares	Ministry of Agriculture, Fisheries and Food	—	—	2,923	2,630	3,694
Amersham International plc special rights preference share	Department of Energy	—	—	—	—	1
Bank of England capital stock	Treasury	—	58,212,000	14,553,000	14,553,000	14,553,000
Beagle Aircraft Ltd £1 ordinary shares	Department of Industry	—	—	1,000,000	1,000,000	—
Birmingham District Council Bond	Department of Health and Social Security	—	—	—	1,000	—

503

British Aerospace plc 50p ordinary shares	Department of Trade and Industry	—	—	—	48,426,373
British Airways plc £1 ordinary shares	Department of Transport	—	—	—	180,050,000
British Channel Tunnel Company plc (a) £1 founder shares (b) £1 'A' ordinary shares	Department of Transport	—	—	(a) 1,086,957 (b) 3,652,174	(a) 1,086,957 (b) 3,652,174
British Electricity 3% guaranteed stock, 1968–73	Ministry of Technology	—	16,064	—	—
British Leyland plc 50p ordinary shares	Department of Trade and Industry	—	—	—	2,133,131,068
British Nuclear Design & Construction Ltd £1 shares	Ministry of Technology	—	20	—	—
British Nuclear Fuels plc £1 ordinary shares	Department of Energy	—	—	32,668,244	32,668,244
British Petroleum Company plc (previously Anglo-Persian/Anglo-Iranian Oil Co.) (a) ordinary shares (b) preference shares	Treasury	(a) 5,200,000 (b) —	(a) 5,001,000 (b) —	(a) 174,461,538 (b) 1,000	(a) 119,306,716 (b) 1,000	(a) 144,624,223 (b) 1,000

HM Government as shareholder, 1928–85 (contd.)*

Description of holding	Department	Nominal amount at end of financial year							
		1928–9 (£)		1948–9 (£)	1968–9 (£)		1978–9 (£)		1984–5 (£)
British Sugar Corporation Ltd ordinary shares	(i) Treasury (ii) Ministry of Agriculture, Fisheries and Food	— —		— —	(i) 1,125,000 (ii) —	(i) (ii)	2,250,000 5,000,000		— —
British Telecommunications plc (a) £1 preference shares (b) 25p ordinary shares (c) special rights redeemable preference share	Department of Trade and Industry	—		—	—		—	(a) (b) (c)	750,000,000 747,038,421 1
Britoil plc (a) 10p ordinary shares (b) special rights preference share	Treasury	—		—	—		—	(a) (b)	24,458,949 1
Cable and Wireless plc (a) ordinary shares (b) special rights preference share	(i) Treasury (ii) Department of Trade and Industry	—	(i)(a)	30,000,000	(i)(a) 30,000,000	(i)(a)	60,000,000	(i)(a) (b) (ii)(a)	51,249,993 1 9
Chilean schools, holding of shares in	Foreign and Commonwealth Office	—		—	—		1,442		3,275

Cowal Ari Sawmilling Co. Ltd 5% debenture	Forestry Commission	—	—	—	15,000	—	—
Cunard Steamship Co. Ltd ordinary stock	Treasury	—	—	—	66	—	—
Drake and Scull Engineering Ltd £1 preference shares	Department of the Environment	—	—	—	—	598,166	—
Dunford and Elliott Ltd 12½% unsecured loan stock 1980–3	Department of Industry	—	—	—	—	484,574	—
Enterprise Oil Ltd special rights preference share	Department of Energy	—	—	—	—	—	1
Fairfields (Glasgow) Ltd 7% unsecured loan stock, 1975	Department of Industry	—	—	—	940,000	940,000	—
Fast Reactor Technology Ltd £1 ordinary shares	Department of Energy	—	—	—	—	—	49
French 4% rentes	—	3,604,306	—	—	—	—	—
I.C. (Holdings) Ltd £1 'C' ordinary shares	Ministry of Technology	—	—	—	3,500,000	—	—
International Military Services Ltd £1 ordinary shares	Ministry of Defence	—	—	—	—	999,999	19,999,999
Itabira Iron Ore Co. Ltd (a) £1 first preference shares (b) £1 second preference shares (c) £1 ordinary shares	Ministry of Power	—	—	(a) 61,220 (b) 380,000 (c) 493,982	—	—	—

505

HM Government as shareholder, 1928–85 (contd.)*

Nominal amount at end of financial year

Description of holding	Department	1928–9 (£)	1948–9 (£)	1968–9 (£)	1978–9 (£)	1984–5 (£)
John Hastie of Greenock (Holdings) Ltd (a) £1 'B' redeemable participating preference shares (b) £1 'C' redeemable preference shares	Department of Trade and Industry	— 	— 	— 	(a) 40,000 (b) 310,000	(a) 40,000 (b) 310,000
Kearney and Trecker Marwin Ltd (a) £1 cumulative redeemable 13¾% preference 'B' shares (b) £1 cumulative redeemable 13¾% preference 'D' shares	Department of Industry	—	—	—	(a) 800,000 (b) 100,000	—
Kintyre Farmers Ltd £1 shares	Department of Agriculture and Fisheries for Scotland	—	—	5	5	—
KTM Machine Tools (Holdings) Ltd (a) £1 ordinary shares (b) £1 redeemable convertible 'A' preference shares (c) £1 redeemable 'B' preference shares	Department of Industry	—	—	—	(a) 338,141 (b) 950,000 (c) 3,222,200	—

Marathon Shipbuilding Co. (UK) Ltd 7½% redeemable cumulative £100 preference shares	Scottish Economic Planning Department	—	—	—	2,400,000	—
Massey-Ferguson Ltd, Canada Series E preferred shares (unquoted)	Export Credits Guarantee Department	—	—	—	—	47,566,976
Massey-Ferguson Holdings Ltd 1p redeemable convertible preference shares (unquoted)	Export Credits Guarantee Department	—	—	—	—	30,945
Mersey Conservancy Corporation of London 9¼% stock 1984–5	Department of Transport	—	—	—	1,454	1,454
Mersey Docks and Harbour Company (a) redeemable subordinated unsecured loan stock (b) 10p ordinary shares	Department of Transport	—	—	—	(a) 3,806,284 (b) 413,727	(a) 2,937,458 (b) 413,727
National Nuclear Corporation Ltd £10,000 ordinary shares	Department of Energy	—	—	—	3,500,000	3,500,000

HM Government as shareholder, 1928–85 (contd.)*

Nominal amount at end of financial year

Description of holding	Department	1928–9 (£)	1948–9 (£)	1968–9 (£)	1978–9 (£)	1984–5 (£)
National Seed Development Organization £1 shares	Ministry of Agriculture, Fisheries and Food	—	—	—	300,000	400,000
Norton Villiers Triumph Ltd (a) £1 'A' redeemable preference shares (b) £1 'B' convertible redeemable preference shares	Department of Industry	—	—	—	(a) 1,000,000 (b) 1,372,000	—
Parkend Saw Mills Ltd 6% cumulative preference shares	Forestry Commission	—	—	500	—	—
Power Jets (Research and Development) Ltd £1 ordinary shares	Ministry of Technology	—	—	200,000	—	—
The Radiochemical Centre Ltd £1 ordinary shares	Department of Energy	—	—	—	6,266,783	—
Rolls Royce Ltd £1 ordinary shares	Department of Trade and Industry	—	—	—	—	508,000,000

Roumanian 4% Consolidated Bonds, 1922	Treasury	1,910,000	120,000	4,000,000	4,000,000	—
Royal Ordnance plc £1 ordinary shares	Ministry of Defence	—	—	—	—	60,000,000
Sacred Heart School, Kaduna debentures	Foreign and Commonwealth Office	—	—	—	669	706
S.B. (Realizations) Ltd	Ministry of Technology	—	(a) 42,050 (b) 145,326 (c) 62,500	—	—	—
(a) 5% redeemable cumulative £1 preference shares						
(b) 581,302 5s. ordinary shares						
(c) 250,000 5s. 'A' ordinary shares						
Scottish National Housing Co. Ltd share capital	Scottish Development Department	—	170,910	—	—	—
Sealink (UK) Ltd preference share	Department of Transport	—	—	—	—	1
Short Brothers Ltd	Department of Trade and Industry	—	—	(a) 4,840,000 (b) 342,000	(a) 4,840,000 (b) 342,000	4,840,000 342,000
(a) £1 12% 'A' preference shares						
(b) £1 ordinary shares						
Société Anglo-Belge Vulcain S.-A. 11,500 shares of no nominal value	Ministry of Technology	—	(cost) 24,722	—	—	—

HM Government as shareholder, 1928–85 (contd.)*

Nominal amount at end of financial year

Description of holding	Department	1928–9 (£)	1948–9 (£)	1968–9 (£)	1978–9 (£)	1984–5 (£)
Standard Mill (Rochdale) Ltd £1 redeemable 'A' preference shares	Department of Trade and Industry	—	—	—	300,000	300,000
Suez Canal Co. Ltd (a) ordinary shares (b) 'actions de jouissance'	—	(a) 72,258,844† (b)	27,988,440†	—	—	—
Suez Finance Company F.F. 100 capital shares	Treasury	—	—	F.F.64,559,100	F.F.71,015,000	—
Toplis and Harding 997 50p shares	Foreign and Commonwealth Office	—	—	499	499	—
Triang Pedigree (1971) Ltd (a) £1 new cumulative redeemable preference shares (b) £1 ordinary shares	Welsh Office	—	—	—	(a) 1,000,000 (b) 25,000	—
Upper Clyde Shipbuilders Ltd (a) £1 ordinary shares (b) 12,000,000 25p 'A' ordinary shares	Department of Industry	—	—	(a) 875,000	(a) 875,000 (b) 3,000,000	—

Welsh Highland Light Railway Company 5% debenture	Ministry of Transport	—	—	28,172	—
West Highland Crofters and Farmers Ltd £1 shares	Department of Agriculture and Fisheries for Scotland	—	—	10	10
Wolverhampton Industrial Engines Ltd 10p 'A' ordinary shares	Department of Industry	—	—	5,000	—
Proceeds of property sales (a) held in blocked account, Kampala	Department of the Environment	—	—	(a) 118,725	—
(b) invested in Turkish government bonds	Department of the Environment	—	—	(b) 3,054	—
(c) held in blocked account, Ankara	Department of the Environment	—	—	(c) 5,779	—
Holdings of miscellaneous foreign bonds, shares, etc.	Inland Revenue	—	—	1,934	1,599,444
Total		82,973,150	121,321,440	232,177,896‡	281,884,166‡	4,781,280,154

Sources: Finance Accounts of the United Kingdom for the financial years 1928–9 and 1948–9; Consolidated Fund and National Loans Fund Accounts, Supplementary Statements, for 1968–9, 1978–9, and 1984–5. I am grateful to Mr M. T. Barnshaw of the Treasury and Cabinet Office Library for drawing my attention to these papers. Securities held and interest received in respect of government loans are excluded as are investments held by some surrogate like a public corporation or other fringe body. The details for the earlier years may be incomplete as no full list of direct nominal holdings appears to have been published before 1968. It would be interesting to see a complete, cumulative list of all government shareholdings since, say, the turn of the century whether these were held directly or indirectly. It would have to take account, for instance, of Securities Trust Ltd, a body set up to manage investments acquired during the Great War and which was still in existence in 1946: see PRO, T160/1391/F.7314/01/2. The departmental title indicated in the table is that appropriate to the latest year of holding.
† Estimated market value. Dividend earned in 1928–9 was £1,696,932 8s 2d and in 1948–9 was £1,580,680 16s 11d.
‡ Excluding Suez Finance Co. holding.

APPENDIX 2

Privatization, 1979–86[a]

Name	Authorizing Statute	Successor company (date of registration)	Percentage of equity sold or transferred (date and receipts)	Subsidiaries or assets sold (date and receipts)	Competitive elements introduced (date)	Future intention

Nationalized industries[b]

British Aerospace	British Aerospace Act (1980)	British Aerospace plc (January 1981)	51.57% (February 1981; £43m) 48.43% (May 1985; £350m)			
British Airports Authority						Airports Bill introduced January 1986 – BAA assets to be vested in a successor company as a first step to privatization with each of the seven airports under a holding company

British Airways Board	Civil Aviation Act (1980)	British Airways plc (April 1984)	International Aeradio (March, 1983; £60m) College of Air Training (April, 1984; £5m)	CAA refusal of British Midland's application to operate a Heathrow – Scotland service overturned by government	Privatization of BA now intended during financial year 1986–7
British Coal					No present plans to privatize BC mining activities Private open-cast mining to be permitted under licence
British Gas Corporation	Oil and Gas Enterprise Act (1982)		Enterprise Oil (June 1984; £380m)		Gas Bill introduced to authorize creation of a private sector company shares in which will be sold by 1986–7. Subject to safety requirements competition would be allowed in gas supply
British National Oil Corporation[c]	Oil and Gas Enterprise Act (1982)	(i) BNOC – oil trading (November 1982)	(i) sale of oil licences (1980–3; £349m)		
	Oil and Gas Enterprise Act (1982)	(ii) Britoil plc – exploration and production (November 1982)	(ii) 51.2% (November 1982; £627m) 48.8% (August 1985; £434m)		

513

Privatization, 1979–86 (contd.)[a]

Name	Authorizing Statute	Successor company (date of registration)	Percentage of equity sold or transferred (date and receipts)	Subsidiaries or assets sold (date and receipts)	Competitive elements introduced (date)	Future intention
British Railways Board	Transport Act (1981)			Hotels (1981–3; £130.5m) Sealink (July 1984; £66m) Seaspeed (September, 1981)		Introduction of private capital into rail investment programmes a possibility
British Shipbuilders	British Shipbuilders Act (1983)			Warship yards (1984–6) Repair and equipment subsidiaries (1984–5)		As much as possible of the industry to be returned to the private sector; companies to be floated separately if sale of whole not feasible
British Steel Corporation	Iron and Steel Act (1981)			Numerous shareholdings in other steel companies; peripheral subsidiaries in construction and engineering	Joint ventures with private sector	To be privatized as quickly as practicable with priority being given to the areas of overlap with the private sector and non-mainstream activities

British Telecom[d]	British Telecommunications Act (1984)	British Telecom plc (August 1984)	50.2% (November 1984; £3915.6m)	Mercury Consortium established (1982) – later became a wholly owned subsidiary of Cable and Wireless	In supply of handsets and other phone equipment; maintenance of PABX; other transmission systems licensed
British Transport Docks Board	Transport Act (1981)	Associated British Ports Holdings plc (December 1982)	49% (February 1983; £46m) 48.3% (April 1984; £51m)		
British Waterways Board					
Civil Aviation Authority				Reduce dependence on government grant in long term	Airfields owned in Scottish Highlands and Islands to remain in CAA ownership but to operate within a separate plc administration (a previous attempt to sell these airfields having failed)

Privatization, 1979–86 (contd.)[a]

Name	Authorizing Statute	Successor company (date of registration)	Percentage of equity sold or transferred (date and receipts)	Subsidiaries or assets sold (date and receipts)	Competitive elements introduced (date)	Future intention
Electricity Council, area boards, and CEGB	Electricity Act (1983)					No present plans to privatize the electricity supply industry
London Regional Transport	London Regional Transport Act (1984)	London Buses Ltd; London Underground Ltd; LRT Bus Engineering Ltd (all April 1985)			44 bus routes put out to tender (1985–6)	Further route tenders to be invited; involvement of private capital in the subsidiary companies; their possible disposal; docklands light railway to be owned and operated by private sector
National Bus Company	Transport Acts (1980–5)	Various			Competition allowed on express routes; deregulation of buses in all areas by Oct. 1986; local control over taxi licences restricted; BR permitted to run alternative bus services in lieu of trains	Full programme of disposals to be implemented within three years. NBC subsidiaries to be sold

516

National Freight Corporation	Transport Act (1980)	National Freight Company (1982)	100% (February 1982; £53.5m)
National Girobank		Girobank plc (October 1985)	
North of Scotland Hydro-electric Board			
Post Office	British Telecommunications Act (1981)		Express mail, document, exchange, and other services (July 1985)	Basic letter monopoly to remain Crown Offices may be sold or put out to tender
Scottish Transport Group	Transport Act (1984)		Road haulage subsidiary sold (July 1985; £.45m)	Deregulation of bus services; subsidized services put out to competitive tender
South of Scotland Hydroelectricity Board			

Privatization, 1979–86 (contd.)[a]

Name	Authorizing Statute	Successor company (date of registration)	Percentage of equity sold or transferred (date and receipts)	Subsidiaries or assets sold (date and receipts)	Competitive elements introduced (date)	Future intention

Major utilities and services

National Health Service					Contracting out of laundry and other services	Increase in competitive tendering for e.g. cleaning, laundry, catering, security services, and some maintenance work
New towns				Sale of commercial and industrial assets (1979–85; £490m)		
Water authorities in England and Wales						The 10 authorities to be put on the market as soon as possible after the necessary legislation has been passed (though certain responsibilities like flood protection will remain in the public sector)

UK Atomic Energy Authority	Atomic Energy Authority Act (1985)	Trading Fund basis from April 1986		

Other public departments and agencies

British Leyland (NEB)			Alvis, Prestcold, and S. African assembly plants; Jaguar (August 1984; £297m)	Joint venture with Honda (1981)	To sell BL and its constituent businesses (either together or separately) as soon as possible
British Petroleum[e]		7.31% (November 1980; £276m)[e] 5.17% (September 1983; £543m) nil paid rights (1981–2; £8m)			No further sales planned
British Sugar Corporation		24.17% (1981–2; £44m)			
British Technology Group/National Enterprise Board		Various shareholdings (1979–85; £264m)			To continue to dispose of equity holdings as soon as commercially possible

Privatization, 1979–86 (contd.)[a]

Name	Authorizing Statute	Successor company (date of registration)	Percentage of equity sold or transferred (date and receipts)	Subsidiaries or assets sold (date and receipts)	Competitive elements introduced (date)	Future intention
Cable and Wireless Ltd[f]	British Telecommunications Act (1981)	n.a.[g]	50% (October 1981; £182m) 22% (December 1983; £263m) 22.7% (December 1985; £933m)	Subsidiaries in Hong Kong and Bahrain (1981; £129.4m)		
Crown Agents for Overseas Governments and Administration	Crown Agents Act (1979)	Incorporated January 1980		Sale of property (1982; £7m)		Privatization on the basis of reorganization begun in 1984 and which is now largely complete
Crown Agents Holding and Realization Board	Crown Agents Act (1979)			Most of the assets of the old unincorporated Crown Agents now disposed of (1982–4; £18m)		

520

Crown Suppliers[h]	Government Trading Funds Act (1973)	Trading Fund basis from 1976	
Department of the Environment			Property Services Agency: sale of land and buildings (1979–82; £10m)	Hydraulics Research Station; maintenance tests at monument sites; domestic services at police and prison training establishments; miscellaneous (total saving of 809 staff and £1.1m [net] p.a.)	To be reviewed to see whether the whole or part may be transferred to the private sector
Forestry Commission	Forestry Act (1981) and earlier legislation		Woodland and other assets (1979–85; £65m)
Her Majesty's Stationery Office	Government Trading Funds Act (1975)	Trading Fund basis from April 1980	

Privatization, 1979–86 (contd.)[a]

Name	Authorizing Statute	Successor company (date of registration)	Percentage of equity sold or transferred (date and receipts)	Subsidiaries or assets sold (date and receipts)	Competitive elements introduced (date)	Future intention
Land Settlement Association Ltd				Sale of land (1983–5; £15m)		
Ministry of Defence					Contracting out of support services (cleaning, catering, printing, storage, transport, training, etc. e.g. 95% of MOD cleaning and laundry services now contracted out); Meteorological Office ocean weather ships (total saving of 2903 staff and £6.3 millions [net] p.a.)	

National Film Finance Corporation	NFFC Act (1981); Films Act (1985)	British Screen Finance Consortium Ltd (December 1985)
Public Trust Ports	Ports Finance Act (1985)	Classified as in private sector as from 1985–6 and government controls removed
Rolls Royce (NEB)		Intention is to return to private sector before 1988 after registration as a plc
Royal Dockyards		Dockyard Services Bill introduced November 1985 by which from April 1987 the government would retain ownership of fixed assets at the naval dockyards of Devonport and Rosyth but would put out their operation to commercial management after competitive tender

Privatization, 1979–86 (contd.)[a]

Name	Authorizing Statute	Successor company (date of registration)	Percentage of equity sold or transferred (date and receipts)	Subsidiaries or assets sold (date and receipts)	Competitive elements introduced (date)	Future intention
Royal Mint	Government Trading Funds Act (1973)	Trading Fund basis from April 1985				
Royal Ordnance Factories (plus some R & D establishments)	Ordnance Factories and Military Services Act (1984)	Royal Ordnance plc (January 1985)				Company to move to private sector by mid-1986 subject to appropriate trading performance and stock market conditions

Local authorities

| | Housing Act (1980); Transport Act (1985) | | | Council house sales (1979–84; £6,251m) | Some 37% of all local authorities have contracted out at least | Bus undertakings outside London to become plc's and will be deregulated from October 1986; when the Airports Bill is passed, 16 major municipal airports |

one service (the range includes various cleaning services, refuse collection and disposal, catering, pest control, car park management, ground and vehicle maintenance, etc.)

will become plc's with the possible introduction of private capital or sale; wider private sector involvement in ownership and management of council housing; extension of contracting out of services

a *Sources: KCA* (1980–6); *Whitaker's Almanack* (1980–6); The Government's Expenditure Plans 1986–87 to 1988–89, 1985–6, Cmnd. 9702-II; Treasury and Civil Service, Sel. Cttee. 7th Rep., 1980–1, HC 423 and 1st Special Rep., 1982–3, HC 46; *Municipal Year Book* (1986).
b For further details of the nationalized sector as it was in 1979, see Table 8, p. 394 above.
c Ceased to operate on 1 December 1985 under Oil and Pipelines Act (1985), assets being transferred to the Oil and Pipelines Agency.
d Established as a public corporation separate from the Post Office on 1 October 1981.
e For earlier sales to the public, see *KCA* (1977), p. 28476A (where the origin and nature of the government's involvement with BP is described).
f Conversion was not necessary as Cable and Wireless was already a limited company with, since 1969, shares vested in the Post Office.
g For an account of the government's involvement with the company, see *KCA* (1982), p. 31289A.
h A branch of the Property Services Agency acting as the central purchasing agency for government departments, the armed forces, and other public bodies.

APPENDIX 3

Central privatization proceeds,[a] 1979–85[b]

Sale	1979–80	1980–1	1981–2	1982–3	1983–4	1984–5
			(£ millions)			
Amersham International plc – sale of shares			64			
Associated British Ports Holdings plc – sale of shares				46		51
British Aerospace plc – sale of shares		43				
British Petroleum plc – sale of shares	276		8		543	
British Sugar Corporation – sale of shares			44			
British Telecommunications plc – sale of shares						1,357
Britoil plc – sale of shares				334	293	
Cable and Wireless plc – sale of shares			182		263	
Crown Agents – sale of property			7			
Crown Agents Holding and Realisation Board – sale of property				16	2	
Drake and Scull Holding Ltd – sale of shares	1					
Enterprise Oil plc – sale of shares						380
Forestry Commission – sale of land, plantations, and buildings			7	14	23	21
Land Settlement Association – sale of land					2	13

Central privatization proceeds,[a] 1979–85 (contd.)[b]

Sale	1979–80	1980–1	1981–2	1982–3	1983–4	1984–5
			(£ millions)			
Lease on motorway service areas – sale of land and buildings		28	19	4	1	
National Freight Company – sale of shares			5			
NEB/BTG – sale of shareholdings	37	83	2			142
New Town Development Corporations and Commission for the New Towns – sale of land and buildings	26	52	73	1		
North Sea Oil Licence Premia		195		33		121
Property Services Agency – sale of land and buildings	5	4	1			
Regional Water Authority – sale of land	3					
Sale of commodity stocks			19	7	4	6
Sale of oil stockpiles			63	33	11	
Suez Finance Company – sale of shares	22					
Total	370	405	494	488[c]	1,142[d]	2,091[e,f]

a Previously described as 'Special Sales of Assets'.
b Sources: The Government's Expenditure Plans 1981–82 to 1983–84, 1980–1, Cmnd. 8175, Table 4.11 p.215; The Government's Expenditure Plans 1986–87 to 1988–89, 1985–6, Cmnd. 9702-II, Table 2.23 p.29.
c Excludes receipts from sale of BR Hotels (£30 millions) and of the BA subsidiary International Aeradio Ltd (£60 millions) which were retained by the nationalized industries concerned.
d Excludes receipts from the sale of BR Hotels (£15 millions) retained by the industry.
e Excludes receipts from the sale of Jaguar Cars (£297 millions), British Gas Corporation Onshore Oil Assets (£82 millions), and Sealink (£40 millions) which were retained by the industries concerned.
f The estimated outturn for 1985–6 is £2,622 millions; and for 1986–9 £4,750 millions: see The Government's Expenditure Plans 1986–87 to 1988–89, loc. cit., Table 2.1 p.5.